$16.99

Fodor's **2010**

CARIBBEAN PORTS OF CALL

Where to Stay and Eat
for All Budgets

Must-See Sights
and Local Secrets

Ratings You Can Trust

Fodor's Travel Publications   New York

www.fodors.com

D1416747

FODOR'S CARIBBEAN PORTS OF CALL 2010

Editor: Douglas Stallings

Editorial Contributors: Carol M. Bareuther, John Bigley, Linda Coffman, Michelle Delio, Michael de Zayas, David Dudenhoefer, Lynne Helm, Clint Hill, Michele Joyce, Marlise Kast, Lynda Lohr, Richard McColl, Maribeth Mellin, Elise Meyer, Tim Moloney, Paris Permenter, Alice Powers, Vernon O'Reilly Ramesar, Jessica Robertson, Sam Sessa, Ramona Settle, Jordan Simon, Lan Sluder, Eilen Robinson Smith, Roberta Sotonoff, Kerry Speckman, Mark Sullivan, Cynthia Tourigny, Jim Tunstall, Jeff Van Fleet, Chelle Koster Walton, Melanie Wetzel, Jane E. Zarem

Production Editor: Carrie Parker

Maps & Illustrations: David Lindroth, Mark Stroud, cartographers; Bob Blake, Rebecca Baer, map editors; William Wu, information graphics

Design: Fabrizio LaRocca, creative director; Guido Caroti, Siobhan O'Hare, art directors; Tina Malaney, Chie Ushio, Ann McBride, Jessica Walsh, designers; Melanie Marin, senior picture editor

Cover Photo: (Deadman's Bay, Peter Islands, British Virgin Islands): Karl Weatherly/ Photographer's Choice, RF/Getty Images

Production Manager: Angela L. McLean

ISBN 978-1-4000-0846-9

ISSN 1090-7343

SPECIAL SALES

This book is available at special discounts for bulk purchases for sales promotions or premiums. Special editions, including personalized covers, excerpts of existing books, and corporate imprints, can be created in large quantities for special needs. For more information, write to Special Markets/Premium Sales, 1745 Broadway, MD 6-2, New York, New York 10019, or e-mail specialmarkets@randomhouse.com.

AN IMPORTANT TIP & AN INVITATION

Although all prices, opening times, and other details in this book are based on information supplied to us at press time, changes occur all the time in the travel world, and Fodor's cannot accept responsibility for facts that become outdated or for inadvertent errors or omissions. So **always confirm information when it matters,** especially if you're making a detour to visit a specific place. Your experiences—positive and negative— matter to us. If we have missed or misstated something, **please write to us.** We follow up on all suggestions. Contact the Caribbean Ports of Call editor at editors@fodors.com or c/o Fodor's at 1745 Broadway, New York, NY 10019.

PRINTED IN THE UNITED STATES OF AMERICA

10 9 8 7 6 5 4 3 2 1

Be a Fodor's Correspondent

Your opinion matters. It matters to us. It matters to your fellow Fodor's travelers, too. And we'd like to hear it. In fact, we need to hear it.

When you share your experiences and opinions, you become an active member of the Fodor's community. That means we'll not only use your feedback to make our books better, but we'll publish your names and comments whenever possible. Throughout our guides, look for "Word of Mouth," excerpts of your unvarnished feedback.

Here's how you can help improve Fodor's for all of us.

Tell us when we're right. We rely on local writers to give you an insider's perspective. But our writers and staff editors—who are the best in the business—depend on you. Your positive feedback is a vote to renew our recommendations for the next edition.

Tell us when we're wrong. We're proud that we update most of our guides every year. But we're not perfect. Things change. Hotels cut services. Museums change hours. Charming cafés lose charm. If our writer didn't quite capture the essence of a place, tell us how you'd do it differently. If any of our descriptions are inaccurate or inadequate, we'll incorporate your changes in the next edition and will correct factual errors at fodors.com immediately.

Tell us what to include. You probably have had fantastic travel experiences that aren't yet in Fodor's. Why not share them with a community of like-minded travelers? Maybe you chanced upon a beach or bistro or B&B that you don't want to keep to yourself. Tell us why we should include it. And share your discoveries and experiences with everyone directly at fodors.com. Your input may lead us to add a new listing or highlight a place we cover with a "Highly Recommended" star or with our highest rating, "Fodor's Choice."

Give us your opinion instantly at our feedback center at www.fodors.com/feedback. You may also e-mail editors@fodors.com with the subject line "Caribbean Ports of Call Editor." Or send your nominations, comments, and complaints by mail to Caribbean Ports of Call Editor, Fodor's, 1745 Broadway, New York, NY 10019.

You and travelers like you are the heart of the Fodor's community. Make our community richer by sharing your experiences. Be a Fodor's correspondent.

Bon voyage!

Tim Jarrell, Publisher

CONTENTS

ABOUT THIS BOOK

Our Ratings

Sometimes you find terrific travel experiences and sometimes they just find you. But usually the burden is on you to select the right combination of experiences. That's where our ratings come in.

As travelers we've all discovered a place so wonderful that its worthiness is obvious. And sometimes that place is so experiential that superlatives don't do it justice: you just have to be there to know. These sights, properties, and experiences get our highest rating, **Fodor's Choice** indicated by orange stars throughout this book.

Black stars highlight sights and properties we deem **Highly Recommended** places that our writers, editors, and readers praise again and again for consistency and excellence.

By default, there's another category: any place we include in this book is by definition worth your time, unless we say otherwise. And we will.

Disagree with any of our choices? Care to nominate a place or suggest that we rate one more highly? Visit our feedback center at www.fodors.com/feedback.

Budget Well

Hotel and restaurant price categories from ¢ to $$$$ are defined in the opening pages of each chapter. For attractions, we always give standard adult admission fees; reductions are usually available for children, students, and senior citizens. Want to pay with plastic? **AE, D, DC, MC, V** following restaurant and hotel listings indicate if American Express, Discover, Diners Club, MasterCard, and Visa are accepted.

Restaurants

Unless we state otherwise, restaurants are open for lunch and dinner daily. We mention dress only when there's a specific requirement and reservations only when they're essential or not accepted—it's always best to book ahead.

Hotels

Hotels have private bath, phone, TV, and air-conditioning and operate on the European Plan (aka EP, meaning without meals), unless we specify that they use the Breakfast Plan (BP, with a full breakfast), Continental Breakfast Plan (CP), or Modified American Plan (MAP, with breakfast and dinner daily), or Full American Plan (FAP, with three meals a day). We always list facilities but not whether you'll be charged an extra fee to use them, so when pricing accommodations, find out what's included.

Many Listings

★	Fodor's Choice
★	Highly recommended
⊠	Physical address
⊹	Directions
⬠	Mailing address
☎	Telephone
🖷	Fax
⊕	On the Web
✐	E-mail
⊡	Admission fee
☉	Open/closed times
Ⓜ	Metro stations
▭	Credit cards

Hotels & Restaurants

🏨	Hotel
⤵	Number of rooms
⚲	Facilities
🍽	Meal plans
✕	Restaurant
⟰	Reservations
⟍	Smoking
🆎	BYOB
✕🏨	Hotel with restaurant that warrants a visit

Outdoors

🏌	Golf
⛺	Camping

Other

☾	Family-friendly
⇨	See also
⊠	Branch address
☞	Take note

Cruise Primer

WORD OF MOUTH

"[K]eeping in mind that I would like to keep the cruise on a lower budget, I have a few questions being a first-time cruiser: 1) Is a room with a window important, or would it be better to pick a room on a middle to higher floor with no window? 2) Is there an advantage to booking on the phone vs online? 3) Is there an advantage to booking airfare through the cruise line . . .? Anything else I should consider before booking?"

—mmd1

By Linda Coffman

If you're considering a cruise but can't decide whether it's really for you, it's tempting to ask, "What's so special about a cruise vacation?" It's a good question. Until the age of the airplane, ocean travel was simply a means to get to your far-flung destination—often the only way. But even in the early decades of the 20th century, venerable ocean liners such as the *Normandie* offered the occasional round-trip cruise to an exotic locale.

Passengers on those earliest cruises didn't have a fun-in-the-sun mindset as they sailed to faraway ports. They sailed to broaden their horizons and learn about ports of call that couldn't be reached by overland travel. Perhaps they booked a cruise to Panama to observe the construction of the canal or, like the *Normandie*'s passengers, were bound for Brazil and the daring excitement of Carnival.

Regardless of *why* they were cruising, early cruisers steamed toward the unfamiliar with many fewer comforts than contemporary passengers enjoy. On the *Normandie*, air-conditioned comfort was available only in the ship's first-class dining room, though at least passengers could find relief from Rio's heat by taking a dip in one of the era's few outdoor swimming pools at sea. In those days, if an ocean liner had a permanent swimming pool, it was often indoors and deep in the hull.

Carnival Cruise Lines executives like to reminisce about the tiny "gyms" on their early ships, which were converted ocean liners, and then point to how far ship designs have evolved. I remember the old ships well. It was even difficult to find the casino on Carnival's first "Fun Ship" *Mardi Gras,* let alone locate the indoor swimming pool. That's hardly the case today. Designed for contemporary travelers and tastes, modern cruise ships carry passengers amid conveniences unheard of in the heyday of the North Atlantic ocean liner or even in the earliest vessels permanently dedicated to cruises. As more than 12 million passengers discovered when they went to sea in 2007, there's a lot to like on ships these days.

The allure of a modern sea cruise is its ability to appeal to a wide range of vacationers as a safe and convenient way to travel. Today's cruise ships are lively and luxurious floating resorts that offer something to satisfy the expectations of almost everyone. The first thing you'll find is that although cruise ships differ dramatically in the details and how they craft and deliver the cruise experience, most ships have the same basic features. And although the decisions and considerations in booking one cruise over another can be complex, the more you know about cruise travel in general, the better prepared you will be when it comes to making your choices.

BEFORE YOU GO

To expedite your preboarding paperwork, most cruise lines have convenient forms on their Web sites. As long as you have your reservation number, you can provide the required immigration information, pre-reserve shore excursions, and even indicate any special requests from the comfort of your home. Less "wired" cruise lines might mail preboarding paperwork to you or your travel agent for completion after you make your final payment and request that you return the forms by mail or fax. No matter how you submit them, be sure to make hard copies of any forms you fill out and bring them with you to the pier to smooth the embarkation process.

DOCUMENTS

It is every passenger's responsibility to have proper identification. If you arrive at the port without it, you may not be allowed to board, and the line will issue no fare refund. Most travel agents know the requirements and can guide you to the proper agency to obtain what you need if you don't have it.

Everyone must have proof of citizenship and identity to travel abroad. Effective June 1, 2009, travelers will be required to present a passport or other approved document denoting citizenship and identity for all land *and* sea travel into the United States. Like most rules, there is a confusing exception—U.S. citizens traveling within the Caribbean on closed-loop cruises (cruises that begin and end in the same port) will still be permitted to depart from or enter the U.S. with proof of identity, which includes a government-issued photo ID, such as a driver's license, along with proof of citizenship, such as a birth certificate. However, you may still be required to present a passport when you dock at a foreign port, depending on the islands or countries that your cruise ship is visiting. And if your cruise begins in one U.S. port and ends in a different port, you will be required to have a passport. Check with your cruise line to ensure you have the appropriate documents for the stops you'll be making on your cruise.

Even for cruises that begin and end in the same port, cruise lines strongly recommend that all passengers travel with a valid passport. That will enable you to fly from the U.S. to meet your ship at the first port should you miss the scheduled embarkation, as well as allow you to leave the ship without significant delays and complications before the cruise ends if you must fly back to the U.S. due to an emergency.

Children under the age of 18, when they are not traveling with both parents, almost always require a letter of permission from the absent parent(s). Airlines, cruise lines, and immigration agents can deny minor children initial boarding or entry to foreign countries without proper proof of identification and citizenship *and* a notarized permission letter from absent or noncustodial parents. Your travel agent or cruise line can help with the wording of such a letter.

WHAT TO PACK

In terms of your wardrobe, cruise wear falls into three categories: casual, informal, and formal. Cruise documents should include information indicating how many evenings fall into each category. You will know when to wear what by reading your ship's daily newsletter—each evening's dress code will be prominently announced.

For the day, you'll need casual wear. For warm-weather cruises, you'll typically need swimwear, a cover-up, and sandals for pool and beach. Time spent ashore touring and shopping calls for shorts topped with T-shirts or polo shirts and comfy walking shoes. Conservative is a rule to live by in the Caribbean (most Caribbean islands are very socially conservative), and mix-and-match will save room in your suitcase. Forget denim, which is too hot, and concentrate on lighter fabrics that will breathe in the Caribbean heat. Although jeans are allowed in the dining rooms of most mainstream ships, at night casual generally means khaki-type slacks and nice polo or sport shirts for men. Ladies' outfits are sundresses, skirts and tops, or pants outfits. By sticking to two or three complementary colors and a few accessories, you can mix up tops and bottoms for a different look every night.

Informal dress—sometimes called "resort" or "smart" casual—is a little trickier. It applies only to evening wear, and can mean different things depending on the cruise line. Informal for women is a dressier dress or pants outfit; for men it almost always includes a sport coat and sometimes a tie. Check your documents carefully.

Formal night means dressing up, but these days even that is a relative notion. You will see women in everything from simple cocktail dresses to elaborate glittering gowns. A tuxedo (either all black or with white dinner jacket) or dark suit is required for gentlemen. If you have been a "Mother-of-the-Bride" lately, chances are your outfit for the wedding is just perfect for formal night. For children, Sunday-best is entirely appropriate.

Men can usually rent their formal attire from the cruise line, and if they do so, it will be waiting when they board. Be sure to make these arrangements in advance; your travel agent can get the details from the cruise line. But if you are renting a tux, buy your own studs: a surefire way to spot a rented tuxedo is by the inexpensive studs that come with it. Also, many men with a little "girth" consider a vest more comfortable than a cummerbund.

An absolute essential for women is a shawl or light sweater. Aggressive air-conditioning can make public rooms uncomfortable, particularly if you are sunburned from a day at the beach.

Put things you can't do without—such as prescription medication, spare eyeglasses, toiletries, a swimsuit, and change of clothes for the first day—in your carry-on. Most cruise ships provide soap, shampoo, and conditioner, so you probably won't need those.

And plan carefully. In fact, we'd strongly advise you to make a list so you don't forget anything.

ACCESSIBILITY ISSUES

As recently as the early 1990s, "accessibility" on a cruise ship meant little more than a few inside staterooms set aside for passengers with mobility issues. Most public restrooms and nearly all en suite bathrooms had a "step-over" threshold. Newer ships are more sensitive to the needs of passengers with disabilities, but many older ships still have physical barriers in both cabins and public rooms. And once you get off the ship—particularly in some Caribbean ports—your problems will be compounded.

All cruise lines offer a limited number of staterooms designed to be wheelchair- and scooter-accessible. Booking a newer vessel will generally assure more choices. On newer ships, public rooms are generally more accessible, and more facilities have been planned with wheelchair users in mind. Auxiliary aids, such as flashers for the hearing impaired and buzzers for visually impaired passengers, as well as lifts for swimming pools and hot tubs, are available upon request. However, more than the usual amount of preplanning is necessary for smooth sailing if you have special needs.

For example, when a ship is unable to dock—as is the case in Grand Cayman, for instance—passengers are taken ashore on tenders that are sometimes problematic even for the able-bodied to negotiate under adverse conditions. Some people with limited mobility may find it difficult to embark or disembark the ship when docked due to the steep angle of gangways during high or low tide at certain times of day. In some situations, crew members may offer assistance that involves carrying guests, but if the sea is choppy when tendering is a necessity, that might not be an option.

Passengers who require continuous oxygen or have service animals have further hurdles to overcome. You can bring both aboard a cruise ship, but your service animal may not be allowed to go ashore with you if the port has strict laws regarding animal quarantines.

INSURANCE

We believe that comprehensive trip insurance is especially valuable if you're booking a very expensive or complicated trip (particularly to an isolated region) or if you're booking far in advance. Who knows what could happen six months down the road? But whether or not you get insurance has more to do with how comfortable you are assuming all that risk yourself.

Comprehensive travel policies typically cover trip-cancellation and interruption, letting you cancel or cut your trip short because of a personal emergency, illness, or, in some cases, acts of terrorism in your destination. Such policies also cover emergency evacuation and medical care. Some also cover you for trip delays because of bad weather or mechanical problems as well as for lost or delayed baggage. Another type of coverage to look for is financial default—that is, when your trip is disrupted because a tour operator, airline, or cruise line goes out of business. Generally you must buy this when you book your trip or shortly thereafter, and it's only available to you if your operator isn't on a list of excluded companies.

If you're going abroad, consider buying medical-only coverage at the very least. Neither Medicare nor some private insurers cover medical expenses anywhere outside of the United States (including time aboard a cruise ship, even if it leaves from a U.S. port). Medical-only policies typically reimburse you for medical care (excluding that related to preexisting conditions) and hospitalization abroad, and provide for evacuation. You still have to pay the bills and await reimbursement from the insurer, though.

Expect comprehensive travel insurance policies to cost about 4% to 7% or 8% of the total price of your trip (it's more like 8%–12% if you're over age 70). A medical-only policy may or may not be cheaper than a comprehensive policy. Always read the fine print of your policy to make sure that you are covered for the risks that are of most concern to you. Compare several policies to make sure you're getting the best price and range of coverage available.

U.S. Travel Insurers Access America (☎ *800/284–8300* ⊕ *www.access america.com*). **CSA Travel Protection** (☎ *800/711–1197* ⊕ *www.csatravel protection.com*). **HTH Worldwide** (☎ *610/254–8700 or 888/243–2358* ⊕ *www.hthworldwide.com*). **Travelex Insurance** (☎ *800/228–9792* ⊕ *www. travelex-insurance.com*). **Travel Guard International** (☎ *715/345–0505 or 800/826–4919* ⊕ *www.travelguard.com*). **Travel Insured International** (☎ *800/243–3174* ⊕ *www.travelinsured.com*).

ARRIVING AND EMBARKING

Most cruise-ship passengers fly to the port of embarkation. If you book your cruise far enough in advance, you'll be given the opportunity to purchase an air-and-sea package, which may, or may not, save you money on your flight. You might get a lower fare by booking your flight independently, so it's a good idea to check for the best fare available.

If you buy an air-and-sea package from your cruise line, a uniformed cruise-line agent will meet you (usually in the baggage claim area) to smooth your way from airport to pier. You will need to claim your own bags and give them to the transfer driver so they can be loaded on the bus. Upon arrival at the pier, luggage is automatically transferred to the ship for delivery to your cabin. The cruise line ground transfer system can also be available to independent fliers. However, be sure to ask your travel agent how much it costs; you may find that a taxi or shuttle service is less expensive and more convenient.

In addition to the busiest embarkation ports such as Miami, Fort Lauderdale, and New York City, cruises now leave from less-familiar port cities all around the East and Gulf coasts. Galveston, Texas, and Port Canaveral, Florida, have become major home ports in recent years and are considered now to be among the nation's top 10 cruise ports. Many people prefer to drive to these ports if they are close enough to home; happily, secure parking is always available, either within the port itself or nearby.

BOARDING

1

Once the planning, packing, and anticipation are behind them, veteran cruise passengers sometimes view embarkation day as anticlimactic. However, for first-time cruise travelers, embarking on their first ship can be more than exhilarating—it can be downright intimidating. What exactly can you expect?

CHECK-IN

Once inside the cruise terminal, you'll see a check-in line. Actual boarding time is often scheduled for noon, but some cruise lines will begin processing early arrivals and then direct them to a "holding" area. During check-in you will be asked to produce your documents and any forms you were sent to complete ahead of time, plus proof of citizenship and a credit card (to cover onboard charges). You are issued a boarding card that often also doubles as your stateroom "key" and shipboard charge card. At some point—either before you enter the check-in area or before proceeding to the ship—you and your hand luggage will pass through a security procedure similar to those at airports.

Check-in lines can be long, particularly at peak times. If check-in starts at noon but continues to 4 PM, you can expect lines to trail off as the boarding deadline approaches. Everyone is anxious to get on board and begin their vacation, so if you arrive at one of the busy periods, keep in mind that this is not the time to get cranky if you have to wait.

While the gangway is generally not removed until 30 minutes before sailing, U.S. government security regulations require cruise lines to submit certain passenger information to law enforcement authorities at least 60 minutes prior to departure. To meet that requirement, they must have the necessary information in their records at least 90 minutes before departure. If you arrive too late and your information is not in the system before the deadline, you run the risk being denied boarding even if the ship hasn't sailed.

BOARDING THE SHIP

Once boarding begins, you will inevitably have your first experience with the ship's photographer and be asked to pose for an embarkation picture. It only takes a second, so smile. Later, you'll find those photos for purchase in the ship's photo center.

Procedures vary somewhat once you are greeted by staff members lined up just inside the ship's hull; however, you'll have to produce your boarding card for the security officer. At some point—either at the check-in desk or when boarding the ship for the first time—you will be photographed for security purposes; your image will display when your boarding card is "swiped" into a computer as you leave and reboard the ship in ports of call. Depending on the cruise line, you will be directed to your cabin, or a steward will relieve you of your carry-on luggage and accompany you. Stewards on high-end cruise lines not only show you the way, but hand you a glass of champagne as a welcome-aboard gesture. However, if you board early, don't be surprised if you are told cabins are not "ready" for occupancy—passageways to accommodations may even be roped off. In that case you can explore the ship, have lunch, or simply relax until an announcement is made that you can go to your cabin.

ON BOARD

Check out your cabin to make sure that everything is in order. Try the plumbing and set the air-conditioning to the temperature you prefer. Your cabin may feel warm while docked but will cool off when the ship is underway. You should find a copy of the ship's daily schedule in the cabin. Take a few moments to look it over—you will want to know what time the muster drill takes place (a placard on the back of your cabin door will indicate directions to your emergency station; the drill will happen within the first 24 hours of your cruise), as well as meal hours and the schedule for various activities and entertainments.

Rented tuxedoes are either hanging in the closet or will be delivered sometime during the afternoon; bon voyage gifts sent by your friends or travel agent usually appear as well. Be patient if you are expecting deliveries, particularly on mega-ships. Cabin stewards participate in the ship's turnaround and are extremely busy, although yours will no doubt introduce himself at the first available opportunity. It will also be a while before your checked luggage arrives, so your initial order of business is usually the buffet, if you haven't already had lunch. Bring along the daily schedule to check over while you eat.

While making your way to the Lido buffet, you may see bar waiters offering trays of colorful and exotic drinks, often in souvenir glasses that you can keep. Beware—on most lines they are not complimentary! If you choose one, you will be asked to sign for it.

Do your plans for the cruise include booking shore excursions and indulging in spa treatments? The most popular tours sometimes sell out, and spas can be very busy during sea days, so your next stops should be the Shore Excursion Desk to book tours and the spa to make appointments.

Dining-room seating arrangements are another matter for consideration. Some people like to check the main dining room to determine where their table is located. If it is not to your liking, or if you requested a large table and find yourself assigned to a small one, you will want to see the head waiter. He or she will be stationed in a lounge with the seating charts handy to make changes. The daily schedule will indicate where and when to meet with him or her. If you plan to dine in the ship's specialty restaurant, make those reservations as soon as possible to avoid disappointment.

PAYING FOR THINGS ON BOARD

Let's step back a moment and take a look at what happened when you checked in at the pier. Because a cashless society prevails on cruise ships, an imprint was made of your credit card, or you had to place a cash deposit for use against your onboard charges. Then you were issued a charge card that usually doubles as your stateroom "key." Most onboard expenditures are charged to your shipboard account with your signature as verification, with the possible exception of casino gaming—even so, you can often get "cash advances" against your account from the casino cashier.

An itemized bill is provided at the end of the voyage listing your purchases. In order to avoid surprises, it is a good idea to set aside your charge slips and request an interim printout of your bill from the purser to ensure accuracy. Should you change your mind about charging onboard purchases, you can always inform the purser and pay in cash or traveler's checks instead. If your cash deposit was more than you spent, you will receive a refund.

TIPPING

One of the most delicate—yet frequently debated—topics of conversation among cruise passengers involves the matter of tipping. Who do you tip? How much? What's "customary" and "recommended?" Should parents tip the full amount for children or is just half adequate? Why do you have to tip at all?

When transfers to and from your ship are a part of your air-and-sea program, gratuities are generally included for luggage handling. In that case, do not worry about the interim tipping. However, if you take a taxi to the pier and hand over your bags to a stevedore, be sure to tip him. Treat him with respect and pass along at least $5.

During your cruise, room-service waiters generally receive a cash tip of $1 to $3 per delivery. A 15% to 18% gratuity will automatically be added to each bar bill during the cruise. If you use salon and spa services, a similar percentage might be added to the bills there as well. If you dine in a specialty restaurant, you may be asked to provide a one-time gratuity for the service staff.

There will be a "Disembarkation Talk" on the last day of the cruise that explains tipping procedures. If you are expected to tip in cash, small white "tip" envelopes will appear in your stateroom that day. If you tip in cash, you usually give the tip envelope directly to each person on the last night of the cruise, but this practice is becoming increasingly rare. Most cruise lines now either automatically add gratuities to passengers' onboard charge accounts or offer the option. If that suits you, then do nothing further. However, you are certainly free to adjust the amounts up or down to more appropriate levels or ask that the charge be removed altogether if you prefer distributing cash gratuities.

Tips generally add up to about $10 to $15 per person per day. You tip the same amount for each person who shares the cabin, including children, unless otherwise indicated.

DINING

All food, all the time? Not quite, but it is possible to literally eat away the day and most of the night on a cruise. A popular cruise directors' joke is, "You came on as passengers, and you will be leaving as cargo." Although it is meant in fun, it does contain a ring of truth.

Food—tasty and plentiful—is available 24 hours a day on most cruise ships, and the dining experience at sea has reached almost mythical proportions. Perhaps it has something to do with legendary midnight buffets, the absence of menu prices, or maybe it's the vast selection and availability.

RESTAURANTS

Every ship has at least one main restaurant and a Lido, or casual, buffet alternative. Increasingly important are specialty restaurants. Meals in the primary and buffet restaurants are included in the cruise fare, as are midday tea and snacks, late-night buffets, and most round-the-clock room service. Most mainstream cruise lines levy a surcharge for dining in alternative restaurants that may, or may not, also include a gratuity. With the exception of some connoisseur-wine-and-gourmet-food dining experiences, generally there is no additional charge on luxury cruise lines.

You may also find a pizzeria or a specialty coffee bar on your ship—increasingly popular favorites cropping up on ships old and new. Although pizza is complimentary, expect an additional charge for specialty coffees at the coffee bar and, quite likely, in the dining room as well. You will also likely be charged for sodas and drinks during meals other than iced tea, regular coffee, tap water, and fruit juice.

There is often a direct relationship between the cost of a cruise and the quality of its cuisine. The food is very sophisticated on some (mostly expensive) lines, among them Crystal, Cunard, Seabourn, SeaDream, Regent Seven Seas, and Silversea. In the more moderate price range, Celebrity Cruises has gained renown for its culinary stylings. The trend toward featuring specialty dishes and even entire menus designed by acclaimed chefs has spread throughout the cruise industry; however, on most mainstream cruise lines, the food is the quality that you would find in any good hotel banquet—perfectly acceptable but certainly not great.

DINNER SEATINGS

If your cruise ship has traditional seatings for dinner, the one decision that may set the tone for your entire cruise is your dinner seating. Which is best? Early dinner seating is generally scheduled between 6 and 6:30 PM, while late seating can begin from 8:15 to 8:45 PM. So the "best" seating depends on you, your lifestyle, and your personal preference.

Families with young children and older passengers often choose an early seating. Early seating diners are encouraged not to linger too long over dessert and coffee because the dining room has to be readied for late seating. Late seating is viewed by some passengers as more romantic and less rushed.

Cruise lines understand that strict schedules no longer satisfy the desires of all modern cruise passengers. Many cruise lines now include alternatives to the set schedules in the dining room, including casual dinner menus in their buffet facilities where more flexibility is allowed in dress and mealtimes. À la carte restaurants are showing up on more ships and offer yet another choice, though usually for an additional charge.

Open seating is primarily associated with more upscale lines; it allows passengers the flexibility to dine any time during restaurant hours and be seated with whomever they please.

Led by Norwegian Cruise Line and Princess Cruises, more contemporary and premium cruise lines, including Holland America Line, Royal Caribbean, and Carnival Cruise Lines are exploring adaptations of open seating to offer variety and a more personalized experience for their passengers. Most cruise lines also offer casual evening meals in the Lido buffet, some with limited table service.

CHANGING TABLES

Cruise lines will never guarantee that you receive your preferred dinner seating, and table assignments are generally not confirmed until embarkation; however, every effort is made to satisfy all guests. Should there be a problem, see the maître d' for assistance. Changes after the first evening are generally discouraged, so if you want to change your seating or table, meet with dining room staff and iron out problems on embarkation day. Check the daily program for time and location.

SPECIAL DIETS

Cruise lines make every possible attempt to ensure dining satisfaction. If you have special dietary considerations—such as low-salt, kosher, or food allergies—be sure to indicate them well ahead of time and check to be certain your needs are known by your waiter once on board. In addition to the usual menu items, "spa," vegetarian, low-calorie, low-carbohydrate, or low-fat selections, as well as children's menus are usually available. Requests for dishes not featured on the menu can often be granted if you ask in advance.

WINE

Wine typically costs about what you would expect to pay at a nice lounge or restaurant in a resort or a large U.S. city. Wine by the bottle is sometimes a more economical choice at dinner than ordering it by the glass. Any wine you don't finish will be kept for you and served the next night. Gifts of wine or champagne ordered from the cruise line (either by you, a friend, or your travel agent) can be taken to the dining room. Wine from any other source will incur a "corkage" fee of approximately $10 to $15 per bottle.

THE CAPTAIN'S TABLE

Legend has it that a nouveau riche passenger's response to an invitation to dine with the captain during a round-the-world cruise was, "I didn't shell out all those bucks to eat with the help!" Although there are some cruise passengers who decline invitations to dine at the captain's table, there are far more who covet such an experience. You will know you have been included in that exclusive coterie when an embossed invitation arrives in your stateroom on the day of a formal dinner. RSVP as soon as possible—if you are unable to attend, someone else will be invited in your place.

Who is invited? If you are a frequent repeat cruiser, the occupants of an owner's suite, or if you hail from the captain's hometown or speak his native language, you may be considered. Honeymoon couples are sometimes selected at random, as are couples celebrating a golden wedding

Drinking on Board

It's hard to avoid the ship's bars since they are social centers, but alcoholic drinks are not usually included in your cruise fare, and bar bills can add up quickly. Drinks at the captain's welcome-aboard cocktail party and at cocktail parties held specifically for past-cruisers are usually free. But if you pick up that boldly colored welcome-aboard cocktail as your ship pulls away from the dock, you may very well be asked to sign for it, and the cost will then be added to your shipboard account.

You should expect to pay about the same for a drink on board a cruise ship that you would pay in a bar at home: $5 to $6 for a domestic beer, $5 to $9 for a cocktail, $6 to $9 for a glass of wine, $1.25 to $2 for a soft drink. On virtually all ships, an automatic 15% gratuity will be added to your tab. What most people don't consider is that specialty coffees are also added to your bar tab, so if you order a cappuccino—and on some ships that applies even if it's in the dining room after dinner—you'll see a charge of $4 to $6 on your bar bill.

To save money on your bar bill, you can follow a few simple strategies. In lounges, request the less-expensive bar brands or the reduced-price drink-of-the-day. On some ships, discounted "beverage cards" for unlimited fountain soft drinks and/or a set number of mixed drinks are available.

In international waters there are, technically, no laws against teenage drinking, but almost all ships now require passengers to be over 21 to purchase alcoholic beverages.

anniversary. Attractive, unattached female passengers often round out an uneven number of guests. Requests made by travel agents on behalf of their clients sometimes do the trick.

ENTERTAINMENT

It's hard to imagine, but in the early years of cruise travel shipboard entertainment consisted of little more than poetry readings and recitals that exhibited the talents of fellow passengers. Those bygone days of sedate amusements in an intimate setting have been replaced by lavish showrooms where sequined and feathered showgirls strut their stuff on stage amid special effects not imagined in the past.

Seven-night Caribbean cruises usually include two original production shows. One of these might be a Las Vegas–style extravaganza and the other a best-of-Broadway show featuring old and new favorites from the Great White Way. Other shows highlight the talents of individual singers, dancers, magicians, comedians, and even acrobats. Don't be surprised if you are plucked from the audience to take the brunt of a comedian's jokes or act as the magician's temporary assistant. Sit in the front row if appearing onstage appeals to you.

Whether it is relegated to a late-afternoon interlude between bingo and dinner, or a featured evening highlight, the passenger talent show is often a "don't miss" production. From pure camp to stylishly slick, what passes for talent is sometimes surprising but seldom boring. Stand-up comedy is generally discouraged; however, passengers who want their performance skills to be considered should answer the call for auditions and plan to rehearse the show at least once.

Enrichment programs have become a popular pastime at sea. It may come as a surprise that port lecturers on many large contemporary cruise ships offer more information on shore tours and shopping than insight into the ports of call. If more cerebral presentations are important to you, consider a cruise on a line that features stimulating enrichment programs and seminars at sea. Speakers can include destination-oriented historians, popular authors, business leaders, radio or television personalities, and even movie stars.

LOUNGES AND NIGHTCLUBS

If you find the show lounge stage a bit intimidating and want to perform in a more intimate venue, look for karaoke. Singing along in a lively piano bar is another shipboard favorite for would-be crooners. Some passengers even take the place of the ship's pianist during breaks to demonstrate their skill.

Other lounges might feature easy-listening music, jazz, or combos for pre- and postdinner social dancing. Later in the evening, lounges pick up the pace with music from the 1950s and '60s; clubs aimed at a younger crowd usually have more contemporary dance music during the late-night hours.

CASINOS

A sure sign that your ship is in international waters is the opening of the casino. On most ships, lavish casinos pulsate with activity. The most notable exceptions are the family-oriented ships of Disney Cruise Line, which shun gaming in favor of more wholesome pastimes.

On ships that feature them, the rationale for locating casinos where most passengers must pass either through or alongside them is obvious—the unspoken allure of winning. In addition to slot machines in a variety of denominations, cruise-ship casinos might feature roulette, craps, and a variety of poker games—Caribbean Stud Poker, Let It Ride, Texas Hold 'Em, and blackjack, to name a few. Cruise lines strive to provide fair and professional gambling entertainment and supply gaming guides that set out the rules of play and betting limits for each game.

Casino hours vary based on the itinerary or location of the ship; most are required to close while in port, while others may be able to offer 24-hour slot machines and simply close table games. Every casino has a cashier, and you may be able to charge a cash advance to your onboard account, for a fee.

OTHER ENTERTAINMENT

Most vessels have a room for screening movies. On older ships and some newer ones, this is often a genuine cinema-style movie theater, while on other ships it may be just a multipurpose room. Over the course of a weeklong voyage a dozen films may be screened, each repeated several times. Theaters are also used for lectures, culinary demonstrations, religious services, and private meetings. The latest twist in video programming can be found on some Princess, Disney, and Carnival ships—huge outdoor LED screens where movies, music video concerts, news channels, and even the ship's activities are broadcast for passengers lounging poolside.

With a few exceptions, cruise ships equip their cabins with closed-circuit TVs showing movies (continuously on some newer ships), shipboard lectures, news channels, and regular programs (thanks to satellite reception). Pay-per-view movies (for a charge) are available on some ships. Ships with in-cabin VCRs or DVDs usually provide a selection of movies at no charge (a deposit is sometimes required).

Most medium and large ships have video arcades, and nearly all ships now have computer centers.

SPORTS AND FITNESS

Onboard sports facilities might include a court for basketball, volleyball, tennis—or all three—a jogging track, or even an in-line skating track. Some ships are even offering innovative and unexpected features, such as rock-climbing walls, bungee trampolines, and surfing pools on some Royal Caribbean ships. You'll even be able to bowl on certain NCL ships. For the less adventurous, there's always table tennis and shuffleboard.

Naturally, you will find at least one swimming pool and, possibly, several. Cruise-ship pools are generally on the small side—more appropriate for cooling off than doing laps—and the majority contain filtered salt water. But some are elaborate affairs with waterslides. Princess Grand-class ships have challenging, freshwater "swim against the current" pools for swimming enthusiasts who want to get their low-impact exercise while on board.

Golf is a perennial seagoing favorite of players who want to take their games to the next level and include the Caribbean's most beautiful and challenging courses on their scorecards. Shipboard programs can include clinics, use of full-motion golf cages, and even individual instruction from resident pros using state-of-the-art computer analysis. Once ashore, escorted excursions include everything needed for a satisfying round of play, including equipment and tips from the pro, and the ability to schedule tee times at exclusive courses.

FITNESS CENTERS

Cruise vacations can be hazardous to your waistline if you are not careful. Eating "out" for all meals and sampling different cuisines tend to pile on unaccustomed calories. But shipboard fitness centers have become ever more elaborate, offering state-of-the-art exercise machines, treadmills, and stair steppers, not to mention weights and weight machines. As a bonus, many fitness centers with floor-to-ceiling windows have the world's most inspiring sea views.

For guests who prefer a more social atmosphere as they burn off sinful chocolate desserts, there are specialized fitness classes for all levels of ability. High-impact, energetic aerobics are not for everyone, but any class that raises the heart rate can be toned down and tailored to

CLOSE UP

Health and Safety at Sea

1

Safety begins with you, the passenger. Once settled into your cabin, locate life vests and review posted emergency instructions. Make sure vests are in good condition and learn to secure them properly. If you have a physical infirmity that may hamper a speedy exit from your cabin, make certain the ship's purser knows, so that in an emergency he or she can quickly dispatch a crew member to assist you. If you're traveling with children, be sure that child-size life jackets are placed in your cabin.

Within 24 hours of embarkation, you'll be asked to attend a mandatory lifeboat drill. Do so and listen carefully. If you're unsure about how to use your vest, now is the time to ask. Only in the most extreme circumstances will you need to abandon ship—but it has happened. The time you spend learning the procedure may serve you well in a mishap.

In actuality, the greatest danger facing cruise-ship passengers is fire. All cruise lines must meet international standards for fire safety, which require sprinkler systems, smoke detectors, and other safety features. Fires on cruise ships are not common, but they do happen, and these rules have made ships much safer. You can do your part by *not* using an iron in your cabin and taking care to properly extinguish smoking materials. Never throw a lit cigarette overboard—it could be blown back into an opening in the ship and start a fire.

All large ships have an infirmary to deal with minor medical emergencies, but these infirmaries are not suitable for dealing with major procedures. The ship's doctor should be able to treat you as well as any general practitioner or clinic ashore for minor problems. For really complicated medical conditions, such as a heart attack or appendicitis, the ship's medical team evacuates passengers to the nearest hospital ashore. While at sea, evacuation expenses can rise as fast as the helicopter that whisks the patient away. You'll need supplementary insurance to cover evacuation costs.

Two of the most prevalent diseases that spread through cruise-ship populations are influenza and noroviruses that cause intestinal and stomach upsets. Annual influenza vaccination is the primary method for preventing influenza and its complications. But to prevent all kinds of infections—including noroviruses—frequent hand-washing is also essential; take advantage of the dispensers of hand-sanitizer, and use it when entering any dining room. Or slip into the restroom to wash your hands with soap and hot water.

individual capabilities. Stretching classes help you warm up for a light jog or brisk walk on deck, and there are even sit-for-fitness classes for mature passengers or those with delicate joints. Fees are usually charged for specialty classes, such as Pilates, spinning, and yoga. Personal trainers are usually on board to get you off on the right foot, also for a fee.

SPAS

With all the usual pampering and service in luxurious surroundings, simply being on a cruise can be a stress-reducing experience. Add to that the menu of spa and salon services at your fingertips and you have a recipe for total sensory pleasure. Spas have also become among the most popular of shipboard areas.

Some spa offerings sound good enough to eat. A Milk-and-Honey Hydrotherapy Bath, Coconut Rub and Milk Ritual Wrap or Float, and a Javanese Steam Wrap incorporating cinnamon, ginger, coffee, sea salt, and honey are just a few of the tempting items found on spa menus. Not quite as exotic sounding, other treatments and services are nonetheless therapeutic for the body and soul. Steiner Leisure is the largest spa and salon operator at sea (the company also operates the Mandara- and the Greenhouse-brand spas), with facilities on more than 100 cruise ships worldwide.

In addition to facials, manicures, pedicures, massages, and sensual body treatments, other hallmarks of Steiner Leisure are salon services and products for hair and skin. Founded in 1901 by Henry Steiner of London, a single salon prospered when Steiner's son joined the business in 1926 and was granted a Royal Warrant as hairdresser to Her Majesty Queen Mary in 1937. In 1956 Steiner won its first cruise-ship contract to operate the salon on board the ships of the Cunard Line. By the mid-1990s, Steiner Leisure began taking an active role in creating shipboard spas offering a wide variety of wellness therapies and beauty programs for both women and men.

SHIPBOARD SERVICES

COMMUNICATIONS

Just because you are out to sea does not mean you have to be out of touch. Ship-to-shore telephone calls can cost $5 to $15 a minute, so it makes more economic sense to use e-mail to remain in contact with your home or office. Most ships have basic computer systems, while some newer vessels offer more high-tech connectivity—even in-cabin hookups or wireless connections for either your own laptop computer or one you can rent on board. Expect charges in the 50¢- to $1-per-minute range for the use of these Internet services. Ships usually offer some kind of package so that you get a reduced per-minute price if you pay a fee up front.

The ability to use your own mobile phone from the high seas is a relatively new alternative that is gaining popularity. It's usually cheaper than using a cabin phone if your ship offers the service, but it can still cost up to $4 or $5 a minute. It's a rather ingenious concept, with the ship acting as a cell "tower" in international waters—you use your own cell phone and your own number when roaming at sea. If using your cell phone is essential, contact your mobile service carrier before leaving home to enable international roaming and dialing, and be sure to understand their roaming agreements to be certain that your carrier has one with your cruise line. When in port, depending on the

Crime on Ships

CLOSE UP

1

Crime aboard cruise ships has occasionally become headline news, thanks in large part to a few well-publicized cases. Most people never have any type of problem, but you should exercise the same precautions aboard ship that you would at home. Keep your valuables out of sight—on big ships virtually every cabin has a small safe. Don't carry too much cash ashore, use your credit card whenever possible, and keep your money in a secure place, such as a front pocket that's harder to pick. Single women traveling with friends should stick together, especially when returning to their cabins late at night. When assaults occur, it often comes to light that excessive drinking of alcohol is a factor. Be careful about befriending anyone, as you would anywhere, whether it's a fellow passenger or a member of the crew. Don't be paranoid, but do be prudent.

Your cruise is a wonderful opportunity to leave everyday responsibilities behind, but don't neglect to pack your common sense. After a few drinks it might seem like a good idea to sit on a railing or lean over the rail to get a better view of the ship's wake. Passengers have been known to fall. "Man overboard" is more likely to be the result of carelessness than criminal intent.

agreements your mobile service provider has established, you may be able to connect to local networks. Rates for using the maritime service, as well as any roaming charges from Caribbean islands, are established by your mobile service carrier and are worth checking into before you leave home. They can be substantial (i.e., up to $2 or $4 per minute); text messages are cheaper but are usually charged at the higher international roaming rate of 25¢ to 50¢ per message and will be charged separately, even if you have a text-message plan. Most GSM tri-band phones from the U.S. will work in the Caribbean if your carrier has a roaming agreement.

LAUNDRY AND DRY CLEANING

Most cruise ships offer valet laundry and pressing (and some also offer dry-cleaning) service. Expenses can add up fast, especially for laundry, since charges are per item and the rates are similar to those charged in hotels. If doing laundry is important to you and you do not want to send it out to be done, many cruise ships have a self-service laundry room (which usually features an iron and ironing board in addition to washer and dryer). If you book one of the top-dollar suites, laundry service may be included for no additional cost. Upscale ships, such as those in the Regent Seven Seas Cruises, Silversea Cruises, and Seabourn fleets, have complimentary self-service launderettes. On other cruise lines, such as Princess Cruises, Oceania Cruises, Carnival Cruise Lines, Disney Cruise Line, and Holland America Line (except Vista- and Signature-class ships), you can do your own laundry for about $3 or less per load; Norwegian Cruise Lines' laundry facilities are free, but you have to purchase your own laundry products. None of the vessels in the Royal Caribbean or Celebrity Cruises fleets has self-service laundry facilities.

SHORE EXCURSION DESK

Manned by a knowledgeable staff, the Shore Excursion Desk can not only book ship-sponsored tours, but may also be the place to learn more about ports of call and garner information to tour independently. Although staff members and the focus of their positions vary widely, the least you can expect is basic information and port maps. Happily, some shore excursion staff members possess a wealth of information and share it without reservation. On some ships the port lecturer may emphasize shopping and "recommended" merchants, with little to impart regarding sightseeing or the history and culture of ports.

DISEMBARKATION

All cruises come to an end eventually, and it hardly seems fair that you have to leave when it feels like your vacation has just begun, but leave you must. The disembarkation process actually begins the day before you arrive at your ship's home port. During that day your cabin steward delivers special luggage tags to your stateroom, along with customs forms and instructions.

The night before you disembark, you'll need to set aside clothing to wear the next morning when you leave the ship. Many people dress in whatever casual outfits they wear for the final dinner on board, or change into travel clothes after dinner. Also, do not forget to put your passport or other proof of citizenship, airline tickets, and medications in your hand luggage.

After you finish packing, attach your new luggage tags (they are color- or number-coded according to postcruise transportation plans and flight schedules). Follow the instructions provided and place the locked luggage outside your stateroom door for pickup during the hours indicated.

A statement itemizing your onboard charges is delivered before you arise on disembarkation morning. Plan to get up early enough to check it over for accuracy, finish packing your personal belongings, and vacate your stateroom by the appointed hour. Any discrepancies in your onboard account should be taken care of before leaving the ship, usually at the purser's desk.

Room service is not available on most ships on the last day; however, breakfast is served in the main restaurant as well as the buffet. After breakfast there is not much to do but wait comfortably in a lounge or on deck for your tag color or number to be called. Disembarkation procedures can sometimes be drawn out by passengers who are unprepared. This is no time to abandon your patience or sense of humor.

Remember that all passengers must meet with customs and immigration officials before disembarkation, either on the ship or in the terminal. Procedures vary and are outlined in your instructions. In some ports passengers must meet with the officials at a specified hour (usually very early) in an onboard lounge; in other ports, customs forms are collected in the terminal and passports/identification papers are examined there as well.

Once in the terminal, locate your luggage and proceed to your bus or taxi, or retrieve your vehicle from the parking lot.

CUSTOMS AND DUTIES

U.S. CUSTOMS

Before a ship docks, each individual or family must fill out a customs declaration. If your purchases total less than the limit for your destination, you will not need to itemize them. Be prepared to pay whatever duties are owed directly to the customs inspector, with cash or check. Be sure to keep receipts for all purchases; and you may be asked to show officials what you've bought.

U.S. Customs preclears ships sailing into and out of some ports—it's done on the ship before you disembark. In other ports you must collect your luggage from the dock, then stand in line to pass through the inspection point. This can take up to an hour.

ALLOWANCES

You're always allowed to bring goods of a certain value back home without having to pay any duty or import tax. There's also a limit on the amount of tobacco and liquor you can bring back duty-free, and some countries have separate limits for perfumes; for exact figures, check with your customs department. The values of so-called "duty-free" goods are included in these amounts. When you shop abroad—and in the Caribbean, this means all islands except for Puerto Rico, which is considered a part of the U.S. for customs purposes—save all your receipts, as customs inspectors may ask to see them as well as the items you purchased. If the total value of your goods is more than the duty-free limit, then you'll have to pay a tax (most often a flat percentage) on the value of everything beyond that limit.

Individuals entering the United States from the Caribbean are allowed to bring in $800 worth of duty-free goods for personal use ($1,600 from the U.S. Virgin Islands), including 1 liter of alcohol (2 liters if one was produced in the Caribbean and 5 liters from the USVI), one carton of cigarettes (or five if four were purchased in the U.S. Virgin Islands), and 100 non-Cuban cigars. Antiques and original artwork are also duty-free.

SENDING PACKAGES HOME

Although you probably won't want to spend your time looking for a post office, you can send packages home duty-free, with a limit of one parcel per addressee per day (except alcohol or tobacco products or perfume worth more than $5). You can mail up to $200 worth of goods for personal use; label the package "personal use" and attach a list of the contents and their retail value. If the package contains your used personal belongings, mark it "personal goods returned" to avoid paying duty on your laundry. You may also send up to $100 worth of goods as gifts, with the same limit of one parcel per addressee per day ($200 from the U.S. Virgin Islands); mark the package "unsolicited gift." Items you mailed do not affect your duty-free allowance on your return.

NONCITIZENS

Non–U.S. citizens who are returning home within hours of docking may be exempt from all U.S. Customs duties. Everything you bring into the United States must leave with you when you return home, though. When you reach your own country, you will have to pay duties there.

Cruising the Caribbean

WORD OF MOUTH

"To just select a cruise line without doing some research or talking to a knowledgeable cruise [travel agent] is just asking for trouble. Cruise lines are different. They are not all the same. They offer different passenger demographics, different activities, different service, etc."

—golfette

By Linda
Coffman

More cruise ships ply the waters of the Caribbean than any other spot on Earth. Some are huge ships carrying more than 3,000 passengers; some are "midsize" ships welcoming about 1,500 cruisers; and others are comparatively small ships on which you'll find yourself with 300 or fewer other passengers. There are fancy ships and party ships, ships with sails, ships that pride themselves on the numbers of ports they visit, and ships that provide so much activity right on board that you hardly have time or inclination to go ashore. In peak season it's not uncommon for thousands of passengers to disembark from several ships into a small island port on the same day—a phenomenon not always enjoyed by locals. With such an abundance of cruise ships in this area, however, you can choose the ship and the itinerary that suit you best.

CHOOSING YOUR CRUISE

Some of the best "islands" in the Caribbean are the ones that float and move—they are called cruise ships. Just as Caribbean islands have distinct histories and cultures, cruise ships also have individual personalities. Determined by their size, the year they were built, and their style, on one hand, they can be bold, brassy, and exciting—totally unlike home, but a great place to visit. Big ships offer stability and a huge variety of activities and facilities. On the other hand, small ships feel intimate, like private clubs or, more appropriately, personal yachts. For every big-ship fan there is someone who would never set foot aboard a "floating resort." Examine your lifestyle—there's sure to be a cruise ship to match your expectations.

After giving some thought to your itinerary and where in the Caribbean you might wish to go, the ship you select is the most vital factor in your Caribbean cruise vacation, since it will not only determine which islands you will visit, but also how you will see them. Big ships visit major ports of call such as St. Thomas, St. Maarten/St. Martin, Nassau, and San Juan; when they call at smaller islands with shallower ports, passengers must disembark aboard shore tenders (small boats that ferry dozens of passengers to shore at a time). Or they may skip these smaller ports entirely. Small and midsize ships can visit smaller islands, such as St. Barths, St. Kitts, or Tortola, more easily; passengers are often able to disembark directly onto the pier without having to wait for tenders to bring them ashore.

ITINERARIES

You'll want to give some consideration to your ship's Caribbean itinerary when you are choosing your cruise. The length of the cruise will determine the variety and number of ports you visit, but so will the type of itinerary and the point of departure. **Round-trip cruises** start and end at the same point and usually explore ports close to one another; **one-way cruises** start at one point and end at another and range farther afield.

Almost all cruises in the Caribbean are round-trip cruises. On Caribbean itineraries you often have a choice of U.S. mainland departure points. Ships sailing out of San Juan can visit up to five ports in seven days, while cruises out of Florida can reach up to four ports in the same length of time. The Panama Canal can also be combined with a Caribbean cruise: the 50-mi (83-km) canal is a series of locks, which make up for the height difference between the Caribbean and the Pacific. Increasingly popular are partial transit cruises that enter the Panama Canal, anchor in Gatún Lake for a short time, and depart through the same set of locks.

EASTERN CARIBBEAN ITINERARIES

Eastern Caribbean itineraries consist of two or three days at sea as well as stops at some of the Caribbean's busiest cruise ports. A typical cruise will usually take in three or four ports of call, such as St. Thomas in the U.S. Virgin Islands, San Juan, or St. Maarten/St. Martin, along with a visit to the cruise line's "private" island for beach time. Every major cruise line has at least two of those popular islands on its itineraries. Some itineraries might also include others, such as Tortola, Dominica, Barbados, St. Kitts, or Martinique.

WESTERN CARIBBEAN ITINERARIES

Western Caribbean itineraries embarking from Galveston, Ft. Lauderdale, Miami, Port Canaveral, New Orleans, Mobile, or Tampa might include Belize, Cozumel or the Costa Maya Cruise Port in Mexico, Key West, Grand Cayman, or Jamaica—all perfect choices for passengers who enjoy scuba diving and snorkeling and look forward to exploring Mayan ruins. Ships often alternate itineraries in the Western Caribbean with itineraries in the Eastern Caribbean on a weekly basis, offering the ability to schedule a 14-night back-to-back cruise without repeating ports.

SOUTHERN CARIBBEAN ITINERARIES

Southern Caribbean cruises tend to be longer in duration, with more distant ports of call. They often originate in a port that is not on the U.S. mainland. Embarking in San Juan, for example, allows you to reach the lower Caribbean on a seven-day cruise with as many as four or five ports of call. Southern Caribbean itineraries might leave Puerto Rico for the Virgin Islands, Guadeloupe, Grenada, Curaçao, Barbados, Antigua, St. Lucia, Martinique, or Aruba. Smaller ships leave from embarkation ports as far south as Bridgetown, Barbados, and cruise through the Grenadines. Every major cruise line offers some Southern Caribbean itineraries, but these cruises aren't as popular as Western and Eastern Caribbean cruises.

OTHER ITINERARIES

In recent years shorter itineraries have grown in appeal to time-crunched and budget-constrained travelers. If you are planning your first cruise in the tropics, a short sailing to the Bahamas allows you to test your appetite for cruising before you take a chance on a longer and more expensive cruise. Embarking at Fort Lauderdale, Miami, Jacksonville, or Port Canaveral, you will cruise for three to five days, taking in at least one port of call (usually Nassau or Freeport in the Bahamas) and possibly a visit to a "private" island or Key West. Four- and five-night cruises may also include a day at sea. Cruises also depart from ports farther north on the east coast; you might depart from Charleston, Baltimore, or New York City and cruise to Bermuda or the Bahamas.

WHEN TO GO

Average year-round temperatures throughout the Caribbean are 78°F–85°F, with a low of 65°F and a high of 95°F; downtown shopping areas always seem to be unbearably hot. Low season runs from approximately mid-September through mid-April. Many travelers, especially families with school-age children, make reservations months in advance for the most expensive and most crowded summer months and holiday periods; however, with the many new cruise ships that have entered the market, you can often book fairly close to your departure date and still find room, although you may not get exactly the kind of cabin you would prefer. A summer cruise offers certain advantages: temperatures are virtually the same as in winter (cooler on average than in parts of the U.S. mainland), island flora is at its most dramatic, the water is smoother and clearer, and although there is always a breeze, winds are rarely strong enough to rock a ship. Some Caribbean tourist facilities close down in summer, however, and many ships move to Europe, Alaska, or the northeastern United States.

Hurricane season runs a full six months of the year—from June 1 through November 30. Although cruise ships stay well out of the way of these storms, hurricanes and tropical storms—their less-powerful relatives—can affect the weather throughout the Caribbean for days, and damage to ports can force last-minute itinerary changes.

CRUISE COSTS

The average daily price for Caribbean itineraries varies dramatically depending on several circumstances. The cost of a cruise on a luxury line such as Silversea or Seabourn may be three to four times the cost of a cruise on a mainstream line such as Carnival or even premium lines like Princess. When you sail will also affect your costs: published brochure rates are usually highest during the peak summer season and holidays. When snow blankets the ground and temperatures are in single digits, a

Saving Money on Your Cruise Fare

You can save on your cruise fare in several ways. Obviously, you should shop around. Some travel agents will discount cruise prices, though this is becoming a thing of the past. One thing never changes—do not ever, under any circumstances, pay brochure rate. You can do better, often as much as half off published fares. These are a few simple strategies you can follow:

■ **Book early:** Cruise lines discount their cruises if you book early, particularly during the annual "Wave" season between January and March.

■ **Cruise during the off-season:** If you take a cruise during the later months of hurricane season (especially October and November) or the period between Thanksgiving and Christmas, you'll often find specials.

■ **Book late:** Sometimes you can book a last-minute cruise at substantial savings if the ship hasn't filled all its cabins.

■ **Choose accommodations with care:** Cabins are usually standardized, and location determines the fare. Selecting a lower category can result in savings while giving up nothing in terms of cabin size and features.

■ **Book a "guarantee":** You won't be able to select your own cabin because the cruise line will assign you one in the category you book, but a "guarantee" fare can be substantially lower than a regular fare.

■ **Cruise with friends and family:** Book a minimum number of cabins, and your group can generally receive a special discounted fare.

■ **Reveal your age and affiliations:** Fare savings may be available for seniors and members of certain organizations, as well as cruise-line stockholders.

■ **Cruise often:** Frequent cruisers usually get discounts from their preferred cruise lines.

Caribbean cruise can be a welcome respite and less expensive than land resorts, which often command top dollar in winter months.

Solo travelers should be aware that single cabins have virtually disappeared from cruise ships. Taking a double cabin can cost twice the advertised per-person rates (which are based on double occupancy). Some cruise lines will find same-sex roommates for singles; each then pays the per-person, double-occupancy rate.

EXTRAS

In addition to the cost of your cruise there are further expenses to consider, such as airfare to the port city. These days, virtually all cruise lines offer air add-ons, which are sometimes, but not always, less expensive than the lowest available airline fare. Shore excursions can also be a substantial expense; the best shore excursions are not cheap. But if you skimp too much on your excursion budget you'll deprive yourself of an important part of the Caribbean cruising experience. Finally, there will be many extras added to your shipboard account during the cruise, including drinks (both alcoholic and nonalcoholic), activity fees (you pay to use that golf simulator), dining in specialty restaurants, spa services, and even cappuccino and espresso on most ships. These add-ons are no longer nominal fees, either; you pay top-dollar for most extras onboard mainstream ships, and the average post-cruise bill may be as much as 50% of the base cost of your cruise.

TIPPING

Tipping is another add-on. At the end of the cruise, it's customary to tip your room steward, dining room waiter, and the person who buses your table. You should expect to pay an average of $10 to $15 per person per day in tips. Most major cruise lines are moving away from the traditional method of tipping the service staff in cash at the end of the cruise, instead adding the recommended amount per day to your onboard account to cover tips, which you may adjust upward or downward according to the level of service you receive. Bar bills generally include an automatic 15%–18% gratuity, so the one person you don't need to tip is your bartender. Some cruise lines have gratuities-included policies, though some passengers tip for any extra services received anyway. Each cruise line offers guidelines.

CRUISE LINES

Seated in an airplane after a week of enjoying an exceptionally nice cruise, I overheard the couple behind me discussing their "dreadful" cruise vacation. What a surprise when they mentioned the ship's name. It was the one I'd just spent a glorious week on. I never missed a meal; they hated the food. My cabin was comfortable and cheery, if not large; their identical accommodations resembled a "cave." One size definitely does not fit all in cruising. What's appealing to one passenger may be unacceptable to another. Ultimately, most cruise complaints arise from passengers whose expectations were not met. The couple I eavesdropped on were on the wrong cruise line and ship for them.

I enjoy cruises. Some have suited me more than others, but I've never sailed on a cruise that was completely without merit. Make no mistake about it: cruise lines have distinct personalities, but not all luxury or mainstream cruise lines are alike, although they will share many basic similarities. The cruise industry is a fluid one—that means that when new features are introduced, they may not be found on all ships, even those within the same cruise line. For instance, you won't find an ice-skating rink on any but the biggest Royal Caribbean ships. However, most cruise lines attempt to standardize the overall experience throughout their fleets, which is why you'll find a waterslide on every Carnival ship.

Just as trends and fashion evolve over time, cruise lines embrace the ebb and flow of change. To keep pace with today's lifestyles, some cruise lines strive to include something that will appeal to everyone on their ships. Others focus on narrower elements and are more traditional. Today's passengers have higher expectations, and they sail on ships that are far superior to their predecessors. And they often do so at a much lower comparable fare than in the past.

So which cruise line is best? Only you can determine which is best for you. You won't find ratings by Fodor's—either quality stars or value scores. Why? Think of those people seated behind me on the airplane. Ratings are personal and heavily weighted to the reviewer's opinion. Your responsibility is to select the right cruise for you—no one knows your expectations better than you do yourself. It's your time, money, and vacation that are at stake. No matter how knowledgeable your travel agent it, how sincere your friends are, or what any expert can tell you, you are the only one who really knows what you like. The short wait for a table might not bother you because you would prefer a casual atmosphere with open seating; however, some people want the security of a set time at an assigned table served by a waiter who gets to know their preferences. You know what you are willing to trade off in order to get what you want.

The following cruise line profiles offer a general idea of what you can expect in terms of overall experience, quality, and service from each major cruise line that operates in the Caribbean and the Bahamas. You will want to compare the features of several cruise lines to determine which ones come closest to matching your needs. Then narrow them down further to a few that appeal most to you. Keep in mind that not all ships belonging to the cruise lines described in the following profiles are deployed in the Caribbean year-round; some head for Alaska and Europe during summer months; others call port cities on the Pacific coast their home for part of the year.

LUXURY CRUISE LINES
Comprising only 5% of the market, the exclusive luxury cruise lines, which include Crystal, Cunard, Regent Seven Seas, Seabourn, SeaDream, Silversea, and Windstar, offer high staff-to-guest ratios for personal service, superior cuisine in a single seating (except Crystal, with two assigned seatings and Cunard, with dual-class dining assignments), and a highly inclusive product with few onboard charges. These small and midsize ships offer much more space per passenger than you will find on the mainstream lines' vessels. Lines differ in what they emphasize, with some touting luxurious accommodations and entertainment and others focusing on exotic destinations and onboard enrichment.

If you consider travel a necessity rather than a luxury and frequent posh resorts, then you will appreciate the extra attention and the higher level of comfort that luxury cruise lines offer.

Itineraries on these ships often include the big casino and most popular island beach resorts, but luxury ships also visit some of the more uncommon Caribbean destinations. With a shallow draft and intimate size, the smaller luxury ships can visit such ports as Anguilla, St. Barths, Tobago, and Jost Van Dyke and Virgin Gorda in the British Virgin Islands.

MAINSTREAM CRUISE LINES
More than 85% of the Caribbean is covered by nearly a dozen mainstream cruise lines. They offer the advantage of something for everyone and nearly every available sports facility imaginable. Some ships even

have ice-skating rinks, 18-hole miniature golf courses, bowling alleys, and rock-climbing walls.

Generally speaking, the mainstream lines have two basic ship sizes— large cruise ships and mega-ships—in their fleets. These cruise ships have plentiful outdoor deck space, and many have a wraparound outdoor promenade deck that allows you to stroll or jog the ship's perimeter. In the newest vessels, traditional meets trendy. You'll find atrium lobbies and expansive sun and sports decks, picture windows instead of portholes, and cabins that open onto private verandahs. For all their resort-style innovations, they still feature cruise-ship classics—afternoon tea, complimentary room service, and lavish pampering. The smallest ships carry 1,000 passengers or fewer, while the largest accommodate more than 3,000 passengers and are filled with diversions.

If you're into big, bold, brassy, and nonstop activity, these huge ships offer it all. The centerpiece of most mega-ships is a 3-, 5-, or even 11-story central atrium. However, these giant vessels are most readily distinguished by their profile: the boxy hull and superstructure rise as many as 14 stories out of the water and are capped by a huge sun- or sports deck with a jogging track and one or more swimming pools. Some mega-ships have a traditional wraparound promenade deck. Picture windows are standard equipment, and cabins in the top categories have private verandahs. From their casinos and discos to their fitness centers, everything is bigger and more extravagant than on other ships. You may want to rethink a cruise aboard one of these ships if you want a little downtime, since you'll be joined by 1,500 to 3,000 fellow passengers.

OTHER CRUISE LINES

A few small cruise lines sail through the Caribbean and offer boutique to nearly bed-and-breakfast experiences. Notably, Cruise West and Star Clippers appeal to passengers who eschew mainstream cruises. Most of these niche vessels accommodate 200 or fewer passengers, and their focus is on soft adventure. Cruising between nearby ports and anchoring out so passengers can swim and snorkel directly from the ship, their itineraries usually leave plenty of time for exploring and other activities on- or offshore. Many of these cruises schedule casual enrichment talks that often continue on decks, at meals, and during trips ashore.

AZAMARA CRUISES

"The adventuresome (yet pampered) soul has met its match" is the catchy new slogan for this ultra-premium cruise line newly launched by parent company Royal Caribbean in 2007. The line is comprised of two ships, both built for now-defunct Renaissance Cruises and refitted for the deluxe-cruise crowd. Designed to offer exotic, destination-driven itineraries, Azamara offers a more-intimate onboard experience, while allowing access to the more unusual ports of call experienced travelers want to visit.

Enrichment programs, from culinary demonstrations to seminars by guest speakers and experts on a wide variety of topics, are some of the best on offer. The ships are designated resort casual, so there is no necessity to weigh down your luggage with formal attire—even though your butler is on hand to unpack for you. Evening entertainment leans toward sophisticated cabaret and jazz. Azamara ships are some of the most smoke-free at sea. Only two small sections are designated for smokers—one in a section of the observation lounge and the other in a forward area of the pool deck. No other areas on the ships allow smoking, including cabins and balconies.

Your Shipmates. Azamara is designed to appeal to discerning travelers, primarily American couples of any age who appreciate a high level of service in an unstructured atmosphere. The ships are not family oriented and do not have facilities or programs for children.

Food. Expect all the classic dinner favorites but with an upscale twist, such as gulf shrimp with cognac and garlic, or a filet mignon with black truffle sauce. In addition to the open-seating main dining room, each Azamara ship offers two specialty restaurants: the Mediterranean-influenced Aqualina and the stylish steak-and-seafood restaurant Prime C. While complimentary, the specialty restaurants require reservations. Daily in-cabin afternoon tea service and delivery of canapés are available to all passengers.

Fitness and Recreation. In addition to a well-equipped gym and an outdoor jogging track, Azamara's fitness program includes yoga at sunset, Pilates, and access to an onboard wellness consultant. Both ships offer a full menu of spa treatments, an outdoor spa relaxation lounge, and an aesthetics suite featuring acupuncture, laser hair removal, and micro-dermabrasion.

Service and Tipping. Gracious and polished service throughout the ships affords everyone an exclusive experience. Azamara offers butler service in every stateroom and suite. Gratuities are automatically charged to onboard accounts at the daily rate of $12.25 per person per day. Guests in suites experience superior Head Butler service in addition to Butler & Stateroom Attendant service and are charged an additional gratuity of $4 per person, per day. Amounts may be adjusted according to the level of service received. A standard 15% gratuity is added to beverage charges. It is recommended that a $5 per person gratuity be extended when dining in the specialty restaurants.

Contact **Azamara Cruises** ☎*877/999–9553* ⊕*www.azamaracruises.com.*

CARNIVAL CRUISE LINES

The world's largest cruise line originated the "Fun Ship" concept in 1972 with the relaunch of an aging ocean liner that got stuck on a sandbar during its maiden voyage. Sporting red-white-and-blue flared funnels, which are easily recognized from afar, new ships are continuously added to the fleet and rarely deviate from a successful pattern. Decor tends to be over the top; each ship features theme public rooms and huge casinos, spas, and lavish entertainment in massive show lounges.

Cabins are spacious and comfortable, often as much as 50% larger than on other ships in this price category, and feature the "Carnival Comfort

Bed" sleep system consisting of plush mattresses, luxury duvets, high-quality linens, and cushy pillows.

Your Shipmates. Carnival's passengers are mostly American couples in their mid-30s to mid-50s. During holidays and school vacation periods you'll see many families with kids on board. "Camp Carnival" offers year-round programs for children and teens from age 2 to 17. Daytime group babysitting is offered for infants two and under until noon on all port days, as well as from 10 PM to 3 AM, when slumber party–style group babysitting is available for ages 4 months to 11 years. As long as diapers and supplies are provided, toddlers do not have to be toilet trained to participate.

Food. Carnival ships have both flexible dining options and casual alternative restaurants. While the tradition of two set meal times for dinner prevail on Carnival ships, the line is experimenting with an open-seating concept, which, if successful, will be implemented fleet-wide. Upscale supper clubs on the newest ships serve cuisine comparable to high-end steak houses and seafood restaurants ashore. "Georges Blanc Signature Selections" expand main dining room, Lido restaurant, and Supper Club menus with a variety of gourmet-quality choices. In addition to the regular menu, vegetarian, low-calorie, low-carbohydrate, low-salt, no-sugar, and children's selections are available. If you don't feel like dressing up for dinner, the Lido buffet serves full meals and excellent pizza.

Fitness and Recreation. Carnival's trademark spas and fitness centers are some of the largest and best equipped at sea. State-of-the-art cardiovascular and strength-training equipment, a jogging track, and basic exercise classes are available at no charge in the fitness centers. There's a fee for personal training and specialized classes such as yoga and Pilates.

Service and Tipping. Service on Carnival ships is friendly but not polished. Stateroom attendants are not only recognized for their attention to cleanliness, but also for their expertise in creating towel animals that appear most nights during turn-down service. Gratuities of $10 per passenger, per day, are automatically added to onboard accounts. A 15% gratuity is automatically added to bar and beverage tabs.

Contact Carnival Cruise Lines ☎ *305/599–2600 or 800/227–6482* ⊕ *www. carnival.com.*

CELEBRITY CRUISES

Founded in 1989, Celebrity has gained a reputation for fine food and professional service. The cruise line has built premium, sophisticated ships and developed signature amenities, including a specialty coffee shop, martini bar, large standard staterooms with generous storage, spas, and butler service for passengers booking the top suites. ConciergeClass makes certain premium ocean-view and balcony staterooms almost the equivalent of suites in terms of amenities and service.

Entertainment choices range from Broadway-style productions, captivating lounge shows, and lively discos to Monte Carlo–style casinos and specialty lounges. Multimillion-dollar art collections grace the entire fleet, which merged with Royal Caribbean International in 1997.

Your Shipmates. Celebrity caters to Americans, primarily couples from their mid-30s to mid-50s. During summer months and holiday periods you'll see many families with kids aboard. Each vessel has a dedicated playroom and offers planned activities for children and teens ages 3 to 17, plus Toddler Time for parents and their children under age 3. Some activities have additional fees; evening in-cabin babysitting can also be arranged for a fee.

Food. In early 2007 Celebrity announced plans to advance its already distinguished fleetwide culinary program to the next level. Las Vegas–based Blau & Associates, a strategic restaurant planning and development firm, now consults on shipboard cuisine on all ships. Alternative restaurants on some ships offer fine dining in classic ocean-liner splendor.

Fitness and Recreation. Celebrity's fitness centers and AquaSpa by Elemis are some of the most tranquil and nicely equipped at sea. State-of-the-art exercise equipment, a jogging track, and some fitness classes are available at no charge. Spa treatments include a variety of massages, body wraps, and facials. Each ship has an Acupuncture at Sea program administered by a specialist in Oriental medicine. Hair and nail services are offered in the salons.

Service and Tipping. Service on Celebrity ships is unobtrusive and polished. ConciergeClass adds an unexpected level of service and amenities that are usually reserved for passengers in top-category suites on other premium cruise lines. Gratuities can be added to shipboard accounts or personally distributed in cash by passengers on the last night of the cruise. Suggested guidelines are per person, per day: each waiter and cabin steward $3.50 ($4 in Concierge class); butler: $3.50 (suites only); assistant waiter $2; assistant chief housekeeper 50¢; assistant maître d' $1. An automatic gratuity of 15% is added to all beverage tabs.

Contact **Celebrity Cruises** ☎ *800/647–2251* ⊕ *www.celebritycruises.com.*

COSTA CRUISES

The Genoa-based Costa Crociere, parent company of Costa Cruises, had been in the shipping business for more than 100 years and in the passenger business for almost 50 years when Carnival Corporation gained sole ownership of the line in 2000, but the ships retain their original flavor. Costa's Italian-inspired vessels bring the Mediterranean vitality of *La Dolce Vita* to far-flung regions of the Caribbean. The ships are a combination of classic and modern design. A new vessel-building program has brought Costa ships into the 21st century with innovative, large-ship designs that reflect their Italian heritage and style without overlooking the amenities expected by modern cruisers.

Festive shipboard activities include games of boccie and a wacky toga party, yet there is also a nod to the traditional cruise-ship entertainment expected by North Americans. Supercharged social staffs work overtime to get everyone in the mood and encourage everyone to be a part of the action.

Your Shipmates. Passengers tend to be a little older than average—the average age is 54—and have an interest in all things Italian. Up to 80% of passengers are North Americans, and many of them are of Italian descent. You don't find a lot of first-time cruisers on Costa ships. Youth programs provide daily age-appropriate activities for children age 3 to 17. Group evening babysitting for youngsters ages 3 and up (children must be toilet trained) is available on request for a fee.

Food. Dining features regional Italian cuisines, a variety of pastas, chicken, beef, and seafood dishes, as well as authentic pizza. Costa dining is notable for its delicious, properly prepared pasta courses. Vegetarian and healthy diet choices are also offered. Alternative dining is by reservation only in the upscale supper clubs, which serve choice steaks and seafood from a Tuscan Steakhouse menu as well as traditional Italian specialties. Costa chefs celebrate the tradition of several lavish midnight buffets during Caribbean cruises.

Fitness and Recreation. Costa places continuing emphasis on wellness and sybaritic pleasures. Spa treatments include a variety of massages, body wraps, and facials. Hair and nail services are available in the salons. State-of-the-art exercise equipment in the terraced gym, a jogging track, and basic fitness classes for all levels of ability are available.

Service and Tipping. Service in dining areas can be spotty and rushed, but is adequate—if not always overly friendly. Gratuities are added to onboard accounts in the following amounts: $10 per adult per day for cruises up to eight nights; $7.50 per adult per day on longer cruises; 50% of that amount for teens between the ages of 14 and 17; and no charge for children under the age of 14. A 15% is automatically added to all beverage tabs.

Contact **Costa Cruises** ☎ 954/266–5600 or 800/462–6782 ⊕ www.costa cruises.com.

CRYSTAL CRUISES

Crystal's midsize ships stand out for their modern design, amenities, and spaciousness. Built to deliver the first-rate service and amenities expected from a luxury line, these vessels nevertheless carry upward of 900 passengers—and have many big-ship facilities. Beginning with ship designs based on the principles of feng shui, no detail is too small to overlook to provide passengers with the best imaginable experience.

Crystal ships have long set standards for pampering—one reason these vessels often spend several days at sea rather than in port. To the typical litany of cruise-ship diversions, Crystal adds enrichment opportunities that include destination-oriented lectures and talks by scholars, political figures, and diplomats; hands-on classes in music and art; and deluxe theme cruises that emphasize such topics as food and wine or the fine arts.

Your Shipmates. Affluent, well-traveled couples, from their late-30s to retirees, are typical. While the cruises are adult-oriented, there are dedicated facilities for children from 3 to 17 that are staffed for some sailings, especially during holiday periods and the summer season; however, Crystal limits the number of children under three and does not allow infants less than six months of age without a signed waiver of parental consent.

Food. The food is a good enough reason to book a Crystal cruise. Dining in the main restaurants is an event starring Continental-inspired cuisine served by European-trained waiters. Off-menu requests are honored when possible, and special dietary considerations are handled with ease. Unlike most luxury lines, Crystal still has only two assigned dinner seatings. Casual poolside dining from the grills is offered on some evenings in a relaxed, no-reservations-required option. A variety of hot and cold hors d'oeuvres are served in bars and lounges every evening before dinner and again during the wee hours. Where service and the dishes really shine are in the specialty restaurants; each ship has Asian-inspired and Italian specialty restaurants.

Fitness and Recreation. Large spas offer innovative treatments. Fitness centers feature a range of exercise and weight-training equipment and workout areas for aerobics classes, plus complimentary yoga and Pilates. Utilizing Le Monde Life Fitness bikes, Crystal ships offer "Tour de Spin," a complimentary indoor cycling program. In addition, golfers enjoy extensive shipboard facilities, including a driving-range practice cage and putting green.

Service and Tipping. Crystal's European-trained staff members provide gracious service in an unobtrusive manner. Tips are either personally distributed by passengers on the last night of the cruise or charged to onboard accounts. Suggested guidelines for stateroom and dining service gratuities (per person, per day) are: stewardess $5 (single travelers, $6 per day); senior waiter $5; waiter $3; butler (Penthouse Decks) $4. For specialty restaurants, the suggested gratuity is $7 per person per dinner. A 15% gratuity is automatically added to bar checks; the same is suggested for spa and beauty treatments.

Contact **Crystal Cruises** ☎ 310/785–9300 or 888/799–4625 ⊕ www.crystal cruises.com.

CUNARD LINE

One of the world's most distinguished names in ocean travel since 1840, Cunard Line has a history of deluxe transatlantic crossings and worldwide cruising that is legendary for comfortable accommodations, excellent cuisine, and personal service. Though the line is now owned by Carnival Corporation, its high-end ships retain a distinctly British sensibility. Cunard offers a short season of Caribbean cruises, which are highly prized by fans of the line.

Entertainment includes nightly production shows or cabaret-style performances and even plays. An authentic pub adds to the British ambience, while a wide variety of musical styles can be found for dancing and listening in other bars and lounges. Cunard's fine enrichment programs are presented by expert guest lecturers. You can preplan your activities prior to departure by consulting the syllabus of courses available online at Cunard Line's Web site.

Your Shipmates. Discerning, well-traveled British and American couples from their late-30s to retirees are drawn to Cunard's traditional style. The availability of spacious accommodations and complimentary self-service laundry facilities make Cunard liners a good option for families, but the number of kids on board is usually fairly limited. Kid-friendly features include a dedicated play area for children one to six. Separate programs are reserved for older children ages 7 to 12 and teens up to 17. Toddlers are supervised by English nannies, and complimentary group babysitting is available in the evenings.

Food. In the tradition of multiclass ocean liners, dining room assignments are made according to the accommodation category booked, so you get the luxury you pay for. Passengers in Junior Suites are assigned to single-seating Princess Grill, while the posh Queen's Grill serves passengers booked in the most lavish suites. All other passengers are assigned to one of two seatings in the dramatic Britannia Restaurant. Menus also include vegetarian and low-calorie selections. Specialty restaurants require reservations, and there is an additional charge.

Fitness and Recreation. Swimming pools, golf driving ranges, table tennis, paddle tennis, shuffleboard, and jogging tracks barely scratch the surface of onboard facilities dedicated to recreation. Fitness centers offer high-tech workout equipment, a separate weight room, and classes ranging from aerobics to healthy living workshops. The spas are top-notch, with a long menu of treatments and salon services for women and men.

Service and Tipping. Service is formal and sophisticated. Suggested gratuities of $13 per person per day (for Grill Restaurant accommodations) or $11 per person per day (all other accommodations) are automatically charged to shipboard accounts. A 15% gratuity is added to bar tabs. Direct gratuities for special service are allowed.

Contact **Cunard Line** ☎661/753–1000 or 800/728–6273 ⊕ www.cunard.com.

DISNEY CRUISE LINE

Disney Cruise Line launched its ships in 1998 and 1999. Dozens of the best ship designers, industry veterans, and Disney creative minds planned intensely for three years to produce these vessels, which make a positive impression on adults and children alike. Exteriors are reminiscent of the great ocean liners of the early 20th century, resplendent with two funnels and black hulls, but interiors are technologically up-to-the-minute and full of novel developments in dining, cabin, and entertainment facilities. Accommodations are especially family-friendly, and most have a split-bathroom configuration with a sink and bathtub in one section and a sink and toilet in the other.

Entertainment leans heavily on popular Disney themes and characters. Parents are actively involved in the audience with their children at production shows, movies, "live" character meetings, deck parties, and dancing in the family nightclub. Teens have a supervised, no-adults-allowed club space. For adults, there are traditional no-kids-allowed bars and lounges with live music, dancing, theme parties, and late-night comedy as well as daytime wine-tasting sessions, game shows, culinary-arts and home-entertaining demonstrations, and behind-the-scenes lectures.

Your Shipmates. The young and not so young all find Disney Cruises appealing. Multigenerational family groups are the core clientele for these ships. As expected, Disney ships have extensive, age-appropriate programs for children and teens. A nursery for infants as young as three months is available for an hourly fee, and the diapers you supply will be changed by attendants—a service not available on most cruise lines. You might be surprised at the number of honeymooners on board.

Food. Don't expect top chefs and gourmet food; the fare is all-American for the most part. Naturally, all restaurants have children's menus. In a novel twist on dining, passengers "rotate" between theme dining rooms, accompanied each night by their waitstaff. Palo, the adults-only Italian restaurant, requires reservations and has a cover charge. Fountain drinks at beverage stations are complimentary.

Fitness and Recreation. Three swimming pools are designated for different groups: children, families, and adults. The salon and spa rival any afloat. Unique to Disney ships are Spa Villas, indoor/outdoor treatment suites, each with a verandah with a hot tub and open-air shower. In addition to a nicely equipped fitness center and aerobics studio are a jogging track and basketball court.

Service and Tipping. Service is friendly, and particular importance is placed on treating children with the same courtesy extended to adults. Suggested gratuities are calculated on a per-person/per-cruise basis, and can be added to onboard accounts or offered in cash on the last night. For the dining room server, assistant server, head server, and stateroom host/hostess, guidelines are $36 for three-night cruises, $48 for four-night cruises, and $84 for seven-night cruises. A 15% gratuity is added to bar service tabs.

Contact **Disney Cruise Line** ☎407/566–3500 or 888/325–2500. ⊕www.disneycruise.com.

HOLLAND AMERICA LINE

Founded in 1873, Holland America Line (HAL) is one of the oldest names in cruising. Its cruises are classic, conservative affairs renowned for their grace and gentility. As its ships attract a more youthful clientele, Holland America has taken steps to shed its "old folks" image, now offering stops at a private island in the Bahamas, trendier cuisine, a culinary arts center, and an expanded children's program. Still, these are not party cruises, and Holland America has managed to preserve the refined and relaxing qualities that have always been its hallmark, even on sailings that cater more to younger passengers and families.

Luxury bedding, magnifying makeup mirrors, robes, fresh-fruit baskets, flat-screen TVs, and DVD players are found in all cabins. In addition, suites have duvets, fully stocked minibars, personalized stationery, and access to the exclusive Neptune Lounge. Explorations Café, powered by the *New York Times,* combines a coffee bar, computer center, and cozy library-reading room complete with tabletop versions of the *Times*' crossword puzzles.

Your Shipmates. No longer your grandparents' cruise line, today's Holland America also attracts families and discerning couples, mostly from their late 30s and up. Retirees are often still in the majority; however, during holidays and summer months you'll find more families with kids. Group activities are planned for children ages 3 to 7 and 8 to 12 in Club HAL. After Hours offers late-night activities from 10 PM until midnight for an hourly fee. Teens ages 13 to 17 have their own lounge with activities.

Food. You have your choice of two assigned seatings or open seating for evening meals in the formal dining room. In the reservations-required Pinnacle Grill alternative restaurant ($20 dinner; $10 lunch), fresh seafood and premium cuts of beef are used to prepare creative specialty dishes. Delicious onboard traditions are afternoon tea, a Dutch Chocolate Extravaganza, and Holland America Line's signature bread pudding. Casual evening dining in the Lido restaurants offers a combination of buffet and waiter service.

Fitness and Recreation. Well-equipped and fully staffed fitness facilities contain state-of-the-art exercise equipment; basic fitness classes are available at no charge, though you pay for personal training, yoga, and Pilates. You'll also find a jogging track, multiple swimming pools, and sports courts. Promenade decks encircle each ship and are popular for walking. The Greenhouse Spa offers a variety of treatments and salon services.

Service and Tipping. Professional, unobtrusive service by the Indonesian and Filipino staff is a fleetwide standard on Holland America Line. A standard gratuity of $11 per passenger per day is automatically added to shipboard accounts and is distributed to stewards and waitstaff. Room-service tips are offered in cash. An automatic 15% gratuity is added to bar-service tabs.

Contact Holland America Line ☎ *206/281–3535 or 800/577–1728.* ⊕ *www. hollandamerica.com.*

MSC CRUISES

With several seasons of Caribbean sailing behind them, MSC Cruises has outgrown its newcomer status. More widely known as one of the world's largest cargo shipping companies, parent company Mediterranean Shipping Company has operated cruises with an eclectic fleet since the late 1980s, but expanded its cruising reach by introducing graceful, modern ships in the Caribbean.

While sailing Caribbean itineraries, MSC Cruises adopts activities that appeal to American passengers without abandoning those preferred by Europeans—prepare for announcements in several languages in addition to English. In addition to trivia games, Bingo, and cooking demonstrations, a popular option is Italian language classes. Nightly shows accentuate MSC Cruises' Mediterranean heritage—there might be an opera presentation in the main showroom and live music in the smaller lounges.

Your Shipmates. On Caribbean itineraries you will find about half of your fellow passengers are American couples in the 35- to 55-year-old range and families. Children from ages 3 to 17 are welcome to participate in age-appropriate youth programs; the Teenage Club is for youths 13 years and older.

Food. Dinner on MSC ships is centered around authentic Italian fare. Menus list Mediterranean regional specialties and classic favorites prepared from scratch. "Healthy Choice" and vegetarian items are offered as well as sugar-free desserts. In a nod to American tastes, chicken, sirloin steak, grilled salmon, and Caesar salad are always available in addition to the regular dinner menu. A daily highlight is the bread and pasta, freshly made on board. Midnight buffets are a retro food feature missing from most of today's cruises. Alternative restaurants are featured throughout the fleet, but vary by ship class. Coffee bars and ice-cream bars charge for specialty coffee drinks and frozen treats.

Fitness and Recreation. Up-to-date exercise equipment, a jogging track, and basic fitness classes for all levels are available. Spa treatments include a variety of massages, body wraps, and facials that can be scheduled à la carte or combined in packages to encompass an afternoon or the entire cruise.

Service and Tipping. Service can be inconsistent, but is more than acceptable—if not overly gracious. The mainly Italian staff are sometimes still befuddled by American habits and expectations. Customary gratuities are automatically charged to onboard accounts in the amount of $12 per person per day for adults and $6 for children. Gratuities are included in all bar purchases.

Contact **MSC Cruises** ☎ *800/666–9333* ⊕ *www.msccruises.com.*

NORWEGIAN CRUISE LINE

Norwegian Cruise Line (NCL) was established in 1966, when one of Norway's oldest and most respected shipping companies, Oslo-based Klosters Rederi A/S, acquired the *Sunward* and repositioned the ship from Europe to the then-obscure Port of Miami. With the formation of a company called Norwegian Caribbean Lines, the cruise industry as we know it today was born. NCL launched an entirely new concept with its regularly scheduled cruises to the Caribbean on a single-class ship. No longer simply a means of transportation, the ship became a destination unto itself, offering guests an affordable alternative to land-based resorts.

Always a cruise industry innovator, Norwegian Cruise Line's "Freestyle" cruising introduced a wider variety of dining options in a casual, free-flowing atmosphere. Noted for top-quality, high-energy entertainment and emphasis on fitness facilities and programs, NCL combines action, activities, and a resort-casual atmosphere.

Your Shipmates. NCL's mostly American cruise passengers are active couples ranging from their mid-30s to mid-50s; some passengers may be in the over-55 age group. Many families enjoy cruising on NCL ships during summer months. Each NCL vessel offers the "Kid's Crew" program of supervised entertainment for young cruisers ages 2 to 17. For 13- to 17-year-olds there are clubs where they can hang out in adult-free zones.

Food. Main dining rooms serve what is traditionally deemed Continental fare, although it's about what you would expect at a really good hotel banquet. Where NCL stands above the ordinary is in their specialty restaurants, especially the French-Mediterranean Le Bistro (on all ships), the Pan-Asian restaurants, and steak houses (on the newer ships). In addition, you may find a Spanish tapas bar and an Italian trattoria. Most, but not all, specialty restaurants carry a cover charge and require reservations. An NCL staple, the late-night Chocoholic Buffet continues to be a favorite event.

Fitness and Recreation. Mandara Spa offers a long list of unusual and exotic spa treatments fleet-wide on NCL. State-of-the-art exercise equipment, jogging tracks, and basic fitness classes are available at no charge. There's a fee for personal training and specialized classes such as yoga and Pilates.

Service and Tipping. Although somewhat inconsistent, service is nonetheless congenial. A fixed service charge of $12 per person, per day, is added to shipboard accounts for passengers age three and up. An automatic 15% gratuity is added to bar tabs and 18% for spa services. Staff members are permitted to accept cash gratuities. Passengers in suites are asked to offer a cash gratuity to their concierge and butlers.

Contact **Norwegian Cruise Line** ☎ 305/436–4000 or 800/327–7030 ⊕ www. ncl.com.

OCEANIA CRUISES

This distinctive cruise line, founded by cruise-industry veterans with the know-how to satisfy inquisitive passengers with interesting ports of call and upscale touches for fares much lower than you would expect, is now owned by Prestige Cruise Holdings. Oceania uses midsize "R-class" ships from the now-defunct Renaissance Cruises fleet and is set to launch a new ship class in fall 2010. Varied, destination-rich itineraries are an important characteristic of Oceania Cruises, and most Caribbean sailings are in the 10- to 12-night range. Before arrival in ports of call, lectures are presented on the historical background, culture, and traditions of the islands.

Intimate and cozy public spaces reflect the importance of socializing on Oceania ships. Evening entertainment leans toward light cabaret, solo artists, music for dancing, and conversation with fellow passengers; however, you'll find lively karaoke sessions as well. On sea days jazz or easy-listening melodies are played poolside.

Your Shipmates. Oceania Cruises appeal to singles and couples from their late-30s to well-traveled retirees who have the time for and prefer longer cruises. Most are attracted to the casually refined atmosphere, creative cuisine, and European service. Oceania Cruises are adult-oriented and not a good choice for most families; there are no dedicated children's facilities.

Food. Master chef Jacques Pépin designed the menus for Oceania, and the results are sure to please the most discriminating palate. Oceania simply serves some of the best food at sea, particularly impressive for a cruise line that charges far less than luxury rates. The main open-seating restaurant offers trendy French-Continental cuisine with an always-on-the menu steak, seafood, or poultry choice and vegetarian option. Intimate specialty restaurants require reservations, but there is no additional charge.

Fitness and Recreation. While small, the spa, salon, and well-equipped fitness center are adequate for the number of passengers on board. There is a walking/jogging track circling the top of the ship. Spa menus list massages, body wraps, and facials. Forward of the locker rooms you will find a large therapy pool and quiet deck for relaxation and sunning on padded wooden steamer chaises.

Service and Tipping. Highly personalized service by a mostly European staff is crisp and efficient without being intrusive. Butlers are on hand to satisfy the needs of suite guests and will even assist with packing and unpacking upon request. A charge of $12.50 per person, per day is added to onboard accounts, and an additional $4 per person, per day is added for suite occupants. An 18% gratuity is automatically added to all beverage purchases and spa and salon services.

Contact Oceania Cruises ☎ 305/514-2300 or 800/531-5658 ⊕ www.oceania cruises.com.

PRINCESS CRUISES

Rising from modest beginnings in 1965, when it began offering cruises to Mexico with a single ship, Princess has become one of the world's best-known cruise lines. Catapulted to stardom in 1977, when its flagship became the setting for *The Love Boat* television series, Princess introduced millions of viewers to the still-new concept of a seagoing vacation. While the line does have some medium-size vessels, Princess more often follows the "big is better" trend. Its fleet sails to more destinations each year than any other major line, though many cruises depart from the West Coast.

All Princess ships feature the line's innovative "Personal Choice Cruising" program that gives passengers choice and flexibility in customizing their cruise experience—multiple dining locations, flexible entertainment, and affordable private balconies are all highlights. Enrichment programs feature guest lecturers and opportunities to learn new skills or crafts, but you'll still find staples such as bingo and art auctions. You can even earn PADI scuba-diving certification in just one week during select sailings.

Your Shipmates. Princess Cruises attract mostly American passengers ranging from their mid-30s to mid-50s. Longer cruises appeal to well-

Drinking and Gambling Ages

CLOSE UP

Many underage passengers have learned to their chagrin that the rules that apply on land are also adhered to at sea. On most mainstream cruise ships you must be 21 in order to imbibe alcoholic beverages. There are exceptions—for instance, on cruises departing from countries where the legal drinking age is typically lower than 21. By and large, if you haven't achieved the magic age of 21, your shipboard charge card will be coded as booze-free, and bartenders won't risk their jobs to sell you alcohol.

Gambling is a bit looser, and 18 year olds can try their luck on cruise lines such as Carnival, Celebrity, Azamara, Silversea, Norwegian, and Royal Caribbean; most other cruise lines adhere to the age-21 minimum. Casinos are trickier to patrol than bars, though, and minors who look "old enough" may get away with dropping a few coins in an out-of-the-way slot machine before being spotted on a hidden security camera. If you hit a big jackpot, you may have a lot of explaining to do to your parents.

traveled retirees. Families can be found cruising together on the Princess fleet, particularly during summer months, when many children are on board. For young passengers ages 3 to 17, each Princess vessel (except Ocean, Royal, and Pacific Princess) allows parents independent time ashore, youth centers operate as usual during port days.

Food. Personal choices regarding where and what to eat abound, but unless you opt for traditional assigned seating, you might have to wait for a table in one of the open-seating dining rooms. Menus are varied and extensive, and the results are good to excellent. A special menu is designed especially for children. Alternative restaurants are a staple throughout the fleet, but vary by ship class. Lido buffets on all ships are almost always open, and a pizzeria and grill offer casual daytime snack choices. The fleet's patisseries and ice-cream bars charge for specialty coffee, pastries, and ice-cream treats. With balcony accommodations, you can enjoy a private Champagne Breakfast or Ultimate Balcony Dinner.

Fitness and Recreation. Spa and salon rituals include massages, body wraps, facials, and numerous hair and nail services, including treatments designed specifically for men, teens, and couples. Modern exercise equipment, a jogging track, and basic fitness classes are available at no charge. Grand-class ships have a resistance pool for lap swimming.

Service and Tipping. Professional service by an international staff is efficient and friendly. Princess suggests tipping $11 per person per day for passengers in suites and minisuites and $10.50 per person, per day for all other passengers (including children). Gratuities are automatically added to onboard accounts; spa personnel are tipped at your discretion; 15% is added to bar bills.

Contact Princess Cruises ☎ *661/753-0000 or 800/774-6237* ⊕ *www. princess.com.*

REGENT SEVEN SEAS CRUISES

Regent Seven Seas Cruises sails an elegant fleet of vessels that offer a nearly all-inclusive cruise experience in sumptuous, contemporary surroundings. The line's spacious ocean-view staterooms have the industry's highest percentage of private balconies, and almost all drinks (except some premium brands) are now included.

Subtle improvements throughout the fleet are ongoing, such as computer service with Wi-Fi capability for your own laptop and cell phone access. New luxury bedding, Regent-branded bath amenities, flat-screen TVs, DVD players, and new clocks have been added to all cabins. Top suites also feature iPods and Bose speakers. Delightful ships feature exquisite service, generous staterooms with abundant amenities, a variety of dining options, and superior enrichment programs. Cruises are destination focused, and most sailings host guest lecturers—historians, anthropologists, naturalists, and diplomats.

Your Shipmates. Regent Seven Seas Cruises are inviting to active, affluent, well-traveled couples ranging from their late 30s to retirees who enjoy the ships' elegance and destination-rich itineraries. Longer cruises attract passengers in the over-60 age group. Regent vessels are adult oriented and do not have dedicated children's facilities; however, youth programs are offered on some sailings.

Food. Menus may appear to include the usual cruise-ship staples, but the results are some of the most outstanding meals at sea. Specialty dining varies within the fleet; when available, the sophisticated Signatures features the cuisine of Le Cordon Bleu of Paris; Prime 7 offers menus that rival the finest shoreside steak and seafood restaurants. In addition, Mediterranean-inspired bistro dinners are served in the daytime casual Lido buffet restaurants. Wines chosen to complement dinner menus are freely poured each evening.

Fitness and Recreation. Although gyms and exercise areas are well equipped, these are not large ships, so the facilities tend to be on the small side. Each ship has a jogging track, and the larger ones feature a variety of sports courts. Exclusive to Regent Seven Seas, the spa and salon are operated by high-end Carita of Paris.

Service and Tipping. The efforts of a polished European staff go almost unnoticed, yet special requests are handled with ease. Butlers provide an additional layer of personal service to guests in the top-category suites. Gratuities are included in the fare, and none are expected. Passengers are allowed to donate to a crew welfare fund that benefits the ship's staff.

Contact **Regent Seven Seas Cruises** ☎ *954/776–6123 or 877/505–5370* ⊕ *www.rssc.com.*

ROYAL CARIBBEAN INTERNATIONAL

Big, bigger, biggest! More than a decade ago, Royal Caribbean launched the first of the modern mega-cruise ships for passengers who enjoy traditional cruising with a touch of daring and whimsy tossed in. These large-to-giant vessels are indoor-outdoor wonders, with every conceivable activity in a resortlike atmosphere, including atrium lobbies, shopping arcades, large spas, expansive sundecks, and rock-climbing walls. Several ships have such elaborate facilities as 18-hole miniature-golf courses, ice-skating rinks, and in-line skating tracks. Freedom-class ships, RCI's latest additions, and presently the world's largest cruise ships, even have the first surf parks at sea. Plush new bedding has been installed fleetwide.

The centerpiece of Royal Caribbean mega-ships is the multideck atrium, a hallmark that has been duplicated by many other cruise lines. The brilliance of this design is that all the major public rooms radiate from this central point, so you can learn your way around these huge ships within minutes of boarding. Ships in the Vision class are especially bright and airy, with sea views almost anywhere you happen to be. The main problem with RCI's otherwise well-conceived vessels is that there are often too many people on board, making embarkation, tendering, and disembarkation exasperating. However, Royal Caribbean is still one of the best-run and most popular cruise lines.

Your Shipmates. Royal Caribbean cruises have a broad appeal for active couples and singles, mostly in their 30s to 50s. Families are partial to the newer vessels that have larger staterooms, excellent kids' facilities, and seemingly endless choices of activities and dining options. Supervised age-appropriate activities are designed for children ages 3 through 17. For infants and toddlers 6 to 36 months of age, interactive playgroup sessions are planned, while a teen center with a disco is an adult-free gathering spot. "Family-size" staterooms are available on most newer ships, but there are no self-service laundry facilities.

Food. Royal Caribbean offers the choice of an early or late dinner seating and has been testing an open-seating program that is expected to be available across the fleet by 2010. Windjammer Café and, on certain ships, the sunny Seaview Café are casual dining options. Each ship has a pizzeria, coffee bar, and ice-cream parlor, and Johnny Rockets 1950s-style diners (extra fee) can be found on most ships. Royal Caribbean doesn't place emphasis on celebrity chefs or specialty alternative restaurants, although the line has introduced a more upscale and intimate dinner experience in the form of an Italian-specialty restaurant and a steak house on some ships.

Fitness and Recreation. Fabled for its range of top-of-the-line recreations, Royal Caribbean also delivers on the basics: most exercise classes, aimed at sweating off those extra calories, are included in the fare (although there's a fee for spinning, yoga, and Pilates classes, as well as personal training). Each ship has multiple swimming pools and a rock-climbing wall. Spas feature extensive treatment menus and full services for pampering adults and teens.

Service and Tipping. Service on Royal Caribbean ships is friendly but not consistent. Assigned meal seatings assure that most passengers get to know the waiters and their assistants, who in turn get to know the passengers' likes and dislikes; however, that can lead to a level of familiarity that some find uncomfortable. Tips can be prepaid when the cruise is booked, added onto shipboard accounts, or given in cash on the last night of the cruise. Suggested gratuities per passenger, per day, are: $3.50 for the cabin steward (or $5.75 for suite attendant); $3.50 for the waiter; $2 for the assistant waiter; and $0.75 for the head waiter. A 15% gratuity is automatically added to all bar tabs.

Contact **Royal Caribbean International** ☎ *305/539–6000 or 800/327–6700* ⊕ *www.royalcaribbean.com.*

SEABOURN CRUISE LINE

Ultraluxury pioneer Seabourn was founded on the principle that dedication to personal service in elegant surroundings would appeal to sophisticated, independent-minded passengers whose lifestyles demand the best. Its fleet of three nearly identical, all-suites ships received extensive makeovers in 2008 and were joined by a newly launched larger vessel in 2009. The "yachts" remain favorites with people who can take care of themselves but would rather do so aboard a luxury ship. Dining and evening socializing are generally more stimulating to Seabourn passengers than splashy song-and-dance reviews; however, proportionately scaled production and cabaret shows are presented in the main showroom and smaller lounge. The library stocks not only books but also movies.

You can expect complimentary wines and spirits, elegant amenities, and even the pleasure of minimassages while lounging poolside. Guest appearances by luminaries in the arts and world affairs highlight the enrichment program. Wine tasting, trivia contests, and other quiet pursuits might be scheduled, but most passengers prefer to simply do what pleases them.

Your Shipmates. Seabourn attracts mostly affluent, 50-plus and retired couples who are accustomed to evening formality. The ships are adult oriented, with no children's programs or facilities, and are unable to accommodate children under six months (one year for voyages of 15 days or longer).

Food. Exceptional cuisine created by celebrity chef-restaurateur Charlie Palmer is prepared to order and served in open-seating dining rooms. Creative menu offerings include foie gras, quail, and fresh seafood. Vegetarian dishes and offerings low in cholesterol, salt, and fat are prepared with the same care. Wines are chosen to complement each day's lunch and dinner menus and caviar is always available. Evening dining alternatives include "Restaurant 2," which serves dinner nightly, and a second—even more laid-back—"Sky Grill," offering sizzling steaks and seafood, is sometimes offered in the open-air Sky Bar. Both require reservations but no additional charge.

Fitness and Recreation. Complimentary "massage moments" offered poolside are mini-previews of the soothing treatments available in the spa. A full array of cardio, strength, and weight-training equipment and basic fitness classes are available in the small gym, while some specialized fitness sessions are offered for a fee. The water-sports marina is popular with active passengers who want to jet-ski, windsurf, kayak, or swim in the integrated saltwater "pool" while anchored in calm waters.

Service and Tipping. Personal service and attention by the professional staff are the order of the day. Your preferences are noted and fulfilled without the necessity of reminders. Tipping is neither required nor expected.

Contact **Seabourn Cruise Line** ☏ *305/463–3000 or 800/929–9391*
🖷 *305/463–3010* ⊕ *www.seabourn.com.*

SEADREAM YACHT CLUB

Launched in 1984 as Sea Goddess mega-yachts, these boutique ships have changed hands through the years, becoming SeaDream Yacht Club in 2002. Passengers enjoy an unstructured holiday at sea doing whatever pleases them, giving the diminutive vessels the feel of true private yachts with a select guest list. Other than a pianist in the tiny piano bar, a small casino, and movies in the main lounge, there is no roster of activities. The rocking late-night place to be is the Top of the Yacht Bar, where passengers gather to share the day's experiences and kick their shoes off to dance on the teak deck. The Captain hosts welcome-aboard and farewell cocktail receptions in the Main Salon each week. Otherwise, you are on your own to do as you please. A well-stocked library has books and movies for those who prefer quiet pursuits in the privacy of their staterooms.

Ports of call almost seem an intrusion on socializing amid the chic surroundings, although a picnic on a secluded beach adds the element of a private island paradise to each Caribbean cruise. While the ambience is sophisticated, all cruises are "yacht" casual, and you can leave your formal clothing at home. You can also leave your charge card in your pocket, as all beverages, including select wines and spirits are complimentary.

Your Shipmates. SeaDream yachts appeal to energetic, affluent travelers of all ages, as well as groups. Passengers tend to be couples from 45 year olds and up to retirees. No children's facilities or organized activities are available, and these ships are not really suitable for passengers confined to wheelchairs. Although one stateroom on each vessel is designated "accessible," public facilities have thresholds, and the elevator doesn't reach the uppermost deck.

Food. Every meal is prepared to order using the freshest seafood and prime cuts of beef. Menus include vegetarian alternatives and Asian wellness cuisine for the health-conscious. Cheeses, petits fours, and chocolate truffles are offered with after-dinner coffee, and desserts are to die for. All meals are open seating, either in the main restaurant or, weather permitting, alfresco in the canopied Topsider Restaurant daily for breakfast, lunch, and special dinners. Wines are chosen to complement each luncheon and dinner menu.

Fitness and Recreation. Small gyms on each ship are equipped with treadmills, elliptical machines, recumbent bikes, and free weights. A personal trainer is available. SeaDream's unique Asian Spa facilities are also on the small side, yet offer a full menu of individualized gentle pampering treatments including massages, facials, and body wraps utilizing Eastern techniques. Mountain bikes are available for use ashore.

Service and Tipping. Personal service and attention to detail are amazing—you will be greeted by name within hours of boarding. Passenger preferences are shared among staff members who all work hard to assist one another. You seldom, if ever, have to repeat a request. Tipping is neither required nor expected.

Contact SeaDream Yacht Club ☎ 305/856–5622 or 800/707–4911 ⊕ www. seadreamyachtclub.com.

SILVERSEA CRUISES

Intimate ships, paired with exclusive amenities and unparalleled hospitality, are the hallmarks of Silversea luxury cruises. Personalization is a Silversea maxim. Ships offer more activities than other comparably sized luxury vessels, with guest lecturers on nearly every cruise. A multitiered show lounge is the setting for classical concerts, big-screen movies, and folkloric entertainers from ashore. All accommodations are spacious outside suites, most with private verandas. Silversea ships have large swimming pools in expansive Lidos. Silversea's third generation of ships will introduce even more luxurious features when the 36,000-ton Silver Spirit launches late in 2009.

Although these ships schedule more activities than other comparably sized luxury vessels, you can either take part or opt instead for a good book and any number of quiet spots to read or snooze in the shade. Silversea is so all-inclusive that you'll find your room key/charge card is seldom used for anything but opening your suite door.

Your Shipmates. Silversea Cruises appeal to sophisticated, affluent couples who enjoy the country club–like atmosphere, exquisite cuisine, and polished service. You might see the occasional child, but children less than six months old are not permitted, and the cruise line limits the number of children under the age of three on board.

Food. Dishes from the galleys of Silversea's master chefs are complemented by those of La Collection du Monde, created by Silversea's culinary partner, the world-class chefs of Relais & Châteaux. Perhaps more compelling is the line's flair for originality. The pasta chef's daily special is a passenger favorite, as is the galley brunch, held just once each cruise, when the galley is transformed into a buffet restaurant. Special off-menu orders are prepared whenever possible. Nightly alternative theme dinners in La Terrazza (by day, the buffet restaurant) feature regional specialties from the Mediterranean; an intimate dining experience aboard each vessel is Le Champagne—the Wine Restaurant, which is run by Relais & Châteaux.

Fitness and Recreation. The rather small gyms are well equipped with cardiovascular and weight-training equipment, and fitness classes are held in the mirror-lined, but somewhat confining, exercise room. South Pacific–inspired Mandara Spa offers numerous treatments, including exotic-sounding massages, facials, and body wraps.

Service and Tipping. Personalized service is exacting and hospitable, yet discreet; staff members strive for perfection and often achieve it. Personal preferences are remembered and satisfied. Tipping is neither required nor expected.

Contact **Silversea Cruises** ☎ *954/522–4477 or 800/722-9955* ⊕ *www.silver sea.com.*

STAR CLIPPERS

In 1991 Star Clippers presented a new tall-ship alternative to sophisticated travelers whose wants included adventure at sea, but not on board a conventional cruise ship. Star Clippers vessels are the world's largest barkentine and full-rigged sailing ships—four- and five-masted sailing beauties filled with modern, high-tech equipment as well as amenities more often found on private yachts. The ships rely on sail power while at sea unless conditions require the assistance of the engines. Minimum heeling, usually less than 6%, is achieved through judicious control of the sails.

Star Clippers are not cruise ships in the ordinary sense, with strict agendas and pages of activities. You can lounge on deck and simply soak in the nautical ambience or learn about navigational techniques from the captain. Cabins, which are very compact, do include such amenities as hair dryers, TVs, and telephones. Star Clippers ships also have swimming pools. Other features fall somewhere between those of a true sailing yacht and the high-tech Windstar ships. The differences are more than just in the level of luxury—Star Clippers are true sailing vessels. Prices, however, are a bit more affordable and often less than you would pay on a high-end cruise ship.

Your Shipmates. Star Clippers cruises appeal to active, upscale American and European couples from their 30s on up who enjoy sailing, but in a casually sophisticated atmosphere with modern conveniences. Many sailings are split nearly equally between North American and European passengers. This is not a cruise line for the physically challenged; there are no elevators or ramps, nor are any staterooms or bathrooms wheelchair-accessible. Star Clippers ships are adult oriented, and while children are allowed, there are no dedicated youth facilities.

Food. Not noted for gourmet fare, the international cuisine is what you would expect from a trendy shoreside bistro, albeit an elegant one. Fresh fruits and fish are among the best choices from Star Clippers' galleys. In a nod to American tastes, dinner menus include an alternative steak selection. Lunch buffets are quite a spread of seafood, salads, and grilled items. Room service is only available to occupants of suites aboard *Royal Clipper.*

Fitness and Recreation. Formal exercise sessions take a backseat to water sports, although aerobics classes and swimming are featured on all ships. Only *Royal Clipper* has a marina platform that can be lowered in calm waters to access water sports and diving, however, the smaller ships replicate the experience by using launches. A gym/spa with an array of exercise equipment, free weights, spa treatments, and unisex hair services are found only on *Royal Clipper*.

Service and Tipping. Service is friendly and gracious, similar to what you would find in a boutique hotel or restaurant. Star Clippers recommends the following gratuities (always in euros): room steward, €3 per day; dining-room staff, €5 per day. Tips are pooled and shared; individual tipping is discouraged. A 15% gratuity is added to bar bills. Gratuities may be charged to your shipboard account.

Contact Star Clippers ☏ *305/442-0550 or 800/442-0551* ⊕ *www.star clippers.com.*

WINDSTAR CRUISES

Are they cruise ships with sails or sailing ships designed for cruises? In actuality they are masted sailing yachts, pioneers in the upscale sailing niche. Although the sails add speed, Windstar ships seldom depend on wind alone to sail. However, if you are fortunate and conditions are perfect, the total silence of pure sailing is a thrill. Although the ships' designs may be reminiscent of sailing vessels of yore, the amenities and shipboard service are among the best at sea.

In keeping with the line's exacting standards, all ocean-view staterooms and suites provide the comforts of home with sitting area, luxury linens and mattresses, DVD/CD player, Apple iPod Nano and Bose Sound-Dock speakers, wireless Internet, safe, minibar/refrigerator, international direct dial phones, L'Occitane bath toiletries, hair dryer, plenty of closet space, and plush robes and slippers. An array of international newspapers, books, and games can be found in the library, and a wide selection of DVD titles and CDs are available for complimentary use. Life on board is unabashedly sybaritic, attracting a sophisticated, relatively young crowd who are happy to sacrifice bingo and pool games for the attractions of remote islands and water sports; even motorized water sports are included, and passengers pay extra only for scuba diving. Unfortunately, only basic beverages are included in the fare.

Your Shipmates. Windstar cruises appeal to upscale professional couples in their late 30s to 60s. These ships are especially popular with honeymooners. The ships were not designed for accessibility, and are not a good choice for the physically challenged. *Wind Surf,* for example, has only two elevators, and the smaller ships have none. There are no staterooms or bathrooms deemed "accessible," and gangways can be difficult to navigate, depending on the tide and angle of ascent. The unregimented atmosphere is adult oriented; children are not encouraged, and dedicated children's facilities are nonexistent.

Food. Windstar menus feature dishes with tropical accents, using fresh local ingredients whenever possible. In a nod to healthful dining, low-calorie and low-fat spa cuisine and vegetarian dishes are always available in the open-seating restaurants. A mid-cruise deck barbecue featuring grilled seafood and other favorites is offered on all cruises. Aboard *Wind Surf,* the specialty restaurant serves a steak-house menu four nights a week; on other nights menus feature northern Italian,

French, and Indonesian cuisine. Reservations are required, but there is no additional charge.

Fitness and Recreation. Windstar's massage and exercise facilities are quite small on *Wind Star* and *Wind Spirit,* as would be expected on ships that carry fewer than 150 passengers. However, on the larger *Wind Surf,* the WindSpa and fitness areas are surprisingly large. An array of exercise equipment, free weights, and basic fitness classes are available in the gym and Nautilus room. A wide variety of massages, body wraps, and facial treatments are offered in the spa, while hair and nail services are available for women and men in the salon. Stern-mounted water-sports marinas are popular with active passengers who want to kayak, windsurf, and water-ski.

Service and Tipping. Personal service is comprehensive, competent, and designed to create an elite and privileged atmosphere. Expect to be addressed by name within a short time of embarking. A service charge of $12 per person, per day is automatically added onto shipboard accounts. An automatic 15% gratuity is automatically added to all bar tabs.

Contact Windstar Cruises ☎ *206/281–3535 or 800/258–7245* ⊕ *www.wind starcruises.com.*

Ports of Embarkation

WORD OF MOUTH

"[The Fort Lauderdale airport] is only 45 minutes from the Port [of Miami], and you can grab a shared shuttle outside FLL baggage claim. . . . (Then to return to FLL, we just booked a private ride and the driver was waiting when we left the ship.)"

—cruisin_tigger

Miami is the world's cruise capital, and more cruise ships are based here year-round than anywhere else. Caribbean cruises depart for their itineraries from several ports on either of Florida's coasts, as well as from cities on the Gulf Coast and East Coast of the United States.

Generally, if your cruise is on an Eastern Caribbean itinerary, you'll likely depart from Miami, Fort Lauderdale, Jacksonville, or Port Canaveral; short three- and four-day cruises to the Bahamas also depart from these ports. Most cruises on Western Caribbean itineraries depart from Tampa, Mobile, New Orleans, Galveston, or Houston, though some depart from Miami as well. Cruises from farther up the East Coast of the United States, including such ports as Baltimore, Maryland, Charleston, South Carolina, and even New York City, usually go to the Bahamas or Key West and often include a private-island stop or a stop elsewhere in Florida. Cruises to the Southern Caribbean might depart from Miami if they are 10 days or longer, but more likely they will depart from San Juan, Puerto Rico, or some other port deeper in the Caribbean.

Regardless of which port you depart from, air connections may prevent you from leaving home on the morning of your cruise or going home the day you return to port. Or you may wish to arrive early simply to give yourself a bit more peace of mind, or you may just want to spend more time in one of these interesting port cities. Many people choose to depart from New Orleans just to have an excuse to spend a couple of days in the city before or after their cruise.

PORT ESSENTIALS

CAR RENTAL

Major Agencies Alamo (☎ 800/462-5266 ⊕ www.alamo.com). **Avis** (☎ 800/230-4898 ⊕ www.avis.com). **Budget** (☎ 800/527-0700 ⊕ www.budget.com). **Hertz** (☎ 800/654-3131 ⊕ www.hertz.com). **National Car Rental** (☎ 800/227-7368 ⊕ www.nationalcar.com).

SURCHARGES   To avoid a hefty refueling fee, fill the tank just before you turn in the car, but be aware that gas stations near the rental outlet may charge more than those farther away. It's almost never a deal to buy the tank of gas that's in the car when you rent it; the understanding is that you'll return it empty, but some fuel usually remains. Surcharges may apply if you are under 25 or over 75, if you want to add an additional driver to the contract, or if you want to drive over state borders or out of a specific radius from your point of rental. You'll pay extra for child seats (about $6 a day), which are compulsory for children under five, and usually for additional drivers (about $10 per day).

DINING

Unless otherwise noted, all prices are given in U.S. dollars. The following price categories are used in this book.

WHAT IT COSTS IN U.S. DOLLARS				
¢	$	$$	$$$	$$$$
AT DINNER under $8	$8–$12	$12–$20	$20–$30	over $30

Prices are per person for a main course at dinner and do not include any service charges or taxes.

LODGING

Whether you are driving or flying into your port of embarkation, it is often more convenient to arrive the day before or to stay for a day after your cruise. For this reason we offer lodging suggestions for each port of embarkation.

The lodgings we list are convenient to the cruise port and the cream of the crop in each price category. We always list the facilities that are available, but we don't specify whether they cost extra; when pricing accommodations, always ask what's included. Properties are assigned price categories based on the range between their least expensive standard double room in high season (excluding holidays) and the most expensive. But if you find everything sold out or wish to find a more predictable place to stay, there are chain hotels at almost all ports of embarkation.

Assume that hotels operate on the European Plan (EP, with no meals) unless we specify that they use either the **Continental Plan** (CP, with a Continental breakfast), **Breakfast Plan** (BP, with a full breakfast), or the **Modified American Plan** (MAP, with breakfast and dinner). The following price categories are used in this book.

WHAT IT COSTS IN U.S. DOLLARS				
¢	$	$$	$$$	$$$$
FOR 2 PEOPLE under $70	$70–$120	$120–$175	$175–$250	over $250

Prices are for a double room in high season, excluding service and taxes.

BALTIMORE, MARYLAND

Sam Sessa

Baltimore's charm lies in its neighborhoods. While stellar downtown attractions such as the National Aquarium and Camden Yards draw torrents of tourists each year, much of the city's character can be found outside the Inner Harbor. Scores of Baltimore's trademark narrow red-brick row houses with white marble steps line the city's east and west sides. Some neighborhood streets are still made of cobblestone, and grand churches and museums and towering, glassy high-rises fill out the growing skyline. Now the city's blue-collar past mixes with present urban professional revitalization. Industrial waterfront properties are giving way to high-end condos, and corner bars formerly dominated

CLOSE UP

Security

All cruise lines have instituted stricter security procedures in recent years; however, you may not even be aware of all the changes.

Some of the changes will be more obvious to you. For example, only visitors who have been authorized well in advance are allowed onboard. Proper identification (a government-issued photo ID) is required in all instances to board the ship, whether you are a visitor or passenger. Ship security personnel are stationed at all points of entry to the ship. All hand-carried items are searched by hand in every port (this applies to both crew and passengers).

Some of the changes are more behind the scenes. All luggage is scanned, whether you carry it aboard with you or not, and all packages and provisions brought onboard are scanned.

In addition, every ship has added professionally trained security officers and taken many other measures to ensure the safety of all passengers. Many cruise-line security personnel are former navy or marine officers with extensive maritime experience. Some cruise lines recruit shipboard security personnel from the ranks of former British Gurkha regiments. From Nepal, the Gurkhas are renowned as soldiers of the highest caliber.

by National Bohemian beer—once made in the city—are adding micro-brews to their beverage lists. And with more and more retail stores replacing old, run-down buildings and parking lots, Baltimore is one of the nation's up-and-coming cities.

ESSENTIALS

Hours During the summer tourist season, most of Baltimore's stores and attractions usually open around 9 AM and close around 9 PM.

Internet Enoch Pratt Free Library (✉ *400 Cathedral St., Mount Vernon* ☎ *410/396-5500* ⊕ *www.pratt.lib.md.us* ☉ *June–Sept., Mon.–Wed. 10-8, Thurs. 10-5:30, Fri. and Sat. 10-5, Sun. 1-5; Oct.–May, Mon.–Wed. 11-7, Thurs. 10-5:30, Fri. and Sat. 10-5, Sun. 1-5).*

Visitor Information Baltimore Visitor Center (✉ *401 Light St., Inner Harbor* ☎ *877/225-8466* ⊕ *www.baltimore.org*).

THE CRUISE PORT

Well marked and easily accessible by major highways, the South Locust Point Cruise Terminal is about a mile from center city. Several cruise lines offer seasonal cruises from the port, and *Carnival Pride* is based here permanently. Ships dock near the main cruise building, which itself is little more than a hub for arrivals and departures. There are few facilities for passengers in the immediate port area, which is out of walking distance to Baltimore's attractions.

During cruise season, taxis are the best transportation to the downtown area. They cost about $5 one way and frequent the port. Taxis to Baltimore–Washington International Airport charge a flat rate of

Exploring ▼

B&O Railroad Museum 5

Fort McHenry 1

Maryland Science Center 2

National Aquarium in Baltimore 4

Oriole Park at Camden Yards ...6

Port Discovery— The Baltimore Children's Museum 3

Restaurants ▼

Amicci's 7

Attman's 6

Bo Brooks 8

Rusty Scupper ...3

Hotels ▼

Celie's Waterfront B&B ..5

Hyatt Regency ...2

Marriott Baltimore Waterfront 4

Renaissance Harborplace Hotel 1

$27. Rental cars are generally not necessary; if you fly into Baltimore, you can see the majority of Baltimore by taxi. Guided tours of the city range from $20 to $60.

INFORMATION **Port of Baltimore** (✉*2001 E. McComas St.* ☎*410/962–8701* ⊕*www. cruisemaryland.com*).

AIRPORTS **Baltimore-Washington International Airport** (*BWI* ✉*10 mi south of Baltimore off Rte. 295/Baltimore-Washington Pkwy.* ☎*410/859–7111 for information and paging* ⊕*www.bwiairport.com*).

AIRPORT TRANSFERS **Airport Taxis** (☎*410/859–1100* ⊕*www.bwiairporttaxi.com*). **Arrow Taxicab** (☎*410/358–9696*). **BWI Airport rail station** (☎*410/672–6167* ⊕*www.mtamaryland.com*). **BWI SuperShuttle** (☎*800/258–3826* ⊕*www. supershuttle.com*). **Carey Limousines** (☎*410/880–0999 or 888/880– 0999* ⊕*www.carey.com*). **Maryland Area Rail Commuter** (*MARC* ☎*800/325– 7245 or 410/539–5000* ⊕*www.mtamaryland.com*). **Penn Station** (✉*Charles St. at Mt. Royal Ave., Mount Vernon* ☎*800/523–8720*). **Private Car/RMA Worldwide Chauffeured Transportation** (☎*410/519–0000 or 800/878–7743* ⊕*www.rmalimo.com*).

PARKING There's a secure parking lot next to the cruise terminal, where parking costs $15 per day. Drop off your luggage before parking.

EXPLORING BALTIMORE

Numbers in the margin correspond to points of interest on the Baltimore map.

B&O Railroad Museum. The famous Baltimore & Ohio Railroad was founded on the site that now houses this museum, which contains more than 120 full-size locomotives and a great collection of railroad memorabilia, from dining-car china and artwork to lanterns and signals. The 1884 roundhouse (240 feet in diameter and 120 feet high) adjoins one of the nation's first railroad stations. Train rides are available every day but Monday. The Iron Horse Café serves food and drinks. ⊠*901 W. Pratt St., West Baltimore* ☎*410/752–2490* ⊕*www.borail.org* 🎟*$14* ⊗*Mon.–Sat. 10–4, Sun. 11–4.*

Fort McHenry. This star-shaped brick fort is forever associated with Francis Scott Key and "The Star-Spangled Banner," which Key penned while watching the British bombardment of Baltimore during the War of 1812. A visit to the fort includes a 15-minute history film, guided tour, and frequent living-history displays on summer weekends. To see how the formidable fortifications might have appeared to the bombarding British, catch a water taxi from the Inner Harbor to the fort instead of driving. ⊠*E. Fort Ave., from Light St., take Key Hwy. for 1½ mi and follow signs, Locust Point* ☎*410/962–4290* ⊕*www.nps.gov/fomc* 🎟*$7* ⊗*Memorial Day–Labor Day, daily 8–8; Labor Day–Memorial Day, daily 8–5.*

Maryland Science Center. Originally known as the Maryland Academy of Sciences, this 200-year-old scientific institution is one of the oldest in the United States. Now housed in a contemporary building, the three floors of exhibits on the Chesapeake Bay, Earth science, physics, the body, dinosaurs, and outer space are an invitation to engage, experiment, and explore. The center has a planetarium, a simulated dinosaur dig, an IMAX movie theater with a screen five stories high, and a playroom especially designed for young children. ⊠*601 Light St., Inner Harbor* ☎*410/685–5225* ⊕*www.mdsci.org* 🎟*$14.50, IMAX $8* ⊗*Memorial Day–Labor Day, Thurs.–Sat. 10–8, Sun.–Wed. 10–6; Labor Day–Memorial Day, Tues.–Fri. 10–5, Sat. 10–6, Sun. 11–5.*

National Aquarium in Baltimore. The most-visited attraction in Maryland has more than 10,000 fish, sharks, dolphins, and amphibians dwelling in 2 million gallons of water. Animal Planet Australia: Wild Extremes, a new exhibit built to mimic a river running through a gorge (with all its native wildlife), opened in 2006. The aquarium also features reptiles, birds, plants, and mammals in its rain-forest environment inside a glass pyramid 64 feet high. The aquarium's famed shark tank and Atlantic coral-reef exhibits are spectacular; you can wind through an enormous glass enclosure on a spiral ramp while hammerheads and brightly hued tropical fish glide by. ■TIP➔ **Arrive early to ensure admission, which is by timed intervals; by noon the wait is often two or three hours.** ⊠*Pier 3, Inner Harbor* ☎*410/576–3800* ⊕*www.aqua.org* 🎟*$21.95* ⊗*Nov.–Feb., Sat.–Thurs. 10–5, Fri. 10–8; Mar.–June, Sept., and Oct., Sat.–Thurs. 9–5, Fri. 9–8; July–Aug. 19, daily 9–8; Aug. 20–31, Sat.–Thurs. 9–6, Fri. 9–8; visitors may tour for up to 1½ hrs after closing. Timed*

FodorsChoice

FodorsChoice

tickets may be required on week-ends and holidays; purchase these early in the day.

6 Oriole Park at Camden Yards. Home ☾ ★ of the Baltimore Orioles, Camden Yards and the nearby area bustle on game days. Since it opened in 1992, this nostalgically designed baseball stadium has inspired other cities to emulate its neotraditional architecture and amenities. The Eutaw Street promenade, between the warehouse and the field, has a view of the stadium; look for the brass baseballs embedded in the sidewalk that mark where home

runs have cleared the fence, or visit the Orioles Hall of Fame display and the monuments to retired Orioles. Daily 90-minute tours take you to nearly every section of the ballpark, from the massive JumboTron scoreboard to the dugout to the state-of-the-art beer delivery system. ✉ *333 W. Camden St., Downtown* ☎ *410/685–9800 general information, 410/547–6234 tour times, 888/848–2473 tickets to Orioles home games* ⊕ *www.theorioles.com* ✉ *Eutaw St. promenade free; tour $7* ☾ *Eutaw St. promenade daily 10–3, otherwise during games and tours; tours Mar.–Sept., Mon.–Sat. at 11, noon, 1, and 2; Oct., weekdays at 11:30 and 1:30, Sat. at 11, noon, 1, and 2, Sun. at 12:30, 1, 2, and 3; Nov., Mon.–Sat. at 11:30 and 1:30, Sun. at 12:30 and 2:30.*

3 Port Discovery—The Baltimore Children's Museum. At this interactive ☾ museum adults are encouraged to play every bit as much as children. A favorite attraction is the three-story KidWorks, a futuristic jungle gym on which the adventurous can climb, crawl, slide, and swing their way through stairs, slides, ropes, zip-lines, and tunnels, and even cross a narrow footbridge three stories up. Changing interactive exhibits allow for even more play. ✉ *35 Market Pl., Inner Harbor* ☎ *410/727–8120* ⊕ *www.portdiscovery.com* ✉ *$11.75* ☾ *Memorial Day–Labor Day, Mon.–Sat. 10–5, Sun. noon–5; Labor Day–Memorial Day, Tues.–Fri. 9:30–4:30, Sat. 10–5, Sun. noon–5.*

SHOPPING

Baltimore isn't the biggest shopping town, but it does have some malls and good stores here and there. Hampden (the "p" is silent), a neighborhood west of Johns Hopkins University, has funky shops selling everything from housewares to housedresses along its main drag, 36th Street (better known as "The Avenue"). Some interesting shops can be found along Charles Street in Mount Vernon and along Thames Street in Fells Point. Federal Hill has a few fun shops, particularly for furnishings and vintage items. At the Inner Harbor, the Pratt Street and Light Street pavilions of **Harborplace and the Gallery** (☎ *410/332–4191*) contain almost 200 specialty shops that sell everything from business attire to children's toys. The Gallery has J. Crew, Banana Republic, and the Gap, among others.

NIGHTLIFE

Both Fells Point, just east of the Inner Harbor, and Federal Hill, due south, have hosts of bars, restaurants, and clubs that draw a rowdy, largely collegiate, crowd. If you're seeking quieter surroundings, head for the upscale comforts of downtown or Mount Vernon clubs and watering holes.

BARS AND LOUNGES

Upstairs at **The Brewer's Art** (⊠*1106 N. Charles St., Mount Vernon* ☎*410/547–6925* ⊕*www.belgianbeer.com*) is an elegant bar and lounge with armchairs, marble pillars, and chandeliers, plus a dining room with terrific food; downstairs, the dark basement bar specializes in Belgian-style beers. With its stylized art deco surroundings, the funky **Club Charles** (⊠*1724 N. Charles St., StationNorth Arts District* ☎*410/727–8815*) is a favorite hangout for an artsy crowd, moviegoers coming from the Charles Theater across the street, and, reputation has it, John Waters. **Club Hippo** (⊠*1 W. Eager St., Mount Vernon* ☎*410/547–0069* ⊕*www.clubhippo.com*) is Baltimore's longest-reigning gay bar. A dance club, martini bar, and pub have all helped make **Grand Central** (⊠*1003 N. Charles St., Mount Vernon* ☎*410/752–7133*) into a hip gay hot spot. Beer lovers should visit **Max's Taphouse** (⊠*737 S. Broadway, Fells Point* ☎*410/675–6297* ⊕*www.maxs.com*), which has more than 70 brews on tap and about 300 more in bottles. **Red Maple** (⊠*930 N. Charles St., Mount Vernon* ☎*410/547–0149* ⊕*www.930redmaple.com*) is one of the city's most stylish spots for drinks and tapas. At the top of the Belvedere Hotel, the **13th Floor** (⊠*1 E. Chase St., Mount Vernon* ☎*410/347–0888*) offers a great view, a long martini list, and live dance music. The **Tusk Lounge** (⊠*924 N. Charles St., Mount Vernon* ☎*410/547–8480*), above the Brass Elephant restaurant, is a cozy, classy place for drinks.

COMEDY CLUBS

The Comedy Factory (⊠*36 Light St., Inner Harbor* ☎*410/752–4189*) is the best local spot to see live standup.

WHERE TO EAT

Baltimore loves crabs. Soft- or hardshell crabs, crab cakes, crab dip—the city's passion for clawed crustaceans seems to have no end. Flag down a Baltimore native and ask them where the best crab joint is and you'll get a list of options. In addition to crabs and seafood, Baltimore's restaurant landscape also includes Italian, Afghan, Greek, American, tapas, and other cuisines. The city's dining choices may not compare with those of New York, or even Washington, but it does have some real standouts. Note that places generally stop serving by 10 PM, if not earlier.

For price categories, see ⇨ Dining at the beginning of this chapter.

$–$$ ✕**Amicci's.** At this self-proclaimed "very casual eatery," you don't have
ITALIAN to spend a fortune to get a satisfying taste of Little Italy. Blue jean–clad

diners and walls hung with movie posters make for a fun atmosphere. Service is friendly and usually speedy, and the food comes in large portions. Try the chicken Lorenzo: breaded chicken breast covered in a marsala wine sauce, red peppers, prosciutto, and provolone. ✉ *231 S. High St., Little Italy* ☎ *410/528–1096* ✆ *www.amiccis.com* ⊟ *AE, D, DC, MC, V.*

¢–$ × **Attman's.** Open since 1915, this authentic New York–style deli near
ISRAELI the Jewish Museum is the king of Baltimore's "Corned Beef Row." Of
★ the three delis on the row, Attman's has the longest waits and steepest prices, but delivers the highest-quality dishes. Don't be put off by the long lines—they move fairly quickly, and the outstanding corned beef sandwiches are worth the wait, as are the pastrami, homemade chopped liver, and other oversize creations. Attman's closes at 6:30 PM daily. ✉ *1019 Lombard St., Historic Jonestown* ☎ *410/563–2666* ✆ *www. attmansdeli.com* ⊟ *AE, DC, MC, V* ⊘ *Closed Sat.*

$$–$$$ × **Bo Brooks.** Picking steamed crabs on Bo Brooks's waterfront deck
SEAFOOD with a pitcher of cold beer at hand as sailboats and tugs ply the harbor
★ is a quintessential Baltimore pleasure. Locals spend hot summer days cracking into warm, spicy crabs while a cool breeze blows in from the harbor. Brooks serves its famous crustaceans year-round, along with a menu of Chesapeake seafood classics. Locals know to stick to the Maryland crab soup, crab dip, jumbo lump crab cakes, and fried oysters. ✉ *2701 Boston St., Canton* ☎ *410/558–0202* ✆ *www.bobrooks. com* ⊟ *AE, D, MC, V.*

$$–$$$ × **Rusty Scupper.** A tourist favorite, the Rusty Scupper undoubtedly has
SEAFOOD the best view along the waterfront; sunset here is magical, with the sun sinking slowly into the harbor as lights twinkle on the city's skyscrapers. The interior is decorated with light wood and windows from floor to ceiling; the house specialty is seafood, particularly the jumbo lump crab cake, but the menu also includes beef, chicken, and pasta. Reservations are essential on Friday and Saturday, and service can be spotty. ✉ *402 Key Hwy., Inner Harbor* ☎ *410/727–3678* ⊟ *AE, D, DC, MC, V.*

WHERE TO STAY

When booking a hotel or bed-and-breakfast in Baltimore, focus on the Inner Harbor, where you're likely to spend a good deal of time. The downside to staying in hotels near downtown is the noise level, which can rise early in the morning and stay up late into the night—especially if there's a baseball or football game. For quieter options, head to neighborhoods like Fells Point and Canton.

$$–$$$ ▦ **Celie's Waterfront Bed & Breakfast.** Proprietors Nancy and Kevin Kupec oversee every detail of this small inn in the heart of Fells Point. Guest rooms, all with private bath, are furnished in Early American style; two suites accommodate large groups. Upscale amenities include down comforters, terry robes, fireplaces, and whirlpool baths. Continental breakfast is served in the cozy dining room. The rooftop deck provides a wonderful view of Baltimore's skyline and harbor. **Pros:** intimate accommodations; situated next to an entertainment district. **Cons:** prices high for what you get; it can get noisy late at night. ✉ *1714 Thames St., Fells*

Point ☎410/522–2323 or 800/432–0184 ⊕*www.celieswaterfront.com* ⌂7 rooms, 2 suites ♿In-room: Wi-Fi. In-hotel: restaurant, parking (paid) ⊟AE, D, MC, V ❢◎❩CP.

$$$$ ⌂**Hyatt Regency.** This stretch of Light Street is practically a highway, but the unenclosed skyways allow ready pedestrian access to both Inner Harbor attractions and the convention center. Rooms have rich gold and black-purple prints and cherrywood furniture; most rooms have views of the harbor or the city. The lobby has glass elevators and the chain's trademark atrium. The 12th floor is the Club level, with complimentary breakfast, evening hors d'oeuvres, and a private concierge available. Atop the hotel, the Pisces restaurant and lounge provides stunning city views, especially at night. **Pros:** the Inner Harbor is just a skywalk away. **Cons:** service can be slow and unhelpful. ⊠*300 Light St., Inner Harbor* ☎410/528–1234 or 800/233–1234 ⊕*baltimore. hyatt.com* ⌂488 rooms, 26 suites ♿In room: Wi-Fi. In-hotel: 2 restaurants, bars, tennis courts, pool, gym, parking (paid), no-smoking rooms ⊟AE, D, DC, MC, V.

$$$–$$$$ ⌂**Marriott Baltimore Waterfront.** The city's tallest hotel and the only one directly on the Inner Harbor itself, this upscale 31-story Marriott has a neoclassical interior that uses multihue marbles, rich jewel-tone walls, and photographs of Baltimore architectural landmarks. Although it's at the eastern end of the Inner Harbor, all downtown attractions are within walking distance; there's also a water-taxi stop right by the front door. Most rooms offer unobstructed views of the city and harbor; ask for one that faces west toward downtown for a splendid panorama of the waterfront and skyscrapers. **Pros:** nice amenities; great location and view. **Cons:** pricey, compared to nearby hotels. ⊠*700 Aliceanna St., Inner Harbor East* ☎410/385–3000 ⊕*www.marriotthotels.com/ bwiwf* ⌂751 rooms ♿In-room: safe, refrigerator, Internet. In-hotel: restaurant, bar, pool, gym, parking (paid), no-smoking rooms ⊟AE, D, DC, MC, V.

$$$–$$$$ ⌂**Renaissance Harborplace Hotel.** The most conveniently located of the Inner Harbor hotels—across the street from the shopping pavilions—the Renaissance Harborplace meets the needs of tourists, business travelers, and conventioneers. Guest rooms are light and cheerful, with amenities that include coffeemakers, terry robes, hair dryers, and ironing boards. Some rooms have a view of the harbor, the downtown landscape, or the indoor courtyard. The hotel adjoins the Gallery, a four-story shopping mall. **Pros:** snappy service. **Cons:** some rooms can be a bit threadbare. ⊠*202 E. Pratt St., Inner Harbor* ☎410/547–1200 or 800/468–3571 ⊕*www.renaissancehotels.com/bwish* ⌂562 rooms, 60 suites ♿In-room: Internet. In-hotel: restaurant, bar, pool, gym, Wi-Fi, parking (paid), no-smoking rooms ⊟AE, D, DC, MC, V.

CHARLESTON, SOUTH CAROLINA

Eileen Robin-
son Smith

Charleston looks like a movie set, an 18th-century etching brought to life. The spires and steeples of more than 180 churches punctuate her low skyline, and tourists ride in horse-pulled carriages that pass grandiose, centuries-old mansions and antique gardens brimming with heirloom plants. Preserved through the poverty following the Civil War, and natural disasters like fires, earthquakes, and hurricanes, much of Charleston's earliest public and private architecture still stands. And thanks to a rigorous preservation movement and strict Board of Architectural Review, the city's new structures blend with the old ones. If you're boarding your cruise ship here, it's worth coming a few days early to explore the historic downtown and to eat in one of the many superb restaurants. In late spring, plan in advance for the Spoleto U.S.A. Festival. For more than 30 memorable years, arts patrons have gathered to enjoy both international and regional concerts, dance performances, operas, improv shows, and plays at creative venues citywide.

> ## CHARLESTON BEST BETS
>
> ■ **Viewing Art.** The city is home to more than 133 galleries, so you'll never run out of places to see world-class art. The Charleston Museum and dozens of others add to the mix.
>
> ■ **The Battery.** The views from the point—both natural and man-made—are the loveliest in the city. Look west to see the harbor; to the east you'll find elegant Charleston mansions.
>
> ■ **Historic Homes.** Charleston's preserved 19th-century houses, including the Nathaniel Russell House, are highlights.

ESSENTIALS

Hours Most shops are open from 9 or 10 AM to at least 6 PM, but some are open later. A new city ordinance requires bars to close by 2 AM.

Internet While almost all hotels (and even B&Bs) offer some kind of Internet service, Internet cafés are rare in the Charleston historic district; however, many coffee shops, including all the local Starbucks, offer Wi-Fi for a fee.

Visitor Information Charleston Visitor Center (✉ *375 Meeting St., Upper King* 🖳 *423 King St., 29403* ☎ *843/853–8000 or 800/868–8118* ⊕ *www. charlestoncvb.com*).

THE CRUISE PORT

Cruise ships sailing from Charleston leave from the Union Pier Terminal, which is in Charleston's historic district. If you are driving, however, and need to leave your car parked, take the East Bay Street exit off the new, majestic Arthur Ravenel, Jr. Bridge on I–17 and follow the signs to the Charleston Aquarium. On ship embarkation days police officers will direct you to the ship terminal from the intersection of Calhoun and Washington streets. Parking is near Union Pier (you can't park in the aquarium garage).

INFORMATION **Port of Charleston** (✉ *196 Concord St., Market area, at foot of Market St.* ☎ *843/577–8776 for Union Pier* ⊕ *www.port-of-charleston.com*).

AIRPORT TRANSFERS Several cab companies service the airport, including the new Charleston Black Cab Company, which operates a fleet of genuine London cabs with uniformed drivers and costs about $10 more than calling a regular cab—about $50 to downtown. Airport Ground Transportation arranges shuttles, which cost $15 per person to the downtown area,

Charleston, SC

TO MOUNT
PLEASANT
AND U.S. 17N

KEY

Cruise Ship Terminal

Exploring sights

Hotels & Restaurants

Charleston
Maritime
Center

Reid St.
South St.
Mary St.
Wragg St.
Ann St.
Judith St.
America St.
Drake St.
East Bay St.
Washington
Chapel St.
Alexander St.
Charlotte St.
Elizabeth St.
John St.
Hutson St.
Henrietta St.
Calhoun St.
Marsh St.
Concord St.

UPPER KING

Marion
Square

TO ASHLEY RIVER RD.

Burns Ln.
Meeting St.
King St.
George St.
Society St.
Wentworth St.
Glebb St.
St. Phillips St.
Coming St.
Beaufain St.
Archdale St.
Magazine St.
King St.
Legare St.
Logan St.
New St.
Orange St.
Greenhill St.
Limehouse St.
Gibbes St.
Laurens St.

NORTH
OF
BROAD

Hasell St.
Pinckney St.
Hayne St.
N. Market St.
S. Market St.
Market St.
Princess St.
Fulton St.
Clifford St.
Horlbeck Al.
Cumberland St.
Meeting St.
Queen St.
Chalmers St.
Phil Al.
State St.
Anson St.
East Bay St.
Pritchard St.

MARKET AREA

Vendue
Range

Broad St.
St. Michael's
Alley
Elliot St.
Exchange St.

SOUTH OF
BROAD

Tradd St.
Prices
Al.
Water St.
Ladson St.
Atlantic St.
Church St.
East Bay St.
Lamboll St.
South Battery

THE BATTERY

East Battery

Cooper River

Murray Blvd.

Ashley River

0   1/4 mile

0   400 meters

$40 to $45 for a reurn trip to the airport. CARTA's bus #11, a public bus, now goes to the airport for a mere $1.25; it leaves downtown from the Meeting/Mary St. parking garage every 50 minutes, starting at 5:45 AM until 11:09 PM.

PARKING An outdoor parking lot is near the pier and patrolled 24 hours a day. Parking costs $15 per day ($105 per week) for regular vehicles, $25 per day ($150 per week) for RVs or other vehicles more than 20 feet in length. You pay in advance (credit cards are not accepted). A free shuttle bus takes you to the cruise-passenger terminal. Be sure to drop your large luggage off at Union Pier before you park your car; only carry-on size luggage is allowed on the shuttle bus, so if you have any bags larger than 22 inches by 14 inches, they will have to be checked before you park. You'll need your cruise tickets to board the shuttle bus.

EXPLORING CHARLESTON

Numbers in the margin correspond to points of interest on the Charleston map.

The heart of the city is on a peninsula, sometimes just called "downtown" by the nearly 60,000 residents who populate the area. Walking Charleston's peninsula is the best way to get to know the city. The main downtown historic district is roughly bounded by Lockwood Boulevard to the west, Calhoun Street to the north, the Cooper River to the east, and the Battery to the south. Nearly 2,000 historic homes and buildings occupy this fairly compact area divided into South of Broad (Street) and North of Broad. King Street, the main shopping street in town, cuts through Broad Street, and the most trafficked tourist area ends a few blocks south of the Crosstown, where U.S. 17 cuts across Upper King. If you don't wish to walk, there are bikes, pedicabs, and trolleys. Street parking is irksome, as meter readers are among the city's most efficient public servants. Parking garages, both privately and publicly owned, charge around $1.50 an hour.

❸ Aiken-Rhett House. This stately 1818 mansion still has its original wallpaper, paint schemes, and even some of its furnishings. The kitchen, slave quarters, and work yard are much as they were when the original occupants lived here, making this one of the most complete examples of urban slave life. Confederate general P. G. T. Beauregard made his headquarters here in 1864. ⊠ *48 Elizabeth St., Upper King* ☎ *843/723–1159* ⊕ *www.historiccharleston.org* 🖃 *$10; $16 with admission to Nathaniel Russell House* ☉ *Mon.–Sat. 10–5, Sun. 2–5.*

❻ Avery Research Center for African-American History and Culture. This center, part museum and part archive, was once a school for freed slaves. Collections include slavery artifacts like badges, manacles, and bills of sale. A riveting mural chronicles the Middle Passage—the journey slaves made from Africa to Charleston's shores. The free tours include a brief film. ⊠ *125 Bull St., College of Charleston Campus* ☎ *843/953–7609* ⊕ *www. cofc.edu* 🖃 *Free* ☉ *Weekdays noon–5, mornings by appointment.*

❷ Charleston Museum. Founded in 1773, the country's oldest museum is housed in a contemporary complex. The museum's decorative-arts holdings and its permanent Civil War exhibit are extraordinary. There are more than 500,000 items in the collection, including silver, toys, and snuffboxes. There are also fascinating exhibits on natural history, archaeology, and ornithology. ■ TIP→ **Combination tickets that give you admission to the Joseph Manigault House and the Heyward-Washington House are a bargain at $22.** ✉ *360 Meeting St., Upper King* ☎ *843/722–2996* ⊕ *www.charlestonmuseum.org* ➜ *$10* ⊙ *Mon.–Sat. 9–5, Sun. 1–5.*

❶ **Charleston Visitors Center.** The center's 20-minute film *Forever Charleston* is a fine introduction to the city. ■ TIP→ **The first 30 minutes are free at the parking lot, making it a real bargain.** ✉ *375 Meeting St., Upper King* ☎ *843/853–8000 or 800/868–8118* ⊕ *www.charlestoncvb.com* ➜ *Free* ⊙ *Apr.–Oct., daily 8:30–5:30; Nov.–Mar. 31, daily 8:30–5.*

❺ **Children's Museum of the Lowcountry.** Hands-on exhibits at this top-notch
Ⓒ museum keep kids up to 12 occupied for hours. They can climb on a
★ replica of a local shrimp boat, play in exhibits that show how water evaporates, and wander the inner workings of a medieval castle. ✉ *25 Ann St., Upper King* ☎ *843/853–8962* ⊕ *www.explorecml.org* ➜ *$7* ⊙ *Tues.–Sat. 10–5, Sun. 1–5.*

⓭ **Edmondston-Alston House.** First built in 1825 in late-Federal style, the Edmondston-Alston House was transformed into the imposing Greek Revival structure you see today during the 1840s. Tours of the home— furnished with antiques, portraits, silver, and fine china—are informative. ✉ *21 E. Battery, South of Broad* ☎ *843/722–7171* ⊕ *www. middletonplace.org* ➜ *$10; $41 with combination ticket for Middleton Place* ⊙ *Tues.–Sat. 10–4:30, Sun. and Mon. 1:30–4:30.*

⓫ **Fort Sumter National Monument.** The first shot of the Civil War was fired
Ⓒ at Fort Sumter on April 12, 1861. After a 34-hour battle, Union forces
★ surrendered the fort, which became a symbol of Southern resistance. The Confederacy held it, despite almost continual bombardment, from August of 1863 to February of 1865. When it was finally evacuated, the fort was a heap of rubble. Today the National Park Service oversees it. The **Fort Sumter Liberty Square Visitor Center,** next to the South Carolina Aquarium, contains exhibits on the Civil War. This is a departure point for ferries headed to the island where you can find Fort Sumter itself. ✉ *340 Concord St., Upper King* ☎ *843/577–0242* ➜ *Free* ⊙ *Daily 8:30–5.* Rangers conduct guided tours of the restored **Fort Sumter.** To reach the fort, you have to take a ferry; boats depart from Liberty Square Visitor Center and from Patriot's Point in Mount Pleasant. There are six crossings daily between mid-March and mid-August. The schedule is abbreviated the rest of the year, so call ahead for details. ✉ *Charleston Harbor* ☎ *843/577–0242* ⊕ *www.nps.gov/fosu* ➜ *Fort free; ferry $15, kids 9 and under $5* ⊙ *Mid-Mar.–early Sept., daily 10–5:30; early Sept.–Mar., daily 10–4 (11:30–4 Jan.–Feb.).*

❹ **Joseph Manigault House.** An outstanding example of Federal architecture, this home was designed by Charleston architect Gabriel Manigault in 1803. It's noted for its carved-wood mantels, elaborate plasterwork, and garden "folly." The pieces of rare tricolor Wedgwood are noteworthy. ✉ *350 Meeting St., Upper King* ☎ *843/722–2996* ⊕ *www.charleston museum.org* ➜ *$10* ⊙ *Mon.–Sat. 10–5, Sun. 1–5.*

7 **Market Hall.** Built in 1841, this imposing landmark was modeled after the Temple of Nike in Athens. The hall contains the **Confederate Museum,** in which the United Daughters of the Confederacy display flags, uniforms, swords, and other Civil War memorabilia. ⊠ *188 Meeting St., Market area* 🕾 *843/723–1541* 🔊 *$5* ☉ *Tues.–Sat. 11–3:30.*

12 **Nathaniel Russell House.** One of the nation's finest examples of Adamstyle architecture, the Nathaniel Russell House was built in 1808. The interior is distinguished by its ornate detailing, its lavish period furnishings, and the "free-flying" staircase that spirals three stories with no visible support. The garden is well worth a stroll. ⊠ *51 Meeting St., South of Broad* 🕾 *843/724–8481* ⊕ *www.historiccharleston.org* 🔊 *$10; $16 with admission to Aiken-Rhett House* ☉ *Mon.–Sat. 10–5, Sun. 2–5.*

Fodor's Choice ★

8 **Old City Market.** This area is often called the Slave Market because it's where house slaves once shopped for produce and fish. Today stalls are lined with restaurants and shops selling children's toys, leather goods, and regional souvenirs. Local "basket ladies" weave and sell sweetgrass, pine-straw, and palmetto-leaf baskets—a craft passed down through generations from their West African ancestors. ⊠ *N. and S. Market Sts., between Meeting and E. Bay Sts., Market area* 🕾 *No phone* ☉ *Daily 9–dusk.*

9 **St. Philip's (Episcopal) Church.** The namesake of Church Street, this graceful late-Georgian building is the second on its site: the congregation's first building burned down in 1835 and was replaced in 1838. During the Civil War the steeple was a target for shelling; one Sunday a shell exploded in the churchyard. The minister bravely continued his sermon. Afterward, the congregation gathered elsewhere for the duration of the war. Notable Charlestonians like John C. Calhoun are buried in the graveyard. ⊠ *146 Church St., Market area* 🕾 *843/722–7734* ⊕ *www.stphilipschurchsc.org* ☉ *Church weekdays 9–11 and 1–4; cemetery daily 9–4.*

Fodor's Choice ★

10 **South Carolina Aquarium.** The 380,000-gallon Great Ocean Tank has the tallest aquarium window in North America. Exhibits display more than 10,000 creatures, representing more than 500 species. You travel through the five major regions of the Southeast Appalachian Watershed: the Blue Ridge Mountains, the Piedmont, the coastal plain, the coast, and the ocean. Little ones can pet stingrays at one touch tank and horseshoe crabs and conchs at another. ⊠ *100 Aquarium Wharf, Upper King* 🕾 *843/720–1990 or 800/722–6455* ⊕ *www.scaquarium. org* 🔊 *$16* ☉ *Mid-Apr.–mid-Aug., Mon.–Sat. 9–5, Sun. noon–5; mid-Aug.–mid-Apr., Mon.–Sat. 9–4, Sun. noon–4.*

SHOPPING

The Market area is a cluster of shops and restaurants centered around the **Old City Market** (⊠ *E. Bay and Market Sts., Market area*). Sweetgrass basket weavers work here, and you can buy the resulting wares. **King Street** is the major shopping street in town. Lower King (from Broad to Market streets) is lined with high-end antiques dealers. Middle King (from Market to Calhoun streets) is a mix of national chains like Banana Republic and Pottery Barn. Upper King (from Calhoun Street to Cannon street) is the up-and-coming area where fashionistas like the alternative shops such as Putumayo.

NIGHTLIFE

At **Mistral** (✉ *99 S. Market St., Market area* ☎ *843/722–5709*) live blues and jazz make patrons feel good on Monday, Tuesday, Thursday, and Saturday nights. On Wednesday, two French musicians sing their renditions of pop and folk songs. On Friday, a Dixieland band really animates those who grew up with this music. During Spoleto, fabulous groups, like a Brazilian combo, electrifies the room. Mistral's French onion soup is fabulous if you want a late-night refuel. **Southend Brewery** (✉ *161 E. Bay St., Market area* ☎ *843/853–4677*) has a lively bar serving beer brewed on the premises. Try the wood-oven pizzas and the smokehouse barbecue. Thursday is salsa night, Friday showcases a bluegrass band, and Saturday night a guitarist. You can dance if the music moves you; in fact, it is encouraged. Listen to authentic Irish music at **Tommy Condon's** (✉ *15 Beaufain St., Market area* ☎ *843/577–3818*).

WHERE TO EAT

For price categories, see ⇨ *Dining at the beginning of this chapter.*

$$

SEAFOOD

×**Bubba Gump.** If you loved Forrest, Jenny, Lieutenant Dan, and the others from the movie *Forrest Gump*, then head to this chain eatery. The food, particularly the shrimp with mango-pineapple salsa, can be surprisingly good. You won't be able

> **WAITER KNOWS BEST**
>
> If your waiter frowns when you make a menu selection, follow his lead. He knows what's good on the dining room menu and what isn't.

to resist the chocolate-chip-cookie sundae. Children who weren't even born when the movie came out in 1994 adore the "Gumpisms" scrawled on the walls of the indoor dining room, and that if you flip the license plate on the table, the server will come back. Young kids love to race the rubber duckies in the mock creek and to get a slushy drink in a glowing plastic cup that is available in the cutesy gift shop. ✉ *96 S. Market St., Market area* ☎ *843/723–5665* ☐ *AE, DC, MC, V.*

$$$–$$$$

SOUTHERN

★

×**Slightly North of Broad.** This former warehouse with brick-and-stucco walls has a chef's table that looks directly into the open kitchen. It's a great place to perch if you can "take the heat," as chef Frank Lee, who wears a baseball cap instead of a toque, is one of the city's culinary characters. Known for his talent in preparing game, his venison is exceptional. Many of the items come as small plates, which make them perfect for sharing. The braised lamb shank with a ragout of white beans, arugula and a red demi-glace is divine. Lunch can be as inexpensive as $9.95 for something as memorable as mussels with spinach, grape tomatoes, and smoked bacon. ✉ *192 E. Bay St., Market area* ☎ *843/723–3424* ☐ *AE, D, DC, MC, V* ☺ *No lunch weekends.*

$$

SOUTHERN

×**Sticky Fingers.** The sound of blues and the aroma of ribs reach the street—where you may have to wait to get seated. This family-oriented local chain was founded by three Charleston buddies who admired

Memphis barbecue. The pulled pork is popular, but the ribs are *it*. You have your choice of five different sauces, including some made with honey or bourbon. ⊠*235 Meeting St., Market area* ☎*843/853–7427* ⊠*341 Johnnie Dodds Blvd., Mount Pleasant* ☎*843/856–9840* ⊠*1200 N. Main St., Summerville* ☎*843/875–7969* ▤*AE, DC, MC, V.*

WHERE TO STAY

While the city's best hotels and B&Bs are in the historic district, most of them do not have free parking. If you stay outside of downtown in a chain hotel, you will give up much in charm and convenience but pay significantly less. High-season rates are traditionally in effect March through May and September through November.

$$$–$$$ **Andrew Pinckney Inn.** The lobby of this boutique inn has a homey ambience that blends South Carolina and the West Indies. The two-story town-house suites, which sleep four, are ideal for longer stays. A heavenly breakfast with fresh-baked pastries and biscuits with sausage gravy is taken on its fourth floor terrace, which overlooks the church spires. It's in the bustling market area, so ask for an interior room. **Pros:** great place if you are looking for quaint Southern charm in the heart of Charleston; afternoon gourmet tea and coffee service with fresh-baked cookies. **Cons:** elevator accesses regular rooms only, not town houses; near the horse stables, which can be smelled. ⊠*40 Pinckney St., Market area* ☎*843/937–8800 or 800/505–8983* ⊕*www.andrewpinckneyinn.com* ⇄*41 rooms, 3 town houses, 1 suite* &*In-room: refrigerator (some), Wi-Fi. In-hotel: laundry service, Internet terminal, Wi-Fi, parking (paid), no-smoking rooms* ▤*AE, MC, V* ❍|*BP.*

$$$$ **Charleston Place.** Even casual passersby enjoy gazing up at the hand-
★ blown Murano glass chandelier in the hotel's open lobby, clicking across the Italian marble floors, and admiring the antiques from Sotheby's. A gallery of upscale shops completes the ground-floor offerings. Rooms are furnished with period reproductions. The impeccable service is what you would expect from an Orient-Express property, particularly on the Club Level, where rooms carry a $100 surcharge that gets you a breakfast spread, afternoon tea, and cocktails and pastries in the evening. A truly deluxe day spa, with an adjacent fitness room, has an inviting indoor salt- and mineral-water pool with a retractable roof and illuminated skylight for night swimming. ■**TIP**→ **Even if you aren't staying here, stop by for afternoon tea at the equestrian-theme Thoroughbred Club.** **Pros:** two great restaurants; located in the historic district on the best shopping street; pet-friendly. **Cons:** no Wi-Fi; rooms aren't as big as one would expect for the price; much of the business is conference groups in shoulder seasons. ⊠*130 Market St., Market area* ☎*843/722–4900 or 800/611–5545* ⊕*www.charlestonplacehotel.com* ⇄*400 rooms, 42 suites* &*In-room: safe, refrigerator, Internet. In-hotel: 2 restaurants, bars, pool, gym, spa, Internet terminal, parking (paid), some pets allowed, no-smoking rooms* ▤*AE, D, DC, MC, V* ❍|*EP.*

$$$ **Hampton Inn–Historic District.** Hardwood floors and a fireplace in the lobby of what was once an 1800s warehouse help elevate this chain hotel a bit above the rest. Spindle posts on the headboards give guest

rooms a little personality. Rooms are not large but have little perks like coffeemakers. The location is perfect for exploring downtown. There is always something to eat and drink in the lobby. **Pros:** hot breakfast; located near the business and retail district of Upper King and near a couple of really good restaurants. **Cons:** a long walk to the Market area; rooms are smallish and not atmospheric. ⊠*373 Meeting St., Upper King* ☎*843/723–4000 or 800/426–7866* ⊕*www.hamptoninn. com* ⊅*166 rooms, 5 suites* ⚒*In-room: refrigerator, Wi-Fi. In-hotel: pool, laundry facilities, parking (paid), no-smoking rooms* ⊟*AE, D, DC, MC, V* ⦶*BP.*

FORT LAUDERDALE, FLORIDA

Lynne Helm

In the 1960s Fort Lauderdale's beachfront was lined with T-shirt shops interspersed with quickie-food outlets, and downtown consisted of a lone office tower, some dilapidated government buildings, and motley other structures waiting to be razed. Today the beach is home to upscale shops and restaurants, while downtown has exploded with new office and luxury residential development. The entertainment and shopping areas—Las Olas Boulevard, Las Olas Riverfront, and Himmarshee Village—are thriving. And Port Everglades is giving Miami a run for its money in passenger cruising, with a dozen cruise-ship terminals hosting more than 20 cruise ships with some 3,000 departures annually. A captivating shoreline with wide ribbons of sand for beachcombing and sunbathing makes Fort Lauderdale and Broward County a major draw for visitors and often tempts cruise-ship passengers to spend an extra day or two in the sun. Fort Lauderdale's 2-mi (3-km) stretch of unobstructed beachfront has been further enhanced with a sparkling promenade designed more for the pleasure of pedestrians than vehicles.

ESSENTIALS

Hours Many museums close on Monday.

Internet If you have your own laptop, Broward County has created a fairly extensive wireless broadband network with numerous Wi-Fi hotspots in downtown Fort Lauderdale, providing free Internet access to anyone using suitably equipped laptops. There's also free Wi-Fi in the airport.

Boat Tours Water Bus (☎*954/467–6677* ⊕ *www.watertaxi.com*) provides service along the intracoastal waterway in Fort Lauderdale between the 17th Street Causeway and Oakland Park Boulevard daily from 10:30 AM until midnight. A day-pass costs $13.

Visitor Information Greater Fort Lauderdale Convention and Visitors Bureau (☎*954/765–4466* ⊕ *www.broward.org*).

THE CRUISE PORT

Port Everglades, Fort Lauderdale's cruise port (nowhere near the Everglades, but happily near the beach and less than 2 mi [3 km] from the airport), is among the world's largest, busiest ports. It's also the straightest, deepest port in the southeastern United States, meaning you'll be out to sea in no time flat once your ship sets sail. The port is south of downtown Fort Lauderdale, spread out over a huge area and actually extending into Dania Beach and Hollywood. A few words of caution: Schedule plenty of time to navigate the port from the airport, your hotel, or wherever else you might be staying, especially if you like to be among the first to embark for your sailing. Increased security (sometimes you'll be asked for a driver's license and/or other identification upon entering the port, other times not) combined with increased traffic, larger parking facilities, construction projects, roadway improvements, and other obstacles mean the old days of popping over to Port Everglades and running up a gangplank in the blink of an eye are history.

If you are driving, there are two entrances to the port. One is from 17th Street, west of the 17th Street Causeway Bridge, turning south at the traffic light onto Eisenhower Boulevard. Or to get to the main entrance, take either State Road 84, running east–west, to the intersection of Federal Highway and cross into the port, or take I–595 East straight into the Port (I–595 becomes Eller Drive once inside the Port). I–595 runs east–west with connections to the Fort Lauderdale–Hollywood International Airport, U.S. 1, I–95, State Road 7 (441), Florida's Turnpike, Sawgrass Expressway, and I–75.

CONTACT **Port Everglades** (⊠*1850 Eller Dr.* ☎*954/523–3404* ⊕*www.portev erglades.org*).

AIRPORT
TRANSFERS Fort Lauderdale–Hollywood International Airport is 4 mi (6 km) south of downtown and 2 mi (3 km) (about 5 to 10 minutes) from the docks. If you haven't arranged an airport transfer with your cruise line, you can take a taxi to the cruise-ship terminals. The ride in a metered taxi costs about $12 to $15, depending on your departure terminal. Taxi fares are $4.50 for the first mile and $2.40 for each additional mile, and 40¢ per minute for waiting time. If you are staying over, Airport Express provides limousine service to all parts of Broward County; fares to most Fort Lauderdale beach hotels are in the $25 range.

> **FORT LAUDERDALE BEST BETS**
>
> ■ **The Beach.** With more than 20 mi of ocean shoreline, don't miss soaking up the scene at Greater Fort Lauderdale's best beaches including those along Lauderdale-by-the-Sea and Fort Lauderdale.
>
> ■ **The Everglades.** Take in the wild reaches in or near the Everglades with an airboat ride. Mosquitos are friendly, so arm yourself accordingly.
>
> ■ **The Riverwalk.** This is a great place to stroll before and after performances, dinner, libations, and other entertainment.

PARKING Two covered parking facilities close to the terminals are Northport (with 2,500 spaces, expanding to 4,250) and Midport (for 2,000 cars). Use the Northport garage if your cruise leaves from Piers 1, 2, or 4; use Midport if your cruise leaves from Piers 18, 19, 21, 22/24, 25, 26, 27, or 29. The cost is $15 per day for either garage ($19 for oversize vehicles up to 40 feet). To save a few bucks on your parking tab, Park 'N Fly provides remote parking just outside Port Everglades, at the exit off I–595, with shuttle service assistance to all cruise terminals. Rates are $12 per day. **Park 'N Fly** (⊠*2200 N.E. 7th Ave., at the Port Everglades exit off I–595* ☎*954/779–1776* ⊕*www.pnf.com*).

EXPLORING FORT LAUDERDALE

Like its southeast Florida neighbors, Fort Lauderdale has been busily revitalizing for several years. In a state where gaudy tourist zones often stand aloof from workaday downtowns, Fort Lauderdale is unusual in that the city exhibits consistency at both ends of the 2-mi (3-km) Las Olas corridor. The sparkling look results from efforts to thoroughly improve both beachfront and downtown. Matching the downtown's innovative arts district, cafés, and boutiques is an equally inventive beach area with its own share of cafés and shops facing an undeveloped shoreline.

Numbers in the margin refer to points of interest on the Fort Lauderdale map.

❻
☾ A stretch from Fort Lauderdale's beaches, but worth the hour-plus drive, is the **Big Cypress Seminole Reservation** with its two very different attractions. At the **Billie Swamp Safari,** experience the majesty of the Everglades firsthand. Daily tours of the wetlands and hammocks, where

wildlife abounds, promise sightings of deer, water buffalo, bison, wild hogs, hawks, eagles, alligators, and occasionally the rare Florida panther. Animal and reptile shows are entertaining. Ecoheritage tours are conducted aboard motorized swamp buggies, and airboat rides are available, too. On the property is Swamp Water Café, serving gator nuggets, frogs' legs, catfish,

> **IT'S A GIRL**
>
> Even as far back as ancient times, mariners have traditionally referred to their ships as "she." To a seaman, a ship is as beautiful and comforting as his mother or sweetheart. You could say a good ship holds a special place in his heart.

3

and Indian fry bread with honey, along with burgers and more. ✉ *19 mi north of I–75 Exit 49* ☎ *863/983–6101 or 800/949–6101* ⊕ *www. seminoletribe.com* ✉ *Free; combined ecotour, reptile or critter show, and airboat ride, $43* ⊙ *Daily 8–5.*

Not far from the Billie Swamp Safari is the **Ah-Tah-Thi-Ki Museum**, whose name means "a place to learn, a place to remember." It is just that. The museum documents and honors traditions and culture of the Seminole tribe of Florida through artifacts, exhibits, and reenactments of rituals and ceremonies. The 60-acre site includes a living-history Seminole village, nature trails, and a wheel chair–accessible boardwalk through a cypress swamp. ✉ *17 mi north of I–75 Exit 49* ☎ *863/902–1113* ⊕ *www.seminoletribe.com* ✉ *$6* ⊙ *Tues.–Sun. 9–5.*

❷ Bonnet House. A 35-acre oasis in the heart of the beach area, this sub-★ tropical estate stands as a tribute to the history of Old South Florida. The charming home was the winter residence of the late Frederic and Evelyn Bartlett, artists whose personal touches and small surprises are evident throughout. Whether you're interested in architecture, artwork, or the natural environment, this is a special place. Be on the lookout for playful monkeys swinging from trees, a source of amusement at even some of the most solemn weddings on the grounds. Hours can vary, so call first. ✉ *900 N. Birch Rd.* ☎ *954/563–5393* ⊕ *www.bonnethouse. org* ✉ *$20 for house tours, $10 for grounds only* ⊙ *Tues.–Sat. 10–4, Sun. noon–4.*

❶ Butterfly World. As many as 80 butterfly species from South and Central ⌘ America, the Philippines, Malaysia, Taiwan, and other Asian nations are typically found within the serenity of this 3-acre site inside Tradewinds Park (itself a delight, with fishing, an educational farm, horseback riding, and sports-equipment rental). A screened aviary called North American Butterflies is reserved for native species. The Tropical Rain Forest Aviary is a 30-foot-high construction, with observation decks, waterfalls, ponds, and tunnels where thousands of colorful butterflies flutter. Kids bug out on the bug zoo. ✉ *3600 W. Sample Rd., Coconut Creek* ☎ *954/977–4400* ⊕ *www.butterflyworld.com* ✉ *$21.95* ⊙ *Mon.–Sat. 9–5, Sun. 11–5.*

❺ Museum of Art. In an Edward Larrabee Barnes–designed building that's ★ considered an architectural masterpiece, this newly renovated museum, which started in a storefront and now makes a habit of hosting world-class touring exhibits, has an impressive permanent collection of

20th-century European and American art, including works by Picasso, Calder, Dalí, Mapplethorpe, Warhol, and Stella, as well as celebrated Ashcan School artist William Glackens. ☒*1 E. Las Olas Blvd.* ☎*954/763–6464* ⊕*www.moafl.org* ☜*$10* ☾*Feb.–mid-Dec., Wed.–Mon. 11–5, Thurs. open until 9; mid-Dec.–Jan. daily 11–5, Thurs. open until 9.*

❸ **Museum of Discovery and Science/AutoNation IMAX Theater.** Open 365 days
★ barring weather-related events, this museum aims to show children—
☾ *and* adults—the wonders of science in an entertaining fashion. The courtyard's 52-foot-tall Great Gravity Clock lets arrivals know a cool experience awaits. Inside, exhibits include Kidscience, encouraging youngsters to explore the world; and Gizmo City, a look at how gadgets work. Florida Ecoscapes has a living coral reef, plus sharks, stringrays, and eels. The AutoNation IMAX theater, part of the complex, shows films (some 3-D) on a five-story-high screen. ☒*401 S.W. 2nd St.* ☎*954/467–6637 museum, 954/463–4629 IMAX* ⊕*www.mods. org* ☜*Museum $10, $15 with one IMAX show* ☾*Mon.–Sat. 10–5, Sun. noon–6.*

❹ **Riverwalk.** Fantastic views and entertainment prevail on this lovely,
★ paved promenade on the New River's north bank. On the first Sunday of every month a free jazz brunch attracts visitors. The walk has been extended 2 mi on both sides of the beautiful urban stream, connecting the facilities of the Arts and Science District.

BEACHES

Fort Lauderdale's **beachfront** offers the best of all possible worlds, with easy access not only to a wide band of beige sand but also to restaurants and shops. For 2 mi (3 km) heading north, beginning at the Bahia Mar yacht basin, along Route A1A you'll have clear views, typically across rows of colorful beach umbrellas, of the sea and ships passing into and out of nearby Port Everglades. If you're on the beach, gaze back on an exceptionally graceful promenade.

Pedestrians rank above cars in Fort Lauderdale. Broad walkways line both sides of the beach road, and traffic has been trimmed to two gently curving northbound lanes, where in-line skaters skim past slow-moving cars. On the beach side, a low masonry wall doubles as an extended bench, separating sand from the promenade. At night the wall is accented with ribbons of fiber-optic color, quite pretty when working, although outages are frequent. The most crowded portion of beach is between Las Olas and Sunrise boulevards. Tackier aspects of this onetime strip—famous for the springtime madness spawned by the film *Where the Boys Are*—are now but a fading memory, with the possible exception of the icon Elbo Room, an ever-popular bar at the corner of Las Olas and A1A.

North of the redesigned beachfront are another 2 mi (3 km) of open and natural coastal landscape. Much of the way parallels the **Hugh Taylor Birch State Recreation Area,** preserving a patch of primeval Florida.

SHOPPING

When you're downtown, check out **Las Olas Riverfront** (⊠*1 block west of Andrews Ave. along New River*), a shopping, dining, and entertainment complex with constantly evolving shops for everything from meals and threads to cigars and tattoos. If only for a stroll and some window-shopping, don't miss **Las Olas Boulevard** (⊠*1 block off New River east of Andrews Ave.*). The city's best boutiques plus top restaurants and art galleries line a beautifully landscaped street.

Just north of Las Olas Boulevard on Route A1A is **The Gallery at Beach Place** (⊠*17 S. Fort Lauderdale Beach Blvd.*). Browse shops, enjoy lunch or dinner, or carouse at assorted nightspots. Lower-level eateries tend toward the more upscale, whereas upper-level prices are lower (go figure), with superior ocean views. ■TIP➔**Beach Place has covered parking, but you can pinch pennies by using a nearby municipal lot.** Just west of the Intracoastal Waterway, the split-level **Galleria Mall** (⊠*2414 E. Sunrise Blvd.*) entices with Neiman Marcus, Dillard's, Macy's, and Saks Fifth Avenue, plus 150 specialty shops for anything from cookware to exquisite jewelry. Chow down at Capital Grille, Blue Martini, Mama Sbarro's, and Seasons 52, or head for the food court, a decided cut above at this upscale mall open 10 AM–9 PM Monday through Saturday, noon–5:30 Sunday. The **Swap Shop** (⊠*3291 W. Sunrise Blvd.*) is the South's largest flea market, with 2,000 vendors open daily. While exploring this indoor–outdoor entertainment and shopping complex, hop on the carousel or stick around for Swap Shop drive-in movies.

NIGHTLIFE

Automatic Slims (⊠*15 W. Las Olas Blvd.* ☎*954/522–8585*) is neon-lit and plenty loud; hordes jam in to do shots and hang out. **Coyote Ugly** (⊠*220 S.W. 2nd St.* ☎*954/764–8459*) continues a tradition of being one of the hottest spots in Broward. **Howl at the Moon Saloon/Sloppy Joe's** (⊠*The Gallery at Beach Place, 17 S. Fort Lauderdale Beach Blvd.* ☎*954/522–5054*) has dueling piano players and sing-alongs Wednesday through Sunday. Sloppy Joe's, a take-off on the iconic Key West bar, is open nightly.

Around since 1948, **Kim's Alley Bar** (⊠*1920 E. Sunrise Blvd.* ☎*954/763–2143*) has two bar areas, a jukebox, and pool tables that provide endless entertainment. **Maguire's Hill 16** (⊠*535 N. Andrews Ave.* ☎*954/764–4453*) hosts live music in classic Irish-pub surroundings. **O'Hara's Jazz & Blues Café** (⊠*722 E. Las Olas Blvd.* ☎*954/524–1764*) takes pride in giving good sax nightly, with live jazz, blues, R&B, and funk. Its crowd spills onto this prettiest of downtown streets. **Parrot Lounge** (⊠*911 Sunrise La.* ☎*994/563–1493*) favored by Philadelphia Eagles fans, backs up libations and revelry with wings, fingers, poppers, and skins.

WHERE TO EAT

For price categories, see ⇨ Dining at the beginning of this chapter.

$$$$ ✕**Blue Moon Fish Company.** Most tables have stellar views of the Intra-
SEAFOOD coastal Waterway, but Blue Moon's true magic comes from the kitchen,
★ where chefs Baron Skorish and Bryce Statham create moon-and-stars-
worthy seafood dishes. Start with the raw bar, a sushi sampler, or pan-
seared fresh-shucked oysters. Salads include hydroponic lettuce with
candied walnuts, and among the entrée favorites are lump crab and
corn-roasted grouper with asparagus risotto and peppercorn-crusted
big-eye tuna with sticky rice. Carnivores might opt for prosciutto-
stuffed veal tenderloin. Wrap up an evening with the tartelette of
bananas Foster. For Sunday champagne brunches book early, even in
the off-season. ⊠*4405 W. Tradewinds Ave.* ☎*954/267–9888* ⊟*AE,
D, DC, MC, V.*

$$ ✕**Floridian.** This Las Olas landmark is plastered with photos of Monroe,
AMERICAN Nixon, and local notables past and present in a succession of brightly
painted rooms with funky chandeliers. The kitchen dishes up some
of the best breakfasts around, with oversize omelets that come with
biscuits, toast, or English muffins, plus a choice of grits or tomato.
With sausage or bacon on the side, you'll forget about eating again
soon. Count on savory sandwiches and hot platters for lunch, tempting
meat-loaf plates for dinner, and friendly, efficient service. It's open 24
hours—even during hurricanes, as long as the power holds out. Feeling
flush? Try the Fat Cat Breakfast (New York strip steak, hash browns
or grits, toast, and worthy champagne) or the Not-So-Fat-Cat, with
the same grub and a lesser-quality vintage. ⊠*1410 E. Las Olas Blvd.*
☎*954/463–4041* ⊟*No credit cards.*

$–$$ ✕**Southport Raw Bar.** You can't go wrong at this unpretentious spot
SEAFOOD where the motto, on bumper stickers for miles around, proclaims EAT
FISH, LIVE LONGER, EAT OYSTERS, LOVE LONGER, EAT CLAMS, LAST LONGER.
Raw or steamed clams, raw oysters, and peel-and-eat shrimp are market
priced. Side orders range from Bimini bread to key lime pie, with conch
fritters, beer-battered onion rings, and corn on the cob in between.
Order wine by the bottle or glass and beer by the pitcher, bottle, or
can. Eat outside overlooking a canal, or inside at booths, tables, or the
bars, in front and back. Limited parking is free, and a grocery-store
parking lot is across the street. ⊠*1536 Cordova Rd.* ☎*954/525–2526*
⊟*MC, V.*

WHERE TO STAY

Fort Lauderdale has a growing and varied roster of lodging options,
from beachfront luxury suites to intimate B&Bs to chain hotels along
the Intracoastal Waterway. If you want to be on the beach, be sure to
mention this when booking your room, since many hotels advertise
"waterfront" accommodations that are actually on inland waterways,
not the beach.

For price categories, see ⇨ Lodging at the beginning of this chapter.

$$$–$$$$
FodorsChoice
★
Hyatt Regency Pier Sixty-Six Resort & Spa. Unfortunately, the trademark of this high-rise resort—the rooftop Pier Top Lounge—has closed. Happily, that space with the most eye-popping views around is open to the public for a pricey Sunday brunch ($65 per head). The iconic 17-story tower dominates a lovely 22-acre spread that includes the full-service Spa 66. Each room has a balcony with views of the 142-slip marina, pool, ocean, or the Intracoastal Waterway. Some guests prefer the ground-level lanai rooms. Lush landscaping and convenience to the beach, shopping, and restaurants add to overall allure. Hail the Water Bus at the resort's dock for access to downtown or the beach. **Pros:** great views; plenty of activities; ideal location. **Cons:** not on the beach; spa's location seems like an afterthought. ✉2301 S.E. 17th St. Causeway ☎954/525–6666 or 800/327–3796 ⊕www.pier66.com ⬅380 rooms, 8 suites ♿In-room: safe, refrigerator, Wi-Fi. In-hotel: 6 restaurants, bars, tennis courts, pools, gym, spa, water sports ▤AE, D, DC, MC, V.

$$$–$$$$
☾
★
Pelican Grand Beach Resort. Smack on the beach, this already lovely property has transformed with a restaurant and lounge, an old-fashioned ice-cream parlor, and a circulating lazy river pool that allows guests to float round and round. Most of the rooms and one-bedroom suites in the newer building have ocean views. The original Sun Tower has gotten a makeover. **Pros:** you can't get any closer to the beach in Fort Lauderdale. **Cons:** you'll need wheels to access Las Olas beach-area action. ✉2000 N. Atlantic Blvd. ☎954/568–9431 or 800/525–6232 ⊕www.pelicanbeach.com ⬅180 rooms ♿In-room: safe, refrigerator, Internet. In-hotel: restaurant, bar, pools ▤AE, DC, MC, V.

GALVESTON, TEXAS

Tim Moloney

A thin strip of an island in the Gulf of Mexico, Galveston is big sister Houston's beach playground—a year-round coastal destination just 50 mi away. Many of the first public buildings in Texas, including a post office, bank, and hotel, were built here, but most were destroyed in the Great Storm of 1900. Those that endured have been well preserved, and the Victorian character of the Strand shopping district and the neighborhood surrounding Broadway is still evident. On the Galveston Bay side of the island (northeast), quaint shops and cafés in old buildings are near the Seaport Museum, harbor-front eateries, and the cruise-ship terminal. On the Gulf of Mexico side (southwest), resorts and restaurants line coastal Seawall Boulevard. The 17-foot-high seawall abuts a long ribbon of sand and provides a place for rollerblading, bicycling, and going on the occasional surrey ride. The city was badly damaged from flooding during Hurricane Ike in 2008; at this writing, most of the businesses that had been closed were beginning to reopen.

Galveston is a port of embarkation for cruises on Western Caribbean itineraries; some Panama Canal cruises leave from here as well. It's an especially popular port of embarkation for people living in the southeastern states who don't wish to fly to their cruise. At this writing, both Carnival and Royal Caribbean have ships based in Galveston.

ESSENTIALS

Hours Shops in the historic district are usually open until at least 7, but some stay open later. This is also the city's nightlife district, and that is hopping until late.

Internet The best place to check your e-mail is at your hotel. Most of the hotels in Galveston offer some kind of Internet service, though usually for a fee. If you have a laptop, the city has a relatively extensive network of free Wi-Fi zones, including several spots on The Strand.

Visitor Information Strand Visitors Center (⊠ *2215 Strand* ⊕ *www.galveston. com*).

THE CRUISE PORT

The relatively sheltered waters of Galveston Bay are home to the Texas Cruise Ship Terminal. It's only 30 minutes to open water from here. Driving south from Houston on I–45, you cross a long causeway before reaching the island. Take the first exit, Harborside Drive, left after you've crossed the causeway onto Galveston Island. Follow that for a few miles to the port. Turn left on 22nd Street (also called Kemnper Street); there is a security checkpoint before you continue down a driveway. The drop-off point is set up much like an airport terminal, with pull-through lanes and curbside check-in.

INFORMATION **Port of Galveston** (⊠ *Harborside Dr. and 22nd St.* ☎ *409/765–9321* ⊕ *www.portofgalveston.com*).

AIRPORT TRANSFERS The closest airports are in Houston, 50 mi from Galveston. Houston has two major airports: Hobby Airport, 9 mi (15 km) southeast of downtown, and George Bush Intercontinental, 15 mi (24 km) northeast of the city. Traffic into Galveston can be delayed because of ongoing construction and demolition work from Hurricane Ike.

Unless you have arranged airport transfers through your cruise line, you'll have to make arrangements to navigate the miles between the Houston airport at which you land and the cruise-ship terminal in Galveston. Galveston Limousine Service provides scheduled transportation (return reservations required) between either airport and Galveston hotels or the cruise-ship terminal. Hobby is a shorter ride (1 hour, $45 one-way, $80 round-trip), but Intercontinental (2 hours, $55 one-way, $100 round-trip) is served by more airlines, including international carriers. Taking a taxi allows you to set your own schedule, but can cost twice as much (it's also important to note that there aren't always enough taxis to handle the demands of disembarking passengers, so you might have to wait after you leave your ship). Negotiate the price before you get in.

INFORMATION **Galveston Limousine Service** (☎ *800/640–4826* ⊕ *www.galvestonlimousineservice.com*).

PARKING Parking is coordinated by the Port Authority. After you drop off your checked luggage and passengers at the terminal, you receive a color-coded parking pass from the attendant, with directions to a parking lot for your cruise departure. The lots are approximately ½ mi (1 km) from

Galveston

GALVESTON BAY

Pelican Island

Pelican Island Causeway

see inset

Cruise Ship Terminal

Moody Mansion ◆

GULF OF MEXICO

GALVESTON SEAWALL

Galveston Island Trolley Route

Cruise Ship Terminal

Harborside Drive

Strand
Mechanic
Market
Post Office

14th 15th 16th 17th 18th 19th 20th 21st 22nd Church

KEY

1 Exploring sights

1 Hotels & Restaurants

Exploring
Broadway **1**
Moody Gardens **2**
Pier 21 Theater **5**
The Strand **3**
Texas Seaport Museum **4**

Restaurants
Fisherman's Wharf **4**
Mosquito Café **5**

Hotels
Hotel Galvez **2**
San Luis Resort **1**
Tremont House **3**

0 ___ 1 mile
0 ___ 1 km

the terminal. Check-in, parking, and boarding are generally allowed four hours prior to departure. A shuttle bus (carry-on luggage only) runs back and forth between the lots and the terminal every 7 to 12 minutes on cruise arrival and departure days (be sure to drop off your luggage *before* you park the car). The lot is closed other days. Port Authority security checks the well-lighted, fenced-in lots every two hours; there is also a limited amount of covered parking. Parking for a 5-day cruise is $50 ($60 covered), 7-day is $70 ($80 covered). Cash, traveler's checks, and credit cards (Visa and MasterCard only) are accepted for payment, which must be made in advance.

EXPLORING GALVESTON

❶ **Broadway.** The late 1800s were the heyday of Galveston's port (before Houston's was dug out). Victorian splendor is evident in the meticulously restored homes of this historic district, some of which are now museums. If you're in town the first two weekends of May, don't miss the **Galveston Historic Homes Tour.** In addition to visiting the neighborhood's museums, you can walk through privately owned homes dating from the 1800s. For more information about area house museums or the tour, contact the Heritage Visitors Center. **Moody Mansion** (⊠ *2618 Broadway* ☎ *409/762–7668* ⊕ *www.moodymansion.org*), the residence of generations of one of Texas's most powerful families, was completed in 1895. Tour its interiors of exotic woods and gilded trim filled with family heirlooms and personal effects. It's open from 11 to 3 daily, charging $7 admission. **Ashton Villa** (⊠ *2328 Broadway* ☎ *409/762–3933* ⊕ *www.galvestonhistory.org*), a formal Italianate villa, was built in 1859 of brick. Look for the curtains that shielded the more modest Victorian guests from the naked cupids painted on one wall. At this writing, it was closed to visitors because of damage from Hurricane Ike in 2008; check for opening dates before visiting. ⊠ *2328 Broadway* ☎ *409/765–7834* ⊕ *www.galvestonhistory.org* ⊠ *Visitor center free, museums $7 each* ⊙ *Visitor Center Mon.–Sat. 10–4, Sun. noon–4.*

❷ **Moody Gardens** is a multifaceted entertainment and educational com-
☾ plex inside pastel-color glass pyramids. Attractions include the 13-story **Aquarium Pyramid,** showcasing marine life from four oceans in tanks and touch pools; **Rainforest Pyramid,** a 40,000-square-foot tropical habitat for exotic flora and fauna; **Discovery Pyramid,** a joint venture with NASA featuring more than 40 interactive exhibits; and two **IMAX theaters,** one of which has a space adventure ride. Outside, **Palm Beach** has white-sand beach, landscaped grounds, man-made lagoons, a kid-size waterslide and games, and beach chairs. ⊠ *1 Hope Blvd.* ☎ *409/741–8484 or 800/582–4673* ⊕ *www.moodygardens.com* ⊠ *$8.95–$15.95 per venue, $35.95 day pass or $40.95 2-day pass* ⊙ *Daily 10–6.*

❺ **Pier 21 Theater.** At this theater on the Strand, watch the Great Storm of 1900 come back to life in a multimedia presentation that includes video clips of archival drawings, still photos, and narrated accounts from survivors' diaries. Also playing is a film about the exploits of pirate Jean Lafitte, who used the island as a base. ⊠ *Pier 21, Harborside*

Dr. and 21st St. ☎*409/763–8808* ⊕*www.galveston.com/pier21the-atre* ✆*Great Storm $5, Pirate Island $4* ☉*Sun.–Thurs. 11–6, Fri. and Sat. 11–8.*

❸ **The Strand.** This shopping area is defined by the architecture of its 19th- and early-20th-century buildings, many of which survived the storm of 1900 and are on the National Register of Historic Places. When Galveston was still a powerful port city—before the Houston Ship Channel was dug, diverting most boat traffic inland—this stretch, formerly the site of stores, offices, and warehouses, was known as the Wall Street of the South. As you stroll up the Strand, you'll pass dozens of shops and cafés. ⊠*Between Strand and Postoffice St., 25th and 19th Sts.*

❹ **Texas Seaport Museum.** Aboard the restored 1877 tall ship *Elissa*, detailed interpretive signs provide information about the shipping trade in the 1800s, including the routes and cargoes this ship carried into Galveston. Inside the museum building is a replica of the historic wharf and information about the ethnic groups that immigrated through this U.S. point of entry after 1837. ⊠*Pier 21* ☎*409/763–1877* ⊕*www.tsm-elissa.org* ✆*$8* ☉*Daily 10–5.*

BEACHES

The **Seawall** (⊠*Seawall Blvd. from 61st St. to 25th St.*) on the Gulf-side waterfront attracts runners, cyclists, and rollerbladers. Just below it is a long, free beach near many big hotels and resorts. **Stewart Beach Park** (⊠*6th St. and Seawall Blvd.* ☎*409/765–5023* ✆*$5 per vehicle*) has a bathhouse, amusement park, bumper boats, miniature-golf course, and a water coaster in addition to salt water and sand. It's open weekdays 9 to 5, weekends 8 to 6 from March through May; weekdays 8 to 6 and weekends 8 to 7 from June through September; and weekends 9 to 5 during the first two weekends of October. **Galveston Island State Park** (⊠*3 Mile Rd., 10 mi (16 km) southwest on Seawall Blvd.* ☎*409/737–1222* ✆*Free*), on the western, unpopulated end of the island, is a 2,000-acre natural beach habitat ideal for birding, walking, and renewing your spirit. At this writing, it is open only on weekends from sunrise to sunset and is not currently charging admission (formerly $3).

SHOPPING

The **Strand** (⊠*Bounded by Strand and Postoffice St. [running east–west] and 25th and 19th Sts. [running north–south]*) is the best place to shop in Galveston. Old storefronts are filled with gift shops, antiques stores, and one-of-a-kind boutiques. More than 50 antiques dealers are represented at the **Emporium at Eibands** (✉ *2201 Postoffice St.* ☎ *409/515–1517*), an upscale showroom filled with custom upholstery, bedding and draperies, antique furniture, and interesting architectural finds. The **Firm** (✉ *2218 Postoffice St.* ☎ *409/762–8300*) was the first retail business along quaint Postoffice Street. Today it is a favorite place to shop for trendy, unique women's fashions from Los Angeles, while reveling in the boutique's shabby-chic decor. **Old Strand Emporium** (✉ *2112 Strand* ☎ *409/515–0715*) is a charming deli and grocery reminiscent of an old-fashioned ice-cream parlor and sandwich shop, with candy bins, packaged nuts, and more.

> **BOARDING PASSES**
>
> Modern ID cards and scanning equipment record passenger comings and goings on the majority of cruise ships these days. With a swipe through a machine (it looks much like a credit card swipe at the supermarket), security personnel know who is on board the vessel at all times. On most large ships passengers' pictures are recorded digitally at check-in.

NIGHTLIFE

For a relaxing evening, choose any of the harborside restaurant-bars on piers 21 and 22 to sip a glass of wine or a frozen Hurricane as you watch the boats go by. The **Grand 1894 Opera House** (✉ *2020 Postoffice St.* ☎ *409/765–1894 or 800/821–1894* ⊕ *www.thegrand.com*) stages musicals and hosts concerts year-round. It's worth visiting for the ornate architecture alone. Sarah Bernhardt and Anna Pavlova both performed on this storied stage.

WHERE TO EAT

For price categories, see ⇨ Dining at the beginning of this chapter.

$$$–$$$$
SEAFOOD
✕ **Fisherman's Wharf.** Even though Landry's has taken over this harborside institution, locals keep coming here for the reliably fresh seafood and reasonable prices. Dine indoors or watch the boat traffic (and waiting cruise ships) from the patio. Start with a cold combo, like boiled shrimp and grilled rare tuna. For entrées, the fried fish, shrimp, and oysters are hard to beat. ✉ *Pier 22, Harborside Dr. and 22nd St.* ☎ *409/765–5708* 🗐 *AE, D, DC, MC, V.*

$$–$$$
AMERICAN
✕ **Mosquito Café.** This chichi eatery in Galveston's historic East End serves fresh, contemporary food—including some vegetarian dishes—in a hip, high-ceilinged dining room and on an outdoor patio. Wake up to a fluffy egg frittata or a homemade scone topped with whipped cream, or try a large gourmet salad for lunch. The grilled snapper with Parmesan grits is a hit in the evening. ✉ *628 14th St.* ☎ *409/763–1010* 🗐 *AE, D, DC, MC, V* ☉ *Closed Mon. No dinner Sun.*

WHERE TO STAY

For price categories, see ⇨ Lodging at the beginning of this chapter.

$$$–$$$$
🏨 **Hotel Galvez: A Wyndham Historic Hotel.** This renovated six-story Spanish colonial hotel, built in 1911, was once called "Queen of the Gulf."

Teddy Roosevelt and Howard Hughes are just two of the many well-known guests who have stayed here. Traditional dark wood and plush upholstery pieces furnish both the public and private areas. A pool, swim-up bar, and outdoor grill have been added to the tropical garden facing the sea. **Pros:** directly on beach; incredible pool area; beautiful grounds. **Cons:** rooms can be small (especially the bathrooms). ⊠*2024 Seawall Blvd.* ☎*409/765–7721* ⊕*www.wyndham.com* ↩*231 rooms* ⚹*In-hotel: Wi-Fi. In-hotel: restaurant, pool, gym, laundry service, Internet terminal, no-smoking rooms* ⊟*AE, DC, MC, V.*

$$–$$$ 🖼 **San Luis Resort, Spa and Conference Center.** A long marble staircase alongside a slender fountain with sculpted dolphins welcomes you to the beachfront elegance of this resort. The upper-floor facade isn't much to look at, but don't let that fool you; inside, the colors of cool, cream marble and taupe stone in the lobby are echoed in the guest rooms. The sculptural lines of pink granite on the headboards and armchairs say "Italian villa." All rooms have balconies facing the Gulf, and prices rise with the floor height. New Club Ten guest rooms on the 10th floor offer upgraded linens, down comforters, iPod docking stations, and huge plasma TVs. Back on ground level, step into the meandering (and heated) grotto pool with a rock waterfall set amid coconut palms and bougainvillea; then have a Balinese massage (or a wildflower compress) at the Spa San Luis. The resort offers free parking for the duration of a cruise as well as transportation to the cruise terminal. **Pros:** great Gulf views; nice pool area. **Cons:** public parking (nonvalet) is not convenient. ⊠*5222 Seawall Blvd.* ☎*409/744–1500 or 800/445–0090* ⊕*www.sanluisresort.com* ↩*244 rooms* ⚹*In-room: Internet. In-hotel: restaurant, room service, bars, tennis courts, pools, gym, spa, children's programs (ages 4–12), laundry service, Internet terminal, parking (free), no-smoking rooms* ⊟*AE, D, DC, MC, V.*

$$–$$$ 🖼 **Tremont House: A Wyndham Historic Hotel.** A four-story atrium lobby, with ironwork balconies and full-size palm trees, showcases an 1872 hand-carved rosewood bar in what was once a busy dry-goods warehouse. This actually is a historic place: Republic of Texas president Sam Houston presented his last speech at this hotel, both Confederate and Union soldiers bunked here, and Great Storm victims took refuge under this roof. Rooms have high ceilings and 11-foot windows. Period reproduction furniture and Victorian-pattern wallpapers add to the authenticity. It's the closest full-service lodging to the port, just a short walk from shopping on the Strand—and it's also a completely no-smoking environment. Damaged heavily during Hurricane Ike, the hotel was expected to reopen at this writing in June 2009. **Pros:** beautiful, historic environment; great location. **Cons:** not a fun scene for young single travelers. ⊠*2300 Ship's Mechanic Row* ☎*409/763–0300* 🖷*409/763–1539* ⊕*www.wyndham.com* ↩*119 rooms* ⚹*In-room: Internet. In-hotel: restaurant, room service, bar, laundry service, Internet terminal, parking (paid), no-smoking rooms* ⊟*AE, D, DC, MC, V.*

Jacksonville

KEY

❶ Exploring sights

① Hotels & Restaurants

JACKSONVILLE, FLORIDA

Kerry
Speckman

One of Florida's oldest cities and at 730 square mi (1,891 square km) the largest city in the continental United States, Jacksonville is underrated and makes a worthwhile vacation spot for an extra day or two before or after your cruise. It offers appealing downtown riverside areas, handsome residential neighborhoods, the region's only skyscrapers, a thriving arts scene, and, for football fans, the NFL Jaguars and the NCAA Gator Bowl. Remnants of the Old South flavor the city, especially in the Riverside/Avondale historic district, where moss-draped oak trees frame prairie-style bungalows and Tudor Revival mansions, and palm trees, Spanish bayonet, and azaleas populate Jacksonville's landscape.

ESSENTIALS

Hours Many museums close on Monday.

Internet Most people access the Internet in their hotel, and most hotels offer some kind of Internet access, often Wi-Fi.

Visitor Information Jacksonville and The Beaches Convention & Visitors Bureau (✉ *550 Water St., Suite 1000, Jacksonville* ☎ *904/798–9100 or 800/733–2668* ⊕ *www.visitjacksonville.com*).

THE CRUISE PORT

Limited in the sizes of ships it can berth, JAXPORT currently serves as home port to the *Carnival Fascination,* which departs weekly on four- and five-night cruises to Key West and the Bahamas during the fall and winter cruising seasons. The facility is fairly sparse, consisting basically of some vending machines and restrooms, but the embarkation staff receives high marks. The terminal itself is a temporary structure; a permanent cruise terminal has been under consideration for some time, but its fate is uncertain at this writing.

> ### JACKSONVILLE BEST BETS
>
> ■ **Jacksonville Zoo.** One of the best midsize zoos you'll visit.
>
> ■ **Kids Kampus.** If you are traveling with your family, this park may become your favorite place in the city.
>
> ■ **Museum of Contemporary Art Jacksonville.** Though small, this is excellent museum is an unexpected treat in northeast Florida.

JAXPORT is about 15 minutes from the Jacksonville International Airport. Take I–95 S to S.R. 9-A E. Follow 9-A to Heckscher Drive (S.R. 105) west until you reach August Drive. Head south on August Drive, and follow the signs to the cruise terminal.

INFORMATION **Jacksonville Port Authority** (⊠ *9810 August Dr., Jacksonville* ☎ *904/630–3006* ⊕ *www.jaxport.com*).

AIRPORT TRANSFERS The transfer from Jacksonville airport takes about 15 minutes and costs $32 to $35 for up to three passengers by taxi. **Gator City Taxi** (☎ *904/741–0008*). **Yellow Cab–Jacksonville** (☎ *904/260–1111*).

PARKING There is a fenced and guarded parking lot next to the cruise terminal, within walking distance. Parking costs $15 per day for regular vehicles, $25 for RVs. You must pay in advance by cash or major credit card.

EXPLORING JACKSONVILLE

Because Jacksonville was settled along both sides of the twisting St. Johns River, a number of attractions are on or near a riverbank. Both sides of the river, which is spanned by myriad bridges, have downtown areas and waterfront complexes of shops, restaurants, parks, and museums; some attractions can be reached by water taxi or the Skyway Express monorail system—scenic alternatives to driving back and forth across the bridges—but a car is generally necessary.

❻ **Anheuser-Busch Jacksonville Brewery Tour.** Beer lovers will appreciate this behind-the-scenes look at how barley malt, rice, hops, and water form the "King of Beers." Guided tours take guests through the entire brewing and bottling process. Or you can hightail it through the self-guided tour and head straight to the free beer tastings (for those guests 21 years and older, that is). ⊠ *111 Busch Dr.* ☎ *904/696–8373* ⊕ *www. budweisertours.com* ☑ *Free* ☉ *Mon.–Sat. 10–4; guided tours Mon.– Sat. 10–3 on the ½ hr.*

❶ **Cummer Museum of Art and Gardens.** The world-famous Wark Collection of early-18th-century Meissen porcelain is just one reason to visit this former riverfront estate, which includes 13 permanent galleries with more than 5,000 items spanning more than 8,000 years and 3 acres of riverfront gardens reflecting Northeast Florida's blooming seasons and indigenous varieties. For the kids, Art Connections allows them to experience art through hands-on, interactive exhibits. One of the museum's latest additions, the Thomas H. Jacobsen Gallery of American Art, focuses on works by American artists, including Max Weber, N.C. Wyeth, and Paul Manship. ✉*829 Riverside Ave.* ☎*904/356–6857* ⊕*www.cummer.org* ✑*$10, free Tues. 4–9* ◷*Tues. 10–9, Wed., Thurs., Fri., and Sat. 10–5, Sun. noon–5.*

❸ Jacksonville Landing. During the week, this riverfront festival marketplace caters to locals and tourists alike, with more than 20 specialty shops with home furnishings, apparel, and toys, nine full-service restaurants—including a sushi bar, Italian bistro, and steak house—and an internationally flavored food court. On the weekends, the Landing hosts more than 250 events each year, ranging from the good clean fun of the American Cancer Society Duck Race to the just plain obnoxious Florida/Georgia game after-party, as well as live music (usually of the local cover band variety) in the courtyard. ✉*2 Independent Dr.* ☎*904/353–1188* ⊕*www.jacksonvillelanding.com* ✑*Free* ◷*Mon.–Thurs. 10–8, Fri. and Sat. 10–9, Sun. noon–5:30; restaurants hrs vary.*

❺ Jacksonville Zoo and Gardens. Encompassing more than 120 acres on Jacksonville's north side, this midsize zoo is home to thousands of amphibians, birds, invertebrates, mammals, and reptiles, from barking tree frogs and Madagascar hissing cockroaches to dusky pygmy rattlesnakes and giant anteaters. Among the zoo's outstanding exhibits is its collection of rare waterfowl and the Serona Overlook, which showcases some of the world's most venomous snakes. The Florida Wetlands is a 2½-acre area with black bears, bald eagles, white-tailed deer, and other animals native to Florida. The African Veldt has alligators, elephants, and white rhinos, among other species of African birds and mammals; and the Range of the Jaguar, winner of the Association of Zoos and Aquarium's Exhibit of the Year, includes 4 acres of exotic big cats as well as 20 other species of animals. One of the zoo's newest addition is its Play Park, complete with a splash park, forest play area, maze, and discovery building. ✉*370 Zoo Pkwy., off Heckscher Dr. E* ☎*904/757–4463* ⊕*www.jaxzoo.org* ✑*$13* ◷*Daily 9–5.*

*Fodor's*Choice
★

❹ Museum of Contemporary Art Jacksonville. In this loftlike downtown building, the former headquarters of the Western Union Telegraph Company, a permanent collection of 20th-century art shares space with traveling exhibitions. The museum encompasses five galleries and ArtExplorium, a highly interactive educational exhibit for kids, as well as a funky gift shop and Café Nola, open for lunch, Sunday brunch, and dinner on Wednesday. MOCA Jacksonville (previously known as the Jacksonville Museum of Modern Art) also hosts film series, lectures, and workshops throughout the year. Big-city visitors often remark that they're impressed with the facility and exhibitions, but with MOCA Jacksonville comprising just 14,000 square feet (compared with the 630,000 at New York's Museum of Modern Art), they wonder where the rest is. Sunday is free for kids and their accompanying adults. ✉*Hemming Plaza,*

*Fodor's*Choice
★

333 N. Laura St. ☎*904/366–6911*
⊕*www.mocajacksonville.org* ✉*$8*
☉*Tues., Wed., Fri., and Sat. 10–4,*
Thurs. 10–8, Sun. noon–4; hrs sub-
ject to change.

② **Museum of Science and History.** You
Ⓒ won't find any mad scientists here,
but you'll probably find lots of gig-
gling ones. Targeted at the elemen-

tary and middle school set, MOSH aims to educate and entertain kids
about science and history through a variety of interactive exhibits like
the JEA Science Theatre, where they'll participate in live experiments
related to electricity and electrical safety; the Florida Naturalist's Center, where they can explore Northeast Florida wildlife (like American
alligators, gopher turtles, and various native snakes and birds); and the
Universe of Science, where they'll learn about properties of physical
science through hands-on demonstrations. Other permanent exhibits
include Atlantic Tails, a hands-on exploration of whales, dolphins, and
manatees; Currents of Time, chronicling 12,000 years of Northeast
Florida history; and Prehistoric Park, featuring a life-size Allosaurus
skeleton. The Alexander Brest Planetarium hosts daily shows on astron-
omy (request your seating pass from the front desk 30 minutes before
any showing) and, on weekends, Cosmic Concerts, 3-D laser shows
set to pop music. ✉*1025 Museum Circle* ☎*904/396–6674* ⊕*www.
themosh.org* ✉*$9 adult, planetarium $1 and Extreme Science Show
$1 (in addition to admission), Cosmic Concerts $7–$9* ☉*Weekdays
10–5, Sat. 10–6, Sun. 1–6.*

SHOPPING

At **Five Points** (✉*Intersection of Park, Margaret, and Lomax Sts., Riverside*) you'll find a small but funky shopping district of new and vin-
tage-clothing boutiques, shoe stores, and antiques shops, as well as a
handful of eateries and bars, not to mention some of the most colorful characters in the city. The **Shoppes of Avondale** (✉*St. Johns Ave.,
between Talbot Ave. and Dancy St.*) highlight upscale clothing and
accessories boutiques, art galleries, home-furnishing shops, a choco-
latier, and trendy restaurants. **San Marco Square** (✉*Intersection of San
Marco and Atlantic Blvds.*) has dozens of interesting apparel, home,
and jewelry stores and restaurants in 1920s Mediterranean-revival–style
buildings. One of northeast Florida's newest shopping destinations, **St.
Johns Town Center** (✉*4663 River City Dr., Southside* ☎*904/642–8339*)
is an outdoor "lifestyle center" with shops not found anywhere else in
northeast Florida, including Anthropologie, Apple, Lucky Brand Jeans,
and Sephora, as well as the Cheesecake Factory, P. F. Changs, and Mag-
giano's Little Italy.

NIGHTLIFE

Technically, **Eclipse** (⊠ *4219 St. Johns Ave.* ☎ *904/387–3582*) is a dance club, but it's the kind that only indie hipster kids—and their thirty-something counterparts—would appreciate. Wine snobs, rejoice! You, too, have a place to hook up: the **Grotto** (⊠ *2012 San Marco Blvd.* ☎ *904/398–0726*). **Harmonious Monks** (⊠ *10550 Old St. Augustine Rd.* ☎ *904/880–3040*) claims to have "the world's most talented waitstaff," who perform throughout the night and encourage customers to dance on the bar. **Jack Rabbits** (⊠ *1528 Hendricks Ave.* ☎ *904/398–7496*) welcomes the latest and greatest indie bands and budding rock stars. The "neighborhood lounge with a dash of dance club style," **Mark's** (⊠ *315 E. Bay St.* ☎ *904/355–5099*) attracts the beautiful people for theme nights like Funkalicious Fridays. **Metro** (⊠ *2929 Plum St.* ☎ *904/388–8719*) is more than just a gay bar: it's like seven gay bars rolled into one, including a piano bar, dance club, lounge, and drag-show cabaret. Fans of Christian music flock to the **Murray Hill Theatre** (⊠ *932 Edgewood Ave. S* ☎ *904/388–7807*), a no-smoking, no-alcohol club. At 12,000 square feet, **Plush** (⊠ *845 University Blvd. N* ☎ *904/743–1845*) is certainly Jacksonville's largest nightclub; it's also the loudest. **Square One** (⊠ *1974 San Marco Blvd.* ☎ *904/306–9004*) has an upscale singles scene, with live music on weekends.

WHERE TO EAT

JAXPORT's location on Jacksonville's Westside means there aren't too many nearby restaurants. But by taking a 10- to 15-minute drive south, you'll find a wealth of restaurants for all tastes and price categories.

For price categories, see ⇨ Dining at the beginning of this chapter.

$$–$$$
AMERICAN
✕**Biscottis.** The local artwork on the redbrick walls is a mild distraction from the jovial crowds (from yuppies to soccer moms to metrosexuals) jockeying for tables in this midsize restaurant. Elbows almost touch, but no one seems to mind. The menu offers the unexpected: wild mushroom ravioli with a broth of corn, leek, and dried apricot; or curry-grilled swordfish with cucumber-fig bordelaise sauce. Be sure to sample from Biscottis' decadent dessert case (we hear the peanut butter ganache is illegal in three states). Brunch served until 3 on weekends. ⊠ *3556 St. Johns Ave., Avondale* ☎ *904/387–2060* ⌂ *Reservations not accepted* ▤ *AE, MC, V.*

$$$–$$$$
ECLECTIC
★
✕**Bistro Aix.** When a Jacksonville restaurant can make Angelinos feel like they haven't left home, that's saying a lot. With its slick black-leather booths, 1940s brick work, velvet drapes, and intricate marbled globes, Bistro Aix (pronounced "X") is just that place. Regulars can't get enough of the creamy onion soup, crispy calamari, and house-made potato chips with warm blue-cheese appetizers or entrées like oak-fired fish Aixoise, grilled salmon, and filet mignon. (Diners on a budget may want to stop by for lunch or try a wood-fired pizza for dinner.) Aix's resident pastry chef ensures no sweet tooth leaves unsatisfied. For the most part, waitstaff are knowledgeable and pleasant, though some patrons find their demeanor snooty, except, of course, the ones from L.A. Call for preferred seating. ⊠ *1440 San Marco Blvd., San Marco*

☎ 904/398–1949 ⚓ *Reservations not accepted* ▤ *AE, D, DC, MC, V* 🕒 *No lunch weekends.*

WHERE TO STAY

Hotels near the cruise terminals are few and far between, so most cruisers needing a room make the drive to Downtown (15 minutes) or to the Southbank or Riverside (20 minutes).

For price categories, see ⇨ Lodging at the beginning of this chapter.

3

$$–$$$ 🏨**Crowne Plaza Jacksonville Riverfront.** A staple on Jacksonville's south bank for decades, the former Hilton Jacksonville Riverfront maintains its commanding presence but now as a Crowne Plaza property. Its location on the south side of the St. Johns River puts it within walking distance of restaurants, the Automated Skyway Express, and the water taxi; Ruth's Chris Steak House is one of the on-site restaurants. Guests wanting to live like a king can book the San Marco (aka the Elvis Room), a premier suite with Jacuzzi tub and two balconies that Presley called home during numerous trips to Jacksonville. **Pros:** newly renovated rooms; riverfront balconies; friendly staff. **Cons:** small bathrooms; loud air-conditioning units; no free parking. ✉ *1201 Riverplace Blvd.* ☎ *904/398–8800* ⊕ *www.cpjacksonville.com* ↪ *292 rooms, 30 suites* ♿ *In-room: refrigerator (some), Wi-Fi. In-hotel: 2 restaurants, room service, bars, pool, gym, laundry service, Wi-Fi, parking (paid), no-smoking rooms* ▤ *AE, D, MC, V.*

$$$ 🏨**Hyatt Regency Jacksonville Riverfront.** In Jacksonville it doesn't get much more convenient than this downtown waterfront hotel. Perched on the north bank of the St. Johns River, the 19-story property is within walking distance of the Jacksonville Landing, Florida Theatre and Times-Union Center, corporate office towers, and the county courthouse. The former Adam's Mark Hotel has undergone some significant changes, including the addition of the Plaza III Steakhouse and a complete room overhaul with Florida-style decor, triple-sheeted beds, pillow-top mattresses, and sliding glass doors. Since northeast Florida's largest hotel encompasses 110,000 square feet of meeting space, chances are pretty good you'll share an elevator with someone wearing a name tag (if you're not wearing one yourself). **Pros:** riverfront location; newly renovated; rooftop pool and gym. **Cons:** not all rooms are riverfront; slow valet service; no minibars. ✉ *225 E. Coastline Dr.* ☎ *904/588–1234* ⊕ *www.jacksonville. hyatt.com* ↪ *966 rooms, 21 suites* ♿ *In-room: refrigerator (some), DVD (some), Internet. In-hotel: 3 restaurants, room service, bar, pool, gym, laundry facilities, laundry service, Wi-Fi, parking (paid), some pets allowed, no-smoking rooms* ▤ *AE, D, DC, MC, V.*

MIAMI, FLORIDA

Updated by
Michelle Delio
and Michael
de Zayas

Miami is the busiest of Florida's very busy cruise ports. Because there's so much going on here, you might want to schedule an extra day or two before and/or after your cruise to explore North America's most Latin city. Downtown is a convenient place to stay if you are meeting up with a cruise ship, but at night, except for Bayside Marketplace, the

American Airlines Arena, and a few ever-changing clubs in warehouses, the area is deserted. Travelers spend little time here, since most tourist attractions are in other neighborhoods. Miami Beach, particularly the 1-square-mi Art Deco District in South Beach—the section south of 24th to 28th streets—is the heart of Miami's vibrant nightlife and restaurant scene. But you may also want to explore beyond the beach, including the Little Havana, Coral Gables, and Coconut Grove sections of the city.

THE CRUISE PORT

The Port of Miami, in downtown Miami near Bayside Marketplace and the MacArthur Causeway, justifiably bills itself as the Cruise Capital of the World. Home to 9 cruise lines and the largest year-round cruise fleet in the world, the port accommodates more than 3 million passengers a year. It has 12 air-conditioned terminals, duty-free shopping, and limousine service. You can get taxis at all the terminals, and car-rental agencies offer shuttles to off-site lots.

If you are driving, take I–95 north or south to I–395. Follow the directional signs to the Biscayne Boulevard exit. When you get to Biscayne Boulevard, make a right. Go to 5th Street, which becomes Port Boulevard (look for the AmericanAirlines Arena); then make a left and go over the Port Bridge. Follow the directional signs to your terminal.

INFORMATION **Port of Miami** (✉ *1015 North American Way, Miami* ☎ *305/371–7678* ⊕ *www.co.miami-dade.fl.us/portofmiami*).

AIRPORT TRANSFERS If you have not arranged an airport transfer through your cruise line, you have a couple of options for getting to the cruise port. The first is a taxi, and the fares are reasonable. The fare between MIA and the Port of Miami is a flat fare of $24. This fare is per trip, not per passenger, and includes tolls and $1 airport surcharge but not tip. SuperShuttle vans transport passengers between MIA and local hotels, as well as the Port of Miami. At MIA the vans pick up at the ground level of each concourse (look for clerks with yellow shirts, who will flag one down). Service from MIA is available on demand; for the return it's best to make reservations 24 hours in advance. The cost from MIA to the cruise port is $15 per person, or $55 if you want the entire van to yourselves.

INFORMATION **SuperShuttle** (☎ *305/871–2000 from MIA, 954/764–1700 from Fort Lauderdale, 800/258–3826 elsewhere* ⊕ *www.supershuttle.com*).

PARKING Street-level lots are right in front of each of the cruise terminals. The cost is $20 per day ($40 for RVs), payable in advance. You can pay with a credit card at most terminals (except for numbers 2 and 10), though it's MasterCard and Visa only.

VISITOR INFORMATION **Greater Miami Convention & Visitors Bureau** (✉ *701 Brickell Ave., Suite 2700, Miami* ☎ *305/539–3000, 800/933–8448 in U.S.* ⊕ *www.gmcvb. com*).

Miami

KEY

▶ ① Exploring sights

▶ ① Hotels & Restaurants

Exploring

▶ Art Deco District
Welcome Center **3**
Bass Museum of Art **1**
Fairchild Tropical
Botanic Garden. **7**
Jungle Island **4**
Lincoln Road Mall **2**
Little Havana **5**
Vizcaya Museum
& Gardens **6**

Restaurants

▶ Azul **3**
Big Pink **5**
Nemo **6**

Hotels

▶ Doubletree Grand Hotel
Biscayne Bay **1**
Loews Miami Beach **4**
The Standard **2**

0 ——— 2 mile
0 ——— 2 kilometer

EXPLORING MIAMI

In the 1950s Miami was best known for alligator wrestlers and you-pick strawberry fields or citrus groves. Well, things have changed. Miami on the mainland is South Florida's commercial hub, while its sultry sister Miami Beach (America's Riviera) encompasses 17 islands in Biscayne Bay. Seducing winter refugees with its sunshine, beaches, palms, and nightlife, this is what most people envision when planning a trip to what they think of as Miami. If you want to do any exploring, you'll have to drive.

❸ Art Deco District Welcome Center. Run by the Miami Design Preservation League, the center provides information about the buildings in the district. A gift shop sells 1930s–1950s art deco memorabilia, posters, and books on Miami's history. Several tours—covering Lincoln Road, Española Way, North Beach, and the entire Art Deco District, among others—start here. You can rent audiotapes for a self-guided tour, join one of the regular morning (Wednesday and Friday through Sunday) or Thursday-evening walking tours, or take a bicycle tour. All of the options provide detailed histories of the art deco hotels. Don't miss the special boat tours during Art Deco Weekend, in early January. ✉ *1001 Ocean Dr., at Barbara Capitman Way (10th St.)* ☎ *305/531–3484* ✉ *Tours $20* ☼ *Sun.–Thurs. 10–7, Fri. and Sat. 10–6.*

❶ Bass Museum of Art. The Bass, in historic Collins Park, is part of the Miami Beach Cultural Park, which includes the Miami City Ballet's Arquitectonica-designed facility and the Miami Beach Regional Library. The original building, constructed of keystone, has unique Maya-inspired carvings. The expansion designed by Japanese architect Arata Isozaki houses another wing and an outdoor sculpture garden. Special exhibitions join a diverse collection of European art. Works on permanent display include *The Holy Family,* a painting by Peter Paul Rubens; *The Tournament,* one of several 16th-century Flemish tapestries; and works by Albrecht Dürer and Henri de Toulouse-Lautrec. Special exhibits often cost a little extra. ✉ *2121 Park Ave., at 21st St.* ☎ *305/673–7530* ⊕ *www.bassmuseum.org* ✉ *$8* ☼ *Tues.–Sat. 10–5, Sun. 11–5.*

❼ Fairchild Tropical Botanic Garden. With 83 acres of lakes, sunken gardens, a 560-foot vine pergola, orchids, bellflowers, coral trees, bougainvillea, rare palms, and flowering trees, Fairchild is the largest tropical botanical garden in the continental United States. The tram tour highlights the best of South Florida's flora; then set off exploring on your own. A 2-acre rain-forest exhibit showcases tropical rain-forest plants from around the world, complete with a waterfall and stream. The conservatory, Windows to the Tropics, houses rare tropical plants, including the Titan Arum (*Amorphophallus titanum*), a fast-growing variety that attracted thousands of visitors when it bloomed in 1998. (It was only the sixth documented bloom in this country in the 20th century.) The excellent bookstore–gift shop carries books on gardening and horticulture, and the Garden Café serves sandwiches and, seasonally, smoothies made from the garden's own crop of tropical fruits. ✉ *10901 Old Cutler Rd., Coral Gables* ☎ *305/667–1651* ⊕ *www.fairchildgarden.org* ✉ *$20* ☼ *Daily 9:30–5.*

Fodor'sChoice
★

4 Jungle Island. South Florida's original tourist attraction—it opened in 1936 in South Miami—closed in 2002 but reopened in 2003 on an island between Miami and Miami Beach. The park is home to more than 1,100 exotic birds, a few orangutans and snakes, a squadron of flamingos, a rare albino alligator, a liger (lion and tiger mix) and a

> **CAUTION**
>
> Airline carry-on restrictions are being updated continuously. Check with your airline before packing, and be aware that large purses will sometimes be counted as a carry-on item!

28-foot-long "crocosaur," plus amazing orchids and other flowering plants. There's also the Hippo, but in this case, it's a three-story water-slide open on weekends. Kids enjoy the hands-on (make that wings-on) experience of having parrots perch on their shoulders. The Japanese garden that once stood on this site is next door—it's open on weekends and free to enter. ■TIP➔**You can eat at the indoor-outdoor lakeside café, overlooking the Caribbean flamingos, without paying the park's admission fee.** ⊠*1111 Parrot Jungle Trail, off MacArthur Causeway (I–395)* ☎*305/400–7000* ⊕*www.parrotjungle.com* ✆*$22.95 plus $7 parking* ⊙*Daily 10–6.*

2 Lincoln Road Mall. The Morris Lapidus–renovated Lincoln Road, just a few blocks from the beach and convention center, is fun, lively, and friendly for people old, young, gay, and straight—and their dogs. Folks skate, scoot, bike, or jog here past the electronics stores at the Collins Avenue end toward the chichi boutiques and outdoor cafés heading west. An 18-screen movie theater anchors the west end of the street. The best times to hit the road are during Sunday-morning farmers' markets and on weekend evenings when cafés are bustling; art galleries, like Romero Britto's Britto Central, schedule openings; street performers take the stage; and bookstores, import shops, and clothing stores are open late. ⊠*Lincoln Rd., between Collins Ave. and Alton Rd.*

Fodor'sChoice
★

5 Little Havana. More than 40 years ago the tidal wave of Cubans fleeing the Castro regime flooded into an older neighborhood west of downtown Miami. Don't expect a sparkling and lively reflection of 1950s Havana, however. What you will find are ramshackle motels and cluttered storefronts. With a million Cubans and other Latinos—who make up more than half the metropolitan population—dispersed throughout Greater Miami, Little Havana and neighboring East Little Havana remain magnets for Hispanics and Anglos alike, who come to experience the flavor of traditional Cuban culture. That culture, of course, functions in Spanish. Many Little Havana residents and shopkeepers speak little or no English. Two blocks in the heart of Little Havana, which are known as **Cuban Memorial Boulevard,** are filled with monuments to Cuba's freedom fighters. Among the memorials are the *Eternal Torch of the Brigade 2506,* commemorating those who were killed in the failed Bay of Pigs invasion of 1961; a bust of 19th-century hero Antonio Maceo; and a bas-relief map of Cuba depicting each of its *municipios.* There's also a bronze statue in honor of Tony Izquierdo, who participated in the Bay of Pigs invasion. ⊠*S.W. 13th Ave., south of S.W. 8th St., Little Havana.*

Through the giant storefront windows of **El Credito Cigar Factory** you can see cigars being rolled. Many of the workers at this family business dating back three generations learned their trade in prerevolutionary Cuba. Today the tobacco leaf they use comes primarily from the Dominican Republic and Mexico, and the wrappers from Connecticut, making theirs a truly multinational product. A walk-in humidor has more than 40 brands favored by customers such as Arnold Schwarzenegger, Bill Clinton, Robert De Niro, and Bill Cosby. ⊠ *1106 S.W. 8th St., near S.W. 11th Ave., Little Havana* ☎ *305/858–4162* ⊙ *Mon.–Sat. 9–4. Factory closed Sat.*

6 **Vizcaya Museum & Gardens.** Of the 10,000 people living in Miami
Fodor'sChoice between 1912 and 1916, about 1,000 of them were gainfully employed
★ by Chicago industrialist James Deering to build this Italian Renaissance–style winter residence. Once comprising 180 acres, the grounds now occupy a 30-acre tract that includes a native hammock and more than 10 acres of formal gardens with fountains overlooking Biscayne Bay. The house, open to the public, contains 70 rooms, 34 of which are filled with paintings, sculpture, antique furniture, and other fine and decorative arts. The pieces date from the 15th through the 19th century and represent the Renaissance, baroque, rococo, and neoclassical movements. So unusual and impressive is Vizcaya that visitors have included many major heads of state. Guided tours are available. Moonlight tours, in particular, offer a unique look at the gardens; call for reservations. ⊠ *3251 S. Miami Ave.* ☎ *305/250–9133* ⊕ *www.vizcayamuseum.org* ☜ *$12* ⊙ *Daily 9:30–4:30.*

BEACHES

Fodor'sChoice The stretch of beach along **Ocean Drive**—primarily the 10-block stretch
★ from 5th to 15th streets—is one of the most talked-about beachfronts in America. The beach is wide, white, and bathed by warm aquamarine waves. Separating the sand from the traffic of Ocean Drive is palm-fringed Lummus Park, with its volleyball nets and chickee huts for shade. The beach also plays host to some of the funkiest lifeguard stands you'll ever see, pop stars shooting music videos, and visitors from all over the world. The beach at 12th Street is popular with gays. Locals hang out on 3rd Street Beach, where they watch fit Brazilians play foot volley, a variation of volleyball that uses everything but the hands! Because much of South Beach has an adult flavor—women are often casually topless—many families prefer Mid- and North Beach. Unless you're parking south of 3rd Street, metered spaces near the waterfront are rarely empty. Instead, opt for a public garage and walk; you'll have lots of fun people-watching, too. ⊠ *Ocean Dr., between 1st and 22nd Sts., Miami Beach* ☎ *305/673–7714.*

SHOPPING

In Greater Miami you're never more than 15 minutes from a major commercial area that serves as both a shopping and entertainment venue for tourists and locals. The shopping is great on a two-block stretch of **Collins Avenue** between 6th and 8th streets. The busy **Lincoln**

Road Mall is just a few blocks from the beach and convention center, making it popular with locals and tourists. There's an energy to shopping here, especially on weekends, when the pedestrian mall is filled with locals. Creative merchandise, galleries, and a Sunday-morning antiques market can be found among the art galleries and cool cafés. An 18-screen movie theater anchors the west end of the street.

> **PACK IT, POST IT**
>
> Pack a pad of Post-It notes when you take a cruise. They come in handy when you need to leave messages for your cabin steward, family, and shipboard friends.

NIGHTLIFE

Most of the city's nightlife scene is concentrated in South Beach. The best, most complete source is the *New Times,* a free weekly distributed throughout Miami–Dade County each Thursday. Greater Miami's English-language daily newspaper, the *Miami Herald,* publishes reliable reviews and comprehensive listings in its "Weekend" section on Friday and in the "IN South Florida" section on Sunday. Various tabloids reporting on South Beach entertainment and the Miami social scene come and go, but *Ocean Drive Magazine* remains the most reliable glossy monthly publication for what's new and hot in the city's fashion, nightlife, and dining scenes. Buy it on the newsstands at Publix or Books & Books, or pick it up for free in South Beach's high-end hotels, salons, and boutiques. *Wire* covers the gay scene.

WHERE TO EAT

At many of the hottest spots you'll need a reservation to avoid a long wait for a table. And when you get your check, note whether a gratuity is included; most restaurants add 15% (ostensibly for the convenience of—and protection from—Latin-American and European tourists who are used to this practice in their homelands and would not normally tip), but you can reduce or supplement it depending on your opinion of the service.

For price categories, see ⇨ Dining at the beginning of this chapter.

$$$$
ECLECTIC
Fodor's Choice
★

✕**Azul.** Azul has sumptuously conquered the devil in the details, from chef Clay Conley's exotically rendered Asian-Mediterranean cuisine to the thoughtful service staff who graciously anticipate your broader dining needs. Does your sleeveless blouse leave you too cold to properly appreciate the Moroccan lamb and seared red snapper? Ask for one of the house pashminas, available in a variety of fashionable colors. Forgot your reading glasses and can't decipher the hanger steak with foie-gras sauce? Request a pair from the host. Want to see how the other half lives? Descend the interior staircase to Café Sambal, the all-day casual restaurant downstairs. ✉*Mandarin Oriental Hotel, 500 Brickell Key Dr., Downtown Miami* ☎*305/913–8358* ⌂*Reservations essential* ▭*AE, MC, V* ✆*Closed Sun. No lunch weekends.*

$–$$

AMERICAN

Fodor'sChoice

★

✕**Big Pink.** The decor in this innovative, super-popular diner may remind you of a roller-skating rink—everything is pink Lucite, stainless steel, and campy (think sports lockers as decorative touches)—and the menu is 3 feet tall, complete with a table of contents. Food is solidly all-American, with dozens of tasty sandwiches, pizzas, turkey or beef burgers, and side dishes, each and every one composed with gourmet flair. Big Pink also makes a great spot for brunch. ⊠*157 Collins Ave., South Beach* ☎*305/532–4700* ▤*AE, MC, V*

$$$$

SEAFOOD

✕**Nemo.** The SoFi (South of 5th Street) neighborhood may have emerged as a South Beach hot spot, but Nemo's location is not why this casually comfortable restaurant receives rave reviews. It's the menu, which often changes but always delivers, blending Caribbean, Asian, Mediterranean, and Middle Eastern influences and providing an explosion of cultures in each bite. Popular appetizers include citrus-cured salmon rolls with tobiko caviar and wasabi mayo, and crispy duck leg confit served with lentils in a tangy pineapple sauce. Main courses might include wok-charred salmon or grilled Indian-spice pork chop. Bright colors and copper fixtures highlight the tree-shaded courtyard. ⊠*100 Collins Ave., South Beach* ☎*305/532–4550* ▤*AE, DC, MC, V*

WHERE TO STAY

Staying in downtown Miami will put you close to the cruise terminals, but there is little to do at night. South Beach is the center of the action in Miami Beach, but it's fairly distant from the port. Staying in Miami Beach, but north of South Beach's Art Deco District, will put you on the beach but nominally closer to the port.

For price categories, see ⇨ *Lodging at the beginning of this chapter.*

$$$

🏨 **Doubletree Grand Hotel Biscayne Bay.** Like the Biscayne Bay Marriott, this elegant waterfront option is at the north end of downtown off a scenic marina, and near many of Miami's headline attractions: the Port of Miami, Bayside, the Arena, and the Carnival Center. Rooms are spacious, and most have a view of Biscayne Bay and the port. Some suites have full kitchens. You can rent Jet Skis or take deep-sea-fishing trips from the marina. **Pros:** great bay views; deli and market on-site. **Cons:** need a cab to get around. ⊠*1717 N. Bayshore Dr., Downtown Miami* ☎*305/372–0313 or 800/222–8733* ⊕*www.doubletree.com* ⤵*152 suites* ♿*In-room: safe, kitchen (some), Wi-Fi. In-hotel: restaurant, room service, bar, pool, gym, spa* ▤*AE, D, DC, MC, V.*

$$$$

🏨 **Loews Miami Beach Hotel.** The oldest of South Beach's "new hotels," Loews Miami Beach is marvelous for families, businesspeople, and groups. The 800-room megahotel combines top-tier amenities, a massive new spa, a great pool, and a direct beachfront setting in its pair of enormous 12- and 18-story towers. When it was built in 1998, Loews managed not only to snag 99 feet of beach, but also to take over the vacant St. Moritz next door and restore it to its original 1939 art deco beauty. The entire complex combines boutique charm with updated opulence. How big is it? The Loews has 85,000 square feet of meeting space and an enormous ocean-view grand ballroom. Emeril Lagasse opened a restaurant here, and a three-story spa has 15 treatment rooms and a state-of-the-art fitness center. In the grand lobby you'll find a dozen black-suited staffers behind the counter, and a half-dozen other bellboys and valets. Rooms are great: contemporary and very comfortable, with flat-screen TVs and high-end amenities. If you like big hotels with all the services, this is your choice in South Beach. **Pros:** top-notch amenities include a beautiful oceanfront pool and immense spa. **Cons:** intimacy is lost due to its large size. ⊠*1601 Collins Ave.* ☎*305/604–1601 or 800/235–6397* ⊕*www.loewshotels.com/miamibeach* ⇄*733 rooms, 57 suites* ♿*In-room: Internet. In-hotel: 3 restaurants, room service, bars, pool, gym, spa, beachfront, laundry service, Internet terminal, Wi-Fi, parking (paid), some pets allowed, no-smoking rooms* ▤*AE, D, DC, MC, V*

$$$–$$$$ **The Standard.** An extension of André Balazs's trendy, budget hotel chain, the Standard is a Hollywood newcomer that set up shop a few minutes from South Beach on an island just over the Venetian Causeway. The message: we'll do what we please, and the cool kids will follow. The scene is trendy 30- and 40-year-olds interested in the hotel's many "do-it-yourself" spa activities, including mud bathing, scrubbing with sea salts, soaking in hot or arctic-cold waters, and yoga. An 8-foot, 103-degree cascade into a Roman hot tub is typical of the handful of adult pleasures spread around the pool deck. An informal restaurant overlooks the bay's Mediterranean-style mansions and the cigarette boats that float past. If you choose, you can go kayaking around the island. On the hotel facade you'll see the monumental signage of a bygone occupant, the Lido Spa Hotel, and the much smaller sign of its current occupant, hung, with a wink, upside down. The rooms are small and simple, though they have thoughtful touches like a picnic basket and embroidered fabric covers for the small flat-screen TVs. First-floor rooms have outdoor soaking tubs but very limited privacy, so few take that plunge. **Pros:** interesting island location; free bike and kayak rentals; swank pool scene; great spa; inexpensive. **Cons:** removed from South Beach nightlife; small rooms with no views; outdoor tubs are gimmicks; mediocre service. ⊠*40 Island Ave., Belle Isle* ☎*305/673–1717* ⊕*www.standardhotel.com* ⇄*104 rooms, 1 suite* ♿*In-room: safe, refrigerator, DVD, Internet. In-hotel: restaurant, room service, bars, pool, gym, spa, water sports, bicycles, laundry service, Wi-Fi, parking (paid), some pets allowed, no children under 14, no-smoking rooms* ▤*AE, D, DC, MC, V*

MOBILE, ALABAMA

Updated by
Clint Hill

Fort Condé was the name given by the French in 1711 to the site known today as Mobile; around it blossomed the first white settlement in what is now Alabama. For eight years it was the capital of the French colonial empire, and it remained under French control until 1763, long after the capital had moved to New Orleans. Mobile, known as the "Port City"—not to mention the birthplace of Mardi Gras—is noted for its tree-lined boulevards fanning westward from the riverfront. In the heart of busy downtown is Bienville Square, a park with an ornate cast-iron fountain and shaded by centuries-old live oaks. One of the city's main thoroughfares, Dauphin Street, has many thriving restaurants, bars, and shops.

THE CRUISE PORT

The *Carnival Holiday* is based in Mobile at this writing, and it does shorter (four- and five-day) Western Caribbean itineraries. The cruise terminal is near the downtown area. Free shuttles from Mobile's public transit system, Moda, are provided to the cruise terminal from throughout downtown Mobile on days when ships are in port. It's a good home port to consider if you want to drive, but it's less convenient by air, with just a few airlines flying to the Mobile Regional Airport; however, the Biloxi and Pensacola airports are a relatively short drive away.

INFORMATION **Mobile Alabama Cruise Terminal** (✉ *201 S. Water St., Mobile* ☎ *251/338–7447* ⊕ *www.shipmobile.com*).

AIRPORT TRANSFERS Taxis are available to the cruise terminal, or you can call the Mobile Regional Airport Shuttle, which will transport you for $13 per person ($25 round-trip). Mobile Bay Transportation Company also operates airport transfers. A taxi costs about $30 each way, but that is for the trip not per-passenger. **Mobile Bay Transportation Company** (☎ *251/633–5693* or *800/272–6234* ⊕ *www.mobilebaytransportation.com*). **Mobile Regional Airport Shuttle** (☎ *251/633–0313 or 800/357–5373* ⊕ *www.mobairport.com*).

PARKING Parking is available in a garage next to the cruise terminal. It costs $15 a day for cars, $30 for RVs. You can pay by cash or credit card.

VISITOR INFORMATION **Mobile Bay Convention & Visitor's Bureau** (✉ *1 S. Water St., Mobile* ☎ *251/208–2000 or 800/566–2453* ⊕ *www.mobilebay.org*).

EXPLORING MOBILE

Numbers in the margin refer to points of interest on the Mobile map.

❸ **Battleship Memorial Park.** Mobile Bay, east of downtown, is the site of the 155-acre park where the battleship USS *Alabama* is anchored. A self-guided tour gives a fascinating glimpse into the World War II vessel, which had a crew of 2,500. Dry-docked next to it is the USS *Drum*, a World War II submarine. Other exhibits include the B-52 bomber *Calamity Jane*. ✉ *2703 Battleship Pkwy., Mobile* ☎ *251/433–2703 or 800/426–4929* ⊕ *www.ussalabama.com* 🎟 *$12* ⊘ *Apr.–Sept., daily 8–6; Oct.–Mar., daily 8–4.*

❻ **Bellingrath Gardens & Home.** One of the most popular gardens in the South is Bellingrath, famous for its magnificent azaleas, which are part of 65 acres of gardens set amid a 905-acre semitropical landscape. Showtime for the azaleas is mid- to late-March, when some 250,000 plantings of 200 different species are ablaze with color. But Bellingrath is a year-round wonder, with more than 75 varieties of roses blooming in summer, 60,000 chrysanthemum plants cascading in fall, and red fields of poinsettias brightening winter. Countless species and flowering plants spring up along the Fowl River, surround streams, and a lake populated by ducks and swans. A free map lets you plan your own strolls along flagstone paths

Fodor's Choice
★

across charming bridges. In April and October large numbers of migratory birds drop by. You can also visit the home of Coca-Cola bottling pioneer Walter D. Bellingrath. Forty-five-minute boat cruises on the Fowl River aboard the *Southern Belle* leave from the dock next to the home daily at 10, noon, and 2 from mid-February through Thanksgiving. Take I–10 West to Exit 15, then follow CR 59 South to Theodore. ✉*12401 Bellingrath Gardens Rd., Theodore* 🕾*251/973–2217, 800/247–8420, 251/973–1244 for boat cruises* ⊕*www.bellingrath.org* 🖾*Gardens $11; gardens and home $19; gardens, home, and cruise $27* ⊙*Gardens daily 8–5, home daily 9–4.*

❹ **Ft. Condé.** In 1711 France built this fort that would one day expand and become Mobile. The city's French origins endure in its creole cuisine. Now, 150 years after the fort was destroyed, its remains were discovered during construction of the I–10 interchange. A reconstructed portion houses the city's **visitor center,**

MOBILE BEST BETS

■ **Bellingrath Gardens.** One of the finest gardens in the South is just outside Mobile.

■ **Battleship Memorial Park.** Many people come to Mobile just to tour the USS *Alabama.*

■ **Oakleigh.** This well-preserved antebellum home is furnished with period antiques; it's a great experience if you like history.

as well as a museum. Costumed guides conduct tours. ✉*150 S. Royal St., Mobile* ☎*251/208–7304* ⊕*www.museumofmobile.com* ✉*Free* ☉*Daily 8–5.*

❷ **Gulf Coast Exploreum Science Center.** Near Ft. Condé, Mobile's science museum for children hosts traveling exhibits and an IMAX dome theater. ✉*65 Government St., Mobile* ☎*251/208–6883 or 877/625–4386* ⊕*www.exploreum.net* ✉*Museum $10, IMAX $8, both $14; admission charges are sometimes increased for special exhibitions* ☉*Weekdays 9–5, Sat. 10–5, Sun. noon–5.*

> **FRESH, WRINKLE-FREE**
>
> You can tuck fabric-softener sheets between garments as you pack to keep your clothing smelling fresh during travel. Dry-cleaning bags are good for keeping out wrinkles.

❺ **Mobile Carnival Museum.** Mobile celebrates its heritage in this converted 1870 town house dedicated to all things Mardi Gras. The pre-Lenten festival was first celebrated in the New World here in Mobile in 1703, and the museum allows the party to continue 365 days a year. Displays include regal costumes of past kings and queens, traditional Mardi Gras "throws" (items that are thrown from the floats during parades), and even full-sized floats. ✉*355 Government St.* ☎*251/432–3324* ⊕*www. mobilecarnivalmuseum.com* ✉*$5* ☉*Mon., Wed., Fri., Sat. 9–4.*

❶ **Museum of Mobile.** The museum opened in 2001 in the renovated circa-1857 Southern Market/Old City Hall building next to the Exploreum. Interactive exhibits and special collections of antique silver, weapons, and more tell the 300-year history of Mobile. ✉*111 S. Royal St., Mobile* ☎*251/208–7569* ⊕*www.museumofmobile.com* ✉*$5* ☉*Mon.–Sat. 9–5, Sun. 1–5.*

❼ **Oakleigh.** About 1½ mi (2 ½ km) from Ft. Condé, in the heart of the ★ historic Oakleigh Garden District, is an antebellum Greek Revival–style mansion built between 1833 and 1838. Costumed guides give tours of the home, which has fine period furniture, portraits, silver, jewelry, kitchen implements, toys, and more. Tickets include a tour of neighboring **Cox-Deasy House,** an 1850s cottage furnished with simple 19th-century pieces. ✉*350 Oakleigh Pl., Mobile* ☎*251/432–1281* ⊕*www. historicmobile.org* ✉*$7* ☉*Oakleigh: daily 10–4.*

SHOPPING

Most shopping in Mobile is in malls and shopping centers in the suburbs. Stores are generally open Monday to Saturday 10–9, Sunday noon–6. Antiques buffs may be interested in Mobile's many antiques stores that are in the Loop area of midtown (where Government Street, Airport Boulevard, and Dauphin Island Parkway converge); several shops are within walking distance of each other.

Bel Air Mall (✉*3299 Bel Air Mall* ☎*251/478–1893*) has more than 130 stores, including Parisian, Dillard's, Sears, JCPenney, and Target. **Eastern Shore Centre** (✉*30500 State Hwy. 181, at I–10, Spanish Fort* ☎*251/625–0060*) is the newest shopping complex in Mobile, with 70 stores, including a large Dillard's. It's about 10 minutes from downtown.

NIGHTLIFE

Most of Mobile's nightlife centers around the downtown's former commercial district, Dauphin Street, which today has a number of restaurants and nightspots spread out over several blocks. Mobilians have taken to calling the area LoDa, short for Lower Dauphin. In midtown Mobile the **Double Olive** (⊠ *2033 Airport Blvd.* ☎ *251/450–5001*) is an artsy, urbane martini bar that draws hip crowds. **Monsoon's** (⊠ *210 Dauphin St.* ☎ *251/433–3500*) is one of several almost indistinguishable bars that host local bands as well as a few national ones, drawing crowds of twentysomethings on Friday and Saturday nights.

WHERE TO EAT

For price categories, see ⇨ *Dining at the beginning of this chapter.*

CAUTION

Notify the cruise line of any special dietary restrictions when booking your cruise, and then follow up on the arrangements a couple of months before boarding.

$–$$
BARBECUE
✗ **Brick Pit.** It's "the best damn barbecue in the state of Alabama," owner Bill Armbrecht insists. Chicken, ribs, and pork are smoked for hours over a blend of hickory and pecan to achieve a distinct flavor. Barbecue sauce comes spicy or sweet, with soft white bread for dipping. Be sure to add your name to the graffiti scrawled in red marker all over the walls and ceiling. Try the smoked pulled-pork plate. ⊠ *5456 Old Shell Rd.* ☎ *251/343–0001* ▤ *AE, DC, MC, V* ⊘ *Closed Sun. and Mon.*

$–$$
SEAFOOD
✗ **Wintzell's Oyster House.** "Oysters—fried, steamed, or nude" is the motto for this downtown Mobile institution. Founded in 1938 by Oliver Wintzell, the restaurant is in the same location and with few cosmetic changes since it was founded, the walls still covered by Oliver's homespun sayings. You can get your oysters by the dozen or half-dozen, but won't go wrong sampling any of the seafood on the menu or simply enjoying a cup of homemade gumbo. ⊠ *605 Dauphin St.* ☎ *251/432–4605* ▤ *AE, D, DC, MC, V.*

WHERE TO STAY

Several local hotels offer cruise packages that include lodging, parking for the duration of your cruise, and a shuttle to the cruise terminal.

For price categories, see ⇨ *Lodging at the beginning of this chapter.*

$–$$
▦ **Malaga Inn.** A delightful, romantic getaway, this place comprises two town houses built by a wealthy landowner in 1862. The lobby is furnished with 19th-century antiques and opens onto a landscaped central courtyard with a fountain. The rooms are large, airy, and furnished with antiques. The Malaga is on a quiet street downtown, within walking distance of the Museum of Mobile and the Gulf Coast Exploreum, and offers a cruise package. ⊠ *359 Church St.* ☎ *251/438–4701 or 800/235–1586* ⊕ *www.malagainn.com* ⬐ *35 rooms, 3 suites* ⬧ *In-room: Wi-Fi. In-hotel: pool, Wi-Fi* ▤ *AE, D, MC, V.*

$-$$ :::Radisson Admiral Semmes Hotel. This restored 1940 hotel in the historic district is a favorite with local politicians. It's also popular with party-goers, particularly during Mardi Gras, because of its excellent location directly on the parade route. The spacious, high-ceiling rooms have a burgundy-and-green color scheme and are furnished in Queen Anne and Chippendale styles. ✉ *251 Government St.* ☎ *251/432–8000 or 800/333–3333* ⊕ *www.radisson.com* ➘ *148 rooms, 22 suites* ⚴ *In-room: refrigerator, Internet. In-hotel: restaurant, bar, pool, laundry service, Wi-Fi* ⊟ *AE, D, DC, MC, V.*

NEW ORLEANS, LOUISIANA

Tucked between the Mississippi River and Lake Ponchartrain, New Orleans is mostly below sea level, and when Hurricane Katrina struck in August 2005 the city's levees strained under the force of the strong storm's wind and rain, finally breaking. The resulting floods covered 80% of New Orleans. Fortunately, much of the Big Easy that is well known to tourists was relatively untouched by the floods, including most of the French Quarter, the River Walk, the Garden District, and most of Uptown. Within months, these areas rebounded. Although the city is still recovering, all the aforementioned areas are up and running and eager to welcome visitors.

ESSENTIALS

Hours Shops in the French Quarter tend to be open late, but stores in most of the malls close by 9. Restaurants tend to be open late as well.

Internet French Quarter Postal Emporium (✉ *1000 Bourbon St.* ☎ *504/525–6651* ⊕ *www.frenchquarterpostal.com*) offers Internet service and is also a mailing center.

Visitor Information New Orleans Convention & Visitors Bureau (✉ *2020 St. Charles Ave.* ☎ *800/672–6124 or 504/566–5011* ⊕ *www.neworleanscvb. com*). **New Orleans Multicultural Tourism Network** (✉ *1520 Sugar Bowl Dr.* ☎ *800/725–5652 or 504/523–5652* ⊕ *www.soulofneworleans.com*).

THE CRUISE PORT

The Julia Street Cruise Terminal is at the end of Julia Street on the Mississippi River; the Erato Street Terminal is just to the north. Both terminals are behind the Ernest M. Morial Convention Center. You can walk to the French Quarter from here in about 10 minutes; it's a short taxi ride to the Quarter or nearby hotels. Carnival and Norwegian base ships here at least part of the year.

If you are driving, you'll probably approach New Orleans on I–10. Take the Business 90 West/Westbank exit, locally known as Pontchartrain Expressway, and proceed to the Tchoupitoulas Street/South Peters Street exit. Continue to Convention Center Boulevard, where you will take a right turn. Continue to Henderson Street, where you will turn left, and then continue to Port of New Orleans Place. Take a left on Port of New Orleans Place to Julia Street Terminals 1 and 2, or take a right to get to the Robin Street Wharf.

New Orleans

CBD/Warehouse District

Mississippi River

TO FRENCH QUARTER

Canal Street Ferry Terminal

Poydras Street Wharf

Cruise Ship Terminal

Riverwalk Marketplace

Girod Street Wharf

Julia Street Wharf

St. Joseph Street Wharf

Convention Center Blvd.

Water St. (Front St.)

Girod St.

Tchoupitoulas St.

Julia St.

SEE INSET ↙

Mississippi River

Canal St. Ferry Terminal

Café du Monde

Moon Walk

Madison St.

Esplanade Ave.
Barracks St.
Gov. Nicholls St.
Ursulines St.
St. Philip St.
Dumaine St.
St. Ann St.
Orleans St.
St. Peter St.
Wilk Row
Toulouse St.
St. Louis St.
Conti St.
Bienville St.
Iberville St.
Canal St.
Common St.
Gravier St.
Union St.
Perdido St.
Poydras St.
Lafayette St.
Natchez St.
Commercial St.

French Market Pl.
Decatur St.
Chartres St.
N. Peters St.
Dauphine St.
Bourbon St.
Royal St.
Exchange Alley
Chartres St.
Decatur St.
Clinton St.
N. Peters St.
Clay St.
N. Front St.
Dorsiere St.
Baronne St.
St. Charles Ave.
Carondelet St.
Camp St.
Magazine St.
Constance St.
Tchoupitoulas St.
S. Peters St.
Fulton St.
North St.
Girod St.
Commerce St.

1/2 mile
0
0
1/2 kilometer

INFORMATION **Port of New Orleans** (⊠*Port of New Orleans Pl. at foot of Julia St.* ☎*504/522–2551* ⊕*www.portno.com*).

AIRPORT
TRANSFERS
Shuttle-bus service to and from the airport and the cruise port is available through Airport Shuttle New Orleans. Buses leave regularly from the ground level near the baggage claim. Return trips to the airport need to be booked in advance. The cost one-way is $13 per person, and the trip takes about 45 minutes.

A cab ride to or from the airport from uptown or downtown New Orleans costs $28 for the first two passengers and $12 for each additional passenger. At the airport, pick-up is on the lower level, outside the baggage claim area. There may be an additional charge for extra baggage.

> **NEW ORLEANS BEST BETS**
>
> ■ **Aquarium of the Americas.** Especially good for families is this fantastic aquarium near the city's convention center.
>
> ■ **Eating Well.** A highlight in New Orleans is dining. If you ever wanted to splurge on a great restaurant meal, this is the place to do it. At the very least, have a beignet at Café du Mond.
>
> ■ **Hermann-Grima House.** This is one of the best-preserved historic homes in the French Quarter.

Airport Shuttle New Orleans (☎*504/522–3500*).

PARKING If you are spending some time in the city before or after your cruise, finding a parking space is fairly easy in most of the city, except for the French Quarter, where meter maids are plentiful and tow trucks eager. If in doubt about a space, pass it up and pay to use a parking lot. Avoid parking spaces at corners and curbs: less than 15 feet between your car and the corner will result in a ticket. Watch for temporary NO PARKING signs, which pop up along parade routes and film shoots. Long-term and overnight parking are extremely expensive at hotels and garages. Parking for the duration of your cruise is available for $14 per night and is on Erato Street; if you want, SeaCaps will take your bags directly to the ship so you just have to deal with your hand luggage.

EXPLORING NEW ORLEANS

Bullets in the margins refer to points of interest on the New Orleans map.

The **French Quarter,** the oldest part of the city, lives up to all you've heard: it's alive with the sights, sounds, odors, and experiences of a major entertainment hub. At some point, ignore your better judgment and take a stroll down **Bourbon Street,** past the bars, restaurants, music clubs, and novelty shops that have given this strip its reputation as the playground of the South. Be sure to find time to stop at Café du Monde for chicory-laced coffee and beignets. With its beautifully landscaped gardens surrounding elegant antebellum homes, the **Garden District** is mostly residential, but most home owners do not mind your enjoying the sights from outside the cast-iron fences surrounding their magnificent properties.

7 **Aquarium of the Americas.** Power failures during Hurricane Katrina resulted in the major loss of the Aquarium's collection of more than 7,000 aquatic creatures. In a dramatic gesture of solidarity, aquariums around the country joined together to repopulate its stock. Each of the four major exhibit areas—the Amazon Rain Forest, the Caribbean Reef, the Mississippi River, and the Gulf Coast—has fish and animals native to that environment. A fun exhibit called Beyond Green houses more than 25 frog species and includes informative displays. The aquarium's spectacular design allows you to feel part of the watery worlds by providing close-up encounters with the inhabitants. A gift shop and café are on the premises. You can get a combined ticket for the aquarium and the Audubon Zoo, including a round-trip cruise down the river. ⊠*1 Canal St., French Quarter* ☎*504/581–4629 or 800/774–7394* ⊕*www. auduboninstitute.org* ⊠*Aquarium $18; combination ticket with IMAX $23.50; combination ticket for aquarium, zoo, and round-trip cruise $41* ⊙*Aquarium Tues.–Sun. 10–5.*

3 **Beauregard-Keyes House.** This stately 19th-century mansion with period furnishings was the temporary home of Confederate general P. G. T. Beauregard. The house and grounds had severely deteriorated by the 1940s, when the well-known novelist Frances Parkinson Keyes moved in and helped restore it. Her studio at the back of the large courtyard remains intact, complete with family photos, original manuscripts, and her doll, fan, and teapot collections. Keyes wrote 40 novels in this studio, all in longhand, among them the local favorite, *Dinner at Antoine's.* The house suffered some roof damage during the storm, resulting in water stains along the dining-room ceiling. Undaunted, the staff has reopened the site and continues its normal tour schedule. If you do not have time to tour the house, take a peek through the gates at the beautiful walled garden at the corner of Chartres and Ursulines streets. Landscaped in the same sun pattern as Jackson Square, the garden is in bloom throughout the year. ⊠*1113 Chartres St., French Quarter* ☎*504/523–7257* ⊠*$5* ⊙*Mon.–Sat. 10–3, tours on the hr.*

8 **Garden District.** The Garden District is divided into two sections by Jackson Avenue. Upriver from Jackson is the wealthy **Upper Garden District,** where the homes are meticulously kept. Below Jackson, the **Lower Garden District** is considerably rougher. Though the homes here are often just as structurally beautiful, most of them lack the recent restorations of those of the Upper Garden District. The streets are also less well patrolled; wander cautiously. **Magazine Street,** lined with antiques shops and coffeehouses (ritzier along the Upper Garden District, hipper along the Lower Garden District), serves as a southern border to the Garden District, and St. Charles Avenue forms the northern border.

5 **Hermann-Grima House.** One of the largest and best-preserved examples of American architecture in the Quarter, this Georgian-style house has the only restored private stable and the only working 1830s Creole kitchen in the Quarter. American architect William Brand built the house in 1831. The house fortunately sustained only minor damage during the storm and is open for visits and tours. Cooking demonstrations on the open hearth are held here all day Thursday from October through May. You'll want to check the gift shop, which has many local crafts and books. ✉ *820 St. Louis St., French Quarter* ☎ *504/525–5661* 💵 *$10, combination ticket with the Gallier House $18* 🕐 *Tours Thurs.–Tues. 10, 11, noon, 2, 3.*

❶ **Jackson Square.** Surrounded by historic buildings and filled with plenty
🕐 of the city's atmospheric street life, the heart of the French Quarter
★ is today a beautifully landscaped park. Originally called the Place d'Armes, the square was founded in 1718 as a military parade ground. It was also the site of public executions carried out in various styles, including burning at the stake, beheading, breaking on the wheel, and hanging. A **statue of Andrew Jackson,** victorious leader of the Battle of New Orleans in the War of 1812, commands the center of the square; the park was renamed for him in the 1850s. President George W. Bush made a major address to the nation here after Katrina, in which he celebrated the importance of the city in the history of the country and the federal government's commitment to its recovery.

Among the notable buildings around the square are **St. Louis Cathedral** and **Faulkner House.** Two Spanish colonial–style buildings, the **Cabildo** and the **Presbytère,** flank the cathedral. The handsome rows of brick apartments on each side of the square are the **Pontalba Buildings.** The park is landscaped in a sun pattern, with walkways set like rays streaming out from the center, a popular garden design in the royal court of King Louis XIV, the Sun King. In the daytime, dozens of artists hang their paintings on the park fence and set up outdoor studios where they work on canvases or offer to draw portraits of passersby. These artists are easy to engage in conversation and are knowledgeable about many aspects of the Quarter and New Orleans. You can also be entertained by musicians, mimes, tarot-card readers, and magicians who perform on the flagstone pedestrian mall surrounding the square, many of them day and night. ✉ *French Quarter* 🕐 *Park daily 8 AM–dusk; flagstone paths on park's periphery open 24 hrs.*

❻ **Jean Lafitte National Park Visitor Center.** This center has free visual and
★ sound exhibits on the customs of various communities throughout the state, as well as information-rich daily history tours of the French Quarter. The one-hour daily tour leaves at 9:30 AM; tickets are handed out one per person (you must be present to get a ticket), beginning at 9 AM, for that day's tours only. Arrive at least 15 minutes before tour time to be sure of a spot. The office also supervises and provides information on Jean Lafitte National Park Barataria Unit, a nature preserve (complete with alligators) across the river from New Orleans, and the Chalmette Battlefield, where the Battle of New Orleans was fought in the War of 1812. Each year in January, near the anniversary of the battle, a reenactment is staged at the Chalmette site. ✉ *419 Decatur St., French Quarter* ☎ *504/589–2636* 🕐 *Daily 9–5.*

❹ **Old Mint.** Minting began in 1838 in this ambitious, Ionic structure, a proj-
★ ect of President Andrew Jackson. The New Orleans mint was to provide currency for the South and the West, which it did until the Confederacy began minting its own currency here in 1861. When supplies ran out, the building served as a barracks, then a prison, for Confederate soldiers; the production of U.S. coins recommenced only in 1879. It stopped again,

for good, in 1909. After years of neglect, the federal government handed the Old Mint over to Louisiana in 1966; the state now uses the quarters to exhibit collections of the Louisiana State Museum. At the Barracks Street entrance, notice the one remaining sample of the mint's old walls—it'll give you an idea of the building's deterioration before its restoration. Hurricane Katrina ripped away a large section of the copper roof, and for months the twisted metal remained on the ground here, one of the most dramatic reminders of the storm in the French Quarter. Repairs to the building have begun in earnest, but the museum's reopening date remains in question. At the foot of Esplanade Avenue, notice the memorial to the French rebels against early Spanish rule, the first instance of a New World rebellion against a European power. The rebel leaders were executed on this spot and give nearby Frenchmen Street its name. The principal exhibit here is the **New Orleans Jazz Collection,** a brief but evocative tour through the history of traditional New Orleans jazz. In addition to informative written explanations, a wealth of artifacts movingly tells the story of the emergent art form. Among the gems are the soprano saxophone owned by Sidney Bechet, the trumpets of Pops Celestin and Dizzy Gillespie, and the cornet given to Louis Armstrong at the juvenile home where he spent much of his youth. Across the hall from the jazz exhibit are a few rooms filled with the beautiful and locally treasured Newcomb pottery. ⊠*400 Esplanade Ave., French Quarter* ☎*504/568–6968* ⊠*Old US Mint $5.*

❷ **St. Louis Cathedral.** The oldest active cathedral in the United States, this church at the heart of the Old City is named for the 13th-century French king who led two crusades. The current building, which replaced two structures destroyed by fire, dates from 1794 (although it was remodeled and enlarged in 1851). The austere interior is brightened by murals covering the ceiling and stained-glass windows along the first floor. Pope John Paul II held a prayer service for clergy here during his New Orleans visit in 1987; to honor the occasion, the pedestrian mall in front of the cathedral was renamed Place Jean Paul Deux. Nearly every evening in December brings a free concert held inside the cathedral. The statue of the Sacred Heart of Jesus dominates **St. Anthony's Garden,** which extends behind the rectory to Royal Street. This statue was damaged during the storm, losing the thumb and forefinger of one hand. The pieces have been recovered, but the statue's injuries have yet to be repaired. The garden is also the site of a monument to 30 members of a French ship who died in a yellow-fever epidemic in 1857. ⊠*615 Père Antoine Alley, French Quarter* ☎*504/525–9585* ⊠*Free.*

SHOPPING

The fun of shopping in New Orleans is in the regional items available throughout the city, in the smallest shops or the biggest department stores. You can take home some of the flavor of the city: its pralines (pecan candies), seafood (packaged to go), Louisiana red beans and rice, coffee (pure or with chicory), and creole and Cajun spices (cayenne pepper, chili, and garlic). There are even packaged mixes of such local favorites as jambalaya, gumbo, beignets, and the sweet red local cocktail called the Hurricane. Cookbooks also share the secrets of preparing distinctive New Orleans dishes. The French Quarter is well known for its fine antiques shops, located mainly on Royal and Chartres streets. The main shopping areas in the city are the French Quarter, with narrow, picturesque streets lined with specialty, gift, fashion, and antiques shops and art galleries; the Central Business District (CBD), populated mostly with jewelry, specialty, and department stores; the Warehouse District, best known for contem-

> ### YOUR CARD PLEASE
>
> Print cards with your name, address, phone number, and e-mail address to share with new friends. Stiff, business card–style paper can be purchased at nearly any office supply store, and you can make the cards on your computer at home. Having your cards handy sure beats hunting for pens and scribbling on scraps of paper to swap addresses.

porary arts galleries and cultural museums; Magazine Street, home to antiques shops, art galleries, home-furnishing stores, dining venues, fashion boutiques, and specialty shops; and the Riverbend/Maple Street area, filled with clothing stores and some specialty shops.

Jax Brewery (✉ *600 Decatur St., French Quarter* ☎ *504/566–7245* ⊕ *www.jacksonbrewery.com.*) was a factory for Jax beer, but now holds a Jax Beer museum and an upscale mall filled with both local shops and national chains. **Riverwalk Marketplace** (✉ *1 Poydras St., Warehouse District* ☎ *504/522–1555* ⊕ *www.riverwalkmarketplace.com*), with 180-some stores, was built in what once was the International Pavilion of the 1984 World's Fair.

NIGHTLIFE

No American city places such a premium on pleasure as New Orleans. From swank hotel lounges to sweaty dance clubs, refined jazz clubs and raucous Bourbon Street bars, this city is serious about frivolity. And famous for it. Partying is more than an occasional indulgence in this city—it's a lifestyle. Bars tend to open in the early afternoon and stay open into the morning hours; live music, though, follows a more restrained schedule. Some jazz spots and clubs in the French Quarter stage evening sets around 6 PM or 9 PM; at a few clubs, such as the Palm Court, the bands actually finish by 11 PM. But this is the exception: for the most part, gigs begin between 10 and 11 PM, and locals rarely emerge for an evening out before 10. Keep in mind that the lack of legal closing time means that shows advertised for 11 may not start until after midnight.

Crescent City Brewhouse. This convivial brewpub makes five specialty brews on the premises and one seasonal selection. The suds pair well with oysters on the half shell and other pub grub. Jazz combos set up near the entrance most afternoons, and seating on a second-floor balcony affords a nice view of the Mississippi River and busy Decatur Street. ✉ *527 Decatur St., French Quarter* ☎ *504/522–0571.*

Harrah's New Orleans. Commanding the foot of Canal Street, this beaux arts–style casino is the largest such facility in the South. Its 100,000 square feet hold 2,900 slots and 120 gaming tables. The casino's dining options include an upscale steak restaurant run by local celebrity-chef John Besh and the French brasserie Riche. Valet parking is available. ⊠*4 Canal St., CBD* ☎*504/533–6000 or 800/427–7247* ⊕*www.harrahs.com.*

Mulate's. Across the street from the Convention Center, this large restaurant seats 400, and the dance floor quickly fills with couples twirling and two-stepping to authentic Cajun bands from the countryside. Regulars love to drag first-timers to the floor for impromptu lessons. The home-style Cajun cuisine is quite good, and the bands play until 10:30 or 11 PM. ⊠*201 Julia St., Warehouse District* ☎*504/522–1492.*

> ### GET MUGGED
>
> Take along an insulated mug with a lid that you can fill at the beverage station in the buffet area. Your drinks will stay hot or cold, and you won't have to worry about spills. Most bartenders will fill the mug with ice and water or a soft drink. With a straw, your ice will not melt instantly while you lounge at the pool.

Pat O'Brien's. Sure, it's touristy, but there are reasons Pat O's has been a must-stop on the New Orleans cocktail trail for so long. For one thing, there's plenty of room to spread out, from the elegant side bar and piano bar that flank the carriageway entrance to the lush (and in winter, heated) patio. Friendly staff, an easy camaraderie among patrons, and a signature drink—the pink, cloying, and extremely potent Hurricane, which comes with a souvenir glass—make this French Quarter stalwart a pleasant afternoon diversion. ⊠*718 St. Peter St., French Quarter* ☎*504/525–4823.*

★ **Preservation Hall.** The jazz tradition that flowered in the 1920s is enshrined in this cultural landmark by a cadre of distinguished New Orleans musicians, most of whom were schooled by an ever-dwindling group of elder statesmen. There is limited seating on benches—many patrons end up squatting on the floor or standing in back—and no beverages are served or allowed. Nonetheless, the legions of satisfied customers regard an evening here as an essential New Orleans experience. Cover charge is $10, but can run a bit higher for special appearances. ⊠*726 St. Peter St., French Quarter* ☎*504/522–2841 or 504/523–8939.*

★ **Tipitina's.** A bust of legendary New Orleans pianist Professor Longhair, or "Fess," greets visitors at the door of this Uptown landmark, which takes its name from one of his most popular songs. As the concert posters pinned to the walls attest, Tip's hosts a wide variety of touring bands and local acts. The long-running Sunday-afternoon Cajun dance still packs the floor. The Tipitina's Foundation has an office and workshop upstairs, where local musicians affected by Hurricane Katrina can network, gain access to resources, and search for gigs. ⊠*501 Napoleon Ave., Uptown* ☎*504/895–8477.*

SIGHTSEEING TOURS

Several local tour companies give two- to four-hour city tours by bus that include the French Quarter, the Garden District, uptown New Orleans, and the lakefront. Prices range from $25 to $125 per person, depending on the kind of experience. Both Gray Line and New Orleans Tours offer a longer tour that combines a two-hour city tour by bus with a two-hour steamboat ride on the Mississippi River. Gray Line and Tours by Isabelle both offer tours of Hurricane Katrina devastation as well.

Information Gray Line ☎800/535–7786 or 504/569–1401 ⊕ www.graylinenew orleans.com. **New Orleans Tours** ☎504/592–1991 ⊕www.notours.com. **Tours by Isabelle** ☎877/665–8687 or 504/398–0365 ⊕www.toursbyisabelle.com.

WHERE TO EAT

For price categories, see ⇨ *Dining at the beginning of this chapter.*

Don't miss beignets and rich, chicory-laced coffee at **Café du Monde** (⊠*800 Decatur St., French Quarter* ☎*504/525–4544* ⊟*No credit cards*) in the French Quarter, though there's also an outlet in the Riverwalk.

$$$
SOUTHERN
Fodor'sChoice
★

✕**Bayona.** "New World" is the label Louisiana native Susan Spicer applies to her cooking style, which results in such signature dishes as the Caribbean pumpkin soup with coconut, and Niman ranch pork chop with a spicy adobo glaze. The lunch omelet of andouille, smoked cheddar, and fried oysters is about as authentic as Louisiana cooking can be. These and other imaginative dishes are served in an early-19th-century Creole cottage that glows with flower arrangements, elegant photographs, and trompe l'oeil murals suggesting Mediterranean landscapes. Don't skip pastry chef Christy Phebus's sweets, such as a dark chocolate banana torte with espresso crème caramel. ⊠*430 Dauphine St., French Quarter* ☎*504/525–4455* ⊛*Reservations essential* ⊟*AE, DC, MC, V* ⊗*Closed Sun. No lunch Mon. or Tues.*

$
CAFÉ
Fodor'sChoice
★

✕**Central Grocery.** This old-fashioned Italian grocery store produces authentic muffulettas, one of the gastronomic gifts of the city's Italian immigrants. Good enough to challenge the po'boy as the local sandwich champs, they're made by filling round loaves of seeded bread with ham, salami, mozzarella, and a salad of marinated green olives. Sandwiches, about 10 inches in diameter, are sold in wholes and halves. You can eat your muffuletta at a counter, or get it to go and dine on a bench on Jackson Square or the Moon Walk along the Mississippi riverfront. The Grocery closes at 5:30 PM. ⊠*923 Decatur St., French Quarter* ☎*504/523–1620* ⊟*D, MC, V* ⊗*No dinner.*

$$$$
SOUTHERN
Fodor'sChoice
★

✕**Commander's Palace.** No restaurant captures New Orleans's gastronomic heritage and celebratory spirit as well as this one, long considered the grande dame of New Orleans's fine dining. The recent renovation has added new life, especially upstairs, where the Garden Room's glass walls have marvelous views of the giant oak trees on the patio below; other rooms promote conviviality with their bright pastels. The menu's classics include sugarcane grilled pork chops; a spicy and meaty turtle soup; terrific bourbon-laquered Mississippi Quail; and a wonderful griddle-seared gulf fish. Among the addictive desserts is the bread-pudding soufflé. Weekend brunches are a New Orleans tradition. Jackets are preferred at dinner. ⊠*1403 Washington Ave., Garden District* ☎*504/899–8221* ⩊*Reservations essential* ▤*AE, D, DC, MC, V.*

> **CAUTION**
>
> Items confiscated by airport security will not be returned to you. If you are uncertain whether something will pass the security test, pack it in your checked luggage.

$$$$
SOUTHERN
Fodor'sChoice
★
✕**Galatoire's.** Galatoire's has always epitomized the old-style French-creole bistro. Many of the recipes date to 1905. Fried oysters and bacon en brochette are worth every calorie, and the brick-red rémoulade sauce sets a high standard. Other winners include veal chops in béarnaise sauce, and seafood-stuffed eggplant. The setting downstairs is a single, narrow dining room lighted with glistening brass chandeliers; bentwood chairs and white tablecloths add to its timelessness. You may reserve a table in the renovated upstairs rooms, though the action is on the first floor, where partying regulars inhibit conversation but add good people-watching entertainment value. Friday lunch starts early and continues well into early evening. A jacket is required. ⊠*209 Bourbon St., French Quarter* ☎*504/525–2021* ▤*AE, D, DC, MC, V* ✆*Closed Mon.*

$$–$$$
SOUTHERN
Fodor'sChoice
★
✕**Herbsaint.** Upscale food and moderate prices are among Herbsaint's assets. Chef Donald Link turns out food that sparkles with robust flavors and top-grade ingredients. "Small plates" and side dishes such as charcuterie, a knock-'em-dead shrimp bisque, house-made pasta, and cheese- or nut-studded salads are mainstays. Don't overlook the rich and flavorful Louisiana cochon with turnips, cabbage, and cracklins. Also irresistible: smoked beef brisket with horseradish potato salad. For dessert, the layered spice cake with figs and pecans will ensure future return trips. The plates provide most of the color in the lighthearted, often noisy, rooms. The wine list is expertly compiled and reasonably priced. ⊠*701 St. Charles Ave., CBD* ☎*504/524–4114* ⩊*Reservations essential* ▤*AE, D, DC, MC, V* ✆*Closed Sun. No lunch Sat.*

WHERE TO STAY

You can stay in a large hotel near the cruise-ship terminal or in more intimate places in the French Quarter. Hotel rates in New Orleans tend to be on the high end, though deals abound.

For price categories, see ⇨ *Lodging at the beginning of this chapter.*

$$$
🛏**Ambassador Hotel.** Guest rooms at this hotel bordering the CBD and Warehouse District have real character, with hardwood floors, oversize windows, and high ceilings. Four-poster iron beds, armoires, and local jazz prints are among the furnishings. Exposed brick walls and ceiling fans add to the ambience of the pre–Civil War building. This is a good alternative to the huge convention hotels; you're just steps from the major downtown attractions and the Convention Center, and Harrah's New Orleans Casino is a five-minute walk. **Pros:** distinctive decor; urban/chic atmosphere. **Cons:** some first-floor rooms let in too

much noise from street and lobby area. ✉ *535 Tchoupitoulas St., CBD* ☎ *504/527–5271 or 800/455–3417* ⊕ *www.ambassadorneworleans. com* ↘ *165 rooms* ⚙ *In-room: Wi-Fi. In-hotel: restaurant, bar, parking (paid)* ⊟ *AE, D, DC, MC, V.*

$$$–$$$$ ⊞ **New Orleans Hilton Riverside.** The sprawling multilevel Hilton complex sits right on the Mississippi, with superb views. Guest rooms have French-provincial furnishings, and the 180 rooms that share a concierge have fax machines. The lavish Sunday brunch is consistently outstanding. Adjacent to Riverwalk Shopping Center, the hotel is directly across the street from Harrah's New Orleans Casino; the Riverfront streetcar stops out front. The health club is among the best in town, and the hotel has a resident golf pro and a four-hole putting green. Designed for large convention groups, this hotel is also a great choice for independent travelers. **Pros:** well-maintained facilities; hotel runs like a well-oiled machine. **Cons:** the city's biggest hotel; typical chain service and surroundings; garage needs better lighting and security. ✉ *Poydras St. at the Mississippi River, CBD* ☎ *504/561–0500 or 800/445–8667* ⊕ *www. hilton.com* ↘ *1,600 rooms, 67 suites* ⚙ *In-room: Wi-Fi. In-hotel: 3 restaurants, tennis courts, pools, gym, parking (paid), no-smoking rooms* ⊟ *AE, D, DC, MC, V.*

$$$–$$$$ ⊞ **New Orleans Marriott Hotel.** The Marriott has a fabulous view of the Quarter, the CBD, and the river. It's an easy walk from the Canal Place mall, the Riverwalk, and the Convention Center. Rooms are comfortable, service is friendly (if uneven), and nightly jazz enlivens the lobby— but the hotel lacks New Orleans charm. The Canal Street streetcar line provides convenient access to most parts of the city. Keep in mind that this high-rise convention hotel is located on Canal Street, the busiest street in the downtown area. **Pros:** good location; very clean; stunning city and river views. **Cons:** typical chain hotel; inconsistent service. ✉ *555 Canal St., French Quarter* ☎ *504/581–1000 or 800/228–9290* ⊕ *www.neworleansmarriott.com* ↘ *1,290 rooms, 54 suites* ⚙ *In-room: Internet. In-hotel: restaurant, bar, pool, gym, Wi-Fi, parking (paid)* ⊟ *AE, D, DC, MC, V.*

NEW YORK, NEW YORK

A few cruise lines now base Caribbean-bound ships in New York City year-round, though most of the market is made up of ships doing seasonal cruises to New England and Bermuda. If you're coming to the city from the immediate area, you can easily arrive the day before and do a bit of sightseeing and perhaps take in a Broadway show. The cruise port in Manhattan is fairly close to Times Square and Midtown hotels and theaters. But the New York City region now has three major cruise ports. You can also leave from Cape Liberty Terminal in Bayonne, New Jersey, on both Celebrity and Royal Caribbean ships. In 2006 a new cruise-ship terminal opened in Red Hook, Brooklyn, and this terminal serves Carnival and Princess ships as well as Cunard's *Queen Mary 2.*

New York City (Midtown)

ESSENTIALS

Hours They say that New York never sleeps, and that's particularly true around Times Square, where some stores are open until 11 PM or later even during the week. But most stores outside of the immediate Times Square area are open from 9 or 10 until 6 or 7. Many museums close on Monday.

Internet Internet service is offered by most New York hotels, and there are independent Internet cafés all over town. You might even see cheap Internet service in pizzerias and delis. Starbucks offers wireless service for a fee, but if you have your own laptop you can use the free outdoor Wi-Fi network in Bryant Park (6th Avenue, between 42nd and 41st streets).

Visitor Information **NYC & Company Convention & Visitors Bureau** (⊠ *810 7th Ave., between W. 52nd and W. 53rd Sts., 3rd fl., Midtown West* ☎ *212/484–1222* ⊕ *www.nycvisit.com*). **Times Square Information Center** (⊠ *1560 Broadway, between 46th and 47th Sts., Midtown West* ☎ *212/768–1560* ⊕ *www.timessquarenyc.org*).

THE CRUISE PORT

The New York Passenger Ship Terminal is on the far west side of Manhattan, five very long blocks from the Times Square area, between 48th and 52nd streets; the vehicle entrance is at 55th Street. Traffic can be backed up in the area on days that cruise ships arrive and depart, so allow yourself enough time to check in and go through security. There are no nearby subway stops, though city buses do cross midtown at 50th and 42nd streets. If you don't have too much luggage, it is usually faster and more convenient to have a taxi drop you off at the intersection across the street from the entrance to the lower-level of the terminal area between 48th and 49th streets; then you can walk right in and take the elevators up to the embarkation level.

Cape Liberty Terminal in Bayonne is off Route 440. From the New Jersey Turnpike, take Exit 14A, then follow the signs for 440 South, and make a left turn into the Cape Liberty Terminal area (on Port Terminal Boulevard). If you are coming from Long Island, you cross Staten Island, and after crossing the Bayonne Bridge take 440 North, making a right into the terminal area. If you are coming from Manhattan, you can also reach the terminal by public transit. Take the New Jersey Transit light-rail line that connects to the PATH trains in Hoboken; get off at the Bayonne stop, and from there you can take a taxi to the terminal (about 2 mi [3 km] away); there may be free shuttle bus on cruise sailing dates, but confirm that with your cruise line.

The Brooklyn cruise terminal at Pier 12 in Red Hook, which opened in April 2006, is not convenient to public transportation, so you should plan to take a taxi, drive, or take the bus transfers offered by the cruise lines (the cost for this is about $40 per person from either LaGuardia or JFK). There is a secure, 500-car outdoor parking lot on-site. To reach the terminal from La Guardia Airport, take I–278 W (the Brooklyn-Queens Expressway), Exit 26, Hamilton Avenue; the terminal entrance is actually off Browne Street. From JFK, take I–278 E (again, the Brooklyn-Queens Expressway), and then the same exit. If you arrive early, there's not much in the neighborhood, but there are a few neighborhood delis and restaurants within a 10- to 15-minute walk; the area is a safe place to walk around during daylight hours. Red Hook is the home of ships from the Carnival, Princess, and Cunard cruise lines.

INFORMATION **Cape Liberty Terminal** (⊠14 Port Terminal Blvd., Bayonne, NJ ☎201/823–3737 ⊕www.cruiseliberty.com).

New York Passenger Ship Terminal (⊠711 12th Ave., Midtown West, New York, NY ☎212/246–5450 ⊕www.nycruiseterminal.com ⊠Pier 12, Bldg. 112, Red Hook, Brooklyn, NY ☎718/858–3450).

NEW YORK BEST BETS
■ **An Art Museum.** Take your pick: the Met, MOMA, or the Frick, but this is a true highlight of New York.
■ **A Broadway Show.** The theater experience in New York is better than almost anywhere else in the world.
■ **Statue of Liberty.** Just the sight of Lady Liberty will melt the coldest heart, though the highlight of the trip is actually the Ellis Island museum, not the statue itself.

AIRPORT TRANSFERS A cab to or from JFK to the passenger-ship terminal in **Manhattan** will cost $45 (a flat fare) plus toll and tip; expect to pay at least $35 on the meter if you are coming from LaGuardia and at least $50 or $60 (not including tolls of about $10 and the tip) from Newark in a regular taxi (from Newark airport, it's usually more cost-effective to call for a car service to pick you up; these services have a flat fare of about $48, not including the tolls and tip.

From Newark Airport it's approximately $30 to **Cape Liberty,** $75 from JFK (plus toll and tip), and $80 from La Guardia (plus toll and tip). Royal Caribbean offers bus service from several Mid-Atlantic and Northeast cities on sailing dates, but confirm that with the cruise line.

If your cruise is leaving from **Red Hook,** the taxi fare will be much cheaper if you fly into either La Guardia (about $30) or JFK (about $40); you'll pay at least $70 from Newark Airport. Cruise lines provide bus transfers from all three of the area's airports, but it may be cheaper to take a taxi if you are traveling with more than one other person. Note that all these taxi fares do not include tolls and tips. From Newark, the tolls to Brooklyn can be substantial, adding almost $20 to the fare.

PARKING You can park at the New York Passenger Ship Terminal for a hefty $30 a day; the fee is payable in advance in cash or traveler's checks (no credit cards).

Parking at Cape Liberty Terminal in Bayonne is $19 per day, payable only in cash, traveler's checks, and major credit cards.

Parking at Red Hook, Brooklyn, costs $23 for the first 24 hours and then $20 per day.

TOP ATTRACTIONS

There's no way to do justice to even the most popular tourist stops in New York. Below is information about several top attractions. If you have only a day in the city, choose one or two attractions and buy a daily unlimited subway pass to get around. There's a moving series of panels about the World Trade Center at the so-called "Ground Zero" site across from the Millennium Hotel (take the 1 train to Cortlandt Street or the E to World Trade Center); there's another series of memorial panels underneath at the World Trade Center PATH station, which is accessible from the main, streetside memorial area.

Bullets in the margins refer to points of interest on the Midtown Manhattan map.

① American Museum of Natural History. With 45 exhibition halls and more than 32 million artifacts and specimens, the world's largest and most important museum of natural history can easily occupy you for half a day. The dioramas might seem dated, but are fun. The dinosaur exhibits are probably the highlight. Attached to the museum is the **Rose Center for Earth and Space,** with various exhibits and housing the **Hayden Planetarium** and an **IMAX Theater.** ⊠ *Central Park W. at W. 79 St., Upper West Side* ☎ *212/769–5200* ⊕ *www.amnh.org* ✉ *$20 suggested donation, includes admission to Rose Center for Earth and Space* ☉ *Daily 10–5:45. Rose Center until 8:45 on Fri.*

② Central Park. Without Central Park's 843 acres of meandering paths, tranquil lakes, ponds, and open meadows, New Yorkers might be a lot less sane. You can drop by the zoo (near 64th Street, on the east side) or the famous Bethesda Fountain (mid-park, at around 72nd Street), but the main draw is just to wander the lanes. Central Park has one of the lowest crime rates in the city. Still, use common sense and stay within sight of other park visitors, and don't go into the park after dark. Directions, park maps, and events calendars can be obtained from volunteers at two 5th Avenue **information booths,** at East 60th Street and East 72nd Street. ☎ *212/408–0266 for schedule of park events, 212/360–2727 for schedule of walking tours* ⊕ *www.nycgovparks.org* Ⓜ *Subway: A, C, or 1 to Columbus Circle.*

③ Frick Collection. Coke-and-steel baron Henry Clay Frick (1849–1919)
★ amassed this superb art collection far from the soot and smoke of Pittsburgh, where he made his fortune. The mansion was designed by Thomas Hastings and built in 1913–14. It opened in 1935, but still resembles a gracious private home, albeit one with bona fide masterpieces in almost every room. This is the best small museum in town by a mile. ⊠ *1 E. 70th St., at 5th Ave., Upper East Side* ☎ *212/288–0700* ⊕ *www.frick.org* ✉ *$15* ☉ *Tues.–Sat. 10–6, Sun. 11–5* Ⓜ *6 to 68th St./Hunter College.*

⑧ Grand Central Terminal. Grand Central is not only the world's largest (76
Fodor's Choice acres) and the nation's busiest (500,000 commuters and subway riders
★ use it daily) railway station, but also one of the world's greatest public spaces ("justly famous," as critic Tony Hiss noted, "as a crossroads, a noble building . . . and an ingenious piece of engineering"). A massive four-year renovation completed in October 1998 restored the 1913 landmark to its original splendor—and then some. *Main entrance* ⊠ *E. 42nd St. at Park Ave., Midtown East* ☎ *212/935–3960* ⊕ *www.grand centralterminal.com* Ⓜ *4, 5, 6, 7, S to 42nd St./Grand Central.*

3

❺ *Intrepid* **Sea-Air-Space Museum.** Formerly the USS *Intrepid*, this 900-foot aircraft carrier is serving out its retirement as the center-piece of Manhattan's only floating museum. An A-12 Blackbird spy plane, lunar landing modules, heli-copters, seaplanes, and two dozen other aircraft are on deck. Docked

alongside, and also part of the museum, are the *Growler*, a strategic-missile submarine; the *Edson*, a Vietnam-era destroyer; and several other battle-scarred naval veterans. Children can explore the ships' skinny hallways and winding staircases, as well as manipulate countless knobs, buttons, and wheels. The museum reopened in November 2008 after a major renovation. ✉*Hudson River, Pier 86, 12th Ave. at W. 46th St., Midtown West* ☎*212/245-0072 or 877/957-7447* ⊕*www.intrepid museum.org* ✑*$19.50; free to active and retired U.S. military personnel* ⊗*Apr.–Sept., weekdays 10–5, weekends 10–6; Oct.–Mar., Tues.–Sun. 10–5; last admission 1 hr before closing* Ⓜ*A, C, E to 42nd St.; M42 bus to pier.*

❹ **The Metropolitan Museum of Art.** If the city held no other museum than the colossal Metropolitan Museum of Art, you could still occupy yourself for days roaming its labyrinthine corridors. Because the Metropolitan Museum has something approaching 3 million works on display over its more than 7 square mi, you're going to have to make some hard choices. Looking at everything here could take a week. ✉*5th Ave. at 82nd St., Upper East Side* ☎*212/535-7710* ⊕*www.metmuseum.org* ✑*$20 suggested donation* ⊗*Tues.–Thurs. and Sun. 9:30–5:30, Fri. and Sat. 9:30–9.*

❿ **Museum of Jewish Heritage—A Living Memorial to the Holocaust.** In a granite hexagon rising 85 feet above Robert F. Wagner Jr. Park at the southern end of Battery Park City, this museum pays tribute to the 6 million Jews who perished in the Holocaust. It's one of the best such museums in the country. ✉*36 Battery Pl., Battery Park City, Lower Manhattan* ☎*646/437-4200* ⊕*www.mjhnyc.org* ✑*$10* ⊗*Thurs. and Sun.–Tues. 10–5:45, Wed. 10–8, Fri. and eve of Jewish holidays 10–3* Ⓜ*4, 5 to Bowling Green.*

❻ **Museum of Modern Art (MoMA).** The masterpieces—Monet's Water Lilies, Picasso's Les Demoiselles d'Avignon, Van Gogh's Starry Night—are still here, but for now the main draw at MoMA is, well, MoMA. A "mod-ernist dream world" is how critics described the museum after its $425 million face-lift. Unfortunately, the museum was an instant success, which means lines are sometimes down the block. For the shortest wait, get here before the museum opens; you can avoid some of the crowd-ing by entering through the 54th Street side. Be prepared for sticker shock when you buy your ticket. ✉*11 W. 53rd St., between 5th and 6th Aves., Midtown East* ☎*212/708-9400* ⊕*www.moma.org* ✑*$20* ⊗*Sat.–Mon., Wed., and Thurs. 10:30–5:30, Fri. 10:30–8* Ⓜ*Subway: E, V to 5th Ave./53rd St.; B, D, E to 7th Ave.; B, D, F, V to 47th–50th Sts./Rockefeller Center.*

9 **Staten Island Ferry.** The best transit deal in town is the Staten Island Ferry, a free 20- to 30-minute ride across New York Harbor providing great views of the Manhattan skyline, the Statue of Liberty, the Verrazano-Narrows Bridge, and the New Jersey coast. Ferries embark on various schedules: every 15 minutes during rush hours, every

> **CAUTION**
>
> Store any irreplaceable valuables in the ship purser's safe rather than the one in your cabin. Some insurance policies will not cover the loss of items left in your cabin.

20–30 minutes most other times, and every hour on weekend nights and mornings. If you can manage it, catch one of the older blue-and-orange ferries, which have outside decks. ⊠ *State and South Sts., Lower Manhattan* ☎ *718/390–5253* Ⓜ *Subway: 4, 5 to Bowling Green; 1, 9 to South Ferry.*

10 **Statue of Liberty & Ellis Island.** Though you must endure a long wait and onerous security, it's worth the trouble to see one of the iconic images of New York. But the truth is there's not much to see in the statue itself. You can no longer climb up to the crown, just view the inside from the base. There's a small museum on-site. Much more interesting—and well worth exploring—is the Ellis Island museum, which traces the story of immigration in New York City with moving exhibits throughout the restored processing building. Other parts of the island are still ruins. Make reservations and go early if you want to see everything. The ferry stops first at the statue and then continues to Ellis Island. ⊠ *Castle Clinton, Battery Park, Lower Manhattan* ☎ *212/363–3200 for park service, 877/523–9849 for ferry information and ticket reservations* ⊕ *www.nps.gov/stli, www.statuecruises.com for reservations* ☑ *Statue and museums free, ferry $12 round-trip* ⊙ *Daily 9:30–5; extended hrs in summer* Ⓜ *Subway: 5 to Bowling Green; 1, 9 to South Ferry; or W to Whitehall.*

7 **Top of the Rock.** Rockefeller Center's multifloor observation deck, first

Fodor's Choice opened in 1933, and closed in the early 1980s, reopened in 2005.

★ The experience is infinitely better than that at the Empire State Building, where interminable lines spoil most of the fun. Arrive just before sunset for the best views (which include the Empire State Building). ⊠ *Entrance on 50th St., between 5th and 6th Aves., Midtown West* ☎ *877/692–7625 or 212/698–2000* ⊕ *www.topoftherocknyc.com* ☑ *$17.50* ⊙ *Daily 8–midnight; last elevator at 11 PM* Ⓜ *B, D, F, V to 47th–50th Sts./Rockefeller Center.*

SHOPPING

You can find almost any major store from virtually any designer or chain in Manhattan. High-end designers tend to be along **Madison Avenue,** between 55th and 86th streets. Some are along **57th Street,** between Madison and 7th avenues. **Fifth Avenue,** starting at Saks Fifth Avenue (at 50th Street) and going up to 59th Street, is a hodgepodge of high-end stores and more accessible options, including the high-end department store Bergdorf-Goodman, at 58th Street. More interesting and individual stores can be found in **SoHo** (between Houston and Canal, West Broadway and Lafayette), and the **East Village** (between 14th Street and Houston, Broadway and Avenue A). **Chinatown** is chock-full of designer knockoffs, crowded streets, and dim sum palaces; though frenetic during the day, it's a fun stop. The newest group of stores in Manhattan is at the **Time-Warner Center,** at Columbus Circle (at 8th Avenue and 59th Street); the high-rise mall has upscale stores and some of the city's best-reviewed and most expensive new restaurants.

BROADWAY SHOWS

Scoring tickets to Broadway shows is fairly easy except for the very top draws. For the most part, the top ticket price for Broadway musicals is now over $120; the best seats for Broadway plays can run as high as $100. **Telecharge** (☎212/239–6200 ⊕*www.telecharge.com*). **Ticketmaster** (☎*212/307–4100* ⊕*www.ticketmaster.com*).

For seats at 25%–50% off the usual price, go to **TKTS** (⊠*Duffy Sq., at W. 47th St. and Broadway, Midtown West* Ⓜ*1, 2, 3, 7, N, Q, R, W, S to 42nd St./Times Sq.; N, R, W to 49th St.; 1 to 50th St.* ⊠*South St. Seaport, at Front and John Sts., Lower Manhattan* Ⓜ*2, 3, 4, 5, A, C, E, J, M, Z to Fulton St./Broadway-Nassau* ⊕*www.tdf.org*).

WHERE TO EAT

The restaurants we recommend below are all in Midtown West, near Broadway theaters and hotels. Make reservations at all but the most casual places or face a numbing wait.

For price categories, see ⇨ *Dining at the beginning of this chapter.*

$$$ ✕**Becco.** An ingenious concept makes Becco a prime Restaurant Row
ITALIAN choice for time-constrained theatergoers. There are two pricing scenarios: one includes an all-you-can-eat selection of antipasti and three pastas served hot out of pans that waiters circulate around the dining room; the other adds a generous entrée to the mix. The pasta selection changes daily but often includes gnocchi, fresh ravioli, and fettuccine in a cream sauce; it's fairly mediocre pasta but filling. The much better entrées include braised veal shank, grilled double-cut pork chop, and rack of lamb, among other selections. ⊠*355 W. 46th St., between 8th and 9th Aves., Midtown West* ☎*212/397–7597* ⊕*www.becco-nyc.com* ⌂*Reservations essential* ⊟*AE, D, DC, MC, V* Ⓜ*A, C, E to 42nd St.*

¢ ✕**Burger Joint.** What's a college burger bar, done up in particleboard and
BURGER rec-room decor, doing hidden inside of a five-star Midtown hotel? This
Fodor'sChoice tongue-in-cheek lunch spot buried in the Parker Meridien does such
★ boisterous midweek business that lines often snake through the lobby. Stepping behind the beige curtain you can find baseball cap–wearing grease-spattered cooks dispensing paper-wrapped cheeseburgers and crisp thin fries. Forget Kobe beef or foie gras—these burgers are straightforward, cheap, and delicious. ⊠*118 W. 57th St., between 6th and 7th Aves., Midtown West* ☎*212/245–5000* ⊕*www.parkermeridien. com* ⊟*No credit cards* Ⓜ*F, N, Q, R, W to 57th St.*

$$$ ✕**Marseille.** With great food and a convenient location near several
MEDITERRANEAN   Broadway theaters, Marseille is perpetually packed. Executive Chef
and partner Andy d'Amico's Mediterranean creations are continually
impressive. The daube is classic: a hunk of beef is slowly braised into
submission in red wine, then plated on a crispy square of fried polenta
with diced sautéed root vegetables. Leave room for the spongy beignets
with chocolate and raspberry dipping sauces. ✉*630 9th Ave., at W.
44th St., Midtown West* ☎*212/333–2323* ⊕*www.marseillenyc.com*
⌒*Reservations essential* ⊟*AE, MC, V* Ⓜ*A, C, E to 42nd St./Port
Authority Bus Terminal.*

$$–$$$ ✕**Serafina.** Mediterranean-hue friezes, a most inviting upstairs terrace,
PIZZA   and a steady stream of tourists and office workers grace this very Ital-
☾   ian café. Scene aside, the real draw here is some authentic Neopoli-
tan pizza—they even filter the water for the pizza dough to make it
more closely resemble the water in Naples. Beyond the designer pizzas
(Nutella, mascarpone, and robiola cheese; mozzarella, smoked salmon,
and dill) are antipasti, salads, pastas including a number of ravioli
dishes, and second courses like bass fillet pinot grigio. ✉*210 W. 55th
St. at Broadway, Midtown West* ☎*212/315–1700* Ⓜ*N, Q, R, W to
57th St.–7th Ave.*

WHERE TO STAY

There are no real bargains in the Manhattan hotel world, and you'll
find it difficult to get a decent room for under $250. However, occa-
sional weekend deals can be found. All the hotels we recommend for
cruise passengers are on the west side due to the area's relatively easy
proximity to the cruise ship terminal.

For price categories, see ⇨ *Lodging at the beginning of this chapter.*

$$–$$$ ▦**The Hotel at Times Square.** Yes, there really is a Super 8 in Times
Square—though it no longer goes by that name. The rooms are motel
plain with an unfortunate sea-foam color scheme, but most are well
maintained and clean. However, if you're an unfussy traveler who
wants to be in the thick of the madness, it's not a bad option, and it's
not too far from Manhattan's cruise-ship terminal. This small prewar
hotel shares its block with a plethora of Brazilian restaurants and is
near many theaters and Rockefeller Center. The peculiar lobby has
a narrow corridor that snakes off around a corner and is decorated
with some rather handsome art deco Bakelite lamps. **Pros:** free break-
fast; free wireless; free local calls. **Cons:** peremptory, low-frills service;
noisy area. ✉*59 W. 46th St., between 5th and 6th Aves., Midtown
West* ☎*212/719–2300 or 800/848–0020* ⊕*www.applecorehotels.com*
⇥*209 rooms* ⌒*In-room: Wi-Fi. In-hotel: bar, gym, Internet terminal,
parking (paid), no-smoking rooms* ⊟*AE, D, DC, MC, V* Ⓜ*B, D, F, V
to 47th–50th Sts./Rockefeller Center.*

$$$$ ▦**The Time Hotel.** One of the neighborhood's first boutique hotels, this
spot half a block from the din of Times Square tempers trendiness with
a touch of humor. A ridiculously futuristic glass elevator—eggshells line
the bottom of the shaft—transports guests to the second-floor lobby. In
the adjoining bar, nature videos lighten up the low-slung, serious, gray-

3

scale furnishings while homegrown New York City DJs spin a fresh selection of music in the trendy Time Lounge. The smallish guest rooms, each themed on one of the primary colors—red, yellow, or blue—have mood lighting and even specific "color" aromas that create a unique, if contrived, hotel experience. Whatever your primary color, they boast iPod docks, large flat-screens, and modern, if not especially comfortable, beds and couches. **Pros:** acclaimed and popular Serafina restaurant downstairs; surprisingly quiet for Times Square location; good turndown service. **Cons:** decor makes the rooms seem a little dated; service is inconsistent; water pressure is lacking. ⊠ *224 W. 49th St., between Broadway and 8th Ave., Midtown West* ☎ *212/320–2900 or 877/846–3692* ⊕ *www.thetimeny.com* 🛏 *164 rooms, 29 suites* ♿ *In-room: safe, Internet. In-hotel: restaurant, room service, bar, gym, laundry service, Internet terminal, parking (paid), no-smoking rooms* ▤ *AE, D, DC, MC, V* Ⓜ *1, C, E to 50th St.*

$$$$ 🏨 **Westin New York at Times Square.** The Westin changed the skyline of Midtown with this soaring skyscraper that subtly mimics the flow of the city—look for subway patterns in the carpets and the city reflected on the building's exterior. A thoughtful staff helps make the cavernous lobby and throngs of guests tolerable. Exceptionally large rooms are blissfully quiet and built to give you optimal views, which will probably be the most memorable part of your stay. Try especially for the light-filled corner rooms. Decor is sleek and amenities like flat-screen TVs are up to the latest standards. Bathrooms are stylish, with two-tone tiling, and have fun double showerheads. For even more comfort, spa-floor rooms come with massage chairs, aromatherapy candles, and other pampering pleasures. **Pros:** busy Times Square location; big and stylish rooms and baths. **Cons:** busy Times Square location; small bathroom sinks. ⊠ *270 W. 43rd St., at 8th Ave., Midtown West* ☎ *212/201–2700 or 866/837–4183* ⊕ *www.westinny.com* 🛏 *737 rooms, 126 suites* ♿ *In-room: safe, refrigerator, Wi-Fi. In-hotel: restaurant, room service, bars, gym, spa, laundry service, Internet terminal, Wi-Fi, parking (paid), some pets allowed, no-smoking rooms* ▤ *AE, D, DC, MC, V* Ⓜ *A, C, E to 42nd St./Times Sq.*

NORFOLK, VIRGINIA

Alice Powers   Founded in 1680, Norfolk is no newcomer to the cruise business. One famous passenger, Thomas Jefferson, arrived here in November 1789 after a two-month crossing of the Atlantic. More than 200 years later, this historic seaport welcomes more than 300,000 cruise passengers annually. Situated at the heart of nautical Hampton Roads, Norfolk is home to the largest Naval Base in the world and is also a major commercial port.

ESSENTIALS

Hours Most stores are open weekdays from 10 to 9. Some museums close on Monday and/or Tuesday.

Internet Most of the hotels offer free Wi-Fi service if you have your own laptop. If not, you may be able to find an Internet café, but the local Norfolk Public

Norfolk

KEY
- **1** Exploring sights
- (1) Hotels & Restaurants

Scope Arena

Town Point Park

Elizabeth River

Eastern Branch
Elizabeth River

Southern Branch
Elizabeth River

BERKLEY

Crawford Pkwy.

PORTSMOUTH

0   1/4 mile
0   1/4 kilometer

Exploring ▼
Chrysler Museum of Art **1**
MacArthur Memorial **3**
Moses Myers House **2**
Nauticus **4**
Norfolk Naval Station **5**

Restaurants ▼
Doumar's **2**
Freemason Abbey
Restaurant and Tavern **1**
No Frill Bar and Grill **7**
Vintage Kitchen **6**

Hotels ▼
Marriott Courtyard
Downtown **3**
Norfolk Marriott
Waterside **4**
Sheraton Norfolk
Waterside Hotel **5**

Library has free Internet access, so why pay? **Norfolk Public Library** (✉ *235 E. Plume St.* ☎ *757/664–7323* ⊕ *www.npl.lib.va.us*).

Visitor Information Hampton Roads Transit kiosk (✉ *Waterfront, 333 Waterside Dr.* ☎ *757/623–3222* ⊕ *www.watersidemarketplace.com*) is the launching point for tours of the city. **Norfolk Convention & Visitors Bureau** (✉ *End of 4th View St.* ☎ *757/441–1852 or 800/368–3097* ⊕ *www.norfolkcvb.com*).

THE CRUISE PORT

The new Half Moone Cruise and Celebration Center, as Norfolk calls its cruise terminal is in the center of the attractive, downtown waterfront. It's within walking distance of numerous attractions and amenities. From I–264, take the City Hall exit (Exit 10). At the light, turn right on St. Paul's Boulevard, and follow the signs to the Cedar Grove parking lot.

INFORMATION **Half Moone Cruise and Celebration Center** (✉ *1 Waterside Dr.* ☎ *757/664–1000 for cruise hotline* ⊕ *www.cruisenorfolk.org*).

AIRPORT TRANSFERS Norfolk International Airport (ORF) is 9 mi (15 km) and 20 minutes away from the cruise terminal. One-way, shared shuttle costs range from $7.50 to $22 per person, and a taxi costs about $18 to $25. **Norfolk Airport Express** (☎ *800/643–2197* ⊕ *www.norfolkairportexpress.com*). **Norfolk International Airport (ORF)** (✉ *200 Norview Ave.* ☎ *757/857–3200* ⊕ *www.norfolkairport.com*).

PARKING Cedar Grove Parking is the designated facility for cruise passengers. The parking fee ($10 daily) is paid upon entering the lot; Visa, MasterCard, American Express, cash, and traveler's checks are accepted. Less than 1 mi (1½ km) from I–264, this lot is located on Monticello Avenue between Virginia Beach Boulevard and Princess Anne Road in Downtown Norfolk. Shuttles run regularly to the cruise terminal.

EXPLORING NORFOLK

History meets high-tech in this waterfront city. From 18th-century historic homes and a major art museum to 20th-century battleships and nuclear-powered aircraft carriers, Norfolk has many interesting sites to explore, several of them free and most within walking distance of the cruise terminal.

Bullets in the margins refer to points of interest on the Norfolk map.

❶ ★ By any standard, the **Chrysler Museum of Art** downtown qualifies as one of America's major art museums. The permanent collection includes works by Rubens, Gainsborough, Renoir, Picasso, Cézanne, Matisse, Warhol, and Pollock, a list that suggests the breadth available here. Classical and pre-Columbian civilizations are also represented. The decorative-arts collection includes exquisite English porcelain and art nouveau furnishings. The Chrysler is home to one the most important glass collections in America, which includes glass objects from the 6th century BC to the present, with particularly strong holdings in Tiffany, French art glass, and English cameo, as well as artifacts from ancient Rome and the Near and Far East. ✉ *245 W. Olney Rd.* ☎ *757/664–6200* ⊕ *www.chrysler.*

org ✉*$7; Wed. by voluntary contribution* ⊙ *Wed. 10–9, Thurs.–Sat. 10–5, Sun. 1–5.*

❸ The **MacArthur Memorial** is the burial place of one of America's most distinguished military officers. General Douglas MacArthur (1880–1964) agreed to this navy town as the site for his monument because it was his mother's birthplace. In the rotunda of the old City Hall, converted according to MacArthur's design, is the mausoleum; 11 adjoining galleries house mementos of MacArthur's career, including his signature corncob pipe and the Japanese instruments of surrender that concluded World War II. However,

this is a monument not only to General MacArthur but to all those who served in wars from the Civil to the Korean War. Its Historical Center holds 2½ million documents and more than 100,000 photographs, and assists scholars, students, and researchers from around the world. The general's staff car is on display in the gift shop, where a 24-minute biography is shown. ✉*Bank St. at City Hall Ave., MacArthur Square* ☎*757/441–2965* ⊕*www.macarthurmemorial.org* ✉*By donation* ⊙*Mon.–Sat. 10–5, Sun. 11–5.*

❷ **Moses Myers House.** The Federal redbrick house built by its namesake between 1792 and 1796, is exceptional, and not just for its elegance. The furnishings, 70% of them original, include family portraits by Gilbert Stuart and Thomas Sully. A transplanted New Yorker as well as Norfolk's first Jewish resident, Myers made his fortune in Norfolk in shipping, then served as a diplomat and a customhouse officer. His grandson married James Madison's grandniece; his great-grandson served as mayor; and the family kept the house for five generations. ✉*323 E. Free Mason St.* ☎*757/333–1086* ⊕*www.chrysler.org/houses. asp* ✉*Free* ⊙ *Wed.–Sat. 10–4, Sun. noon–4.*

❹ **Nauticus,** a popular attraction on Norfolk's redeveloped downtown ☾ waterfront, is a maritime science museum featuring hand-on exhibits, ★ interactive theaters and high-definition films that celebrate the local connection to the seaport. Visitors can touch a shark, learn about weather and underwater archaeology, and explore the mysteries of the Elizabeth River. A NOAA Environmental Resource Center is an invaluable stop for education materials. Temporary exhibits in both the Changing Gallery and Forecastle Gallery keep things fresh. The Hampton Roads Naval Museum on the second floor and the Battleship *Wisconsin* adjacent to the building are also popular attractions operated by the U.S. Navy, and are included in the Nauticus admission. ✉*1 Waterside Dr.* ☎*757/664–1000* ⊕*www.nauticus.org* ✉*$10* ⊙*Memorial Day–Labor Day, daily 9–5; Labor Day–Memorial Day, Tues.–Sat. 10–5, Sun. noon–5.*

5 The **Norfolk Naval Station,** on the northern edge of the city, is an impressive sight, home to more than 100 ships of the Atlantic Fleet. The base was built on the site of the Jamestown Exposition of 1907; many of the original buildings survive and are still in use. Several large aircraft carriers, built at nearby

Fodor's Choice
★

> **BEACH AND BUY**
>
> A nylon tote bag that folds compactly into its own pocket can be used as a beach bag during your cruise and as an extra carry-on for your return home.

Newport News, call Norfolk home port and can be seen from miles away, especially at the bridge-tunnel end of the base. You may see two, each with a crew of up to 6,300, beside slightly smaller amphibious carriers that discharge marines in both helicopters and amphibious assault craft. The submarine piers, floating dry docks, supply center, and air station are all worth seeing. The *Victory Rover* and *Carrie B.* provide boat tours from downtown Norfolk to the naval station, and Hampton Roads Transit operates tour trolleys most of the year, departing from the naval-base tour office. Visitor access is by tour only, and photo ID is required to enter the base. ✉ *9079 Hampton Blvd.* ☎ *757/444–7955* ⊕ *www.cnic.navy.mil/norfolksta/* ✉ *Tour $7.50 (cash only and there is no ATM on premises)* ⊙ *Tours: Jan. 1–Mar. 15, Tues.–Sun. at 1:30; Mar. 16–May 17, every ½ hr 11–2; May 18–Aug. 30, every 30 min 10–2; Aug. 31–Nov. 1, hourly 11–2; Nov. 2–Dec. 31, Tues.–Sun. at 1:30.*

SHOPPING

If you forget to pack something for your cruise, you'll find stores galore within walking distance of the cruise terminal at the handsome MacArthur Center Mall. A car is helpful if you want to visit **Ghent,** where you'll find an eclectic mix of shops, including antiques stores and restaurants. It's a turn-of-the-20th-century neighborhood that runs from the Elizabeth River to York Street, to West Olney Road and Llewellyn Avenue. Colley Avenue and 21st Street is the hub.

You can meet painters, sculptors, glassworkers, jewelers, photographers, and other artists at work in their studios at **d'Art Center** (✉ *Selden Arcade, 208 E. Main St.* ☎ *757/625–4211*); the art is for sale. An eclectic mix of chic shops, including antiques stores, bars, and eateries, lines the streets of **Ghent,** a turn-of-the-20th-century neighborhood that runs from the Elizabeth River to York Street, to West Olney Road and Llewellyn Avenue. The intersection of Colley Avenue and 21st Street is the hub. The center of Norfolk's downtown, the **MacArthur Center** (✉ *300 Monticello Ave.* ☎ *757/627–6000*) has more than 100 stores, including anchors Nordstrom and Dillard's. There are restaurants downstairs and numerous fast-food outlets upstairs offering a variety of reasonably tolerable food. In Ghent the upscale clothing and shoe boutiques at the **Palace Shops** (✉ *21st St. at Llewellyn Ave.*) are a good place to search out some finery.

WHERE TO EAT

In addition to hotel restaurants, downtown Norfolk has many fine-dining restaurants as well as casual eateries in Waterside Festival Marketplace, where there's a versatile food court, and in the MacArthur Center Mall, including Johnny Rockets and Castaldi's—good food values for the price.

For price categories, see ⇨ Dining at the beginning of this chapter.

¢ ⊠**Doumar's.** After he introduced the world to its first ice-cream cone at
BARBECUE the 1904 World's Fair in St. Louis, Abe Doumar founded this drive-in institution in 1934. It's still operated by his family. Waitresses carry to your car the specialties of the house: barbecue, limeade, and ice cream in waffle cones made according to an original recipe. For breakfast, try the Egg-O-Doumar, a bargain at $2.70. The Food Network's "Diners, Drive-Ins, and Dives" featured Doumars twice in 2008. ⊠*20th St. at Monticello Ave.* ☎*757/627–4163* ⊕*www.doumars.com* ⊟*MC, V* ⊗*Closed Sun.*

$ ⊠**Freemason Abbey Restaurant and Tavern.** This former church near the
AMERICAN historic business district has been drawing customers for a long time, and not without reason. It has 40-foot-high cathedral ceilings and large windows, making for an airy, and dramatic, dining experience. You can sit upstairs, in the large choir loft, or in the main part of the church downstairs. Beside the bar just inside the entrance is an informal sort of "diner" area, but with the whole menu to choose from. Regular appetizers include artichoke dip and Santa Fe shrimp. There's a dinner special every weeknight, such as lobster, prime rib, and wild game (wild boar or alligator, for example). ⊠*209 W. Freemason St.* ☎*757/622–3966* ⊕*www.freemasonabbey.com* ⊟*AE, D, DC, MC, V.*

$ ⊠**No Frill Bar and Grill.** This expansive café is in an antique building in
CAFÉ the heart of Ghent. Beneath a tin ceiling and exposed ductwork, a cen-
★ tral bar is surrounded by several dining spaces with cream-and-mustard walls and wooden tables. Signature items include its ribs; the Funky Chicken Sandwich, a grilled chicken breast with bacon, tomato, melted Swiss cheese, and Parmesan pepper dressing on rye; and the Spotswood Salad of baby spinach, Granny Smith apples, and blue cheese. ⊠*806 Spotswood Ave., at Colley Ave.* ☎*757/627–4262* ⊕*www.nofrillgrill. com* ⊟*AE, MC, V.*

$$–$$$ ⊠**Vintage Kitchen.** In its short life, the Vintage Kitchen has racked up
AMERICAN many accolades for its focus on local foods, artisan cheeses, and micro-brews. The chef is Paris trained, but local, and knows the specialties of the area. It's a place where you can order "Five Spice Duck Breast" and also a superb cheeseburger. A special seven-course tasting meal is available by appointment Monday through Wednesday. ⊠*Dominion Tower, 999 Waterside Dr.* ☎*757/625–3370* ⊕*www.vintage-kitchen.com* ⚑*Reservations essential* ⊟*AE, D, MC, V* ⊗*No dinner Mon.–Wed.*

WHERE TO STAY

There are hotels within walking distance of the cruise port, or if you have a car, there are numerous chain motels on the outskirts of town where you can save a little money.

For price categories, see ⇨ Lodging at the beginning of this chapter.

$$ **⊞Marriott Courtyard Downtown.** Built in 2005, this eight-story hotel is near everything visitors want to see and where business travelers need to be. It's next door to the MacArthur Memorial and near the MacArthur Center and Nauticus. A handsome, inviting lobby has a tailored look; the modern guest rooms have a large desk, comforters, hair dryers, coffeemakers, irons, ironing boards, and a free daily newspaper. **Pros:** convenient downtown location. **Cons:** the hotel has a smoke-free policy. ✉*520 Plume St.* ☎*757/963–6000 or 800/321–2211* ⊕*www. marriott.com* ↩*137 rooms, 3 suites* ♿*In-room: refrigerator, Wi-Fi. In-hotel: restaurant, room service, pool, laundry facilities, laundry service, parking (paid)* ▤*AE, D, DC, MC, V.*

$$$ **⊞Norfolk Marriott Waterside.** This hotel in the redeveloped downtown area is connected to the Waterside Festival Marketplace shopping area by a ramp and is close to Town Point Park, site of many festivals. The handsome lobby, with wood paneling, a central staircase, silk tapestries, and Federal-style furniture, sets a high standard that continues throughout the hotel. Rooms are somewhat small, but each has most everything the business traveler could ask for—including two telephones, voice mail, and Internet access. **Pros:** great central location; two blocks from the Waterside Festival Marketplace. **Cons:** parking is pricey. ✉*235 E. Main St.* ☎*757/627–4200 or 800/228–9290* ⊕*www.marriott.com* ↩*396 rooms, 8 suites* ♿*In-room: Wi-Fi. In-hotel: 2 restaurants, bar, pool* ▤*AE, D, DC, MC, V.*

$$$ **⊞Sheraton Norfolk Waterside Hotel.** Modern is the word for this hotel's furnishings, from the bright, spacious lobby to the ample rooms and large suites. A ground-floor bar with dramatic 30-foot windows overlooks the Elizabeth—many rooms also have a beautiful view over the water. This property is convenient to the Waterside Festival Marketplace shopping area. **Pros:** the only hotel that is truly on the waterfront. **Cons:** again, parking—for Norfolk—is pricey. ✉*777 Waterside Dr.* ☎*757/622–6664* ⊕*www.sheraton.com* ↩*426 rooms, 20 suites* ♿*In-hotel: restaurant, bar, pool* ▤*AE, D, DC, MC, V.*

PORT CANAVERAL, FLORIDA

Kerry
Speckman

This once-bustling commercial fishing area is still home to a small shrimping fleet, charter boats, and party fishing boats, but its main business these days is as a cruise-ship port. Cocoa Beach itself isn't the spiffiest place around, but what *is* becoming quite clean and neat is the north end of the port where the Carnival, Disney, and Royal Caribbean cruise lines set sail, as well as Sun Cruz and Sterling casino boats. Port Canaveral is now Florida's second-busiest cruise port. Because of Port Canaveral's proximity to Orlando theme parks (about an hour away), many cruisers combine a short cruise with a stay in the area. The port is also convenient to popular Space Coast attractions such as the Kennedy Space Center and United States Astronaut Hall of Fame in Titusville.

ESSENTIALS

Hours Most of the area's attractions are open every day.

Internet Most people choose to go online at their hotel.

Visitor Information Space Coast Office of Tourism (⊠ *430 Brevard Ave.,*
Suite 150, Cocoa ☎ *321/433–4470* ⊕ *www.space-coast.com).*

THE CRUISE PORT

Port Canaveral is the second-busiest cruise port in the world, with more
than 4.6 million passengers passing through its terminals annually. The
port has six cruise terminals and is home to Carnival Cruise Lines,
Disney Cruise Line, and Royal Caribbean International. Other cruise
lines, such as Holland America and Norwegian Cruise Line, operate
seasonally. The port serves as the embarkation point for three-, four-,
and seven-day cruises to the Bahamas, Key West, Mexico, Jamaica,
and the Virgin Islands.

In Brevard County, Port Canaveral is on State Road (S.R.) 528, also
known as the Beeline Expressway, which runs straight to Orlando,
which has the nearest airport. To drive to Port Canaveral from there,
take the north exit out of the airport, staying to the right, to S.R. 528
(Beeline Expressway) East. Take S.R. 528 directly to Port Canaveral;
it's about a 45-minute drive.

INFORMATION **Canaveral Port Authority** (⊠*9150 Christopher Columbus Dr., Cape Canaveral* ☎*321/783–7831 or 888/767–8226* ⊕*www.portcanaveral.org*).

AIRPORT TRANSFERS If you are flying into the area, the Orlando airport is 45 minutes away from the docks. If you have not arranged airport transfers with your cruise line, then you will need to make your own arrangements. Taxis are expensive, but many companies offer minivan and bus shuttles to Port Canaveral. They are all listed on the Canaveral Port Authority Web site. Some shuttles charge for the entire van, which is a good deal for groups but not for individuals or couples; some will charge a per-person rate. Expect to pay at least $48 per person round-trip. But you will need to make a reservation in advance regardless of which service you use. Some cruisers who want to do some exploring before the cruise rent a car at the airport and drop it off at the port, which houses several major rental-car agencies.

AAA Cruise Line Connection (☎*407/908–5566* ⊕*www.aaasuperride. com*). **Busy Traveler Transport Service** (☎*321/453–5278 or 800/496–7433* ⊕*www.abusytraveler.com*).

PARKING Outdoor, gated lots and a six-story parking garage are near the terminals and cost $15 per day for vehicles up to 20 feet in length and $26 per day for vehicles over 20 feet, which must be paid in advance, either in cash, traveler's checks, or by major credit card (MasterCard and Visa only).

> ### PORT CANAVERAL BEST BETS
>
> ■ **Kennedy Space Center.** Kennedy Space Center in Titusville is the region's biggest attraction.
>
> ■ **Merritt Island.** If you want to get out and commune with nature, this is the place, especially for bird-watchers.
>
> ■ **Orlando Theme Parks.** With Orlando just an hour away, many cruisers combine a theme-park visit with their cruise.

3

EXPLORING THE CAPE CANAVERAL AREA

With the Kennedy Space Center just 20 minutes away, there is plenty to do in and around Cape Canaveral, though many folks opt to travel the extra hour into Orlando to visit the popular theme parks.

❺ **Brevard Museum of History & Natural Science.** To see what the lay of the local land looked like in other eras, check out this local science museum. Hands-on activities for children are the draw here. Not to be missed is the Windover Archaeological Exhibit of 7,000-year-old artifacts indigenous to the region. In 1984 a shallow pond revealed the burial ground of more than 200 Native Americans who lived in the area about 7,000 years ago. Preserved in the muck were bones and, to the archaeologists' surprise, the brains of these ancient people. Don't overlook the hands-on discovery rooms and the collection of Victoriana. The museum's nature center has 22 acres of trails encompassing three distinct ecosystems—sand pine hills, lake lands, and marshlands. ⊠*2201 Michigan Ave.* ☎*321/632–1830* ⊕*www.brevardmuseum.org* ✎*$6* ☉*Mon.–Sat. 10–4.*

④ Brevard Zoo. It took 20,000 volunteers two weeks to turn 56 acres of forest and wetlands into the only American Zoo and Aquarium Association–accredited zoo built by a community. Stroll along the shaded boardwalks and get a close-up look at alligators, crocodiles, giant anteaters, marmosets, jaguars, eagles, river otters, kangaroos, exotic birds, and kookaburras. Alligator, crocodile, and river-otter feedings are held on alternate afternoons—although the alligators do not dine on the otters. Stop by Paws-On, an interactive learning playground where kids and adults can crawl into human-size gopher burrows, beehives, and spiderwebs; get cozy with several domestic animals in Animal Encounters; hand-feed a giraffe in Expedition Africa or a lorrikeet in the Australian Free Flight Aviary; and step up to the Wetlands Outpost, an elevated pavilion that's a gateway to 22 acres of wetlands through which you can paddle kayaks and keep an eye open for the 4,000 species of wildlife that live in these waters and woods. ⊠ *8225 N. Wickham Rd.* 🕾 *321/254–9453* ⊕ *www.brevardzoo.org* 🖃 *$11.50; train ride $3, kayaking $6* ⊙ *Daily 9:30–5, last admission at 4:15.*

❶ Kennedy Space Center Visitor Complex. This "must-see" sight is just southeast of Titusville. Following the lead of the theme parks, they've switched to a one-price-covers-all admission. To get the most out of your visit to the space center, take the basic bus tour (included with admission), which makes stops at several facilities. Buses depart every 15 minutes, and you can get on and off any bus whenever you like. If you want a more special experience, you can pay for many different add-ons. As you approach the Kennedy Space Center grounds, tune your car radio to AM1320 for attraction information.

The Shuttle Launch Experience uses a sophisticated motion-based platform, special-effects seats, and high-fidelity visual and audio components to simulate the sensations experienced in an actual Space Shuttle launch. It's included in the basic admission price, which also includes whatever film is showing in the IMAX theater. The basic bus tour includes many different exhibits and activities, including a stop at the **Launch Complex 39 Observation Gantry,** which has an unparalleled view of the twin space-shuttle launchpads. An outdoor display includes examples of many different rockets. The most moving exhibit is the **Astronaut Memorial,** a tribute to those who have died while in pursuit of space exploration. You can pay for many different additional experiences, including a daily Q&A session, a lunch with an astronaut, or a NASA Up Close tour. ⊠ *S.R. 405, Kennedy Space Center* 🕾 *321/449–4444* ⊕ *www.kennedyspacecenter.com* 🖃 *General admission includes bus tour, IMAX movies, Visitor Complex shows and exhibits, and the Astronaut Hall of Fame, $38* ⊙ *Space Center opens daily at 9, closing times vary according to season (call for details), last regular tour 3 hrs before closing; closed certain launch dates.*

❸ Merritt Island National Wildlife Refuge. Adjoining the Canaveral National Seashore, this refuge acts as a buffer around Kennedy Space Center, while protecting 500 species of wildlife, including 10 considered threatened or endangered. It's an immense area dotted by brackish estuaries and marshes and patches of land consisting of coastal dunes, scrub oaks, pine forests and flatwoods, and palm and oak hammocks. You can borrow field guides and binoculars at the visitor center to track down various types of falcons, ospreys, eagles, turkeys, doves, cuckoos, loons, geese, skimmers, terns, warblers, wrens, thrushes, sparrows, owls, and woodpeckers. A 20-minute video about refuge wildlife and accessibility—only 10,000 acres are developed—can help orient you. You might take a self-guided tour along the 7-mi **Black Point Wildlife Drive**. On the **Oak Hammock Foot Trail** you can see wintering migratory waterfowl and learn about the plants of a hammock community. If you exit the north end of the refuge, look for the **Manatee Observation Area** just north of the Haulover Canal (maps are at the visitor center). They usually show up in spring and fall. The refuge is closed four days before a shuttle launch. ⊠ *Rte. 402, across Titusville Causeway* ☎ *321/861–0667, visitor center 321/861–0668* ⊕ *www.fws.gov/merritt island* ☒ *Free* ⊙ *Daily sunrise–sundown; visitor center weekdays 8–4:30, weekends 9–5 (Nov.–Mar.).*

❷ United States Astronaut Hall of Fame. The original Mercury 7 team and the later Gemini, Apollo, Skylab, and shuttle astronauts contributed to make this the world's premium archive of astronauts' personal stories. Authentic memorabilia and equipment from their collections tell the story of human space exploration. You'll watch videotapes of historic moments in the space program and see one-of-a-kind items like Wally Schirra's relatively archaic Sigma 7 Mercury space capsule, Gus Grissom's spacesuit (colored silver only because NASA thought silver looked more "spacey"), and a flag that made it to the moon. The exhibit **First on the Moon** focuses on crew selection for *Apollo 11* and the Soviet Union's role in the space race. Definitely don't miss the **Astronaut Adventure,** a hands-on discovery center with interactive exhibits that help you learn about space travel. One of the more challenging activities is a space-shuttle simulator that lets you try your hand at landing the craft—and afterward replays a side view of your rolling and pitching descent. ⊠ *S.R. 405, Kennedy Space Center* ☎ *321/449–4444, 321/449–4400 ATX* ⊕ *www.kennedyspacecenter.com* ☒ *$17 adults, $13 children 3–11* ⊙ *Hall of Fame opens daily at 9, closing times vary according to season (call for details).*

ORLANDO THEME PARKS

☺ **SeaWorld Orlando.** In the world's largest marine adventure park, every attraction is devoted to demonstrating the ways that humans can protect the mammals, birds, fish, and reptiles that live in the ocean and its tributaries. The presentations are gentle reminders of our responsibility to safeguard the environment, and you'll find that SeaWorld's use of humor plays a major role in this education. The park is small enough that, armed with a map that lists show times, you can plan a chronological approach that flows easily from one attraction to the next. Near the intersection of I–4 and the Beeline Expressway; take I–4 to Exit 71 or 72 and follow signs. ⊠ *7007 Sea Harbor Dr., International Drive Area, Orlando* ☎ *407/351–3600 or 800/327–2424* ⊕ *www.seaworld. com* ☒ *$74.95 for a 1-day ticket* ⊙ *Daily 9–6 or 7, until as late as 11* *summer and holidays; educational programs daily, some beginning as early as 6:30 AM.*

🜨 **Universal Orlando.** The resort consists of **Universal Studios** (the original movie theme park), **Islands of Adventure** (the second theme park), and **CityWalk** (the dining-shopping-nightclub complex). Although it's bordered by residential neighborhoods and thickly trafficked International Drive, Universal Orlando is surprisingly expansive yet intimate and accessible, with two massive parking complexes, easy walks to all attractions, and a motor launch that cruises to the hotels. Universal Orlando emphasizes "two parks, two days, one great adventure," but you may find the presentation, creativity, and cutting-edge technology brings you back for more. ✉ *1000 Universal Studios Plaza, Orlando* ☎ *407/363–8000 or 888/331–9108* ⊕ *www.universalorlando.com* 🎟 *1-day, 1-park ticket $75; 1-day, 2-park ticket $84.99* ⊙ *Usually daily 9–9, but hrs vary seasonally; CityWalk restaurants and bars have individual open hrs.*

🜨 **Walt Disney World.** Walt Disney World is a huge complex of theme parks and attractions, each of which is worth a visit. Parks include the **Magic Kingdom,** a family favorite and the original here; **Epcot,** Disney's international, educational park; **Disney–MGM Studios,** a movie-oriented theme park; and **Disney's Animal Kingdom,** which is much more than a zoo. Beyond these, there are water parks, elaborate minigolf courses, a sports center, resorts, restaurants, and nightlife. If you have only one day, you'll have to concentrate on a single park; Disney–MGM Studios or Animal Kingdom are easiest to do in a day, but arrive early and expect to stay until park closing, which might be as early as 5 PM for Animal Kingdom or as late as 11 PM during busy seasons at the Magic Kingdom. The most direct route to the Disney Parks from Port Canaveral is S.R. 528 (the Beeline Expressway) to I–4; when you get through Orlando, follow the signs to Disney and expect traffic. ✉ *Lake Buena Vista* ☎ *407/824–4321* ⊕ *disneyworld.disney.go.com* 🎟 *1-day, 1-park pass $75* ⊙ *Most parks open by 9 AM; closing hrs vary, but usually 5 PM for Animal Kingdom and 6–11 PM for other parks, depending on season.*

BEACHES

After crossing a long and high bridge just east of Cocoa Village, you'll be dropped down upon a barrier island. A few miles farther and you'll reach the Atlantic Ocean and picture-perfect **Cocoa Beach** at Route A1A. This is one of the Space Coast's nicest beaches, with many wide stretches that are excellent for biking, jogging, power walking, or strolling. In some places there are dressing rooms, showers, playgrounds, picnic areas with grills, snack shops, and surf-side parking lots. Beach vendors offer necessities, and guards are on duty in summer. Cocoa Beach is considered the capital of Florida's surfing community. At the opposite end of the seashore from New Smyrna Beach's Apollo Beach, remote **Playalinda Beach** (⊠ *Rte. 402/Beach Rd.* ☎ *321/867–4077* ⊕ *www.nps.gov/cana* ☒ *$3 per person, admission to National Seashore* ☉ *Nov.–Mar., daily 6–6; Apr.–Oct., daily 6* AM *–8* PM) has pristine sands and is the

BATTERY ALERT

Even if you don't think you'll need them, bring along extra camera batteries and change them before you think the old ones are dead.

longest stretch of undeveloped coast on Florida's Atlantic seaboard. Its isolation explains why there are limited services (i.e., no phones, food service, drinking water, or lifeguards from September through May) and why a remote strand of the beach is popular with nude sunbathers. Aside from them, hundreds of giant sea turtles come ashore here from May through August to lay their eggs. Eight parking lots anchor the beach at 1-mi intervals. Take bug repellent in case of horseflies. To get here, take I–95 Exit 220 east and follow the signs. The 10-acre oceanfront **Sidney Fischer Park** (⊠ 2100 block of Rte. A1A ☎ 321/868–3252) has showers, playgrounds, changing areas, picnic areas with grills, snack shops, and plenty of well-maintained, inexpensive surf-side parking lots. Beach vendors carry necessities for sunning and swimming. The parking fee is $5 for cars and RVs.

SHOPPING

You could spend hours browsing in the more than 50 boutiques and shops of **Cocoa Village** (⊠ *Rte. 520 and Brevard Ave.* ☎ *321/631–9075*) along Brevard Avenue and Harrison Street, which has the densest concentration of shops. Although most are of the gift and clothing variety, the village is also home to several antiques shops, art galleries, florists, bookstores, and even a tattoo parlor and a spa.

Fodor's Choice ★ It's impossible to miss the **Ron Jon Surf Shop** (⊠ *4151 N. Atlantic Ave., Rte. A1A* ☎ *321/799–8888*). With a giant surfboard and an aqua, teal, and pink art deco facade, Ron Jon takes up nearly two blocks along Route A1A. What started in 1963 as a small T-shirt and bathing suit shop has evolved into a 52,000-square-foot superstore that's open every day 'round the clock. The shop has water-sports gear as well as chairs and umbrellas for rent and sells every kind of beachwear, surf wax, plus the requisite T-shirts and flip-flops. ■ TIP➔ **For up-to-the-minute surfing conditions, call the store and press 3 and then 7 for the Ron Jon Surf and Weather Report.**

WHERE TO EAT

The Cove at Port Canaveral has several restaurants if you are looking for a place to eat right at the port.

For price categories, see ⇨ *Dining at the beginning of this chapter.*

$$$–$$$$
GERMAN
✕ **Heidelberg.** As the name suggests, the cuisine here is definitely German, from the sauerbraten served with potato dumplings and red cabbage to the beef Stroganoff and spaetzle to the classically prepared Wiener schnitzel. All the soups and desserts are homemade; try the

Viennese-style apple strudel and the rum-zapped almond-cream tortes. Elegant interior touches include crisp linens and fresh flowers. There's live music Friday and Saturday evenings. You can also dine inside the jazz club, Heidi's, next door. ⊠ *7 N. Orlando Ave., opposite City Hall, Cocoa Beach* ☎ *321/783–6806* ⊟ *AE, MC, V* ⊘ *Closed Mon. Closed Tues. in summer. No lunch Sun.*

$–$$ ✗ **Oh Shucks Seafood Bar.** At the only open-air seafood bar on the beach,
SEAFOOD   at the entrance of the Cocoa Beach Pier, the main item is oysters, served on the half shell. You can also grab a burger here, crab legs by the pound, or Oh Shucks' most popular item, coconut beer shrimp. Some diners complain that the prices don't jibe with the ultracasual atmosphere (e.g., plastic chairs), but they're also paying for the "ex-Pier-ience." There's live entertainment on Friday and Saturday. ⊠ *401 Meade Ave., Cocoa Beach Pier, Cocoa Beach* ☎ *321/783–7549* ⊟ *AE, D, MC, V.*

WHERE TO STAY

Many local hotels offer cruise packages that include one night's lodging, parking for the duration of your cruise, and transportation to the cruise port.

For price categories, see ⇨ Lodging at the beginning of this chapter.

$$ 🏨 **Inn at Cocoa Beach.** One of the area's best, this charming oceanfront
★   inn has spacious, individually decorated rooms with four-poster beds, upholstered chairs, and balconies or patios; most have ocean views. Deluxe rooms are much larger, with a king-size bed, sofa, and sitting area; most also have a dining table. Jacuzzi rooms are different sizes. Included in the rate are afternoon socials in the breezeway, evening wine and cheese, and a Continental breakfast. **Pros:** quiet; romantic; honor bar. **Cons:** no on-site restaurant; "forced" socializing. ⊠ *4300 Ocean Beach Blvd., Cocoa Beach* ☎ *321/799–3460, 800/343–5307 outside Florida* ⊕ *www.theinnatcocoabeach.com* ⇗ *50 rooms* ⚬ *In-room: safe, DVD (some), Wi-Fi. In-hotel: pool, beachfront, Wi-Fi, parking (free), no-smoking rooms* ⊟ *AE, D, MC, V* ⦿ *CP.*

$$–$$$ 🏨 **Radisson Resort at the Port.** For cruise-ship passengers who can't wait to get under way, this splashy resort, done up in pink and turquoise, already feels like the Caribbean. Guest rooms have wicker furniture, hand-painted wallpaper, tropical-theme decor, and ceiling fans. The pool is lushly landscaped and features a cascading 95-foot mountain waterfall, tiki bar, and occasional appearances by the "Radisson parrots," about a dozen renegade birds who call the resort home (can you blame them?). This resort, directly across the bay from Port Canaveral, is not on the ocean, but it does provide complimentary transportation to the beach, Ron Jon Surf Shop, and the cruise-ship terminals at Port Canaveral. **Pros:** cruise-ship convenience; pool area; free shuttle. **Cons:** three-day cancellation policy; rooms around the pool can be noisy; loud air-conditioning in some rooms. ⊠ *8701 Astronaut Blvd., Cape Canaveral* ☎ *321/784–0000 or 888/201–1718* ⊕ *www.radisson.com/cape canaveralfl* ⇗ *284 rooms, 72 suites* ⚬ *In-room: refrigerator (some), kitchen (some), Internet. In-hotel: restaurant, bar, tennis court, pool, gym, laundry facilities, laundry service, Wi-Fi* ⊟ *AE, D, MC, V.*

SAN JUAN, PUERTO RICO

By Mark
Sullivan

In addition to being a major port of call, San Juan is also a common port of embarkation for cruises on Southern Caribbean itineraries. For information on dining, shopping, nightlife, and sightseeing see ⇨ San Juan, Puerto Rico *in* Chapter 4.

THE CRUISE PORT

Most cruise ships dock within a couple of blocks of Old San Juan. The Paseo de la Princesa, a tree-lined promenade beneath the city wall, is a nice place for a stroll—you can admire the local crafts and stop at the refreshment kiosks. A tourist information booth is in the cruise terminal area. Major sights in the Old San Juan area are mere blocks from the piers, but be aware that the streets are narrow and steeply inclined in places. Even if you have only a few hours before your cruise, you'll have time to do a little sightseeing. A few ships dock across the bay, which will require you to take a taxi everywhere.

AIRPORT
TRANSFERS

The ride from the Luis Muñoz Marín International Airport, east of downtown San Juan, to the docks in Old San Juan takes about 20 minutes. The white TAXI TURISTICO cabs, marked by a logo on the door, have a fixed rate of $19 to the cruise-ship piers; there is a 50¢ charge for luggage. Other taxi companies charge by the mile, which can cost a little more. Be sure the driver starts the meter, or agree on a fare beforehand.

VISITOR
INFORMATION

Puerto Rico Tourism Company (⊠*Plaza de la Dársena, near Pier 1, Old San Juan* ☎*787/721–2400 or 787/722–1709* ⊕*www.gotopuertorico. com*).

WHERE TO STAY

If you are planning to spend one night in San Juan before your cruise departs, you'll probably find it easier to stay in Old San Juan, where the cruise-ship terminals are. But if you want to spend a few extra days in the city, there are other possibilities near good beaches a bit farther out. We make some nightlife suggestions in the San Juan port of call section (*see* ⇨ *San Juan in Chapter 4*).

For price categories, see ⇨ *Lodging at the beginning of this chapter.*

$$$–$$$$
★

Chateau Cervantes. There's nothing like this hotel anywhere else in San Juan—or Puerto Rico, for that matter. The brainchild of local fashion icon Nono Maldonado, this luxury lodging has a look that's completely au courant. Bursts of color from red pillows or gold upholstery on the banquettes add considerable warmth. And the amenities are above and beyond other hotels. Splurge for one of the larger suites and you get a butler who'll come to mix cocktails; the two-level presidential suite comes with a car and driver. The rooftop terrace has a bar, a hot tub, and an area for massages. Only one downside: this colonial-era building is on a side street, so it doesn't have a view of the water. But with such a gorgeous interior, you may not even notice. **Pros:** historic property; boutique-hotel feel; doting staff. **Cons:** no view; street noise on weekends. ⊠*329*

Calle Recinto Sur, Old San Juan ☎ *787/724–7722* ⊕ *www.cervantespr. com* ↩ *6 rooms, 6 suites* ♿ *In-room: safe, Wi-Fi. In-hotel: restaurant, bar, laundry service* ▭ *AE, D, DC, MC, V* ⌖ *EP.*

$$–$$$ 🏨 **Numero Uno.** The name refers to the address, but Numero Uno is also
★   how this small hotel rates with its guests. It's not unusual to hear people trading stories about how many times they've returned to this relaxing retreat. Behind a whitewashed wall is a patio where you can catch some rays beside the pool, dine in the restaurant, or enjoy a cocktail at the bar. A few steps away, a sandy beach beckons; guests are provided with beach chairs and umbrellas. Rooms are decorated in sophisticated shades of cream and taupe; several have ocean views. **Pros:** sophisticated rooms; beautiful beach; friendly staff. **Cons:** neighborhood is too quiet for some. ✉ *1 Calle Santa Ana, Ocean Park* ☎ *787/726–5010* ⊕ *www.numero1guesthouse.com* ↩ *11 rooms, 2 apartments* ♿ *In-room: kitchen (some), refrigerator, Internet. In-hotel: restaurant, bar, pool, beachfront* ▭ *AE, MC, V* ⌖ *CP.*

$$$ 🏨 **Sheraton Old San Juan.** This hotel's triangular shape subtly echoes the cruise ships docked nearby. Rooms facing the water have dazzling views of these behemoths as they sail in and out of the harbor. Others have views over the rooftops of Old San Juan. The rooms have been plushly renovated and have nice touches like custom-designed beds. On the top floor you can find a sunny patio with a pool and whirlpool bath, as well as a spacious gym with the latest equipment; the concierge level provides hassle-free check-ins, Continental breakfasts, and evening hors d'oeuvres. **Pros:** great views of cruise ships; shimmering rooftop pool; only casino in neighborhood. **Cons:** chain-hotel feel;, not all rooms have views. ✉ *100 Calle Brumbaugh, Old San Juan* ☎ *787/721–5100 or 866/376–7577* ⊕ *www.sheratonoldsanjuan.com* ↩ *200 rooms, 40 suites* ♿ *In-room: safe, Internet. In-hotel: restaurant, room service, bar, pool, gym, laundry service, Internet terminal, Wi-Fi, parking (paid), no-smoking rooms* ▭ *AE, D, DC, MC, V* ⌖ *EP.*

TAMPA, FLORIDA

By Christina
Tourigny and
Jim Tunstall

Although glitzy Miami seems to hold the trendiness trump card and Orlando is the place your kids want to visit annually until they hit middle school, the Tampa Bay area has that elusive quality that many attribute to the "real Florida." The state's second-largest metro area is less fast-lane than its biggest (Miami), or even Orlando, but its strengths are just as varied, from broad cultural diversity to a sun-worshipping beach culture. Florida's third-busiest airport, a vibrant business community, world-class beaches, and superior hotels and resorts—many of them historic—make this an excellent place to spend a week or a lifetime. Several ships are based here year-round and seasonally, most doing Western Caribbean itineraries.

ESSENTIALS

Hours Some museums are closed on Monday.

Internet Most people choose to access the Internet through their hotels. Most Starbucks outlets offer Internet service for a fee if you have your own laptop.

Visitor Information Tampa Bay & Company (✉ *401 E. Jackson St., Suite 2100, Tampa* ☎ *800/368–2672 or 813/223–1111* ⊕ *www.visittampabay.com*). **Ybor City Chamber Visitor Bureau** (✉ *1600 E. 8th Ave., Ste. B104, Tampa* ☎ *813/241–8838* ⊕ *www.ybor.org*).

THE CRUISE PORT

Tampa is the largest shipping port in the state of Florida, and it's becoming ever more important to the cruise industry, now with three passenger terminals. In Tampa's downtown area, the port is linked to nearby Ybor City and the rest of the Tampa Bay Area by the TECO streetcar line.

To reach the port by car, take I–4 West to Exit 1 (Ybor City), and go south on 21st Street. To get to Terminals 2 and 6, turn right on Adamo Drive (Highway 60), then left on Channelside Drive.

INFORMATION **Tampa Port Authority** (✉ *1101 Channelside Dr.* ☎ *813/905–7678, 813/ 905–5045, or 800/741–2297* ⊕ *www.tampaport.com*).

AIRPORT
TRANSFERS Both Bay Shuttle and Super Shuttle provide shared van service to and from the airport and the cruise terminal. Expect to pay about $12 per person.

INFORMATION **Bay Shuttle** (☎ *813/259–9998* ⊕ *www.tampabayshuttle.com*). **Super Shuttle** (☎ *727/572–1111 or 800/282–6817* ⊕ *www.supershuttle.com*).

PARKING   Parking is available at the port directly across from the terminals. For Terminals 2 and 3 (Carnival and Royal Caribbean), parking is in a garage across the street. For Terminal 6 (Holland America), parking is outdoors in a guarded, enclosed lot. The cost is $14 a day, payable by credit card (MasterCard or Visa) or in cash.

EXPLORING THE TAMPA BAY AREA

Florida's west coast crown jewel as well as its business and commercial hub, Tampa has high-rises and heavy traffic. Amid the bustle is the region's greatest concentration of restaurants, nightlife, stores, and cultural events.

Numbers in the margin refer to points of interest on the Tampa Bay Area map.

❹ Adventure Island. From spring until mid-fall, rides named Tampa Typhoon, Gulf Scream, and Key West Rapids promise heat relief at this corporate cousin and neighbor of Busch Gardens. Tampa's most popular "wet" park features waterslides and artificial wave pools in a 30-acre package. One of the attraction's headliners, Riptide, challenges you to race three other riders on a sliding mat through twisting tubes and hairpin turns. Planners of this park also took the younger kids into account, with offerings such as Fabian's Funport, which has a scaled-down wave pool and interactive water gym. Along with a volleyball complex and a surf pool, there are cafés, snack bars, picnic and sunbathing areas, and changing rooms. ✉ *1001 Malcolm McKinley Dr., less than 1 mi north of Busch Gardens, Central Tampa* ☎ *813/987–5660 or 888/800–5447* ⊕ *www.adventureisland.com* 💲 *$37.95; parking $6* ⊙ *Mid-Mar.–late Oct., daily 10–5.*

❸ Busch Gardens. Nearly 4½ million vacationers and locals flock here each year. The hook: five roller coasters are an irresistible lure for thrill-ride jockeys. But this state-of-the-art attraction also is a world-class zoo, with more than 2,000 animals, and a live-entertainment venue that provides a full day (or more) of entertainment for the whole family. The 335-acre adventure park's habitats offer views of some of the world's most endangered and exotic animals. You can experience up-close animal encounters (for an extra charge), and there are many individual shows and special exhibit areas to bring you up close and personal with a wide variety of animals. Not to mention those rides. Allow six to eight hours to experience Busch Gardens. ✉ *3000 E. Busch Blvd., 8 mi northeast of downtown Tampa and 2 mi east of I–275 Exit 50, Central Tampa* ☎ *813/987–5000 or 888/800–5447* ⊕ *www.buschgardens.com* 💲 *$67.95; parking $10* ⊙ *Daily 10–6.*

FodorsChoice
★

❶ Florida Aquarium. While eels, sharks, and stingrays are the headliners, this much more than a giant fishbowl. It is a dazzling architectural landmark with an 83-foot-high multitier glass dome and 200,000 square feet of air-conditioned exhibit space. It has more than 10,000 aquatic plants, and animals representing species native to Florida and the rest of the world. The major exhibit areas reflect the diversity of Florida's natural habitats—Wetlands, Bays and Beaches, and Coral Reef. Creature-specific exhibits are the No Bone Zone (lovable invertebrates) and

Sea Hunt, with predators ranging from sharks to exotic lion fish. The aquarium's most impressive single exhibit is the Coral Reef Gallery, in a 500,000-gallon tank ringed with viewing windows, including an awesome 43-foot-wide panoramic opening. Part of the tank is a walkable tunnel, almost giving the illusion of venturing into underwater depths. There you see a thicket of elkhorn coral teeming with tropical fish. A dark cave reveals sea life you would normally see only on night dives. ✉*701 Channelside Dr., Downtown, Tampa* ☎*813/273–4000* ⊕*www.flaquarium.org* ✍*Aquarium $17.95, Ecotour $19.95; Aquarium/Ecotour combo $32.95; parking $5* ☉*Daily 9:30–5.*

> ### TAMPA BEST BETS
>
> ■ **Busch Gardens.** The area's best theme park is a good family destination.
>
> ■ **Florida Aquarium.** The aquarium is next to the cruise port, so you can just walk, making it a good option even if you have a couple of hours to kill before boarding (they'll even store your luggage if you want to visit after disembarking).
>
> ■ **Ybor City.** For nightlife and restaurants, this historic district is Tampa's hot spot.

❼ **Museum of Fine Arts.** Outstanding examples of European, American, pre-Columbian, and Far Eastern art are at St. Petersburg's major art museum. There are also photographic exhibits. Staff members give narrated gallery tours two to five times a day. ✉*255 Beach Dr. NE* ☎*727/896–2667* ⊕*www.fine-arts.org* ✍*$12* ☉*Tues.–Sat. 10–5, Sun. 1–5.*

❺ **Museum of Science and Industry (MOSI).** This is a fun and stimulating scientific playground, though at times some exhibits aren't working properly. When it's hitting on all cylinders, you learn about Florida weather, anatomy, flight, and space by seeing *and* by doing. At the Gulf Coast Hurricane Exhibit, you can experience what a hurricane and its 74-mph winds feel like, though crowds sometimes mean a long wait. The BioWorks Butterfly Garden is a 6,400-square-foot engineered ecosystem project that demonstrates how wetlands can clean water plus serve as a home for butterflies. The 100-seat Saunders Planetarium—Tampa's only planetarium—has afternoon and evening shows, one of them a trek through the universe. For adventurous spirits, there's a high-wire bicycle ride 30 feet above the floor. There's also an impressive IMAX theater, where films are projected on a hemispherical 82-foot dome. ✉*4801 E. Fowler Ave., 1 mi north of Busch Gardens, Northeast Tampa* ☎*813/987–6100 or 800/995–6674* ⊕*www.mosi.org* ✍*$23.95* ☉*Weekdays 9–5, weekends 9–6.*

❽ **Salvador Dalí Museum.** The collection includes 95 oils, more than 100 watercolors and drawings, and 1,300 graphics, sculptures, photographs, and objets d'art, including floor-to-ceiling murals. Frequent tours are led by well-informed docents. How did the collection end up here? A rich northern industrialist and friend of Dalí, Ohio magnate A. Reynolds Morse, was looking for a museum site after his huge personal Dalí collection began to overflow his mansion. The people of St. Petersburg vied admirably for the collection, and the museum was established here as a

Fodor's Choice ★

result. ⊠ *1000 3rd St. S* ☎ *727/823–3767 or 800/442–3254* ⊕ *www. salvadordalimuseum.org* ⊡ *$15* ⊙ *Mon.–Wed. and Sat. 9:30–5:30, Thurs. 9:30–8, Fri. 9:30–6:30, Sun. noon–5:30.*

❻ Seminole Hard Rock Hotel & Casino. The latest buzz at the casino is about the much-anticipated upgrade that may add blackjack and baccarat to the gaming areas. Until the formalities are addressed (including legislative action and a possible legal challenge), gamers can still get their kicks at the casino's poker tables, slot machines, and video gaming machines. The casino lounge serves drinks 24 hours a day. Floyd's restaurant has dinner and nightlife. ⊠ *5223 N. Orient Rd., off I–4 at N. Orient Rd. Exit* ☎ *813/627–7625 or 866/502–7529* ⊕ *www.seminolehardrock. com* ⊡ *Free* ⊙ *Daily 24 hrs.*

❷ Lively **Ybor City,** Tampa's Latin quarter, is one of only four National
Fodor'sChoice Historic Landmark districts in Florida. It has antique-brick streets and
★ wrought-iron balconies. Cubans brought their cigar-making industry to Ybor (pronounced *ee*-bore) City in 1886, and the smell of cigars—hand-rolled by Cuban immigrants—still wafts through the heart of this east Tampa area, along with the strong aroma of roasting coffee. These days the neighborhood is emerging as Tampa's hot spot, as empty cigar factories and historic social clubs are transformed into trendy boutiques, art galleries, restaurants, and nightclubs that are a microcosm of Miami's sizzling South Beach. Take a stroll past the ornately tiled **Columbia** restaurant and the stores lining 7th Avenue. Step back into the past at **Centennial Park** (⊠ *8th Ave. and 18th St.*), which re-creates a period streetscape and hosts the Fresh Market every Saturday. The **Ybor City Museum State Park** provides a look at the history of the cigar industry. Admission includes a tour of La Casita, one of the shotgun houses occupied by cigar workers and their families in the late 1890s. ⊠ *1818 E. 9th Ave., between Nuccio Pkwy. and 22nd St., from 7th to 9th Ave., Tampa* ☎ *813/247–6323* ⊕ *www.ybormuseum.org* ⊡ *$3* ⊙ *Daily 9–5; walking tours Sat. 10:30, $6.*

BEACHES

Spread over five small islands, or keys, 1,136-acre **Fort De Soto Park** (⊠ *3500 Pinellas Bayway S, Tierra Verde* ☎ *727/582–2267* ⊡ *Free*) lies at the mouth of Tampa Bay. It has 7 mi of beaches, two fishing piers, a 4-mi hiking-skating trail, picnic and camping grounds, and a historic fort that kids of any age can explore. The fort for which it's named was built on the southern end of Mullet Key to protect sea lanes in the gulf during the Spanish-American War. Roam the fort or wander the beaches of any of the islands within the park. **Pass-A-Grille Beach** (⊠ *Off Gulf Blvd. [Rte. 699], St. Pete Beach*), at the southern end of St. Pete Beach, has parking meters, a snack bar, restrooms, and showers. It and Clearwater Beach are two of the area's most popular saltwater swimming holes.

SHOPPING

Ybor City's destination within a destination is the dining and entertainment palace **Centro Ybor** (⊠*1600 E. 7th Ave., Ybor City*). It has shops, trendy bars and restaurants, a 20-screen movie theater, and GameWorks, an interactive playground developed by Steven Spielberg. **Channelside** (⊠*615 Channelside Dr., Downtown*) offers movie theaters, shops, restaurants, and clubs. The official Tampa Bay visitor center is also here. If you want to grab something at Neiman Marcus or Nordstrom on your way to the airport, the upscale **International Plaza** (⊠*2223 N. West Shore Blvd., Airport Area*) has Betsey Johnson, J. Crew, L'Occitane, Louis Vuitton, Tiffany & Co., and many other shops. **Old Hyde Park Village** (⊠*Swan Ave. near Bayshore Blvd., Hyde Park*) is a gentrified shopping district like the ones you find in every major American city. Williams-Sonoma and Brooks Brothers are mixed in with bistros and sidewalk cafés.

NIGHTLIFE

Although there are more boarded storefronts than in the past, the biggest concentration of nightclubs, as well as the widest variety, is found along 7th Avenue in Ybor City. It becomes a little like Bourbon Street in New Orleans on weekend evenings. Popular **Adobe Gilas** (⊠*1600 E. 8th Ave., Ybor City* ☎*813/241–8588*) has a balcony overlooking the crowds on 7th Avenue. There's live music Thursday through Sunday nights, a large selection of margaritas, and more than 30 brands of tequila. Food is served until 2 AM. International Plaza's **Bay Street** (⊠*2223 N. West Shore Blvd., Airport Area*) has become one of Tampa's dining and imbibing hot spots. Considered something of a dive—but a lovable one—by a loyal and young local following that ranges from esteemed jurists to nose-ring-wearing night owls, the **Hub** (⊠*719 N. Franklin St., Downtown* ☎*813/229–1553*) is known for having one of Tampa's best martinis and one of its most eclectic jukeboxes.

WHERE TO EAT

For price categories, see ⇨ *Dining at the beginning of this chapter.*

$$$$
STEAK
Fodor'sChoice
★

✕**Bern's Steak House.** With the air of an exclusive club, this is one of Florida's finest steak houses. Rich mahogany paneling and ornate chandeliers define the legendary Bern's, where the chef ages his own beef, grows his own organic vegetables, roasts his own coffee, and maintains his own saltwater fish tanks. Cuts of topmost beef are sold by weight and thickness. There's a 60-ounce, 3-inch porterhouse that's big enough to feed your pride (of lions), but for our taste the veal loin chop or 8-ounce chateaubriand is more than enough. The wine list includes some 6,500 selections (with 1,800 dessert wines). After dinner, tour the kitchen and wine cellar before having dessert upstairs in a cozy booth. The dessert room is a hit. For a real jolt, try the Turkish coffee with an order of Mississippi mud pie. Casual business attire is recommended. ⊠*1208 S. Howard Ave., Hyde Park* ☎*813/251–2421* ⊕*www.berns steakhouse.com* ⟨*Reservations essential* ⊟*AE, D, MC, V.*

$$ ✕**Columbia.** Make a date for some of the best Latin cuisine in Tampa.
SPANISH A fixture since 1905, this magnificent structure with an old-world air,
Fodor'sChoice spacious dining rooms, and a sunny courtyard takes up an entire city
★ block and seems to feed the entire city—locals as well as travelers—
throughout the week, but especially on weekends. The paella, bursting
with seafood, chicken, and pork, arguably is the best in Florida, and
the 1905 salad—with ham, olives, cheese, and garlic—is legendary. The
menu has Cuban classics such as *boliche criollo* (tender eye of round
stuffed with chorizo sausage), *ropa vieja* (shredded beef with onions,
peppers, and tomatoes), and *arroz con pollo* (chicken with yellow rice).
Don't miss the flamenco dancing show every night but Sunday. ✉*2117
E. 7th Ave., Ybor City* ☎*813/248–4961* ⊕*www.columbiarestaurant.
com* ▭*AE, D, DC, MC, V.*

$$ ✕**Kojak's House of Ribs.** Few barbecue joints can boast the staying power
SOUTHERN of this family-owned and -operated pit stop, which had its debut in
1978. In the last three decades, it has earned a following of sticky-fin-
gered regulars who have turned it into one of the most popular barbecue
stops in central Florida. It could pass for a century-old Cracker house
complete with verandah, pillars supporting the overhanging roof, and
brick steps. Day and night, three indoor dining rooms and an outdoor
dining porch have a steady stream of hungry patrons digging into tender
pork spareribs that are dry-rubbed and tanned overnight before visiting the smoker for a couple hours. Then they're bathed in the sauce of
your choice. Kojak's also has a nice selection of sandwiches, including
sloppy chicken and country-style sausage. ✉*2808 Gandy Blvd., South
Tampa* ☎*813/837–3774* ⊕*www.kojaksbbq.com* ▭*AE, D, MC, V*
⊗*Closed Mon.*

WHERE TO STAY

If you want to be close to the cruise-ship terminal, then you'll have to
stay in Tampa, but if you want to spend more time in the area and perhaps stay on the beach, St. Petersburg and the beaches are close by.

For price categories, see ⇨ *Lodging at the beginning of this chapter.*

$$ ▦**Don Vicente de Ybor Historic Inn.** Built as a home in 1895 by town
★ founder Don Vicente de Ybor, this inn shows that the working-class
cigar city had an elegant side, too. From the beige-stucco exterior to
the white marble staircase in the main lobby, this boutique hotel is an
architectural tour de force. Rooms have parquet floors, canopy beds,
and private baths; most have wrought-iron balconies. Common areas
have crystal chandeliers, Tiffany lamps, and Persian carpets. **Pros:** ele-
gant rooms; rich in history; walking distance to nightlife. **Cons:** rowdy
neighborhood on weekend nights. ✉*1915 Republica de Cuba, Ybor
City* ☎*813/241–4545 or 866/206–4545* ⊕*donvicenteinn.com* ⏎*13
rooms, 3 suites* ⏃*In-room: Internet. In-hotel: restaurant, bar, laundry
service, Wi-Fi* ▭*AE, D, DC, MC, V* ⏃O⏃*BP.*

$$–$$$ ▦**Hilton Garden Inn Tampa Ybor Historic District.** Although its modern
★ architecture makes it seem out of place in this historic district, this
chain hotel's location across from Centro Ybor is a plus. There is an
on-site restaurant that serves breakfast, but be sure to take at least one

day off to visit one of the nearby eateries for a traditional breakfast of *café cubano* or *café con leche* with a wedge of Cuban bread slathered with butter. **Pros:** good location for business travelers; reasonable rates. **Cons:** chain-hotel feel; far from downtown. ✉*1700 E. 9th Ave., Ybor City* ☎*813/769–9267* ⊕*www.hiltongardeninn.com* ⟳*93 rooms, 2 suites* ♿*In-room: refrigerator, Internet. In-hotel: restaurant, pool, Wi-Fi, laundry facilities, laundry service* ▭*AE, D, DC, MC, V.*

$$$–$$$$ 🏨**Tampa Marriott Waterside Hotel & Marina.** Across from the Tampa Convention Center, this downtown hotel was built for conventioneers but is also convenient to tourist spots such as the Florida Aquarium and the Channelside and Hyde Park shopping districts. At least half the rooms and most of the suites overlook the concrete-walled channel to Tampa Bay, which has sparse boat traffic except on weekends; the bay itself is visible from the higher floors of the 27-story tower. The pillared lobby has real palm trees growing out of the gleaming tile floors, and the coffee bar overlooks the water. Il Terrazzo is the hotel's formal dining room. **Pros:** great downtown location; near shopping. **Cons:** gridlock during rush hour; area sketchy after dark; chain-hotel feel. ✉*700 S. Florida Ave., Downtown* ☎*888/268–1616* ⊕*www.marriott. com* ⟳*681 rooms, 36 suites* ♿*In-room: safe, kitchen (some), Internet. In-hotel: 3 restaurants, room service, bars, pool, gym, spa, laundry facilities, laundry service, Wi-Fi, parking (paid), no-smoking rooms* ▭*AE, D, DC, MC, V.*

Ports of Call

WORD OF MOUTH

"I research the ports, select what we want to do, and engage a cab driver when we get off the ship to take us around. It's much cheaper than the ship's shore excursion and personalized to our interests. Other people book excursions through private companies, and seem quite happy with that."

—abram

Nowhere in the world are conditions better suited to cruising than in the Caribbean Sea. Tiny island nations, within easy sailing distance of one another, form a chain of tropical enchantment that curves from Cuba in the north all the way down to the coast of Venezuela. There's far more to life here than sand and coconuts, however. The islands are vastly different, with a variety of cultures, topographies, and languages represented. Colonialism has left its mark, and the presence of the Spanish, French, Dutch, Danish, and British is still felt. Slavery, too, has left its cultural legacy, blending African overtones into the colonial/Indian amalgam. The one constant, however, is the weather. Despite the islands' southerly latitude, the climate is surprisingly gentle, due in large part to the cooling influence of the trade winds.

The Caribbean is made up of the Greater Antilles and the Lesser Antilles. The former consist of those islands closest to the United States: Cuba, Jamaica, Hispaniola (Haiti and the Dominican Republic), and Puerto Rico. (The Cayman Islands lie south of Cuba.) The Lesser Antilles, including the Virgin, Windward, and Leeward islands and others, are greater in number but smaller in size, and constitute the southern half of the Caribbean chain.

GOING ASHORE

Traveling by cruise ship presents an opportunity to visit many places in a short time. The flip side is that your stay in each port of call will be brief. For this reason cruise lines offer shore excursions, which maximize passengers' time. There are a number of advantages to shore excursions arranged by your ship: in some destinations, transportation may be unreliable, and a ship-packaged tour is the best way to see distant sights. Also, you don't have to worry about missing the ship. The disadvantage of a shore excursion is the cost—you usually pay more for the convenience of having the ship do the legwork for you, but it's not always a lot more. Of course, you can always book a tour independently, hire a taxi, or use foot power to explore on your own. For each port of call included in this guide, we've provided some suggestions for the best ship-sponsored excursions—in terms of both quality of experience and price—as well as some suggestions for what to do if you want to explore on your own.

ARRIVING IN PORT

When your ship arrives in a port, it will tie up alongside a dock or anchor out in a harbor. If the ship is docked, passengers walk down the gangway to go ashore. Docking makes it easy to move between the shore and the ship.

TENDERING

If your ship anchors in the harbor, you will have to take a small boat—called a launch or tender—to get ashore. Tendering is a nuisance; however, participants in shore excursions are given priority. Passengers wishing to disembark independently may be required to gather in a public room, get sequenced boarding passes, and wait until their numbers are called. The ride to shore may take as long as 20 minutes. If you don't like waiting, plan to go ashore an hour or so after the ship drops its anchor. On a very large ship, the wait for a tender can be quite long and frustrating.

Because tenders can be difficult to board, passengers with mobility problems may not be able to visit certain ports. The larger ships are more likely to use tenders. It is usually possible to learn before booking a cruise whether the ship will dock or anchor at its ports of call.

Before anyone is allowed to walk down the gangway or board a tender, the ship must be cleared for landing. Immigration and customs officials board the vessel to examine passports and sort through red tape. It may be more than an hour before you're allowed ashore. You will be issued a boarding pass, which you'll need to get back on board.

RETURNING TO THE SHIP

Cruise lines are strict about sailing times, which are posted at the gangway and elsewhere and announced in the daily schedule of activities. Be sure to be back on board (not on the dock waiting to get a tender back to the ship) at least a half-hour before the announced sailing time or you may be stranded. If you are on a shore excursion that was sold by the cruise line, however, the captain will wait for your group before casting off. That is one reason many passengers prefer ship-packaged tours.

If you're not on one of the ship's tours and the ship sails without you, immediately contact the cruise line's port representative, whose phone number is often listed on the daily schedule of activities. You may be able to hitch a ride on a pilot boat, although that is unlikely. Passengers who miss the boat must pay their own way to the next port.

CARIBBEAN ESSENTIALS

CURRENCY

The U.S. dollar is the official currency on Puerto Rico, the U.S. Virgin Islands, the Turks and Caicos, and the British Virgin Islands. On Grand Cayman you will usually have a choice of Cayman or U.S. dollars when you take money out of an ATM, and you may even be able to get change in U.S. dollars. In Cozumel, Calica, Costa Maya, and Progreso, the Mexico peso is the official currency. The euro is used in a handful of

4

ATLANTIC OCEAN

LEEWARD ISLANDS

DOMINICAN
REPUBLIC

SANTO
DOMINGO

SAN JUAN

Puerto
Rico

St. Thomas
St. John
Tortola
Virgin Gorda
Anguilla
St. Barthélemy
St. Maarten/
St. Martin
Saba
Barbuda
St.
Croix
St. Eustatius
Antigua
St. Kitts
Nevis
Montserrat
Marie
Galante
Guadeloupe

ANTILLES

Dominica

WINDWARD

Martinique
Fort-de-France

St. Lucia

Sea

Barbados

St. Vincent

Bequia
The
Grenadines
Carriacou
St. George's
Grenada

Bridgetown

LESSER ANTILLES

Aruba
WILLEMSTAD
Bonaire
Curaçao
Islas Los
Roques

Tobago

LESSER ANTILLES

Port of Spain
Trinidad

La Guaira

CARACAS

VENEZUELA

| 0 | | 200 miles |
| 0 | | 300 km |

The Mayan Riviera

TO PROGRESO

Isla Holbox

Isla Contoy

Reserva de la Biósfera Ría Lagartos

Río Lagartos

El Cuyo

Isla Mujeres

San Felipe

295

Chiquilá

Cancún

Sucilá

176

Yucatán

Kantunilkin

Tizimin

X-can

180

Puerto Morelos

EK Balam

Valladolid

Playa del Carmen

San Miguel

Chemax

180

Cobá

Akumal

Cozumel

Tihosuco

Xel-Há

Palancar Reef

Tulum

Boca Paila

295

Muyil

Punta Allen

Vigia Chico

QUINTANA ROO

184

Punta Pájaros

Felipe Carrillo Puerto

Tupak

307

Punta Herrero

Reserva de la Biosfera Sian Ka'an

293

Chacchoben

Limónes

Banco Chinchorro

Punto Bravo

Puerto Costa Maya

Bacalar

307

Bahía de Chetumal

Majahual

Dzibanché & Kinichná

Cayo Centro

Chetumal

Bahía de Corozal

Kohunlich

Xcalac

BELIZE

Caribbean Sea

0   30 miles
0   30 km

KEY

Ferry

Mayan Ruins

Area of Detail

U.S.A.

MEXICO

BELIZE

French island (St. Barths, St. Martin, Martinique, Guadeloupe). In most Caribbean ports, U.S. paper currency (not coins) is accepted readily. When you pay in dollars you'll almost always get change in local currency, so it's best to carry bills in small denominations. If you need local currency (say, for a trip to one of the French islands that uses the euro), change money at a local bank or use an ATM for the best rate. Most major credit cards are accepted all over the Caribbean, except at local market stalls and small establishments.

> **BUYING LIQUOR & PERFUME**
>
> If you buy duty-free liquor or perfume while in a Caribbean port, don't forget that you may not bring it aboard your flight home. You will have to put it in your checked bags. Many liquor stores will pack your bottles in bubble wrap and pack them in a good cardboard box. Take advantage of this service.

KEEPING IN TOUCH

Internet cafés are now fairly common on many islands, and you'll sometimes find Internet cafés in the cruise-ship terminal itself—or perhaps in an attached or nearby shopping center. If you want to call home, most cruise-ship facilities have phones that accept credit cards or local phone cards (local phone cards are almost always the cheapest option). And on most islands, GSM multi-band mobile phones will work, though roaming charges may be steep (some plans include Puerto Rico and the U.S. Virgin Islands in their nationwide calling regions).

WHERE TO EAT

Cuisine on the Caribbean's islands is as varied as the islands themselves. The region's history as a colonial battleground and ethnic melting pot creates plenty of variety and adds lots of unusual tropical fruit and spices. In fact, the one quality that defines most Caribbean cooking is its spiciness, acquired from nutmeg, mace, allspice, peppers, saffron, and many other seasonings grown in the islands. Dress is generally casual, although throughout the islands beachwear is inappropriate most anywhere except on the beach. Unless otherwise noted, prices are given in U.S. dollars. The following price categories are used in this book.

WHAT IT COSTS IN U.S. DOLLARS					
	¢	$	$$	$$$	$$$$
At Dinner	Under $8	$8–$11	$12–$19	$20–$30	Over $30

Prices are per person for a main course at dinner and do not include any service charges.

SHORE EXCURSIONS

Typical excursions include an island or town bus tour, a visit to a beach or rum factory, a boat trip, a snorkeling or diving trip, and charter fishing. In recent years, however, shore excursions have gotten more adventurous, with mild river rafting, parasailing, jet-skiing, hiking, and biking added to the mix. It's often easier to take a ship-arranged excursion, but it's almost never the cheapest option.

If you prefer to break away from the pack, find a knowledgeable taxi driver or tour operator—they're usually within a stone's throw of the pier—or wander around on your own. A group of four to six people will usually find this option more economical and practical than will a single person or a couple.

Renting a car is also a good option on many islands—again, the more people, the better the deal. But get a good island map before you set off, and be sure to find out how long it will take you to get around.

Conditions are ideal for water sports of all kinds—scuba diving, snorkeling, windsurfing, sailing, waterskiing, and fishing excursions abound. Your shore-excursion director can usually arrange these activities for you if the ship offers no formal excursion.

PRIVATE ISLANDS

Linda Coffman   When evaluating the "best" Caribbean ports of call, many repeat cruise passengers often add the cruise Lines' own private island to their lists of preferred destinations.

The cruise lines established "private" islands to provide a beach break on an island (or part of one) reserved for their exclusive use. While most passengers don't select an itinerary based solely upon calling at a private island, they usually consider them a highlight of their cruise vacation. The very least you can expect of your private island is lush foliage and a wide swath of beach surrounded by azure water. Facilities vary, but a beach barbecue, water-sports equipment rental, lounge chairs, hammocks, and restrooms are standard. Youth counselors come ashore to conduct sand castle building competitions and lead junior pirates on swashbuckling island treasure hunts.

The use of strollers and wheelchairs equipped with all-terrain wheels may be offered on a complimentary first-come, first-served basis. However, with the exception of some participation sports on the beach, plan to pay for most water toys and activities. Costs associated with private island fun and recreation can range from $8 for use of a snorkel vest (you may use your own snorkel equipment; however, in the event a floatation vest is required for safety, you must rent one) to $30 for rental of an entire snorkeling outfit for the day (mask, fins, snorkel vest, a mesh bag, fish identification card, and fish food). You can often take a banana boat ride for $16 to $19 (15-minute ride), sail a small boat or catamaran for $30 to $50 (one hour), paddle a kayak for $18 to $38 (half-hour to hour-and-a-half), ride Jet Skis for $59 to $95 (45 minutes to one hour), parasail for a hefty $79 to $84 (10 minutes or less), or fly through the treetops on a zip line for $85. Floating mats are a relative bargain at $10 to $12 for all day lounging in the water. You might also find open-air massage cabanas with pricing comparable to the spa charges onboard.

There is generally no charge for food or basic beverages such as those served on board ship. While soft drinks and tropical cocktails can usually be charged to your shipboard account, you might want to bring a small amount of cash ashore for souvenir shopping, which is usually possible from vendors set up on or near the beach. You will also want to bring beach towels ashore and return them to the ship at the end of the day because, as Princess Cruises reminds passengers, "Although the locals may offer to do this for you, unfortunately we seldom see the towels again!"

Even if you do nothing more than lie in a shaded hammock and sip fruity tropical concoctions, the day can be one of the most fun and relaxing of your entire cruise.

ISLANDS BY CRUISE LINE

Carnival Cruise Lines is currently the only major cruise line without an extensive private island experience available to the entire fleet. However, select Carnival itineraries include calls at Half Moon Cay, Holland America Line's private paradise, where "Fun Ship" passengers can use all the facilities and participate in organized activities. Similarly, certain Regent Seven Seas cruises include beach days at Princess Cays or Cayo Levantado.

Although they do not stop at "private islands" in the strictest sense, the yachts of Seabourn and SeaDream offer passengers a day ashore on secluded private beaches where they can enjoy lavish barbecues and take a break from swimming and snorkeling to indulge in champagne and caviar served in the surf.

COSTA CRUISES

An unspoiled island paradise, Costa's **Catalina Island** is located just off the coast of the Dominican Republic. Passengers can participate in Costa's "Beach Olympics," schedule a seaside massage, or just kick back on a chaise lounge or a complimentary water float. Water-toy rentals, banana-boat rides, and sailing tours are available from independent concessionaires. Local vendors set up souvenir shops offering crafts and T-shirts. The ship provides the food for a lunch barbecue and tropical beverages at the beach bar.

Activities: Snorkeling, sailing, jet-skiing, waterskiing, hiking, volleyball, organized games, massages, shopping.

DISNEY CRUISE LINE

Disney's **Castaway Cay** has a dock so passengers simply step ashore (rather than tendering, as is required to reach most cruise lines' private islands). Like everything associated with Disney, the line's private island is almost too good to be true. Located in the Abacos, a chain in the Bahamas, only 10% of Castaway Cay is developed, leaving plenty of unspoiled area to explore in Robinson Crusoe fashion. Trams are provided to reach separate beaches designated for children, teens, families, and adults, and Disney is the only line to offer age-specific activities and extensive, well-planned children's activities. Biking and hiking are so popular that a second nature trail, complete with an observation tower, has been added. Excursions range from as passive as a glass-bottom boat tour to the soaring excitement of parasailing. An interactive experience with stingrays is educational and safe—the gentle creatures' barbs are blunted for safety. In addition to barbecue fare and several beverage stations, beach games, island-style music, and a shaded game pavilion, there are shops, massage cabanas by the sea, and even a post office.

Activities: Snorkeling, kayaking, parasailing, sailing, jet-skiing, paddleboats, water cycles, fishing, bicycles, basketball, billiards, hiking, Ping-Pong, shuffleboard, soccer, volleyball, organized games, massages, shopping.

HOLLAND AMERICA LINE

Little San Salvador, one of the Bahamian out-islands, was renamed **Half Moon Cay** by Holland America Line to honor Henry Hudson's ship (depicted on the cruise line's logo) as well as to reflect the beach's crescent shape. Even after development, the island is still so unspoiled that it has been named a Wild Bird Preserve by the Bahamian National Trust. Passengers, who are welcomed ashore at a West Indies Village complete with shops and straw market, find Half Moon Cay easily accessible—all facilities are connected by hard-surfaced and packed-sand pathways and meet and exceed ADA requirements. An accessible tram also connects the welcome center with the food pavilion; wheelchairs with balloon tires are available. In addition to the beach area for lazing in the sun or shade, the island has a post office, Bahamian-style chapel, a lagoon where you can interact with stingrays, and, for family fun, you'll find a beachfront water park with waterslides and fanciful sea creatures tethered to the sandy bottom of the shallow water. Massage services are available, as are fitness activities. Air-conditioned cabanas can be rented for the day, with or without the services of your own butler.

Activities: Scuba diving, snorkeling, windsurfing, kayaking, parasailing, sailing, jet-skiing, Aqua Bikes, fishing, bicycles, basketball, hiking, horseback riding, shuffleboard, volleyball, massages, shopping.

MSC CRUISES

Cayo Levantado, roughly translated as "Floating Island," is located off the Samaná Peninsula on the northeast coast of the Dominican Republic. The unspoiled cay, which can be accessed only by tenders, is leased by a development company that has installed beach chairs, bars, a dining facility, and acres of walking paths through the topical rain forest. A flagstone path from the pier passes the arts and crafts marketplace and affords accessibility for strollers and wheelchairs, though you'll have to bring your own as none are provided. Not owned outright by MSC Cruises, the island is also available to other cruise lines. All food and beverage concessions ashore are privately operated, and there is a charge for refreshments and the beach buffet. In addition to lazing in the sun, swimming in the warm surf, and participating in spirited beach games, you can opt to feed a playful sea lion, get a massage in an open air cabana, or relax in the shade and watch a folkloric show. Many ships now tender passengers ashore to the town of Santa Barbara de Samaná for shore excursions. (*For more information on this port, see* ⇨ *Samaná, Dominican Republic, below.*)

Activities: Snorkeling, sailing, kayaking, parasailing, hiking, volleyball, massages, shopping.

NORWEGIAN CRUISE LINE

Only 120 mi east of Fort Lauderdale in the Berry Island chain of the Bahamas, much of **Great Stirrup Cay** looks as it did when it was acquired by Norwegian Cruise Line in 1977. The first uninhabited island purchased to offer cruise-ship passengers a private beach day, Great Stirrup Cay's white-sand beaches are fringed by coral and ideal for snorkeling but become very crowded when a large number of passengers are ashore. Permanent facilities have been added to and improved in the intervening years, but bougainvillea, sea grape, and coconut palms are still as abundant as the colorful tropical fish that inhabit the reef. To reduce beach erosion and preserve the environment, a seawall was erected. A straw market, water-sports centers, bars, volleyball courts, beachside massage stations, and a food pavilion round out the facilities.

Activities: Snorkeling, kayaking, parasailing, sailing, paddleboats, Ping-Pong, hiking, volleyball, organized games, massages, shopping.

PRINCESS CRUISES

Princess Cays is a 40-acre haven on the southern tip of Eleuthera Island in the Bahamas. Not quite an uninhabited island, it nevertheless offers a wide ribbon of beach, long enough for passengers to splash in the surf, relax in a hammock, or limbo to the beat of local music and never feel crowded. In a similar fashion to booking shore excursions, water-sports equipment can be reserved ahead of time, either onboard the ship or through the Princess Web site. Nestled in a picturesque palm grove, private bungalows with air-conditioning and ceiling fans and a deck for lounging can be rented for parties of up to six. A pirate-theme play area for children is supervised. In addition to three tropical bars and the area where a Bahamian barbecue is served, permanent facilities include small shops that sell island crafts and trinkets, but if you head around the back and through the fence, independent vendors sell similar goods for lower prices.

Activities: Snorkeling, kayaking, parasailing, sailing, paddleboats, Aqua Bikes, hiking, organized games, shopping.

ROYAL CARIBBEAN, CELEBRITY CRUISES, AND AZAMARA CRUISES

Royal Caribbean, Azamara Cruises, and Celebrity Cruises passengers have twice as many opportunities to visit a private island. The lines share two, and many Caribbean itineraries include one or the other.

Coco Cay is a 140-acre island in the Berry Island chain between Nassau and Freeport. Originally known as Little Stirrup Cay, it's within view of Great Stirrup Cay (NCL's private island) and the snorkeling is just as good, especially around a sunken airplane and a replica of Blackbeard's flagship, *Queen Anne's Revenge*. In addition to activities and games ashore, Coco Cay boasts the largest Aqua Park in the Caribbean, where children and adults alike can jump on an in-water trampoline or climb a floating sand castle before they dig into a beach barbecue or explore a nature trail. The newest attractions include an inflatable 40-foot waterslide (fun for adults and kids alike) and a Power Wheels track where youngsters age three to eight can take a miniature car for a spin at a sedate 3 mph.

Activities: Scuba diving, snorkeling, jet-skiing, kayaking, parasailing, hiking, volleyball, organized games, shopping.

Labadee is a 260-acre peninsula approximately 6 mi (10 km) from Cap Haitien on the secluded north coast of Haiti (the port of call is sometimes called "Hispaniola"). New for 2010 is a dock, from which water taxis and five different walking paths, trails, and avenues lead to many areas throughout the peninsula, including the Labadee Town Square and Dragon's Plaza where a welcome center and central tram station are located. In addition to swimming, water sports, an Aqua Park with floating trampolines and waterslides, and nature trails to explore, bonuses on Labadee are an authentic folkloric show presented by island performers and a market featuring work of local artists and crafters, where you might find an interesting painting or unique wood carving. One of the most exciting—and at 2,600 feet in length the longest—zipline experiences in the Caribbean takes place 500 feet above the beaches of Labadee, where riders can reach speeds of 40 to 50 mph over the water. Due to the proximity of Labadee to mainland Haiti, in the past it has occasionally been necessary to cancel calls there due to political unrest. In that event, an alternate port is usually scheduled.

Activities: Snorkeling, jet-skiing, kayaking, parasailing, hiking, volleyball, organized games, shopping.

ANTIGUA (ST. JOHN'S)

Jordan Simon

Some say Antigua has so many beaches that you could visit a different one every day for a year. Most have snow-white sand, and many are backed by lavish resorts that offer sailing, diving, windsurfing, and snorkeling. The largest of the British Leeward Islands, Antigua was the headquarters from which Lord Horatio Nelson (then a mere captain) made his forays against the French and pirates in the late 18th century. You may wish to explore English Harbour and its carefully restored Nelson's Dockyard, as well as tour old forts, historic churches, and tiny villages. Appealing aspects of the island's interior include a small tropical rain forest ideal for hiking, ancient Native American archaeological digs, and restored sugar mills. Due to time constraints, it's best to make trips this far from port with an experienced tour operator. But you can easily take a taxi to any number of fine beaches on your own and escape from the hordes descending from the ship.

ESSENTIALS

Currency Eastern Caribbean (EC) dollar (EC$2.67 to US$1). U.S. dollars are generally accepted, but change is given in EC.

Internet There are some small Internet cafés in St. John's and English Harbour; ask at the tourist information booth at the cruise-ship pier.

Telephones A GSM tri-band mobile phone will usually work in Antigua. You can use a LIME (formerly Cable & Wireless) Phone Card (available in $5, $10, and $20 denominations in most hotels and post offices) for local and long-distance calls. To call the United States and Canada, dial 1 + the area code + the seven-digit number, or use the phone card or one of the CALL USA phones, which are

Antigua

available at several locations, including the cruise terminal at St. John's and the English Harbour Marina.

COMING ASHORE

Though some ships dock at the deepwater harbor in downtown St. John's, most use Heritage Quay, a multimillion-dollar complex with shops, condominiums, a casino, and a food court. Most St. John's attractions are an easy walk from Heritage Quay; the older part of the city is eight blocks away. A tourist information booth is in the main docking building.

If you intend to explore beyond St. John's, consider hiring a taxi driver–guide. Taxis meet every cruise ship. They're unmetered; fares are fixed, and drivers are required to carry a rate card. Agree on the fare before setting off, and plan to tip drivers 10%. Some cabbies may take you from St. John's to English Harbour and wait for a "reasonable" amount of time (about a half-hour) while you look around, for about $50; you can usually arrange an island tour for around $25 per hour. Renting your own car isn't usually practical, since you must purchase a $20 temporary driving permit in addition to the car-rental fee, which is usually about $50 per day in the high season.

EXPLORING ANTIGUA

Falmouth. This town sits on a lovely bay backed by former sugar plantations and sugar mills. The most important historic site here is St. Paul's Church, which was rebuilt on the site of a church once used by troops during the Horatio Nelson period.

Ft. George. East of Liberta—one of the first settlements founded by freed slaves—on Monk's Hill, this fort was built from 1689 to 1720. Among the ruins are the sites for 32 cannons, water cisterns, the base of the old flagstaff, and some of the original buildings.

Fodor'sChoice   **Nelson's Dockyard.** Antigua's most famous attraction is the world's only ★   Georgian-era dockyard still in use, a treasure trove for history buffs and nautical nuts alike. In 1671 the governor of the Leeward Islands wrote to the Council for Foreign Plantations in London, pointing out the advantages of this landlocked harbor. By 1704 English Harbour was in regular use as a garrisoned station.

In 1784, 26-year-old Horatio Nelson sailed in on the HMS *Boreas* to serve as captain and second-in-command of the Leeward Island Station. Under him was the captain of the HMS *Pegasus,* Prince William Henry, duke of Clarence, who was later crowned King William IV. The prince acted as best man when Nelson married Fannie Nisbet on Nevis in 1787.

When the Royal Navy abandoned the station at English Harbour in 1889, it fell into a state of decay, though adventuresome yachties still lived there in near-primitive conditions. The Society of the Friends of English Harbour began restoring it in 1951; it reopened with great fanfare as Nelson's Dockyard, November 14, 1961. Within the compound are crafts shops, restaurants, and two splendidly restored 18th-century hotels, the Admiral's Inn and the Copper and Lumber Store Hotel, worth peeking into. (The latter, occupying a supply store for Nelson's Caribbean fleet, is a particularly fine example of Georgian architecture and has an interior courtyard evoking Old England.) The Dockyard is a hub for oceangoing yachts and serves as headquarters for the annual Sailing Week Regatta in late April and early May. Water taxis will ferry you between points for EC$5. The Dockyard National Park also includes serene nature trails accessing beaches, rock pools, and crumbling plantation ruins and hilltop forts.

The **Dockyard Museum,** in the original Naval Officer's House, presents ship models, mock-ups of English Harbour, displays on the people who worked there and typical ships that docked, silver regatta trophies, maps, prints, antique navigational instruments, and Nelson's very own telescope and tea caddy. ⊠*English Harbour* ☎*268/481–5022, 268/463–1060, 268/460–1379 for the National Parks Authority* ⊕*www.antiguamuseums.org* 🖃*$2 suggested donation* ⊙*Daily 8–5.*

St. John's. Antigua's capital, with some 45,000 inhabitants (approximately half the island's population), lies at sea level at the inland end of a sheltered northwestern bay. Although it has seen better days, a couple of notable historic sights and some good waterfront shopping areas make it worth a visit.

Signs at the **Museum of Antigua and Barbuda** say PLEASE TOUCH, encouraging you to explore Antigua's past. Try your hand at the educational video games or squeeze a cassava through a *matapi* (grass sieve). Exhibits interpret the nation's history, from its geological birth to its political independence in 1981. There are fossil and coral remains from some 34 million years ago; models of a sugar plantation and a wattle-and-daub house; an Arawak canoe; and a wildly eclectic assortment of objects from cannonballs to 1920s telephone exchanges. The museum occupies the former courthouse, which dates from 1750. The superlative museum gift shop carries such unusual items as calabash purses, seed earrings, warri boards,

and lignum vitae pipes, as well as historic maps and local books (including engrossing, detailed monographs on varied subjects by longtime resident, the late Desmond Nicholson). ✉*Long and Market Sts.* ☎*268/462–1469* ⊕*www.antiguamuseums.org* ✉*$2 suggested donation* ☉*Sun.–Thurs. 8:30–4, Fri. 8:30–3, Sat. 10–2.*

At the south gate of the **Anglican Cathedral of St. John the Divine** are figures of St. John the Baptist and St. John the Divine, said to have been taken from one of Napóleon's ships and brought to Antigua. The original church was built in 1681, replaced by a stone building in 1745, and destroyed by an earthquake in 1843. The present neo-baroque building dates from 1845; the parishioners had the interior completely encased in pitch pine, hoping to forestall future earthquake damage. The church attained cathedral status in 1848. Tombstones bear eerily eloquent testament to the colonial days. ✉*Between Long and Newgate Sts.* ☎*268/461–0082.*

Redcliffe Quay, at the water's edge just south of Heritage Quay, is the most appealing part of St. John's. Attractively restored (and superbly re-created) buildings in a riot of cotton-candy colors house shops, restaurants, and boutiques, and are linked by courtyards and landscaped walkways. At the far south end of town, where Market Street forks into Valley and All Saints roads, haggling goes on every Friday and Saturday, when locals jam the **Public Market** to buy and sell fruits, vegetables, fish, and spices. Ask before you aim a camera; your subject may expect a tip. This is old-time Caribbean shopping, a jambalaya of sights, sounds, and smells.

Shirley Heights. This bluff affords a spectacular view of English Harbour. The heights are named for Sir Thomas Shirley, the governor who fortified the harbor in 1787. At the top is Shirley Heights Lookout, a restaurant built into the remnants of the 18th-century fortifications.

Most notable for its boisterous Sunday barbecues that continue into the night with live music and dancing, it serves dependable burgers, pumpkin soup, grilled meats, and rum punches.

Not far from Shirley Heights is the **Dows Hill Interpretation Centre,** where observation platforms provide still more sensational vistas of the English Harbour area. A multimedia sound-and-light presentation on island history and culture, spotlighting lifelike figures and colorful tableaux accompanied by running commentary and music, results in a cheery, if bland, portrait of Antiguan life from Amerindian times to the present. *☎268/460–2777 for National Parks Authority* *✉EC$15* *⊙Daily 9–5.*

⊙ **Stingray City Antigua** (✉*Seaton's Village* *☎268/562–7297*) is a carefully reproduced "natural" environment nicknamed by staffers the "retirement home," though the 30-plus stingrays, ranging from infants to seniors, are frisky. You can stroke, feed, even hold the striking gliders, as well as snorkel in deeper, protected waters. The tour guides do a marvelous job of explaining the animals' habits, from feeding to breeding, and their predators (including man).

SHOPPING

Redcliffe Quay, on the waterfront at the south edge of St. John's, is by far the most appealing shopping area. Several restaurants and more than 30 boutiques, many with one-of-a-kind wares, are set around landscaped courtyards shaded by colorful trees. **Heritage Quay,** in St. John's, has 35 shops—including many that are duty-free—that cater to the cruise-ship crowd, which docks almost at its doorstep. Outlets here include Benetton, the Body Shop, Sunglass Hut, Dolce and Gabbana, and Oshkosh B'Gosh. There are also shops along **St. John's, St. Mary's, High,** and **Long streets.** The tangerine-and-lilac-hue four-story **Vendor's Mall** at the intersection of Redcliffe and Thames streets gathers the pushy, pesky vendors that once clogged the narrow streets. It's jammed with stalls; air-conditioned indoor shops sell some higher-price, if not higher-quality, merchandise. On the west coast the Mediterranean-style, arcaded **Jolly Harbour Marina** holds some interesting galleries and shops, as do the marinas and Main Road snaking around English and Falmouth Harbours.

★ The **Goldsmitty** (✉*Redcliffe Quay, St. John's* *☎268/462–4601*) is Hans Smit, an expert goldsmith who turns gold, black coral, and precious and semiprecious stones into one-of-a-kind works of art. **Isis** (✉*Redcliffe Quay, St. John's* *☎268/462–4602*) sells island and international bric-a-brac, such as antique jewelry, hand-carved walking sticks, and glazed

★ pottery. **Noreen Phillips** (✉*Redcliffe Quay, St. John's* *☎268/462–3127*) creates glitzy appliquéd and beaded evening wear—inspired by the colors of the sea and sunset—in sensuous fabrics ranging from chiffon and silk to Italian lace and Indian brocade.

★ At **Galley Boutique** (✉*Nelson's Dockyard, English Harbour* *☎268/460–1525*), Janey Easton personally seeks out exclusive creations from both international (Calvin Klein, Adrienne Vittadini) and local Caribbean designers, ranging from swimwear to evening garb. She also sells handicrafts and lovely hammocks.

ACTIVITIES

ADVENTURE TOURS

★ **Adventure Antigua** (☎*268/727–3261* ⊕*www.adventureantigua.com*) is run by enthusiastic Eli Fuller, who is knowledgeable not only about the ecosystem and geography of Antigua but also about its history and politics (his grandfather was the American consul). His thorough seven-hour excursion (Eli dubs it "re-creating my childhood explorations") includes stops at Guiana Island (for lunch and guided snorkeling; turtles, barracuda, and stingrays are common sightings), Pelican Island (more snorkeling), Bird Island (hiking to vantage points to admire the soaring ospreys and frigate and red-billed tropic birds), and "Hell's Gate" (a striking limestone rock formation where the more intrepid may hike and swim through sunken caves and tide pools painted with pink and maroon algae). The company also offers a fun, shorter "amusement park ride" variation on a racing boat catering to adrenaline junkies who "feel the need for speed." **"Paddles" Kayak Eco Adventure** (⊠*Seaton's Village* ☎*268/463–1944 or 268/560–3782* ⊕*www.antiguapaddles. com*) takes you on a 3½-hour tour of serene mangroves and inlets with informative narrative about the fragile ecosystem of the swamp and reefs and the rich diversity of flora and fauna. The tour ends with a hike to sunken caves and snorkeling in the North Sound Marine Park. Experienced guides double as kayaking and snorkeling instructors, making this an excellent opportunity for novices.

DIVING

Antigua is an unsung diving destination, with plentiful undersea sights to explore, from coral canyons to sea caves. Barbuda alone features roughly 200 wrecks on its treacherous reefs. The most accessible wreck is the 1890s bark *Andes,* not far out in Deep Bay, off Five Islands Peninsula. Among the favorite sites are **Green Island, Cades Reef,** and **Bird Island** (a national park). Memorable sightings include turtles, stingrays, and barracuda darting amid basalt walls, hulking boulders, and stray 17th-century anchors and cannon. One advantage is accessibility in many spots for shore divers and snorkelers. Double-tank dives run about $90. **Dockyard Divers** (⊠*Nelson's Dockyard, English Harbour* ☎*268/460–1178*), owned by British ex-merchant seaman Captain A. G. "Tony" Fincham, is one of the island's most-established outfits and offers diving and snorkeling trips, PADI courses, and dive packages with accommodations. They're geared to seasoned divers, but staff work patiently with novices.

BEACHES

Dickenson Bay, a lengthy stretch of powder-soft white sand and exceptionally calm water, is the closest good beach to St. John's. You can find small and large hotels, water sports, concessions, and beachfront restaurants. There's decent snorkeling at either point. **Half Moon Bay,** a ¾-mi (1-km) ivory crescent, is a prime snorkeling and windsurfing area. On the Atlantic side of the island, the water can be quite rough at times, attracting a few intrepid hard-core surfers and wakeboarders. Half Moon is a real trek (you might end up asking locals directions several times) but one of Antigua's show-case beaches. Follow signs for the villages of St. Philips or Freetown, and pray: all roads are unmarked, and the island's hinterland has no landmarks to guide you. **Johnson's Point/Crab Hill** is a series of con-nected, deliciously deserted beaches

on the southwest coast looking out toward Montserrat, Guadeloupe, St. Kitts, and Nevis. You can explore a ruined fort at one end. Notable beach bar-restaurants include OJ's (try the snapper) and Turner's. **Pigeon Point**, near Falmouth Harbour, has two fine white-sand beaches. The leeward side is calmer, the windward side is rockier, and there are sen-sational views and snorkeling around the point. **Runaway Beach**, an often unoccupied stretch of bone-white sand, is still rebuilding after years of hurricane erosion, with just enough palms left for shelter. Both the water and the scene are relatively calm.

WHERE TO EAT

$$$–$$$$
CONTINENTAL
★
✕**Coconut Grove.** Coconut palms grow through the roof of this open-air thatched restaurant, flickering candlelight illuminates colorful local murals, waves lap the white sand, and the warm waitstaff provides just the right level of service. Jean-François Bellanger's superbly pre-sented dishes fuse French culinary preparations with island ingredients. Top choices include pan-seared snapper medallions served with roasted sweet potato in a saffron white-wine curry; kingfish tartare accented by tapenade with molasses drizzle and guacamole; marvelously tex-tured Caribbean bouillabaisse with coconut milk and pumpkin aioli; and chicken stuffed with creole vegetables in mango-kiwi sauce. The kitchen can be uneven, the wine list is merely serviceable, and the buzz-ing happy-hour bar crowd lingering well into dinnertime can detract from the otherwise romantic atmosphere. Nonetheless, Coconut Grove straddles the line between casual beachfront boîte and elegant eatery with aplomb. ⊠*Siboney Beach Club, Dickenson Bay* ☎*268/462–1538* ▭*AE, D, MC, V.*

$$–$$$
CARIBBEAN
✕**Commissioner Grill.** White-tile floors, powder-blue chairs, floral table-cloths, glass buoys, Antiguan pottery, conch shells, and historic maps give this converted, 19th-century tamarind warehouse a timeless island feel. Specials might include whelks in garlic butter, bacon-wrapped plan-tains in mustard sauce, snapper in lobster sauce, or mahimahi creole. Local seafood is the obvious choice, although beef and poultry are also reliable. Lunch is considerably cheaper and more authentic. ⊠*Com-missioner Alley and Redcliffe St., St. John's* ☎*268/462–1883* ▭*AE, D, MC, V.*

ARUBA (ORANJESTAD)

Vernon
O'Reilly
Ramesar

Few islands can boast the overt dedication to tourism and the quality of service that Aruba offers. The arid landscape is full of attractions to keep visitors occupied, and the island offers some of the most dazzling beaches in the Caribbean. Casinos and novelty nightclubs abound in Oranjestad, giving the capital an almost Las Vegas appeal. To keep tourists coming back year after year, the island boasts a tremendous variety of restaurants ranging from upscale French eateries to toes-in-the-sand casual dining. Aruba may not be an unexplored paradise, but hundreds of thousands of tourists make it a point to beat a path here every year. Because it's not a very large island, cruise-ship visitors can expect to see a large part of the island on their day ashore. Or they can simply see a lot of the beautiful beaches. Whether you're planning to be active or to simply relax, this is an ideal cruise port.

ESSENTIALS

Currency The Aruban florin (AFl 1.77 to US$1). The florin is pegged to the U.S. dollar, and Arubans accept U.S. dollars readily, so you need only acquire local currency for pocket change. Note that the Netherlands Antilles florin used on Bonaire and Curaçao is not accepted on Aruba.

Internet **Café Internet** (✉ 8 Royal Plaza Mall, Oranjestad ☎ 297/582–4609).

Telephones When making calls to anywhere in Aruba, simply dial the seven-digit number. AT&T customers can dial 800–8000 from special phones at the cruise dock and in the airport's arrival and departure halls. Otherwise dial 121 to contact the international operator to place an international call.

COMING ASHORE

The Port of Oranjestad is a busy place and is generally full of eager tourists looking for souvenirs or a bite to eat. The port can accommodate up to five ships at a time (and frequently does). The Renaissance Mall is located right on the port, as are a number of souvenir shops and some decent and inexpensive eating places. The main shopping areas of Oranjestad are all within 10 minutes' walk from the port.

Taxis can be flagged down on the street that runs alongside the port (look for license plates with a TX tag). Rates are fixed (i.e., there are no meters; the rates are set by the government and displayed on a chart), though you and the driver should agree on the fare before your ride begins. Rides to Eagle Beach run about $10; to Palm Beach, about $15. If you want to rent a car, you can do so for a reasonable price; driving is on the right, just as in the U.S., and it's pretty easy to get around, though a four-wheel drive vehicle does help in reaching some of the more out-of-the-way places.

EXPLORING ARUBA

Alto Vista Chapel. Alone near the island's northwest corner sits the scenic little Alto Vista Chapel. The wind whistles through the simple mustard-color walls, eerie boulders, and looming cacti. Along the side of the

Aruba

KEY
Beaches
Cruise Ship Terminal
Dive Sites

C a r i b b e a n   S e a

0   4 mi
0   6 km

California Lighthouse
Californian Wreck
California Pt.
Malmok Beach
Antilla Shipwreck
Debbie II
Fisherman's Hut
Tierra del Sol Golf Course
Mt. Altovista
Pedernalis Wreck
Palm Beach
Alto Vista Chapel
Bushiribana
Andicouri
Butterfly Farm
Noord
Tanki Leendert
Paradera
Aruba Ostrich Farm
Rock Formations
Mt. Hooiberg
Santa Cruz
Eagle Beach
Manchebo Beach
Harbour Reef
J.E. Irausquin Blvd.
Druif Bay
L.G. Smith Blvd.
Surfside Beach
Cruise Ship Terminal
Reina Beatrix International Airport
Jane Sea Wreck
Mt. Yamanota
Spanish Lagoon
Miralamar
Mt. Arikok
Fontein Cave
Boca Prins (sand dunes)
Guadikiri Cave
Baranca Sunu
Boca Grandi
Bachelor's Beach
Colorado Pt.
Grapefield Beach
Coco's Beach
Captain Wreck
Baby Beach
Mangel Halto Reef (Pos Chiquito Reef)

1 A/B
2 A/B
4 A/B
6 A/B
7 A/B
1 A/B
7 A/B

Oranjestad
see inset map

Oranjestad (inset)

Faeschweg
Paramiraweg
Heiligerweg
De Windtweg
De Graafweg
Fort Oranjestr.
Prinsesweg
Cottageweg
Post Office
Archaeological Museum
Honen Dalim
De Ruyterweg
Kerkweg
Van Tonningenweg
Fort Oranje
Dutch Reformed Church
Wilhelmina Park
L.G. Smith Blvd.
Oranjestad Bay

0   1/8 mile
0   200 meters

road back to civilization are miniature crosses with depictions of the stations of the cross and hand-lettered signs exhorting PRAY FOR US, SINNERS and the like—a simple yet powerful evocation of faith. To get here, follow the rough, winding dirt road that loops around the island's northern tip, or, from the hotel strip, take Palm Beach Road through three intersections and watch for the asphalt road to the left just past the Alto Vista Rum Shop.

★ **Aruba Ostrich Farm.** Everything you ever wanted to know about the world's largest living birds can be found at this farm. A large palapa houses a gift shop and restaurant (popular with large bus tours), and tours of the farm are available every half hour. This operation is virtually identical to the facility in Curaçao; it's owned by the same company. ⊠ *Makividiri Rd., Paradera* ☎ *297/585–9630* ⊕ *www.arubaostrichfarm.com* ⊠ *$12* ⊙ *Daily 9–5.*

Butterfly Farm. Hundreds of butterflies from around the world flutter about this spectacular garden. Guided 20- to 30-minute tours (included in the price of admission) provide an entertaining look into the life cycle of these insects, from egg to caterpillar to chrysalis to butterfly. There's a special deal offered here: after your initial visit, you can return as often as you like for free during your vacation. ⊠ *J. E. Irausquin Blvd., Palm Beach* ☎ *297/586–3656* ⊕ *www.thebutterflyfarm.com* ⊠ *$13* ⊙ *Daily 9–4:30; last tour at 4.*

California Lighthouse. The lighthouse, built by a French architect in 1910, stands at the island's far northern end. Although you can't go inside, you can ascend the hill to the lighthouse base for some great views. In this stark landscape you might feel as though you've just landed on the moon. The lighthouse is surrounded by huge boulders that look like extraterrestrial monsters and sand dunes embroidered with scrub that resemble undulating sea serpents.

Mt. Hooiberg. Named for its shape (*hooiberg* means "haystack" in Dutch), this 541-foot peak lies inland just past the airport. If you have the energy, climb the 562 steps to the top for an impressive view of Oranjestad (and Venezuela on clear days).

Oranjestad. Aruba's charming capital is best explored on foot. L. G. Smith Boulevard, the palm-lined thoroughfare in the center of town, runs between pastel-painted buildings, old and new, of typical Dutch design. You'll find many malls with boutiques and shops here.

The **Archaeological Museum of Aruba** has two rooms chock-full of fascinating artifacts from the indigenous Arawak people, including farm

---

ARUBA BEST BETS

■ **Oranjestad.** Aruba's capital is pretty and easy to explore on foot, and it's impossible to get lost.

■ **Eagle Beach.** One of the most beautiful beaches in the Caribbean, with miles of white sand.

■ **Nightlife.** If your ship stays in port late, take advantage of the island's great bar scene and its many casinos.

■ **Snorkeling.** Though you can't dive here, you can snorkel to get a glimpse of what's under the sea.

■ **Windsurfing.** Constant wind allows this adrenaline sport to thrive in Aruba.

4

and domestic utensils dating back hundreds of years. ✉ *J. E. Irausquin Blvd. 2A* ☎ *297/582-8979* 🔖 *Free* ⊙ *Weekdays 8–noon and 1–4.*

Learn all about aloe—its cultivation, processing, and production—at **Aruba Aloe,** Aruba's own aloe farm and factory. Guided tours lasting about a half hour will show you how the gel—revered for its skin-soothing properties—is extracted from the aloe vera plant and used in a variety of products, including after-sun creams, soaps, and shampoos. Though not the most exciting tour on the island—and unlikely to keeps kids entertained—it might be a good option in the event of a rainy day. You can purchase the finished goods in the gift shop. ✉ *Pitastraat 115* ☎ *297/588-3222* 🔖 *$8* ⊙ *Weekdays 8:30–4:30, Sat. 9–1.*

One of the island's oldest edifices, **Ft. Zoutman** was built in 1796 and played an important role in skirmishes between British and Curaçao troops in 1803. The Willem III Tower, named for the Dutch monarch of that time, was added in 1868 to serve as a lighthouse. Over time, the fort has been a government office building, a police station, and a prison; now its historical museum displays Aruban artifacts in an 18th-century house. ✉ *Zoutmanstraat* ☎ *297/582-6099* 🔖 *Free* ⊙ *Weekdays 8–noon and 1–4.*

★ The **Numismatic Museum** displays more than 40,000 historic coins and paper money from around the world. A few pieces were salvaged from shipwrecks in the region. Some of the coins circulated during the Roman Empire, the Byzantine Empire, and the ancient Chinese dynasties; the oldest dates to the 3rd century BC. The museum had its start as the private collection of an Aruban who dug up some old coins in his garden. It's now run by his granddaughter. ✉ *Weststraat, Oranjestad* ☎ *297/582-8831* 🔖 *$5* ⊙ *Mon.–Thurs. 9–4, Fri. 9–1, Sat. 9–noon.*

Rock Formations. The massive boulders at Ayo and Casibari are a mystery, as they don't match the island's geological makeup. You can climb to the top for fine views of the arid countryside. On the way you'll doubtless pass Aruba whiptail lizards—the males are cobalt blue, and the females are blue-gray with light-blue dots. The main path to Casibari has steps and handrails the entire way (except on one side), and you must move through tunnels and along narrow steps and ledges to reach the top. At Ayo you can find ancient pictographs in a small cave (the entrance has iron bars to protect the drawings from vandalism). Access to Casibari is via Tanki Highway 4A; you can reach Ayo via Route 6A. Watch carefully for the turnoff signs near the center of the island on the way to the windward side.

SHOPPING

★ Oranjestad's **Caya G. F. Betico Croes** is Aruba's chief shopping street, lined with several shops advertising "duty-free prices" (again, these are not truly duty-free), boutiques, and jewelry stores noted for the aggressiveness of their vendors on cruise-ship days. Five minutes from the cruise-ship terminal, the **Renaissance Mall** (✉ *L. G. Smith Blvd. 82, Oranjestad*), also known as Seaport Mall, has more than 120 stores selling merchandise to meet every taste and budget; the Crystal Casino is also here. The **Royal Plaza Mall** (✉ *L. G. Smith Blvd. 94, Oranjestad*), across from the cruise-ship terminal, has cafés, a post office (open weekdays 8 to 3:30), and such stores as Nautica, Benetton, Tommy Hilfiger, and Gandelman Jewelers. There's also a Cyber Café for those who want to send e-mail and get their caffeine fix all in one stop.

> **CAUTION**
>
> Pack and wear a hat to protect your scalp, ears, and face from sun damage and premature aging. Excessive sun exposure contributes to wrinkles and dark spots.

★ **Art and Tradition Handicrafts** (⊠ *Caya G. F. Betico Croes 30, Oranjestad* ☎ *297/583–6534* ⊠ *Royal Plaza Mall, L. G. Smith Blvd. 94, Oranjestad* ☎ *297/582–7862*) sells intriguing souvenirs. Buds from the *mopa mopa* tree are boiled to form a resin, which is colored using vegetable dyes, then stretched by hand and mouth. Tiny pieces are cut and layered to form intricate designs—these are truly unusual gifts. Filling 6,000 square feet of space, **Boolchand's** (⊠ *Renaissance Mall, L. G. Smith Blvd. 82, Oranjestad* ☎ *297/583–0147*) sells jewelry and watches. It also stocks leather goods, cameras, and electronics. A venerated name in Aruba, **J. L. Penha and Sons** (⊠ *Caya G. F. Betico Croes 11/13, Oranjestad* ☎ *297/582–4160 or 297/582–4161*) sells high-end perfumes and cosmetics. It stocks such brands as Boucheron, Cartier, Dior, and Givenchy.

ACTIVITIES

BIKING

Pedal pushing is a great way to get around the island; the climate is perfect, and the trade winds help to keep you cool. **Melchor Cycle Rental** (⊠ *Bubali 106B, Noord* ☎ *297/587–1787*) rents ATVs and bikes. **Rancho Notorious** (⊠ *Boroncana, Noord* ☎ *297/586–0508* ⊕ *www.rancho notorious.com*) organizes mountain-biking tours and provides the bikes as well.

DIVING AND SNORKELING

With visibility of up to 90 feet, the waters around Aruba are excellent for snorkeling and diving. Advanced and novice divers alike will find plenty to occupy their time, as many of the most popular sites—including some interesting shipwrecks—are found in shallow waters ★ ranging from 30 to 60 feet. **De Palm Watersports** (⊠ *L. G. Smith Blvd. 142, Oranjestad* ☎ *297/582–4400 or 800/766–6016* ⊕ *www.depalm. com*) is one of the best choices for your undersea experience, and the options go beyond basic diving. You can don a helmet and walk along the ocean floor near De Palm Island, home of huge blue parrot fish. You can even do Snuba—which is like scuba diving but without the heavy air tanks—from either a boat or from an island; it costs $56.

GOLF

The **Links at Divi Aruba** (⊠ *J. E. Irausquin Blvd. 93, Oranjestad* ☎ *297/581–4653*), is a 9-hole course designed by Karl Litten and Lorie Viola. The par-36 paspalum grass course (best for seaside courses) takes you past beautiful lagoons. Amenities include a golf school with professional instruction, a swing analysis station, a driving range, and a two-story golf clubhouse with a pro shop. Two restaurants are available: Windows on Aruba for fine dining and Mulligan's for a casual and quick lunch. Greens fees are $85 for 9 holes, $124 for 18 from December to April.

KAYAKING

Kayaking is a popular sport on Aruba, especially along the south coast, where the waters are calm. It's a great way to explore the coastline. **Aruba Kayak Adventure** (✉*Ponton 90, Oranjestad* ☎*297/587–7722* ⊕*www.arubakayak.com*) has excellent half-day kayak trips, which start with a quick lesson before you paddle through caves and mangroves and along the scenic coast. The tour makes a lunch stop at De Palm Island, where snorkeling is included as part of the $99 package.

BEACHES

The beaches on Aruba are beautiful, clean, and easily reached from the cruise-ship terminal in Oranjestad.

Fodor'sChoice
★
Eagle Beach (✉*J. E. Irausquin Blvd., north of Manchebo Beach*), on the southwestern coast, is one of the Caribbean's—if not the world's—best beaches. Not long ago it was a nearly deserted stretch of pristine sand dotted with the occasional thatched picnic hut. Now that the resorts have been completed, this mile-plus-long beach is always hopping. **Manchebo Beach** (✉*J. E. Irausquin Blvd., at the Manchebo Beach Resort*)is impressively wide; the shoreline in front of the Manchebo Beach Resort is where officials turn a blind eye to the occasional topless sunbather. This beach merges with Druif Beach, and most locals use the name Manchebo to refer to both. **Palm Beach** (✉*J. E. Irausquin Blvd. between the Westin Aruba Resort, Spa and Casino and the Marriott Aruba Ocean Club*) from the Westin Aruba to the Marriott Aruba Ocean Club is the center of Aruban tourism, offering good opportunities for swimming, sailing, and other water sports. In some spots you might find a variety of shells that are great to collect, but not as much fun to step on barefoot—bring sandals just in case.

WHERE TO EAT

$$–$$$ ✕**MooMba Beach Bar and Restaurant.** Drop by anytime—this festive eatery
AMERICAN   serves breakfast, lunch, and dinner, and the menu includes a wide selection of seafood and meat specialties. It is probably best to stick with the grilled seafood courses as the quality of other items can be erratic and especially so during busy periods. By day, you can sit beneath the giant palapa if you want to beat the heat or plant yourself at a table in the sand if you haven't had enough sun. Come straight from the beach—bare feet are *expected* here. MooMba is popular with locals, so you can learn a bit about Aruban culture over sunset cocktails. Once a month, the place is rollicking after hours with a full-moon dance party that lures all the island's night owls. It's on Palm Beach between the Marriott Surf Club and the Holiday Inn. The restaurant participates in AGA's Dine-Around program. ✉*J. E. Irausquin Blvd. 230, Palm Beach* ☎*297/586–5365* ⊕*www.moombabeach.com* ⊟*AE, D, MC, V.*

$$–$$$ ✕**Rumba Bar and Grill.** In the heart of Oranjestad, this lively bistro has an
CARIBBEAN   open kitchen where you can watch the chef prepare tasty international

fare (mostly grilled seafood and beef) over a charcoal grill, with such highlights as coconut shrimp, rack of lamb, and Caribbean lobster. The presentations are fanciful, with entrées forming towering shapes over beds of colorful vegetables and sauces. You can dine on the terrace and soak up the local color or inside amid wicker and warm pink hues; the crowd is always worth watching. It's an AGA Dine-Around member. ⊠*Havenstraat 4, Oranjestad* ☎*297/588–7900* ⊕*www.rumba-aruba. com* ⊟*AE, D, MC, V* ☺*Closed Sun.*

BARBADOS (BRIDGETOWN)

Jane E. Zarem

Barbadians (Bajans) are a warm, friendly, and hospitable people, who are genuinely proud of their country and culture. Although tourism is the island's number one industry, the island has a sophisticated business community and stable government, so life here doesn't skip a beat after passengers return to the ship. Barbados is the most "British" island in the Caribbean. Afternoon tea is a ritual, and cricket is the national sport. The atmosphere, though, is hardly stuffy. This is still the Caribbean, after all. Beaches along the island's south and west coasts are picture-perfect, and all are available to cruise passengers. On the rugged east coast, the Atlantic Ocean attracts world-class surfers. The northeast is dominated by rolling hills and valleys, while the interior of the island is covered by acres of sugarcane and dotted with small villages. Historic plantations, a stalactite-studded cave, a wildlife preserve, rum distilleries, and tropical gardens are among the island's attractions. Bridgetown is the capital city, and its downtown shops and historic sites are a short walk or taxi ride from the pier.

ESSENTIALS

Currency The Barbados dollar (BDS$) is pegged to the U.S. dollar at the rate of BDS$1.99 to US$1. U.S. dollars are accepted universally across the island, but change is given in Barbados dollars.

Internet You'll find Internet cafés in and around Bridgetown and at St. Lawrence Gap on the south coast. Rates range from $2 for 15 minutes to $8 or $9 per hour. **Bean-n-Bagel Internet Cafe** (⊠ *St. Lawrence Gap, Dover*). **Connect Internet Cafe** (⊠*Shop #9, 27 Broad St., Bridgetown*).

Telephone Your cell phone should work in Barbados, although roaming charges can be costly. Alternatively, you can purchase phone cards at the cruise-ship terminal. Direct-dialing to the United States, Canada, and other countries is efficient and reasonable. Some toll-free numbers cannot be accessed in Barbados. To charge your overseas call on a major credit card or U.S. calling card without incurring a surcharge, dial 800/225–5872 (1-800/CALL-USA) from any phone.

COMING ASHORE

Up to eight ships at a time can dock at Bridgetown's Deep Water Harbour, on the northwest side of Carlisle Bay near Bridgetown. The cruiseship terminal has duty-free shops, handicraft vendors, a post office, a telephone station, a tourist information desk, and a taxi stand. To get

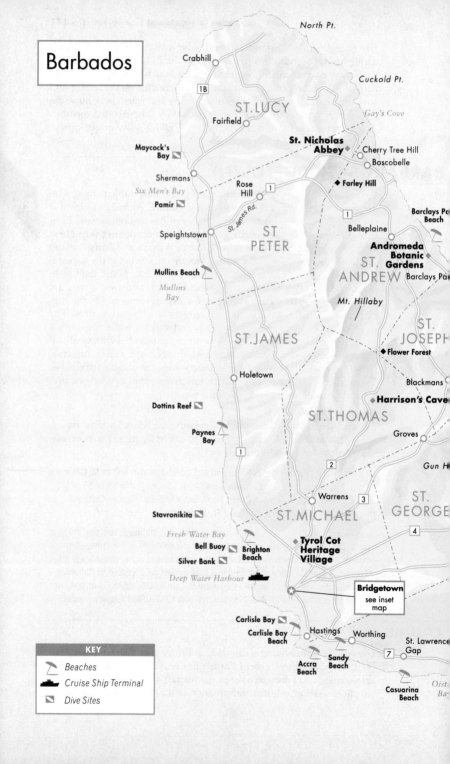

Barbados

North Pt.

Crabhill

1B

Cuckold Pt.

ST. LUCY

Fairfield

Gay's Cove

St. Nicholas Abbey ◆   Cherry Tree Hill

Maycock's Bay 🤿

Boscobelle

Shermans

Rose Hill

1

◆ **Farley Hill**

Six Men's Bay

Pamir 🤿

1

Barclays Beach ⛱

Speightstown

Belleplaine

ST PETER

Andromeda Botanic Gardens

ST. ANDREW

Mullins Beach

Barclays Pa

Mullins Bay

Mt. Hillaby

ST. JAMES

ST. JOSEPH

◆ **Flower Forest**

Holetown

Blackmans

Dottins Reef 🤿

◆ **Harrison's Cave**

ST. THOMAS

Paynes Bay

Groves

1

Gun H

2

Stavronikita 🤿

Warrens

3

ST. MICHAEL

ST. GEORGE

Fresh Water Bay

4

Bell Buoy 🤿   Brighton Beach

Silver Bank 🤿

◆ **Tyrol Cot Heritage Village**

Deep Water Harbour 🚢

Bridgetown see inset map

Carlisle Bay 🤿

Carlisle Bay Beach

Hastings

Worthing

St. Lawrence Gap

Accra Beach

Sandy Beach

7

Casuarina Beach

Oist Ba

KEY

- ⚓ *Beaches*
- 🚢 *Cruise Ship Terminal*
- 🤿 *Dive Sites*

downtown, follow the shoreline to the Careenage. It's a 15-minute walk or a $3 taxi ride.

Taxis await ships at the pier. Drivers accept U.S. dollars and appreciate a 10% tip. Taxis are unmetered and operate at a fixed hourly rate of $25 per carload (up to three passengers). Most drivers will cheerfully

> **TIP**
>
> If you don't want to rely on shipboard wake-up calls, be sure to bring your own travel alarm clock; most staterooms do not have clocks.

narrate an island tour. You can rent a car with a valid driver's license, but rates are steep—up to $85 per day during the high season—and some agencies require a two-day rental at that time.

EXPLORING BARBADOS

BRIDGETOWN

This bustling capital city is a major duty-free port with a compact shopping area. The principal thoroughfare is Broad Street, which leads west from National Heroes Square.

Nidhe Israel Synagogue. Providing for the spiritual needs of one of the oldest Jewish congregations in the western hemisphere, this synagogue was formed by Jews who left Brazil in the 1620s and introduced sugarcane to Barbados. The adjoining cemetery has tombstones dating from the 1630s. The original house of worship, built in 1654, was destroyed in an 1831 hurricane, rebuilt in 1833, and restored with the assistance of the Barbados National Trust in 1987. Friday-night services are held during the winter months, but the building is open to the public year-round. Shorts are not acceptable during services but may be worn at other times. ✉ *Synagogue La., St. Michael* ☎ *246/426–5792* 🖅 *Donation requested* ☉ *Weekdays 9–4.*

Parliament Buildings. Overlooking National Heroes Square in the center of town, these Victorian buildings were constructed around 1870 to house the British Commonwealth's third-oldest parliament. A series of stained-glass windows depicts British monarchs from James I to Victoria. ✉ *Broad St., St. Michael* ☎ *246/427–2019* 🖅 *Donations welcome* ☉ *Tours weekdays at 11 and 2, when parliament isn't in session.*

CENTRAL AND WEST

☼ **Gun Hill Signal Station.** The 360-degree view from Gun Hill, 700 feet
★ above sea level, was what made this location of strategic importance to the 18th-century British army. Using lanterns and semaphore, soldiers based here could communicate with their counterparts at the Garrison, on the south coast, and at Grenade Hill, in the north. Time moved slowly in 1868, and Captain Henry Wilkinson whiled away his off-duty hours by carving a huge lion from a single rock—which is on the hillside just below the tower. Come for a short history lesson but mainly for the view; it's so gorgeous, military invalids were once sent here to convalesce. ✉ *Gun Hill, St. George* ☎ *246/429–1358* 🖅 *$5* ☉ *Weekdays 9–5.*

Harrison's Cave. This limestone cavern, complete with stalactites, stalagmites, subterranean streams, and a 40-foot waterfall, is a rare find in the Caribbean—and one of Barbados's most popular attractions. The cave reopened in 2007, following extensive renovations comprising a new visitor center with interpretative displays, life-size models and sculptures, a souvenir shop, improved restaurant facilities, and access for people with disabilities. The one-hour tours are conducted via electric trams, which fill up fast; reserve ahead of time. ⊠ *Hwy. 2, Welchman Hall, St. Thomas* ☎ *246/438–6640* ⊕ *www.harrisonscave.com* ☒ *$20* ⊗ *Wed.–Sun. 9–3:45 (last tour).*

Fodor's Choice ★

BARBADOS BEST BETS

■ **The East Coast.** The island's windward coast, with its crashing surf, is striking.

■ **Harrison's Cave.** This extensive cave system is in the limestone deep beneath Barbados.

■ **Mount Gay Rum Visitors Centre.** Take a tour and a tasting.

■ **Flower Gardens.** Andromeda Botanic Gardens and the Flower Forest are both scenic and fragrant.

■ **St. Nicholas Abbey.** Not an abbey at all, this is one of the oldest Jacobean-era houses still standing in the western hemisphere.

4

NORTH AND EAST

★ **Andromeda Botanic Gardens.** Beautiful and unusual plant specimens from around the world are cultivated in 6 acres of gardens nestled among streams, ponds, and rocky outcroppings overlooking the sea above the Bathsheba coastline. The gardens were created in 1954 with flowering plants collected by the late horticulturist Iris Bannochie. They're now administered by the Barbados National Trust. The Hibiscus Café serves snacks and drinks. ⊠ *Bathsheba, St. Joseph* ☎ *246/433–9384* ☒ *$8.75* ⊗ *Daily 9–5.*

★ **St. Nicholas Abbey.** There's no religious connection here at all. The island's oldest greathouse (circa 1650) was named after the original British owner's hometown, St. Nicholas Parish near Bristol, and Bath Abbey nearby. Its stone-and-wood architecture makes it one of only three original Jacobean-style houses still standing in the western hemisphere. It has Dutch gables, finials of coral stone, and beautiful grounds that include an old sugar mill. The first floor, fully furnished with period furniture and portraits of family members, is open to the public. Fascinating home movies, shot by a previous owner's father, record Bajan life in the 1930s. ⊠ *Cherry Tree Hill, St. Peter* ☎ *246/422–5357* ☒ *$12.50* ⊗ *Weekdays 10–3:30.*

SOUTH

Barbados Concorde Experience. Opened to the public in April 2007, the Concorde Experience revolves around the British Airways Concorde G-BOAE (Alpha Echo, for short), that for many years flew between London and Barbados and has now made its permanent home here. Besides boarding the sleek supersonic aircraft itself, you'll learn about how the technology was developed and how this plane differed from other jets. ⊠ *Grantley Adams International Airport, Christ Church*

☎246/253–6257 ⊕*www.barbadosconcorde.com* ◌$17.50 ⊙*Daily*
9–5.

☼ **Tyrol Cot Heritage Village.** This coral-stone cottage just south of Bridgetown
was constructed in 1854 and is preserved as an example of period architecture. In 1929 it became the home of Sir Grantley Adams, the first
premier of Barbados and the namesake of its international airport.
Part of the Barbados National Trust, the cottage is now filled with
the late Sir Grantley and Lady Adams's antiques and memorabilia. It's
also the centerpiece of an outdoor "living museum," where artisans
and craftsmen have their workshops in a cluster of traditional chattel
houses. The crafts are for sale, and refreshments are available at the
"rum shop." ⊠*Rte. 2, Codrington Hill, St. Michael* ☎246/424–2074
or 246/436–9033 ◌$6 ⊙*Weekdays 9–5.*

SHOPPING

Duty-free shopping is found in Bridgetown's Broad Street stores and
their branches in Holetown and at the cruise-ship terminal. Stores are
generally open weekdays 8:30–4:30, Saturday 8:30–1. ■ TIP➔**To purchase items duty-free, you must show your passport and cabin key card.**

Best of Barbados (⊠*Worthing, Christ Church* ☎246/421–6900), was
the brainchild of architect Jimmy Walker as a place to showcase the
works of his artist wife. Now with seven locations, the shops offer
products that range from Jill Walker's frameable prints, housewares,
and textiles to arts and crafts in both "native" style and modern designs.
Fodor's Choice Everything is made or designed on Barbados. **Earthworks Pottery** (⊠*No.
★ 2, Edgehill Heights, Edgehill Heights, St. Thomas* ☎246/425–0223)
is a family-owned and -operated pottery shop where you can purchase
anything from a dish or knickknack to a complete dinner service or
one-of-a-kind art piece. You can find the characteristically blue or green
pottery decorating hotel rooms for sale in gift shops throughout the
island, but the biggest selection (including some "seconds") is at Earthworks, where you also can watch the potters work. **Pelican Craft Centre**
(⊠*Princess Alice Hwy., Bridgetown, St. Michael* ☎246/427–5350) is
a cluster of workshops halfway between the cruise-ship terminal and
downtown Bridgetown where craftspeople create and sell locally made
leather goods, batik, basketry, carvings, jewelry, glass art, paintings,
pottery, and other items. It's open weekdays 9 to 5 and Saturday 9 to
2, with extended hours during holidays or cruise-ship arrivals.

ACTIVITIES

FISHING

Billfisher II (☎246/431–0741), a 40-foot Pacemaker, accommodates up
to six guests with three fishing chairs and five rods. Captain Winston
("The Colonel") White has been fishing these waters since 1975. Full-
day charters include a full lunch and guaranteed fish (or a 25% refund);
all trips include drinks and transportation to and from the boat. **Blue
Jay** (☎246/429–2326 ⊕*www.bluemarlinbarbados.com*) is a spacious,
fully equipped, 45-foot Sport Fisherman with a crew that knows the

water's denizens—blue marlin, sailfish, barracuda, and kingfish. Four to six people can be accommodated—it's the only charter boat on the island with four chairs. Most fishing is done by trolling. Drinks, snacks, bait, tackle, and transfers are provided.

GOLF

Barbados Golf Club (✉ *Hwy. 7, Durants, Christ Church* ☎246/428–8463 ⊕ *www.barbadosgolfclub.com*), the first public golf course on Barbados, is an 18-hole championship course (6,805 yards, par 72) redesigned in 2000 by golf-course architect Ron Kirby. Greens fees are $130 for 18 holes, plus a $25 per-person cart fee, or $78 for 9 holes, plus a $20 per-person cart fee. Unlimited three-day and seven-day golf passes are available. Club and shoe rentals are available.

Fodor'sChoice
★ At the prestigious **Country Club at Sandy Lane** (✉ *Hwy. 1, Paynes Bay, St. James* ☎246/444–2500 ⊕ *www.sandylane.com/golf*), golfers can play on the Old Nine or the Tom Fazio–designed Country Club Course (the spectacular Green Monkey Course is reserved for hotel guests and club members only). Golfers have complimentary use of the club's driving range. The Country Club Restaurant and Bar, which overlooks the 18th hole, is open to the public. Greens fees in high season are $150 for 9 holes or $235 for 18 holes. Golf carts, caddies, or trolleys are available for hire, as well as clubs and shoes. Carts are equipped with GPS, which alerts you to upcoming traps and hazards, provides tips on how to play the hole, and allows you to order refreshments!

BEACHES

All beaches on Barbados are open to cruise-ship passengers. The west coast has the stunning coves and white-sand beaches dear to the hearts of postcard publishers, plus calm, clear water for snorkeling and swimming. Waterskiing and parasailing are also available on most beaches along the south and west coasts. Windsurfing is best on the south coast.

Accra Beach, also known as Rockley Beach, is next to the Accra Beach Hotel. Look forward to gentle surf and a lifeguard, plenty of nearby restaurants for refreshments, a children's playground, and beach stalls for renting chairs and equipment for snorkeling and other water sports. Parking is available at an on-site lot. **Carlisle Bay,** adjacent to the Hilton Barbados and Grand Barbados hotels just south of Bridgetown, is a broad half-circle of white sand and one of the island's best beaches—but it can become crowded on weekends and holidays. Park at Harbour Lights or the Boatyard, both on Bay Street, where you can also rent umbrellas and beach chairs and buy refreshments. **Crane Beach,** an exquisite crescent of pink sand on the southeast coast, is protected by steep cliffs on the land side and a reef on the water side. Changing rooms are available at the Crane resort for a small fee (which you can apply toward drinks or a meal at the restaurant). Access is through the hotel and down to the beach via either a cliff-side elevator or 98 steps. **Mullins Beach,** just south of Speightstown, is a perfect place to spend the day. The water is safe for swimming and snorkeling, there's easy parking on the main road, and Mannie's Suga Suga restaurant serves snacks, meals, and drinks—and rents chairs and umbrellas. **Paynes Bay**

is lined with luxury hotels. It's a pretty area, with plenty of beach to go around and good snorkeling. Public access is available at several locations along Highway 1; parking is limited. Grab a bite to eat and liquid refreshments at Bomba's Beach Bar.

WHERE TO EAT

$$–$$$ ╳**Cliffside Restaurant.** The outdoor deck of this restaurant in the New
CARIBBEAN Edgewater hotel provides one of the prettiest, breeziest ocean views in all Barbados and, therefore, is a good stop for lunch when touring the east coast. From noon to 3 PM, choose the Bajan buffet or select from the menu. Either way, you might enjoy fried flying fish, roast or stewed chicken, local lamb chops, rice and peas, steamed root vegetables, sautéed plantains, and salad. ⊠*Bathsheba Beach, Bathsheba, St. Joseph* ☎*246/433–9900* ⚐*Reservations essential* ⊟*AE, MC, V.*

$$ ╳**Waterfront Cafe.** This friendly bistro alongside the Careenage is the
CARIBBEAN perfect place to enjoy a drink, snack, or meal—and to people-watch. Locals and tourists alike gather for all-day alfresco dining on sandwiches, salads, fish, pasta, pepper-pot stew, and tasty Bajan snacks such as *buljol* (a salad of shredded salt cod, tomatoes, and hot peppers), fish cakes, or plantation pork (plantains stuffed with spicy minced pork). The panfried flying-fish sandwich is especially popular. ⊠*The Careenage, Bridgetown, St. Michael* ☎*246/427–0093* ⊟*AE, DC, MC, V* ⊘*Closed Sun.*

BELIZE CITY, BELIZE

Lan Sluder   Belize probably has the greatest variety of flora and fauna of any country of its size in the world. Here you'll often find more iguanas or howler monkeys than humans. A few miles off the mainland is the Belize Barrier Reef, a great wall of coral stretching the entire 200-mi (333-km) length of the coast. Over 200 cayes (pronounced keys) dot the reef like punctuation marks, and three coral atolls lie farther out to sea. All are superb for diving and snorkeling. Many, like Ambergris Caye (pronounced Am-bur-griss Key) and Caye Caulker, are jolly resort islands with ample supplies of bars and restaurants, easily reachable on day trips from Belize City. The main choice you'll have to make is whether to stay in Belize City for a little shopping, a little walking, and perhaps lunch or a dram at one of the Fort George hotels or restaurants, or alternatively to head out by boat, rental car, taxi, or tour on a more active adventure.

ESSENTIALS

Currency The Belize dollar (BZ$2 to US$1). Since the U.S. dollar is universally accepted, there's no need to acquire Belize currency.

Flights Especially if you are going to Ambergris Caye, you may prefer to fly, or you can water-taxi over and fly back to maximize your time. There are hourly flights on two airlines. The flight to Caulker takes about 15 minutes and that to San Pedro about 25 minutes. The cost is about BZ$140 round-trip to either island. Be sure you fly out of Belize City's Municipal, not out of the international airport north of the city. **Maya Island Airways** (🖅 *Box 458, Municipal Airport,*

Belize City ☎ 223/1140, 800/225-6732 in U.S. ⊕ www.mayaislandair.com).
Tropic Air (🏠 Box 20, San Pedro ☎ 226/2012, 800/422-3435 in U.S. ⊕ www.tropicair.com).

Internet Click and Sip Internet Café (✉ Fort St. in Tourist Village ☎ 223/1305). **Mail Boxes Etc.** (✉ 166 N. Front St., Belize City ☎ 227/6046).

Telephones Calling locally or internationally is easy, but rates are high; around BZ$1.50 a minute for calls to the U.S. To call the United States, dial 001 or 10-10-199 plus the area code and number. Pay phones, which are located in the Tourist Village where you are tendered, and elsewhere downtown, accept only prepaid Belize Telecommunications Ltd. phone cards, available in shops in denominations from $5 to $50. Special "USA Connect" prepaid cards, for sale at some stores in Belize City, in denominations of $5 to $20, claim discounts of as much as 57% for calls to the U.S. only. Your U.S.-based GSM phone will probably work on Belize's GSM 1900 system. Foreign calling cards are generally blocked in Belize. Call 113 for local directory assistance, and 115 for an operator.

COMING ASHORE

Because Belize City's harbor is shallow, passengers are tendered in. If you're going the independent route, try to get in line early for the tenders, as it sometimes takes 90 minutes or more for all the passengers to be brought ashore. You arrive at the Fort Pointe Tourist Village, which opened in 2002. It has an antiseptic collection of gift shops, restaurants, and tour operators nicely situated along the harbor. Bathrooms are spick-and-span, too. At this writing, a much-delayed $50-million cruise terminal is under construction south of the city center; this new terminal may open sometime in 2010.

Taxis, tour guides, and car-rental desks are readily available. Taxi trips—official taxis have green license plates—within Belize City are supposed to be set at BZ$7 to BZ$10 for one person between any two points in the city, plus BZ$1 for

> **BELIZE CITY BEST BETS**
>
> ■ **Belize Zoo.** Though small, this collection of native Belize wildlife is excellent.
>
> ■ **Cave Tubing.** If you are not claustrophic, this is an unforgettable excursion.
>
> ■ **Diving.** Belize is becoming known as one of the world's best dive destinations. For the certified, this is a must.
>
> ■ **Snorkeling in Hol Chan.** The water is teeming with fish, and you don't need to be certified to enjoy the underwater world here.

each additional person. Outside the city, and from downtown to the suburbs, you're charged by the distance you travel. Hourly rates are negotiable, but expect to pay around $30, or $150 for the day. There's no need to tip cab drivers. You can also rent a car at the Tourist Village, but rates can be high (at least $75 per day), and gas is also expensive. Green directional signs point you to nearby destinations such as the Belize Zoo. The Wet Lizard, next to the Tourism Village also organizes tours for cruise-ship passengers.

EXPLORING BELIZE

Numbers in the margin correspond to points of interest on the Belize City map.

Belize City. Many Belize hands will tell you that the best way to see Belize City is through a rearview window. But, with an open mind to its peculiarities, and with a little caution (the city has a crime problem, but the tourist police keep a close watch on cruise-ship passengers), you may decide Belize City has a raffish, atmospheric charm rarely found in other Caribbean ports of call. You might even see the ghost of Graham Greene at a hotel bar. A 5- to 10-minute stroll from the perky Tourist Village brings you into the other worlds of Belize City. On the north side of Haulover Creek is the colonial-style world of the Fort George section, where large old homes, stately but sometimes down at the heels, take the breezes off the sea and share their space with hotels and restaurants. On the south side is the bustling world of Albert Street, the main commercial thoroughfare. But don't stroll too far. Parts of Belize City are unsafe by night or day. During the daylight hours, as long as you stay within the main commercial district and the Fort George area—and ignore the street hustlers—you should have no problem.

House of Culture, the city's finest colonial structure, is said to have been designed by the illustrious British architect Sir Christopher Wren.

Built in 1814, it was once the residence of the governor-general, the queen's representative in Belize. ⊠*Regent St. at Southern Foreshore* ☎*227/3050* ☜*BZ$10* ⊙*Weekdays 9–4.*

From the **Marine Terminal** you can catch a boat to Ambergris Caye, Caye Caulker, St. George's Caye, and Caye Chapel. Go to the white clapboard building, which was a firehouse in the 1920s. While waiting for a water taxi, you can wander around the **Marine Museum,** where downstairs there are displays on marine life, and upstairs are models of boats that have sailed these waters and tools used by shipwrights. ⊠*10 N. Front St., at Queen St.* ☎*223/1969* ☜*Museum, BZ$4* ⊙*Daily 8–5.*

This small but interesting **Museum of Belize** was a Belize City jail from the 1850s to 1993. Displays on Belize history and culture include ancient Mayan artifacts, eclectic memorabilia, colorful Belize postage stamps, and an actual jail cell. Exhibitions change frequently. ⊠*Gabourel La.* ☎*223/4524* ☜*BZ$10* ⊙*Weekdays 9–5.*

St. John's Cathedral, at the south end of Albert Street, is the oldest Anglican church in Central America and the only one outside England where kings were crowned. From 1815 to 1845 four kings of the Mosquito Coast (a British protectorate along the coast of Honduras and Nicaragua) were crowned here. ⊠*Albert St.* ☎*227/2137.*

🕐 **Altun Ha.** If you've never visited an ancient Maya site, make a trip to Altun Ha, 28 mi (45 km) north of Belize City. ✛*From Belize City, take the Northern Hwy. north to Mile 18.9. Turn right (east) on the Old Northern Hwy., which is only partly paved, and go 10½ mi (17 km) to the signed entrance road to Altun Ha on the left. Follow this paved road 2 mi (3 km) to the visitor center* ☎*609/3540* ☜*BZ$10* ⊙*Daily 9–5.*

🕐 **Belize Zoo.** One of the smallest, but arguably one of the best, zoos in the world, this park houses only animals native to Belize. Highlights including spotted and rare black jaguars, the pumas, margays, ocelots, jaguarondi, and the Baird's tapir, the national animal of Belize. ⊠*Western Hwy., 30 mi (49 km) west of Belize City* ☎*220/8004* ⊕*www.belizezoo. org* ☜*BZ$16 adults, BZ$8 children* ⊙*Daily 8–5.*

Fodor'sChoice
★

🕐 **Community Baboon Sanctuary.** This interesting wildlife conservation project is actually a haven for nearly 1,000 black howler monkeys and numerous other species of birds and mammals. ⊠*Community Baboon Sanctuary, 31 mi (50 km) northwest of Belize City* ☎*220/2181* ☜*BZ$10* ⊙*Daily 8–5.*

Crooked Tree Wildlife Sanctuary. A paradise for birders and animal lovers, this wildlife sanctuary encompasses a chain of inland waterways around the Northern Lagoon covering about 3,000 acres. Traveling through by canoe, you're likely to see iguanas, crocodiles, coatis, and turtles. The sanctuary's most prestigious visitors, however, are the jabiru storks, several of which usually visit between November and May. ⊠*Turn west off Northern Hwy. at Mile 30.8, then drive 2 mi (3 km)* ☎*223/4987* *for Belize Audubon Society* ⊕*www.belizeaudubon.org/parks/ctws.htm* ☜*BZ$8.*

4

Hummingbird Highway. At Belmopan, the paved Hummingbird Highway is Belize's most scenic road, cutting 54 mi (90 km) southeast through the Maya Mountains to Dangriga, passing Five Blues Lake and Blue Hole national parks. Mile markers on the Hummingbird start in Dangriga.

Ⓢ Less than a half-hour south of Belmopan, the 575-acre **St. Herman's Blue Hole Natural Park** has a natural turquoise pool surrounded by mosses and lush vegetation, excellent for a cool dip. ⊠ *Mile 42.5, Hummingbird Hwy.* ⊕ *www.belizeaudubon.org* 🏷 *BZ$8* 🕐 *Daily 8–4:30*

THE CAYES

Ambergris Caye. Ambergris is the queen of the cayes. With a population around 5,000, the island's only town, San Pedro, remains a small, friendly, and prosperous village. It has one of the highest literacy rates in the country and an admirable level of awareness about the fragility of the reef. The large number of substantial private houses being built on the edges of town is proof of how much tourism has enriched San Pedro. A water taxi from the Marine Terminal takes about 75 minutes and costs BZ$20 each way. You can also fly.

Fodor's Choice **Hol Chan Marine Reserve** (Maya for "little channel") is 4 mi (6 km)
★ from San Pedro at the southern tip of Ambergris. Because fishing is forbidden here, snorkelers and divers can see teeming marine life. You can also snorkel with nurse sharks and rays (which gather here to be fed) at Shark-Ray Alley, a sandbar that is part of the reserve. You need above-average swimming skills, as the current is often strong. ⊠ *Southern tip of Ambergris Caye* ⊕ *www.holchanbelize.org* 🏷 *BZ$20 marine reserve fee.*

Caye Caulker. On Caye Caulker, where the one village is home to around 800 people, brightly painted houses on stilts line the coral-sand streets. Although the island is being developed more each year, flowers still outnumber cars 10 to 1 (golf carts, bicycles, and bare feet are the preferred means of transportation). The living is easy, as you might guess from all the NO SHIRT, NO SHOES, NO PROBLEM signs at the bars. This is the kind of place where most of the listings in the telephone directory give addresses like "near football field." A water taxi from the Marine Terminal costs about BZ$15 each way and takes about 45 minutes.

SHOPPING

Belize does not have the crafts tradition of its neighbors, Guatemala and Mexico, and imported goods are expensive due to high duties, but hand-carved items of zircote or other local woods make good souvenirs. Near the Swing Bridge at Market Square is the **Commercial Center,** which has some food and craft vendors on the first floor, and a restaurant and shops on the second. The **Fort Pointe Tourist Village,** where the ship tenders come in, is a collection of bright and clean gift shops selling T-shirts and Belizean and Guatemalan crafts. Beside the Tourist Village is an informal **Street Vendor Market,** with funkier goods and performances by a "Brukdown" band or a group of Garifuna drummers.

National Handicraft Center (⊠ *2 South Park St., in Fort George section* ☎ *223/3636*) has Belizean souvenir items, including hand-carved figurines, handmade furniture, pottery, and woven baskets. The prices are about as good as you'll find anywhere in Belize, and the sales clerks are friendly. It faces the small Memorial Park, which commemorates the Battle of St. George's Caye and is just a short stroll from the harbor front, the Tourist Village, and many of the hotels in the Fort George area, including the Radisson, Chateau Caribbean, and Great House.

ACTIVITIES

CANOPY TOURS

You may feel a little like Tarzan as you dangle 80 feet above the jungle floor, suspended by a harness, moving from one suspended platform to another. **Jaguar Paw Lodge** (☎820/2023 ⊕*www.jaguarpaw.com*), off Mile 37 of the Western Highway, has eight platforms set 100 to 250 feet apart. At the last platform you have to rappel to the ground. The cost is BZ$110 to BZ$150, depending on whether lunch and transportation are included. There's a 240-pound weight limit.

CAVE TUBING

Very popular with cruise passengers are river-tubing trips that go through a cave, where you'll turn off your headlamp for a minute of absolute darkness, but these are not for the claustrophic or those afraid of the dark. **Cave-Tubing in Belize** (☎605/1573 ⊕*www.cave-tubing.com*) specializes in cave tubing trips. The cost is BZ$90 (not including transportation from the cruise pier); for BZ$150, you can do both the cave-tubing and an ATV trip in the jungle.

DIVING AND SNORKELING

Most companies on Ambergris Caye offer morning and afternoon single-tank dives; snorkel trips begin mid-morning or early afternoon. Dive and snorkeling trips that originate in Caye Caulker are a bit cheaper. **Amigos del Mar** (✉*Off Barrier Reef Dr. near Mayan Princess Hotel, Ambergris Caye* ☎226/2706 ⊕*amigosdive.com*) is perhaps the island's most consistently recommended dive operation. It offers a range of local dives as well as trips to Turneffe Atoll and Lighthouse Reef in a fast 48-foot dive boat.

Go out for a snorkel on a sailboat with **Raggamuffin Tours** (✉*Front St., Caye Caulker* ☎226/0348 ⊕*www.raggamuffintours.com*), which goes to Hol Chan for BZ$90, including the park entrance fee.

INDEPENDENT TOURS

Several Belize City–based tour guides and operators offer custom trips for ship passengers; companies will usually meet you at the Tourist Village. Katie Valk, who owns **Belize Trips** (✉*Box 1108, Belize City* ☎223/0376 *in Belize,* 561/210–7015 *in U.S.* ⊕*www.belize-trips.com*), is a transplanted New Yorker. Her company can organize a custom trip to just about anywhere in the country. **Ecological Tours and Services.** (✉*Box 473, Belize City* ☎223/4874 ⊕*www.ecotoursbelize.com*), based in Belize City, specializes in organizing independent tours for cruise-ship passengers.

BEACHES

Although the barrier reef just offshore limits the wave action, which, over eons, builds classic wide sandy beaches, and there is a good deal of seagrass on the shore bottom, Ambergris Caye's beaches are among the best in Belize. All beaches in Belize are public. **Mar de Tumbo,** 1½ mi (3 km) south of town near the Tropica Hotel, is the best beach on the south end of the island. **North Ambergris,** accessible by water taxi from San Pedro or by golf cart over the new bridge to the north, has miles of narrow beaches and fewer people. **Ramon's Village's beach,** right across from the airstrip, is the best in the town area. The beaches on Caulker are not as good as those on Ambergris. Along the front side of the island is a narrow strip of sand, but the water is shallow and swimming conditions are poor. The **Split,** on the north end of the village (turn to your right from the main public pier), is the best place on Caye Caulker for swimming.

WHERE TO EAT

$$$–$$$$ ✕**Harbour View.** For the most romantic setting in the city, ask for a table
SEAFOOD   on the wraparound balcony overlooking the harbor. The friendly staff
★   and consistently excellent food also make the Harbour View a favorite of Belize's power brokers. The seafood is especially good; try the snapper with mango chutney, cooked in a banana leaf. Pork dishes, especially Pork Picasso with a hot pepper relish, are also delicious. ⊠*Fort St., near Tourist Village* ☎*223/6420* ▤*AE, D, MC, V* ⊘*Closed for lunch weekends.*

$–$$ ✕**Wet Lizard.** Right next to the Tourism Village, overlooking the board-
AMERICAN   walk where cruise-ship tenders drop off passengers, there's no question of the target market of the Wet Lizard. Even so, it's become a popular bar and a place to grab a sandwich or hamburger, even for those not on a cruise ship. An expansion added a gift shop, snack bar, and tour operation aimed at cruise passengers who don't want to take ship-sponsored excursions. ⊠*1 Fort St.* ☎*223/2664* ▤*MC, V* ⊘*Weekdays 9–4.*

BERMUDA

Basking in the Atlantic, 508 mi (817 km) due east of Cape Hatteras, North Carolina, restrained, polite Bermuda is a departure from other sunny, beach-strewn isles. You won't find laid-back locals wandering around barefoot proffering piña coladas. Bermuda is somewhat formal, and despite the gorgeous weather, residents wearing stockings and heels or jackets, ties, Bermuda shorts, and knee socks are a common sight, whether on the street by day or in restaurants at night. On Bermuda's 22 square mi (57 square km) you will discover that pastel cottages, quaint shops, and manicured gardens betray a more staid, suburban way of life. A self-governing British colony since 1968, Bermuda has maintained some of its English character even as it is increasingly influenced by American culture. Most cruise ships make seven-night loops from U.S. embarkation ports, with four nights at sea and three tied up in port. Increasingly popular are round-trip itineraries originating in northeastern embarkation ports that include a single day or overnight port call in Bermuda before continuing south to the Bahamas or the Caribbean.

ESSENTIALS

Currency The Bermuda dollar (B$) is on par with the U.S. dollar. You can use American money anywhere, but change is often given in Bermudian currency. ATMs are common.

Internet Expect to pay as much as $12 per hour to check your e-mail on Bermuda. **Internet Lane** (⊠ *The Walkway, 22 Reid St., Hamilton* ☎ *441/296–9972*).

Telephones To make a local call, simply dial the seven-digit number. You'll find specially marked AT&T USADirect phones at the airport, the cruise-ship dock in Hamilton, and King's Square and Ordnance Island in St. George's. Destination-specific international calling cards from North Rock Communications in Hamilton offer the cheapest way of calling. You can use them on any phones, including public pay phones and mobile phones. You can also get standard international cards from pharmacies, some supermarkets, and many gas stations. You can also make international calls with a calling card from the main post office.

COMING ASHORE

Three Bermuda harbors serve cruise ships: Hamilton (the capital), St. George's, and King's Wharf at the Royal Naval Dockyard.

In Hamilton, cruise ships tie up right on the city's main street, Front Street. A Visitors Service Bureau is next to the ferry terminal, also on Front Street and nearby; maps and brochures are displayed in the cruise terminal itself.

St. George's actually has two piers that accommodate cruise ships. One is on Ordnance Island, which is in the heart of the city; another pier is nearby. Visitors Service Bureau offices are at each pier.

King's Wharf, in the Royal Naval Dockyard at the westernmost end of the island, is the most isolated of the three cruise-ship berthing areas, and it is where the largest vessels dock. But it is well connected to the rest of the island by taxi, bus, and ferry. The nearby Cooperage has a Visitors Service Bureau office, and bus stops and the ferry pier are clearly marked.

Taxis are the fastest and easiest way to get around the island, but they are also quite expensive. Four-seaters charge $6.40 for the first mile and $2 for each subsequent mile. You can hire taxis for around $40 per hour (three-hour minimum for up to four passengers) if you want to do some exploring, and if you can round up a group of people, this is often cheaper than an island tour offered by your ship. Tip drivers 15%. Rental cars are prohibited, but the island has a good bus and ferry system. You can also rent scooters, but this can be dangerous for the unitiated and is not recommended.

Hamilton

Victoria Park

City Hall & Arts Centre

Dundonald Street

Cathedral of the Most Holy Trinity

Union Street

Church Street

Victoria Street

King Street

Happy Valley Road

Washington Street

Burnaby Street

Parliament Street

Court Street

Church Street

Church Street

Bermudiana Road

Par-La-Ville Road

Par-La-Ville Park

Washington Lane

Queen Street

Museum of the Bermuda Histocial Society

Reid Street

Fort Hamilton

Front Street

Cavendish Road

Visitors Service Bureau

The Birdcage

Ferry Terminal

Crow Lane

Bermuda Underwater Exploration Institute

Point Pleasant Rd.

| 0 | | 200 miles |
| 0 | | 200 kilometers |

KEY

Beaches

Cruise Ship Dock

Ferry

Railway Trail

WEST END — **Royal Naval Dockyard**

Ireland Island N.

Bermuda Maritime Museum

Cruise Ship Dock

Ireland Island S.

Boaz Island

Cobbler's Island

Admiralty House Park

Clarence Cove

Devonshire Dock

Watford Is.

Malabar Rd.

Spanish Point

Spanish Pt.

Hamilton see inset map

DEVONSHI

Somerset Long Bay

Daniel's Head

SAI

Somerset Village

Watford Bridge

PEMBROKE

Front St.

Somerset Island

Somerset Rd.

Great Sound

Hawkins Island

Hamilton Harbour

Cruise Ship Dock

Somerset Bridge

Paget Marsh

Middle Rd.

Harbour Rd.

PAGET

Spring Benny's Bay

Middle Rd.

Little Sound

Spicelands Riding Center

WARWICK

Whale Bay Fort

West Whale Bay

Middle Rd.

South Shore Rd.

Warwick Long Bay

SOUTHAMPTON

Gibb's Hill Lighthouse

Church Bay

Horseshoe Bay Beach

Bermuda

0 — 2 miles
0 — 3 km

Tobacco Bay Beach
Fort St. Catherine
ST. GEORGE'S
Fort St. Catherine Beach
Town of St. George

St. George's Island

Mullet Bay Rd.
Cruise Ship Dock

St.George's see inset map

St. George's Harbour

Ferry Rd.

Kindley Field Rd.

St. David's Rd.

Bermuda Airport

St. David's Island

The Causeway

Crystal Caves

Castle Harbour

ATLANTIC OCEAN

Crawl Hill North

HAMILTON

Harrington Sound Rd.

Shelly Bay

Harrington Sound

Tucker's Town

Bermuda Aquarium, Museum & Zoo

Flatts Village

Harrington Sound Rd.

North Shore Rd.

SMITH'S

John Smith's Bay

♦**Verdmont**

ATLANTIC OCEAN

South Shore Rd.

St. George's

Printer's Alley

Broad A...

Featherbed Alley

Bermudian Heritage Museum

Nea's Alley

Church Street

Clarence St.

Duke of York Street

Old Maid's Lane

Petticoat La. (Silk Alley)

Queen St.

St. Peter's Church

Bridge St.

Pound Alley

Princess St.

One Gun Alley

King St.

Duke of York Street

Bermuda National Trust Museum

Tucker House

Barber's Alley

Water Street

Visitors Service Bureau

Convict Bay

Ordnance Island

0 — 50 yards
0 — 50 meters

Cruise Ship Dock

St. George's Harbour

EXPLORING BERMUDA

Numbers in the margin correspond to points of interest on the Bermuda map.

HAMILTON

Bermuda's capital since 1815, the city of Hamilton is a small, bustling harbor town. It's the economic and social center of Bermuda, with busy streets lined with shops and offices. International influences, from both business and tourism, have brought a degree of sophistication unusual in so small a city. There are several museums and galleries to explore, but the favorite pastimes are shopping in Hamilton's numerous boutiques and dining in its many upscale restaurants.

☼ **Bermuda Underwater Exploration Institute (BUEI).** The 40,000-square-foot
★ Ocean Discovery Centre has numerous multimedia and interactive displays designed to acquaint you with the deep sea and its inhabitants. Never heard of a bathysphere? See a replica of this deep-sea diving vehicle, which allowed oceanographer William Beebe and Otis Barton to venture ½ mi down into the deep in 1934. ⊠*40 Crow La., off E. Broadway* ☎*441/292–7219* ⊕*www.buei.org* ☐*$12.50* ⊙*Weekdays 9–5, weekends 10–5, last admission at 4.*

★ **Cathedral of the Most Holy Trinity.** Designed in early Greek Revival flourishes, the cathedral was constructed out of Bermuda limestone and materials imported from France, Nova Scotia, and Scotland. The cathedral was completed in 1911. It has a copper roof, unusual in Bermuda's sea of white-topped buildings. After exploring the interior, you can purchase tickets to climb the 150-odd steps (143 feet) of the tower ⊠*Church St.* ☎*441/292–4033* ⊕*www.anglican.bm* ☐*Cathedral free; tower $3* ⊙*Church daily 7:30–5 and for Sun. services, tower weekdays 10–4.*

★ **City Hall and Arts Centre.** Set back from the street behind a fountain and
☼ lily pond, City Hall contains Hamilton's administrative offices as well as two art galleries and a performance hall. Instead of a clock, its tower is topped with a bronze wind vane—a prudent choice in a land where the weather is as important as the time. Massive cedar doors open into a large lobby with beautiful chandeliers and high ceilings. On the first landing, in the East Exhibition Room, is the **Bermuda National Gallery**, the home of Bermuda's national art collection. Farther up the stairs, in the West Wing, the **Bermuda Society of Arts Gallery** displays work by its members. ⊠*17 Church St.* ☎*441/292–1234* ☐*Galleries free* ⊙*City Hall weekdays 9–5; National Gallery and Society of the Arts Mon.–Sat. 10–4.*

★ **Fort Hamilton.** This imposing moat-ringed fortress has underground pas-
☼ sageways that were cut through solid rock by Royal Engineers in the 1860s. Built to defend the West End's Royal Naval Dockyard from land attacks, it was outdated even before its completion, but remains a fine example of a polygonal Victorian fort. Even if you're not a big fan of military history, the hilltop site's stellar views and stunning gardens make the trip worthwhile. ⊠*Happy Valley Rd.* ☎*441/292–1234* ☐*Free* ⊙*Daily 9:30–5.*

★ **Museum of the Bermuda Historical Society/Bermuda Public Library.** This building was once the home of Hamilton's first postmaster, William Bennet Perot, and his family. Mark Twain once lamented that the rubber tree in the front yard didn't bear fruit in the form of hot-water bottles and rubber overshoes. The library was founded in 1839, and its reference section has virtually every book ever written about Bermuda. The museum depicts Bermuda history with household goods and other artifacts, including an 18th-century sedan chair. ✉ *13 Queen St.* ☎ *441/295–2905 library, 441/295–2487 museum* ⊕ *www.bermudanationallibrary.bm* ✉ *Donations accepted* ☉ *Library Mon.–Thurs. 8:30–7, Fri. 10–5, Sat. 9–5, Sun. 1–5; closed Sun. in July and Aug.; museum Mon.–Sat. 9:30–3:30* ☞ *Tours by appointment.*

> **BERMUDA BEST BETS**
>
> ■ **Gibb's Lighthouse.** Make the climb to the top, where the reward is an expansive view of the inlets and harbors.
>
> ■ **Bermuda Maritime Museum.** Absorb Bermuda's nautical and military history in this Royal Navy Dockyard museum.
>
> ■ **St. George's.** Attend the pierside show hosted by the town crier, where gossips and nagging wives are drenched in a dunking stool.

ST. GEORGE'S

The settlement of Bermuda began in what is now the town of St. George nearly 400 years ago, when the *Sea Venture* was shipwrecked on Bermuda's treacherous reefs on its way to the colony of Jamestown, Virginia. No trip to Bermuda is complete without a visit to this historic town and UNESCO World Heritage Site.

★ **Bermuda National Trust Museum at the Globe Hotel.** This building was erected in 1700. During the American Civil War, Confederate Major Norman Walker was stationed in the building, where he coordinated the flow of guns, ammunition, and war supplies through Union blockades in American ports. The house saw service as the Globe Hotel during the mid-19th century and became a National Trust property in 1951. ✉ *32 Duke of York St.* ☎ *441/297–1423* ⊕ *www.bnt.bm* ✉ *$5; $10 combination ticket includes admission to Tucker House and Verdmont* ☉ *Nov.–Mar., Wed.–Sat. 10–4; Apr.–Oct., Mon.–Sat. 10–4.*

Bermudian Heritage Museum. The history, trials, and accomplishments of black Bermudians are highlighted in this converted 1840s warehouse. A model of the slave ship *Enterprise* is part of a display that describes how the ship, with its load of human "cargo," was blown off its course from Virginia to South Carolina in 1835; it landed in Bermuda, where slavery had already been abolished, so most of the slaves accepted freedom in Bermuda. ✉ *Water and Duke of York Sts.* ☎ *441/297–4126* ✉ *$4* ☉ *Tues.–Sat. 10–3.*

★ **Ordnance Island.** A splendid bronze statue of Sir George Somers dominates the island. The dunking stool is a replica of the one used to dunk gossips, nagging wives, and suspected witches. Demonstrations are sometimes given, although volunteers report that getting dunked is no picnic. Also on the island is the *Deliverance II*, a replica of one of two ships—the other was the *Patience*—built by the survivors of the 1609 wreck of the *Sea Venture* to carry them to Jamestown, Virginia, their original destination. ⊠*Across from King's Sq.* ☎*441/297–1459* ⬚*$3* ☉*Apr.–Oct., weekdays 9:30–5.*

Fodor'sChoice ★ **St. Peter's Church.** Because parts of this church date back to 1620, it holds the distinction of being the oldest continuously operating Anglican church in the western hemisphere. It was not the first church to stand on this site, however. It replaced a 1612 structure of posts and palmetto leaves that was destroyed in a storm. The present church was extended in 1713, and the galleries on either side were added in 1833. ⊠*33 Duke of York St.* ☎*441/297–2459* ⬤*www.anglican.bm* ⬚*Donations accepted* ☉*Mon.–Sat. 10–4, Sun. service at 11:15.*

★ **Tucker House.** Constructed out of native limestone, Tucker House is typical of many early Bermudian houses. It was built in 1711 for a merchant who used the basement as storage space for his wares, and it was originally close to the shore—landfill has since moved the water back. The house is at the corner of Barber's Alley, named for Joseph Haine Rainey, a freed slave from South Carolina who fled to Bermuda at the outbreak of the American Civil War and made his living here as a barber. After the war, Rainey returned home and, in 1870, became the first black man to be elected to the U.S. House of Representatives. ⊠*5 Water St.* ☎*441/297–0545* ⬤*www.bnt.bm* ⬚*$5; $10 combination ticket includes admission to National Trust Museum in Globe Hotel and Verdmont* ☉*Nov.–Mar., Wed.–Sat.; Apr.–Oct., Mon.–Sat. 10–4.*

ELSEWHERE ON THE ISLAND

☾ Fodor'sChoice ★ **Bermuda Aquarium, Museum and Zoo.** The aquarium has always been a pleasant diversion, but thanks to an ambitious expansion project it has become truly great. The 145,000-gallon tank holding the North Rock Exhibit, in the main gallery, gives you a diver's view of Bermuda's famed living coral reefs and colorful marine life. ⊠*40 N. Shore Rd., Flatts Village, Hamilton Parish* ☎*441/293–2727* ⬤*www.bamz.org* ⬚*$10* ☉*Daily 9–5, last admission at 4; North Rock dive talk and seal feeding 1:10 daily Apr.–Sept.; Oct.–Mar., weekends only.*

☾ Fodor'sChoice ★ **Bermuda Maritime Museum and Dolphin Quest.** Inside Bermuda's largest fort, built between 1837 and 1852, the Maritime Museum exhibits its collections in six old stone munitions warehouses, which surround the parade grounds and the Keep Pond. On top of the hill is the Commissioner's House, an unusual cast-iron building constructed from 1823 to 1828 in England and shipped to Bermuda for the chief administrator of the Dockyard.

The Maritime Museum's most popular attraction is **Dolphin Quest** (☎*441/234–4464* ⬤*www.dolphinquest.org*) within the fortress's historic keep. Several programs designed for adults and/or children age five and older let you get into the water and touch, play with, and swim alongside dolphins. ⊠*Maritime Museum, Dockyard* ☎*441/234–1418* ⬤*www.bmm.bm* ⬚*$10; Dolphin Quest programs $60–$299* ☉*Daily 9:30–5, last admission 4.*

○ **Crystal Caves.** This fantastic cavern 120 feet underground, which was
Fodor'sChoice discovered in 1907, has spectacular stalactite formations. ⊠ *8 Crys-*
★ *tal Caves Rd., off Wilkinson Ave., Bailey's Bay, Hamilton Parish*
⊞*441/293–0640* ⊕*www.bermudacaves.com* ⊡*One cave $14; com-*
bination ticket $20 ⊙*Daily 9:30–4:30, last combination tour at 4.*

○ **Fort St. Catherine.** This restored fortress is one of the most impressive
★ on the island. The original fort was built around 1613, but it was
remodeled and enlarged at least five times. As you travel through the
tunnels, you'll come across some startlingly lifelike figures tucked into
niches. ⊠*15 Coot Pond Rd., St. George's Parish* ⊞*441/297–1920*
⊡*$5* ⊙*Daily 10–4.*

○ **Gibb's Hill Lighthouse.** The second cast-iron lighthouse ever built soars
★ above Southampton Parish. Designed in London and opened in 1846,
the tower stands 117 feet high and 362 feet above the sea. It's a long
haul up the 185 spiral stairs, but you can stop to catch your breath at
platforms along the way, where photographs and drawings of the lighthouse divert your attention. ⊠*68 St. Anne's Rd., Southampton Parish*
⊞*441/238–8069* ⊕*www.bermudalighthouse.com* ⊡*$2.50* ⊙*Daily*
9–5. Closed Feb.

Fodor'sChoice **Paget Marsh.** This small, easily walkable slice of unspoiled native Ber-
★ muda is just minutes from bustling Hamilton. Listen for the cries of the
native and migratory birds who visit this natural wetland, jointly owned
and preserved by the Bermuda National Trust and the Bermuda Audubon Society. ⊠*Lover's La., Paget Parish* ⊞*441/236–6483* ⊕*www.bnt.*
bm ⊡*Free* ⊙*Daily dawn–dusk.*

○ **Verdmont.** Though it was used as a home until the mid-20th century, the
★ house has had virtually no structural changes since it was built in about
1710. Verdmont holds a notable collection of historic furnishings. Some
are imported from England—such as the early-19th-century piano—
but most of the furniture is 18th-century cedar, crafted by Bermudian
cabinetmakers. ⊠*6 Verdmont La., off Collector's Hill, Smith's Parish*
⊞*441/236–7369* ⊕*www.bnt.bm* ⊡*$5; $10 combination ticket with*
Bermuda National Trust Museum in Globe Hotel and Tucker House
⊙*Nov.–Mar., Wed.–Sat. 10–4; Apr.–Oct., Tues.–Sat. 10–4.*

SHOPPING

Hamilton has the greatest concentration of shops in Bermuda, and Front
Street is its pièce de résistance. Lined with small, pastel-color buildings,
this most fashionable of Bermuda's streets houses sedate department
stores and snazzy boutiques, with several small arcades and shopping
alleys spinning away from it. A smart canopy shades the entrance to the
55 Front Street Group, which houses Crisson Jewellers. Modern But-
terfield Place has galleries and boutiques selling, among other things,
Louis Vuitton leather goods. The Emporium, a renovated building with
an atrium, has a range of shops, from antiques to souvenirs.

In **St. George's,** Water Street, Duke of York Street, Hunters Wharf, Pen-
no's Wharf, and Somers Wharf are the sites of numerous renovated
buildings that house branches of Front Street stores, as well as artisans'

studios. Historic King's Square offers little more than a couple of T-shirt and souvenir shops.

In the West End, **Somerset Village** has a few shops, but they hardly merit a special shopping trip. However, the **Clocktower Mall,** in a historic building at the Royal Naval Dockyard, has a few more shopping opportunities, including branches of Front Street shops and specialty boutiques. The **Dockyard** is also home to the Craft Market, the Bermuda Arts Centre, and Bermuda Clayworks.

ACTIVITIES

BICYCLING

The best and sometimes only way to explore Bermuda's nooks and crannies—its little hidden coves and 18th-century tribe roads—is by bicycle or motor scooter. A popular option for biking in Bermuda is the **Railway Trail,** a dedicated cycle path blissfully free of cars. Running intermittently the length of the old Bermuda Railway (old "Rattle 'n' Shake"), this trail is scenic, paved, and restricted to pedestrian and bicycle traffic. You can ask the staff at any bike-rental shop for advice on where to access the trail. **Wheels Cycles** (⊠ *Front St., near docks, Hamilton* ☎*441/292–2245* ⊕*www.bermuda.com/wheels*) has 13 branches all over the island, including one near the cruise-ship pier in Hamilton. You can rent mountain bikes for children and adults.

GOLF

Golf courses make up nearly 17% of the island's 21.6 square mi. The scenery on the courses is usually spectacular, with flowering trees and shrubs decked out in multicolor blossoms against a backdrop of brilliant blue sea and sky. The layouts are remarkably challenging, thanks to capricious ocean breezes, daunting natural terrain, and the clever work of world-class golf architects.

Fairmont Southampton Golf Club is known for its steep terrain. ⊠*Fairmont Southampton, South Rd., Southampton Parish* ☎*441/239–6952* ⊕*www. fairmont.com/southampton* 🏌*Greens fees $59 with mandatory cart.*

★ **Mid Ocean Club,** a classic 1921 Charles Blair Macdonald design revamped by Robert Trent Jones Sr. in 1953, is ranked as one of the top 50 courses outside the U.S. by *Golf Digest.* ⊠*Mid Ocean Dr., off S. Shore Rd., Tucker's Town* ☎*441/293–0330* ⊕*www.themidoceanclubbermuda. com* 🏌*Greens fees $210 ($70 when playing with a member). Nonmembers must be sponsored by a club member (your hotelier can arrange this); nonmember starting times available Mon., Wed., and Fri. until noon, except holidays. After noon, every second tee time is available to nonmembers. Caddies $30 per bag, single, or $35 per bag, double (tip not included). Cart rental $25 per person.*

St. George's Golf Club, short but daunting, dominates a secluded headland at the island's northeastern end. In 2005 the course revamped its greens, which are small and were perpetually thin from constant buffeting by salty air. ⊠*1 Park Rd., St. George's Parish* ☎*441/297–8353 pro shop, 441/234–4653 tee times* ⊕*www.stgeorgesgolf.bm* 🏌*Greens fees $90 including cart, sunset $70 including cart. The same fees apply to walking, which is not allowed on weekends and holidays until after 3* PM.

SNORKELING

Snorkeling cruises are generally offered from April through November. Smaller boats, which limit capacity to 10 to 16 passengers, offer more personal attention and focus more on the beautiful snorkeling areas themselves. Guides on such tours often relate interesting historical and ecological information about the island. Some larger boats take up to 40 passengers.

Jessie James Cruises (⊠ *47 Front St., Hamilton* ☎ *441/236–4804* ⊕ *www. jessiejames.bm*) offers half-day trips aboard the 31-foot glass-bottomed boat *Pisces*, which holds up to 17 people, cost $65, $45 for children (ages 8–10). The boat takes you to three different sites, including at least two shipwrecks.

4

BEACHES

☺ **Elbow Beach.** Swimming and bodysurfing are great at this beach, which
★ is bordered by the prime strand of sand reserved for guests of the Elbow Beach Hotel on the left, and the ultraexclusive Coral Beach Club beach area on the right. Protective coral reefs make the waters the safest on the island, and a good choice for families. A lunch wagon sells fast food and cold drinks during the day, and Mickey's beach bar (part of the Elbow Beach Hotel) is open for lunch and dinner, though it may be difficult to get a table. ⊠ *Off South Rd., Paget Parish* Ⓜ *Bus 2 or 7 from Hamilton.*

☺ **Horseshoe Bay Beach.** When locals say they're going to "the beach,"
Fodor'sChoice they're generally referring to Horseshoe Bay Beach, the island's most
★ popular. With clear water, a -m crescent of pink sand, a vibrant social scene, and the uncluttered backdrop of South Shore Park, Horseshoe Bay has everything you could ask of a Bermudian beach. A snack bar, changing rooms, beach-rental facilities, and lifeguards add to its appeal. The undertow can be strong, especially on the main beach. ⊠ *Off South Rd., Southampton Parish* ☎ *441/238–2651* Ⓜ *Bus 7 from Hamilton.*

Tobacco Bay Beach. The most popular beach near St. George's—about 15 minutes northwest of the town on foot—this small north-shore strand is huddled in a coral cove. Its beach house has a snack bar, equipment rentals, toilets, showers, changing rooms, and ample parking. It's a 10-minute hike from the bus stop in the town of St. George's, or you can flag down a St. George's Minibus Service van and ask for a lift ($2 per person). In high season the beach is busy, especially midweek, when the cruise ships are docked. ⊠ *Coot Pond Rd., St. George's Parish* ☎ *441/297–2756* Ⓜ *Bus 1, 3, 10, or 11 from Hamilton.*

WHERE TO EAT

$$–$$$ ✗ **Cafe Gió.** This is waterside dining at its best, with great views of St.
ITALIAN George's Harbor. It's not unusual to see hungry boaters pull up and
☺ tie their vessels alongside the restaurant's sundeck. The popular spot offers tasty Italian cuisine, with the addition of a few Asian dishes, in a pleasant, romantic setting. The fettuccine is good and the Caesar salad is great. ⊠ *36 Water St., St. George's* ☎ *441/297–1307* ▭ *MC, V.*

$$ ✕**Docksider.** Locals come to mingle at this sprawling Front Street sports
BRITISH bar. It's generally more popular as a drinking venue, as it can get quite overcrowded and rowdy. But if you want to catch the game on the big screen with everyone else, standard pub fare is available, as well as local fish. Go for the English beef pie, fish-and-chips, or a fish sandwich, and sip your dessert—a Dark 'n Stormy—out on the porch as you watch Bermuda stroll by. The pub has a good jukebox and there's often a DJ or a band on summer weekends. ⊠*121 Front St., Hamilton* ☎*441/296–3333* ▭*MC, V.*

BONAIRE (KRALENDIJK)

Vernon
O'Reilly
Ramesar

Starkly beautiful Bonaire is the consummate desert island. Surrounded by pristine waters, it is a haven for divers and snorkelers who flock here from around the world to take advantage of the excellent visibility, easily accessed reefs, and bountiful marine life. Bonaire is the most rustic of the three ABC islands and despite its dependence on tourism it manages to maintain its identity and simple way of life. There are many good restaurants, most of which are located within walking distance of the port. Most of the island's 14,000-some inhabitants live in and around Kralendijk, which must certainly qualify as one of the cutest and most compact capitals in the Caribbean. The best shopping is to be found along the very short stretch of road that constitutes "downtown." Bonaire's beaches tend to be small and rocky, but there is a nice stretch of sandy beach at Lac Bay. It is entirely possible to see almost all of the sights and sounds of the island in one day by taking one of the island tours on offer.

ESSENTIALS

Currency The NAf guilder (NAF 1.78 to US$1); U.S. currency is accepted almost everywhere on the island, and the island has several ATMs, particularly in Kralendijk.

Internet Bonaire Access (⊠*Harbourside Mall, Kralendijk* ☎*No phone*). **Cyber City** (⊠*City Café, Kaya Grandi 7, Kralendijk* ☎*599/717–8286*).

Telephones You can make international calls from from the Telbo central phone company office (next to the tourism office in Kralendijk), which is open 24 hours a day. The country code for Bonaire is 599; 717 is the exchange for every four-digit telephone number on the island. When making interisland calls, dial 717 plus the local four-digit number.

COMING ASHORE

One of the great benefits of Bonaire to cruise passengers is that the port is right in downtown Kralendijk. Ships usually tender passengers ashore. A four-minute walk takes you to most of the best shopping and restaurants on the island.

Bonaire lives for tourism, so upon the arrival of a cruise ship the locals are ready. Taxis wait right at the port and operate on fixed government rates. All the sights of Kralendijk are within easy walking distance, and

Bonaire

KEY

⬧ Beaches
◧ Dive Sites

0 ————— 4 miles
0 ————— 4 kilometers

Boca Kokalishi

Washington

Mt. Brandaris ▲

Playa Funchi ◧

Boca Slagbaai ◧

Main Park Enterance

Washington-Slagbaai National Park

Caribbean Sea

Fontein

Spelonk

Karpata ◧

Rappel ◧

Small Wall ◧

Bari Reef ◧

Something Special ◧

Lagoen

Boven Bolivia ◧

Antriol

Kralendijk
see inset map

Klein Bonaire

Forest ◧

Calabas Reef ◧

Windsock Steep ◧

Nikiboko

Flamingo Airport ✈

Angel City ◧

Alice in Wonderland ◧

Wanapa

Trans-World Radio Tower

Mangrove Forest

Cai ◯

Lac Bay Beach

Sorobon Beach ⬧

Slave Huts ⬧

Salt Flats

Pink Beach ◧

Flamingo Sanctuary

Willemstoren Lighthouse

Lacre Pt.

Inset map (Kralendijk):

Karel's Pier

K. Gob.
Nic. Debrot
K. J. N. F. Crane

Kaya L.D. Gerhardts

Harborside Mall ◆

Kaya Grandi
Kaya C. E. B. Hellmund

Kaya Simon Bolivar

Town Pier

Kaya Lulio A. Abraham

Stadium

South Pier

Fort Oranje ◆

Kaya G.F. Croes

Kaya Industria

---

a taxi ride to one of the larger resorts on the island will run between $9 and $12. A half-day island tour by taxi costs about $25 per hour for up to four passengers.

EXPLORING BONAIRE

Two routes, north and south from Kralendijk, the island's small capital, are possible on the 24-mi-long (39-km-long) island; either route will take from a few hours to a full day, depending on whether you stop to snorkel, swim, dive, or lounge. Those pressed for time will find that it's easy to explore the entire island in a day if stops are kept to a minimum.

Kralendijk. Bonaire's small, tidy capital city (population 3,000) is five minutes from the airport. The main drag, J.A. Abraham Boulevard, turns into **Kaya Grandi** in the center of town. Along it are most of the island's major stores, boutiques, and restaurants. Across Kaya Grandi, opposite the Littman jewelry store, is Kaya L.D. Gerharts, with several small supermarkets, a handful of snack shops, and some of the better restaurants. Walk down the narrow waterfront avenue called Kaya C.E.B. Hellmund, which leads straight to the **North and South piers.** In the center of town, the Harbourside Mall has chic boutiques. Along this route is **Ft. Oranje,** with its cannons. From December through April, cruise ships dock in the harbor once or twice a week. The diminutive ocher-and-white structure that looks like a tiny Greek temple is the **fish market**; local anglers no longer bring their catches here (they sell out of their homes these days), but you can find plenty of fresh produce brought over from Columbia and Venezuela. Pick up the brochure *Walking and Shopping in Kralendijk* from the tourist office to get a map and full listing of all the monuments and sights in the town.

⟲ **Rooi Lamoenchi Kunuku.** Owner
★ Ellen Herrera restored her family's homestead north of Lac Bay, in the Bonairean *kadushi* (cactus) wilderness, to educate tourists and residents about the history and tradition of authentic kunuku living and show

unspoiled terrain in two daily tours. You must make an appointment in advance and expect to spend a couple of hours. ⊠ *Kaya Suiza 23, Playa Baribe* ☎ *599/717–8490* ⊕ *www.webpagecur.com/rooilamoenchi* ⊠ *$20* ☺ *By appointment only.*

Salt Flats. You can't miss the salt flats—voluptuous white drifts that look something like mountains of snow. Harvested once a year, the "ponds" are owned by Cargill, Inc., which has reactivated the 19th-century salt industry with great success (one reason for that success is that the ocean on this part of the island is higher than the land—which makes irrigation a snap). Keep a lookout for the three 30-foot obelisks—white, blue, and red—that were used to guide the trade boats coming to pick up the salt. Look also in the distance across the pans to the abandoned solar saltworks that's now a designated **flamingo sanctuary**. With the naked eye you might be able to make out a pink-orange haze just on the horizon; with binoculars you will see a sea of bobbing pink bodies. The sanctuary is completely protected, and no entrance is allowed (flamingos are extremely sensitive to disturbances of any kind).

⟲ **Slave Huts.** The salt industry's gritty history is revealed in Rode Pan, the site of two groups of tiny slave huts. The white grouping is on the right side of the road, opposite the salt flats; the second grouping, called the red slave huts (though they appear yellow), stretches across the road toward the island's southern tip. During the 19th century, slaves working the salt pans by day crawled into these huts to rest. Each Friday afternoon they walked seven hours to Rincon to weekend with their families, returning each Sunday. Only very small people will be able to enter, but walk around and poke your head in for a look.

♻ **Washington–Slagbaai National Park.** Once a plantation producing divi-divi trees (the pods were used for tanning animal skins), aloe (used for medicinal lotions), charcoal, and goats, the park is now a model of conservation. It's easy to tour the 13,500-acre tropical desert terrain on the dirt roads. As befits a wilderness sanctuary, the well-marked, rugged routes force you to drive slowly enough to appreciate the animal life and the terrain. There are two hiking routes: the long one (22 mi [35.5 km]) is marked by yellow arrows, the short one (15 mi [24 km]) by green arrows. Goats and donkeys may dart across the road, and if you keep your eyes peeled you may catch sight of large iguanas camouflaged in the shrubbery. A useful guide to the park is available at the entrance for about $6. To get here, take the secondary road north from the town of Rincon. The Nature Fee for swimming and snorkeling also grants you free admission to this park. ☎599/717–8444 ⊕*www. washingtonparkbonaire.org ✉Free but requires payment of Nature Fee of $10* ⊗ *Daily 8–5; you must enter before 3.*

Willemstoren Lighthouse. Bonaire's first lighthouse was built in 1837 and is now automated (but closed to visitors). Take some time to explore the beach and notice how the waves, driven by the trade winds, play a crashing symphony against the rocks. Locals stop here to collect pieces of driftwood in spectacular shapes and to build fanciful pyramids from objects that have washed ashore.

SHOPPING

Although it is a relatively small town, Kralendijk offers a good range of high-end items like watches and jewelry at attractive prices. There are a number of souvenir shops offering T-shirts and trinkets lining the main street of Kaya Grandi.

★ **Atlantis** (⊠*Kaya Grandi 32B, Kralendijk* ☎599/717–7730) carries a large range of precious and semiprecious gems. The tanzanite collection is especially beautiful. You will also find Sector, Raymond Weil, and Citizen watches, among others, all at great savings. Since gold jewelry

★ is sold by weight here, it's an especially good buy. **Bon Tiki** (⊠*Kaya C. E. B. Hellmund 3, Kralendijk* ☎599/717–6877) sells unique works from Bonaire's finest artists. **JanArt Gallery** (⊠*Kaya Gloria 7, Kralendijk* ☎599/717–5246), on the outskirts of town, sells unique watercolor paintings, prints, and art supplies; artist Janice Huckaby also hosts art classes. Whatever you do, make a point of visiting **Jenny's Art** (⊠*Kaya Betico Croes 6, near post office, Kralendijk* ☎599/717–5004). Roam around her house, which is a replica of a traditional Bonaire town complete with her handmade life-size dolls and the skeletons of all her dead pets. Lots of fun (and sometimes kitschy) souvenirs made out of driftwood, clay, and shells are all handmade by Jenny. **Littman's** (⊠*Kaya Grandi 33, Kralendijk* ☎599/717–8160 ✉*Harbourside Mall, Kaya Grandi 31, Kralendijk* ☎599/717–2130) is an upscale jewelry and gift shop where many items are handpicked by owner Steven Littman on his regular trips to Europe. Look for Rolex, Omega, Cartier, and Tag Heuer watches; fine gold jewelry; antique coins; nautical sculptures; resort clothing; and accessories.

4

ACTIVITIES

BICYCLING

Bonaire is generally flat, so bicycles are an easy way to get around. Because of the heat it's essential to carry water if you're planning to cycle for any distance and especially if your plans involve exploring the deserted interior. There are more than 180 mi (290 km) of unpaved routes (as well as the many paved roads) on the island.

Cycle Bonaire (⊠ *Kaya Gobernador N. Debrot 77A, Kralendijk* ☎ *599/717–2229*) rents mountain bikes and gear (trail maps, water bottles, helmets, locks, repair and first-aid kits) for $20 a day or $100 for six days; half-day and full-day guided excursions start at $55, not including bike rental.

DIVING AND SNORKELING

Diving and snorkeling are almost a religion on Bonaire, and are by far the most popular activities for cruise passengers. Bonaire has some of the best reef diving this side of Australia's Great Barrier Reef. It takes only 5 to 25 minutes to reach many sites, the current is usually mild, and although some reefs have sudden, steep drops, most begin just offshore and slope gently downward at a 45-degree angle. General visibility runs 60 to 100 feet, except during surges in October and November. You can see several varieties of coral: knobby-brain, giant-brain, elkhorn, staghorn, mountainous star, gorgonian, and black.

☾ ★ **Larry's Shore and Wild Side Diving** (☎ *599/790–9156* ⊕ *www.larryswild sidediving.com*) is run by a former army combat diver and offers a variety of appealing options ranging from the leisurely to downright scary. This company has become an extremely popular choice, so try to book as early as possible. The **Mushi Mushi** (☎ *599/790–5399*) is a catamaran offering a variety of two- and three-hour cruises starting at $35 per person. It departs from the Bonaire Nautico Marina in downtown Kralendijk (opposite the restaurant It Rains Fishes).

BEACHES

Don't expect long stretches of glorious powdery sand. Bonaire's beaches are small, and though the water is blue (several shades of it, in fact), the sand isn't always white. Bonaire's National Parks Foundation requires all nondivers to pay a $10 annual Nature Fee in order to enter the water anywhere around the island (divers pay $25). The fee can be paid at most dive shops.

Klein Bonaire. Just a water-taxi hop across from Kralendijk, this little island offers picture-perfect white-sand beaches. The area is protected, so absolutely no development has been allowed. Make sure to pack everything before heading to the island, including water and an umbrella to hide under, because there are no refreshment stands, no changing facilities, and almost no shade to be found. Boats leave from the Town Pier, across from the City Café, and the round-trip water-taxi ride costs roughly $14 per person.

Lac Bay Beach. It's a bumpy drive (10 to 15 minutes on a dirt road) to get here, but you'll be glad when you arrive. It's a good spot for diving, snorkeling, and kayaking (as long as you bring your own), and there are public restrooms and a restaurant for your convenience. ⊠ *Off Kaminda Sorobon, Lac Cai.*

Windsock Beach. Near the airport (just off E. E. G. Boulevard), this pretty little spot, also known as Mangrove Beach, looks out toward the north side of the island and has about 200 yards of white sand along a rocky shoreline. It's a popular dive site, and swimming conditions are also good. ⊠ *Off E. E. G. Blvd., near Flamingo Airport.*

WHERE TO EAT

$$–$$$ ✕**City Café/City Restaurant.** This busy waterfront eatery is also one of
ECLECTIC   the most reliable nightspots on the island, so it's always hopping day or night. Breakfast, lunch, and dinner are served daily at reasonable prices. Seafood is always featured, as are a variety of sandwiches and salads. The pita sandwich platters are a good lunchtime choice for the budget challenged. Weekends, there's always live entertainment and dancing. ⊠ *Hotel Rochaline, Kaya Grandi 7, Kralendijk* ☎ *599/717–8286* ▤ *AE, MC, V.*

$$–$$$ ✕**Le Flamboyant.** This intimate restaurant offers good food at affordable
CONTINENTAL   prices. The cozy historic house—conveniently downtown—also has a
★   small gourmet food shop, espresso bar, and lovely cocktail bar. The main attraction is the tree-covered courtyard in the back. Lunch offers a selection of ample sandwiches and salads; dinner is mostly seafood and pastas. There's also a comprehensive vegetarian menu. ⊠ *Kaya Grandi 12, Kralendijk* ☎ *599/717–3919* ▤ *AE, MC, V* ⊙ *Closed Sun.*

CALICA (PLAYA DEL CARMEN), MEXICO

Marlise Kast   Just minutes away from Calica, Playa del Carmen has become one of Latin America's fastest-growing communities, with a pace almost as hectic as Cancún's. Hotels, restaurants, and shops multiply here faster than you can say "Kukulcán." Some are branches of Cancún establishments whose owners have taken up permanent residence in Playa—or who commute daily between the two places; others are owned by American and European expats who came here years ago, as early adopters. It makes for a varied, international community. Avenida 5, the first street in town parallel to the beach, is a long, colorfully tiled pedestrian walkway with shops, cafés, and street performers; small hotels and stores stretch north from this avenue. Avenida Juárez, running east–west from the highway to the beach, is the main commercial zone for the Riviera Maya corridor. Here locals visit the food shops, pharmacies, auto-parts and hardware stores, and banks that line the curbs. People traveling the coast by car usually stop here to stock up on supplies—its banks, grocery stores, and gas stations are the last ones until Tulum.

ESSENTIALS

Currency The Mexican peso (MX$13.82 to US$1). U.S. dollars and credit cards are widely accepted in the area, from the port to Playa del Carmen, but it's best to have pesos—and small bills—when you visit ruins, where cashiers often run out of change. There is no advantage to paying in dollars, but there may be an advantage to paying in cash.

Internet There are several Internet cafés on Avenida 5 in Playa del Carmen. **24 Com Center** (✉ *Av. 24, between Calle 1 and Calle 8, Playa del Carmen,* ☎ *984/803–5778*).

Telephones Most pay phones accept prepaid Ladatel cards, sold in 30-, 50-, or 100-peso denominations. To use the card, insert it in the pay phone's slot, dial 001 (for calls to the U.S.) or 01 (for calls within Mexico), followed by the area code and number. Credit is deleted from the card as you use it, and the balance is displayed on the small screen on the phone.

COMING ASHORE

The port at Calica, about 3 mi south of the town of Playa del Carmen (between Playa del Carmen and Xcarat), is small. Sometimes ships actually dock, and other times passengers are tendered to shore. There is a makeshift market at the port, where locals sell crafts. Beyond that, there is not much to do, and you'll need to head into Playa del Carmen proper to find restaurants and even tour operators. If you really want to shop, skip the vendors at the port and head to Playa del Carmen's

Avenida 5, where you can easily spend an afternoon browsing shops and enjoying restaurants.

Taxis and tour buses are available at the port to take you to Playa del Carmen and other destinations, but lines often form as passengers wait for taxis, so hurry to the front of the line if you really want to pack a lot of activity into your day. Your taxi will have you in Playa del Carmen or in Xcaret in under 10 minutes, but you'll pay a whopping $10 for the short trip.

EXPLORING CALICA

Muyil. This photogenic archaeological site at the northern end of the Reserva de la Biosfera Sian Ka'an is underrated. Once known as Chunyaxché, it's now called by its ancient name, Muyil (pronounced *mool-hill*). It dates from the late preclassic era, when it was connected by road to the sea and served as a port between Cobá and the Mayan centers in Belize and Guatemala. The most notable site at Muyil today is the remains of the 56-foot **Castillo**—one of the tallest on the Quintana Roo coast—at the center of a large acropolis. During excavations of the Castillo, jade figurines representing the moon and fertility goddess Ixchel were found. Recent excavations at Muyil have uncovered some smaller structures. The ruins stand near the edge of a deep-blue lagoon and are surrounded by almost impenetrable jungle—so be sure to bring bug repellent. You can drive down a dirt road on the side of the ruins to swim or fish in the lagoon. The bird-watching is also exceptional here. ✛ *15 mi (24 km) south of Tulum, 53 mi (86 km) south of Playa del Carmen ⊕muyil.smv.org ≅$4, free Sun. ⊙Daily 8–5.*

Playa del Carmen. Once upon a time, Playa del Carmen was a fishing village with a ravishing deserted beach. The villagers fished and raised coconut palms to produce copra, and the only foreigners who ventured here were beach bums. That was a long time ago, however. These days, although the beach is still delightful—alabaster-white sand, turquoise-blue waters—it's far from deserted. In fact, Playa has become one of Latin America's fastest-growing communities, with a population of more than 135,000 and a pace almost as hectic as Cancún's. The ferry pier, where the hourly boats arrive from and depart for Cozumel, is another busy part of town. The streets leading from the dock have shops, restaurants, cafés, a hotel, a basketball court, and food stands. If you take a stroll north from the pier along the beach, you'll find the serious sun worshippers. On the pier's south side is the edge of the sprawling Playacar complex. The development is a labyrinth of residences and all-inclusive resorts bordered by an 18-hole championship golf course. ✛ *3 mi (5 km) north of Calica.*

The excellent 32-acre **Xaman Ha Aviary** (⊠*Paseo Xaman-Ha, Mza 13-A Lote 1, Playacar* ☎984/873–0330), in the middle of the Playacar development, is home to more than 30 species of native birds. It's open daily 9–5, and admission is $20.

The **Tres Ríos Eco Park** (⊠*Carretera Cancún–Tulum, Km 54* ☎998/850–4849 ≅$18 ⊙*Daily 9–5*), located just 7 mi (11 km) north of Playa, is a great place to get a sense of this region's ecology and natural wonders.

Three rivers converge in the expansive 800-acre property (a lush rarity in the dry Yucatán landscape), and you can explore them by kayaking, canoeing, or snorkeling. You can also take horseback rides along the beach or bike along jungle paths. Keep an eye out for birds and animals. If you're lucky, you might spot a white-fronted parrot, or even a coati. Day Passes can be be purchased at the main entrance or at Hacienda Tres Rios Resort, located near the park gate.

Tulum. Tulum (pronounced tool-*lum*) is the Yucatán Peninsula's most-visited Mayan ruin. This means you have to share the site with roughly half of the tourist population of Quintana Roo on any given day, even if you arrive early. Though most of the architecture is of unremarkable postclassic (1000–1521) style, the amount of attention that Tulum receives is not entirely undeserved. Its location by the blue-green Caribbean is breathtaking. Tulum is one of the few Mayan cities known to have been inhabited when the conquistadores arrived in 1518. In the 16th century it functioned as a safe harbor for trade goods from rival Mayan factions; it was considered neutral territory, where merchandise could be stored and traded in peace. When the Spaniards arrived, they forbade the Mayan traders from sailing the seas, and commerce among the Maya died. Tulum has long held special significance for the Maya. A key city in the League of Mayapán (AD 987–1194), it was never conquered by the Spaniards, although it was abandoned about 75 years after the conquest. For 300 years thereafter it symbolized the defiance of an otherwise subjugated people; it was one of the last outposts of the Maya during their insurrection against Mexican rule in the War of the Castes, which began in 1846. Uprisings continued intermittently until 1935, when the Maya ceded Tulum to the government. ⊠*Carretera 307 Km 133, Tulum* ☎*983/837–2411* ☜*$5 entrance, $3 parking, $3 video fee, $1 shuttle from parking to ruins* ☉*Daily 8–5.*

☾ **Xcaret.** Once a sacred Mayan city and port, Xcaret (pronounced *ish-car-et*) is now a 250-acre ecological theme park on a gorgeous stretch of coastline. It's the coast's most heavily advertised attraction, billed as "nature's sacred paradise," with its own network of buses, its own published magazines, and a whole collection of stores. The park has done a good job showcasing, celebrating, and helping to preserve the natural environment of the Caribbean coast. ■TIP➜**You can easily spend at least a full day here; there's tons to see and do.** Among the most popular attractions are the Paradise River raft tour that takes you on a winding, watery journey through the jungle; the Butterfly Pavilion; and an ocean-fed aquarium where you can see local sealife drifting through coral heads and sea fans without getting wet. The list of

FodorsChoice
★

CALICA BEST BETS

■ **A Day at Xcaret.** Particularly for families, this ecological theme park is a great way to spend the day.

■ **Beaches.** The beaches in the Riviera Maya are stellar.

■ **Diving.** From Playa del Carmen, you're a short hop from some of the Yucatan's best dive sites.

■ **Shopping.** Playa del Carmen's Avenida 5 can easily keep you occupied for your day in port if you are a shopaholic.

Xcaret's attractions goes on and on. The entrance fee covers only access to the grounds and the exhibits; all other activities and equipment—from horseback riding to lockers to snorkel and swim gear—are extra. You can buy tickets from any travel agency or major hotel along the coast. ☎984/871–5200, 998/883–0470 in Cancun ⊕www.xcaret.com ☞$59 ⊘Daily 8:30 AM–10 PM.

SHOPPING

Playa del Carmen's Avenida 5 between Calles 4 and 10 is the best place to shop along the coast. Boutiques sell folk art and textiles from around Mexico, and clothing stores carry lots of sarongs and beachwear made from Indonesian batiks. A shopping area called Calle Corazon, between Calles 12 and 14, has a pedestrian street, art galleries, restaurants, and boutiques.

ACTIVITIES

DIVING

The PADI and SSI-affiliated **Abyss** (⊠Av. 1 between Calles 10 and 12 ☎984/873–2164 ⊕www.abyssdiveshop.com) offers introductory courses and dive trips ($50 for one tank, $70 for two tanks). The oldest shop in town, **Tank-Ha Dive Center** (⊠Calle 10 between Av 5 and 10 Playa del Carmen ☎984/873–0302 ⊕www.tankha.com), has PADI-certified teachers and runs diving and snorkeling trips to the reefs and caverns. A one-tank dive costs $45; for a two-tank trip it's $75. Dive packages are also available.

GOLF

Playa del Carmen's golf course is an 18-hole, par-72 championship course designed by Robert von Hagge. The greens fee is $180; there's also a special twilight fee of $120. Information is available from the **Casa Club de Golf** (☎984/873–0624 or 998/881–6088).

WHERE TO EAT

$$
ECLECTIC
★ ✕**Babe's Noodles & Bar.** Photos and paintings of old Hollywood pinup models decorate the walls and are even laminated onto the bar of this Swedish-owned Asian restaurant, known for its fresh and interesting fare. Everything is cooked to order—no prefab dishes here. Try the spring rolls with peanut sauce, or the sesame noodles, made with chicken or pork, veggies, lime, green curry, and ginger. In the Buddha Garden you can sip a mojito or sit at the bar and watch the crowds on nearby 5th Avenue. The lemonade, blended with ice and mint, is incredibly refreshing. If the place is crowded, head to their second location on Av 5 between Calles 28 and 30. ⊠Calle 10 between Avs. 5 and 10 ☎984/120–2592 ⊠Av. 5 between Calles 28 and 30 ☎984/803–0056 ▭No credit cards.

¢–$
CAFÉ
✕**Hot.** This café is a great place to get an early start before a full day of sightseeing, shopping—or even sunbathing. It opens at 7 AM and whips up great egg dishes (the chili-and-cheese omelet is particularly good),

baked goods, and hot coffee. Everything, including delicious bagels and bread, is made on the premises. Salads and sandwiches are available at lunch. ⊠ *Calle 14 Norte, between Avs. 5 and 10* ☎ *984/116–3020* 🖃 *No credit cards.*

CARTAGENA, COLOMBIA

Richard
McColl

Ever wondered what the "Spanish Main" refers to? This is it. Colombia's Caribbean coast invokes ghosts of conquistadors, pirates, and missionaries journeying to the New World in search of wealth, whether material or spiritual. Anchoring this shore is Cartagena—poetically, officially *Cartagena de Indias* (Cartagena of the Indies)—founded in 1533 and one of Latin America's magnificent colonial cities. Gold and silver passed through here en route to Spain, making the city an obvious target for pirates, hence the construction of Cartagena's trademark walls and fortresses. Outside the *Ciudad Amurallada* (walled city) lie less historic (but no less interesting) beaches and water excursions. If Colombia conjures up images of drug lords and paramilitary guerillas, think again; security is quite visible (without being oppressive) here in the country's top tourist destination. Take the same precautions you'd follow visiting any city of 800,000 people, and you should have a grand time.

ESSENTIALS

Currency The Colombian peso (COP 2,457 to US$1). In Colombia, peso prices are denoted with the "$" sign, too. If they carry a lot of zeros, they likely are not dollar prices, but always ask. ATMs are ubiquitous around town.

Internet Upon arrival or before departure, you can check your e-mail at the bank of computers in the Terminal de Cruceros. In town, you can check your e-mail at **CaribeNet** (⊠ *Calle Santo Domingo 3-54*).

Precautions Security is tighter in Cartagena than elsewhere in Colombia, so you certainly can navigate the city on your own. (Knowing some Spanish helps.) However, the scarcity of English speakers or English signage at the city's tourist attractions and the persistence of vendors, street touts, and the periodic con artist—they *do* speak English—mean that many cruise passengers opt for the reassurance of an organized shore excursion. If you set out on your own, under no circumstances should you deal with anyone who approaches you on the street offering to change money; rip-offs are guaranteed.

Telephones The Terminal de Cruceros has ample phones for your use. Local numbers in Cartagena have seven digits. For international calls, dial 009 followed by country and area codes and local number. The U.S. mobile carrier AT&T offers roaming options in this region of Colombia for calls back to the United States; if you have a tri-band GSM phone it should work.

COMING ASHORE

Cruise ships dock at the modern Terminal de Cruceros (cruise terminal) on Isla de Manga, an island connected by a bridge to the historic city center, about 2 mi (3 km) northwest of the docks. You'll find telephones, Internet computers, and a duty-free shop in the terminal.

Cartagena

A small army of taxis waits in front of the terminal. Expect to pay 5,000 pesos for the 10-minute drive to the walled city; about 8,000 pesos will get you to the nearby beaches at Bocagrande. Drivers are all too happy to take you on your own do-it-yourself guided tour. Most charge around 10,000 to 15,000 pesos for an hour of waiting time. There's little need to rent a car here. Cartagena, at least that of tourist interest, is so compact, and walking the labyrinth of cobblestone streets in the Old City is far more enjoyable than driving them.

EXPLORING CARTAGENA

Numbers in the margin correspond to points of interest on the Cartagena map.

Nothing says Cartagena quite like a ride in a horse-drawn carriage, or *coche*, as it known locally. Drivers are a wealth of information about Cartagena, and many do speak English. The downside for you is that the rides begin near dusk—it's a far cooler time of the day, after all—and your need to be back on ship may not coincide with that schedule. Do check. You can pick up carriages at many places, including the Plaza de los Coches, near the Puerta del Reloj in the walled city, or the Hotel Caribe in Bocagrande. Expect to pay around $170 to $200 for a two-hour tour (this kind of excursion is best when the cost is split among a group).

Castillo de San Felipe de Barajas. Designed by Antonio de Arévalo in 1639, the Fort of St. Philip's steep-angled brick and concrete battlements were arranged so that if part of the castle were conquered, the rest could still be defended. A maze of tunnels, minimally lit today to allow for spooky exploration, still connects vital points of the fort. Acoustics were perfect in the tunnels, allowing occupants of the fort to hear the footsteps of the approaching enemy. You can walk here from the walled city in about 30 minutes; an 8,000-peso taxi ride is an easier option. ⊠*Avenida Pedro de Heredia at Carrera 17* ☎*575/666–4790* ⚟*13,000 pesos* ⊙*Daily 8–6.*

> ## CARTAGENA BEST BETS
>
> ■ **Cruise the Harbor.** A boat trip around the city's inner bay allows to you appreciate the city's formidable walls and fortresses.
>
> ■ **Islas del Rosario.** The beaches of nearby Islas del Rosario are an hour away by boat.
>
> ■ **Ride a Coche.** Take the quintessential horse-and-buggy ride through the streets.
>
> ■ **Walk Las Murallas.** Walking the city's massive stone walls is a favorite tourist pastime.
>
> ■ **Visit Palacio de la Inquisición.** Cartagena's most-visited sight is this historic—and creepy—center for the Spanish Inquisition.

Catedral. Any Latin American city centers on its cathedral and main square. Cartagena's Plaza de Bolívar is a shady place from which to admire the 16th-century cathedral, with its colorful bell tower and 20th-century dome. Inside is a massive gilded altar. A statue of South American liberator Simón Bolívar stands watch over his namesake plaza. ⊠*Plaza de Bolívar.*

Fodor'sChoice   **Cerro de la Popa.** For spectacular views of Cartagena, ascend this hill,
★   the highest ground around. Because of its strategic location, the 17th-century hilltop convent did double duty as a fortress during the colonial era. It now houses a museum and a chapel dedicated to the Virgin de la Candelaria, Cartagena's patron saint. There is no public transport to get you here; taxis charge about 6,000 pesos. ⊠*2 mi (3 km) southeast of Ciudad Amurallada* ☎*575/666–2331* ⚟*6,000 pesos* ⊙*Daily 8:30–5.*

Las Murallas. Cartagena survived only because of its walls, and its murallas remain today the city's most distinctive feature. Repeated sacking by pirates and foreign invaders convinced the Spaniards of the need to enclose the region's most important port. Construction began about 1600 and was completed in 1796. Walking along the thick walls remains one of Cartagena's time-honored tourist pastimes. The Puerta del Reloj is the principal gate to the innermost sector of the Ciudad Amurallada. Its four-sided clock tower was a relatively late addition (1888), and has become the best-known symbol of the city. ⊠*Area bounded by Bahía de las Ánimas, Caribbean Sea, and Laguna de San Lázaro* ⊙*24 hrs.*

Museo del Oro y Arqueología. The Gold and Archaeological Museum, a project of Colombia's Central Bank, displays an assortment of artifacts culled from the Sinús, an indigenous group that lived in the region 2,000 years ago. ⊠ *Carrera 4 No. 33–26* ☎ *575/660–0778* 🕾 *Free* 🕙 *Tues.– Fri. 10–1 and 3–7, Sat. 10–1 and 2–5.*

Fodor's Choice ★ **Palacio de la Inquisición.** Arguably Cartagena's most-visited tourist attraction documents the darkest period in the city's history. The 1770 Palace of the Inquisition served as the second headquarters of the repressive arbiters of political and spiritual orthodoxy who once exercised jurisdiction over northern South America. Although the museum also displays benign colonial and pre-Columbian artifacts, everyone heads to the ground floor to "Eeeewww" over the implements of torture—racks and thumbscrews, to name but two. ⊠ *Carrera 4 No. 33–26* ☎ *575/664–7381* 🕾 *3,000 pesos* 🕙 *Daily 9–5.*

4

SHOPPING

Think "Juan Valdez" if you're looking for something to take the folks back home. Small bags of fine Colombian coffee, the country's signature souvenir, are available in most tourist-oriented shops. Colombia also means emeralds, and you'll find plenty in the jewelry shops on or near Calle Pantaleón, beside the cathedral. Don't forget the duty-free shop in the Terminal de Cruceros for those last-minute purchases. The name of **Las Bóvedas** (⊠ *North of Plaza Fernández de Madrid*) translates as "the vaults," and the city's best crafts shops occupy this row of storerooms built in the 18th century to hold gunpowder and other military essentials. Your stockpile here will consist of hats, hammocks and leather goods.

ACTIVITIES

DIVING

Coral reefs line the coast south of Cartagena, although warm-water currents have begun to erode them in recent years. There is still good diving to be had in the Islas del Rosario, an archipelago of 27 coral islands about 21 mi (35 km) southwest of the city. **Buzos de Barú** (⊠ *Laguito Edificio Belmar L-103* ☎ *575/665–7675* ⊕ *www.buzosdebaru. com*) organizes snorkeling trips to the Islas del Rosario and scuba diving at underwater wrecks, as well as dive instruction.

BEACHES

For white sand and palm trees, your best bet is **Playa Blanca,** about 15 minutes away by boat. Many people opt for a visit to the **Islas del Rosario,** a verdant archipelago surrounded by aquamarine waters and coral reefs. Tour boats leave from the Muelle de los Pegasos, the pier flanked by statues of two flying horses that is just outside the city walls. Plenty of men with boats will also offer to take you on the one-hour journey. A final option is **Bocagrande,** the resort area on a 3 mi- (5 km-) long peninsula south of the walled city. High-rise hotels and condos front the gray-sand beach. It gets quite crowded and is very lively, but Bocagrande is probably not the Caribbean beach of which you've always dreamed.

WHERE TO EAT

$–$$ ✕ **Café San Pedro.** Although it serves Colombian fare, this restaurant's
CAFÉ   eclectic menu includes dishes from Thailand, Italy, and Japan. You can
also drop by to have a drink and to watch the activity on the plaza
from one of the outdoor tables. ⊠ *Plaza San Pedro* ☎ *575/664–5121
or 575/664–1433* ⊟ *DC, MC, V* ⊗ *Closed Sun.*

$–$$ ✕ **Paco's.** Heavy beams, rough terra-cotta walls, wooden benches, and
LATIN AMERICAN   tunes from an aging Cuban band are the hallmarks of this downtown
eatery. Drop by for a drink and some tapas, or try the more substantial
langostinos a la sifú (lobsters fried in batter). You can sit in the dining
room or outside on the Plaza Santo Domingo. ⊠ *Plaza Santo Domingo*
☎ *575/664–4294* ⊟ *V.*

COLÓN, PANAMA

David
Dudenhoefer

When you consider the decades it took to build the canal, not to mention the lives lost and government failures and triumphs involved during its construction, it comes as no surprise that the Panama Canal
is often called the 8th Wonder of the Modern World. Best described
as an aquatic bridge, the Panama Canal connects the Caribbean Sea
with the Pacific Ocean by raising ships up and over Central America,
through artificially created Gatún Lake, the highest point at 85 feet
above sea level, and then lowering them back to sea level by using a
series of locks, or water steps. A masterful engineering feat, three pairs
of locks—Gatún, Pedro Miguel, and Miraflores—utilize gravity to fill
and drain as ships pass through chambers 1,000 feet long by 110 feet
wide that are "locked" by doors weighing 80 tons apiece, yet actually
float into position. Most cruise ships pass through the canal seasonally,
when repositioning from one coast to the other; however, partial transits
have become an increasingly popular "destination" on regularly scheduled 10- and 11-night Caribbean itineraries. These loop cruises enter
the canal from the Caribbean Sea and sail into Gatún Lake, where they
remain for a few hours as passengers are tendered ashore for excursions.
Ships then pass back through the locks, returning to the Caribbean and
stopping at either Cristobal Pier or Colón 2000 Pier to retrieve passengers at the conclusion of their tours.

A day transiting the canal's Gatún Locks begins before dawn as your
passenger ship passes through *Bahia Limon* and lines up with dozens of
other vessels to await its turn to enter. Before your ship can proceed, two
pilots and a narrator will board. The sight of a massive cruise ship being
raised dozens of feet into the air by water is so mesmerizing that passengers eagerly crowd all forward decks at the first lock. If you don't find a
good viewing spot, head for the rear decks where there is usually more
room and the view is just as intriguing. If you remain aboard, as many
passengers do, you'll find plenty of room up front later in the day as your
ship retraces its path down to the sea. Due to the tight scheduling of the
day's activities—it takes at least 90 minutes for a ship to pass through
Gatún Locks—passengers who wish to go ashore early in the day are
advised to sign up for one of the many available shore excursions.

ESSENTIALS

Currency The U.S. dollar, called the balboa, is the currency in Panama; the country does mint its own coins.

Internet There's an Internet café at the Colón 2000 Pier.

Telephones You'll find telephones inside Colón's cruise terminal, where you can purchase phone cards, which are a handy and inexpensive way to make calls.

COMING ASHORE

Colón, Panama's second-largest city, has little to offer of historic interest and is simply a jumping-off point to the rain forest and a wide variety of organized tours. Infrequent cruise itineraries may include a day docked in Colón, rather than a partial canal transit. However, no matter how much time your ship spends in Colón, it is usually easier to take an organized shore excursion, and that's what we recommend. If you don't want to go on a ship-sponsored shore excursion, taxi drivers also await ship arrivals, and some can be acceptable private guides for $70 to $100 per day if you just want to explore Portabelo or San Lorenzo; however, as in any foreign port, before setting out with any unofficial car and driver, you should set a firm price and agree upon an itinerary as well as look over the vehicle carefully.

Although entry time into the canal is always approximate, passenger ships have priority and most pass through Gatún Locks early in the morning. Passengers booked on shore excursions begin the tendering process soon after the ship sets anchor, which can be as early as 8:30 AM. Alternatives to excursions offered by your cruise ship are available from independent tour operators that can be arranged in advance through Web sites or, possibly, travel agents. You will likely be informed that Panamanian regulations restrict passengers going ashore in Gatún Lake to only those who have booked the cruise line's excursions; however, anyone who has a shore-excursion reservation with a local company should be able to leave the vessel. Before making independent tour arrangements, confirm with your cruise line that you will be allowed to go ashore after presenting your private tour confirmation to the shore-excursion staff on board the ship.

Upon completion of either full or partial canal transits, cruise ships generally dock at either Cristobal Pier or Colón 2000 Pier late in the afternoon, where they may remain for several hours. Passengers who remained on board throughout the canal passage have the opportunity to go ashore, and land tours end at the terminals where passengers rejoin the ship. All of Colón is considered a high-crime area, and pickpockets have been known to strike even in the seemingly secure areas of the cruise-ship terminals. If you go ashore, you are well advised to leave jewelry and other valuables aboard your ship and carry only the cash you need.

COLÓN BEST BETS

■ **Explore an Embera Village.** You'll travel through Chagres National Park by dugout canoe.

■ **Kayak on Gatún Lake.** You can paddle among the many islands and mangrove forests.

■ **Panama Railway.** Take a train trip to Panama City for a quick sightseeing tour (you can come back by taxi to save some time).

■ **Portobelo.** Visit historic Panamanian forts.

■ **Rain Forest Aerial Tram.** Travel to Gamboa Rainforest Resort and see the rain forest canopy from above.

EXPLORING THE PANAMA CANAL ZONE

Colón. The provincial capital of Colón, beside the canal's Atlantic entrance, has clearly seen better days, as the architecture of its older buildings attests. Its predominantly Afro-Caribbean population has long had a vibrant musical scene, and in the late 19th and early 20th centuries Colón was a relatively prosperous town. But it spent the second half of the 20th century in steady decay, and things have only gotten worse in the 21st century. For the most part, the city is a giant slum, with unemployment at 15% to 20% and crime on the rise.

⚠ **Travelers who explore Colón on foot are simply asking to be mugged,** and the route between the train station and the bus terminal is especially notorious; do all your traveling in a taxi or rental car. If you do the Panama Railway trip on your own without a tour company, take one of the shuttle vans or hire a taxi to the train station.

Seven miles (12 km) south of Colón are the **Esclusas de Gatún** *(Gatún Locks),* a triple lock complex that's nearly a mile long and raises and lowers ships the 85 feet between sea level and Gatún Lake. There's a small viewing platform at the locks and a simple visitor center that's nothing compared to the center at Miraflores Locks. However, the sheer magnitude of the Gatún Locks is impressive, especially when packed with ships. You have to cross the locks on a swinging bridge to get to San Lorenzo and the **Represa Gatún** *(Gatún Dam),* which holds the water in Gatún Lake. At 1½ mi long, it was the largest dam in the world when it was built, a title it held for several decades. Get there by taking the first left after crossing the locks.

Fuerte San Lorenzo. Perched on a cliff overlooking the mouth of the Chagres River are the ruins of the ancient Spanish *fort* destroyed by pirate Henry Morgan in 1671. The Spaniards built Fort San Lorenzo in 1595, in an effort to protect the South American gold they were shipping down the Chagres River, which was first carried along the Camino de Cruces from Panamá Viejo. The fortress's commanding position and abundant cannons weren't enough of a deterrent for Morgan, whose men managed to shoot flaming arrows into the fort, causing a fire that set off stored gunpowder and forced the Spanish troops to surrender. In the 1980s UNESCO restored the fort to its current condition, which is pretty sparse—it hardly compares to the extensive colonial ruins of Portobelo. Nevertheless, the setting is gorgeous, and the view from that promontory of the blue-green Caribbean, the coast, and the vast jungle behind it is breathtaking. ⊠ *14 mi (23 km) northwest of Gatún Locks* 🕾*No phone* 🎟*Free* 🕙*Daily 8–4.*

Lago Gatún (Gatún Lake). Covering about 163 square mi, an area about the size of the island nation Barbados, Gatún Lake extends northwest from Parque Nacional Soberanía to the locks of Gatún, just south of Colón. The lake was created when the U.S. government dammed the Chagres River, between 1907 and 1910, so that boats could cross the isthmus at 85 feet above sea level. By creating the lake, the United States saved decades of digging that a sea-level canal would have required. It took several years for the rain to fill the convoluted valleys, turning hilltops into islands and killing much forest (some trunks still tower over the water nearly a century later). When it was completed, Gatún Lake was the largest man-made lake in the world. The canal route winds through its northern half, past several forest-covered islands (the largest is Barro Colorado, one of the world's first biological reserves). The lake itself is home to crocodiles, manatees, and peacock bass, a species introduced from South America and popular with fishermen. Fishing charters for bass, snook, and tarpon are out of Gamboa.

★ **Portobelo.** Portobelo is an odd mix of colonial fortresses, clear waters, lushly forested hills, and an ugly little town of cement-block houses crowded higgledy-piggledy amid the ancient walls. It holds some of Panama's most interesting colonial ruins, with rusty cannons still lying in wait for an enemy assault, and is a UNESCO World Heritage Site, together with San Lorenzo.

The forested hills that rise up behind the bay are part of **Parque Nacional Portobelo** *(Portobelo National Park)*, a vast marine and rain-forest reserve contiguous with Chagres National Park. Though several towns lie within the park, and much of its lowlands was deforested years ago, its inaccessible mountains are covered with dense forest that holds plenty of flora and fauna. Extending from offshore coral reefs up to the cloud forest atop 3,212-foot Cerro Brujo, the park comprises an array of ecosystems and is rich in biodiversity. While the coastal area is home to everything from ospreys to sea turtles, the mountains house spider monkeys, brocket deer, harpy eagles, and an array of other endangered wildlife. There is no proper park entrance, but you can explore patches of its forested coast and mangrove estuaries on boat trips from Portobelo, when you might see birds such as the ringed kingfisher and fasciated tiger heron. ⊠*Surrounding Portobelo* ☎*448–2165 or 442–8348* 🖃*Free* ⊙*24 hrs.*

Fuerte San Fernando, one of three **Spanish forts** you can visit at Portobelo, is surrounded by forest and is a good place to see birds. It lies directly across the bay from Batería Santiago, on the left as you drive toward town, a large structure with cannons pointed at the entrance to the bay. The youngest of Portobelo's forts, Batería Santiago was built in the 1860s. The thick walls are coral, which was cut from the reefs that line the coast. Coral was more abundant and easier to cut than the igneous rock found inland, so the Spanish used it for most construction in Portobelo. ■ TIP➜ Local boatmen who are usually sitting near the dock next to Batería Santiago can take you across the bay to explore Fuerte San Fernando for $3. They also offer transportation to several local beaches, as well as a trip into the estuary at the end of the bay.

Portobelo's largest and most impressive fort is Fuerte San Jerónimo, at the end of the bay, which is surrounded by the "modern" town. It was built in the 1600s, but was destroyed and rebuilt to its current state in 1758.

Near the entrance to Fuerte San Jerónimo is the **Real Aduana** *(Royal Customs House)*, where servants of the Spanish crown made sure that the king and queen got their cut from every ingot that rolled through town. Built in 1630, the Real Aduana was damaged during pirate attacks and then destroyed by an earthquake in 1882, only to be rebuilt in 1998. It is an interesting example of colonial architecture—note the carved coral columns on the ground floor—and it holds a limited museum with some old coins, cannonballs, and displays on Panamanian folklore. ⊠*Calle de la Aduana* ☎*No phone* 🖃*$1* ⊙*Weekdays 8–4, weekends 8:30–3.*

One block east of the Real Aduana is the **Iglesia de San Felipe**, a large white church dating from 1814 that's home to the country's most venerated religious figure: the Cristo Negro *(Black Christ)*. According to legend, that statue of a dark-skinned Jesus carrying a cross arrived in Portobelo in the 17th century on a Spanish ship bound for Cartagena, Colombia. Each time the ship tried to leave, it encountered storms and had to return to port, convincing the captain to leave the statue in Portobelo. The statue spends most of the year to the left of the church's altar, but once a year it's paraded through town in the Festival del Cristo Negro. ⊠*Calle Principal* ☎*No phone* 🖃*Free* ⊙*Weekdays 8–4, weekends 8:30–3.*

SHOPPING

Both Cristobal Pier and Colón 2000 Pier have large shopping malls, where you will find Internet access, telephones, refreshments, and duty-free souvenir shopping in relatively secure environments. Stores in both locations feature local crafts such as baskets, wood carvings, and toys, as well as liquor, jewelry, and the ubiquitous souvenir T-shirts. In addition to shops and cafés, Cristobal Pier features an open-air arts and crafts market; Colón 2000 Pier has a well-stocked supermarket. Portobelo has a wide-ranging artisan market next to Iglesia de San Felipe.

The most unique locally made souvenirs are colorful appliquéd *molas,* the whimsical textile artwork created by native Kuna women, who come from the San Blas Islands; they are likely to be at hand stitching new designs while they sell the ones they just completed. The Kuna ladies drive a hard bargain and, considering the intricate nature of their handiwork, prices are quite fair. If you take an excursion to Portobelo, the prices may be better there; several Kuna women are usually there selling their molas in the artisan market next to the church.

COSTA MAYA, MEXICO

Marlise Kast

Puerto Costa Maya is an anomaly. Unlike other tourist attractions in the area (the island of Cozumel being the primary Yucatán cruise port), this port of call near Majahual has been created exclusively for cruise-ship passengers. The shops, restaurants, activities, and entertainment you'll find here aren't open to the general public. After major damage from Hurricane Dean in 2007, the port reopened ahead of schedule (and with an additional berth) in July 2008.

At first glance, the port complex itself may seem to be little more than an outdoor mall. The docking pier (which can accommodate three ships at once) leads to a 70,000 square-foot bazaar-type compound where shops selling local crafts—jewelry, pottery, woven straw hats and bags, and embroidered dresses—are interspersed with duty-free stores and souvenir shops. There are two alfresco restaurants, which serve seafood, American-friendly Mexican dishes like tacos and quesadillas, and cocktails at shaded tables. An outdoor amphitheater stages eight daily performances of traditional music and dance.

The strip of beach edging the complex has been outfitted with colorful lounge chairs and *hamacas* (hammocks), and may tempt you to linger and sunbathe. If you want to have a truly authentic Mexican experience, though, you'll take advantage of the day tours offered to outlying areas. These give you a chance to see some of the really spectacular sights in this part of Mexico, many of which are rarely visited. This is one port where the shore excursion is the point, and there are no options except to purchase what your ship offers. You can preview what excursions may be offered on the Puerto Costa Maya's own Web site.

Among the best tours are those that let you explore the gorgeous (and usually deserted) Mayan ruin sites of Kohunlich, Dzibanche, and Chacchoben. The ancient pyramids and temples at these sites, surrounded by jungle that's protected them for thousands of years, are still dazzling to behold. Since the sites are some distance from the port complex—and require some road travel in one of the port's air-conditioned vans—these tours are all-day affairs.

Prior to a devastating 2007 hurricane, there was no real reason to go into the small, nearby fishing village of Mahahual (pronounced ma-ha-*wal*). Though there are still about 200 residents, post-hurricane renovations have put the village on the map; it now has its own pier as well as a smattering of hotels, restaurants, and shops. The new cement boardwalk along the beach has made Mahahual an ideal spot for a sunset stroll. The crystal clear waters and unspoiled beaches are delightful for snorkeling, diving, and fishing.

ESSENTIALS

Currency The Mexican peso (MX$13.82 to US$1). U.S. dollars and credit cards are accepted by everyone at the port. There is no advantage to paying in dollars, but there may be an advantage to paying in cash.

Information Puerto Costa Maya (⊕ www.puertocostamaya.com).

Telephones Most pay phones accept prepaid Ladatel cards, sold in 30-, 50-, or 100-peso denominations. To use the card, insert it in the pay phone's slot, dial 001 (for calls to the U.S.) or 01 (for calls within Mexico), followed by the area code and number. Credit is deleted from the card as you use it, and the balance is displayed on a small screen on the phone.

COSTA MAYA BEST BETS

■ **Chacchoben.** One of the more recent major archaeological sites to undergo excavation is near the Belize border. The ancient city was a contemporary of Kohunlich.

■ **Kohunlich.** This ruined city is best known for its great temples with sculpted masks.

■ **Majahual.** You might want to go into this small fishing village near the cruise pier; though heavily damaged by Hurricane Dean, it's being spruced up.

■ **Snorkeling at Banco Chinchorro.** Excellent catamaran snorkeling trips go to this nearby reef.

COZUMEL, MEXICO

Maribeth Mellin

Cozumel, with its sun-drenched ivory beaches fringed with coral reefs, fulfills the tourist's vision of a tropical Caribbean island. It's a heady mix of the natural and the commercial. Despite a mini-construction boom in the island's sole city, San Miguel, there are still wild pockets scattered throughout the island where flora and fauna flourish. Smaller than Cancún, Cozumel surpasses its fancier neighbor in many ways. It has more history and ruins, superior diving and snorkeling, more authentic cuisine, and a greater diversity of handicrafts at better prices. The numerous coral reefs, particularly the world-renowned Palancar Reef, attract divers from around the world. On a busy cruise-ship day the island can seem completely overrun, but it's still possible to get away, and some good Mayan sights are within reach on long (and expensive) shore excursions.

ESSENTIALS

Currency The Mexican peso (MX$13.82 to US$1). U.S. dollars and credit cards are widely accepted in the area, from the port to Playa del Carmen, but it's best to have pesos—and small bills—when you visit ruins, where cashiers often run out of change. There is no advantage to paying in dollars, but there may be an advantage to paying in cash.

Internet Calling Station (⊠ Av. Rafael E. Melgar 27, at Calle 3 Sur ☎ 987/872–1417). **The Crew Office** (⊠ Av. 5, No. 201, between Calle 3 Sur and Av. Rosada Salas ☎ 987/869–1485).

Telephones Most pay phones accept prepaid Ladatel cards, sold in 30-, 50-, or 100-peso denominations. To use the card, insert it in the pay phone's slot, dial 001 (for calls to the U.S.) or 01 (for calls within Mexico), followed by the area code and number. Credit is deleted from the card as you use it, and the balance is displayed on a small screen on the phone.

COMING ASHORE

As many as six ships call at Cozumel on a busy day, tendering passengers to the downtown pier in the center of San Miguel or docking at the two international piers 4 mi (6 km) away. From the downtown pier you can walk into town or catch the ferry to Playa del Carmen. Taxi tours are also available. An island tour, including the ruins and other sights, costs about $50 to $70, but negotiate the price before you get in the cab. The international pier is close to many beaches, but you'll need a taxi to get into town. There's rarely a wait for a taxi, but prices are high, and drivers are often aggressive, asking double or triple the reasonable fare. Expect to pay $10 for the ride into San Miguel from the pier. Tipping is not necessary.

Passenger ferries to Playa del Carmen leave Cozumel's main pier approximately every other hour from 5 AM to 10 PM. They also leave Playa del Carmen's dock about every other hour on the hour, from 6 AM to 11 PM (but note that service sometimes varies according to demand). The trip takes 45 minutes. Verify the times: bad weather and changing schedules can prompt cancellations.

EXPLORING COZUMEL

San Miguel is tiny—you cannot get lost—and is best explored on foot. The main attractions are the small eateries and shops that line the streets, and the activity centers at the main square, where the locals congregate in the evening.

Castillo Real. A Mayan site on the coast near the island's northern end, the "royal castle" includes a lookout tower, the base of a pyramid, and a temple with two chambers capped by a false arch. The waters here harbor several shipwrecks. Access to this area was closed at this writing.

El Cedral. Spanish explorers discovered this site, once the hub of Mayan life on Cozumel, in 1518. Later it became the island's first official city, founded in 1847. Today it's a farming community with small, well-tended houses and gardens. Conquistadores tore down much of the Mayan temple and, during World War II the U.S. Army Corps of Engineers destroyed the rest to make way for the island's first airport. All that remains of the Mayan ruins is one small structure with an arch. Nearby is a green-and-white cinder-block church, decorated inside with crosses shrouded in embroidered lace; legend has it that Mexico's first Mass was held here. ⊠ *Turn at Km 17.5 off Carretera Sur or Av. Rafael E. Melgar, then drive 2 mi (3 km) inland to site* ☎ *No phone* ✆ *Free* ☉ *Daily dawn–dusk.*

♺ **Faro Celarain Eco Park.** This 247-acre national preserve at Cozumel's southernmost tip is a protected habitat for numerous birds and animals,

Cozumel

Inset map (San Miguel):

Caribbean Sea
Main Dock
Plaza Villa Mar
Tourist Information
Young Heroes Monument
Plaza
Arts & Crafts Market
Convention Center
Post Office

Avenida Rafael Melgar
5 Av. Norte
10 Av. Norte
15 Av. Norte
20 Av. Norte
25 Av. Norte
Calle 10 Norte
Calle 8 Norte
Calle 6 Norte
Calle 4 Norte
Calle 2 Norte
Av. Benito Juárez
Adolfo Rosada Salas
Calle 1 Sur
5 Av. Sur
10 Av. Sur
15 Av. Sur
20 Av. Sur
25 Av. Sur
Calle 3 Sur
Calle 5 Sur

Main map:

Caribbean Sea

Punta Molas
Castillo Real
Playa Bonita
Isla de Pasión
San Gervasio
Punta Norte
TO PUERTO MORELOS
Playa Santa Pilar
Cozumel Country Club
Playa San Juan
Airport
Playa Los Cocos
TO PLAYA DEL CARMEN
Plaza Central
Av. Benito Juárez
San Miguel see inset map
Punta Este
Punta Morena
Av. Rafael Melgar
La Ceiba
Parque Chankanaab
Playa de San Martín
Playa Corona
Punta Chiqueros
Playa San Clemente
El Trono
Playa San Francisco
El Mirador
Playa Sol
El Cedral
Nachi-Cocom
Parque Punta Sur
Playa Paradiso
Punta Francesca
Playa del Palancar
Laguna Colombia
Laguna Chunchacaab
El Caracol
REEFS
Faro de Punta Celerain
TO PUNTA CELERAIN FARO

0   3 miles
0   3 km

KEY
- Beaches
- Ferry
- Cruise Ship
- Mayan Ruins

including crocodiles, flamingos, egrets, and herons. Cars aren't allowed, so you'll need to use park transportation (rented bicycles or public buses) to get around here. From observation towers you can spot crocodiles and birds in **Laguna Colombia** or **Laguna Chunchacaab.** Or visit the ancient Mayan lighthouse, **El Caracol,** constructed to whistle when the wind blows in a certain direction. At the park's (and the island's) southernmost point is the **Faro de Celarain,** a lighthouse that is now a museum of navigation. Climb the 134 steps to the top; it's a steamy effort, but the views are incredible. Beaches here are wide and deserted, and there's great snorkeling offshore. Without a rental car, expect to pay about $40 for a round-trip taxi ride from San Miguel. ⌧ *Southernmost point of Carretera Sur and coastal road* ☏ *987/872–2940 or 987/872–8462* 🖹 *$10* ⊙ *Daily 9–5.*

COZUMEL BEST BETS

■ **Diving and Snorkeling.** Excellent reefs close to shore make either diving or snorkeling a must-do activity.

■ **Mayan Ruins.** Some of the most famous and dazzling ruins are reachable from Cozumel, and if you have never seen a Mayan pyramid, this is your chance.

■ **Shopping.** Because the dollar is still worth something in Mexico, you can get very good buys, and Cozumel is a major shopping destination.

☍ ★ **Parque Chankanaab.** Chankanaab (which means "small sea") is a national park with a saltwater lagoon, an archaeological park, and a botanical garden. Scattered throughout are reproductions of a Mayan village, and of Olmec, Toltec, Aztec, and Mayan stone carvings. The gardens were severely damaged by Hurricane Wilma in 2005, and are slowly recovering. You can enjoy a cool walk along pathways leading to the sea, where parrotfish and sergeant majors swarm around snorkelers. You can swim, scuba dive, or snorkel at the beach. There's plenty to see: underwater caverns, a sunken ship, crusty old cannons and anchors, and a sculpture of la Virgen del Mar (Virgin of the Sea). Dive shops, restaurants, gift shops, a snack stand, and dressing rooms with lockers and showers are right on the sand. A small museum has exhibits on coral, shells, and the park's history, as well as some sculptures. ⌧ *Carretera Sur, Km 9,* ☏ *987/872–2940* 🖹 *$16* ⊙ *Daily 8–5.*

San Gervasio. Surrounded by a forest, these temples comprise Cozumel's largest remaining Mayan and Toltec site. San Gervasio was once the island's capital and ceremonial center, dedicated to the fertility goddess Ixchel. The classic- and postclassic-style buildings were continuously occupied from AD 300 to 1500. Typical architectural features include limestone plazas and arches atop stepped platforms, as well as stelae and bas-reliefs. Be sure to see the "Manitas" temple with red handprints all over its altar. Plaques clearly describe each structure in Maya, Spanish, and English. ⌧ *From San Miguel take cross-island road (follow signs to airport) east to San Gervasio access road; turn left and follow road 4½ mi (7 km)* 🖹 *$5.75* ⊙ *Daily 7–4.*

★ **San Miguel.** Wait until the cruise ships sail toward the horizon before visiting San Miguel, then stroll along the *malecón* (boardwalk) and take in the ocean breeze. Cozumel's only town feels more traditional the farther you walk away from the water; the waterfront has been taken over by large shops selling jewelry, imported rugs, leather boots, and souvenirs to cruise-ship passengers. Head inland to the pedestrian streets around the plaza, where family-owned restaurants and shops cater to locals and savvy travelers.

> ### SHIP SALES
>
> If you find prices on board too much to bear, shop the ship's boutiques on the last day of your cruise, when they are likely to run special sales.

SHOPPING

Cozumel's main souvenir-shopping area is downtown along Avenida Rafael E. Melgar and on some side streets around the plaza. There are also clusters of shops at **Plaza del Sol** (east side of the main plaza) and **Vista del Mar** (⊠ *Av. Rafael E. Melgar 45*). As a general rule, the newer, trendier shops line the waterfront, and the better crafts shops can be found around Avenida 5a. Malls at the cruise-ship piers aim to please passengers seeking jewelry, perfume, sportswear, and low-end souvenirs at high-end prices.

Most downtown shops accept U.S. dollars; many goods are priced in dollars. To get better prices, pay with cash or traveler's checks—some shops tack a hefty surcharge on credit-card purchases. Shops, restaurants, and streets are always crowded between 10 AM and 2 PM, but get calmer in the evening. Traditionally, stores are open from 9 to 1 (except Sunday) and 5 to 9, but those nearest the pier tend to stay open all day, particularly during high season. Most shops are closed Sunday morning.

ACTIVITIES

DIVING AND SNORKELING

Cozumel is famous for its reefs. In addition to Chankanaab Nature Park, a great dive site is La Ceiba Reef, in the waters off La Ceiba and Sol Caribe hotels. Here lies the wreckage of a sunken airplane blown up for a Mexican disaster movie. Cozumel has plenty of dive shops to choose from. **Aqua Safari** (⊠ *Av. Rafael E. Melgar 429, between Calles 5 and 7 Sur* ☎*987/872–0101* ⊕*www.aquasafari.com*) is one of the oldest and most professional shops and offers PADI certification. **Blue Angel** (⊠ *Caribe Blu Hotel, Carretera Sur, Km 2.3* ☎*987/872–1631* ⊕*www.blueangel-scuba.com*) has an ideal location for both boat and shore dives. **Eagle Ray Divers** (⊠ *La Caleta Marina, near Presidente Inter-Continental Hotel* ☎*987/872–5735* ⊕*www.eagleraydivers.com*) offers snorkeling trips. The company also tracks the eagle rays that appear off Cozumel from December to February and runs trips for advanced divers to walls where the rays congregate.

FISHING

You can charter high-speed fishing boats for about $420 per half-day or $600 per day (with a maximum of six people). Your hotel can help arrange daily charters—some offer special deals, with boats leaving from their own docks. **Albatros Deep Sea Fishing** (☎ *987/872–7904 or 888/333–4643*) offers full-day trips that include boat and crew, tackle and bait, and lunch with beer and soda starting at $575 for up to six persons. **3 Hermanos** (☎ *987/872–6417 or 987/876–8931*) specializes in deep-sea and fly-fishing trips. Their rates for a half-day deep-sea fishing trip start at $350; a full day is $450. They also offer scuba-diving trips, and their boats are available for group charters (a great way to snorkel and cruise around at your own pace) for $400 for up to six passengers.

BEACHES

Cozumel's beaches vary from sandy treeless stretches to isolated coves to rocky shores. Most of the development is on the leeward (western) side. Beach clubs have sprung up on the southwest coast; admission, however, is usually free, as long as you buy food and drinks. Clubs offer typical tourist fare: souvenir shops, *palapa* (thatch-roofed) restaurants, kayaks, and cold beer. A cab ride from San Miguel to most clubs costs about $15 each way. Reaching beaches on the windward (eastern) side is more difficult, but the solitude is worth it.

★ A small parking lot on the side of Carretera Sur just south of town marks the entrance to **Playa Caletita.** There's a rock ledge here and fairly easy access into the water. South of the resorts lies the mostly ignored (and therefore serene) **Playa Palancar.** Offshore is the famous Palancar Reef, easily accessed by the on-site dive shop. There's also a water-sports center, a bar-café, and a long beach with hammocks hanging under coconut palms. The aroma of grilled fish with garlic butter is tantalizing. Playa del Palancar keeps prices low and rarely feels crowded. **Playa San Francisco** is an inviting 3-mi (5-km) stretch of sandy beach, which extends along Carretera Sur, south of Parque Chankanaab at about Km 10. Amenities include two outdoor restaurants, a bar, dressing rooms, gift shops, volleyball nets, beach chairs, and water-sports equipment rentals. Divers use this beach as a jumping-off point for the San Francisco reef and Santa Rosa wall. The abundance of turtle grass in the water, however, makes this a less-than-ideal spot for swimming. **Punta Chiqueros,** a half-moon-shaped cove sheltered by an offshore reef, is the first popular swimming area as you drive north on the coastal road (it's about 8 mi [12 km] north of Parque Punta Sur). Part of a longer beach that some locals call Playa Bonita, it has fine sand, clear water, and moderate waves. This is a great place to swim, watch the sunset, and eat fresh fish at the restaurant, also called Playa Bonita.

WHERE TO EAT

¢–$ × **El Foco.** Locals fuel up before and after partying at this traditional
MEXICAN *taquería* (it's open until midnight, or until the last customer leaves). The soft tacos stuffed with pork, chorizo, cheese, or beef are cheap and

filling; the graffiti on the walls and the late-night revelers provide the entertainment. ⊠*Av. 5 Sur 13B, between Calles Adolfo Rosado Salas and 3 Sur* ☏*987/872–5980* ⊟*No credit cards.*

$$–$$$ ✕**Guido's.** Chef Yvonne Villiger works wonders with fresh fish—if the
ITALIAN   wahoo with capers and black olives is on the menu, don't miss it. But
★   Guido's is best known for its pizzas baked in a wood-burning oven, which makes sections of the indoor dining room rather warm. Sit in the pleasantly overgrown courtyard instead, and order a pitcher of sangria to go with the puffy garlic bread. ⊠*Av. Rafael E. Melgar 23, between Calles 6 and 8 Norte* ☏*987/872–0946* ⊟*MC, V* ☻*Closed Sun.*

CURAÇAO (WILLEMSTAD)

Vernon
O'Reilly-
Ramesar

Try to be on deck as your ship sails into Curaçao. The tiny Queen Emma floating bridge swings aside to allow ships to pass through the narrow channel. Pastel gingerbread buildings on shore look like dollhouses, especially from a large cruise ship. Although the gabled roofs and red tiles show a Dutch influence, the gleeful colors of the facades are peculiar to Curaçao. It's said that an early governor of the island suffered from migraines that were aggravated by the color white, so all the houses were painted in hues from magenta to mauve. Thirty-five miles (56 km) north of Venezuela and 42 mi (68 km) east of Aruba, Curaçao is, at 38 mi (61 km) long and 3 to 7.5 mi (5 to 12 km) wide, the largest of the Netherlands Antilles. Although always sunny, it's never stiflingly hot here because of the constant trade winds. Water sports attract enthusiasts from all over the world, and the reef diving is excellent.

ESSENTIALS

Currency The NAf guilder (NAf 1.78 to US$1); U.S. currency is accepted almost everywhere on the island, and ATMs are plentiful.

Internet Café Internet (⊠*Handelskade 3B, Punda, Willemstad* ☏*5999/465–5088*). **Wireless Internet Café** (⊠*Hanchi Snoa 4, Punda, Willemstad* ☏*5999/461–0590*).

Telephones The telephone system is reliable. To place a local call, dial the seven-digit number. A local call costs NAf 0.50 from a pay phone. Direct-dial access is also available at the AT&T calling center at the cruise-ship terminal and at the megapier in Otrobanda. From other public phones, use phones marked LENSO; many more of these have been added around the island in recent years. You can also call direct from the air-conditioned Digicel center using a prepaid phone card (open 8 AM to 5:30 PM, Monday through Saturday; the center also offers Internet access).

COMING ASHORE

Ships dock at the terminal just beyond the Queen Emma Bridge, which leads to the floating market and the shopping district. The walk to downtown takes less than 10 minutes. Easy-to-read maps are posted dockside and in the shopping area. The terminal has a duty-free shop, telephones, and a taxi stand.

Curaçao

WILLEMSTAD

Kurá Hulanda Museum
Maritime Museum
Scharloo
Floating Market
Mikvé Israel-Emanuel Synagogue
Queen Emma Bridge
Ft. Amsterdam

Sha Caprileskade
Columbusstraat
Wolkstraat
Hendrikplein
Madurostraat
Heerenstraat
Breedestraat
Hanelskade
Heerenstraat
Keukenstraat
Windstraat
Gomezplein
Wilhelmina-plein

PUNDA

Sint Anna Bay

0   50 yards
0   50 meters

Caribbean Sea

North Pt.
Westpunt
Westpunt
Jeremi Bay
Santa Cruz
Savonet
Mt. Christoffel
San Hyronimo
Playa Lagun
Barber
Ascencion
Santa Marta Bay
Soto
Sant Juan Bay
Cas-Abou (Dive Area)
St. Willibrordus
Port Marie Bay
Boca St. Marie
Bullen Bay
Banda Abou (Dive Area)
Christoffel National Park

Hato International Airport
Hato Caves
Brievengat
St. Michiel
St. Michiel Bay
Julianadorp
Piscadera Bay
Central Curaçao

Santa Catarina
Curaçao Aloe Plantation & Factory
St. Joris Bay
Great St. Joris
Little St. Joris
Santa Rosa
Boteljer
Brakkeput
Spanish Water
Caracas Bay
St. Anna Bay
Bopor Kibra
Sea Aquarium Beach
Curaçao Sea Aquarium (Dive Area)
Santa Barbara Beach
Mt. Tafelberg
Nieuwpoort
Ostpunt
Curaçao Underwater Marine Park (Dive Area)

Willemstad
see inset map

0   5 mi
0   5 km

KEY

∠ Beaches
◼ Cruise Ship Terminal
◪ Dive Sites

Taxis, which meet every ship, now have meters, although rates are still fixed from point to point of your journey. The government-approved rates, which do not include waiting time, can be found in a brochure called "Taxi Tariff Guide," available at the cruise-ship terminal and at the tourist board. Rates are for up to four passengers. There's a 25% surcharge after 11 PM. It's easy to see the sights on Curaçao without going on an organized shore excursion. Downtown can be done on foot, and a taxi for up to four people will cost about $35 an hour. Taxi fares to places in and around the city range from $7 to $20. Car rentals are available but are not cheap (about $40 per day, plus $10 compulsory insurance).

EXPLORING CURAÇAO

Willemstad. Willemstad is small and navigable on foot. You needn't spend more than two or three hours wandering around here, although the narrow alleys and various architectural styles are enchanting. English, Spanish, and Dutch are widely spoken. Narrow Santa Anna Bay divides the city into two sides: Punda, where you'll find the main shopping district, and Otrabanda (literally, the "other side"), where the cruise ships dock. Punda is crammed with shops, restaurants, monuments, and markets. Otrabanda has narrow, winding streets full of colonial homes notable for their gables and Dutch-influenced designs.

You can cross from Otrabanda to Punda in one of three ways: walk over the Queen Emma Bridge; ride the free ferry, which runs when the bridge swings open to let seagoing vessels pass; or take a cab across the Juliana Bridge (about $7). On the Punda side of the city, Handelskade is where you'll find Willemstad's most famous sights—the colorful colonial buildings that line the waterfront. The original red roof tiles came from Europe on trade ships as ballast.

★ Each morning dozens of Venezuelan schooners laden with tropical fruits and vegetables arrive at the bustling **Floating Market** on the Punda side of the city. Mangoes, papayas, and exotic vegetables vie for space with freshly caught fish and herbs and spices. The buying is best at 6:30 AM—too early for many people on vacation—but there's plenty of action through the afternoon. Any produce bought here should be thoroughly washed or peeled before being eaten. ⊠ *Sha Caprileskade, Punda, Willemstad.*

Step through the archway of **Fort Amsterdam** and enter another century. The entire structure dates from the 1700s, when it was the center of the city and the island's most important fortification. Now it houses the governor's residence, a church (which has a small museum), and government offices. Outside the entrance, a series of majestic gnarled *wayaka* trees are fancifully carved with human forms—the work of local artist Mac Alberto. ⊠ *Foot of Queen Emma Bridge, Punda, Willemstad* ☎ *5999/461–1139* ⊠ *Free; $1.75 for church museum* ☉ *Weekdays 9–noon and 2–5, Sun. service at 10.*

Fodor'sChoice The fascinating **Kurá Hulanda Museum** reveals the island's diverse roots.
★ Housed in a restored 18th-century village, the museum is built around a former mercantile square (Kurá Hulanda means "Holland courtyard"),

where the Dutch once sold slaves. An exhibit on the transatlantic slave trade includes a gut-wrenching replica of a slave-ship hold. Other sections feature relics from West African empires, examples of pre-Columbian gold, and Antillean art. The complex is the brainchild of Dutch philanthropist Jacob Gelt Dekker, and the museum grew from his personal collection of artifacts. ⊠ *Klipstraat 9, Otrobanda, Willemstad* ☎ *5999/462–1400* ⊕ *www.kurahulanda.com* ⊠ *$9* ⊗ *Daily 10–5.*

The **Maritime Museum**—designed to resemble the interior of a ship—gives you a sense of Curaçao's maritime history, using model ships, historic maps, nautical charts, navigational equipment, and audiovisual displays. Topics explored in the exhibits include the development of Willemstad as a trading city, Curaçao's role as a contraband hub, the remains of *De Alphen* (a Dutch marine freighter that exploded and sank in St. Anna Bay in 1778 and was excavated in 1984), the slave trade, the development of steam navigation, and the role of the Dutch navy on the island. The museum also offers a two-hour guided tour (Wednesday and Saturday, 2 PM) on its "water bus" through Curaçao's harbor—a route familiar to traders, smugglers, and pirates. The museum is wheelchair accessible. ⊠ *Van der Brandhofstraat 7, Scharloo, Willemstad* ☎ *5999/465–2327* ⊕ *www.curacaomaritime.com* ⊠ *Museum $10; museum and harbor tour $15* ⊗ *Tues.–Sat. 10–4.*

★ **Mikvé Israel-Emanuel Synagogue,** the oldest in continuous use in the western hemisphere, is one of Curaçao's most important sights and draws thousands of visitors a year. Enter through the gates around the corner on Hanchi Di Snoa. The Jewish Cultural Museum in the back displays antiques and artifacts from around the world. ⊠ *Hanchi Snoa 29, Punda, Willemstad* ☎ *5999/461–1067* ⊕ *www.snoa.com* ⊠ *$5; donations also accepted* ⊗ *Weekdays 9–4:30.*

Affectionately called the Swinging Old Lady by the locals, the **Queen Emma Bridge** connects the two sides of Willemstad—Punda and Otrobanda—across Santa Anna Bay. The bridge swings open at least 30 times a day to allow passage of ships to and from the sea. The original bridge, built in 1888, was the brainchild of the American consul Leonard Burlington Smith, who made a mint off the tolls he charged for using it: 2¢ per person for those wearing shoes, free to those crossing barefoot. Today it's free to everyone. The bridge was dismantled and completely repaired and restored in 2005. ⊠ *Willemstad.*

CURAÇAO BEST BETS

■ **Diving.** After Bonaire, Curaçao has probably the best diving in the region.

■ **Punda.** Willemstad's chic and beautiful shopping area is a joy to explore on foot.

■ **Curaçao Sea Aquarium.** Explore the wonders of the ocean without getting wet.

■ **Floating Market.** This unique market is a fun destination, even though it's mostly fruits and vegetables.

■ **Kurá Hulanda Museum.** This is the island's best historical museum.

The Wilhelmina Drawbridge connects Punda with the once-flourishing district of **Scharloo**, where the early Jewish merchants built stately homes. The architecture along Scharlooweg (much of it from the 17th century) is magnificent, and, happily, many of the colonial mansions that had become dilapidated have been meticulously renovated. The area closest to Kleine Werf is a red-light district and fairly run-down, but the rest is well worth a visit. ⊠ *Willemstad.*

★ **Christoffel National Park.** This 4,450-acre garden and wildlife preserve with Mt. Christoffel at its center consists of three former plantations. As you drive through the park, watch for deer, goats, and smaller wildlife that might suddenly dart in front of your car. If you skip everything else on the island, it's possible to drive to the park and climb 1,239-foot Mt. Christoffel, which takes two to three strenuous hours. On a clear day you can then see the mountain ranges of Venezuela, Bonaire, and Aruba. The park is an hour from Willemstad but worth a visit. ⊠ *Savonet* ☎ *5999/864–0363 for information and tour reservations, 5999/462–6262 for jeep tours, 5999/864–0535 for horseback tours* 🖃 *$10* ☾ *Mon.–Sat. 8–4, Sun. 6–3; last admission 1 hr before closing.*

Curaçao Aloe Plantation and Factory. Drop in for a fascinating tour that takes you through the various stages of production of aloe vera, renowned for its healing powers. You'll get a look at everything from the fields to the final products. At the gift shop you can buy CurAloe products, including homemade goodies like soap, pure aloe gel, and pure aloe juice, as well as sunscreen and other skin-care products. The plantation is on the way to the Ostrich Farm and run by the same owner. Tours begin throughout the day. ⊠ *Weg Naar Groot St. Joris z/n, Groot St. Joris* ☎ *5999/767–5577* ⊕ *www.aloecuracao.com* 🖃 *$6* ☾ *Mon.–Sat. 9–4; last tour at 3.*

☾ ★ **Curaçao Sea Aquarium.** You don't have to get your feet wet to see the island's underwater treasures. The aquarium has about 40 saltwater tanks filled with more than 400 varieties of marine life. For more up-close interaction, there are several mesmerizing options. You can hand-feed the sharks, stingrays, or sea turtles (or watch a diver do it) at the **Animal Encounters** section, which consists of a 12-foot-deep open-water enclosure. Snorkelers and divers of all skill levels swim freely with tarpon, stingrays, and such. If you prefer to stay dry, there's an underwater observatory in a stationary semi-submarine. It's also possible to swim with the aquarium's six lovable sea lions from Uruguay. Kids as young as three can have their photo taken kissing a sea lion. Reservations for Animal Encounters, including sea-lion programs, must be made 24 hours in advance. A restaurant, a snack bar, two photo centers, and souvenir shops are on-site. *Seaquarium Beach, Bapor Kibra z/n* ☎ *5999/461–6666* ⊕ *www.curacao-sea-aquarium.com* 🖃 *$19; animal encounters $54 for divers, $34 for snorkelers; sea lion programs $49–$169; Dolphin Academy $79–$169* ☾ *Sea Aquarium daily 8:30–5:30; Dolphin Academy daily 8:30–4:30.*

★ **Hato Caves.** Stalactites and stalagmites form striking shapes in these 200,000-year-old caves. Hidden lighting adds to the dramatic effect.

Indians who used the caves for shelter left petroglyphs about 1,500 years ago. More recently, slaves who escaped from nearby plantations used the caves as a hideaway. Hour-long guided tours wind down to the pools in various chambers. Keep in mind that there are 49 steps to climb up to the entrance. To reach the caves, head northwest toward the airport, take a right onto Gosieweg, follow the loop right onto Schottegatweg, take another right onto Jan Norduynweg, a final right onto Rooseveltweg, and follow signs. ⊠ *Rooseveltweg z/n, Hato* ☎ *5999/868–0379* ⊐ *$7* ⊙ *Daily 10–5.*

> ### SUNGLASSES
>
> When selecting sunglasses, the most important considerations are the amount of UV light that is blocked by the lenses and a proper fit. The lenses should shield your eyes from most angles. Darker lenses do not necessarily offer better UV protection. Look for sunglasses that block 99% of harmful UV rays.

SHOPPING

Curaçao has some of the best shops in the Caribbean, but in many cases the prices are no lower than in U.S. discount stores. Hours are usually Monday through Saturday, from 8 to noon and 2 to 6. Most shops are within the six-block area of Willemstad described above. The main shopping streets are Heerenstraat, Breedestraat, and Madurostraat.

Bamali (⊠ *Breedestraat, Punda, Willemstad* ☎ *5999/461–2258*) sells funky, fabulous women's apparel, including Indonesian batik clothing; charming jewelry made of beads, shells, gemstones, and silver; handbags of leather and other fabrics; and lots of other unique accessories. Custom-made clothing is available here, too. **Boolchand's** (⊠ *Heerenstraat 4B, Punda, Willemstad* ☎ *5999/461–6233*) sells electronics, jewelry, Swarovski crystal, Swiss watches, and cameras behind a facade of red-and-white checkered tiles. A sweet aroma permeates **Cigar Emporium** (⊠ *Gomezplein, Punda, Willemstad* ☎ *5999/465–3955*), where you can find the largest selection of Cuban cigars on the island, including H. Upmann, Romeo and Julieta, and Montecristo. Visit the climate-controlled cedar cigar room. However, remember that Cuban cigars cannot be taken back to the United States legally. **New Amsterdam** (⊠ *Gomezplein 14, Punda, Willemstad* ☎ *5999/461–2437* ⊠ *Breedestraat 29, Punda, Willemstad* ☎ *5999/461–3239*) is the place to price hand-embroidered tablecloths, napkins, and pillowcases, as well as blue delft.

ACTIVITIES

BIKING

So you wanna bike Curaçao? **Wanna Bike Curaçao** (☎ *5999/527–3720* ⊕ *www.wannabike-curacao.net*) has the fix: kick into gear and head out for a guided mountain-bike tour through the Caracas Bay peninsula and the salt ponds at the Jan Thiel Lagoon. Although you should be fit to take on the challenge, mountain-bike experience is not required. Tour prices vary depending on skill level and duration, and cover the bike, helmet, water, refreshments, park entrance fee, and guide—but don't forget to bring a camera.

DIVING AND SNORKELING

⟳ **Ocean Encounters** (✉*Lions Dive and Beach Resort, Seaquarium Beach,*
★ *Bapor Kibra z/n* ☎*5999/461–8131* ⊕*www.oceanencounters.com*) is the largest dive operator on the island. Its operations cover the popular east-coast dive sites including the *Superior Producer* wreck, where barracudas hang out, and the tugboat wreck. West-end hot spots—including the renowned Mushroom Forest and Watamula dive sites—are accessible from the company's outlet at Westpunt. Ocean Encounters offers a vast menu of scheduled shore and boat dives and packages, as well as certified PADI instruction. In July, the dive center sponsors
★ a kids' sea camp in conjunction with the Sea Aquarium. **Sunset Divers** (✉*Sunset Waters Beach Resort, Santa Marta Bay* ☎*5999/864–1708* ⊕*www.sunsetdiver.com*), the closest full-service PADI operation to the famous Mushroom Forest, offers daily one- and two-tank dives, 24-hour shore diving, and custom dives. The friendly, expert staff takes you to dive sites along the west-side reef system, which has gently sloping walls with lots of coral growth, soft and hard. Lesser known but no less spectacular sites the company often visits include Harry's Hole and Boca Hulu. The house reef is incredible, too, with common sightings of octopus, eel, frogfish, and sea horses—plus there's a submerged small airplane that makes for a great snorkel. The operator has two boats, including a 44-foot motor-yacht for up to 24 divers that's the largest dive boat on the island. Sunset Divers also rents underwater photography gear.

BEACHES

Cas Abou has the brightest blue water in Curaçao, a treat for swimmers, snorkelers, and sunbathers alike. You can take respite beneath the hut-shaded snack bar. The restrooms and showers are immaculate. The entry fee is $3. Turn off Westpunt Highway at the junction onto Weg Naar Santa Cruz; follow until the turnoff for Cas Abou, and then drive along the winding country road for about 10 minutes to the beach. **Playa Knip** offers crystal clear turquoise waters. Big (Groot) Knip is an expanse of alluring white sand, perfect for swimming and snorkeling. You can rent beach chairs and hang out under the palapas or cool off with ice cream at the snack bar. There are restrooms here but no showers. Just up the road, also in a protected cove, Little (Kleine) Knip is a charmer, too, with picnic tables and palapas. There's no fee for these beaches. **Seaquarium Beach** is divided into separate sections, each uniquely defined by a seaside resort or restaurant as its central draw. By day, no matter where you choose to enter the palm-shaded beach, you can find lounge chairs in the sand, thatched shelters, and restrooms. The island's largest water-sports center (Ocean Encounters at Lion's Dive) caters to nearby hotel guests and walk-ins. Unless you're a guest of a resort on the beach, the entrance fee to any section is $3 until 5 PM, then free.

WHERE TO EAT

$$–$$$ ✕ **Mambo Beach.** Spread over the sand, this open-air bar and grill serves
ECLECTIC   hearty sandwiches and burgers for lunch; steaks, fresh seafood, and
pasta fill the dinner menu. There's an excellent fish buffet on Friday and
dinner with a movie on the beach on Tuesday. ✉*Seaquarium Beach,
Bapor Kibra z/n* ☎*5999/461–8999* ▭*MC, V.*

¢–$ ✕ **Time Out Café.** In the shopping heartland of Punda, this outdoor spot
ECLECTIC   serves up light bites like tuna sandwiches and grilled cheese, as well
as heartier fare like chicken shwarma. From Breedestraat facing Little
Switzerland, take the alley to the left of the store (Kaya A.M. Prince)
and walk about 20 yards, or look for the sign in Gomezplein Square
and follow the arrow. This is more of a place for lunch but they are
open until 7 PM if you're looking for a cheap and cheerful early dinner.
✉*Keukenplein 8, Punda, Willemstad* ☎*5999/524–5071* ▭*No credit
cards* ☉*Closed Sun.*

DOMINICA (ROSEAU)

Roberta
Sotonoff

In the center of the Caribbean archipelago, wedged between the two
French islands of Guadeloupe, to the north, and Martinique, to the
south, Dominica is a wild place. So unyielding is the terrain that colonists surrendered efforts at colonization, and the last survivors of the
Caribbean's original people, the Carib Indians, have made her rugged northeast their home. Dominica—just 29 mi (47 km) long and 16
mi (26 km) wide—is an English-speaking island, though family and
place-names are a mélange of French, English, and Carib. The capital is
Roseau (pronounced rose-oh). If you've had enough of casinos, crowds,
and swim-up bars and want to take leave of everyday life—to hike, bike,
trek, spot birds and butterflies in the rain forest; explore waterfalls;
discover a boiling lake; kayak, dive, snorkel, or sail in marine reserves;
or go out in search of the many resident whale and dolphin species—
this is the place to do it.

ESSENTIALS

Currency The Eastern Caribbean dollar (EC$2.67 to the US$1). U.S. currency is
readily accepted, but you will get change in EC dollars. Most major credit cards
are accepted, as are traveler's checks.

Internet Cornerhouse Café (✉*Old and King George V Sts., Roseau*
☎*767/449–9000*). **Cyber Land Internet Café** (✉*George St., Roseau* ✉*Wood-
stone Shopping Mall, Roseau* ✉*Grandby St., Portsmouth* ☎*767/440–2605*).

COMING ASHORE

In Roseau most ships dock along the bay front. Across the street from
the pier, in the old post office, is a visitor information center. Taxis,
minibuses, and tour operators are available at the berths. If you do
decide to tour with one of them, choose one who is certified, and be
explicit when discussing where you will go and how much you will
pay—don't be afraid to ask questions. The drivers usually quote a fixed
fare, which is regulated by the Division of Tourism and the National

Taxi Association. Drivers also offer their services for tours anywhere on the island beginning at $25 to $30 an hour for up to four persons; a four- to five-hour island tour for up to four persons will cost approximately $150. You can rent a car in Roseau for about $40, not including insurance and a mandatory EC$30 driving permit, but it can be difficult to find things, so you might do better on a guided tour here.

EXPLORING DOMINICA

Most of Dominica's roads are narrow and winding, so you'll need a few hours to take in the sights. Be adventurous, whether you prefer sightseeing or hiking—you'll be amply rewarded.

Carib Indian Territory. In 1903, after centuries of conflict, the Caribbean's first settlers, the Kalinago (more popularly known as the Caribs), were granted a portion of land (approximately 3,700 acres) on the island's northeast coast, on which to establish a reservation with their own chief. Today it's known as Carib Territory, clinging to the northeasterly corner of Dominica, where a group of slightly more than 3,000 Caribs, who resemble native South Americans, live like most other people in rural Caribbean communities. Many are farmers and fishermen; others are entrepreneurs who have opened restaurants, guesthouses, and little shops where you can buy exquisite Carib baskets and other hand-crafted items. The craftspeople retain knowledge of basket weaving, wood carving, and canoe building, which has been passed down from one generation to the next.

Kalinago Barana Autê (☎767/445–7979 ⊕*www.kalinagobaranaaute. com*) is Carib Territory's newest addition and the place to learn about Carib customs, history, and culture. A guided, 45-minute tour explores the village, stopping along the way to learn about plants, dugout canoes, basket weaving, and *kasava* bread making. The path offers wonderful viewpoints of the Atlantic and a chance to see Isukati Falls. There are several site packages, but the basic one—which includes admission, tour, and a drink—is about $10. It's open daily 9–9.

Emerald Pool. Quite possibly the most-visited nature attraction on the island, this emerald-green pool fed by a 50-foot waterfall is an easy trip to make. To reach this spot in the vast Morne Trois Pitons National Park, you follow a trail that starts at the side of the road near the reception center (it's an easy 20-minute walk). Along the way you can pass lookout points with views of the windward (Atlantic) coast and the forested interior. If you don't want a crowd, check whether there are cruise ships in port before going out, as this spot is popular with cruise-ship tour groups.

Morne Trois Pitons National Park. A UNESCO World Heritage Site, this 17,000-acre swath of lush, mountainous land in the south-central interior (covering 9% of Dominica) is the island's crown jewel. Named after one of the highest (4,600 feet) mountains on the island, it contains the island's famous "boiling lake," majestic waterfalls, and cool mountain lakes. There are four types of vegetation zones here. Ferns grow 30 feet tall, wild orchids sprout from trees, sunlight leaks through green canopies, and a gentle mist rises over the jungle floor. A system of trails has

Dominica

Roseau (inset map)

Independence St.
Great George St.
Old St.
J. W. Edwards Building
King George V St.
Roseau River
Bay St.

Botanical Gardens
Bath Rd.

Post Office

Tropicrafts

Dominica Museum/ Old Market Plaza

Fort Young

Main map

Dominica Passage

Capucin Pt.

Toucari Beach and Reef

Morne Aux Diables

Vieille Case

Hampstead

Hodges

L'Anse Tortue

Douglas Bay

Cabrits Drop-Off

Purple Beach

Calibishie

Woodford Hill Bay

Fort Shirley

Portsmouth

Indian Rd.

Bense

Indian R.

Melville Hall Airport

Marigot

ATLANTIC OCEAN

Prince Rupert Bay

Picard Beach

Picard R.

Londonderry Bay

Pt. Ronde

Morne Diablotin

Dublanc

Rd.

Colihaut

Carib Indian Territory

Castle Bruce

Nose Reef

Brain Coral Garden

Salisbury Falls

Salisbury

Mero

Emerald Pool

Petit Soufrière Bay

Layou River

Castaways

Rosalie

Macoucherie River

Rodney's Rock

Mahaut

Pont Casse

Bout Sable Bay

Pringles Bay

Cochrane

Laudat

Morne Trois Pitons National Park

Pt. Giraud

Canefield Airport

Trafalgar

Woodbridge Bay

Wotten Waven Rd.

Roseau see inset map

La Plaine

Petite Savanne Delices Rd.

Caribbean Sea

Pointe Michel

Champagne

Soufrière Bay

Grand Bay

Soufriere Marine Reserve

Scotts Head Village

Scotts Head

Martinique Passage

KEY

- Beaches
- Cruise Ship Terminal
- Dive Sites

0 — 4 miles
0 — 6 km

been developed in the park, and the Division of Forestry and Wildlife works hard to maintain them—with no help from the excessive rainfall and the profusion of vegetation that seems to grow right before your eyes. Access to the park is possible from most points of the compass, though the easiest approaches are via the small mountaintop villages of Laudat (pronounced low-*dah*) and Cochrane.

Fodor'sChoice ★ The undisputed highlight of the park is **Boiling Lake.** Reputedly the world's largest such lake, it's a cauldron of gurgling gray-blue water, 70 yards wide and of unknown depth, with water temperatures from 180°F to 197°F. Although generally believed to be a volcanic crater, the lake is actually a flooded fumarole—a crack through which gases escape from the molten lava

> ## DOMINICA BEST BETS
>
> ■ **Kalinago Barana Autê.** This reserve is a great place to learn about the fierce Caribs.
>
> ■ **Rain-Forest Trips.** Hiking in Dominica's rain forest is the best way to experience its natural beauty.
>
> ■ **Snorkeling in Champagne.** A bubbling volcanic vent makes you feel as if you are snorkeling in champagne.
>
> ■ **Whale-Watching.** November through February offers the best whale-watching in the Caribbean.
>
> ■ **Indian River.** A peaceful rowboat ride on the river is relaxing and peaceful

below. As many visitors discovered in late 2004, the "lake" can sometimes dry up, though it fills again within a few months and, shortly after that, once more starts to boil. The two- to four-hour (one way) hike up to the lake is challenging (on a very rainy day, be prepared to slip and slide the whole way up and back). You'll need attire appropriate for a strenuous hike, and a guide is a must. Most guided trips start early (no later than 8:30 AM) for this all-day, 7-mi (11-km) round-trip trek.

On your way to Boiling Lake you pass through the **Valley of Desolation,** a sight that definitely lives up to its name. Harsh sulfuric fumes have destroyed virtually all the vegetation in what must once have been a lush forested area. Stay on the trail to avoid breaking through the crust that covers the hot lava. At the beginning of the Valley of Desolation trail is the **TiTou Gorge,** where you can swim in the pool or relax in the hot-water springs along one side. If you're a strong swimmer, you can head up the gorge to a cave (it's about a five-minute swim) that has a magnificent waterfall; a crack in the cave about 50 feet above permits a stream of sunlight to penetrate the cavern.

Also in the national park are some of the island's most spectacular waterfalls. The 45-minute hike to **Sari Sari Falls,** accessible through the east-coast village of La Plaine, can be hair-raising. But the sight of water cascading some 150 feet into a large pool is awesome. So large are these falls that you feel the spray from hundreds of yards away. Just beyond the village of Trafalgar and up a short hill is the reception facility, where you can purchase passes to the national park and find guides to take you on a rain-forest trek to the twin **Trafalgar Falls;** the 125-foot high waterfall is called the Father, and the wider, 95-foot high one, the Mother. If you like a little challenge, let your guide take you up the riverbed to the cool pools at the base of the falls (check whether there's a cruise ship in port before setting out; this sight is popular with the tour operators).

Roseau. Although it's one of the smallest capitals in the Caribbean, Roseau has the highest concentration of inhabitants of any town in the eastern Caribbean. Caribbean vernacular architecture and a bustling marketplace transport visitors back in time. Although you can walk the entire town in about an

> **BIBS**
>
> With limited and expensive laundry facilities on ships, you may not want to spend your free time cleaning up after your child. It's convenient to bring along a pack of disposable bibs for mealtimes to keep baby's clothing cleaner and stain-free, avoiding messy garments after meals and a lot of laundry time on board the ship.

hour, you'll get a much better feel for the place on a leisurely stroll.

For some years now, the Society for Historical Architectural Preservation and Enhancement (SHAPE) has organized programs and projects to preserve the city's architectural heritage. Several interesting buildings have already been restored. **Lilac House,** on Kennedy Avenue, has three types of gingerbread fretwork, latticed verandah railings, and heavy hurricane shutters. The **J. W. Edwards Building,** at the corner of Old and King George V streets, has a stone base and a wooden second-floor gallery. The **Old Market Plaza** is the center of Roseau's historic district, which was laid out by the French on a radial plan rather than a grid, so streets such as Hanover, King George V, and Old radiate from this area. South of the marketplace is the Fort Young Hotel, built as a British fort in the 18th century; the nearby state house, public library, and Anglican cathedral are also worth a visit. New developments at the bay front on Dame M. E. Charles Boulevard have brightened up the waterfront.

The 40-acre **Botanical Gardens,** founded in 1891 as an annex of London's Kew Gardens, are a great place to relax, stroll, or watch a cricket match. In addition to the extensive collection of tropical plants and trees, there's also a parrot aviary. At the Forestry Division office, which is also on the garden grounds, you can find numerous publications on the island's flora, fauna, and national parks. The forestry officers are particularly knowledgeable on these subjects and can also recommend good hiking guides. ⊠*Between Bath Rd. and Valley Rd.* ☎*767/448–2401 Ext. 3417* ⊕*www.da-academy.org/dagardens.html* ☎*Free* ☉*Mon. 8–1 and 2–5, Tues.–Fri. 8–1 and 2–4.*

The old post office now houses the **Dominica Museum.** This labor of love by local writer and historian Dr. Lennox Honychurch contains furnishings, documents, prints, and maps that date back hundreds of years; you can also find an entire Carib hut as well as Carib canoes, baskets, and other artifacts. ⊠*Dame M. E. Charles Blvd., opposite cruise-ship berth* ☎*767/448–8923* ☎*$3* ☉*Weekdays 9–4:30 and Sat. 9–1; closed Sun except when a cruise ship is in port.*

SHOPPING

Dominicans produce distinctive handicrafts, with various communities specializing in their specific products. The crafts of the Carib Indians include traditional baskets made of dyed *larouma* reeds and water-proofed with tightly woven *balizier* leaves. These are sold in the Carib Indian Territory and Kalinago Barana Autê as well as in Roseau's shops. Vertivert straw rugs, screw-pine tableware, *fwije* (the trunk of the forest tree fern), and wood carvings are just some examples. Also notable are local herbs, spices, condiments, and herb teas.

One of the easiest places to pick up a souvenir is the Old Market Plaza, just behind the Dominica Museum, in Roseau. Slaves were once sold here, but today handcrafted jewelry, T-shirts, spices, souvenirs, batik, and lacquered and woven bamboo boxes and trays are available from a group of vendors in open-air booths set up on the cobblestones. These are usually busiest when there's a cruise ship berthed across the street. On these days you can also find a vast number of vendors along the bay front.

Baroon International (⊠ *Kennedy Ave. at Old St., Roseau* ☎767/449–2888) sells unusual jewelry from Asia, the United States, and other Caribbean islands; there are also pieces that are assembled in the store, as well as personal accessories, souvenirs, and special gifts. **Dominica Pottery** (⊠ *Bay Front at Kennedy Ave., Roseau* ☎*No phone*) carries products made from various local clays and glazes. **Tropicrafts** (⊠ *Independence St. at Turkey La., Roseau* ☎767/448–2747) has a back room where you can watch local ladies weave grass mats. You can also find arts and crafts from around the Caribbean, local wood carvings, rum, hot sauces, per-fumes, and traditional Carib baskets, hats, and woven mats.

ACTIVITIES

ADVENTURE PARKS

The **Rainforest Aerial Tram** (⊠ *Laudat* ☎767/448–8775, 767/440–3266, 866/759–8726 *in U.S.* ⊕*www.rfat.com*) gives you a bird's-eye view of a pristine forest aboard an open, eight-person gondola. For 90 min-utes to two hours, you slowly skim the tree-top canopy while a guide provides scientific information about the flora and fauna. At the top, there is an optional walking tour, which is worth the steps. The price is $64. Transportation and lunch are extra. This is a popular attraction for cruise-ship passengers, so try to reserve ahead.

Wacky Rollers (⊠ *Front St., Roseau* ⊕ *Box 900, Roseau* ☎767/440–4386 ⊕*www.wackyrollers.com*) will make you feel as if you are training for the Marines as you swing on a Tarzan-style rope and grab onto a ver-tical rope ladder, rappel across zip lines and traverse suspended log bridges, a net bridge, and four monkey bridges (rope loops). It costs $65 for the adult course and should take from 1½ to 3½ hours to conquer the 28 "games." There is also an abbreviated kids' course for $35. Wacky Rollers also organizes adventure tours around the island. Although the office is in Roseau, the park itself is in Hillsborough Estate, about 20 to 25 minutes north of Roseau.

DIVING AND WHALE-WATCHING

Fodor'sChoice Dominica has been voted one of the top 10 dive destinations in the
★ world by *Skin Diver* and *Rodale's Scuba Diving* magazines—and has
won many other awards for its underwater sites. They are truly memorable. There are numerous highlights all along the west coast of the
island, but the best are those in the southwest—within and around
Soufrière/Scotts Head Marine Reserve. There is a $2 fee per person to dive,
snorkel, or kayak in the reserve. The conditions for underwater photography, particularly macrophotography, are unparalleled. The rates
are about $50 for a single tank dive and about $65–$85 for a two-tank
dive or from about $95 for a resort course with one open-water dive.
All scuba-diving operators also offer snorkeling trips; several also offer
whale-watching trips in season; equipment rents for $10 to $25 a day;
trips with gear range from $15 to $35.

The **Anchorage Dive and Whale Watch Center** (⊠ *Anchorage Hotel, Castle
Comfort* ☎ *767/448–2638* ⊕ *www.anchoragehotel.dm*) has two dive
boats that can take you out day or night. It also offers PADI instruction
(all skill levels), snorkeling and whale-watching trips, and shore diving.
One of the island's first dive operations, it has many of the same trips as
Dive Dominica. **Dive Dominica** (⊠ *Castle Comfort Lodge, Castle Comfort* ☎ *954/453–5042 or 888/414–7626* ⊕ *www.divedominica.com*),
one of the island's dive pioneers, conducts NAUI, PADI, and SSI courses
as well as Nitrox certification. With four boats, it offers diving, snorkeling, and whale-watching trips and packages including accommodation
at the Castle Comfort Lodge. Its trips are similar to Anchorage's.

HIKING

★ Dominica's majestic mountains, clear rivers, and lush vegetation conspire to create adventurous hiking trails. The island is crisscrossed by
ancient footpaths of the Arawak and Carib Indians and the Nègres
Maroons, escaped slaves who established camps in the mountains.
Existing trails range from easygoing to arduous. To make the most
of your excursion, you'll need sturdy hiking boots, insect repellent, a
change of clothes (kept dry), and a guide. Hikes and tours run $25 to
$50 per person, depending on destinations and duration. To visit some
of the natural attractions within the island's national parks you need
a site pass. These are sold for varying numbers of visits. A single-entry
site pass costs $2, a day pass $5, and a week pass $10.

Local bird and forestry expert **Bertrand Jno Baptiste** (☎ *767/446–6358*)
leads hikes up Morne Diablotin and along the Syndicate Nature Trail;
if he's not available, ask him to recommend another guide.

Hiking guides can be arranged through the **Discover Dominica Authority**
(⊠ *Valley Rd., Roseau* ☎ *767/448–2045* ⊕ *www.discoverdominica.
com*).

BEACHES

On the west coast, just south of the village of Pointe Michel, **Champagne**
is hailed as one of the best spots for swimming, snorkeling, and diving,
but not for sunning. It gets its name from volcanic vents that constantly

puff steam into the sea, which makes you feel as if you are swimming in warm champagne.

WHERE TO EAT

¢–$ ✕**Cornerhouse Café.** Just off the Old Market Plaza, in a historic, three-
CAFÉ   story stone-and-wood town house, this is Dominica's only true Internet café. An eclectic menu of meals and other treats is on offer to sustain you during your surfing: bagels with an assortment of toppings, delicious soups, fish, sandwiches, salads, cakes, and coffee. Computers are rented by the half hour; relax on soft chairs and flip through books and magazines while you wait. ⊠ *Old and King George V Sts., Roseau* ☎ *767/449–9000* ⊕ *www.avirtualdominica.com/cornerhouse* ⊟ *No credit cards* ⊗ *Closed Sun.*

$ ✕**Pearl's Cuisine.** In a creole town house in central Roseau, chef Pearl,
CARIBBEAN   with her robust and infectious character, prepares some of the island's best local cuisine. On her menu that changes daily, she offers such local delicacies as *sousse* (pickled pigs' feet), blood pudding, and rotis. When sitting down to lunch or dinner, ask for a table on the open-air gallery that overlooks Roseau, and prepare for an abundant portion, but make sure you leave space for dessert. If you're on the go, enjoy a quick meal from the daily, varied menu in the ground-floor snack bar. You're spoiled for choice when it comes to the fresh fruit juices. ⊠ *50 King George V St., Roseau* ☎ *767/448–8707* ⊟ *AE, D, MC, V* ⊗ *Closed Sun. No dinner.*

FREEPORT-LUCAYA, BAHAMAS

Chelle Koster
Walton

Grand Bahama Island, the fourth-largest island in the Bahamas, lies only 52 mi (84 km) off Palm Beach, Florida. In 1492, when Columbus first set foot in the Bahamas, Grand Bahama was already populated. Skulls found in caves attest to the existence of the peaceable Lucayans, who were constantly fleeing the more bellicose Caribs. But it was not until the 1950s, when the harvesting of Caribbean yellow pine trees (now protected by Bahamian environmental law) was the island's major industry, that American financier Wallace Groves envisioned Grand Bahama's grandiose future as a tax-free port for the shipment of goods to the United States. It was in that era that the city of Freeport and later Lucaya evolved. They are separated by a 4-mi (6-km) stretch of East Sunrise Highway, although few can tell you where one community ends and the other begins. Most of Grand Bahama's commercial activity is concentrated in Freeport, the Bahamas' second-largest city. Lucaya, with its sprawling shopping complex and water-sports reputation, stepped up to the role of island tourism capital. Resorts, beaches, a casino, and golf courses make both cities popular with visitors.

ESSENTIALS

Currency The Bahamian dollar, which trades one-to-one with the U.S. dollar, which is universally accepted. There's no need to acquire any Bahamian currency.

Internet Port Lucaya Marina has free Wi-Fi service if you have your own laptop.

Telephones Calling locally or internationally is easy in the Bahamas. To place a local call, dial the seven-digit phone number. To call the United States, dial 1 plus the area code. Pay phones cost 25¢ per call; Bahamian and U.S. quarters are accepted, as are BATELCO phone cards. To place a call using a calling card, use your long-distance carrier's access code or dial 0 for the operator. Be aware that when placing a toll-free call from your hotel, you are charged as if for a regular long-distance call.

COMING ASHORE

Cruise-ship passengers arrive at Lucayan Harbour, which has a clever Bahamian-style look, extensive cruise-passenger terminal facilities, and an entertainment-shopping village. The harbor lies about 10 minutes west of Freeport. Taxis and limos meet all cruise ships. Two passengers are charged $16 and $24 for trips to Freeport and Lucaya, respectively. Fare to Xanadu Beach is $17; it's $24 to Taino Beach. The price per person drops $5 for larger groups. It's customary to tip taxi drivers 15%. A three-hour sightseeing tour of the Freeport-Lucaya area costs $25 to $35. Four-hour West End trips cost about $40.

Grand Bahama's flat terrain and straight, well-paved roads make for good scooter riding. Rentals run $35 a day (about $15 an hour). Helmets are required and provided. Look for small rental stands in parking lots and along the road in Freeport and Lucaya and at the larger resorts. It's usually cheaper to rent a car than to hire a taxi. Automobiles, jeeps, and vans can be rented at the Grand Bahama International Airport. Some agencies provide free pickup and delivery service to the cruise-ship port and Freeport and Lucaya, but prices are still not cheap; cars begin at $50 per day, but insurance of up to $17 per day is also required by law.

EXPLORING FREEPORT-LUCAYA

Grand Bahama is the only planned island in the Bahamas. Its towns, villages, and sights are well laid out but far apart. Downtown Freeport and Lucaya are both best appreciated on foot. Buses and taxis can transport you the 4-mi (6-km) distance between the two. In Freeport shopping is the main attraction. Bolstered by the Westin and Sheraton Grand Bahama Island resort complex, Lucaya has its beautiful beach and water-sports scene, plus more shopping and a big, beautiful new casino. Outside of town, isolated fishing villages, beaches, natural attractions, and the once-rowdy town of West End make it worthwhile to hire a tour or rent a car. The island stretches 96 mi (154 km) from one end to the other.

FREEPORT

★ **Bahamas National Trust Rand Nature Centre.** On 100 acres just minutes from downtown Freeport, ½ mi of self-guided botanical trails show off 130 types of native plants, including many orchid species. The center is the island's birding hot spot, where you might spy a red-tailed hawk or a Cuban emerald hummingbird sipping hibiscus nectar. The flamingo flock was killed off by raccoons, but the center is in the process of replacing

KEY

Beaches
Cruise Ship Terminal
Dive Sites

Lucayan National Park

W. Beach Rd.

Balao Rd.

Taino Beach
Pygmy Caves

Dolphin Experience

Harbour

Midshipman Rd.

UNEXSO

Sea Hunt

Spid City

Our Lucaya Lucaya Golf and Country Club

Sergeant Major

Sea Horse Rd.

E. Sunrise Hwy.

Port Lucaya Marketplace

Royal Palm Way

Lucayan Beach

Settlers Way

Bahamas National Trust Rand Nature Centre

Coral Rd.

Explorers Way

Pioneers Way East

Adventurers Way

Poinciana

Beachway Dr.

Silver Point Beach

The Mall

W. Atlantic Drive

Pioneers Way

W. Mall Dr.

E. Mall Dr.

E Atlantic Dr.

Beach Dr.

East

The Mall South

Perfume Factory

International Bazaar

Emerald Golf Course

Santa Maria Ave.

TO FREEPORT INTERNATIONAL AIRPORT

Ruby Golf Course

W. Sunrise Hwy.

Bahama W.

Yorkshire Rd.

Xanadu Beach

Queens Hwy.

Grand Bahama Hwy.

Grand Bahama Way

Bah Princess Beach

3,000 yards

3,000 m

TO FREEPORT HARBOUR

Pinder's Point Rd.

Northwest Providence Channel

Freeport–Lucaya, Bahamas

the birds. The new visitor center hosts changing local art exhibits and some resident animals, including a Bahama boa. Outside you can visit the caged one-eyed Bahama parrot the center has adopted. On Tuesday and Thursday free guided tours focusing on the use of plants in Bahamian bush medicine depart at 10:30 AM. The reserve is named for philanthropist James H. Rand, the former president of Remington Rand, who donated a hospital and library to the island. ⌧ *E. Settlers Way* ☎*242/352–5438* 🖃*$5* ⊙ *Weekdays 9–4; guided nature walk by advance reservation.*

International Bazaar. Though the 2004 post-hurricane closure of the Royal Oasis Resort and Casino has given this once-vibrant shopping area a down-at-the-heels look, some restaurants and shops, along with the straw market, remain open, especially along the perimeter and in the International Arcade at the west end. At the entrance stands a 35-foot torii arch, a red-lacquered gate that is a traditional symbol of welcome in Japan. ⌧ *W. Sunrise Hwy. and Mall Dr.* ☎*No phone* 🖃*Free* ⊙ *Mon.–Sat. 10–6.*

★ **Perfume Factory.** The quiet and elegant Perfume Factory occupies a replica 19th-century Bahamian mansion—the kind built by Loyalists who settled in the Bahamas after the American Revolution. The interior resembles a tasteful drawing room. This is the home of Fragrance of the Bahamas, a company that produces perfumes, colognes, and lotions using the scents of jasmine, cinnamon, gardenia, spice, and ginger. Take a free five-minute tour of the mixology laboratory. For $30 an ounce you can blend your own perfume using any of the 35 scents ($15 for 1½ ounces of blend-it-yourself body lotion). Sniff mixtures until they hit the right combination, then bottle, name, and take home the personalized potion. ⌧ *Behind International Bazaar, on access road* ☎*242/352–9391* ⊕*www.perfumefactory.com* 🖃*Free* ⊙ *Weekdays 9:30–5:30, Sat. 11–3.*

LUCAYA

Lucaya, on Grand Bahama's southern coast and just east of Freeport, was developed as the island's resort center. These days, it's booming with the megaresort complex called the Westin and Sheraton Grand Bahama Island resort, a fine sandy beach, championship golf courses, a casino, a first-class dive operation, and Port Lucaya's shopping and marina facilities.

FREEPORT-LUCAYA BEST BETS

■ **Diving with UNEXSO.** Simply one of the world's most respected diving facilities.

■ **The Dolphin Experience.** Choose your level of involvement.

■ **East End Eco-adventure.** Venture beyond the city to the quiet fishing settlements east of Freeport.

■ **Lucayan National Park.** The highest peak in the Virgin Islands has breathtaking views and is a great hiking destination.

■ **Shopping.** Duty-free shopping in the Port Lucaya Marketplace is still good; be sure to haggle if you shop at the straw markets.

4

⟳ **The Dolphin Experience.** Encounter
Fodor's Choice   Atlantic bottlenose dolphins in
★   Sanctuary Bay at one of the world's
first and largest dolphin facilities,
about 2 mi east of Port Lucaya. A
ferry takes you from Port Lucaya
to the bay to observe and photo-
graph the animals. If you don't
mind getting wet, you can sit on a
partially submerged dock or stand

> **HANGERS**
>
> Folding or inflatable travel hang-
> ers are useful if you need to dry
> out hand laundry or a bathing
> suit in your cabin. The ones
> in your cabin's closet may not
> be removable.

waist deep in the water, and one of these friendly creatures will swim
up and touch you. You can also engage in one of two swim-with-the-
dolphins programs, but participants must be 55 inches or taller. You
can buy tickets for the Dolphin Experience at the Underwater Explorers
Society (UNEXSO) in Port Lucaya, but be sure to make reservations as
early as possible. ⊠ *Port Lucaya* ☎ *242/373–1244 or 800/992–3483*
🖷 *242/373–8956* ⊕ *www.unexso.com* ✉ *2-hr interaction program
$75, 2-hr swim program $169, dolphin dive $219, open-ocean experi-
ence $199* ⊙ *Daily 8–5.*

★ **Port Lucaya Marketplace.** Lucaya's capacious and lively shopping complex—a dozen low-rise, pastel-painted colonial buildings whose style
was influenced by traditional island homes—is on the waterfront 4 mi
east of Freeport and across the street from a massive resort complex.
The shopping center, whose walkways are lined with hibiscus, bougainvillea, and croton, has about 100 well-kept establishments, among
them waterfront restaurants and bars, and shops that sell clothes, crystal and china, watches, jewelry, perfumes, and local arts and crafts.
⊠ *Sea Horse Rd.* ☎ *242/373–8446* ⊕ *www.portlucayamarketplace.
com* ⊙ *Daily 10–6.*

Fodor's Choice   **Underwater Explorers Society (UNEXSO).** One of the world's most respected
★   diving facilities, UNEXSO welcomes more than 50,000 individuals each
year and trains hundreds of them in scuba diving. Facilities include a
17-foot-deep training pool with windows that look out on the harbor,
changing rooms and showers, docks, equipment rental, a snack bar,
and an air-tank filling station. ⊠ *On wharf at Port Lucaya Marketplace*
☎ *242/373–1244 or 800/992–3483* ⊕ *www.unexso.com* ✉ *Beginner
reef dives $59, dives from $59, night dives $79, dolphin dives $219,
shark dives $99* ⊙ *Daily 8–5.*

BEYOND FREEPORT-LUCAYA

Grand Bahama Island narrows at picturesque West End, once Grand
Bahama's capital and still home to descendants of the island's first settlers. Seaside villages, with concrete-block houses painted in bright blue
and pastel yellow, fill in the landscape between Freeport and West End.
The East End is Grand Bahama's "back-to-nature" side. The road east
from Lucaya is long, flat, and mostly straight. It cuts through a vast
pine forest to reach McLean's Town, the end of the road.

Fodor's Choice   **Lucayan National Park.** In this 40-acre seaside land preserve, trails and
★   elevated walkways wind through a natural forest of wild tamarind and
gumbo-limbo trees, past an observation platform, a mangrove swamp,

sheltered pools containing rare marine species, and what is believed to be the largest explored underwater cave system in the world (7 mi long). You can enter the caves at two access points; one is closed in June and July, the bat nursing season. Twenty miles (32 km) east of Lucaya, the park contains examples of the island's five ecosystems: beach, sandy or whiteland coppice (hardwood forest), mangroves, rocky coppice, and pine forest. Across the road from the caves, trails and rickety, warped boardwalks lead through pine forest and mangrove swamp to Gold Rock Beach, a beautiful, lightly populated strand of white sand edged by some of the island's highest dunes, aquamarine sea, and coral reef. Signs along the trail detail the park's distinctive features. Tickets can be purchased in advance at Rand Nature Centre or on-site. ⊠ *Grand Bahama Hwy.* ☎ *242/352–5438* ⊠ *$5* ⊙ *Daily 8:30–4:30.*

4

SHOPPING

In the stores, shops, and boutiques in Freeport's International Bazaar and at the Port Lucaya Marketplace you can find duty-free goods costing up to 40% less than what you might pay back home. At the numerous perfume shops, fragrances are often sold at a sweet-smelling 25% below U.S. prices. Be sure to limit your haggling to the straw markets. There's a good straw market at the port, just as you come off the ship; many people choose to go no farther on their day in Freeport-Lucaya.

ACTIVITIES

FISHING

Private boat charters for up to four people cost $300 and up for a half day and $350 and up for a full day. Bahamian law limits the catch of game fish to six dolphinfish, kingfish, or wahoo per person per day. **Reef Tours Ltd.** (⊠ *Port Lucaya Marketplace* ☎ *242/373–5880* ⊕ *www. bahamasvacationguide.com/reeftours*) offers sportfishing for four to six people on custom boats. Equipment and bait are provided free. All vessels are licensed, inspected, and insured. Trips run from 8:30 to 12:15 and from 1 to 4:45, weather permitting ($130 per angler, $60 per spectator). Full-day trips are also available, as are bottom fishing excursions, glass-bottom boat tours, snorkeling trips, and sailing-snorkeling cruises. Reservations are essential.

GOLF

Fodor'sChoice **Fortune Hills Golf and Country Club** is a 3,453-yard, 9-hole, par-36 course—
★ a Dick Wilson and Joe Lee design—with a restaurant, bar, and pro shop. ⊠ *E. Sunrise Hwy., Lucaya* ☎ *242/373–4500* ⊠ *$50 for 9 holes, $64 for 18 holes, cart included. Club rental $16 for 9 holes, $20 for 18 holes* ⊙ *Closed Mon.* **Our Lucaya Beach and Golf Resort Lucayan Course,** designed by Dick Wilson, is a dramatic 6,824-yard, par-72, 18-hole course featuring a balanced six straight holes, six classic left-turning doglegs, and six right-turning holes. The 18th hole has a double lake, and a new clubhouse is being built nearby. Its state-of-the-art instruction facilities include a practice putting green with bunker and chipping areas, covered teaching bays, and a teaching seminar area. A shared electric cart is

included in greens fees. ⊠ *Our Lucaya Beach and Golf Resort, Lucaya* ☎ *242/373–2002* ⊠ *Resort guests $120, nonguests $130.*

BEACHES

Some 60 mi of magnificent, pristine stretches of sand extend between Freeport-Lucaya and the island's eastern end. Most are used only by people who live in adjacent settlements. The beaches have no public facilities, so beachgoers often headquarter at one of the local beach bars, which often provide free transportation. **Lucayan Beach** is readily accessible from the town's main drag and is always lively and lovely. **Taïno Beach,** near Freeport, is fun for families, water sports enthusiasts, and partyers. Near Freeport, **Xanadu Beach** provides a mile of white sand.

WHERE TO EAT

$$ ✕ **Caribbean Yard Café and Becky's Diner.** This popular eatery opens at 7
CARIBBEAN AM and may be the best place in the Freeport tourism area to fuel up before a full day of beaching or shopping. Its diner-style booths provide a comfortable backdrop for the inexpensive menu of traditional Bahamian and American food, from conch salad and curried mutton to seafood or a BLT. Pancakes, eggs, and special Bahamian breakfasts— stew fish, boil fish, or chicken souse (the latter two are soups flavored with lime), with johnnycake or grits—are served all day. ⊠ *E. Beach Dr. and E. Sunrise Hwy.* ☎ *242/352–5247* ⊟ *D, MC, V.*

$–$$ ✕ **Pub at Lucaya.** On the Port Lucaya waterfront, this amiable pub has
DOMINICA a reputation for dependable English fare such as bangers 'n' mash and shepherd's and steak-and-ale pies. You also can't go wrong with the frenched lamb chops, Bahamian lobster tail, or strip sirloin. Lunchtime brings burgers, pasta, and deli sandwiches. The nautical decor incorporates antiques, heavy rustic tables, and ersatz Tiffany lamps suspended from a wood-beam ceiling. Ask for a table on the outside terrace. ⊠ *Port Lucaya Marketplace* ☎ *242/373–8450* ⊟ *AE, DC, MC, V.*

GRAND CAYMAN, CAYMAN ISLANDS

Jordan Simon The largest and most populous of the Cayman Islands, Grand Cayman is also one of the most popular cruise destinations in the Western Caribbean, largely because it doesn't suffer from the ailments afflicting many larger ports: panhandlers, hasslers, and crime. Instead, the Cayman economy is a study in stability and the environment is healthy and prosperous. Though the island is rather featureless, Grand Cayman is a diver's paradise, with pristine waters and a colorful variety of marine life. Compared with other Caribbean ports, there are few things to see on land here; instead, the island's most impressive sights are underwater. Snorkeling, diving, and glass-bottom boat and submarine rides top every ship's shore-excursion list and can also be arranged at major aquatic shops if you don't go on a ship-sponsored excursion. Grand Cayman is also famous for the 554 off-shore banks in George Town; not surprisingly, the standard of living is high, and nothing is cheap.

ESSENTIALS

Currency The Cayman Island dollar (CI$ to US$1.25). The U.S. dollar is accepted everywhere, and ATMs often dispense cash in both currencies, though you may receive change in Cayman dollars. Prices are often quoted in Cayman dollars, so make sure you know which currency you're dealing with so you don't end up paying 25% more than you expected.

PLASTIC BAGS
Use Zip-loc bags for all toiletries and anything that might spill. Toss a few extras into your suitcase. You may need them later to pack dirty or damp clothes.

Internet Café del Sol Internet Cafe (⊠ *Marquee Plaza, Seven Mile Beach, Grand Cayman* ☎ *345/946–2233* ⊕ *www.cafedelsol.ky*).

Telephones To dial the United States, dial 1 followed by the area code and telephone number. To place a credit-card call, dial 800/744–7777; credit-card and calling-card calls can be made from any public phone.

COMING ASHORE

Ships anchor in George Town Harbour and tender passengers onto Harbour Drive, the center of the shopping district. If you just want to walk around town and shop or visit Seven Mile Beach, you're probably better off on your own, but the Stingray Sandbar snorkeling trip is a highlight of many Caribbean vacations and fills up quickly on cruise-ship days, so it's often better to order that excursion from your ship, even though it will be more crowded than if you took an independent trip.

A tourist information booth is on the pier, and taxis queue for disembarking passengers. Taxi fares are determined by an elaborate structure set by the government, and although rates may seem high, cabbies rarely try to rip off tourists. Ask to see the chart if you want to check a quoted fare. Taxi drivers won't usually do hourly rates for small-group tours; you must arrange a sightseeing tour with a company. Car rentals are not terribly expensive, beginning at about $40 a day (plus a $7.50 driving permit), so they are a good option if you want to do some independent exploring. You can easily see the entire island and have time to stop at a beach in a single day.

EXPLORING GRAND CAYMAN

ⓒ **Blowholes.** When the easterly trade winds blow hard, crashing waves force water into caverns and send impressive geysers shooting up as much as 20 feet through the ironshore. The blowholes were partially filled during Hurricane Ivan in 2004, so the water must be rough to recapture the elemental drama that they used to have. ⊠ *Frank Sound Rd., roughly 10 mi [16 km]) east of Bodden Town, near East End.*

ⓒ **Boatswain's Beach.** What was Cayman's premier attraction, the Turtle Farm, has been transformed into a marine theme park and rebranded as Boatswain's Beach. The expanded complex now has several shops for souvenirs, jewelry, and cigars as well as restaurants. Still, the turtles remain a central attraction, and you can tour ponds with thousands of

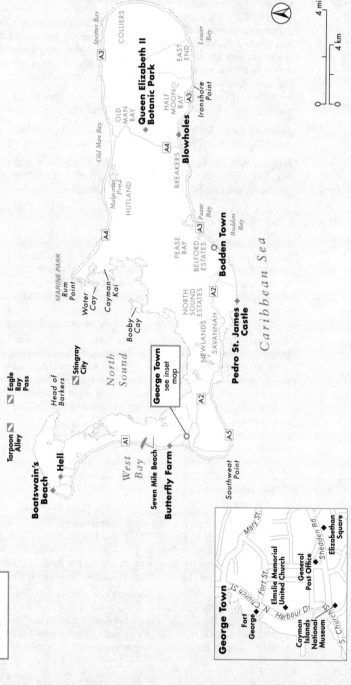

Grand Cayman

KEY

📐 Dive Sites

4 mi
4 km

Colliers Bay

Spotter Bay

COLLIERS

A3

Lower Bay

EAST END

Old Man Bay

OLD MAN BAY

Queen Elizabeth II Botanic Park

HALF MOON BAY

Ironshore Point

A4

Blowholes

Malportas Pond

HUTLAND

BREAKERS

A4

MARINE PARK

Rum Point

PEASE BAY

Pease Bay

A3

BELFORD ESTATES

Bodden Town

Bodden Bay

Water Cay

Cayman Kai

Booby Cay

NORTH SOUND ESTATES

A2

Stingray City

North Sound

NEWLANDS

SAVANNAH

Pedro St. James Castle

Head of Barkers

Tarpoon Alley

Eagle Ray Pass

George Town
see inset map

A2

Caribbean Sea

A5

Southwest Point

Boatswain's Beach

Hell

West Bay

A1

Seven Mile Beach

Butterfly Farm

George Town

Mary St.

N. Church St.

Fort St.

Fort George

Elmslie Memorial United Church

Harbour Dr.

General Post Office

Shedden Rd.

Elizabethan Square

Cayman Islands National Museum

S. Church St.

them in various stages of growth; some can be picked up from the tanks—a real treat for children and adults as the little creatures flap their fins and splash the water. A nature trail affords a 30-minute guided tour through a butterfly garden, bird-watching spot, and displays of Cayman's native reptiles, including iguanas. A snorkel lagoon provides the adventure of swimming with some of the marine life that is found just offshore from the Cayman coastline. These improvements, along with rest areas and refreshment stands, make Boatswain's Beach worthy of a few hours' visit, but the particularly steep new admission price may keep you away. ⊠*825 Northwest Point Rd., West Bay* ☎*345/949–3894* ⊕*www.boats wainsbeach.ky* ⊠*$45 for compre*hensive ticket, $18 for Turtle Farm alone ⊙Daily 8:30–4:30.

Bodden Town. In the island's original south-shore capital you can find an old cemetery on the shore side of the road. Graves with A-frame structures are said to contain the remains of pirates. There are also the ruins of a fort and a wall erected by slaves in the 19th century. A curio shop serves as the entrance to what's called the Pirate's Caves ($8), partially underground natural formations that are more hokey (decked out with fake treasure chests and mannequins in pirate garb plus an outdoor petting zoo) than spooky.

Butterfly Farm. Your entry fee is good for your entire stay, so that you can watch the life-stage changes of the butterflies. It's fun, easy, and interesting and makes a great photo op, particularly early in the morning or on a sunny afternoon. ⊠*Lawrence Rd. across from cinema, Seven Mile Beach* ☎*345/946–3411* ⊕*www.thebutterflyfarm.com* ⊠*$15* ⊙*Daily 8:30–4.*

George Town. Begin exploring the capital by strolling along the waterfront Harbour Drive to **Elmslie Memorial United Church,** named after the first Presbyterian missionary to serve in the Caymans. Its vaulted ceiling, wooden arches, and sedate nave reflect the religious nature of island residents. In front of the court building, in the center of town, names of influential Caymanians are inscribed on the **Wall of History,** which commemorates the islands' quincentennial in 2003. Across the street is the Cayman Islands Legislative Assembly Building, next door to the 1919 Peace Memorial Building. In the middle of the financial district is the **General Post Office,** built in 1939. Let the kids pet the big blue iguana statues.

☉ Built in 1833, the home of the **Cayman Islands National Museum** has had several different incarnations over the years, including that of courthouse, jail (now the gift shop), post office, and dance hall. It's small but fascinating, with excellent displays and videos that illustrate local geology, flora, and fauna, and island history. Pick up a walking-tour map of George Town at the museum gift shop before leaving. At this writing, the museum was expected to reopen sometime in summer 2009, after having been damaged during Hurricane Ivan. ⊠ *Harbour Dr., George Town* ☎ *345/949–8368* ⊕ *www.museum.ky* ☑ *$5* ☉ *Weekdays 9–5, Sat. 10–2.*

☉ **Pedro St. James Castle.** Built in 1780, the greathouse is Cayman's oldest
★ stone structure and the only remaining late-18th-century residence on the island. The buildings are surrounded by 8 acres of natural parks and woodlands. You can stroll through landscaping of native Caymanian flora and experience one of the most-spectacular views on the island from atop the dramatic Great Pedro Bluff. Don't miss the impressive multimedia theater show complete with smoking pots, misting rains, and two film screens where the story of Pedro's Castle is presented. The show plays on the hour; see it before you tour the site. The poignant outdoor Hurricane Ivan Memorial uses text, images, and symbols to represent important aspects of that horrific 2004 natural disaster. If you want a snack, stop by the relocated—and beloved—Durty Reid's, run by an ex-Marine amputee Vietnam vet who advertises "lousy food, surly help." ⊠ *Pedro Castle Rd., Savannah* ☎ *345/947–3329* ⊕ *www. pedrostjames.ky* ☑ *$10* ☉ *Daily 9–5.*

Fodor's Choice **Queen Elizabeth II Botanic Park.** This 65-acre wilderness preserve show-
★ cases a wide range of indigenous and nonindigenous tropical vegetation. Rare blue iguanas are bred and released in the gardens and are a common sight on the trails. If you're lucky, you'll see the brilliant green Cayman parrot—not just here but virtually anywhere in Cayman. ⊠ *Frank Sound Rd., off Frank Sound* ✇ *Box 203, North Side, Grand Cayman* ☎ *345/947–9462, 345/947–3558 info line* ⊕ *www.botanic-park. ky* ☑ *$10* ☉ *Apr.–Sept., daily 9–6:30; Oct.–Mar., daily 9–5:30 (last admission 1 hr prior to closing).*

SHOPPING

The **Anchorage Centre** across from the cruise-ship North Terminal has 10 of the most-affordable stores and boutiques selling duty-free goods from such great brand names as John Hardy, Movado, and Concord, as well as designer ammolite jewelry. Downtown is the **Kirk Freeport Plaza,** known for its boutiques selling fine watches, duty-free china, Gucci goods, perfumes, and cosmetics. Just keep walking—there's plenty of shopping in all directions. Stores in the **Landmark** in George Town sell perfumes, treasure coins, and upscale beachwear; Breezes by the Bay restaurant is upstairs.

Cathy Church's Underwater Photo Centre and Gallery (⊠ *S. Church St., George Town* ☎ *345/949–7415*) has a collection of the acclaimed underwater shutterbug's spectacular color and limited-edition black-and-white underwater photos. Have Cathy autograph her latest coffee-table book and regale you with anecdotes of her latest globe-trotting adventures. She'll schedule private underwater photography

★ instruction as well. **Guy Harvey's Gallery and Shoppe** (⊠ *49 S. Church St., George Town* ☎ *345/943–4891*) is where world-renowned marine biologist, conservationist, and artist Guy Harvey showcases his aquatic-inspired art in nearly every conceivable medium, logo tableware, and sportswear (even logo soccer balls and Zippos). Original paintings,

> ## STROLLERS
>
> Parents should bring along an umbrella stroller for walks around the ship as well as the ports of call; people often underestimate how big ships are. It also comes in handy at the airport. Wheel baby right to the departure gate—the stroller is gate checked and will be waiting for you when you arrive at your port of embarkation.

sculpture, and drawings are expensive, but there's something (tile art, prints, lithographs, and photos) in most price ranges. The shop itself

★ is a virtual Hemingway-esque theme park. **Pure Art** (⊠ *S. Church St., George Town* ☎ *345/949–9133*) purveys wit, warmth, and whimsy right from the wildly colored front steps. About 1.5 mi (2.5 km) south of George Town, its warren of rooms resembles a garage sale run amok or a quirky grandmother's attic spilling over with unexpected finds. The **Tortuga Rum Company** (⊠ *N. Sound Rd., Industrial Park, George Town* ☎ *345/949–7701 or 345/949–7867*) bakes then vacuum-seals more than 10,000 of its world-famous rum cakes daily, adhering to the original "secret" century-old recipe.

ACTIVITIES

DIVING AND SNORKELING

Pristine water (visibility often exceeding 100 feet [30 meters]), breathtaking coral formations, and plentiful and exotic marine life mark the **Great Wall**—a world-renowned dive site just off the north side of Grand Cayman. A must-see for adventurous souls is **Stingray City** in the North Sound, noted as the best 12-foot (3½-meter) dive in the world, where dozens of stingrays congregate, tame enough to suction squid from your outstretched palm. Nondivers gravitate to **Stingray Sandbar,** a shallower part of the North Sound, which has become a popular snorkeling spot; it is also a popular spot for the stingrays. **Don Foster's Dive Cayman Islands** (⊠ *218 S. Church St., George Town* ☎ *345/949–5679 or 800/833–4837* ⊕ *www.donfosters.com*) has a pool with a shower and also snorkeling along the ironshore at Casuarina Point, easily accessed starting at 20 feet, extending to depths of 55 feet. Rates are competitive, and there's free shuttle pickup/drop-off along Seven Mile Beach. **Eden Rock Diving Center** (⊠ *124 S. Church St., George Town* ☎ *345/949–7243* ⊕ *www.edenrockdive.com*), south of George Town, provides easy access to Eden Rock and Devil's Grotto. It features full equipment rental, lockers, shower facilities, and a full range of PADI courses from a helpful, cheerful staff. Costs for guided shore dives and two-tank dives on its Pro 42 jet-boat are cheaper than most outfits,

☾ without sacrificing quality or comfort. **Red Sail Sports** (☎ *345/949–5965 or 877/733–7245* ⊕ *www.redsailcayman.com*) offers daily trips from most of the major hotels. Dives are often run as guided tours, a perfect option for beginners. If you're experienced and your air lasts a long time, consult the boat captain to see if he requires that you come up with the group as determined by the first person who runs low on air. There is a full range of kids' dive options for ages five to 15. The company also operates Stingray City tours, dinner and sunset sails, and just about every major water sport.

FISHING

Cayman waters are abundant with blue and white marlin, yellowfin tuna, sailfish, dolphinfish, bonefish, and wahoo. Two dozen boats are available for charter.

★ **Sea Star Charters** (☎ *345/949–1016, 345/916–5234 after 8* AM), aka Clinton's Watersports, is run by Clinton Ebanks, a fine and very friendly Caymanian who will do whatever it takes to make sure that you have a wonderful time on his three small, 25- to 31-foot cabin cruisers, enjoying light-tackle, bone, and bottom fishing. He's a good choice for beginners, and offers a nice cultural experience, as well as sailing charters and snorkeling with complimentary transportation and equipment. Only cash and traveler's checks are accepted.

HIKING

★ The National Trust's **Mastic Trail** (⊠ *Frank Sound Rd., entrance by fire station at botanic park, Breakers, East End* ☎ *345/949–0121 for guide reservations* ⊕ *www.nationaltrust.org.ky*), used in the 1800s as the only direct path to and from the North Side, is a rugged 2-mi (3-km) slash through 776 dense acres of woodlands, black mangrove swamps, savannah, agricultural remnants, and ancient rock formations. Call the National Trust to determine suitability and to book a guide for $45 ($25 per person for a group); tours are run daily from 9 to 5 by appointment only, regularly on Wednesday at 9 AM. Or walk on the wild side with a $5 guidebook. The trip takes about three hours.

BEACHES

☾ **Seven Mile Beach.** Grand Cayman's west coast is dominated by the famous
Fodor's Choice Seven Mile Beach—actually a 6.5-mi-long (10-km-long) expanse of
★ powdery white sand overseeing lapis water stippled with a rainbow of parasails and kayaks. The width of the beach varies with the season; toward the south end it narrows and disappears altogether south of the Marriott, leaving only rock and ironshore. Free of litter and pesky peddlers, it's an unspoiled (though often crowded) environment. At the public beach toward the north end you can find chairs for rent ($10 for the day, including a beverage), a playground, water toys aplenty, two beach bars, restrooms, and showers. The best snorkeling is at either end, by the Marriott and Treasure Island or off the northern section called Cemetery Reef Beach. ⊠ *West Bay Rd., Seven Mile Beach.*

WHERE TO EAT

$$-$$$
CARIBBEAN
⨉**Breezes by the Bay.** There isn't a bad seat in the house at this nonstop feel-good fiesta festooned with tiny paper lanterns, Christmas lights, and Mardi Gras beads (you're "lei'd" upon entering). Wraparound balconies take in a dazzling panorama from South Sound to Seven Mile Beach. It's a joyous nonstop happy hour all day every day, especially at "Countdown to Sunset." Rum aficionados will find 34 varieties (flights available), and cocktail garnishes are impeccably fresh. Equally fresh food at bargain prices, including homemade baked goods and ice creams, isn't an afterthought. Chunky velvety conch chowder served in a bread bowl or near-definitive conch fritters are meals in themselves. Hefty sandwiches are slathered with yummy jerk mayo or garlicky aïoli. Signature standouts include meltingly moist whole fish escoveitch, curry chicken, popcorn shrimp, and jerk-glazed pork chops. ⌂ *Harbor Dr., George Town* ☎ *345/943–8469* ⊕ *www.breezesbythebay.com* ▭ *AE, MC, V.*

$$
ECLECTIC
★
⨉**Icoa Fine Foods.** Icoa, the goddess of water worshipped by the indigenous people of Venezuela's Paria peninsula, was renowned for her exceptional beauty and alluring perfume; innovative Dutch chef Jurgen Wevers crafts food that likewise stimulates all the senses, drawing his own adoring acolytes. The minimalist (and very white) space allows his cutting-edge cuisine to take center stage. Taste buds tango to such dishes as lump crab cake with marinated melon salad, basil, and yuzu; chicken liver pate with caramelized nuts, golden raisin compote, puffed cereal crisps, and honey; and braised beef short ribs with gremolata (minced garlic, parsley, and lemon peel), roasted potatoes, and saffron-garlic aioli. Fresh-baked breads make a meal in themselves. Desserts are remarkable (you can also buy handcrafted chocolates infused with fresh key limes, passion fruit, pineapple, and Cayman honey). ⌂ *9 Seven Mile Shops, West Bay Rd., Seven Mile Beach* ☎ *345/945–1915* ⊕ *www.icoacafe.com* ▭ *MC, V* ⊗ *No dinner.*

GRAND TURK, TURKS AND CAICOS ISLANDS

Ramona Settle
Just 7 mi (11 km) long and a little over 1 mi (2½ km) wide, Grand Turk, the political capital of the Turks and Caicos Islands, has been a longtime favorite destination for divers eager to explore the 7,000-foot-deep pristine coral walls that drop down only 300 yards out to sea. On shore, the tiny, quiet island is home to white-sand beaches, the National Museum, and a small population of wild horses and donkeys, which leisurely meander past the white-walled courtyards, pretty churches, and bougainvillea-covered colonial inns on their daily commute into town. The main settlement on the island is tranquil Cockburn Town, and that's where most of the small hotels, not to mention Pillory Beach, can be found. Although it has the second-largest number of inhabitants of all the Turks and Caicos Island, Grand Turk's permanent population has still not reached 4,000.

ESSENTIALS

Currency The U.S. dollar. You'll find branches of Scotiabank and FirstCaribbean on Grand Turk, with ATMs; all of these are in tiny Cockburn Town.

Internet There's no Internet café at the cruise center, but if you have a laptop, you might take it to the restaurant at the Osprey Beach Hotel, where you can take advantage of the hotel's free Wi-Fi.

Telephones To make local calls, dial the seven-digit number. To make calls from the Turks and Caicos, dial 0, then 1, the area code, and the number. All telephone service is provided by LIME (formerly Cable & Wireless), and your U.S. cell phone may work on Grand Turk. Calling cards are available, or you can make a call using AT&T's USADirect by dialing 800/872–2881 to charge the call to your credit card or an AT&T prepaid calling card.

COMING ASHORE

Cruise ships dock at the southern end of the island, near the former U.S. Air Force base south of the airport. The purpose-built, $40-million cruise center is about 3 mi (5 km) from tranquil Cockburn Town, Pillory Beach, and the Ridge, and far from most of the western shore dive-sites. The center has many facilities, including shopping, a large, free-form pool, car-rental booths, and even a dock from which many sea-bound excursions depart. Governor's Beach is adjacent to the cruise-ship complex and one of the island's best beaches, but others are right in and around Cockburn Town.

If you want to come into Cockburn Town, it's reachable by taxi. You can also rent a car. However, most cruise-ship passengers can purchase a pass for the Guana "Hop On, Hop Off" Bus Tour of the island, which includes admission to several attractions, including the lighthouse and the old prison in Cockburn Town. This is usually cheaper than renting a car, and drops you near the good beaches in town. Just be aware that not all cruise lines participate in the program. Regent Seven Seas and Oceania, for example, do not offer this as an option at this writing.

Grand Turk Cruise Terminal (⊠*South Base, Grand Turk Cruise Terminal* ☎*649/946–1040* ⊕*www.grandturkcc.com*) has a Web site that shows all the cruise schedules, lists all the shops at the terminal, and outlines options for excursions and transportation. A bonus is the live webcam so you can check the actual weather at any given moment.

EXPLORING GRAND TURK

Pristine beaches with vistas of turquoise waters, small local settlements, historic ruins, and native flora and fauna are among the sights on Grand Turk. Fewer than 4,000 people live on this 7½ square-mi (19-square-km) island, and it's hard to get lost, as there aren't many roads.

Cockburn Town. The buildings in the colony's capital and seat of government reflect a 19th-century Bermudian style. Narrow streets are lined with low stone walls and old street lamps, which are now powered by electricity. The once-vital salinas have been restored, and covered benches along the sluices offer shady spots for observing wading birds,

Grand Turk

KEY

- Beaches
- Cruise Ship Terminal
- Dive Sites

Northwest Point

Little Bluff Point — **Grand Turk Lighthouse**

NORTH WELLS

Corktree Beach

CORK-TREE

North Creek

RIDGE
♦ **Flamingo Cove Marina**

Pillory Beach

North Salina

BREEZY BRAE

Cockburn Town

Town Pond

Victoria Library
St. Mary's Church

Red Salina

ATLANTIC OCEAN

Osprey Beach

Red Salina

Grand Turk International Airport

South Creek

Gibbs Cay

Hawks Pond

WATERLOO

Hawks Nest Plantation

Round Cay

Governor's Beach

Former U.S. A.F.B.

Cruise Ship Port

Hawks Nest Salina

White Sands Beach

Columbus' Landfall

0 ——— 1/2 mi
0 ——— 1/2 km

including flamingos that frequent the shallows. Be sure to pick up a copy of the tourist board's "Heritage Walk" guide to discover Grand Turk's rich architecture.

☼ ★ In one of the oldest stone buildings on the islands, the **Turks and Caicos National Museum** houses the Molasses Reef wreck, the earliest shipwreck—dating to the early 1500s—discovered in the Americas. The natural-history exhibits include artifacts left by Taíno, African, North American, Bermudian, French, and Latin American settlers. The museum has a 3-D coral reef exhibit, a walk-in Lucayan cave with wooden artifacts, and a gallery dedicated to Grand Turk's little-known involvement in the Space Race (former Senator John Glenn made his first landfall back on Earth here after his walk on the moon). An interactive children's gallery keeps knee-high visitors even more "edutained." The museum also claims that Grand Turk was Columbus's first landfall in the New World. ⊠ *Duke St., Cockburn Town* ☎ *649/946–2160* ⊕ *www.tcmuseum.org* 🖃 *$5* ⊙ *Mon., Tues., Thurs., and Fri. 9–4, Wed. 9–5, Sat. 9–1.*

Grand Turk Lighthouse. More than 150 years old, the lighthouse, built in the United Kingdom and transported piece by piece to the island, used to protect ships in danger of wrecking on the northern reefs. Use this panoramic landmark as a starting point for a breezy cliff-top walk by following the donkey trails to the deserted eastern beach. ⊠ *Lighthouse Rd., North Ridge.*

> **GRAND TURK BEST BETS**
>
> ■ **Beaches.** The sand is powdery soft, the water azure blue.
>
> ■ **Diving.** If you're certified, there are several world-class dive sights within each reach.
>
> ■ **Gibb's Cay.** If you're not a diver, take a ship-sponsored trip here; it's an excellent beach.
>
> ■ **Front Street.** Colorful Front Street will give you the feeling you've step back in time.
>
> ■ **Turks and Caicos National Museum.** Small but worthy.

SHOPPING

There's not much to buy in Grand Turk, and shopping isn't a major activity here. However, a duty-free mall is located right at the cruise-ship center, where you'll find the usual array of upscale shops, including Ron Jon's Surf Shop, the largest Margaritaville in the world, and Piranha Joe's. There are also shops in Cockburn Town itself.

ACTIVITIES

CYCLING

The island's mostly flat terrain isn't very taxing, and most roads have hard surfaces. Take water with you: there are few places to stop for refreshment. Most hotels have bicycles available, but you can also rent them for $10 to $15 a day from **Oasis Divers** (⊠ *Duke St., Cockburn Town* ☎ *649/946–1128* ⊕ *www.oasisdivers.com*).

DIVING AND SNORKELING

★ In these waters you can find under-sea cathedrals, coral gardens, and countless tunnels, but note that you must carry and present a valid certificate card before you'll be allowed to dive. As its name sug-

WATER
Tap water on your ship is perfectly safe to drink; purchasing bottled water is only necessary if you prefer the taste.

gests, the **Black Forest** offers stagger-ing black-coral formations as well as the occasional black-tip shark. In the **Library** you can study fish galore, including large numbers of yellowtail snapper. At the Columbus Passage separating South Caicos from Grand Turk, each side of a 22-mi-wide (35-km-wide) channel drops more than 7,000 feet. From January through March, thousands of Atlantic humpback whales swim through en route to their winter breeding grounds. **Gibb's Cay,** a small cay a couple of miles off Grand Turk, makes a great excursion swimming with stingrays.

Dive outfitters can all be found in Cockburn Town. Two-tank boat dives generally cost $60 to $80. **Blue Water Divers** (✉ *Duke St., Cockburn Town* ☎ *649/946–2432* ⊕ *www.grandturkscuba.com*) has been in operation on Grand Turk since 1983, and is the only PADI Gold Palm five-star dive center on the island. Owner Mitch will doubtless put some of your underwater adventures to music in the evenings when he plays at the Osprey Beach Hotel or Salt Raker Inn. **Oasis Divers** (✉ *Duke St., Cockburn Town* ☎ *649/946–1128* ⊕ *www.oasisdivers. com*) specializes in complete gear handling and pampering treatment. It also supplies Nitrox and rebreathers. Besides daily dive trips to the wall, **Sea Eye Diving** (✉ *Duke St., Cockburn Town* ☎ *649/946–1407* ⊕ *www.seaeyediving.com*) offers encounters with friendly stingrays on a popular snorkeling trip to nearby Gibbs Cay.

SOFT ADVENTURE

Jamaica-based Chukka Caribbean Adventures (✉ *Cruise ship terminal shops, Grand Turk Cruise Terminal* ☎ *649/232-1339* ⊕ *www.chukka caribbean.com*) operates most of the ship-sponsored shore excursions, offering a horseback ride and swim, dune buggy safari, and 4x4 safari. You can now book these tours directly with Chukka.

BEACHES

★ Grand Turk is spoiled for choices when it comes to beach options: sun-set strolls along miles of deserted beaches, picnics in secluded coves, beachcombing on the coralline sands, snorkeling around shallow coral heads close to shore, and admiring the impossibly turquoise-blue waters. **Governor's Beach,** a beautiful crescent of powder-soft sand and shallow, calm turquoise waters that fronts the official British Governor's residence, called Waterloo, is framed by tall casuarina trees that provide plenty of natural shade. To have it all to yourself, go on a day when cruise ships are not in port. On days when ships are in port, the beach is lined with lounge chairs. For more of a beachcombing experience, **Little Bluff Point Beach,** just west of the Grand Turk Lighthouse, is a low, limestone-cliff-edged, shell-covered beach that looks out onto shallow waters, mangroves, and often flamingos, especially in spring and summer. **Pillory Beach,** with sparkling neon turquoise water, is the prettiest beach on Grand Turk; it also has great off-the-beach snorkeling.

WHERE TO EAT

$$ ✕**Jimmy Buffet's Margaritaville.** The only chain restaurant (so far) in all
AMERICAN   of the Turks and Caicos is the place to partake in cruise activities even when you're not on a cruise ship. One of the largest Margaritavilles in the world is at the Grand Turk Cruise Terminal and open to all comers (both cruisers and anyone else on the island) when a cruise ship is parked at the dock. Tables are scattered around a large winding pool; there's even a DJ and a FlowRider (a wave pool where you can surf on land—for a fee). You can enjoy 52 flavors of margaritas or the restaurant's own beer, Landshark, while you eat casual bar food such as wings, quesadillas, and burgers. The food is good, the people-watching is great. ⊠ *Grand Turk Cruise Terminal* ☎ *649/946–1880* ⊕ *www. margaritavillecaribbean.com* ⊟ *AE, D, DC, MC, V* ☉ *Closed when no cruise ship is at pier.*

$$ ✕**Sand Bar.** Run by two Canadian sisters, this popular beachside bar is
AMERICAN-   a good value, though the menu is limited to fish-and-chips, quesadillas,
CASUAL   and similarly basic bar fare. The tented wooden terrace jutting out on to the beach provides shade during the day, making it an ideal lunch spot, but it's also a great place to watch the sunset. The service is friendly, and the local crowd often spills into the street. ⊠ *Duke St., Cockburn Town* ☎ *No phone* ⊟ *MC, V.*

GRENADA (ST. GEORGE'S)

Jane E. Zarem   Nutmeg, cinnamon, cloves, cocoa . . . those heady aromas fill the air in Grenada (pronounced gruh-nay-da). Only 21 mi (33½ km) long and 12 mi (19½ km) wide, the Isle of Spice is a tropical gem of lush rain forests, white-sand beaches, secluded coves, exotic flowers, and enough locally grown spices to fill anyone's kitchen cabinet. St. George's is one of the most picturesque capital cities in the Caribbean, St. George's Harbour is one of the most picturesque harbors, and Grenada's Grand Anse Beach is one of the region's finest beaches. The island has friendly, hospitable people and enough good shopping, restaurants, historic sites, and natural wonders to make it a popular port of call. About one-third of Grenada's visitors arrive by cruise ship, and that number continues to grow each year.

ESSENTIALS

Currency Eastern Caribbean (E.C.) dollar (EC$2.67 to US$1). U.S. dollars are generally accepted, but change is given in E.C. dollars.

Internet Java-Kool Internet Cafe (⊠ *The Carenage, St. George's* ☎ *473/435–3506).*

Telephones Prepaid phone cards, which can be used in special card phones throughout the Caribbean for local or international calls, are sold in various denominations at shops, attractions, transportation centers, and other

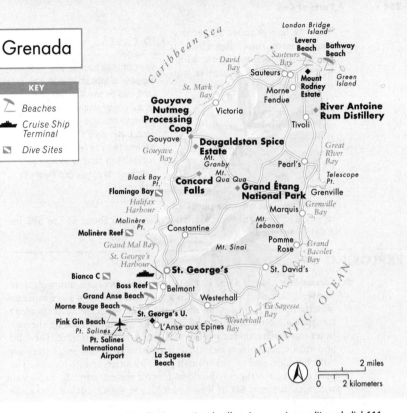

Grenada

KEY

⟋ Beaches

🚢 Cruise Ship Terminal

◳ Dive Sites

Caribbean Sea

London Bridge Island
Levera Beach
Bathway Beach
David Bay
Sauteurs Bay
Sauteurs
Morne Fendue
◆ **Mount Rodney Estate**
Green Island
St. Mark Bay
Gouyave Nutmeg Processing Coop
Victoria
River Antoine Rum Distillery
Tivoli
Gouyave
Gouyave Bay
Dougaldston Spice Estate
Great River Bay
Mt. Granby
Pearl's
Black Bay Pt.
Concord Falls
Mt. Qua Qua
Telescope Pt.
Flamingo Bay ◳
Grand Étang National Park
Grenville
Halifax Harbour
Marquis
Grenville Bay
Molinère Pt.
Constantine
Mt. Lebanon
Molinère Reef ◳
Grand Mal Bay
Mt. Sinai
Pomme Rose
Grand Bacolet Bay
St. George's Harbour
St. George's
St. David's
Bianca C ◳
Belmont
Boss Reef ◳
Grand Anse Beach ⟋
Westerhall
Morne Rouge Beach ⟋
La Sagesse Bay
St. George's U.
Pink Gin Beach ⟋
L'Anse aux Epines
Westerhall Bay
Pt. Salines
Pt. Salines International Airport
La Sagesse Beach

ATLANTIC OCEAN

0 ——— 2 miles
0 ——— 2 kilometers

---

convenient outlets. For international calls using a major credit card, dial 111; to place a collect call or use a calling card, dial 800/225–5872 from any telephone. Pay phones are available at the Cruise Ship Terminal welcome center, the LIME office on the Carenage in St. George's, shopping centers, and other convenient locations.

COMING ASHORE

The Cruise Ship Terminal near Market Square, on the north side of St. George's, allows larger ships to dock rather than anchor outside the harbor. A full range of passenger facilities is available at the terminal, which opens directly into the Esplanade Mall. You can easily tour the capital on foot, but be prepared to climb up and down steep hills. If you don't want to walk up and down through town, you can find a taxi ($3 or $4 each way) or a water taxi ($2 per person each way) right at the terminal to take you around to the Carenage. To explore areas outside St. George's, hiring a taxi or arranging a guided tour is more sensible than renting a car. Taxis are plentiful, and fixed rates to popular island destinations are posted at the terminal's welcome center.

A taxi ride from the terminal to the beach will cost $13, but water taxis are a less expensive and more picturesque way to get there; the one-way fare is about $6 per person to Grand Anse, depending on the number of passengers. Minibuses are the least expensive way to travel between St. George's and Grand Anse; pay EC$1.50 (55¢), but hold on to your hat. They're crowded with local people getting from here to there and often make quick stops and take turns at quite a clip! Still, it's an inexpensive, fun, and safe way to travel around the island. If you want to rent a car and explore on your own, be prepared to pay $12 for a temporary driving permit and about $55 to $75 for a day's car rental.

> **ID CASES**
>
> You can keep track of your boarding pass, shipboard charge/key card, and picture ID when you go ashore by slipping them into a bi-fold business-card carrying case. Cases with a sueded finish are less likely to fall out of your pocket. With security as tight as it is these days, you don't want to lose your ID.

EXPLORING GRENADA

★ **Concord Falls.** About 8 mi (13 km) north of St. George's, a turnoff from the West Coast Road leads to Concord Falls—actually three separate waterfalls. The first is at the end of the road; when the currents aren't too strong, you can take a dip under the cascade. Reaching the two other waterfalls requires an hour's hike into the forest reserve. The third and most spectacular waterfall, at Fountainbleu, thunders 65 feet over huge boulders and creates a small pool. It's smart to hire a guide. The path is clear, but slippery boulders toward the end can be treacherous without assistance. ⊠ *Off West Coast Rd., St. John's* ⊠ *Changing room $2* ⊗ *Daily 9–5.*

☼ **Dougaldston Spice Estate.** Just south of Gouyave, this historic plantation, now primarily a living museum, still grows and processes spices the old-fashioned way. You can see cocoa, nutmeg, mace, cloves, and other spices laid out on giant racks to dry in the sun. A worker will be glad to explain the process (and will appreciate a small donation). You can buy spices for about $2 a bag. ⊠ *Gouyave* ☎ *No phone* ⊠ *Free* ⊗ *Weekdays 9–4.*

☼ **Gouyave Nutmeg Processing Cooperative.** Touring the nutmeg processing
★ co-op, in the center of the west-coast fishing village of Gouyave (pronounced *gwahve*), is a fragrant, fascinating way to spend a half hour. You can learn all about nutmeg and its uses, see the nutmegs laid out in bins, and watch the workers sort them by hand and pack them into burlap bags for shipping worldwide. The three-story plant turned out 3 million pounds of Grenada's most famous export each year prior to Hurricane Ivan's devastating effect on the crop in 2004. Locals estimate it will be 2010 before the nutmeg industry returns to that level. ⊠ *Gouyave* ☎ *473/444-8337* ⊠ *$1* ⊗ *Weekdays 10–1 and 2–4.*

☼ **Grand Étang National Park and Forest Reserve.** Deep in the mountainous
★ interior of Grenada is a bird sanctuary and forest reserve with miles of hiking trails, lookouts, and fishing streams. **Grand Étang Lake** is a 36-acre expanse of cobalt-blue water that fills the crater of an extinct

volcano 1,740 feet above sea level. Although legend has it that the lake is bottomless, maximum soundings are recorded at 18 feet. The informative **Grand Étang Forest Center** has displays on the local wildlife and vegetation. A forest manager is on hand to answer questions. A small snack bar and souvenir stands are nearby. ⊠ *Main interior road, between Grenville and St. George's, St. Andrew's* ☎ 473/440–6160 🖾 $1 ☉ *Daily 8:30–4.*

River Antoine Rum Distillery. At this rustic operation, kept open primarily as a museum, a limited quantity of Rivers rum is produced by the same methods used since the distillery opened in 1785. The process begins with the crushing of sugarcane from adjacent fields. The result is a potent overproof rum, sold only in Grenada, that will knock your socks off. ⊠ *River Antoine Estate, St. Patrick's* ☎ 473/442–7109 🖾 $2 ☉ *Guided tours daily 9–4.*

GRENADA BEST BETS

■ **The Beach.** Grand Anse Beach is one of the Caribbean's most beautiful.

■ **Deep-Sea Fishing.** Fishing is excellent in the waters around Grenada.

■ **Market Square.** Market Square is an excellent bustling produce and spice market.

■ **Nutmeg.** Don't miss a visit to a nutmeg cooperative (and get a pocketful to take home).

■ **Waterfalls.** Concord Falls, just south of Gouyave, and Annandale Falls are among the island's best.

St. George's. Grenada's capital is a bustling West Indian city, most of which remains unchanged from colonial days. Narrow streets lined with shops wind up, down, and across steep hills. Brick warehouses and small shops cling to the waterfront, while pastel-painted homes rise from the waterfront and disappear into steep green hills.

Picturesque **St. George's Harbour,** a submerged volcanic crater, is arguably the prettiest harbor in the Caribbean and the center of town. Schooners, ferries, and tour boats tie up along the seawall or at the small dinghy dock. The **Carenage** (pronounced car-a-*nahzh*), which surrounds horseshoe-shape St. George's Harbour, is the capital's main thoroughfare. Warehouses, shops, and restaurants line the waterfront. The *Christ of the Deep* statue that sits on the pedestrian plaza at the center of the Carenage was presented to Grenada by Costa Cruise Line in remembrance of its ship *Bianca C,* which burned and sank in the harbor in 1961 and is now a favorite dive site.

The **Grenada National Museum** (⊠ *Young and Monckton Sts.* ☎ 473/440–3725 🖾 $1 ☉ *Weekdays 9–4:30, Sat. 10–1*), a block from the Carenage, is built on the foundation of a French army barracks and prison that was originally built in 1704. The small museum has exhibitions of news items, photos, and proclamations relating to the 1983 intervention, along with the childhood bathtub of Empress Joséphine (who was born on Martinique) and other memorabilia from earlier historical periods.

Fodor's Choice ★

Ft. George (⊠ *Church St.*) is high on the hill at the entrance to St. George's Harbour. It's Grenada's oldest fort—built by the French in

1705 to protect the harbor. No shots were ever fired here until October 1983, when Prime Minister Maurice Bishop and some of his followers were assassinated in the courtyard. The fort now houses police headquarters but is open to the public daily; admission is free. The 360-degree view of the capital city, St. George's Harbour, and the open sea is spectacular.

An engineering feat for its time, the 340-foot-long **Sendall Tunnel** was built in 1895 and named for an early governor. It separates the harbor side of St. George's from the Esplanade on the bay side of town, where you can find the markets (produce, meat, and fish), the cruise-ship terminal, the Esplanade Mall, and the public bus station.

Don't miss St. George's picturesque **Market Square** (⊠ *Granby St.*), a block from the cruise-ship terminal. It's open every weekday morning but really comes alive on Saturday from 8 to noon. Vendors sell baskets, spices, brooms, clothing, knickknacks, coconut water, and heaps of fresh produce. A huge renovation project completed in early 2008 provides permanent cover for the vendors. Historically, Market Square is where parades begin and political rallies take place.

Overlooking the city of St. George's and the inland side of the harbor, historic **Ft. Frederick** (⊠ *Richmond Hill*) provides a panoramic view of two-thirds of Grenada. The fort was started by the French and completed in 1791 by the British; it was also the headquarters of the People's Revolutionary Government during the 1983 coup. Today you can get a bird's-eye view of much of Grenada from here.

SHOPPING

Grenada's best souvenirs or gifts for friends back home are spice baskets filled with cinnamon, nutmeg, mace, bay leaves, cloves, turmeric, and ginger. You can buy them for as little as $2 in practically every shop, at the open-air produce market at **Market Square** in St. George's, at the vendor stalls near the pier, and at the **Vendor's Craft and Spice Market** on Grand Anse Beach. Vendors also sell handmade fabric dolls, coral jewelry, seashells, and hats and baskets handwoven from green palm fronds. Bargaining is not appropriate in the shops, and it isn't customary with vendors—although most will offer you "a good price."

★ At **Art Fabrik** (⊠ *Young St., St. George's* ☎ *473/440–0568*), you can find batik fabric created by hand in the next-door studio and sold either by the yard or fashioned into dresses, shirts, shorts, hats, and scarves. **Art Grenada** (⊠ *Grand Anse Shopping Centre, Suite 7, Grand Anse, St. George's* ☎ *473/444–2317*) sells paintings, drawings, and watercolors exclusively by Grenadian artists, among them Canute Caliste, Lyndon Bedeau, and Susan Mains. Exhibitions change monthly, and you can have your purchases shipped. **Tikal** (⊠ *Young St., St. George's* ☎ *473/440–2310*) is known for its exquisite baskets, artwork, jewelry, batik items, and fashions.

ACTIVITIES

DIVING AND SNORKELING

You can see hundreds of varieties of fish and some 40 species of coral at more than a dozen sites off Grenada's southwest coast—only 15 to 20 minutes by boat—and another couple of dozen sites around Carriacou's reefs and neighboring islets. Depths vary from 20 to 120 feet, and visibility varies from 30 to 100 feet.

A spectacular dive is *Bianca C,* a 600-foot cruise ship that caught fire in 1961, sank to 100 feet, and is now encrusted with coral and serves as a habitat for giant turtles, spotted eagle rays, barracuda, and jacks. **Boss Reef** extends 5 mi (8 km) from St. George's Harbour to Point Salines, with a depth ranging from 20 to 90 feet. **Flamingo Bay** has a wall that drops to 90 feet and is teeming with fish, sponges, sea horses, sea fans, and coral. **Molinère Reef** slopes from about 20 feet below the surface to a wall that drops to 65 feet. It's a good dive for beginners, and advanced divers can continue farther out to view the wreck of the *Buccaneer,* a 42-foot sloop.

Aquanauts Grenada (⌂ *Spice Island Beach Resort, Grand Anse Beach, Grand Anse, St. George's* ☎ *473/444–1126, 888/446–9235 in U.S.* ⌂ *True Blue Bay Resort, True Blue* ☎ *473/439–2500* ⊕ *www.aquanauts grenada.com*) has a multilingual staff, so instruction is available in English, German, Dutch, French, and Spanish. Two-tank dive trips, accommodating no more than eight divers, are offered each morning to both the Caribbean and Atlantic sides of Grenada. **EcoDive** (⌂ *Coyaba Beach Resort, Grand Anse, St. George's* ☎ *473/444–7777* ⊕ *www.eco diveandtrek.com*) offers two dive trips daily, both drift and wreck dives, as well as weekly trips to dive Isle de Rhonde. The company also runs Grenada's marine conservation and education center, which conducts coral-reef monitoring and turtle projects.

FISHING

Deep-sea fishing around Grenada is excellent, with marlin, sailfish, yellowfin tuna, and dolphinfish topping the list of good catches. You can arrange sportfishing trips that accommodate up to five people starting at $375 for a half day and $580 for a full day. **True Blue Sportfishing** (☎ *473/444–2048* ⊕ *www.yesaye.com*) offers big-game charters on its 31-foot *Yes Aye.* It has an enclosed cabin, a fighting chair, and professional tackle. British-born Captain Gary Clifford, who has been fishing since the age of six, has run the company since 1998. Refreshments and courtesy transport are included.

BEACHES

Bathway Beach. A broad strip of sand with a natural reef that protects swimmers from the rough Atlantic surf on Grenada's far northern shore, this Levera National Park beach has changing rooms at the park headquarters. ⌂ *Levera, St. Patrick's.*

Fodor'sChoice ★ **Grand Anse Beach.** In the southwest, about 3 mi (5 km) south of St. George's, Grenada's loveliest and most popular beach is a gleaming 2-mi (3-km) semicircle of white sand lapped by clear, gentle surf. Sea grape trees and coconut palms provide shady escapes from the sun. Brilliant rainbows frequently spill into the sea from the high green mountains that frame St. George's Harbour to the north. The Grand Anse Craft and Spice Market is at the midpoint of the beach. ⊠ *Grand Anse, St. George's.*

WHERE TO EAT

Restaurants add an 8% government tax to your bill and usually add a 10% service charge; if not, tip 10% to 15% for a job well done.

$$–$$$ ✕ **Coconut Beach Restaurant.** Take local seafood, add butter, wine, and
CARIBBEAN   Grenadian spices, and you have excellent French-creole cuisine. Throw in a beautiful location on Grand Anse Beach, and this West Indian cottage becomes a perfect alfresco spot. Lobster is a specialty, as lobster thermidor or perhaps wrapped in a crepe, dipped in garlic butter, or added to pasta. Homemade coconut pie is a winner for dessert. Dine "wet or fine," at a table on the beach or inside. On Wednesday and Sunday nights in season, dinner is a beach barbecue with live music. ⊠ *Grand Anse, St. George's* ☎ 473/444–4644 ⊟ *AE, D, MC, V* ⊙ *Closed Tues.*

$$–$$$ ✕ **The Nutmeg.** West Indian specialties, fresh seafood, great hamburgers,
CARIBBEAN   and a waterfront view make this a favorite with locals and visitors alike.
ↄ   It's upstairs on the Carenage (above Sea Change bookstore), with large, open windows from which you can watch the harbor activity as you eat. Try the callaloo soup, curried lambi, spicy crab back, fresh seafood, or a steak—or just stop by for a "famous" Nutmeg rum punch and a roti. It's a busy place, so you may have to share a table. ⊠ *The Carenage, St. George's* ☎ 473/440–2539 ⊟ *AE, D, MC, V.*

GUADELOUPE (POINTE-À-PITRE)

Eileen Robinson Smith   On a map, Guadeloupe looks like a giant butterfly resting on the sea between Antigua and Dominica. Its two wings—Basse-Terre and Grande-Terre—are the two largest islands in the 659-square-mi (1,054-square-km) Guadeloupe archipelago. The Rivière Salée, a 4-mi (6-km) channel between the Caribbean and the Atlantic, forms the "spine" of the butterfly. A drawbridge near Pointe-à-Pitre, the main city, connects the two islands. Gorgeous scenery awaits, as Guadeloupe is one of the most physically attractive islands in the Caribbean. If you're seeking a resort atmosphere, casinos, and nearly white sandy beaches, your target is Grande-Terre. On the other hand, Basse-Terre's Parc National de la Guadeloupe, laced with mountain trails and washed by waterfalls and rivers, is a 74,100-acre haven for hikers, nature lovers, and anyone brave enough to peer into the steaming crater of an active volcano. The tropical beauty suggests the mythical Garden of Eden.

ESSENTIALS

Currency The euro (€1 to US $1.31). Some of the larger liquor and jewelry stores may accept dollars, but don't count on that. You cannot cash traveler's checks or dollars at the bank, only at a bureau de change, so ATMs are your best bet if you need euros; facing the tourist office, there is one just to the right at the bank.

Guadeloupe

KEY

⊿ Beaches

⛴ Cruise Ship Terminal

◿ Dive Sites

La Pointe de la Grande Vigie

Guadeloupe passage

Anse Bertrand
Campêche
Port Louis
Gros-Cap

ATLANTIC OCEAN

Pte. Allègre
Petit-Canal
Vieux-Bourg

La Grande-Anse

GRANDE

Ste-Rose
Morne-à-l'Eau
Le Moule   **Anse de la Gourde**

Deshaies
Pointe-à-Pitre
TERRE

La Désirade
Grande-Anse

Pointe-Noire
Lamentin
Abymes
St-François   **Pointe Tarare**

BASSE   Destrelan
Ft. Fleur   Ste-Anne
d'Épée

Cascade aux Ecrevisses
Gosier
Plage du Helleux
TO LA DÉSIRADE

Mahaut
Ilet de Pigeon
Les Mamelles
Petit-Bourg
Ilet du Gosier
Plage Caravelle

igeon Island ◿
Malendure
Parc National de Guadeloupe
Ste-Marie
Aquarium de la Guadeloupe
Iles de la Petite Terre

Bouillante
La Soufrière
TERRE

Vieux-Habitants
Capesterre-Belle-Eau

Basse-Terre ★
Trois-Rivières

Saint Louis
Marie-Galante

Caribbean Sea
Vieux Fort

Terre-de-Bas
Iles des Saintes (Les Saintes)
Grand-Bourg
Petite-Anse

0 — 10 miles

0 — 10 kilometers

Internet Pointe-à-Pitre has several Internet cafés (there is one right at the new cruise pier); the tourist office can point you in the direction of several more in the immediate vicinity.

Telephones To call the United States from Guadeloupe, dial 001, the area code, and the local number. For calls within Guadeloupe, you now have to put 0590 before the six-digit number. You'll need to purchase a *télécarte* at the post office or at tobacco and grocery shops in order to use the phone booths.

COMING ASHORE

Ships now dock at the new cruise terminal at Pier 5/6, which houses an internet café, duty-free shop, and the colorful Karuland Village, where cruisers can browse and buy spices, pareos, and souvenirs or just sit and listen to the local music while having coconut ice cream. Located in downtown Pointe-à-Pitre, it is about a five-minute walk from the shopping district. Passengers are greeted by local musicians and hostesses, usually dressed in the traditional madras costumes—and often dispensing samplings of local rum and creole specialties. These multilingual staffers operate the information booth and can pair you up with an English-speaking taxi driver for a customized island tour. To get to the main tourist office, walk along the quay to the Place de la Victoire; it is a large white Victorian building with wraparound verandah.

Taxi fares are regulated by the government (but expensive) and posted at taxi stands. The hostesses at the cruise-ship welcome center can pair you with other passengers and put you in a cab with an English-speaking driver. Renting a car is a good way to see Guadeloupe, but it is expensive and best booked in advance. Be aware that traffic around Pointe-à-Pitre can be dreadful during rush-hour, so allow plenty of time to drop off your car rental and get back to the ship. There are many rental agencies at the airport, but that is a €35 taxi ride from the city.

EXPLORING GUADELOUPE

Ⓒ **Aquarium de la Guadeloupe.** Unique in the Antilles, this aquarium in the marina near Pointe-à-Pitre is a good place to spend an hour. The well-planned facility has an assortment of tropical fish, crabs, lobsters, moray eels, coffer fish, and some live coral. It's also a turtle rescue center. New is the spectacular shark tank. ⊠ *Pl. Créole off rte. N4, Pointe-à-Pitre* 🕾 *0590/90–92–38* 🖃 *€8.50* ⊘ *Daily 9–7.*

Ft. Fleur d'Épée. The main attraction in Bas-du-Fort is this 18th-century fortress, which hunkers down on a hillside behind a deep moat. It was the scene of hard-fought battles between the French and the English in 1794. You can explore its well-preserved dungeons and battlements and take in a sweeping view of Iles des Saintes and Marie-Galante. ⊠ *Bas-du-Fort* 🕾 *0590/90–94–61* 🖃 *€6* ⊘ *Mon. 10–5, Tues.–Sun. 9–5.*

★ **Parc National de la Guadeloupe.** This 74,100-acre park has been recognized by UNESCO as a Biosphere Reserve. Before going, pick up a *Guide to the National Park* from the tourist office; it rates the hiking trails according to difficulty, and most are quite difficult indeed. Most mountain trails are in the southern half of the park. The park is bisected by the route de la Traversée, a 16-mi (26-km) paved road lined with masses of tree ferns, shrubs, flowers, tall trees, and green plantains. It's the ideal point of entry to the park. Wear rubber-soled shoes and take along a swimsuit, a sweater, and perhaps food for a picnic. Try to get an early start to stay ahead of the hordes of cruise-ship passengers making a day of it. Check on the weather; if Basse-Terre has had a lot of rain, give it up. In the past, after intense rainfall, rock slides have closed the road for months. ⊠ *Administrative Headquarters, rte. de la Traversée, St-Claude* 🕾 *0590/80–86–00* ⊕ *www.guadeloupe-parcnational.com* 🖃 *Free* ⊘ *Weekdays 8–5:30.*

Within the Parc National de la Guadeloupe, **Cascade aux Ecrevisses** is one of the island's loveliest (and most popular) spots. There's a marked trail (walk carefully—the rocks can be slippery) leading to this splendid waterfall, which dashes down into the Corossol River—a good place for a dip. Come early, though; otherwise you definitely won't have it to yourself.

Pointe-à-Pitre. Although not the capital, it is the island's largest city, a commercial and industrial hub in the southwest of Grande-Terre. The isles of Guadeloupe have 450,000 inhabitants, 99.6% of whom live in the cities. Pointe-à-Pitre is bustling, noisy, and hot—a place of honking horns and traffic jams and cars on sidewalks for want of a parking place. By day its pulse is fast, but at night, when its streets are almost deserted, you don't want to be there.

The city has suffered severe damage over the years from earthquakes, fires, and hurricanes. In recent years it took heavy hits by Hurricanes Frederick (1979), David (1980), and Hugo (1989). On one side of rue Frébault you can see the remaining French colonial structures; on the other, the modern city. Some of the downtown area has been rejuvenated. An impressive terminal serves the ferries that depart for Iles des Saintes, Marie-Galante, Dominica, Martinique, and St. Lucia.

> ## GUADELOUPE BEST BETS
>
> ■ **Beaches.** The southern coast of Grand-Terre has stretches of soft, nearly white sand.
>
> ■ **Diving.** Jacques Cousteau called the reef off Pigeon Island one of the world's top dive sites.
>
> ■ **Hiking.** The Parc National de la Guadeloupe is one of the Caribbean's most spectacular scenic destinations.
>
> ■ **Shopping.** Though Point-à-Pitre itself can be frenetic, it does have a good choice of French goods.

The heart of the old city is **place de la Victoire**; surrounded by wooden buildings with balconies and shutters (including the tourism office) and by sidewalk cafés, it was named in honor of Victor Hugues's 1794 victory over the British. During the French Revolution, Hugues ordered the guillotine set up here so that the public could witness the bloody end of 300 recalcitrant royalists.

Even more colorful is the bustling **marketplace**, between rues St-John Perse, Frébault, Schoelcher, and Peynier. It's a cacophonous place, where housewives bargain for spices, herbs (and herbal remedies), and a bright assortment of papayas, breadfruits, christophenes, and tomatoes.

For fans of French ecclesiastical architecture, there's the imposing **Cathédrale de St-Pierre et St-Paul** (⊠*Rue Alexandre Isaac at rue de l'Eglise*), built in 1807. Although battered by hurricanes, it has fine stained-glass windows and creole-style balconies and is reinforced with pillars and ribs that look like leftovers from the Eiffel Tower.

Anyone with an interest in French literature and culture won't want to miss the **Musée St-John Perse,** which is dedicated to Guadeloupe's most famous son and one of the giants of world literature, Alexis Léger, better known as St-John Perse, winner of the Nobel Prize for literature in 1960. Some of his finest poems are inspired by the history and landscape—particularly the sea—of his beloved Guadeloupe. The museum contains a collection of his poetry and some of his personal belongings. Before you go, look for his birthplace at 54 rue Achille René-Boisneuf. ⊠*At rues Noizières and Achille René-Boisneuf* ☎*0590/90–01–92* 🎫*€2* ⊙*Thurs.–Tues. 8:30–12:30 and 2:30–5:30.*

Musée Schoelcher celebrates Victor Schoelcher, a high-minded abolitionist from Alsace who fought against slavery in the French West Indies in the 19th century. The museum contains many of his personal effects, and exhibits trace his life and work. ⊠*24 rue Peynier* ☎*0590/82–08–04* 🎫*€3* 🕙 *Weekdays 9–5.*

SHOPPING

For serious shopping in Pointe-à-Pitre, browse the boutiques and stores along rue Schoelcher, rue Frébault, and rue Noizières. The multicolored market square and stalls of La Darse are filled mostly with vegetables, fruits, delicious homemade rum liqueurs, and housewares. The air is filled with the fragrance of spices, and they have lovely gift baskets of spices and vanilla lined with madras fabric.

Au Bonheur des Dames (⊠*49 rue Frébault, Pointe-à-Pitre, Grande-Terre* ☎*0590/82–00–30*) sells several different lines of cosmetics and skin-care products in addition to its own perfumes. **Délice Shop** (⊠*45 rue Achille René-Boisneuf, Pointe-à-Pitre, Grande-Terre* ☎*0590/82–98–24*) is the spot for island rum and edibles from France—from cheese to chocolate. Across from the market, **Dody** (⊠*31 rue Frébault, Pointe-à-Pitre, Grande-Terre* ☎*0590/82–18–59*) is the place to go if you want white eyelet (blouses, skirts, dresses, even bustiers). The shop has a high-quality designer line, but you will pay €100 to €300 for a single piece. There's lots of madras, too, which is especially cute in children's clothing. **Vendôme** (⊠*8–10 rue Frébault, Pointe-à-Pitre, Grande-Terre* ☎*0590/83–42–84*) is Guadeloupe's exclusive purveyor of Stendhal and Germaine Monteil cosmetics.

ACTIVITIES

DIVING

The main diving area at the **Cousteau Underwater Park,** just off Basse-Terre near Pigeon Island, offers routine dives to 60 feet. The numerous glass-bottom boats and other craft make the site feel like a marine parking lot; however, the underwater sights are spectacular. Guides and instructors are certified under the French CMAS (some also have PADI, but none have NAUI). Most operators offer two-hour dives three times per day for about €45 to €50 per dive; three-dive packages are €120 to €145. Hotels and dive operators usually rent snorkeling gear.

☾ **Les Heures Saines** (⊠*Le Rocher de Malendure, Plage de Malendure, Bouillante, Basse-Terre* ☎*0590/98–86–63, 0690/31–28–42, or 0690/57–30–07* ⊕*www.plongee-guadeloupe.com*) is the premier operator for dives in the Cousteau Underwater Park. Trips to Les Saintes offer one or two dives for average and advanced divers, with plenty of time for lunch and sightseeing. Wreck, night, and Nitrox diving are also available. The instructors, many of them English speakers, are excellent with children. The company also offers sea kayaking and winter whale- and dolphin-watching trips with marine biologists as guides. These tours, aboard a 60-foot catamaran, cost €53.

HIKING

FodorsChoice ★ With hundreds of trails and countless rivers and waterfalls, the **Parc National de la Guadeloupe** on Basse-Terre is the main draw for hikers. Some of the trails should be attempted only with an experienced guide.

All tend to be muddy, so wear a good pair of boots. Know that even the young and fit can find these outings arduous; the unfit may find them painful. Start off slowly, with a shorter hike, and then go for the gusto. All water sports—even canoeing and kayaking—are forbidden in the center of the park. Scientists are studying the impact of these activities on the park's ecosystem.

Vert Intense (⊠ *Basse-Terre, Basse-Terre* ☎ *0590/99–34–73 or 0690/ 55–40–47* ⊕ *www.vert-intense.com*) organizes fascinating hikes in the national park and to the volcano. You move from steaming hot springs to an icy waterfall in the same hike. Guide Eric Barret is patient and safe, and he can bring you to heights that you never thought you could reach, including the top of Le Soufrière. The volcano hike costs only €25 but must be booked four days in advance. A mixed-adventure package spanning three days costs €210. The French-speaking guides, who also know some English and Spanish, can take you to other tropical forests and rivers, where the sport of canyoning can still be practiced. If you are just one or two people, the company can team you up with a group.

BEACHES

★ **Plage Caravelle.** Just southwest of Ste-Anne is one of Grande-Terre's longest and prettiest stretches of sand, the occasional dilapidated shack notwithstanding. Protected by reefs, it's also a fine snorkeling spot. Club Med occupies one end of this beach, and nonguests can enjoy its beach and water sports, as well as lunch and drinks, by buying a day pass. You can also have lunch at La Toubana, then descend the stairs to the beach below. ⊠ *Rte. N4, southwest of Ste-Anne.*

La Grande-Anse. One of Guadeloupe's widest beaches has soft beige sand sheltered by palms. To the west it's a round verdant mountain. There's a large parking area and some food stands, but no other facilities. The beach can be overrun on Sunday, not to mention littered. Right after the parking lot, you can see signage for the creole restaurant Le Karacoli; if you have lunch there (it's not inexpensive), you can *sieste* on the chaise lounges. ⊠ *Rte. N6, north of Deshaies.*

Malendure. Across from Pigeon Island and the Jacques Cousteau Underwater Park, this long, gray volcanic beach on the Caribbean's calm waters has restrooms, a few beach shacks offering cold drinks and snacks, and a huge parking lot. Don't come here for solitude, as the beach is the starting-off point for dive boats, sportfishing boats, glass-bottom boats, and whale-watching vessels. If you're scheduled to do any of the above, you can hang here afterward. Snorkeling from the beach is good. Le Rocher de Malendure, a fine seafood restaurant, is perched on a cliff over the bay. ⊠ *Rte. N6, Bouillante.*

WHERE TO EAT

$ ✕**Caraïbes Café.** This sidewalk café straight out of Paris is the in place
CAFÉ for lunch and also a spot for a quick breakfast, a fresh juice cocktail—try *corossel with mangue* (soursop with mango), a cappuccino, a sundae

un coupe, or a pastis while you people-watch and listen to French croon-ers. The *formule* (fixed-price menu) is always the best deal. Service is fast and friendly and can even be in English. ⊠*Pl. de la Victoire, Pointe-à-Pitre* ☎*0590/82–92–23* ⊟*MC, V* ⊙*Closed Sun. No dinner.*

$$–$$$ ✕ **Le Rocher de Malendure.** Guests first climb the worn yellow stairs for
FRENCH the panoramic sea views, but return again and again for the food. If
★ you arrive before noon, when the divers pull in, you might snag one of the primo tables in a gazebo, which literally hang over the Caribbean. Begin with a perfectly executed mojito. With fish just off the boat, don't hesitate to try the sushi or grilled crayfish and lobster. ⊠*Bord de Mer, Malendure de Pigeon, Bouillante* ☎*0590/98–70–84* ⊟*AE, MC, V* ⊙*Closed Wed. and Sept.–early Oct.*

KEY WEST, FLORIDA

Chelle Koster Along with the rest of Florida, Key West—the southernmost city in the
Walton continental United States—became part of American territory in 1821. In the late 19th century it was Florida's wealthiest city per capita. The locals made their fortunes from "wrecking"—rescuing people and sal-vaging cargo from ships that foundered on nearby reefs. Cigar mak-ing, fishing, shrimping, and sponge gathering also became important industries. Capital of the self-proclaimed "Conch Republic," Key West today makes for a unique port of call. A genuinely American town, it nevertheless exudes the relaxed atmosphere and pace of a typical Caribbean island. Major attractions include the home of the Conch Republic's most famous residents, Ernest Hemingway and Harry Tru-man; the imposing Key West Museum of Art and History, a former U.S. Customs House and site of the military inquest of the USS *Maine*; and the island's renowned sunset celebrations.

ESSENTIALS
Currency The U.S. dollar.

Internet Get your morning (or afternoon) buzz at **Coffee Plantation** (⊠ *713 Caroline St.* ☎ *305/295–9808* ⊕ *www.coffeeplantationkeywest.com*), where you can also hook up to the Internet in the comfort of a homelike setting in a circa-1890 Conch house. Poets, writers, and minstrels sometimes show up to perform while you munch pastries or luncheon sandwiches and wraps and sip your hot or cold espresso beverage.

Telephones Public phones are found at or near all three cruise docks: Mal-lory Square, Pier B at the Hilton, and Outer Mall (where the Conch Train drops passengers at Duval and Front streets). They're also along the major tourist thoroughfares.

COMING ASHORE

Cruise ships dock at three different locations. Mallory Square and Pier B are within walking distance of Duval and Whitehead streets, the two main tourist thoroughfares. Passengers on ships that dock at Outer Mall are shuttled via Conch Train to Duval and Front streets. Because Key West is so easily explored on foot, there is rarely a need to hire a cab.

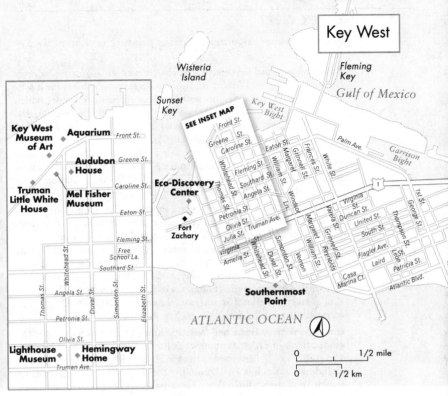

If you plan to venture beyond the main tourist district, a fun way to get around is by bicycle or scooter (rentals begin at about $12 per day). Key West is a cycling town. In fact, there are so many bikes around that cyclists must watch out for one another as much as for cars. You can get tourist information from the Greater Key West Chamber of Commerce, which is just off Mallory Square.

The Conch Tour Train can be boarded at Mallory Square or Flagler Station every half-hour; it costs $27 for the 90-minute tour. The Old Town Trolley operates trolley-style buses starting from Mallory Square every 30 minutes for the same price, but the smaller trolleys go places the train won't fit.

Keys Moped and Scooter (✉523 Truman Ave. ☎305/294–0399) rents beach cruisers with large baskets for $10 a day. Rates for scooters start at $30. Look for the huge American flag on the roof. **Moped Hospital** (✉601 Truman Ave. ☎305/296–3344 or 866/296–1625 ⊕www. mopedhospital.com) supplies balloon-tire bikes with yellow safety baskets for adults and kids ($12 per day), as well as mopeds ($40) and double-seater scooters ($65).

EXPLORING KEY WEST

Numbers in the margin correspond to points of interest on the Key West map.

Audubon House and Gardens. If you've ever seen an engraving by ornithologist John James Audubon, you'll understand why his name is synonymous with birds. See his works in this three-story house, which was built in the 1840s for Captain John Geiger and filled with period furniture. It now commemorates Audubon's 1832 stop in Key West while he was traveling through Florida to study birds. A children's room makes his work accessible to youngsters. Docents lead a guided tour that identifies the rare indigenous plants and trees. ⊠ *205 Whitehead St.* ☎ *305/294–2116 or 877/294–2470* ⊕ *www.audubonhouse. com* ⊠ *$11* ⊙ *Daily 9:30–5, last tour starts at 4:30.*

★ **Eco-Discovery Center.** Walk through a model of Key Largo's Aquarius, the world's only underwater ocean laboratory, to discover what lurks beneath the sea. Opened in 2007, this 6,400-square-foot underwater attraction encourages visitors to venture through a variety of Florida Key habitats, from pinelands, beach dunes, and mangroves to the deep sea. Touch-screen computer displays and live underwater cameras show off North America's only contiguous barrier coral reef. ⊠ *35 E. Quay Rd., at end of Southard St. in Truman Annex* ☎ *305/809–4750* ⊕ *floridakeys.noaa.gov* ⊠ *Free* ⊙ *Tues.–Sat. 9–4.*

★ **Ernest Hemingway Home and Museum.** Amusing anecdotes pepper the guided tours of Ernest Hemingway's home. While living here between 1931 and 1942, Hemingway wrote about 70% of his life's work, including classics like *For Whom the Bell Tolls.* Few of his belongings remain, and there's little about his actual work, but photographs help you visualize his day-to-day life. The supposed descendants of Hemingway's cats—many named for actors, artists, and authors—have free rein of the property. Tours begin every 10 minutes and take 25 to 30 minutes; then you're free to explore on your own. ⊠ *907 Whitehead St.* ☎ *305/294–1136* ⊕ *www.hemingwayhome.com* ⊠ *$12* ⊙ *Daily 9–5.*

Harry S Truman Little White House Museum. In a letter to his wife during one of his visits, President Harry S. Truman wrote, "Dear Bess, you should see the house. The place is all redecorated, new furniture and everything." If he visited today, he'd be similarly impressed. There's a photographic review of visiting dignitaries and permanent audiovisual and artifact exhibits on the Florida Keys as a presidential retreat; Ulysses S. Grant, John F. Kennedy, and Jimmy Carter are among the chief executives who passed through here. Tours lasting 45 minutes begin every 15 minutes until 4:15. On the grounds of **Truman Annex**, a 103-acre former military parade grounds and barracks, the home served as a winter White House for presidents Truman, Eisenhower, and Kennedy. ⊠ *111 Front St.* ☎ *305/294–9911* ⊕ *www.trumanlittlewhitehouse.com* ⊠ *$12* ⊙ *Daily 9–5, grounds sunrise–6, last tour at 4:30.*

ℭ **Key West Aquarium.** Feed a nurse shark and explore the fascinating underwater realm of the Keys without getting wet at this kid-friendly aquarium. Hundreds of tropical fish and sea creatures live here. A touch tank enables you to handle starfish, sea cucumbers, horseshoe and hermit crabs, even horse and queen conchs—living totems of the Conch Republic. Built in 1934 by the Works Progress Administration as the world's first open-air aquarium, most of the building has been enclosed for all-weather viewing. Guided tours, included in the admission price, include shark petting and feedings. ⌂ *1 Whitehead St.* ☎ *305/296–2051* ⊕ *www. keywestaquarium.com* 🔖 *$12 for 2-day pass* ☉ *Daily 10–6; tours at 11, 1, 3, and 4:30.*

Key West Lighthouse Museum and Keeper's Quarters Museum. For the best view in town, climb the 88 steps to the top of this 1847 lighthouse. The 92-foot structure has a Fresnel lens, which was installed in the 1860s at a cost of $1 million. The keeper lived in the adjacent 1887 clapboard house, which now exhibits vintage photographs, ship models, nautical charts, and lighthouse artifacts from all along the Key reefs. ⌂ *938 Whitehead St.* ☎ *305/295–6616* ⊕ *www.kwahs.com* 🔖 *$10* ☉ *Daily 9:30–5, last admission at 4:30.*

Fodor'sChoice ★ **Key West Museum of Art and History in the Custom House.** When Key West was designated a U.S. port of entry in the early 1820s, a customhouse was established. Salvaged cargoes from ships wrecked on the reefs were brought here, causing Key West to become for a time the richest city in Florida. After a $9 million restoration, the imposing redbrick-and-terra-cotta Richardsonian Romanesque–style building has reopened as a museum and art gallery. Smaller galleries have long-term and changing exhibits about the history of Key West, including a Hemingway room and a fine collection of folk artist Mario Sanchez's wood paintings. ⌂ *281 Front St.* ☎ *305/295–6616* ⊕ *www.kwahs.com* 🔖 *$10* ☉ *Daily 9–5.*

Mel Fisher Maritime Museum. In 1622 two Spanish galleons laden with riches from South America foundered in a hurricane 40 mi west of the Keys. In 1985 diver Mel Fisher recovered the treasures from the lost ships, the *Nuestra Señora de Atocha* and the *Santa Margarita*. Fisher's incredible adventure tracking these fabled hoards and battling the state of Florida for rights is as amazing as the loot you'll see, touch, and learn about in this museum. Artifacts include a gold bar worth $15,000 and a 77.76-carat natural emerald crystal worth almost $250,000. Exhibits on the second floor rotate and might cover slave ships, including the excavated 17th-century *Henrietta Marie*, or Florida's maritime history. ⌂ *200 Greene St.* ☎ *305/294–2633* ⊕ *www.melfisher.org* 🔖 *$12* ☉ *Weekdays 8:30–5, weekends 9:30–5.*

KEY WEST BEST BETS

■ **Boat Cruise.** Being out on the water is what Key West is all about.

■ **Conch Train.** Hop aboard for a narrated tour of the town's tawdry past and rare architectural treasures.

■ **Hemingway.** Visit Ernest Hemingway's historic home for a literary treat.

■ **Kayaking.** Kayaking is a great way to spend a few hours.

■ **Sunset in Mallory Square.** The nightly street party is the quintessential Key West experience.

4

The Southernmost Point. Possibly the most-photographed site in Key West, this is a must-see for many visitors. Who wouldn't want their picture taken next to the big striped buoy that marks the southernmost spot in the continental United States? A plaque next to it honors Cubans who lost their lives trying to escape to America. ⊠ *Whitehead and South Sts.* ☎ *No phone.*

> **USED BOOKS**
>
> Leave any paperback novels you have finished for the crew library. You will have more room in your suitcase, and crewmembers will have fresh reading material.

SHOPPING

Passengers looking for T-shirts, trinkets, and other souvenirs will find them along Duval Street and around the cruise-ship piers. **Fast Buck Freddie's** (⊠ *500 Duval St.* ☎ *305/294–2007* ⊕ *www.fastbuckfreddies.com*) sells a classy, hip selection of gifts, including every flamingo item imaginable. It also carries such imaginative items as a noise-activated rat in a trap and a raccoon tail in a bag. The **Key West Island Bookstore** (⊠ *513 Fleming St.* ☎ *305/294–2904*) is a home away from home for the large Key West writers' community. It carries new, used, and rare titles. It specializes in Hemingway, Tennessee Williams, and South Florida mystery writers. **Lucky Street Gallery** (⊠ *1130 Duval St.* ☎ *305/294–3973*) sells high-end contemporary paintings. There are also a few pieces of jewelry by internationally recognized Key West–based artists. Changing exhibits, artist receptions, and special events make this a lively venue.For that unique (but slightly overpriced) souvenir of your trip to Key West head to **Montage** (⊠ *512 Duval St.* ☎ *305/395–9101 or 877/396–4278* ⊕ *montagekeywest.com*), where you'll discover hundreds of handcrafted signs of popular Key West guesthouses, inns, hotels, restaurants, bars, and streets. If you can't find what you're looking for, they'll make it for you.

ACTIVITIES

BOAT TOURS

M/V Discovery (⊠ *Land's End Marina, 251 Margaret St., Key West* ☎ *305/293–0099 or 800/262–0099* ⊕ *www.discoveryunderseatours. com*) offers glass-bottom boats with submerged viewing rooms for 360-degree marine watching ($40). **Lazy Dog Kayak Guides** (⊠ *5114 U.S. 1, Key West* ☎ *305/295–9898* ⊕ *www.lazydog.com*) runs four-hour guided sea-kayak-snorkel tours around the mangrove islands just east of Key West. The $60 charge covers transportation, bottled water, a snack, and supplies, including snorkeling gear. A $35 two-hour guided kayak tour is also available.

DIVING AND SNORKELING

The Florida Keys National Marine Sanctuary extends along Key West and beyond to the Dry Tortugas. Key West National Wildlife Refuge further protects the pristine waters. Most divers don't make it this far out in the Keys, but if you're looking for a day of diving as a break from the nonstop party in Old Town, expect to pay about $45 and upward for a two-tank dive. Serious divers can book dive trips to the Dry Tortugas.

Captain's Corner (⊠*125 Ann St.* ☎*305/296–8865* ⊕*www.captains corner.com*), a PADI–certified dive shop, has classes in several languages and twice-daily snorkel and dive trips ($40–$45) to reefs and wrecks aboard the 60-foot dive boat *Sea Eagle*. Equipment rental *is extra.* Safely dive the coral reefs without getting a scuba certification with **Snuba of Key West** (⊠*Garrison Bight Marina, Palm Ave. between Eaton St. and N. Roosevelt Blvd.* ☎*305/292–4616* ⊕*www.snubakeywest. com*). Ride out to the reef on a catamaran, then follow your guide underwater for a one-hour tour of the coral reefs. You wear a regulator with a breathing hose that is attached to a floating air tank on the surface. No prior diving or snorkeling experience is necessary, but you must know how to swim. The $99 price includes beverages.

FISHING
Any number of local fishing guides can take you to where the big ones are biting, either in the backcountry for snapper and snook or to the deep water for the marlins and shark that brought Hemingway here in the first place.

Key West Pro Guides (⊠*G-31 Miriam St.* ☎*866/259–4205* ⊕*www. keywestproguides.com*) has several different trips, including flats and backcountry fishing ($400 for a half day) and reef and offshore fishing ($600 for half day). **Key West Bait and Tackle** (⊠*241 Margaret St.* ☎*305/292–1961* ⊕*www.keywestbaitandtackle.com*) carries live bait, frozen bait, and fishing equipment. It also has the Live Bait Lounge, where you can sip ice-cold beer while telling fish tales.

BEACHES

Fort Zachary Taylor Historic State Park (⊠*End of Southard St., through Truman Annex* ☎*305/292–6713* ⊕*www.floridastateparks.org/forttaylor* 🖃*$3.50 for 1 person, $6 for 2 people, 50¢ per additional person* ☉*Daily 8–sunset, tours noon and 2*) has the best beach in Key West. There's an adjoining picnic area with barbecue grills and shade trees, a snack bar, and rental equipment, including snorkeling gear and kayaks. **Smathers Beach** (⊠*S. Roosevelt Blvd.* ☎*No phone* 🖃*Free* ☉*Daily 7 AM–11 PM*) has nearly 2 mi of sand, plus restrooms, picnic areas, and volleyball courts, all of which make it popular with the spring-break crowd. Trucks along the road rent rafts, Windsurfers, and other beach "toys." Metered parking is on the street.

WHERE TO EAT

$

AMERICAN

✕**Lobo's Mixed Grill.** If White Castle has attained national cult status with its burgers, then the equivalent among Key West denizens might very well be Lobo's belly buster. The 7-ounce, charcoal-grilled chunk of ground chuck is thick and juicy and served with lettuce, tomato, and pickle on a toasted bun. The 30 wraps (rib eye, oyster, grouper, and others) are equally popular. The menu includes salads and quesadillas, as well as a fried shrimp and oyster combo. Beer and wine are served. This courtyard food stand closes at 6, so eat early. Most of Lobo's business is takeout (it has a half-dozen outdoor picnic tables), and it offers free delivery within Old Town. ⊠ *5 Key Lime Sq., east of intersection of Southard and Duval Sts.* ☎ *305/296–5303* ⊕ *www.loboskeywest. com* ▭ *No credit cards* ⊙ *Closed Sun. Apr.–early Dec.*

$$ ✕ **Turtle Kraals.** Named for the kraals, or corrals, where sea turtles were
SEAFOOD   once kept until they went to the cannery, this place calls to mind the
☾   island's history. Today, much smaller box turtles provide live entertainment at 6 PM on Monday and Friday, when folks cheer on contestants in a turtle race. The menu offers an assortment of marine cuisine that includes seared jerk tuna, seafood enchiladas, lobster Newburg pie, and mango crab cakes. Breakfast offers some interesting options like barbecued hash and eggs or huevos rancheros. The open-walled restaurant overlooks the marina at the Historic Seaport. ⊠ *231 Margaret St.* ☎ *305/294–2640* ⊕ *www.turtlekraals.com* ▭ *AE, MC, V.*

NIGHTLIFE

Three spots stand out for first-timers among the saloons frequented by Key West denizens. All are within easy walking distance of the cruise-ship piers. **Capt. Tony's Saloon** (⊠ *428 Greene St.* ☎ *305/294–1838* ⊕ *www.capttonyssaloon.com*) was the original Sloppy Joe's in the mid-1930s, when Hemingway was a regular. Later, a young Jimmy Buffett sang here and made this watering hole famous in his song "Last Mango in Paris." Bands play nightly. The **Schooner Wharf Bar** (⊠ *202 William St.* ☎ *305/292–3302* ⊕ *www.schoonerwharf.com*), an open-air waterfront bar and grill in the historic seaport district, retains its funky Key West charm. Its margarita ranks among Key West's best. There's more history and good times at **Sloppy Joe's** (⊠ *201 Duval St.* ☎ *305/294–5717* ⊕ *www.sloppyjoes.com*), the successor to a famous 1937 speakeasy named for its founder, Captain Joe Russell. Decorated with Hemingway memorabilia and marine flags, the bar is popular with travelers and is full and noisy all the time. A Sloppy Joe's T-shirt is a de rigueur Key West souvenir, and the gift shop sells them like crazy.

LA ROMANA, DOMINICAN REPUBLIC

Eileen Robinson Smith   Dominicans will extend a gracious welcome, saying, "This is your home!" and, indeed, are happy to share what they have, which is a physically beautiful island bathed by the Atlantic Ocean to the north and the Caribbean Sea to the south. Some of the island's most beautiful beaches are in the area surrounding La Romana, notably Bayahibe Bay, though ironically those at the famed Casa de Campo resort are only middling. A port call here will bring you into the Casa de Campo Marina, from where you can set out to explore the region, stay and enjoy some nice (but expensive) restaurants and shops, or just take advantage of the immediate region's many activities.

ESSENTIALS

Currency The coin of the realm is the Dominican peso ($RD35 to US $1 at this writing). The exchange rate fluctuates continuously, but one thing is certain, the Dominican Republic, although still a good value, is not the cheap date it was up until a couple of years ago.

Telephones Telephones are available at the dock, as soon as passengers disembark, and telephone cards can be purchased there as well. Similarly, at the Casa de Campo Marina, where a shuttle drops passengers off, you'll also find phones. Tele-cards can be bought at the supermarket. To call the U.S. or Canada from the D.R., just punch in 1 plus the area code and number. To make calls on the island, you must tap in the area code (809), plus the seven-digit number; if you are calling a Dominican cell phone, you must first punch in 1. Unfortunately, there is no Internet café where cruise-ship passengers can access their e-mail, either at the dock or at Casa de Campo.

COMING ASHORE

Ships enter the Casa de Campo International Tourist Port (Muelle Turístico Internacional Casa de Campo). A group of folkloric dancers and local musicians, playing merengue, greet passengers as they come down the gangway. An information booth with smiling, English-speaking staffers is there to assist cruise-ship passengers; the desk is open the entire time that the ship is in port.

It is a 15-minute walk into the town of La Romana, or you can jump into a waiting taxi. It's safe to stroll around town, but it's not particularly beautiful, quaint, or even historic; however, it is a real slice of Dominican life. Most people just board the complimentary shuttle and head for the Casa de Campo Marina and/or Altos de Chavón, both of which are at the Casa de Campo resort. Shuttles run all day long.

Taxis line up at the port's docks, and some, but not all, drivers speak English. Staff members from the information kiosk will help to make taxi arrangements. Most rates are fixed and spelled out on a board: $15 to Casa de Campo's Marina, $20 to Altos de Chavón. You may be able to negotiate a somewhat lower rate if a group books a taxi for a tour. You can also rent a car at Casa de Campo (Hertz and Avis have offices near the resort reception area); rates are expensive, usually more than $70 a day. Driving into Santo Domingo can be a hair-raising experience and isn't for the faint of heart.

EXPLORING LA ROMANA

★ **Altos de Chavón.** This re-creation of a 16th-century Mediterranean village sits on a bluff overlooking the Río Chavón, about 3 mi (5 km) east of the main facilities of Casa de Campo. You feel transported to centuries past as you stroll the cobblestoned streets, stopping into the quaint shops, exclusive boutiques, and art galleries located near the archaeological museum, design school, and working artist studios, a new amber museum, medieval-style cathedral, and a row of restaurants, along with a French bakery and coffee bar.

Isla Saona. Off the east coast of Hispaniola lies this island, now a national park inhabited by sea turtles, pigeons, and other wildlife. Caves here were once used by Indians. The beaches are beautiful, and legend has it that Columbus once strayed here.

Spanish civilization in the New World began in the 12-block Zona Colonial of **Santo Domingo.** Strolling its narrow streets, it's easy to imagine this old city as it was when the likes of Columbus, Cortés, and Ponce de León walked the cobblestones, pirates sailed in and out, and colonists were settling themselves. Tourist brochures tout that "history comes alive here"—a surprisingly truthful statement. A fun horse-and-carriage ride throughout the Zone costs $20 for an hour. The steeds are no thoroughbreds, but they clip right along, though any commentary will be in Spanish. The drivers usually hang out in front of the Hostal Nicolas de Ovando. History buffs will want to spend a day exploring the many "firsts" of our continent, which will be included in any cruise-ship excursion. Do wear comfortable shoes.

SHOPPING

Altos de Chavón is a re-creation of a 16th-century Mediterranean village on the grounds of the Casa de Campo resort, where you can find art galleries, boutiques, and souvenir shops grouped around a cobbled square. Extra-special is El Club de Cigaro.

The **Casa de Campo Marina** is home to more than 60 shops and international boutiques, galleries, and jewelers scattered amid restaurants, an ice-cream parlor, Euro-style bars, and a yacht club. It is a great place to spend some hours shopping and sightseeing while you stare at the extravagant yachts. The chic shopping scene at the marina includes Burberry, Bleu Marine, Pucci, Gucci, Cartier, Montblanc, and Versace. Dominican designer Jenny Polanco's boutique here now includes her line of jewelry and handbags. Although upscale is the operative word here, this does not mean that you cannot buy a postcard, a pair of shorts, or a logo T-shirt. Also, the *supermercado* Nacional at the marina has not only groceries but sundries, postcards, and snacks for much less than you would pay at a resort shop.

ACTIVITIES

Most activities available at Casa de Campo are open to cruise-ship passengers. You'll need to make reservations on the ship, particularly for golf.

FISHING

Blue and white marlin, wahoo, sailfish, dorado, and mahimahi are among the most common catches in these waters. **Casa de Campo Marina** (✉ *Casa de Campo, Calle Barlovento 3, La Romana* ☎ *809/523–8646*) is the best charter option in the La Romana area. Yachts are available for charters by day or night for a romantic sunset cruise. Boats for deep-sea and river fishing are available as well. Costs to charter a boat with a crew, refreshments, bait, and tackle generally range from $598 to $2,013 for a half day, from $796 to $3,334 for a full day.

> ### LA ROMANA BEST BETS
>
> ■ **Altos de Chavón.** You'll find shopping and dining as well as great views.
>
> ■ **Golf.** The Teeth of the Dog is one of the Caribbean's best courses despite the cost.
>
> ■ **Horseback Riding.** Casa de Campo has an excellent equestrian center.
>
> ■ **Isla Saona.** The powder-soft beach and beautiful water are excellent.
>
> ■ **Kandela.** The evening Dominican folkloric show is a highlight if your ship stays late in port.

GOLF

Fodor's Choice ★ The famed, 18-hole Teeth of the Dog course at **Casa de Campo** (✉ *La Romana* ☎ *809/523–3333* ⊕ *www.casadecampo.com.do*), with seven holes on the sea, is often ranked as the number-one course in the Caribbean and is among the top courses in the world. Greens fees are $232 per round, per person. Pete Dye has designed this and two other globally acclaimed courses here: Dye Fore, with 18 holes close to Altos de Chavón, hugs a cliff that looks over the sea, a river, and the stunning marina ($203); the Links is an 18-hole inland course ($145). Avid golfers should inquire about the resort's three-day and one-week supplements, or the new Simply Golf Packages. Tee times for all courses must be reserved at least one day in advance by resort guests, earlier for nonguests.

HORSEBACK RIDING

The 250-acre **Equestrian Center at Casa de Campo** (✉ *La Romana* ☎ *809/ 523–3333* ⊕ *www.casadecampo.com.do*) has something for both western and English riders—a dude ranch, a rodeo arena (where Casa's trademark "Donkey Polo" is played), guided trail rides, and jumping and riding lessons. Guided rides run about $35 an hour; lessons cost $56 an hour. There are early morning and sunset trail rides, too. Handsome, old-fashioned carriages are available for hire, as well.

BEACHES

Las Minitas Beach at Casa de Campo is reserved exclusively for hotel guests and villa owners. Cruise passengers must take a beach excursion or make their own arrangements for transportation to nearby beaches. **Catalina Island** is a diminutive, picture-postcard Caribbean island off the coast of the mainland. To get to the island, you'll have to take an excursion. Catalina is about a half-hour away by catamaran, and most excursions offer the use of snorkeling equipment as well as a beach barbecue. **Playa Bayahibe** is a beautiful stretch of beach. Shore excursions are organized by the cruise lines to the beach, which is about 30 minutes away from the cruise port by bus. You can also book your own taxi here, and the trip may be cheaper than the cost of a shore excursion if you come with a group. **Saona Island** was once a pristine, idyllic isle. Now, on a busy cruise-ship day there may be as many as 1,000 bathers there. However, the beach is beautiful. To get here, you'll have to book an excursion with your ship, often a power boat from Altos de Chavón; otherwise, you are bused to Bayahibe and board a boat there.

WHERE TO EAT

$$–$$$ ✕**Peperoni.** Although the name sounds as Italian as *amore*, this res-
ECLECTIC   taurant's menu is much more eclectic than Italian. It has a classy, contemporary, white-dominated decor; waiters are also dressed in white with long aprons. The classic pasta dishes, osso buco, and risottos with rock shrimp or porcinis, or house-made pear and goat cheese raviolis, are authentic and delectable, as are such specialties curried shrimp and jasmine rice. But you can also opt for stylishly simple charcoal-grilled steaks, burgers, gourmet wood-oven pizzas, sandwiches, sushi, and sashimi. ⊠*Plaza Portafolio 16, Casa de Campo Marina* ☎*809/523–2228* ▭*AE, MC, V.*

MARTINIQUE (FORT-DE-FRANCE)

Eileen Robin-   The largest of the Windward Islands, Martinique is 4,261 mi (6,817
son Smith   km) from Paris, but its spirit and language are decidedly French, with more than a soupçon of West Indian spice. Tangible, edible evidence of the fact is the island's cuisine, a superb blend of French and creole. Martinique is lushly landscaped with tropical flowers. Trees bend under the weight of fruits such as mangoes, papayas, lemons, limes, and bright-red West Indian cherries. Acres of banana plantations, pineapple fields, and waving sugarcane stretch to the horizon. The towering mountains and verdant rain forest in the north lure hikers, while underwater sights and sunken treasures attract snorkelers and scuba divers. Martinique is also wonderful if your idea of exercise is turning over every 10 minutes to get an even tan and your taste in adventure runs to duty-free shopping. A popular cruise-ship excursion goes to St-Pierre, which was buried by ash when Mont Pelée erupted in 1902.

ESSENTIALS

Currency The euro (€1 to US$1.31). You will not be able to use dollars, so plan on getting some euros. You cannot cash traveler's checks or dollars at the bank, only at a bureau de change, so ATMs are your best bet if you need euros. Change Caraïbes—which has an office in Fort-de-France at 14 rue Victor Hugo and Le Bord de Mer—will still exchange both dollars and traveler's checks and usually offers fair rates.

Internet Cyber Club Caraïbe (⊠ *16 rue François Arago, Fort-de-France* ☎ *0596/70–31–62* ⊕ *www.cyberclubcaraibe.com*). **Internet Haut Depot** (⊠ *61 rue Victor Hugo, Fort-de-France* ☎ *0596/63–12–20*).

Telephones There are no coin-operated phone booths. Public phones now use a *télécarte*, which you can buy at post offices, café-tabacs, hotels, and *bureaux de change*. To call the United States from Martinique, dial 00 + 1, the area code, and the local seven-digit number. To call locally, you now have to dial 0596 before the six-digit number. You can make collect calls to Canada through the Bell operator; you can get the ATand T or MCI operators from blue, special-service phones at the cruise ports and in town (try Super Sumo snack bar, on rue de la Liberté, near the library).

4

COMING ASHORE

Most cruise ships call either at Tourelles (in the old port, about 1½ mi (2 km) from Fort-de-France) or at Pointe Simon, right in downtown Fort-de-France. (It is rare to have a ship anchor in the Baie des Flamands and tender passengers ashore.) Tourist information offices are at each cruise terminal. Uniformed dispatchers assist passengers in finding English-speaking taxi drivers. Passengers who do not wish to talk 20 minutes into Fort-de-France from Tourelles can take a taxi (set rate of €8 for up to four passengers in a van, or €2 for each additional passenger). Expect to pay about €40 per hour for touring; in larger vans, the price is usually €10 per person per hour. Independent cruisers can explore the capital and the nearby open-air market on their own. Beaming and knowledgeable hostesses in creole dress great cruise passengers. Civilian auxillary police (in blue and orange uniforms) supplement the regular police.

Know that traffic in Fort-de-France can be nightmarish. If you want to go to the beach, a much cheaper option is to take a ferry from Fort-de-France. *Vedettes* (ferries) operate daily between Quai d'Ensnambuc in Fort-de-France and the marina in Pointe du Bout, Anse-Mitan, and Anse-à-l'Ane. Any of the three trips takes about 15 minutes, and the ferries operate about every 30 minutes on weekdays. Renting a car in Fort-de-France is possible, but the heavy traffic can be forbidding. Rates are about €70 per day (high season) for a car with manual transmission;

Martinique

Martinique Passage

ATLANTIC OCEAN

Grand-Rivière
Basse-Pointe
Anse-Céron
Mont Pelée
Le Prêcheur
D21
Le Lorrain
Marigot
N1
N3
Morne Jakob
Havre de la Trinité
Anse Etang
Ste-Marie
Caravelle Peninsula
Rade de St-Pierre
N2
St-Pierre
La Trinité
Tartane
Musée Gauguin
D1
Aqualand
Baie du Galion
Carbet
Morne Vert
Balata
Gros-Morne
Pitons du Carbet
Havre du Robert
N2
Le Robert
Pte. Larose
Bellefontaine
N3
N4
N1
Case-Pilote
Fort-de-France
Le François
Schoelcher
Lamentin International Airport
Mt. Vauclin
Baie de Fort-de-France
Anse-à-l'Ane
Pointe du Bout
N5
Le Vauclin
Les Trois-Îlets
D7
N5
N6
D7
Rivière-Salée
Rivière-Pilote
Anse-d'Arlets
Mt. Bigot
D17
N6
D37
Le Diamant
Ste-Luce
N5
Cap Chevalier
Diamant
Cul-de-Sac du Marin
D9
Baie des Anglais
Lamentin
Grande Anse
Anse-Trabaud
St. Lucia Channel

Caribbean Sea

0   5 mi
0   5 km

KEY
⚓ Beaches
⛴ Ferry

automatics are substantially more expensive and seldom available without reservations.

EXPLORING MARTINIQUE

If you want to see the lush island interior and St-Pierre on your own, take the N3, which snakes through dense rain forests, north through the mountains to Le Morne Rouge, then take the coastal N2 back to Fort-de-France via St-Pierre. You can do the 40-mi (64-km) round-trip in half a day—that is if you don't get lost, can comprehend the road signs, avoid collisions in the roundabouts, drive as fast as the flow of frenetic traffic, and can ask directions in French (probably of someone on the street who only speaks a creole patois). But your best option is to hire an English-speaking driver.

☺ **Aqualand.** This U.S.-style water park is a great place for families to have a wet, happy day. The large wave pool is well tended; little ones love it, as they do the pirate's galleon in their own watery playground. Older kids may prefer to get their thrill from the slides, including the hairpin turns of the Giant Slalom, the Colorado slide, and the Black Hole, which winds around in total darkness. In the best French tradition, the fast-food options are top-notch, including crepes, salads, and even beer. Inquire about catching a weekend Somatour shuttle boat.

Nouvelle Frontier organizes tours that include the park. Phone first during the low season. ⊠*Rte. des Pitons, Carbet* ☎*0596/78–40–00* ⊕*www.aqualand-martinique.fr* 🖃*€17.50* ☽*Daily 10–6.*

Balata. This quiet little town has two sights worth visiting. Built in 1923 to commemorate those who died in World War I, **Balata Church** is an exact replica of Paris's Sacré-Coeur Basilica.

The **Jardin de Balata** *(Balata Gardens)* has thousands of varieties of tropical flowers and plants. There are shaded benches from which to take in the mountain views. You can order anthuriums and other tropical flowers to be delivered to the airport. ⊠*Rte. de Balata, Balata* ☎*0596/64–48–73* ⊕*www. jardindebalata.fr* 🖃*€7* ☽*Daily 9–5.*

MARTINIQUE BEST BETS

■ **Beaches.** If you want to relax, the most beautiful beach is Les Salines.

■ **French culture.** Excellent French food and music make this a *paradis* for Francophiles.

■ **La Route des Rhums.** Visit a distillery and become a rum connoisseur.

■ **Shopping.** Browse Fort-de-France's many upscale boutiques and department stores for French wares.

■ **St-Pierre.** Wander the narrow, winding streets of this hill town.

Fort-de-France. With its historic fort and superb location beneath the towering Pitons du Carbet on the Baie des Flamands, Martinique's capital should be a grand place. It isn't. The most pleasant districts, such as Didier, Bellevue, and Schoelcher, are on the hillside; there are some good shops with Parisian wares and lively street markets. Near the harbor is a marketplace where local crafts and souvenirs are sold.

The **Bibliothèque Schoelcher** is the wildly elaborate Romanesque public library. It was named after Victor Schoelcher, who led the fight to free the slaves in the French West Indies in the 19th century. The eye-popping structure was built for the 1889 Paris Exposition, after which it was dismantled, shipped to Martinique, and reassembled piece by ornate piece. ⊠*Rue de la Liberté at Rue Perrinon (rue de la Liberté runs across the west side of La Savane),* ☎*0596/70–26–67* 🖃*Free* ☽*Mon. 1–5:30, Tues.–Fri. 8:30–5:30, Sat. 8:30–noon.*

★ **Le Musée Régional d'Histoire et d'Ethnographie** is a learning experience that is best undertaken at the beginning of your visit, so you can better understand the history, background, and people of the island. Housed in an elaborate former residence (circa 1888) with balconies and fretwork, it has everything from displays of the garish gold jewelry that prostitutes wore after emancipation to reconstructed rooms of a home of proper, middle-class Martinicans. There's even a display of creole headdresses with details of how they were tied to indicate if a woman was single, married, or otherwise occupied. ⊠*10 bd. Général de Gaulle* ☎*0596/72–81–87* 🖃*€3* ☽*Mon. and Wed.–Fri. 8:30–5, Tues. 2–5, Sat. 8:30–noon.*

Rue Victor Schoelcher runs through the center of the capital's primary shopping district, a six-block area bounded by rue de la République, rue de la Liberté, rue Victor Severe, and rue Victor Hugo. Stores sell Paris fashions and French perfume, china, crystal, and liqueurs, as well as local handicrafts. The Romanesque **St-Louis Cathedral**, with its lovely stained-glass windows, was built in 1878, the sixth church on this site (the others were destroyed by fires, hurricanes, and earthquakes). ⊠ *Rue Victor Schoelcher.*

> **PREPACK**
>
> Set aside a few moments every day to pack up your dirty clothes, then spend the last afternoon of your cruise doing fun things instead of packing.

The heart of Fort-de-France is **La Savane**, a 12.5-acre park filled with trees, fountains, and benches. It's a popular gathering place and the scene of promenades, parades, and impromptu soccer matches. Along the east side are numerous snack wagons. Alas, it's no longer a desirable oasis, what with a lot of litter and other negatives often found in urban parks. Diagonally across from La Savane you can catch the ferries for the 20-minute run across the bay to Pointe du Bout and the beaches at Anse-Mitan and Anse-à-l'Ane. It's relatively cheap, as well as stress-free—much safer, more pleasant, and faster than by car.

The most imposing historic site in La Savane (and in Fort-de-France) is **Fort St-Louis**, which runs along the east side of La Savane. It's open Monday through Saturday from 9 to 3; admission is €4.

Musée Gauguin. Martinique was a brief stop in Paul Gauguin's wanderings, but a decisive moment in the evolution of his art. He arrived from Panama in 1887 with friend and fellow painter Charles Laval and, having pawned his watch at the docks, rented a wooden shack on a hill above Carbet. Dazzled by the tropical colors and vegetation, Gauguin developed a style, his Martinique period, that directly anticipated his Tahitian paintings. Disappointingly, this modest museum has only reproductions and some original letters and documents relating to the painter. Also remembered here is the writer Lafcadio Hearn. In his endearing book *Two Years in the West Indies* he provides the most extensive description of the island before St-Pierre was buried in ash and lava. ⊠ *Anse-Turin, Carbet* ☎ *0596/78–22–66* ⊠ *€6* ⊙ *Daily 9–5:30.*

St-Pierre. The rise and fall of St-Pierre is one of the most remarkable stories in the Caribbean. Martinique's modern history began here in 1635. By the turn of the 20th century St-Pierre was a flourishing city of 30,000, known as the Paris of the West Indies. As many as 30 ships at a time stood at anchor. By 1902 it was the most modern town in the Caribbean, with electricity, phones, and a tram. On May 8, 1902, two thunderous explosions rent the air. As the nearby volcano erupted, Mont Pelée split in half, belching forth a cloud of burning ash, poisonous gas, and lava that raced down the mountain at 250 mph. At 3,600°F, it instantly vaporized everything in its path; 30,000 people were killed in two minutes.

The **Cyparis Express**, a small tourist train, will take you around to the main sights with running narrative (in French) for a half hour on Saturday, an hour on weekdays for €10.

An Office du Tourisme is on the *moderne* seafront promenade. Stroll the main streets and check the blackboards at the sidewalk cafés before deciding where to lunch. At night some places have live music. Like stage sets for a dramatic opera, there are the ruins of the island's first church (built in 1640), the imposing theater, the toppled statues. This city, situated on its naturally beautiful harbor and with its narrow, winding streets, has the feel of a European seaside hill town. Although many of the historic buildings need work, stark modernism has not invaded this burg. As much potential as it has, this is one town in Martinique where real estate is cheap—for obvious reasons.

For those interested in the eruption of 1902, the **Musée Vulcanologique Frank Perret** is a must. Established in 1932 by Frank Perret, a noted volcanologist, the museum houses photographs of the old town, documents, and a number of relics—some gruesome—excavated from the ruins, including molten glass, melted iron, and contorted clocks stopped at 8 AM. ⊠*Rue Victor Hugo* ☎*0596/78–15–16* ⊠*€5* ⊙*Daily 9–5.*

If you want to know more about volcanoes, earthquakes, and hurricanes, check out **Le Centre de Découverte des Sciences de la Terre.** Housed in a sleek building, this earth-science museum has high-tech exhibits and interesting films. ⊠*Habitation Perinelle* ☎*0596/52–82–42* ⊕*www.cdst.cg972.fr* ⊠*€5* ⊙*Wed.–Sun. 9–5.*

★ An excursion to **Depaz Distillery** is one of the island's nicest treats. For four centuries it has sat at the foot of the volcano. In 1902 the greathouse was destroyed in the eruption, but soon afterward it was courageously rebuilt and the fields replanted. A self-guided tour includes the workers' gingerbread cottages and an exhibit of art and sculpture made from wooden casks and parts of distillery machinery. The tasting room sells their rums, including golden and aged rum (notably *rhum doré*) and distinctive liqueurs made from ginger and basil. ⚠ **If you want to buy rum, make sure you have euros. The exchange rate offered if you pay in dollars is very unfavorable.** ⊠*Mont Pelée Plantation* ☎*0596/78–13–14* ⊠*Free* ⊙*Mon.–Sat. 9–5.*

SHOPPING

French products, such as perfume, wines, liquors, designer scarves, leather goods, and crystal, are good buys in Fort-de-France. Luxury goods are discounted 20% when paid for with traveler's checks or major credit cards. Look for creole gold jewelry; white, dark, flavored, and aged rums; and handcrafted straw goods, pottery, madras fabric, and tapestries. Shops that sell luxury items are abundant around the cathedral in Fort-de-France, particularly on rue Victor Hugo, rue Moreau de Jones, rue Antoine Siger, and rue Lamartine.

The work of **Antan Lontan** (⊠ *213 rte. de Balata, Fort-de-France* ☎*0596/64–52–72*) has to be seen. Sculptures, busts, statuettes, and artistic lamps portray the Creole women and the story of the Martiniquaise culture. **Cadet Daniel** (⊠*72 rue Antoine Siger, Fort-de-France* ☎*0596/71–41–48*) sells Lalique, Limoges, and Baccarat. **Roger Albert** (⊠*7 rue Victor Hugo, Fort-de-France* ☎*0596/71–71–71*) carries designer crystal.

ACTIVITIES

FISHING

Deep-sea fishing expeditions in these waters hunt down tuna, barracuda, dolphinfish, kingfish, and bonito, and the big ones—white and blue marlins. You can hire boats from the bigger marinas, particularly in Pointe du Bout, Le Marin, and Le François; most hotels arrange these Hemingwayesque trysts, but will often charge a premium. If you can make advance arrangements, companies can also put you together with other anglers to keep costs down. The **Centre de Peche** (⊠ *Port de Plaisance, bd. Allègre, Le Marin* ☎ *0596/76–24–20 or 0696/28–80–58*), a fully loaded Davis 47-foot fishing boat, is a sportfisherman's dream. It goes out with a minimum of four anglers for €195 per person for a half day, or €390 per person for a full day, including lunch. Nonanglers can come for the ride for €95 and €190, respectively. Captain Yves speaks English fluently and is a fun guy.

GOLF

The 18-hole **Golf Country Club de la Martinique** (⊠ *Les Trois-Ilets* ☎ *0596/68–32–81* ⊕ *www.golfmartinique.com*) has a par-71 Robert Trent Jones course with an English-speaking pro, pro shop, bar, and restaurant. The club offers special greens fees to cruise-ship passengers. Normal greens fees are €32 for 9 holes and €46 for 18; an electric cart costs another €30 for 9, €46 for 18. For those who don't mind walking while admiring the Caribbean view between the palm trees, club trolleys are €6. There are no caddies.

HIKING

Two-thirds of Martinique is designated as protected land. Trails, all 31 of them, are well marked and maintained. At the beginning of each, a notice is posted advising on the level of difficulty, the duration of a hike, and any interesting facts. The **Parc Naturel Régional de la Martinique** (⊠ *9 bd. Général de Gaulle, Fort-de-France* ☎ *0596/73–19–30*) organizes inexpensive guided excursions year-round. If there have been heavy rains, though, give it up. The tangle of ferns, bamboo trees, and vines is dramatic, but during rainy season, the springs and waterfalls and wet, muddy trails will negate any enthusiasm.

HORSEBACK RIDING

Horseback-riding excursions can traverse scenic beaches, palm-shaded forests, sugarcane fields, and a variety of other tropical landscapes. Trained guides often include running commentaries on the history, flora, and fauna of the island.

At **Black Horse Ranch** (⊠ *Les Trois-Ilets* ☎ *0596/68–37–80*), one-hour trail rides (€35) go into the countryside and across waving cane fields; two hours on the trail (€40) bring riders near a river. Only western saddles are used for adults; children can ride English. Semiprivate lessons in French or English are €40 a person, less for kids if they can join a group. Some guides are English-speaking at **Ranch de Caps** (⊠ *Cap Macré, Le Marin* ☎ *0596/74–70–65 or 0696/23–18–18*), where you can take a half-day ride (western) on the wild southern beaches and across the countryside for €45. Rides go out in the morning (8:30 to noon) and afternoon (1:30 to 5) every day but Monday. If you can manage a full day in the saddle, it costs €75. A real treat is the full-moon ride but they need to accrue a group to orchestrate that. Most of the mounts are Anglo-Arabs. Riders are encouraged to help cool and wash their horses at day's end. Reserve in advance. Riders of all levels are welcomed. **Ranch Jack** (✉ *Anse-d'Arlets* ☎ *0596/68–37–69 or 0696/92–26–58* ✐ *ranch.jack@wanadoo.fr*) has trail rides (English style) across some beautiful country for €35 an hour; half-day excursions for €50 (€58 with transfers from nearby hotels) go through the fields and forests to the beach. Short rides can range from €16 to €25. The lessons for kids are recommendable.

BEACHES

Anse-Mitan (✉ *Pointe du Bout, Les Trois-Ilets*) is not the French Riviera, though there are often yachts moored offshore. This long stretch of beach can be particularly fun on Sunday. Small, family-owned seaside restaurants are half hidden among palm trees and are footsteps from the lapping waves. Chaise lounges are available for rent from hotels for about €6. **Pointe du Bout** (✉ *Pointe du Bout, Les Trois-Ilets*) is small, man-made, and lined with resorts, including the Hotel Bakoua (formerly Sofitel Bakoua Martinique). Each little strip is associated with its resident hotel, and security guards and closed gates make access difficult. However, if you take a left across from the main pedestrian entrance to the marina—between the taxi stand and the former Kalenda Hotel—then go left again, you will reach Hotel Bakoua's beach, which has especially nice facilities and several options for lunch and drinks. If things are quiet—particularly during the week—one of the beach boys may rent you a chaise; otherwise, just plop your beach towel down, face forward, and enjoy the delightful view of the Fort-de-France skyline. **Les Salines** (✉ *Ste-Anne*) is a mile-long cove lined with soft white sand and coconut palms. The beach is awash with families and children during holidays and on weekends but quiet during the week. The far end—away from the makeshift souvenir shops—is most appealing. The calm waters are safe for swimming, even for the kids. You can't rent chaise lounges, but there are showers. Food vendors roam the sand. From Le Marin, take the coastal road toward Ste-Anne. You will see signs for Les Salines.

WHERE TO EAT

$$ ✕ **Mille and Une Brindilles.** At this trendy salon you can order anything
CAFÉ from a glass of wine to an aromatic pot of tea in flavors like vanilla or
★ mango. You'll find a litany of tapenades, olive cakes, flans, and coucou on the prix-fixe menu. Fred, the bubbly Parisian who is both chef and proprietress, is the queen of terrines and she makes a delicious tart (like Roquefort and pear) or pâté out of any vegetable or fish. The Saturday brunch (€22) is a very social occasion. The best-ever desserts, like the Amadéus—as appealing as the classical music that plays— and *moelleux au chocolat* (a rich chocolate-and-coffee pudding), are what you would want served at your last meal on Earth. Look for the

sign, for the place is easy to miss. ✉*27 rte. de Didier, Didier, Fort-de-France* ☎*0596/71–75–61* 🚭*No credit cards* 🕘*Closed Sun. and Wed. No dinner.*

$ ✕**Soup Bar du Centre Ville.** A sign reading NO OPIUM SMOKING is just one

ECLECTIC   of the details that make this artsy eatery so much fun. This is one place that the island's colorful characters will tell you about if they think you're hip. Wild-looking art decorates one wall; on the other is a surf-board, signed by its American owner, who added: THANKS FOR THE SOUP. The list of soups is extensive, and includes local specialties like *soupe z'habitant*, a flavorful puree of green vegetables with pigs' tails added for flavor. Because a German owns the place, you can also get goulash and cold cream of cucumber soup. No matter what you order, the price is right: a huge bowl with some rolls is about €8. This place is a venue for art exhibits and live music. And yes, there is German beer. Doors open at 4 PM. ✉*120 rue Martine, Fort-de-France* ☎*0596/60–48–96* 🚭*MC, V* 🕘*Closed Sun. No lunch.*

MONTEGO BAY, JAMAICA

John Bigley and Paris Permenter

Today many explorations of MoBay are conducted from a reclining chair—frothy drink in hand—on Doctor's Cave Beach. As home of Jamaica's busiest cruise pier and the north-shore airport, Montego Bay—or MoBay—is the first taste most visitors have of the island. Travelers from around the world come and go in this bustling community, which ranks as Jamaica's second-largest city. The name Montego is derived from *manteca* (lard in Spanish). The Spanish first named this Bahía de Manteca, or Lard Bay. Why? The Spanish once shipped hogs from this port city. Jamaican tourism began here in 1924, when the first resort opened at Doctor's Cave Beach so that health-seekers could "take the waters." If you can pull yourself away from the water's edge and brush the sand off your toes, you can find some very interesting colonial sights in the surrounding area.

ESSENTIALS

Currency The Jamaican dollar (J$88 to US$1). Currency-exchange booths are set up on the docks at Montego Bay whenever a ship is in port; however, the U.S. dollar is accepted virtually everywhere, though change may be made in Jamaican dollars.

Internet A growing number of Internet cafés have sprung up in recent years in Montego Bay hotels and cafés. A popu-

MONTEGO BAY BEST BETS

■ **Doctor's Cave Beach.** This public beach club is right in the heart of Montego Bay.

■ **Dunn's River Falls.** A visit to the falls is touristy but still exhilarating.

■ **Martha Brae Rafting.** A slow rafting trip down the river is relaxing and very enjoyable.

■ **Shopping.** MoBay has several good shopping centers, as well as bustling craft markets.

■ **Rose Hall Greathouse.** The island's most visited greathouse offers a peek back into the days of the plantations.

Montego Bay

KEY

- Beaches
- Cruise Ship Terminal
- Dive Sites

0   1/2 mi
0   1/2 km

lar option for many cruise passengers is the Internet café at **Doctor's Cave Beach** (✉ *Montego Bay* ☎ *876/971–1050*).

Telephones Public telephones (and faxes) are located at the communications center at the Montego Bay Cruise Terminal. Travelers also find public phones in major Montego Bay malls such as the City Centre Shopping Mall. Some U.S. phone companies won't permit credit-card calls to be placed from Jamaica because they've been victims of fraud, so collect calls are often the top option. GSM cell phones equipped with tri-band or world-roaming service will find coverage throughout the Montego Bay region.

COMING ASHORE

Ships dock at the Montego Cruise Terminal, operated by the Port Authority of Jamaica. Located west of Montego Bay, the cruise terminal has five berths and accommodates both cruise and cargo shipping. The terminal has shops, a communications center, a Jamaica Tourist Board visitor information booth, and a taxi stand supervised by the Jamaica Tourist Board. The cruise port in Montego Bay is not within walking distance of the heart of town; however, there's one shopping center within walking distance of the docks. If you just want to visit a beach, then Doctor's Cave, a public beach, is a very good nearby alternative, and it's right in town.

From the Montego Cruise Terminal both taxis and shuttle buses take passengers downtown. Taxi service is about US$10 each way to downtown. Expect to pay $2 per person each way by shuttle bus to the City Centre Shopping Mall or $3 each way to Doctor's Cave Beach. Jamaica is one place in the Caribbean where it's usually to your advantage to take an organized shore excursion offered by your ship unless you just want to do a bit of shopping in town. Taxis aren't particularly cheap, and a full-day tour for a small group will run $150 to $180 (because of road conditions and the distances in Jamaica, most tours take a full day).

If you take a private taxi, you should know that only some of Jamaica's taxis are metered; rates are per car, not per passenger. You can flag cabs on the street. All licensed and properly insured taxis display red Public Passenger (PP) license plates. Licensed minivans also bear the red PP plates. If you hire a taxi driver as a tour guide, be sure to agree on a price before the vehicle is put into gear. Because of the cost of insurance, which you must buy since most credit cards offering coverage exclude Jamaica, it's expensive to rent a car; you may also find it difficult to arrange a rental on-island. It's far easier to arrange a taxi.

EXPLORING MONTEGO BAY

Fodor'sChoice **Dunn's River Falls.** One of Jamaica's most popular attractions is an eye-
★ catching sight: 600 feet of cold, clear mountain water splashing over a series of stone steps to the warm Caribbean. The best way to enjoy the falls is to climb the slippery steps: don a swimsuit, take the hand of the person ahead of you, and trust that the chain of hands and bodies leads to an experienced guide. The leaders of the climbs are personable fellows who reel off bits of local lore while telling you where to step; you can hire a guide's service for a tip of a few dollars. After the climb, you exit through a crowded market, another reminder that this is one of Jamaica's top tourist attractions. ⊠ *Off Rte. A1, between St. Ann's Bay and Ocho Rios* ☎876/974–4767 ☜*$15* ⊙*Daily 8:30–5.*

★ **Greenwood Great House.** Although this historic home has no spooky legend to titillate, it's much better than Rose Hall at evoking life on a sugar plantation. The Barrett family, from whom the English poet Elizabeth Barrett Browning descended, once owned all the land from Rose Hall to Falmouth; they built this and several other greathouses on it. Highlights of Greenwood include oil paintings of the Barretts, china made for the family by Wedgwood, a library filled with rare books from as early as 1697, fine antique furniture, and a collection of exotic musical instruments. There's a pub on-site as well. It's 15 mi (24 km) east of Montego Bay. ⊠ *Greenwood* ☎876/953–1077 ⊕*www.greenwoodgreathouse. com* ☜*$14* ⊙*Daily 9–6.*

Martha Brae River. This gentle waterway about 25 mi (40 km) southeast of Montego Bay takes its name from an Arawak Indian who killed herself because she refused to reveal the whereabouts of a local gold mine to the Spanish. According to legend, she agreed to take them there and, on reaching the river, used magic to change its course, drowning herself and the greedy Spaniards with her. Her *duppy* (ghost) is said to guard the mine's entrance. Rafting on this river is a very popular activity. Martha Brae River Rafting (⇨ *River Rafting in Activities, below*) arranges trips.

Fodor'sChoice
★ **Rose Hall.** In the 1700s Rose Hall may well have been the greatest of greathouses in the West Indies. Today it's popular less for its architecture than for the legend surrounding its second mistress, Annie Palmer. As the story goes, Annie was born in 1802 in England to an English mother and Irish father. When she was 10, her family moved to Haiti, and soon her parents died of yellow fever. Annie was adopted by a Haitian voodoo priestess and soon became skilled in the practice of voodoo. Annie moved to Jamaica, married, and built Rose Hall, an enormous plantation spanning 6,600 acres with more than 2,000 slaves. According to legend, Annie murdered several of her husbands and her slave lovers. To know more about the tales of Rose Hall, read *The White Witch of Rose Hall,* a novel sold across the island. There's a pub on-site. It's across the highway from the Rose Hall Resort and Country Club, a Hilton Resort. ⊠ *N. Coast Hwy.* ☎ *876/953–9982* ⊠ *$15* ☉ *Daily 9–6.*

SHOPPING

Jamaican artisans express themselves in silk-screening, wood carvings, resort wear, hand-loomed fabrics, and paintings. Jamaican rum makes a great gift, as do Tia Maria (the famous coffee liqueur) and Blue Mountain coffee. Wood carvings are one of the top purchases; the finest carvings are made from the Jamaican national tree, lignum vitae, or tree of life, a dense wood that talented carvers transform into dolphins, heads, or fish. Bargaining is expected with crafts vendors. **Gallery of West Indian Art** (⊠ *11 Fairfield Rd., Montego Bay* ☎ *876/952–4547*) is the place to find Jamaican and Haitian paintings. A corner of the gallery is devoted to hand-turned pottery (some painted) and beautifully carved and painted birds and animals.

ACTIVITIES

DIVING AND SNORKELING

Jamaica isn't a major dive destination, but you can find a few rich underwater regions, especially off the north coast. MoBay, known for its wall dives, has **Airport Reef** at its southwestern edge. The site is known for its coral caves, tunnels, and canyons. The first marine park in Jamaica, the **Montego Bay Marine Park,** was established to protect the natural resources of the bay; a quick look at the area and it's easy to see the treasures that lie beneath the surface. The north coast is on the edge of the Cayman Trench, so it boasts a wide array of marine life.

Scuba Jamaica (⊠ *Half Moon, N. Coast Hwy., Montego Bay* ☎ *876/381– 1113* ⊕ *www.scuba-jamaica.com*) offers serious scuba facilities for dedicated divers. This PADI and NAUI operation also offers Nitrox diving and instruction as well as instruction in underwater photography, night diving, and open-water diving. There's a pickup service for the Montego

Bay, Runaway Bay, Discovery Bay, and Ocho Rios areas.

GOLF

Golfers appreciate both the beauty and the challenges offered by Jamaica's courses, and some of the best are found in the Montego Bay area. Caddies are almost always mandatory throughout the island, and rates are $15 to $45. Cart rentals are available; costs are $20 to $40.

> **BINOCULARS**
>
> Binoculars are as useful indoors as they are outside. You might think they are only for bringing far-off wildlife and sights within view, but take them into museums, churches, and other buildings to examine the details of artwork, sculptures, and architectural elements.

★ **Half Moon** (⊠*Montego Bay* ☎*876/953–2560*), a Robert Trent Jones–designed 18-hole course 7 mi (11 km) east of town, is the home of the Red Stripe Pro Am (greens fees are $105 for guests, $150 for nonguests). In 2005 the course received an upgrade and once again draws international attention. The newest course in Jamaica, which opened in January

★ 2001, is the White Witch course at the **Ritz-Carlton Golf and Spa Resort, Rose Hall** (⊠*1 Ritz Carlton Dr., Rose Hall, St. James* ☎*876/518–0174*). The greens fees at this 18-hole championship course are $179 for resort guests, $199 for nonguests, and $99 for a twilight round. The **Rose Hall Resort and Country Club, A Hilton Resort** (⊠*N. Coast Hwy., Montego Bay* ☎*876/953–2650*), 4 mi (6.5 km) east of the airport, hosts several invitational tournaments (greens fees run $115 for guests, $150 for nonguests) at the 18-hole championship Cinnamon Hill Ocean Course.

RIVER RAFTING

Jamaica's many rivers mean a multitude of freshwater experiences, from mild to wild. Relaxing rafting trips aboard bamboo rafts poled by local boatmen are almost a symbol of Jamaica and the island's first tourist activity outside the beaches. Recently, soft-adventure enthusiasts have also been able to opt for white-water action as well with guided tours through several operators.

Fodor'sChoice Bamboo rafting in Jamaica originated on the **Rio Grande,** a river in the
★ Port Antonio area. Jamaicans had long used the bamboo rafts to transport bananas downriver; decades ago actor and Port Antonio resident Errol Flynn saw the rafts and thought they'd make a good tourist attraction, and local entrepreneurs quickly rose to the occasion. Today the slow rides are a favorite with romantic travelers and anyone looking to get off the beach for a few hours. The popularity of the Rio Grande's trips spawned similar trips down the **Martha Brae River,** about 25 mi (40 km) from MoBay. Near Ocho Rios, the **White River** has lazy river rafting in the daytime, followed by romantic river floats at night with the passage lighted by torches.

★ **Jamaica Tours Limited** (⊠*Providence Dr., Montego Bay* ☎*876/953–3700* ⊕*www.jamaicatoursltd.com*) conducts trips down the River Lethe, approximately 12 mi (19 km; a 50-minute trip) southwest of MoBay; the four-hour excursion costs about $54 per person, includes lunch, and takes you through unspoiled hill country. Bookings can also be made through hotel tour desks. **River Raft Ltd.** (⌧ *66 Claude Clarke Ave., Montego Bay* ☎*876/952–0889* ⊕*www.jamaicarafting.com*) leads trips down the Martha Brae River, about 25 mi (40 km) from most hotels in MoBay. The cost is $45 per person for the 1½-hour river run.

If you're looking for a more rugged adventure, then consider a white-water rafting trip with **Caliche Rainforest** (⌧*Montego Bay* ☎*876/957–5569* ⊕*www.whitewaterraftingmontegobay.com*); you must be at least 14 years old for this trip. The company also offers a less strenuous rafting trip for all ages.

BEACHES

4

★ **Doctor's Cave Beach.** Montego Bay's tourist scene has its roots right on the Hip Strip, the bustling entertainment district along Gloucester Avenue. This is the best beach in Jamaica outside one of the more developed resorts, thanks to its plantation-style clubhouse with changing rooms, showers, gift shops, bar, grill, and even a cybercafé. There's a fee for admission; beach chairs and umbrellas are also for rent. Its location within the Montego Bay Marine Park—where there are protected corals and marine life—makes it a good spot for snorkeling. ⌧*Gloucester Ave., Montego Bay.*

☾ **Walter Fletcher Beach.** Though not as pretty as Doctor's Cave beach, or as tidy, Walter Fletcher Beach is home to Aquasol Theme Park, which offers a large beach (with lifeguards and security), water trampolines, Jet Skis, banana boat rides, Wave Runners, glass-bottom boats, snorkeling, tennis, go-cart racing, a disco at night, a bar, and a grill. Twice a week—on Wednesday and Friday—Aquasol throws a beach bash with a live reggae show and beach party. Near the center of town, the beach has protection from the surf on a windy day. This means you can find unusually fine swimming here; the calm waters make it a good bet for children. ⌧*Gloucester Ave., Montego Bay.*

WHERE TO EAT

$$ ╳**The Native.** Shaded by a large poinciana tree and overlooking Glouc-
JAMAICAN ester Avenue, this open-air stone terrace serves Jamaican and interna-
★ tional dishes. To go native, start with smoked marlin, move on to the *boonoonoonoos* platter (a sampler of local dishes), and round out with coconut pie or *duckanoo* (a sweet dumpling of cornmeal, coconut, and banana wrapped in a banana leaf and steamed). Live entertainment and candlelit tables make this a romantic choice for dinner on weekends. ⌧*29 Gloucester Ave.* ☎*876/979–2769* ⌦*Reservations essential* ▭*AE, MC, V.*

¢ ╳**Pork Pit.** A favorite with many MoBay locals, this no-frills eatery
JAMAICAN serves Jamaican specialties, including some fiery jerk—note that it's spiced to local tastes, not watered down for tourist palates. Many get their food to go, but you can also find picnic tables just outside. ⌧*27 Gloucester Ave.* ☎*876/940–3008* ▭*MC, V.*

NASSAU, BAHAMAS

Jessica
Robertson

Nassau, the capital of the Bahamas, has witnessed Spanish invasions and hosted pirates, who made it their headquarters for raids along the Spanish Main. The heritage of old Nassau blends the Southern charm of British loyalists from the Carolinas, the African tribal traditions of freed slaves, and a bawdy history of blockade-running during the Civil War and rum-running in the Roaring 1920s. The sheltered harbor bustles with crusie-ship hubbub, while a block away, broad, palm-lined Bay Street is alive with commercial activity. Over it all is a subtle layer of civility and sophistication, derived from three centuries of British rule. Nassau's charm, however, is often lost in its commercialism. There's excellent shopping, but if you look past the duty-free shops you'll also find sights of historical significance that are worth seeing.

ESSENTIALS

Currency The Bahamian dollar, which trades one-to-one with the U.S. dollar, which is universally accepted. There's no need to acquire any Bahamian currency.

Internet You'll find Internet kiosks at Prince George Wharf.

Telephones Calling locally or internationally is easy in the Bahamas. To place a local call, dial the seven-digit phone number. To call the United States, dial 1 plus the area code. Pay phones cost 25¢ per call; Bahamian and U.S. quarters are accepted, as are BATELCO phone cards. To place a call using a calling card, use your long-distance carrier's access code or dial 0 for the operator. Be aware that when placing a toll-free call from your hotel you are charged as if for a regular long-distance call.

COMING ASHORE

Cruise ships dock at one of three piers on Prince George's Wharf. Taxi drivers who meet the ships may offer you a $2 "ride into town," but the historic government buildings and duty-free shops lie just steps from the dock area. As you leave the pier, look for a tall pink tower—diagonally across from here is the tourist information office. Stop in for maps of the island and downtown Nassau. On most days you can join a one-hour walking tour ($10 per person) conducted by a well-trained guide. Tours generally start every hour on the hour from 10 AM to 4 PM; confirm the day's schedule in the office. Just outside, an ATM dispenses U.S. dollars.

As you disembark from your ship, you will find a row of taxis and air-conditioned limousines. Fares are fixed by the government by zones. The fare is $6 for trips within downtown Nassau and on Paradise Island, $9 (plus $1 toll) from downtown to Paradise Island, and $18 from downtown to Cable Beach. Fares are for two passengers; each additional passenger is $3, regardless of the destination. It's customary to tip taxi drivers 15%. You also can hire a car or small van for about $50 per hour. These are fixed costs for two passengers; each additional passenger is $3.

The cheapest way to get to Paradise Island on your own is to take the ferry from the dock area ($3 each way).

Nassau, Bahamas

300 yards
300 meters
0

Silver Cay

Arawak Cay

Fort Charlotte

Ardastra Gardens

West Bay St.

Infant View Rd.

Lighthouse

Paradise Island

Paradise Beach

Paradise Beach Dr.

Paradise Lake

Casuarina Dr.

TO BEACHES

Nassau Harbour

Casino Dr.

Paradise Island Bridge

Potter's Cay

TO PARADISE ISLAND GOLF COURSE

Harbor Dr.

Paradise Is. Dr.

Cabbage Beach

Fort Montagu

Lake Waterloo

John Evans

Sutton St.

Kemp Rd.

St. James Rd.

East Bay St.

Mackey St.

Church St.

Montrose Ave.

Mount Royal Ave.

Collins Ave.

Rosetta St.

Madeira St.

Bay St.

Dowdeswell St.

Shirley St.

Queen's Staircase

North St.

Western Esplanade

Nassau St.

Marlborough St.

West Hill St.

Delancy St.

Meeting St.

West St.

Hospital Lane

Blue Hill Rd.

King St.

Market St.

East St.

East Hill St.

Duke St.

King St.

George St.

Cumberland Rd.

Frederick St.

Woodes Rogers Walk

Prince George Wharf

Union Dock

John Alfred Wharf

Parliament Square

Parliament St.

Elizabeth Ave.

Sands Rd.

Fort Fincastle

KEY

Beach

Cruise Ship Terminal

Ferry Lines

4

EXPLORING NASSAU

Numbers in the margins correspond to points of interest on the Nassau map.

Nassau's sheltered harbor bustles with cruise-ship hubbub, while a block away, broad, palm-lined Bay Street is alive with commercial activity. Shops angle for tourist dollars with fine imported goods at duty-free prices, yet you will find a handful of stores overflowing with authentic Bahamian crafts, foods, and other delights. Most of Nassau's historic sites are centered around downtown.

With its thoroughly revitalized downtown—the revamped British Colonial Hilton lead the way—Nassau is recapturing some of its glamour. Nevertheless, modern influence is apparent: fancy restaurants, suave clubs, and trendy coffeehouses have popped up everywhere. This trend comes partly in response to the burgeoning upper-crust crowds that now supplement the spring-breakers and cruise passengers who have traditionally flocked to Nassau.

Today the seedy air of the town's not-so-distant past is almost unrecognizable. Petty crime is no greater than in other towns of this size, and the streets not only look cleaner but feel safer. You can still find a wild club or a rowdy bar, but you can also sip cappuccino while viewing contemporary Bahamian art or dine by candlelight beneath prints of old Nassau, serenaded by soft, island-inspired calypso music.

Arawak Cay. For a literal taste of Bahamian culture throughout the island chain, take the slightly long walk west on Bay Street to this cluster of eateries and shops. You can buy crafts and food, especially squeaky-fresh conch salad, often made before your very eyes. An ice-cold Kalik beer makes the perfect foil. The cay is on the north side of the T-junction of West Bay and Chippingham Road. It's approximately a 5-minute drive or 20-minute walk. ⊠ *W. Bay St.* 🎫 *Free* ⏱ *Shops and restaurants open daily but hrs vary.*

Ⓒ **Ardastra Gardens, Zoo, and Conservation Centre.** Marching flamingos? These national birds of the Bahamas give a parading performance at Ardastra daily at 10:30, 2:10, and 4:10. The zoo, with more than 5 acres of tropical greenery and ponds, also has an aviary of rare tropical birds including the bright green Bahama parrot, native Bahamian creatures such as rock iguanas and the little (and harmless) Bahamian boa constrictors, and a global collection of small animals. ⊠ *Chippingham Rd., south of W. Bay St.* 🎫 *242/323–5806* ⊕ *www.ardastra. com* 🎫 *$15* ⏱ *Daily 9–5.*

NASSAU BEST BETS

■ **Ardastra Gardens.** Flocks of flamingos, the country's national bird, "march" in three daily shows (you can mingle with the flamboyant pink stars afterward).

■ **Atlantis.** Though very costly, the water park here is a must for families.

■ **Shopping.** To many, shopping is one of Nassau's great delights.

■ **Western Esplanade Beach.** Head to this beach (aka Long Wharf Beach) and sit in the shade of a coconut palm (it's a 10-minute walk from the duty-free shops on Bay Street).

CLOSE UP

Saving on Atlantis

Frugal cruisers have long known about **Comfort Suites Paradise Island** (⊕ *www.comfortsuites.com*), which is right across the street from the Atlantis Resort. They use it to avoid paying for expensive and limited ship-sponsored day-passes to the resort, which cost well over $150 per person. Book a room here, and everyone in the room (up to four people, regardless of age) is entitled to a free day-pass to the Atlantis Resort's water park. In addition to the base rate (usually about $300 depending on the season), you will also have to pay (at check-in) an additional energy surcharge of $14 per adult and a housekeeper gratuity of $4.50 per adult on top of the quoted rate,

even if you prepay. Frankly, this isn't as good a deal as it used to be, but families or groups of four can still save some money by going this route, and then you will have a room in which to shower and change before returning to the ship. Of course, it's a better deal if you can get a discounted rate, though these are not often offered. (Be aware that you may not have more than four people on a single reservation regardless of their age, and you may not get access to the room in the morning, but it will be ready when you get back from your day of fun at the water park.) When it's time for lunch, you'll find cheaper restaurants within walking distance of Atlantis.

★ **Fort Charlotte.** Built in 1788, this imposing fort comes complete with a waterless moat, drawbridge, ramparts, and a dungeon, where children love to see the torture device where prisoners were "stretched." Young guides bring the fort to life. (Tips are expected.) Lord Dunmore, who built it, named the massive structure in honor of George III's wife. At the time, some called it Dunmore's Folly because of the staggering expense of its construction. It cost eight times more than was originally planned. (Dunmore's superiors in London were less than ecstatic with the high costs, but he managed to survive unscathed.) Ironically, no shots were ever fired in battle from the fort. It's about 1 mi west of central Nassau. ⊠ *W. Bay St. at Chippingham Rd.* ☜$5 ۞ *Local guides conduct tours daily 8–4.*

Fort Fincastle and the Water Tower. Shaped like the bow of a ship and perched near the top of the **Queen's Staircase**, Fort Fincastle—named for Royal Governor Lord Dunmore (Viscount Fincastle)—was completed in 1793 to be a lookout post for marauders trying to sneak into the harbor. It served as a lighthouse in the early 19th century. ⊠ *Top of Elizabeth Ave. hill, south of Shirley St.* ۞ *Daily 8–5.*

Parliament Square. Nassau is the seat of the national government. The Bahamian Parliament comprises two houses—a 16-member Senate (Upper House) and a 40-member House of Assembly (Lower House)—and a ministerial cabinet headed by a prime minister. Parliament Square's pink, colonnaded government buildings were constructed in the late 1700s and early 1800s by Loyalists who came to the Bahamas from North Carolina. The square is dominated by a statue of a slim young Queen Victoria that was erected on her birthday, May 24, in

1905. In the immediate area are a half-dozen magistrates' courts (open to the public; obtain a pass at the door to view a session). Behind the House of Assembly is the **Supreme Court**. Its four-times-a-year opening ceremonies (held the first weeks of January, April, July, and October) recall the wigs and mace-bearing pageantry of the Houses of Parliament in London. The Royal Bahamas Police Force Band is usually on hand for the event. ⊠ *Bay St.* ☎ *242/322–7500 for information on Supreme Court ceremonies* ☏ *Free* ☉ *Weekdays 10–4.*

Queen's Staircase. These 65 steps are thought to have been carved out of a solid limestone cliff by slaves in the 1790s. The staircase was later named to honor Queen Victoria's 65-year reign. Recent innovations include a waterfall cascading from the top, and an ad hoc straw market along the narrow road that leads to the site. ⊠ *Top of Elizabeth Ave. hill, south of Shirley St.*

SHOPPING

Duty-free shopping is a major pastime in Nassau, and there are plenty of bargains to be found. Most of the stores selling duty-free items are clustered along an eight-block stretch of Bay Street in Old Nassau and on a few downtown side streets. Most stores are open Monday through Saturday from 9 to 5 and accept credit cards.

The **International Bazaar,** a collection of shops under a huge, spreading bougainvillea, sells linens, souvenirs, and offbeat items. This funky shopping row is on Bay Street at Charlotte Street. **Bahamacraft Centre** (⊠ *Paradise Island Dr.* ☎ *No phone*) offers some top-level Bahamian crafts, including a selection of authentic straw work. Dozens of vendors sell everything from baskets to shell collages inside this vibrantly colored building designed by noted architect Jackson Burnside of Doongalik Studios. You can catch a shuttle bus from Atlantis to the center. **Doongalik Studios** (⊠ *18 Village Rd.* ☎ *242/363–1313*) offers dynamic canvases inspired by Junkanoo celebrations, vibrantly painted furniture, Junkanoo masks, and kaleidoscopic sculpture. Don't miss the sculpture garden or the re-creation of a traditional Bahamian home that serves as a display room for handmade Christmas ornaments, art cards, and other inexpensive and unique gifts. You can watch a Junkanoo video while you shop.

ACTIVITIES

FISHING

The waters here are generally smooth and alive with many species of game fish, which is one of the reasons why the Bahamas have more than 20 fishing tournaments open to visitors every year. A favorite spot just west of Nassau is the Tongue of the Ocean, so called because it looks like that part of the body when viewed from the air. The channel stretches for 100 mi. For boat rentals, parties of two to six will pay $600 or so for a half day, $1,600 for a full day. Needless to say, this is an attractive option only if you can share the costs among a group.

Born Free Charters (☎242/393–4144) has three boats and guarantees a catch on full-day charters—if you don't get a fish, you don't pay. **Brown's Charters** (☎242/324–2061) specializes in 24-hour shark-fishing trips, as well as reef and deep-sea fishing. **Chubasco Charters** (☎242/324–3474 ⊕www.chubascocharters.com) has four boats for sportfishing and shark-fishing charters.

> **CAUTION**
>
> Mail overflowing your mailbox is a neon sign to thieves that you aren't home. Have someone pick it up, or better yet, have the post office hold all your mail for you.

GOLF

Cable Beach Golf Club (7,040 yards, par 72), the oldest golf course in the Bahamas, was completely renovated in 2006. It's a somewhat cheaper alternative to the One and Only Ocean Club ⬧Box N-4914, Nassau ☎242/327–6000 Ext. 6189 🔤18 holes $130–$180, cart included. Clubs $30 ⊙Daily 7–5:30; last tee-off at 5:15. **One and Only Ocean Club Golf Course** (6,805 yards, par 72), formerly the Paradise Island Golf Club, had a major face-lift, care of Tom Weiskopf. The championship course is surrounded by the ocean on three sides, which means that winds can get stiff. Call to check on current availability and up-to-date prices (those not staying at Atlantis or the One and Only Ocean Club may find themselves shut out completely). ⬧Paradise Island Dr., next to airport ⬧Box N-4777, Nassau ☎242/363–3925, 800/321–3000 in U.S. 🔤18 holes $190–$260. Clubs $70 ⊙Daily 6 AM–sundown.

BEACHES

New Providence is blessed with stretches of white sand studded with palm and sea grape trees. Some of the beaches are small and crescent-shaped; others stretch for miles. Paradise Island's real showpiece is 3-mi-long **Cabbage Beach,** which rims the north coast from the Atlantis lagoon to Snorkeler's Cove. At the east end you can rent Jet Skis and nonmotorized pedal boats, and go parasailing. **Cable Beach** is on New Providence's north shore, about 3 mi (5 km) west of downtown Nassau. Resorts line much of this beautiful, broad swath of white sand, but there is public access. Jet-skiers and beach vendors abound, so don't expect quiet isolation. Just west of Cable Beach is a rambling pink house on the Rock Point promontory, where much of the 1965 Bond film *Thunderball* was filmed. Right in downtown Nassau is the **Western Esplanade.** Also known as Long Wharf Beach, this stretch of white sand sweeps west from the British Colonial Hilton on Bay Street and offers public restrooms. On Paradise Island, **Paradise Beach,** at the island's far western tip, is a nice stretch of sand.

WHERE TO EAT

$$$
CARIBBEAN

✕**Anthony's Grill.** Color is the standout feature of Anthony's: bright red, yellow, and blue tablecloths spiked with multihued squiggles; yellow-and-green walls with jaunty cloths hanging from the ceilings; booths printed with bright sea themes; and buoyant striped curtains. The lively spirit is reflected in the cheery service you'll receive at breakfast, lunch, or dinner. The extensive menu (68 items to choose from) includes penne pasta, fresh seafood such as herb-crusted red snapper, steaks, burgers, ribs, and salads. ⊠ *Paradise Village Shopping Plaza* ☎ *242/363–3152* ⊕ *www.anthonysgrillparadiseisland.com* ⊟ *AE, MC, V.*

$$
GREEK ✕ **Athena Café and Bar.** A mainstay since 1960, this Greek restaurant provides a break from the Nassau culinary routine. Sit on the second floor among Grecian statuary, or on the balcony overlooking the action below. Enjoy souvlaki, moussaka, and spanakopita, among other specialties, along with Greek beer in a relaxed and friendly atmosphere. Gregarious owner Peter Mousis and his family serve tasty fare at moderate prices, including breakfast seven days a week. ⊠ *Bay St. at Charlotte St.* ☎ *242/326–1296* ⊟ *AE, D, MC, V* ☉ *No dinner Sun.*

NIGHTLIFE

Some ships stay late into the night or until the next day so that passengers can enjoy Nassau's nightlife. You'll find nonstop entertainment nightly along Cable Beach and on Paradise Island. All the larger hotels offer lounges with island combos for listening or dancing and restaurants with soft guitar or piano music.

CASINOS

Crystal Palace Casino. Slots, craps, baccarat, blackjack, roulette, Big Six, and face-up 21 are among the games in this 35,000-square-foot space. There's a Sports Book facility equipped with big-screen TVs that air live sporting events. Both VIPs and low-limit bettors have their own areas. Casino gaming lessons are available for beginners. Tables and slots are open 24 hours daily. ⊠ *Wyndham Nassau Resort and Crystal Palace Casino, Cable Beach* ☎ *242/327–6200* ⊕ *www.wyndhamnassau resort.com.*

Paradise Island Casino. At 50,000 square feet (100,000 if you include the dining and drinking areas), this is the Caribbean–Bahamian area's largest facility. Featuring a spectacularly open and airy design, the casino is ringed with restaurants and offers more than 1,100 slot machines, baccarat, blackjack, roulette, craps tables, and such local specialties as Caribbean stud poker. There's also a high-limit table area, and most of the eateries have additional games. Tables are open from 10 AM to 4 AM daily; slots, 24 hours. ⊠ *Atlantis, Paradise Island* ☎ *242/363–3000.*

NIGHTCLUBS

Club Waterloo. Claiming to be Nassau's largest indoor-outdoor nightclub, this club has five bars and nonstop dancing Monday through Saturday until 4 AM, and live bands on the weekend. Try the spring-break-special "Green Lizard," a tropical mixture of rums and punches. ⊠ *E. Bay St.* ☎ *242/393–7324.*

NEVIS (CHARLESTOWN)

Jordan Simon

In 1493, when Columbus spied a cloud-crowned volcanic isle during his second voyage to the New World, he named it Nieves—the Spanish word for "snows"—because it reminded him of the peaks of the Pyrenees. Nevis rises from the water in an almost perfect cone, the tip of its 3,232-foot central mountain hidden by clouds. Even less developed than sister island St. Kitts—just 2 mi (3 km) away at their closest point, Nevis is known for its long beaches with white and black sand, its lush greenery, the charming if slightly dilapidated Georgian capital of Charlestown, and its restored sugar plantations that now house charming inns. Even on a day trip Nevis feels relaxed and quietly upscale. You might run into celebrities at the Four Seasons (reopening after extensive renovations in November 2009) or lunching at the beach bars on Pinney's, the showcase strand. Yet Nevisians (not to mention the significant expat American and British presence) never put on airs, offering warm hospitality to all visitors.

ESSENTIALS

Currency The Eastern Caribbean dollar (EC$2.67 to US$1). U.S. dollars, major credit cards, and traveler's checks are readily accepted, although large U.S. bills may be difficult to change in small shops—and you'll receive change in the local currency.

Internet Downtown Cybercafe (⊠ *Main St., Charlestown, Nevis* ☎ *869/469–1999*).

Telephones Phone cards, which you can buy in denominations of $5, $10, and $20, are handy for making local phone calls, calling other islands, and accessing U.S. direct lines. To make a local call, dial the seven-digit number. To call Nevis from the United States, dial the area code 869, then access code 465, 466, 468, or 469 and the local four-digit number.

COMING ASHORE

Cruise ships dock in Charlestown harbor; all but the smallest ships bring passengers in by tender to the central downtown ferry dock. The pier leads smack onto Main Street, with shops and restaurants steps away. Taxi drivers often greet tenders, and there's also a stand a block away. Fares are fairly expensive, but a three-hour driving tour of Nevis costs about $80 for up to four people. Several restored greathouse plantation inns are known for their lunches; your driver can provide information and arrange drop-off and pickup. Before setting off in a taxi, be sure to clarify whether the rate quoted is in E.C. or U.S. dollars.

If your ship docks in St. Kitts, Nevis is a 30- to 45-minute ferry ride from Basseterre. You can tour Charlestown, the capital, in a half hour or so, but you'll need three to four hours to explore the entire island. Most cruise ships arrive in port at around 8 AM, and the ferry schedule (figure $18 round-trip) can be irregular, so many passengers sign up for a cruise line–run shore excursion. If you travel independently, confirm departure times with the tourist office to be sure you'll make it back to your ship on time.

Nevis

Charlestown

Alexander Hamilton Birthplace
Chapel St.
Post Office
Library
Market

KEY
2 Beaches
◣ Dive Sites
▬ Ferry

The Narrows
Newcastle Airport ✈
Newcastle Beach
Mosquito Bay
Newcastle
Oualie Beach
Jones Bay
Long Haul Bay
TO ST. KITTS
Cades Bay
Brick Kiln ○
Cotton Ground ○
Pinney's Beach
Jamestown
ST. THOMAS LOWLAND
ST. JAMES WINDWARD
Nevis Peak
Huggins Bay
Charlestown see inset map
ST. PAUL CHARLESTOWN
Zion ○
Nelson Museum
Bath Springs ◆
Fig Tree ○
ST. GEORGE GINGERLAND
White Bay
ST. JOHN FIG TREE
Botanical Gardens of Nevis
Saddle Hill
Red Cliff
Long Pt.
Dogwood Pt.
The Devil's Caves

Saba
St. Eustatius
St. Kitts
Nevis

0 — 3 miles
0 — 3 km

EXPLORING NEVIS

Bath Springs. The Caribbean's first hotel, the Bath Hotel, built by businessmann John Huggins in 1778, was so popular in the 19th century that visitors, including such dignitaries as Samuel Taylor Coleridge and Prince William Henry, traveled two months by ship to "take the waters" in the property's hot thermal springs. It suffered extensive hurricane and probably earthquake damage over the years and languished in disrepair until recently. Local volunteers have cleaned up the spring and built a stone pool and steps to enter the waters; now residents and visitors enjoy the springs, which range from 104°F to 108°F, though signs still caution that you bathe at your own risk, especially if you have heart problems. Upon completion, this promising development will house the Nevis Island Administration offices, massage huts and changing rooms, a restaurant, and a cultural center and historic exhibit on the original hotel property. Follow Main Street south from Charlestown. ⊠ *Charlestown outskirts.*

★ **Botanical Gardens of Nevis.** In addition to terraced gardens and arbors, this remarkable 7.8-acre site in the glowering shadow of Mt. Nevis has natural lagoons, streams, and waterfalls, superlative bronze mermaids, egrets and herons, and extravagant fountains. You can find a proper rose garden, sections devoted to orchids and bromeliads, cacti, and flowering trees and shrubs—even a bamboo garden. The entrance to the Rain Forest Conservatory—which attempts to include every conceivable Caribbean ecosystem and then some—duplicates an imposing Mayan temple. A splendid re-creation of a plantation-style greathouse contains the excellent Bistro 1787 (operated by the exemplary Montpelier Plantation), with sweeping sea views, and the upscale Galleria shop selling art, textiles, jewelry, and Indonesian teak furnishings sourced during the new owner's world travels. ⊠*Montpelier Estate* ☎*869/469–3509* ⊕*www.botanicalgardennevis.com* ☐*$10* ⊗*Mon.–Sat. 9–5.*

★ **Charlestown.** About 1,200 of Nevis's 10,000 inhabitants live in the capital. The town faces the Caribbean, about 12.5 mi (20 km) south of

NEVIS BEST BETS

■ **Charlestown.** The well-preserved little capital is worth a quick stroll.

■ **Golf.** The stunner at the Four Seasons provides challenge aplenty.

■ **Hiking.** Getting out in the countryside on foot is one of the best ways to experience Nevis.

■ **Horseback Riding.** The views from horseback are just as good as those from closer to the ground.

■ **Pinney's Beach.** This long sensuous strand has several beach bars where you can "lime" with locals.

Basseterre on St. Kitts. If you arrive by ferry, as most people do, you'll walk smack onto Main Street from the pier. It's easy to imagine how tiny Charlestown, founded in 1660, must have looked in its heyday. The weathered buildings still have their fanciful galleries, elaborate gingerbread fretwork, wooden shutters, and hanging plants. The stonework building with the clock tower (1825, but mostly rebuilt after a devastating 1873 fire) houses the courthouse and the second-floor **library** (a cool respite on sultry days). The little park next to the library is Memorial Square, dedicated to the fallen of World Wars I and II. Down the street from the square, archaeologists have discovered the remains of a Jewish cemetery and synagogue (Nevis reputedly had the Caribbean's second-oldest congregation), but there's little to see.

The **Alexander Hamilton Birthplace,** which contains the Museum of Nevis History, is on the waterfront, covered in bougainvillea and hibiscus. This Georgian-style house is a reconstruction of what is believed to have been the American patriot's original home, built in 1680 and thought to have been destroyed during an earthquake in the mid-19th century. Hamilton was born here in 1755, and moved to St. Croix when he was about 12. The Nevis House of Assembly occupies the second floor of this building, and the museum downstairs contains Hamilton memorabilia, documents pertaining to the island's history, and displays on island geology, politics, architecture, culture, and cuisine. The gift shop is a wonderful source for historic maps, crafts, and books on Nevis. ⊠*Low St., Charlestown* ☎*869/469–5786* ⊕*www.nevis-nhcs. org* ☐*$5, with admission to Nelson Museum $7* ⊗*Weekdays 9–4, Sat. 9–noon.*

Nelson Museum. This collection merits a visit for its memorabilia of Lord Horatio Nelson, including letters, documents, paintings, and even furniture from his flagship—purportedly the western hemisphere's largest such compilation. Historical archives of the Nevis Historical and Conservation Society are housed here and are available for public viewing. Nelson was based in Antigua, but on military patrol came to Nevis, where he met and eventually married Frances Nisbet, who lived on a 64-acre plantation here. Half the space is devoted to often provocative displays on island life, from leading families to vernacular architecture to the adaptation of traditional African customs, from cuisine to Carnival. ✉ *Bath Rd., outside Charlestown* ☎ *869/469–0408* ⊕ *www.nevis-nhcs. org* 🗅 *$5, with Alexander Hamilton Birthplace $7* 🕙 *Weekdays 9–4, Sat. 9–noon.*

SHOPPING

Nevis is certainly not the place for a shopping spree, but there are some wonderful surprises, notably the island's stamps, fragrant honey, and batik and hand-embroidered clothing. Other than a few hotel boutiques and isolated galleries, virtually all shopping is concentrated on or just off Main Street in Charlestown. The lovely old stonework and wood floors of the waterfront Cotton Ginnery Complex make an appropriate setting for shops of local artisans.

★ Cheryl "Cherrianne" Liburd's **Bocane Ceramics** (✉ *Main St., Stoney Grove* ☎ *869/469–5437*) stocks beautifully designed and glazed local pottery, such as platters painted with marine life, pineapple tea sets, and coffee tables topped with mosaic depictions of chattel houses. The **CraftHouse** (✉ *Pinney's Rd., Charlestown* ☎ *869/469–5505*) is a marvelous source for local specialties from vetiver mats to leather moccasins; there's a smaller branch in the Cotton Ginnery. **Island Fever** (✉ *Main St., Charlestown* ☎ *869/469–0867*) has become the island's classiest shop, with an excellent selection of everything from bathing suits and dresses to straw bags and jewelry. The **Nevis Handicraft Co-op Society** (✉ *Main St., Charlestown* ☎ *869/469–1746*), next to the tourist office, offers works by local artisans (clothing, ceramic ware, woven goods) and locally produced honey, hot sauces, and jellies (try the guava and soursop). The **Philatelic Bureau** (✉ *Off Main St., Charlestown* ☎ *869/469–0617*), opposite the tourist office, is the place to go for stamp collectors. St. Kitts and Nevis are famous for their decorative, and sometimes valuable, stamps. Real beauties include the butterfly, hummingbird, and marine-life series.

ACTIVITIES

GOLF

Fodor's Choice
★
Duffers doff their hats to the beautiful, impeccably maintained Robert Trent Jones Jr.–designed **Four Seasons Golf Course** (✉ *Four Seasons Resort Nevis, Pinney's Beach* ☎ *869/469–1111*). The virtual botanical gardens surrounding the fairways almost qualify as a hazard in themselves. The front 9 holes are fairly flat until the hole 8, which climbs uphill after your tee shot. Most of the truly stunning views are along the back 9.

The signature hole is the 15th, a 660-yard monster that encompasses a deep ravine; other holes include bridges, steep drops, rolling pitches, extremely tight and unforgiving fairways, sugar-mill ruins, and fierce doglegs. Greens fees per 18 holes had been $290 for nonguests but have been discounted to $100 at least through October 2009 for everyone; expect the cost to go back up once the resort reopens.

HIKING

The center of the island is Nevis Peak—also known as Mt. Nevis—which soars 3,232 feet and is flanked by Hurricane Hill on the north and Saddle Hill on the south. If you plan to scale Nevis Peak, a daylong affair, it's highly recommended that you go with a guide. The **Upper Round Road Trail** is a 9-mi (14.5-km) road constructed in the late 1600s that was cleared and restored by the Nevis Historical and Conservation Society. It connects the Golden Rock Plantation Inn, on the east side of the island, with Nisbet Plantation Beach Club, on the northern tip. The trail encompasses numerous vegetation zones, including pristine rain forest, and impressive plantation ruins. The original cobblestones, walls, and ruins are still evident in many places.

★ **Herbert Heights Village Experience** (☎ *869/469–3259 or 869/764–6354* ⊕ *www.herbertheights.com*) is run by the Herbert family, who lead four-hour nature hikes up to panoramic Herbert Heights, where you drink in fresh local juices and the views of Montserrat; the powerful telescope makes you feel as if you're staring right into that island's simmering volcano. Hike prices start at $25 (more for donkey transport). **Sunrise Tours** (☎ *869/469–2758* ⊕ *www.nevisnaturetours.com*), run by Lynell and Earla Liburd, offers a range of hiking tours, but their most popular is Devil's Copper, a rock configuration full of ghostly legends. Local people gave it its name because at one time the water was hot—a volcanic thermal stream. Hikes range from $20 to $40 per person, and you receive a certificate of achievement. **Top to Bottom** (☎ *869/469–9080* ⊕ *www.walknevis.com*), run by Jim and Nikki Johnston, offers ecorambles (slow tours) and hikes that emphasize Nevis's volcanic and horticultural heritage (including pointing out bat caves and folkloric herbal and "murderous" medicines). Three-hour rambles or hikes are $20 per person (snacks and juice included); it's $40 for more strenuous climbs (two are offered) up Mt. Nevis.

HORSEBACK RIDING

Nevis Equestrian Centre (✉ *Cotton Ground, Pinney's Beach* ☎ *869/469–8118* ⊕ *www.ridenevis.com*) arranges leisurely beach rides, more demanding trail rides ($60–$90), and lessons from caring, careful owners Erika and John.

WINDSURFING

★ Waters are generally calm and northeasterly winds steady yet gentle, making Nevis an excellent spot for beginners and intermediates. **Windsurfing Nevis** (✉ *Oualie Beach* ☎ *869/469–9682*) offers top-notch instructors (Winston Crooke is one of the best in the islands) and equipment for $30 per half hour. Groups are kept small (eight maximum), and the equipment is state-of-the-art from Mistral, North, and Tushingham. They also offer mountain bike tours and rentals.

BEACHES

★ All beaches are free to the public (the plantation inns cordon off "private" areas on Pinney's Beach for guests), but there are no changing facilities, so wear a swimsuit under your clothes. **Oualie Beach,** south of Mosquito Bay and north of Cades and Jones bays, is lined with palms and sea grapes, and the folks at Oualie Beach Hotel can mix you a drink and fix you up with water-sports equipment. **Pinney's Beach,** the island's showpiece, has almost 4 mi (6.5 km) of soft, golden sand on the calm Caribbean, lined with a magnificent grove of palm trees.

WHERE TO EAT

$$–$$$ ✕ **Double Deuce.** Mark Roberts, the former chef at Montpelier, decided
SEAFOOD   to chuck the "five-star lifestyle" and now co-owns this jammed, jam-
★   ming beach bar, which lures locals with fine, fairly priced fare, creative cocktails, and a Hemingway-esque feel (the shack is plastered with sailing and fishing pictures, as well as Balinese masks, Sabrett's hot dog umbrellas, and wind chimes). Peer behind the ramshackle bar and you'll find a gleaming modern kitchen where Mark (and fun-loving firebrand partner Lyndy) prepare sublime seafood he often catches himself, as well as organic beef burgers, velvety pumpkin soup, and lip-smacking ribs. The "DD" is as cool and mellow as it gets. Stop by for free Wi-Fi and proper espresso, a game of pool, riotous Thursday-night karaoke, or just to hang out with a Double Deuce Stinger (Lyndy's answer to Sunshine's Killer Bee punch). You'll find more than 4,000 songs on the virtual jukebox—Akon to ZZ Top, Sarah Vaughan to Van Morrison; if you can't find your favorite the "DJ" will download it for you while you take a quick dip. ⊠ *Pinney's Beach* ☎ *869/469–2222* ⚑ *Reservations essential* ▭ *No credit cards* ⊘ *Closed Mon.*

$$–$$$ ✕ **Sunshine's.** Everything about this shack overlooking (and spilling onto)
CARIBBEAN   the beach is larger than life, including the Rasta man Llewelyn "Sunshine" Caines himself. Flags and license plates from around the world complement the international patrons (including an occasional movie star), who wander over from the adjacent Four Seasons. Picnic tables are splashed with bright sunrise-to-sunset colors; even the palm trees are painted, though "it gone upscaled," as locals say, with VIP cabanas. Fishermen cruise up with their catch—you might savor lobster rolls or snapper creole. Don't miss the lethal house specialty, Killer Bee rum punch! As Sunshine boasts, "One and you're stung, two you're stunned, three it's a knockout." ⊠ *Pinney's Beach* ☎ *869/469–1089* ▭ *No credit cards.*

OCHO RIOS, JAMAICA

John Bigley
and Paris
Permenter

About two hours east of Montego Bay lies Ocho Rios (often just "Ochi"), a lush destination that's favored by honeymooners for its tropical beauty. Often called the garden center of Jamaica, this community is perfumed by flowering hibiscus, bird of paradise, bougainvillea, and other tropical blooms year-round. Ocho Rios is a popular cruise port, and the destination where you'll find one of the island's most recognizable attractions: the stairstep Dunn's River Falls, which invites travelers to climb in daisy-chain fashion, hand-in-hand behind a sure-footed guide This spectacular waterfall is actually a series of falls that cascades from the mountains to the sea. That combination of hills, rivers, and sea also means many activities in the area from seaside horseback rides to mountain biking and lazy river rafting.

ESSENTIALS

Currency The Jamaican dollar (J$88 to US$1). Currency-exchange booths are set up on the docks at Ocho Rios whenever a ship is in port. The U.S. dollar is accepted virtually everywhere; at some places, change is made in Jamaican dollars. Prices given are in U.S. dollars unless otherwise indicated.

Internet A growing number of facilities offer Internet service; expect to pay about US$2 for 20 minutes. At the Taj Mahal Centre, **Jerkin @ Taj Internet Bar and Grill** (⊠ *Ocho Rios* ☎ *876/974–7438*) offers numerous terminals for staying in touch by e-mail while traveling.

Telephones Public telephones are located at the communications center at the Ocho Rios Cruise Pier. Travelers also find public phones in major Ocho Rios malls. Some U.S. phone companies won't permit credit-card calls to be placed from Jamaica because they've been victims of fraud, so collect calls are often the top option. GSM cell phones equipped with tri-band or world-roaming service will find coverage throughout the Ocho Rios region.

OCHO RIOS BEST BETS

■ **Chukka Caribbean.** Any of the great adventure tours here is sure to please.

■ **Dunn's River Falls.** A visit to the falls is touristy, yet it's still exhilarating.

■ **Reggae Xplosion.** Reggae fans should check out this museum of the island sound.

■ **Dolphin Cove at Treasure Reef.** Swim with a dolphin, stingray, or shark at this popular stop.

■ **Firefly.** The former home of playwright Noël Coward can be seen on a guided tour.

COMING ASHORE

Most cruise ships are able to dock at this port on Jamaica's north coast, near Dunn's River Falls. Less than 1 mi (2 km) from the Ocho Rios pier are Island Village (within walking distance), Taj Mahal Duty-Free Shopping Center, and the Ocean Village Shopping Center. Getting anywhere else in Ocho Rios will require a taxi; expect to pay $10 for a taxi ride downtown. The pier, which includes a cruise terminal with the basic services and transportation, is also within easy walking distance of Turtle Beach.

Licensed taxis are available at the pier; expect to pay about $35 per hour for a guided taxi tour. Jamaica is one place in the Caribbean where it's usually to your advantage to take an organized shore excursion offered by your ship unless you just want to go to the beach or do a bit of shopping in town. Car rental isn't recommended in Jamaica due to high prices, bad roads, and aggressive drivers.

Ochos Rios

KEY
Beaches
Cruise Ship Terminal
Dive Sites

0   10 miles
0   15 km

Ocho Rios
see inset map

Ocho Rios

Orcho Rios Fort
Ocho Rios Bay
Milla Bay
James Ave.

Main Rd.

Turtle Beach

Reggae Xplosion

A3

Turtle River Park

DaCosta Dr.

Main St.
DaCosta Dr.

Millard Rd.

Eden Bower Rd.

Coyaba

Shaw Park Gardens

Mahoe Bay
Donald Sangster International Airport
Falmouth
Discovery Bay
Duncans
Puerto Seco Beach
Turtle Beach
Dunn's River Falls
Mallard's Beach
James Bond Beach
Galina Pt.
Oracabessa
Port Maria
Blue Lagoon
Clark's Town
Runaway Bay
St. Ann's Bay
Prospect Plantation
B11
FERN GULLY
Annotto Bay
A4
St. Margaret's Bay
San San Beach
Bos Bay
Brown's Town
Albert Town
Alexandria
Walkerswood Factory
B3
Ewarton
Troja
Orange Bay
A3
Port Antonio
Berridale
Moore Town
Rio Grande R.

Balaclava
Christiana
A1
BLUE MOUNTAINS

Middle Quarters
Mandeville
B3
Spanish Town
A1
Kingston
White Horses

Black River
Santa Cruz
A2
May Pen
A2
Norman Manley International Airport
Lyssa Beach

Crane Beach
Treasure Beach
Alligator Pond
Fort Clarence Beach
B12
Port Royal Sites
Mora Bay

Treasure Beach
Great Pedro Bluff
Old Woman's Pt.
Long Bay
Portland Bight
Polink Pt.
Lime Cay
Portland Pt.
Caribbean Sea

EXPLORING OCHO RIOS

Fodor'sChoice ★ **Dunn's River Falls.** One of Jamaica's most popular attractions is an eye-catching sight: 600 feet of cold, clear mountain water splashing over a series of stone steps to the warm Caribbean. The best way to enjoy the falls is to climb the slippery steps: don a swimsuit, take the hand of the person ahead of you, and trust that the chain of hands and bodies leads to an experienced guide. The leaders of the climbs are personable fellows who reel off bits of local lore while telling you where to step; you can hire a guide's service for a tip of a few dollars. After the climb, you exit through a crowded market, another reminder that this is one of Jamaica's top tourist attractions. ⊠ *Off Rte. A1, between St. Ann's Bay and Ocho Rios* ☎ *876/974–4767* ⌨ *$15* ⊙ *Daily 8:30–5.*

Prospect Plantation. To learn about Jamaica's agricultural heritage, a trip to this working plantation, just west of town, is a must. It's not just a place for history lovers, however. Everyone enjoys the views over the White River Gorge and the tour in a tractor-pulled cart. The grounds are full of exotic flowers and tropical trees, some planted over the years by such celebrities as Winston Churchill and Charlie Chaplin. The estate includes a small aviary with free-flying butterflies. You can also saddle up for horseback rides and camel safaris on the plantation's 900 acres.

✉ *Rte. A1, east of Ocho Rios* ☎*876/994–1058* 🎟*$32* ⏱*Daily 8–5; tours Mon.–Sat. 10:30, 2, and 3:30.*

Reggae Xplosion. In the open-air Island Village shopping center, which is owned by Island Records tycoon Chris Blackwell, Reggae Xplosion traces the fascinating history of Jamaican music. Reggae, ska, mento, dancehall, and other genres are featured in a series of exhibits spanning two stories. Special sections highlight the careers of some of Jamaica's best-known talents, including Bob Marley, Peter Tosh, and Bunny Wailer. The museum has an extensive gift shop filled with recordings and collectibles. ✉*Turtle Beach Rd.* ☎*876/675–8895* ⊕*www.islandjamaica. com* 🎟*$15* ⏱*Weekdays 9–5, Sat. 10–5.*

★ **Walkerswood Factory.** To learn more about Jamaican cuisine (as well as the island's bountiful supply of herbs and spices), visit Walkerswood Factory. This company produces everything from jerk seasonings to pepper sauces. A one-hour guided tour provides a look at the herb gardens, a jerk marinade demonstration, and a sampling of local products. The site includes a gift shop and snack bar featuring local dishes (well spiced, of course). The facility is about 6 mi (10 km) south of Ocho Rios. ✉*Rte. A3, Walkerswood* ☎*876/917–2318* 🎟*$15* ⏱*Mon.–Sat. 9–4.*

SHOPPING

Resort wear, jewelry, Jamaican rum, and Blue Mountain coffee are all popular offerings throughout Ocho Rios stores, while the crafts market is filled with wood carvings and paintings. The crafts market is located steps from the cruise-ship dock but, before launching into a shopping expedition, consider your tolerance for pandemonium and price haggling. **Island Village** is a fun mall that also serves as an entertainment center. Located near the cruise port, this mall is home to shops selling Jamaican handicrafts, duty-free goods, and clothing, a Margaritaville restaurant, a Jamaican music museum, and a small beach
★ area with a water trampoline. **Harmony Hall** (✉*Rte. A1, Ocho Rios* ☎*876/975–4222*), an eight-minute drive east of town, is a restored greathouse where Annabella Proudlock sells her unique wooden boxes with covers decorated with reproductions of local art. Also on sale—and magnificently displayed—are larger reproductions of paintings, lithographs, and signed prints of Jamaican scenes.

ACTIVITIES

DOLPHIN-SWIM PROGRAMS

☁ Dolphin lovers will find a well-run operation near Dunn's River Falls. **Dolphin Cove at Treasure Reef** (✉*N. Coast Hwy., Ocho Rios* ☎*876/ 974–5335* ⊕*www.dolphincovejamaica.com*) offers dolphin swims as well as lower-price dolphin encounters for ages eight and up and dolphin touch programs for ages six and up. Programs cost as much as $195, depending on your level of involvement with the dolphins. Advance reservations are required. The facility also has stingray and shark swims available.

GOLF

Ocho Rios courses don't have the prestige of those around Montego Bay, but duffers will find challenges at a few lesser-known courses. The Runaway Bay golf course is found at **Breezes Runaway Bay** (⊠ *N. Coast Hwy., Runaway Bay* ☎ *876/973–7319*). This 18-hole course has hosted many championship events (greens fees are $80 for nonguests; guests play for free) and is also home to an extensive golf academy. The course at **Sandals Dunn's River Villaggio Golf Resort and Spa** (⊠ *N. Coast Hwy., Mammee Bay* ☎ *876/972–1610* ⊕ *www.sandals.com*) sits at 700 feet above sea level, so there are eye-popping views. Greens fees for nonguests are $100.

HORSEBACK RIDING

With its combination of hills and beaches, Ocho Rios is a natural for horseback excursions. Most are guided tours taken at a slow pace and perfect for those with no previous equestrian experience. Many travelers opt to pack long pants for horseback rides, especially those away from the beach.

FodorsChoice Ocho Rios has excellent horseback riding, and the best company is
★ **Chukka Caribbean Adventures** (⊠ *St. Ann's Bay* ☎ *876/972–2506* ⊕ *www. chukkacaribbean.com*). Trainers here once exercised polo ponies by taking them for rides in the sea; soon there were requests from visitors to ride the horses through the surf. The company now offers a three-hour beach ride that ends with a bareback ride in the sea. This experience—a highlight of many people's trip to the island—costs $76 per person. There's also a ride through the White River valley. The ride, priced at $62 per person, takes you through the rain forest and through the mountains. All riders must be six or older. At **Prospect Plantation** (⊠ *Ocho Rios* ☎ *876/994–1058* ⊕ *www.dolphincovejamaica.com*), 90-minute rides take you across the 18th-century estate and along the White River. Tours are $58 per person, and riders must be eight or older. If you're feeling adventurous, you can even book a 90-minute camel ride ($89).

WHITE-WATER RAFTING

White-water rafting is increasingly popular in the Ocho Rios area. **Chukka Caribbean Adventures** (⊠ *St. Ann's Bay* ☎ *876/972–2506* ⊕ *www. chukkacaribbean.com*) offers white-water fun on the White River—an easy trip that doesn't require any previous experience. Rafters travel in a convoy along the river and through some gentle rapids. The 3½-hour tour costs $62 for adults.

BEACHES

Beach World (⊠ *Island Village Shopping Complex, Main St.* ☎ *876/842–9406*)is especially popular with cruise passengers thanks to its proximity to the pier. Admission to the beach is $3; for an extra fee, you can rent umbrellas, towels, and beach chairs. Activities include kayaking, snorkeling, scuba diving, and glass-bottom-boat rides. Changing rooms and lockers are also available.

Dunn's River Falls Beach (⊠*Rte. A1, between St. Ann's Bay and Ocho Rios*). is always crowded. Although tiny—especially considering the masses of people—it's got a great view, as well as a beach bar and grill. Look up from the sands for a spectacular view of the cascading water of the falls, whose roar drowns out the sea as you approach. **James Bond Beach** (⊠*Orcabessa*) is a less crowded alternative near Ocho Rios—if you don't mind traveling—in the community of Orcabessa. This beach is on the former estate of James Bond's creator, the late Ian Fleming. Today record producer Chris Blackwell runs the show, so it's no surprise that the beach often rocks with live music on the bandstand. Admission is $5 per person (closed Monday).

4

WHERE TO EAT

¢ ✕**Ocho Rios Village Jerk Centre.** This blue-canopied, open-air eatery is
JAMAICAN a good place to park yourself for frosty Red Stripe beer and fiery jerk pork, chicken, or seafood. Milder barbecued meats, also sold by weight (typically, ¼ or ½ pound makes a good serving), turn up on the fresh daily chalkboard menu posted on the wall. It's lively at lunch, especially when passengers from cruise ships swamp the place. ⊠*DaCosta Dr.* ☎*876/974–2549* 🖻 *MC, V.*

¢ ✕**Scotchie's Too.** The Ocho Rios branch of the longtime Montego Bay
JAMAICAN favorite has already been lauded by international chefs for its excel-
Fodor'sChoice lent jerk. The open-air eatery offers plates of jerk chicken, sausage,
★ fish, pork, and ribs, all accompanied by *festival* (a rolled bread similar to a Southern hush puppy), *bammy* (fried cassava bread), and some fire-breathing hot sauce. Be sure to step over to the kitchen to watch the preparation of the jerk over the pits. ⊠*N. Coast Hwy., Drax Hall* ☎*876/794–9457* 🖻*AE, D, MC, V.*

PROGRESO, MEXICO

Michele Joyce The waterfront town closest to Mérida, Progreso is not particularly historic. It's also not terribly picturesque; still, it provokes a certain sentimental fondness for those who know it well. On weekdays during most of the year, the beaches are deserted, but when school is out (Easter week, July, and August) and on summer weekends it's bustling with families from Mérida. Progreso's charm—or lack of charm—seems to hinge on the weather. When the sun is shining, the water looks translucent green and feels bathtub-warm, and the fine sand makes for lovely long walks. When the wind blows during one of Yucatán's winter *nortes*, the water churns with whitecaps and looks gray and unappealing. Whether the weather is good or bad, however, everyone ends up eventually at one of the restaurants lining the main street, Calle 19. Across the street from the oceanfront malecón, these all serve up cold beer, seafood cocktails, and freshly grilled fish. Most cruise passengers head immediately for Mérida or one of the nearby archaeological sites.

ESSENTIALS

Currency The Mexican peso (MX$13.82 to US$1). U.S. dollars and credit cards are accepted by everyone at the port. There is no advantage to paying in dollars, but there may be an advantage to paying in cash.

Internet The cruise terminal isn't terribly close to Progreso's downtown area, but if you take a bus or taxi into town, you'll easily find an Internet café with pretty cheap service. If you take an excursion to Mérida, you'll find that Internet cafés there are ubiquitous, particularly on the main square and Calles 61 and 63; most charge $1 to $3 per hour.

Telephones Most pay phones accept prepaid Ladatel cards, sold in 30-, 50-, or 100-peso denominations. To use the card, insert it in the pay phone's slot, dial 001 (for calls to the U.S.) or 01 (for calls within Mexico), followed by the area code and number. Credit is deleted from the card as you use it, and the balance is displayed on the small screen on the phone.

COMING ASHORE

The pier in Progreso is long, and cruise ships dock at its end, so passengers are shuttled to the foot of the pier, where the Progreso Cruise Terminal offers visitors their first stop. The terminal houses small restaurants and shops selling locally produced crafts. These are some of the best shops in sleepy Progreso (a much wider selection is available in nearby Mérida). The beach lies just east of the pier and can easily be reached on foot. If you want to enjoy the sun and a peaceful afternoon, a drink at one of the small palapa-roof restaurants that line the beach is a good option.

If you are looking to explore, there are plenty of taxis around the pier. A trip around town should not cost more than $5, but ask the taxi driver to quote you a price. If you want to see more of Progresso, a cab can also take you to the local sightseeing tour bus, a bright blue, open-air, double-decker bus that travels through town and only costs $2. A taxi ride from Progreso to Mérida runs about $22, and most drivers charge around $12 per hour to show you around. If you plan on renting the cab for a good part of the day, talk about the number of hours the cost with the driver before you take off. It's difficult to rent a car, so most people just band together in a taxi.

EXPLORING MÉRIDA

Numbers in the margin correspond to points of interest on the Mérida map.

Just south of Progreso (about 20 or 30 minutes by taxi), Mérida, the cultural and intellectual hub of the Yucatán, offers a great deal to explore. Mérida is rich in art, history, and tradition. Most streets are numbered, not named, and most run one-way. North-south streets have even numbers, which descend from west to east; east-west streets have odd numbers, which ascend from north to south. One of the best ways to see the city is to hire a *calesa*, a horse-drawn carriage. They congregate on the main square or at the Palacio Cantón, near the anthropology museum.

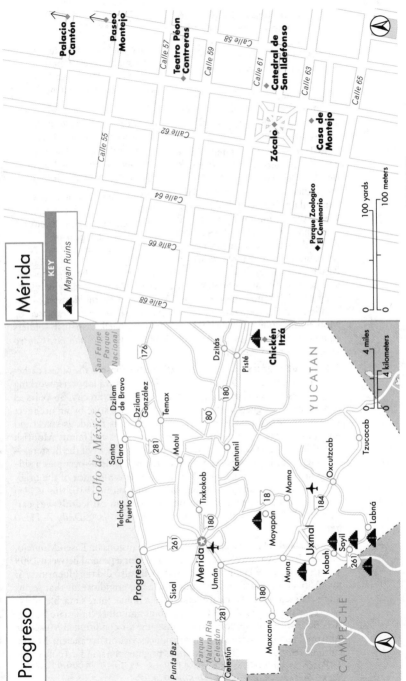

Mérida

KEY

▲ Mayan Ruins

Palacio Cantón
Paseo Montejo
Calle 57
Teatro Péon Contreras
Calle 59
Calle 58
Calle 61
Catedral de San Ildefonso
Calle 63
Calle 55
Calle 62
Zócalo
Casa de Montejo
Calle 65
Calle 64
Calle 66
Calle 68
Parque Zoológico El Centenario

100 yards
100 meters

4

Progreso

Golfo de México
San Felipe Parque Nacional
176
Dzilás
Pisté
Chichén Itzá
YUCATAN
Dzilam de Bravo
Dzilam González
Temax
180
80
Santa Clara
281
Motul
Kantunil
Oxcutzcab
Tzucacab
Telchac Puerto
Tixkokob
180
Mama
18
261
Mayapán
184
Progreso
Mérida
Umán
Uxmal
Labná
Sisal
Muna
Kabah
Sayil
261
Punta Baz
281
180
Maxcanú
Parque Natural Ría Celestún
Celestún
CAMPECHE

4 miles
4 kilometers

Choose your horse and driver carefully as some of the horses look dispirited, but others are fairly well cared for. Drivers charge about $15 for an hour-long circuit around downtown and up Paseo de Montejo, pointing out notable buildings, and providing a little historic background along the way, and $22 for an extended tour.

Casa de Montejo. This stately palace sits on the south side of the plaza, on Calle 63. Francisco de Montejo—father and son—conquered the peninsula and founded Mérida in 1542; they built their "casa" 10 years later. In the late 1970s it was restored by banker Agustín Legorreta and converted to a branch of Banamex bank. Built in the French style, it represents the city's finest—and oldest—example of colonial plateresque architecture, which typically has elaborate ornamentation. A bas-relief on the doorway—the facade is all that remains of the original house—depicts Francisco de Montejo the younger, his wife, and daughter as well as Spanish soldiers standing on the heads of the vanquished Maya. ⊠ *Calle 63, Centro* ⊙ *Weekdays 9–5 and Sat. 9–1.*

Catedral de San Ildefonso. Begun in 1561, St. Ildefonso is the oldest cathedral on the continent. It took several hundred Maya laborers, working with stones from the pyramids of the ravaged Mayan city, 36 years to complete it. Designed in the somber Renaissance style by an architect who had worked on the Escorial in Madrid, its facade is stark and unadorned, with gunnery slits instead of windows and faintly Moorish spires. Inside, the black Cristo de las Ampollas (Christ of the Blisters)—at 7 meters tall, perhaps the tallest Christ in Mexico—occupies a side chapel to the left of the main altar. The statue is a replica of the original, which was destroyed during the revolution in 1910; this is also when the gold that typically decorated Mexican cathedrals was carried off. ⊠ *Calles 60 and 61, Centro* ☎ *No phone* ⊙ *Daily 7–11:30 and 4:30–8.*

Palacio Cantón. The most compelling of the mansions on **Paseo Montejo,** this stately palacio was built as the residence for a general between 1909 and 1911. Designed by Enrique Deserti, who also did the blueprints for the Teatro Peón Contreras, the building has a grandiose air that seems more characteristic of a mausoleum than a home: there's marble everywhere, as well as Doric and Ionic columns and other Italianate Beaux-Arts flourishes. The building also houses the air-conditioned **Museo de Antropología e Historia,** which introduces visitors to ancient Mayan culture. Temporary exhibits sometimes brighten the standard collection. ⊠ *Paseo Montejo 485, at Calle 43, Paseo Montejo* ☎ *999/923–0469* 💳 *$5* ⊙ *Tues.–Sat. 9 AM–8 PM, Sun. 9–2.*

Paseo Montejo. North of downtown, this 10-block-long street was *the* place to reside in the late 19th century, when wealthy plantation owners sought to outdo each other with the opulence of their elegant mansions. Mansion owners typically opted for the decorative styles popular in New Orleans, Cuba, and Paris—imported Carrara marble, European antiques—rather than any style from Mexico. The broad boulevard, lined with tamarind and laurel trees, has lost much of its former panache; some of the mansions have fallen into disrepair. Many are now used as office buildings; others have been or are being restored as part of a citywide, privately funded beautification program. The street is a lovely place to explore on foot or in a horse-drawn carriage.

Teatro Peón Contreras. This 1908 Italianate theater was built along the same lines as grand turn-of-the-20th-century European theaters and opera houses. In the early 1980s the marble staircase, dome, and frescoes were restored. Today, in addition to performing arts, the theater also houses the **Centro de Información Turística** (Tourist Information Center), which provides maps, brochures, and details about attractions in the city and state. The theater's most popular attraction, however, is the café-bar spilling out into the street facing Parque de la Madre. It's crowded every night with people enjoying the balladeers singing romantic and politically inspired songs. ⊠*Calle 60 between Calles 57 and 59, Centro* ☎ *999/924–9290 Tourist Information Center, 999/923–7344 theater, or 999/924–9290* ☺ *Tourist Information Center daily 8–9.*

Zócalo. Méridians traditionally refer to this main square as the Plaza de la Independencia, or the Plaza Principal. Whichever name you prefer, it's a good spot from which to begin a tour of the city, to watch music or dance performances, or to chill in the shade of a laurel tree when the day gets too hot. The plaza was laid out in 1542 on the ruins of T'hó, the Mayan city demolished to make way for Mérida, and is still the focal point around which the most important public buildings cluster. *Confidenciales* (S-shaped benches) invite intimate tête-à-têtes; lampposts keep the park beautifully illuminated at night. ⊠*Bordered by Calles 60, 62, 61, and 63, Centro.*

FARTHER AFIELD

Fodor'sChoice
★ **Chichén Itzá.** One of the most dramatically beautiful of the ancient Mayan cities, Chichén Itzá was discovered by Europeans in the mid-1800s, and much here remains a mystery. Experts have little information about who the Itzás might have been, and the reason why they abandoned the city around 1224 is also unknown. ⊠*Approximately 75 mi (120 km) east of Mérida on Carretera 180* ▦*Site, museum, and sound-and-light show $MX 111; parking $2; use of video camera $3 (keep this receipt if visiting other archaeological sites on same day)* ☺*Daily 8–5; sound-and-light show just after 5 PM (at 8 PM in Spanish with translations for $2.50)* ⊕*www.inah.gob.mx.*

Fodor'sChoice
★ **Uxmal.** If Chichén Itzá is the most expansive Mayan ruin in Yucatán, Uxmal is arguably the most elegant. The architecture here reflects the late classical renaissance of the 7th to the 9th century and is contemporary with that of Palenque and Tikal. ⊠*48 mi (78 km) south of Mérida on Carretera 261* ▦*Site, museum, and sound-and-light show*

$MX 111; parking $1; use of video camera $2 (keep this receipt if visiting other archaeological sites along Ruta Puuc on same day) ☉ *Daily 8–5; sound-and-light show just after dusk (at 7 PM in winter or 8 PM in summer, tickets to only show $3); official English language tour guide $55.*

SHOPPING

In Progreso there is also a small downtown area that is a better place to walk than to shop, between Calle 80 and Calle 31, with small restaurants that serve simple Mexican fare (like *tortas* and *tacos*), small shops with everyday goods for locals, banks, and supermarkets.

Mérida offers more places to shop, including colorful Mexican markets selling local goods. Sunday brings an array of wares into Mérida; starting at 9 AM, the Handicrafts Bazaar, or **Bazar de Artesanías** (⊠ *At main square, Centro*), sells lots of *huipiles* (traditional, white embroidered dresses) as well as hats and costume jewelry. As its name implies, popular art, or handicrafts, are sold at the **Bazar de Artes Populares** (⊠ *Parque Santa Lucía, at Calles 60 and 55, Centro*) beginning at 9 AM on Sunday. If you're interested in handicrafts, **Bazar García Rejón** (⊠ *Calles 65 and 62, Centro*) has rows of indoor stalls that sell items like leather goods, palm hats, and handmade guitars. The **Mercado Municipal** (⊠ *Calles 56 and 67, Centro*) has lots of things you won't need, but which are fascinating to look at: songbirds in cane cages, mountains of mysterious fruits and vegetables, dippers made of hollow gourds (the same way they've been made here for a thousand years). There are also lots of crafts for sale, including hammocks, sturdy leather *huaraches*, and piñatas in every imaginable shape and color. ■ TIP→ **Guides often approach tourists near this market. They expect a tip and won't necessarily bring you to the best deals. You're better off visiting some specialty stores first to learn about the quality and types of hammocks, hats, and other crafts; then you'll have an idea of what you're buying—and what it's worth—if you want to bargain in the market. Also be wary of pickpockets within the markets.**

WHERE TO EAT

¢ ✕**Flamingos.** This restaurant facing Progreso's long cement promenade
SEAFOOD   is a cut above its neighbors. Service is professional and attentive, and soon after arriving you'll get at least one free appetizer—maybe black beans with corn tortillas, or a plate of shredded shark meat stewed with tomatoes. The creamy cilantro soup is a little too cheesy (literally, not figuratively), but the large fish fillets are perfectly breaded and lightly fried. Breakfast is served after 7 AM. There's a full bar, and although there's no air-conditioning, large, glassless windows let in the ocean breeze. ⊠ *Calle 19 No. 144-D, at Calle 72, Progreso* ☎ 969/935–2122 ▭ *MC, V.*

¢ ✕**La Vía Olimpo.** Lingering over coffee and a book is a pleasure at this
CAFÉ   smart Internet café; the outdoor tables are a great place to watch the nonstop parade—or the free Sunday performances—on the main square. In the air-conditioned dining room you can feast on turkey sandwiches, burgers and fries, or *poc chuc* (slices of pork marinated in sour-orange

sauce and spices). Crepes are also popular, and there are lots of salads and juices if you're in the mood for something light. Crowds keep this place hopping from 7 AM to 11 PM daily. Spirits are served, and you'll get an appetizer, like a basket of chips with freshly made guacamole, with most drink orders. ⊠*Calle 62 No. 502, between Calles 63 and 61, Centro* ☎*999/923–5843* ▭*MC, V*

PUERTO LIMÓN, COSTA RICA

Jeff Van Fleet   Christopher Columbus became Costa Rica's first tourist when he landed on this stretch of coast in 1502 during his fourth and final voyage to the New World. Expecting to find vast mineral wealth, he named the region "Costa Rica" (rich coast). Imagine the Spaniards' surprise eventually to find there was none. Save for a brief skirmish some six decades ago, the country *did* prove itself rich in a long tradition of peace and democracy. No other country in Latin America can make that claim. Costa Rica is also abundantly rich in natural beauty, managing to pack beaches, volcanoes, rain forests, and diverse animal life into an area the size of Vermont and New Hampshire combined. It has successfully parlayed those qualities into its role as one the world's great ecotourism destinations. A day visit is short, but time enough for a quick sample.

ESSENTIALS

Currency The colón (¢569 to US$1). Most businesses in port gladly accept U.S. dollars.

Internet A bank of Internet computers is yours to use at the cruise terminal. **Internet Cinco Estrellas** (⊠ *50 meters north of Terminal de Cruceros* ☎ *2758-5752*).

Telephones Telephone numbers have seven digits. Merely dial the number. There are no area codes. You'll find ample phones for use in the cruise terminal. Public phones accept locally purchased calling cards.

COMING ASHORE

Ships dock at Limón's spacious, spiffy Terminal de Cruceros (cruise terminal), one block south of the city's downtown. You'll find telephones, Internet computers, a crafts market, and tourist information and tour operators' desks inside the terminal, as well as a small army of manicurists who do a brisk business. Step outside and walk straight ahead one block to reach Limón's downtown.

A fleet of red taxis waits on the street in front of the terminal. Drivers are happy to help you put together a do-it-yourself tour. Most charge $75 to $100 per carload for a day of touring. There is no place to rent a car here, but you're better off leaving the driving to someone else. Cruise lines offer dozens of shore excursions in Costa Rica, and if you want to go any farther afield than Limón or the coast south, we suggest you take an organized tour. The country looks disarmingly small on a map—it is—but hills give rise to mountains the farther inland you go, and road conditions range from "okay" to "abysmal." Distances are short as the toucan flies, but travel times are longer than you'd expect.

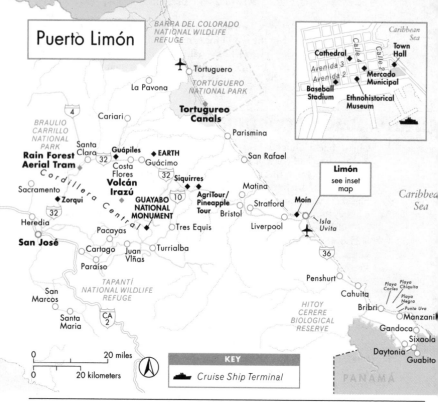

Puerto Limón

BARRA DEL COLORADO
NATIONAL WILDLIFE
REFUGE

Tortuguero
La Pavona
TORTUGUERO
NATIONAL PARK

Cariari
BRAULIO
CARRILLO
NATIONAL
PARK

Tortugureo
Canals

Parismina

San Rafael

Santa
Clara
Rain Forest
Aerial Tram

Guápiles
Costa
Flores
Guácimo

EARTH

Siquirres

Matina

Sacramento
Zorqui

Volcán
Irazú

AgriTour/
Pineapple
Tour
Bristol

Stratford

Moín
Isla
Uvita

Caribbea
Sea

Heredia

GUAYABO
NATIONAL
MONUMENT

Tres Equis

Liverpool

San José

Pacayas

Cartago
Juan
Vlñas
Turrialba

Paraíso

TAPANTÍ
NATIONAL WILDLIFE
REFUGE

Penshurt

San
Marcos

Santa
Maria

Cahuita

HITOY
CERERE
BIOLOGICAL
RESERVE

Bribri

Playa
Cocles
Playa
Chiquita
Playa
Negra
Punta Uva
Manzani

Gandoca

Daytonia

Sixaola

Guabito

PANAMÁ

0   20 miles
0   20 kilometers

KEY
Cruise Ship Terminal

Cordillera Central

Limón
see inset
map

Caribbean
Sea

Cathedral

Calle 4
Calle 2

Town
Hall

Avenida 3
Avenida 2

Mercado
Municipal

Baseball
Stadium

Ethnohistorical
Museum

EXPLORING PUERTO LIMÓN

Limón. "Sultry and sweltering" describes this port community of 90,000. The country's most ethnically diverse city mixes the Latino flavor of the rest of Costa Rica with Afro-Caribbean and Asian populations, descendants of laborers brought to do construction and farming in the 19th century. As in most of the rest of Costa Rica, you'll see no street signs here. Locals use a charmingly archaic system of designating addresses: The place you're looking for may be "100 meters south and 75 meters west of some landmark, "where"100 meters" equals one city block, regardless of actual distance. Just north and east of the cruise terminal lies the city's palm-lined central park, **Parque Vargas**, with a promenade facing the ocean. Nine or so Hoffman's two-toed sloths live in its trees; ask a passerby to point them out, as spotting them requires a trained eye.

Rain Forest Aerial Tram. This 2½-square-mi (4-square-km) preserve houses a privately owned and operated engineering marvel: a series of gondolas strung together in a modified ski-lift pulley system. (To lessen the impact on the jungle, the support pylons were lowered into place by helicopter.) The tram gives you a way of seeing the rain-forest canopy and its spectacular array of epiphyte plant life and birds from just above, a feat you could otherwise accomplish only by climbing the trees yourself. Though purists might complain that it treats the rain forest like an amusement park, it's an entertaining way to learn the value and beauty of rain-forest ecology. ✉*Braulio Carrillo National Park, 76 mi (120 km) west of Limón* ☎*2257–5961, 866/759–8726 in North America* ⊕*www.rainforest rams.com* 🖃*$55* ⏱*Mon. 9–4, Tues.–Sun. 6:30–4.*

San José. Costa Rica's sprawling, congested capital sits in the middle of the country about three hours inland from the coast. Despite the distance, San José figures as a shore excursion—a long one to be sure—on most ships' itineraries. (The vertical distance is substantial, too; the capital sits on a plateau just under a mile above sea level. You'll appre-

PUERTO LIMÓN
BEST BETS

■ **The Rain Forest Tram.** This attraction takes you up into the canopy of the rain forest to see it from a unique angle.

■ **Tortuguero Canals.** Whether you go on a ship-sponsored tour or arrange it on your own, you see a wild part of Costa Rica that isn't reachable by anything but boat.

■ **Zip-Line Tours.** If you have never done one of these thrilling tours, flying from tree to tree, Costa Rica is the original place to do it.

ciate a jacket here after so many days at sea level.) Although the city dates from the mid-18th century, little from the colonial era remains. The northeastern San José suburb of **Moravia** is chock-full of souvenir stores lining a couple of blocks behind the city's church. The **Teatro Nacional** (National Theater) is easily the most enchanting building in Costa Rica, and San José's must-see sight. Coffee barons constructed the Italianate sandstone building, modeling it on a composite of European opera houses, and inaugurating it in 1897. ✉*Plaza de la Cultura, Barrio La Soledad* ☎*221–1329* ⊕*www.teatronacional.go.cr* 🖃*$5* ⏱*Mon.–Sat. 9–4.*

The **Museo Nacional** *(National Museum)* is housed in a whitewashed fortress dating from 1870. Notice the bullet holes: this former army headquarters saw fierce fighting during a brief 1948 civil war. But it was also here that the government abolished the country's military in 1949. ✉*C. 17, between Avdas. Central and 2, Barrio La Soledad* ☎*257–1433* ⊕*www.museocostarica.go.cr* 🖃*$4* ⏱*Tues.–Sat. 8:30–4:30, Sun. 9–4:30* ✚*100 mi (160 km) west of Limón.*

Tortuguero Canals. The largely forested region north of Limón is one of those Costa Rican anomalies: roadless and remote, it's nevertheless one of the country's most-visited places. A system of inland canals runs parallel to the shoreline, providing safer access to the region than a dangerous journey for smaller vessels up the seacoast. Some compare the densely layered greenery highlighted by brilliantly colored flowers, whose impact is doubled by the jungle's reflection in the mirror-smooth canal surfaces, to the Amazon. That might be stretching it, but there's still an Indiana Jones mystique to the journey up here, especially when you get off the main canals and into the narrower lagoons. Your guide will point out the abundant wildlife: sloths hang in the trees; howler monkeys let out their plaintive calls; egrets soar above the river surface; and crocodiles laze on the banks. ⊠*North of Limón.*

🕐 **Veragua Rainforest Adventure Park.** The region's newest attraction is a 4,000-acre nature theme park, about 30 minutes west of Limón. It's popular with cruise-ship passengers in port for the day, but if you're in the area, it's well worth a stop. Veragua's great strength is its small army of enthusiastic, super-informed guides who take you through a network of nature trails and exhibits of hummingbirds, snakes, frogs, and butterflies and other insects. A gondola ride overlooks the complex and transports you through the rain forest canopy. A branch of Monteverde's **Original Canopy Tour** is here, too, and offers you the chance to zip from platform to platform—10 in all—through the rain forest canopy. The $45 tour lasts 1½ hours, and can be done separately from the other attractions. The canopy tour is included in the all-inclusive daylong, walk-in tour, but not the half-day tour or the tour from San José. ⊠*Veragua de Liverpool* ✛*9 mi (15 km) west of Limón* ☎*2296–5056 in San José* ⊕*www.veraguarainforest.com* ⊠*Half-day tour $65, children under 12, $45; full-day tour $99, children under 12, $70; full-day tour with transportation from San José, $139, children under 12, $99* ☉*Tues.–Sun. 8–4.*

Volcán Irazú. Five active volcanoes loom over Costa Rica's territory (as well as many inactive ones). Irazú clocks in at the highest at about 11,000 feet (3,700 meters) and the farthest east and most accessible from Limón, though still a three-hour drive. The volcano last erupted in 1965, but gases and steam have billowed from fumaroles on its northwestern slope ever since. You can go right up to the top, although cloudy days—there are many—can obscure the view. ⊠*84 mi (140 km) southwest of Limón* ☎*2551–9398, 8200–5025 for ranger station* ⊠*$7* ☉*Daily 8–3:30.*

SHOPPING

The cruise-ship terminal contains an orderly maze of souvenir stands. Vendors are friendly; there's no pressure to buy. Many shops populate the restored port building across the street as well. Spelling is not its forte, but the **Caribean Banana** (⊠*50 m north Terminal de Cruceros, west side of Parque Vargas*) stands out from the other shops in the cruise-terminal area with a terrific selection of wood carvings.

ACTIVITIES

WHITEWATER RAFTING

You can experience some of the world's premier white-water rafting in Costa Rica. The Río Reventazón in the eastern part of the country offers a few Class II–III sectors if you've never rafted before. Old standby **Ríos Tropicales** (⊠*On highway in Siquirres* ☎*2233–6455, 866/722–8273 in North America* ⊕*www.riostropicales.com*) has tours on a Class III–IV section of the Pacuare River between Siquirres and San Martín, as well as the equally difficult section between Tres Equis and Siquirres. Not quite so wild, but still with Class III rapids, is the nearby Florida section of the Reventazón. Day excursions normally begin in San José, but if you're out in this part of the country, you can kick off your excursion here at the company's operations center in Siquirres.

ZIP-LINE TOURS

Costa Rica gave birth to the so-called canopy tour, a system of zip lines that transports you from platform to platform in the rain-forest treetops courtesy of a very secure harness. Though billed as a way to get up close with nature, your Tarzan-like yells will probably scare any wildlife away. Think of it more as an outdoor amusement-park ride. The nearest zip-line tour is at Veragua Rainforest Adventure Park.

BEACHES

The dark-sand beaches on this sector of the coast are pleasant enough, but won't dazzle you if you've made previous stops at Caribbean islands with their white-sand strands. Nicer beaches than Limón's Playa Bonita lie farther south along the coast, and can be reached by taxi or organized shore excursion. Strong undertows make for ideal surfing conditions on these shores, but risky swimming. Exercise caution.

Playa Bonita (⊠ *1 mi [2 km] north of Limón*), the name of Limón's own strand, translates as "pretty beach," but it's your typical urban beach, a bit on the cluttered side. **Playa Blanca** (⊠ *26 mi [44 km] southeast of Limón, Cahuita*), one of the coast's only white-sand beaches, lies within the boundaries of Cahuita National Park, right at the southern entrance of the pleasant little town of Cahuita. The park's rain forest extends right to the edge of the beach, and the waters here offer good snorkeling. **Playa Cocles** (⊠ *38 m [63 km] southeast of Limón, Puerto Viejo de Talamanca*), the region's most popular strand of sand, lies just outside Puerto Viejo de Talamanca, one of Costa Rica's archetypal beach towns, with its attendant cafés and bars and all-around good times to be had.

WHERE TO EAT

$ ✕**Brisas del Caribe.** Here's a case study in what happens when cruise

SEAFOOD ships come to town. This old downtown standby, once as charmingly off-kilter as the crooked umbrellas on its front tables, got rid of its video poker machines (and the locals who always hoped to get lucky playing them), tiled the floors, and remodeled. The food is still good—seafood and surprisingly decent hamburgers, a real rarity in Costa Rica, are the fare here—but a bit of the local color has faded. Passenger or not, you can partake of the lunch buffet on cruise days. ⊠*North side of Parque Vargas* ☎*2758–0138* ▤*AE, D, DC, MC, V.*

$ ✕**Hotel Park.** Take refuge from the sweltering midday heat in the air-

SEAFOOD conditioned restaurant of Limón's pastel-and-pink, mid-range business-class hotel. Decent pastas, seafood, and desserts are on the menu, and the pleasant ocean view is tossed in for free. ⊠*Av. 3, Calles 2–3* ☎*2798–0555* ▤*AE, DC, MC, V*

ROATÁN, HONDURAS

Melanie
Wetzel

You'll swear you hear Jimmy Buffett singing as you step off the ship onto Roatán. The flavor is decidedly Margaritaville, but with all there is to do on this island off the north coast of Honduras you'll never waste away here. Roatán is the largest and most important of the Bay Islands, though at a mere 40 mi (65 km) from tip to tip, and no more than 3 mi (5 km) at its widest; "large" is relative here. As happened elsewhere on Central America's Caribbean coast, the British got here first—the Bay Islands didn't become part of Honduras until the mid-1800s—and left an indelible imprint in the form of place names such as Coxen Hole, French Harbour, and West End, and of course, their language, albeit a Caribbean-accented English. The eyes of underwater enthusiasts mist over at the mention of Roatán, one of the world's premier diving destinations, but plenty of topside activity will keep you busy, too.

ESSENTIALS

Currency The Honduran leimpira (L18.9 to US$1). You'll find an ATM at Banco BAC in the town of Coxen Hole, where cruise ships arrive. Credit cards are widely accepted, although merchants frequently add a surcharge to offset the high processing fees they are charged by card companies

Internet Check your e-mail at **Hondusoft Internet** (✉ *Main St., Coxen Hole*), just a couple of blocks from the cruise terminal.

Telephones Phone numbers in Honduras have seven digits. There are no area codes, so just dial the number. You'll find public phones at the cruise terminal, as well as around populated areas on the island.

COMING ASHORE

Ships dock at the Terminal de Cruceros (cruise terminal) in the village of Coxen Hole, the island's administrative center. You'll find telephones, Internet computers, and stands with tour information inside the terminal, as well as a flea market of crafts vendors just outside the gate. At this writing, a public concession has been granted to Royal Caribbean to construct and operate a new $16-million cruise terminal nearby. The current terminal dates only from 2001, but traffic here has outpaced its capacity. The new terminal, which will be open to all cruise lines, is expected to open in 2009.

A fleet of white taxis waits outside the gate, and here is your contact with one of the few negatives about Roatán. Drivers use a two-tier fare system, one for locals, and another, much higher "gringo" level. The $15 you'll be charged for the few miles to West End bears no resemblance to what a resident pays. Negotiate if you feel up to it. The local public-transport system consists of blue minivans that leave from Main Street in Coxen Hole to various points on the island until 6 PM. A collective taxi ride from Coxen Hole to French Harbour or to West End should not cost more than L20 (payable only in leimpira). Look for the cadre of tourist police if you need help with anything. They wear yellow shirts and dark-green trousers and are evident on cruise days. You certainly can rent a car here, but the island's compact size makes it

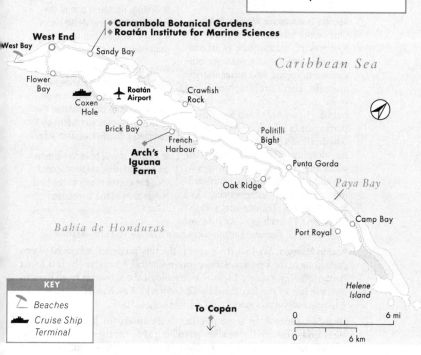

Roatán, Honduras

West End

◆ **Carambola Botanical Gardens**
◆ **Roatán Institute for Marine Sciences**

West Bay

Sandy Bay

Flower Bay

Coxen Hole

✈ **Roatán Airport**

Crawfish Rock

Caribbean Sea

Brick Bay

French Harbour

Arch's Iguana Farm

Politilli Bight

Punta Gorda

Oak Ridge

Paya Bay

Bahía de Honduras

Port Royal

Camp Bay

To Copán

Helene Island

KEY

Beaches

Cruise Ship Terminal

0   6 mi

0   6 km

unnecessary. Taxis will happily take you anywhere; expect to pay $40 to $80 for a day's private tour.

EXPLORING ROATÁN

Arch's Iguana Farm. West of French Harbour you'll find this farm where you can get a close look at the stern-faced lizards. Hundreds of the sleepy creatures roam around the reserve. Drop in around noon to see them have lunch. ⊠*French Harbour* ☎445–1498 ⌨*L75.*

Carambola Botanical Gardens. With one of the country's most extensive orchid collections, this is home to many different varieties of tropical plants. It is also a breeding area for iguanas. There are several trails to follow, and many of the trees and plants are identified by small signs. The longest trail leads up to the top of the hill, where you find an amazing view of the West End and Anthony's Key Resort. ⊠*Sandy Bay, across from Anthony's Key Resort* ☎445–1117 ⌨*$5* ⊙*Daily 7–5.*

Copán. The magnificent Mayan city of Copán easily wins the "Honduras's Most Famous Sight" title, and this mainland destination is included on a few ships' shore-excursion itineraries. Because it includes a flight, the excursion is always an expensive one, but it's well worth doing. You'll marvel at the artistry of a city that many have called the "Paris of

Central America." ✉ ½ mi (1 km) east of Copán Ruinas ☎ No phone 💲$15 ⏲ Daily 8–4.

☯ **Roatán Institute for Marine Sciences.** One of the attractions at Anthony's Key Resort, the institute is an educational center that researches bottlenose dolphins and other marine animals. There are dolphin shows twice a day, which are free to the public. For an additional fee you can participate in a "dolphin encounter," which allows you to interact with the dolphins either swimming or snorkling. There are also programs for children ages five to 14, including snorkeling experiences, and the "Dolphin Trainer for a Day" program. ✉ Anthony's Key Resort ☎ 445–1327 ⊕ www.anthonyskey.com 🚢 L64 ⏲ Daily 8:30–5.

Roatán Museum. Well worth a visit is the tiny museum, which has been called one of the best small museums in Central America. The facility, at Anthony's Key Resort, displays archaeological discoveries from Roatán and the rest of the Bay Islands. ✉ Anthony's Key Resort ☎ 445–1327 ⊕ www.anthonyskey.com 🚢 L64 ⏲ Daily 8:30–5.

West End. One of the most popular destinations for budget travelers, West End offers idyllic beaches stretching as far as the eye can see. One of the loveliest spots is Half Moon Bay, a crescent of brilliant white sand. A huge number of dive shops offer incredibly low-price diving courses. ✉ West End.

SHOPPING

Crafts vendors set up shop outside the cruise-terminal gates, and a small selection of souvenir shops are scattered around the center of Coxen Hole, a short walk from the docks. Few of the souvenirs for sale here—or anywhere else on the island for that matter—were actually made in Roatán; most come from mainland Honduras.

ACTIVITIES

DIVING AND SNORKELING

Most of the activity on Roatán centers on scuba diving and snorkeling, as well as the newest sensation, snuba, a cross between the two, whereby your mask is connected to an air tube above. Warm water, great visibility, and thousands of colorful fish make the island a popular destination. Add to this a good chance of seeing a whale shark, and you'll realize why so many people head here each year. Dive sites cluster off the island's western and southern coasts. Competition among the dive shops is fierce in West End, so check out a few. When shopping around, ask about class size (eight is the maximum), the condition of the diving equipment, and the safety equipment on the dive boat. Just at the entrance to West End, **Coconut Tree Divers** (⊠ *West End* ☎*445–4081* ⊕*www.coconuttreedivers.com*) is a PADI Gold Palm resort, offering a wide range of dives and dive courses. They also have cabins with air-conditioning and fridges, with a discount for their divers. **Native Sons** (⊠ *West End* ☎*445–1335* ⊕*www.nativesonsroatan.com*) is one of the most popular dive shops in town. It's run by a native of Roatán who really knows the area. The popular **Ocean Connections** (⊠ *West End* ☎*445–1925* ⊕*www.ocean-connections.com*) is a well-established dive shop. In business for more than a decade, **West End Divers** (⊠ *West End* ☎*445–1531* ⊕*www.westendivers.com*) has a pair of dive boats. The company is committed to protecting the fragile marine ecology.

4

BEACHES

You almost can't go wrong with any of Roatán's white-sand beaches. Even those adjacent to populated areas manage to stay clean and uncluttered, thanks to efforts of residents. Water is rougher for swimming on the less-protected north side of the island.

Half Moon Bay, Roatán's most popular beach, is also one of its prettiest. Coconut palms and foliage come up to the crescent-shape shoreline. The beach lies just outside the tourist-friendly West End. Crystal clear waters offer abundant visibility for snorkeling. Locals refer to lovely **Tabyana Beach**, simply known as "West Bay," but the travel brochures name it after its prominent Tabyana Beach Resort. It's a de rigueur listing on every shore-excursions list, and the resort sets aside its facilities to cruise passengers as a private beach. The complex also offers zip-line tours, which take you through the treetops courtesy of a series of cables and a very secure harness.

WHERE TO EAT

¢ ✕**Bojangles Chicken/Pizza Inn.** Although you didn't come to Central
AMERICAN America to eat chicken and biscuits, even locals supplement their diet with a little fast food now and then. Sweet tea, your basic fried chicken, and a large variety of cheap pizzas will satisfy most groups or weary travelers. ⊠*At Petrosun Gas Station, main highway outside of Coxen Hole* ☎*445–1208* ▭*MC, V* ☉*Closed Sun.*

¢ ✕**French Harbour Bakery.** The West End branch of this popular bakery
CAFÉ serves great bread, sandwiches, and bagels. ⊠*Beach house at Half Moon Bay, West End* ☎*No phone* ▭*No credit cards* ☉*Closed Sun.*

SAMANÁ, DOMINICAN REPUBLIC

Eileen Robin-
son Smith

Samaná, the name of both a peninsula in the Dominican Republic as well as the largest town on Samaná Bay, is one of the least-known regions of the country, but the new international airport that opened in nearby Catey in late 2006, and the new highway from Santo Domingo that has cut drive-time to two hours, is changing that perception quickly. Much development is planned, so a visit now will be to a place that is not yet geared to a great deal of mainstream, mass tourism. But with the use of the port by some mega-ships, that, too, is changing rapidly. Samaná is one of the Dominican Republic's newest cruise-ship destinations, with one of the island's greatest varieties of shore excursions. You can explore caves and see an amazing waterfall. And since many humpback whales come here each year to mate and give birth, it's a top whale-watching destination from January through March. While some cruise lines still use Cayo Levantado as a private-island type of experience, for other lines it is just one of several options.

ESSENTIALS

Currency The Dominican peso (RD$35 to US$1). Get local currency if you are touring on your own, but most places accept U.S. dollars, though any change will be in pesos. Banks and *cambios* (currency exchange offices) are plentiful.

Internet You'll find several convenient Internet cafés in town. The price of going online ranges between RD$30 and RD$80 per hour, inexpensive to be sure. However, don't be surprised if you go and are told that the computers: *"No sirve, porque no hay electricidad."* Translation: This is still a developing destination, and sometimes half the day is spent without electricity. Although most hotels and restaurants have generators, usually these shops do not. **Centro Llamada Edwards** (✉ *4 Francisco Rosario Sanchez, Samaná* ☎ *809/538-2476*) has five computers and charges only RD$30 an hour to connect. **Deleon Communications** (✉ *13 Maria Trinidad Sanchez, Samaná, across from landmark Palacio Justicia* ☎ *809/538-3538*) has six computers and four phone booths.

Telephones You can call U.S. or Canadian numbers easily; just dial 1 plus the area code and number. **Centro de Communicationes Verizon** (✉ *8 Francisco Rosario Sanchez, Samaná* ☎ *809/538-2901*; ✉ *Maria Trinidad Sanchez, Samaná, next door to Pharmacia Gisella*) is a good place to make phone calls. Only cash is taken, preferably pesos. At the first location, there are public computers for checking your e-mails; at the second, you won't be able to go online, but it is closer to the pier.

COMING ASHORE

Cruise ships anchor at a point equidistant between the town of Samaná and Cayo Levantado, an island at the mouth of Samaná Bay with a great beach and facilities to receive 1,500 cruise-ship passengers. Tenders will take you to one of three docks, located on the malecón, referred to as the Samaná Bay Piers. The farthest is a five-minute walk from the town center. The Verizon office is just before the public market.

Renting a car, although possible, isn't a good option. Driving in the D.R. can be a hectic and even harrowing experience; if you are only in port one day, don't risk it. You'll do better if you combine your resources with friends from the ship and share a taxi to do some independent exploring. Negotiate prices, and settle before getting in the taxi. To give you an idea of what to expect, a minivan that can take eight people will normally charge $90 for the round-trip to Las Terranas, including a two-hour wait while you explore or enjoy the beach. Similarly, you'll pay $80 to travel to Las Galleras or Playa Rincón. Many of the drivers

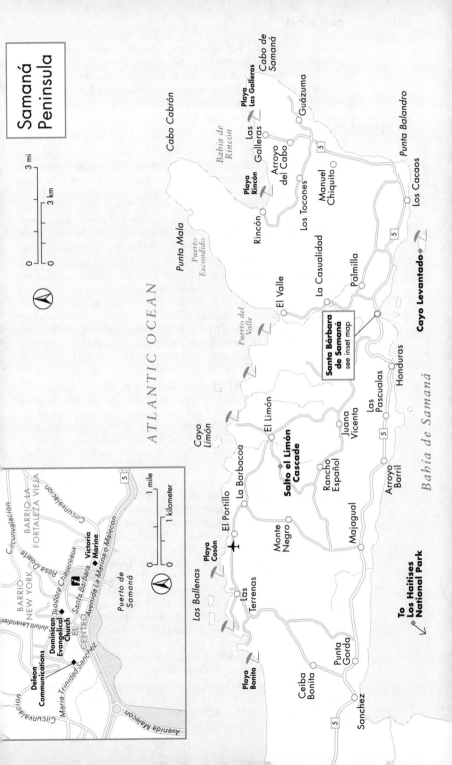

Samaná Peninsula

ATLANTIC OCEAN

Cabo Cabrón

Punta Mala

Puerto Escondido

Bahía de Rincón

Cabo de Samaná

Playa Las Galleras

Las Galleras

Guázuma

Arroyo del Cabo

Punta Balandro

Playa Rincón

Rincón

Los Tocones

Manuel Chiquito

La Casualidad

Palmilla

Los Cacaos

El Valle

Puerto del Valle

Santa Bárbara de Samaná
see inset map

Cayo Levantado

Cayo Limón

El Limón

Salto el Limón Cascade

Honduras

La Barbacoa

Rancho Español

Juana Vicenta

Las Pascualas

Arroyo Barril

El Portillo

Monte Negro

Majagual

Bahía de Samaná

Las Ballenas

Playa Cosón

Las Terrenas

To Los Haitises National Park

Punta Gorda

Playa Bonita

Ceiba Bonita

Sanchez

3 mi
3 km

Inset: Santa Bárbara de Samaná

Circunvalación

BARRIO LA FORTALEZA VIEJA

BARRIO NEW YORK

Julio Lavandier

Rosa Duarte

Teodore Chaseseaux

Victoria ♦ Marine

Dominican Evangelical Church ♦

EL CENTRO

Santa Bárbara

Avenida La Marina o Malecón

Deleon Communications

María Trinidad Sanchez

Puerto de Samaná

Avenida Malecón

Circunvalación

1 mile
1 kilometer

speak some English. Within Samaná, rickshaws are far less costly and are also fun. Called *motoconchos de carretas,* they are not unlike larger versions of the Thai tuk-tuk, but can hold up to six people. The least you will pay is RD$10. They're fine for getting around town, but don't even think about going the distance with them.

EXPLORING SAMANÁ

Samaná. The official name of the city is Santa Barbara de Samaná; alas, that saint's name is falling into disuse, and you'll more often hear simply "Samaná" these days. An authentic port town, not just a touristic zone, it has a typical *malecón* (seaside promenade) with gazebos and park benches, ideal for strolling and watching the boats in the harbor. The main road that borders this green zone, Avenida Malecón, is lined with restaurants, shops, and small businesses. A small but bustling town, Samaná is filled with friendly residents, skilled local craftsmen selling their wares, and many outdoor cafés.

The **Whale Museum and Nature Center** is dedicated to the mighty mammals of the sea, and you will learn everything you have ever wanted to know about whales here. Samaná has one of the largest marine-mammal sanctuaries in the world, and is a center for whale-watching in the migration season. The C.E.B.S.E (Center for Conservation and Ecodevelopment of Samaná Bay and its Environment) manages this facility. ⊠ *Av. La Marina, Tiro Blanco* ☎ *809/538–2042* ⊕ *samana. org.do* ⊠ *RD $50* ⊙ *Daily 8–noon and 2–5.*

The historic **Dominican Evangelical Church** is the oldest original building left in Samaná. It actually came across the ocean from England in 1881 in a hundred pieces and was reassembled here, serving the spiritual needs of African-American freedmen who emigrated here from Philadelphia, Pennsylvania, in 1824. ⊠ *Calle Chaseurox, in front of Catholic church* ☎ *809/538–2579* ⊠ *Donations appreciated* ⊙ *Daily dawn–dusk.*

Cayo Levantado. Residents of Samaná call Cayo Levantado their *pasa dia en la playa* (the place to pass the day on the beach). Today the small island in Samaná Bay has been improved to receive up to 1,500 cruise-ship passengers per day, with dining facilities, bars, restrooms, and lounge chairs on the beautiful beach. The company that runs cruise-ship services on the island has even applied for the coveted "Blue Flag" that designates a beach as clean and unpolluted. Independent restaurants and vendors also ply their wares. This isn't the most tranquil island, but you can quite happily spend the day here if you don't want to go into the town of Samaná. The new Grand Bahía Principe Cayo Levantado, an upscale, all-inclusive resort, claims the eastern two-thirds of the island for its private use. Day-use of the island will either be included in your cruise fare or will be treated as a regular shore excursion, for which the lines usually charge $40 to $60. ⊠ *Samaná Bay* ☎ *809/538–2579* ⊠ *Donations appreciated* ⊙ *Daily dawn–dusk.*

Los Haitises National Park. A guided tour is the only way to explore Los Haitises' (pronounced Hi-*tee*-sis), which is across Samaná Bay from the peninsula. The park is famous for its karst limestone formations, caves, and grottoes filled with pictographs and petroglyphs left by the indigenous Taïno before the discovery of the Americas. Mangrove forests shelter many coastal bird species, including Louisiana night herons and the magnificent American frigate birds, making this a birdwatchers delight as well. Typical trips cruise the coastline dotted with small islands and spectacular cliff faces, finally docking to allow passengers to walk quietly around a mangrove swamp and visit the various caves. Some trips allow you to hike to the village of Crystal in the rain forest, where you can swim in a crystal clear, freshwater lagoon.

Salto el Limón Cascade. Provided that you are fit, an adventurous guided trip to this spectacular waterfall is a delight. The journey is usually done mostly on horseback, but includes walking down rocky, sometimes muddy trails. The well-mannered horses take you across rivers and up mountains to El Limón, where you'll find the waterfall amidst luxuriant vegetation. Some snacks and drinks are usually included in the guided trip. ⊠*Santi Rancho, El Limón.*

> ## SAMANÁ BEST BETS
>
> ■ **Cayo Levantado.** This resort island in the bay does put on an excellent show for day-trippers.
>
> ■ **El Limón Waterfall.** A three-hour round-trip foray on horseback into the forest culminates in dazzling falls into a natural pool.
>
> ■ **Los Haitises National Park.** The caves filled with Taïno drawings and a pristine lagoon.
>
> ■ **Playa Rincón.** This rarely accessed beach packs it all in: a river, unspoiled mountainside, perfect beach, and privacy.
>
> ■ **Whale-watching.** In season, this is the top activity on the Samaná Peninsula.

SHOPPING

Rum, coffee, and cigars are popular local products. You may also find good coconut handicrafts, including coconut-shell candles. Whale-oriented gift items are particularly popular. Most of the souvenir shops are on Samaná's malecón or in the market plaza; you will find more on the major downtown streets in town, all within easy walking distance of the tender piers. A shopping mall called **Plublito Carabeño Plaza** (⊠*20 Francisco Rosario Sanchez, Santa Barbara de Samaná*) is near the piers; it has a bevy of shops and food outlets (including American fast food).

ACTIVITIES

DIVING AND SNORKELING

In 1979 three atolls disappeared following a seaquake off Las Terrenas, providing an opportunity for truly memorable dives. Also just offshore from Las Terrenas are the Islas Las Ballenas ("The Whale Islands"), a cluster of four little islands with good snorkeling. A coral reef is off Playa Jackson, a beach accessible only by boat. **Las Terrenas Divers** (⊠*Playa Bonita, Las Terrenas* ☎*809/889–2422* ⊕*www.lt-divers.com*) offers diving lessons and trips; diving equipment rentals start at $30, snorkeling equipment at $15 per day. It is closed Sunday.

WHALE-WATCHING

Humpback whales come to Samaná Bay to mate and give birth each year, from approximately January 15 through March 30. Samaná Bay is considered one of the top 10 destinations in the world for watching whales. If you're here in season, this can be the experience of a lifetime. You can listen to the male humpback's solitary courting song and witness incredible displays as the whales flip their tails and breach (humpbacks are the most active species of whales in the Atlantic). **Victoria Marine/Whale Samaná** (⊠ *Av. Malecón 3, across street from cement town dock, beside park, Santa Barbara de Samaná* ☎ *809/538–2494* ⊕ *www.whalesamana.com*) is owned by Kim Beddall, a Canadian who is incredibly knowledgeable about whales and Samaná at large, having lived here for 20-some years. Now a certified marine mammal specialist, Kim leads the regions' best trips on board the *Victoria II,* a 50-foot motor vessel. Trips are $58, which includes the Marine Mammal Sanctuary entrance fee. Kim welcomes cruise passengers but requires advance reservations. You must be able to arrive on shore by about 9 AM for the morning trip and by 1:30 PM for the afternoon trip.

BEACHES

There are no recommendable beaches in Samaná de Santa Barbara itself. You will have to travel to one of the beautiful ones elsewhere on the peninsula, another reason why the Cayo Levantado excursion is very popular on most ships.

Playa Bonito, in Las Terrenas, is about an hour away from Samaná. It has become commercialized and can have a frenetic energy, but its beaches are legendary. On Playa Bonito you can bounce between the golden beach (BYO towel—no chaises). There are nearby hotels where you can eat lunch. **Playa Cosón,** the closest good beach to Samaná, is some 15 minutes away from the town of Las Terrenas, and about an hour from Samaná. You can buy a day pass for a reasonable price (about $35) at the resort Viva Wyndham Samaná, which is smack on Bahia Cosón. **Playa Las Galleras,** a 30-minute drive northeast from the port, is lovely, long, and uncluttered. The sand is white, the Atlantic waters generally calm. It has been designated a "Blue Flag" beach, which means that it is crystal-clean with no pollution, though there are several hotels here. Generally, cruisers gravitate toward Casa Marina Bay Resort, and many ★ cruise lines sell day passes for that all-inclusive resort. **Playa Rincón,** a beautiful, white-sand beach, is considered one of the top beaches in the Caribbean. It is relatively undeveloped, and at the far-right end is a sheltered area where you can snorkel. There are no facilities per se, but local ladies will sell you the freshest lobster and fish in coconut sauce with rice, and other creole dishes as well as cold drinks.

WHERE TO EAT

$ ✕ **El Sabor Samanés.** If you want local food, this corner restaurant is
CONTINENTAL your best bet in town, and the quality is a step above what you would expect from the prices. It's also across the street from the bay, and easy to locate with its blue awning. Sit at a range of plastic chairs and tables,

or order from the glass display of Dominican dishes like mofongo. Most fish dishes are 300 pesos. Cocktails are $5. You can also get sandwiches, tacos, and burgers. ⊠ *5 Av. Malecón, Santa Barbara de Samaná* ☎ *809/538–2225* ☐ *No credit cards.*

$

SEAFOOD

✕ **La Mata Rosada.** The French owner/chef Yvonne Bastian has been luring local expats and foodies for 10 years. She sets tables up with white linens in an all-white interior including an army of ceiling fans to keep you cool; breezes sneak in from the bay across the street. There's a plentiful array of flavorful choices, starting with a sea and country salad of conch, potatoes, greens, and bacon; or the "gourmet" plate, a mix of grilled lobster and other shellfish. Ceviche, a specialty of this port town, is made with dorado (mahimahi) and conch. Whether you go local or international, order the creole shrimp or a substantial salad, and you should leave satisfied. But save room: desserts are presented with pride. ⊠ *5 Av. Malecón, Santa Barbara de Samaná* ☎ *809/538–2388* ☐ *AE, MC, V* ☉ *Closed Tues. June–Nov.*

ST. BARTHÉLEMY (GUSTAVIA)

Elise Meyer

Hilly St. Barthélemy, popularly known as St. Barths (or St. Barts) is just 8 square mi (21 square km), but the island has at least 20 good beaches. What draws visitors is its sophisticated but unstudied approach to relaxation: the finest food, excellent wine, high-end shopping, and lack of large-scale commercial development. A favorite among upscale cruise-ship passengers, who also appreciate the shopping opportunities and fine dining, St. Barths isn't really equipped for mega-ship visits, which is why most ships calling here are from smaller premium lines. This is one place where you don't need to take the ship's shore excursions to have a good time. Just hail a cab or rent a car and go to one of the many wonderful beaches, where you will find some of the best lunchtime restaurants, or wander around Gustavia, shopping and eating. It's the best way to relax on this most relaxing of islands.

ESSENTIALS

Currency The euro (€1 to US$1.35); however, U.S. dollars are accepted in almost all shops and in many restaurants. Credit cards are widely accepted.

Internet Centre Alizes (⊠ *Rue de la République, Gustavia* ☎ *0590/29–89–89*).

Telephones Public telephones accept *télécartes,* prepaid calling cards that you can buy at the gas station next to the airport and at post offices in Lorient, St-Jean, and Gustavia. Making an international call using a télécarte is the best way to go.

COMING ASHORE

Even medium-size ships must anchor in Gustavia Harbor and bring passengers ashore on tenders. The tiny harbor area is right in Gustavia, which is easily explored on foot. Taxis, which meet all cruise ships, can be expensive. Technically, there's a flat rate for rides up to five minutes long. Each additional three minutes is an additional amount. In reality, however, cabbies usually name a fixed rate—and will not budge. Fares

St. Barthélemy

ATLANTIC OCEAN

Ile Frégate

Gustavia

Municipal Museum

Fort George

Tourist Office

Les Grenadiers

La Tortue

Pte. à Colombier

Ile Chevreau

Anse à Colombier

La Petite Anse

Anse à Galets

Pte. Milou

Anse Marechal

Ile. Petit Jean

Anse Gros Jean

Colombier

Anse des Cayes

Anse de Lorient

Anse de Marigot

Anse de Grand Cul de Sac

Corossol

Baie de St-Jean

Marigot

Anse Corossol Public Beach

St-Jean Airport

Lorient

Vitet

Anse de Petit Cul de Sac

TO ST. MARTIN

Les Islettes La Baleine

St-Jean

Mt. du Grand Fond

Toiny

♦ Tourist Office

Morne Vitet

Anse à Toiny

Les Petits Saintes

Grand Fond

Anse de Grand Fond

Gustavia
see inset map

Petite Anse de Galet (Shell Beach)

Lurin

Mt. Lurin

Anse de Grande Saline

Morne Rouge

Pt. Gouverneur

Grande Pt.

KEY

Beaches

Dive Sites

Ferry

Caribbean Sea

0   1 mile
0   1 km

---

are 50% higher on Sunday and holidays. St. Barths is one port where it's really worth it to arrange a car rental for a full-day exploration of the island, including the island's out-of-the-way beaches. But be aware that during high season there is often a three-day minimum, so this may not be possible except through your ship (and then you'll pay premium rates indeed). Most car-rental firms operate at the airport; however, renting on your own is usually cheaper than what you'll get if you go with one of the ship's car rentals (you may be able to find a car for €50 per day). The new St. Barth Shuttle service can be convenient and much less expensive than a taxi if you are just one or two people, but it still doesn't completely negate the need for a car.

EXPLORING ST. BARTHS

With a little practice, negotiating St. Barths' narrow, steep roads soon becomes fun. Free maps are everywhere, roads are well marked, and painted signs will point you where you want to be. Take along a towel, sandals, and a bottle of water, and you will surely find a beach upon which to linger.

Corossol. The island's French-provincial origins are most evident in this two-street fishing village with a little rocky beach. Older local women weave lantana straw into handbags, baskets, hats, and delicate strings of birds. Ingenu Magras's **Inter Oceans Museum** has more than 9,000 seashells and an intriguing collection of sand samples from around the world. You can buy souvenir shells. ⊠ *Corossol* ☎ *0590/27–62–97* 🖂*€3* ⊙ *Tues.– Sun. 9–12:30 and 2–5.*

Gustavia. You can easily explore all of Gustavia during a two-hour stroll. Street signs in both French and Swedish illustrate the island's history. Most shops close from noon to 2, so plan lunch accordingly. A good spot to park your car is rue de la République, where catamarans, yachts, and sailboats are moored. The **tourist office**

> ### ST. BARTHÉLEMY BEST BETS
>
> ■ **Soaking up the Atmosphere.** It's the French Riviera transported to the Caribbean.
>
> ■ **Beautiful Beaches.** Pick any of the lovely, uncrowded beaches.
>
> ■ **French Food.** St. Barths has some of the best restaurants in the Caribbean.
>
> ■ **Shopping.** There is no better fashion shopping in the Caribbean, especially if you are young and slim.

(☎*0590/27–87–27* ✉*odtsb@wanadoo.fr*) on the pier can provide maps and a wealth of information. It's open Monday from 8:30 to 12:30, Tuesday through Friday from 8 to noon and 2 to 5, and Saturday from 9 to noon. On the far side of the harbor known as La Pointe is the charming **Municipal Museum,** where you can find watercolors, portraits, photographs, and historic documents detailing the island's history as well as displays of the island's flowers, plants, and marine life. ☎*599/29–71–55* 🖂*€2* ⊙ *Mon., Tues., Thurs., and Fri. 8:30–12:30 and 2:30–6, Sat. 9–12:30.*

Lorient. Site of the first French settlement, Lorient is one of the island's two parishes; a restored church, a school, and a post office mark the spot. Note the gaily decorated graves in the cemetery. One of St. Barths' secrets is **Le Manoir** (☎*0590/27–79–27*), a 1610 Norman manor, now a guesthouse, which was painstakingly shipped from France and reconstructed in Lorient in 1984. Look for the entrance by the Ligne St. Barths building.

St-Jean. The half-mile-long crescent of sand at St-Jean is the island's most popular beach. Windsurfers skim along the water here, catching the strong trade winds. A popular activity is watching and photographing the hair-raising airplane landings. You'll also find some of the best shopping on the island here, as well as several restaurants.

SHOPPING

St. Barths is a duty-free port, and with its sophisticated crowd of visitors, shopping in the island's 200-plus boutiques is a definite delight. In Gustavia boutiques line the three major shopping streets. The **Quai du République,** nicknamed "Rue du Couturier," which is right on the harbor, rivals New York's Madison Avenue, or Paris's Avenue Montaigne for high-end "designer" retail. These shops often carry items that are not available in the United States. Shops are also clustered in **La Savane Commercial Center** (across from the airport), **La Villa Créole** (in St-Jean), and **Espace Neptune** (on the road to Lorient). It's worth working your way from one end to the other at these shopping complexes—just to see or, perhaps, be seen. Boutiques in all three areas carry the latest in French and Italian sportswear and some haute couture. You probably are not going to find any bargains as long as the euro remains high, but you might be able to snag that *pochette* that is sold out stateside, and in any case, you'll have a lot of fun hunting around.

ACTIVITIES

BOATING AND SAILING

St. Barths is a popular yachting and sailing center, thanks to its location midway between Antigua and St. Thomas. Gustavia's harbor, 13 to 16 feet deep, has mooring and docking facilities for 40 yachts. There are also good anchorages available at Public, Corossol, and Colombier. You can charter sailing and motorboats in Gustavia Harbor for as little as a half day. Stop at the Tourist Office in Gustavia for an up-to-the-minute list of recommended charter companies.

Marine Service (✉ *Gustavia* ☎ *0590/27–70–34* ∰ *www.st-barths.com/marine.service*) offers full-day outings, either on a 42- or 46-foot catamaran, to the uninhabited Île Fourchue for swimming, snorkeling, cocktails, and lunch. The cost is $100 per person; an unskippered motor rental runs about $260 a day.

DIVING AND SNORKELING

You can arrange scuba excursions to several local sites. Depending on the weather conditions, you may dive at Pain de Sucre, Coco Island, or even nearby Saba. There's also an underwater shipwreck to explore, plus sharks, rays, sea tortoises, coral, and the usual varieties of colorful fish. The waters on the island's leeward side are the calmest. If you're not a certified diver, there's an accessible shallow reef right off the beach at Anse de Cayes if you want to do snorkeling from the beach. **Plongée Caraïbe** (☎☎ *0590/27–55–94*) is recommended for its up-to-the-minute equipment and dive boat. Marine Service operates the only five-star, PADI-certified diving center on the island, called **West Indies Dive** (☎ *0590/27–70–34* ∰ *www.westindiesdive.com*). Scuba trips, packages, resort dives, night dives, and certifications start at $90, including gear.

BEACHES

There are many *anses* (coves) and nearly 20 *plages* (beaches) scattered around the island, each with a distinctive personality and each open to the general public. Even in season you can find a nearly empty beach. Topless sunbathing is common, but nudism is forbidden—although both Grande Saline and Gouverneur are de facto nude beaches.

★ Because **Anse du Gouverneur** is so secluded, nude sunbathing is popular here; the beach is truly beautiful, with blissful swimming and views of St. Kitts, Saba, and St. Eustatius. Shallow, reef-protected **Anse de Grand Cul de Sac** is especially nice for small children, fly-fishermen, kayakers, and windsurfers; it has excellent lunch spots, water-sports rentals, and lots of the amusing pelicanlike frigate birds that dive-bomb the water

Fodor's Choice ★ fishing for their lunch. Secluded, with its sandy ocean bottom, **Anse de Grande Saline** is just about everyone's favorite beach and great for swimmers, too. Without any major development, it's an ideal Caribbean strand, though it can be a bit windy here, so you can enjoy yourself more if you go on a calm day. In spite of the prohibition, young and old alike go nude. The beach is a 10-minute walk up a rocky dune trail, so be sure to wear sneakers or water shoes. Like a mini–Côte d'Azur—beachside bistros, bungalow hotels, bronzed bodies, windsurfing, and lots of day-trippers—reef-protected **Baie de St-Jean** is divided by Eden Rock promontory, and there's good snorkeling west of the rock.

WHERE TO EAT

A service charge is always added by law, but you should leave the server 5% to 10% extra in cash. It is generally advisable to charge restaurant meals on a credit card, as the issuer will offer a better exchange rate than the restaurant.

$$–$$$
ECLECTIC
★
✕**Le Repaire.** This friendly brasserie, redecorated in 2008, overlooks Gustavia's harbor and is a popular spot from its morning opening to its late-night closing. Its flexible hours are great if you arrive mid-afternoon and need a good snack before dinner. Grab a cappuccino, pull a captain's chair to the street-side rail and watch the pretty girls. The menu ranges from cheeseburgers, which are served only at lunch along with the island's best fries, to simply grilled fish and meat, pasta, and risottos. The composed salads always please. Wonderful ice-cream sundaes round out the menu. ✉ *Quai de la République, Gustavia* ☎ *0590/27-72-48* 🖃 *MC, V.*

$$$$
FRENCH
★
✕**Le Tamarin.** A leisurely lunch here en route to Anse de Grand Saline beach is a St. Barths *must*. But don't discount it for dinner, either. Delicious French cuisine by Maxime Deschamps, formerly of Le Toiny, is served at this sophisticated open-air restaurant. Artistic salads tempt at lunch. Dinner options include a gingerbread-crusted chicken, along with plenty of daily specials. But the real fireworks rock for chocoholics, who swoon for the dessert list. ✉ *Salines* ☎ *0590/27-72-12* 🖃 *AE, MC, V* ⊘ *Closed Mon.*

ST. CROIX (FREDERIKSTED)

Lynda Lohr

St. Croix is the largest of the three U.S. Virgin Islands (USVI) that form the northern hook of the Lesser Antilles; it's 40 mi (64 km) south of its sister islands, St. Thomas and St. John. Christopher Columbus landed here in 1493, skirmishing briefly with the native Carib Indians. Since then, the USVI have played a colorful, if painful, role as pawns in the game of European colonialism. Theirs is a history of pirates and privateers, sugar plantations, slave trading, and slave revolt and liberation. Through it all, Denmark had staying power. From the 17th to the 19th century, Danes oversaw a plantation slave economy that produced molasses, rum, cotton, and tobacco. Many of the stones you tread on in the streets were once used as ballast on sailing ships, and the yellow fort of Christiansted is a reminder of the value once placed on this island treasure. Never a major cruise destination, it is still a stop for several ships each year.

ESSENTIALS

Currency The U.S. dollar is the official currency of St. Croix.

Internet There's a convenient Internet café in Christiansted if you make it there during your day ashore. **A Better Copy**(⊠ *52A Company St., Christiansted, St. Croix* ☎ *340/692–5303*).

Telephones Calling the United States from St. Croix works the same way as calling within the U.S. Local calls from a public phone cost up to 35¢ for every five minutes. You can use your regular toll-free connections for long-distance services.

COMING ASHORE

Cruise ships dock in Frederiksted, on the island's west end. You'll find an information center at the pier, and the town is easy to explore on foot. Beaches are nearby. The only difficulty is that you are far from the island's main town, Christiansted. Some cruise lines offer bus transportation there; otherwise, you are probably better off renting a car to explore the island, since both car-rental rates and gasoline prices are reasonable; just remember to drive on the left. **Midwest** (☎*340/772–0438 or 877/772–0438* ⊕*www.midwestautorental.com*) has an office just outside Frederiksted and will pick you up at the pier.

Taxis of all shapes and sizes are available at the cruise-ship pier and at various shopping and resort areas. Remember, too, that you can hail a taxi that's already occupied. Drivers take multiple fares and sometimes even trade passengers at midpoints. Taxis don't have meters, so you should check the list of official rates (available at the visitor centers or from drivers) and agree on a fare before you start, but there are standard rates for most trips. A taxi to Christiansted will cost about $24 for two people for transportation only; an island tour including Christiansted will cost $100 for two people.

EXPLORING ST. CROIX

Frederiksted speaks to history buffs with its quaint Victorian architecture and historic fort. There's very little traffic, so this is the perfect place for strolling and shopping. Christiansted is a historic Danish-style town that served as St. Croix's commercial center. Your best bet is to see the historic sights in the morning, when it's still cool. This two-hour endeavor won't tax your walking shoes and will leave you with energy to poke around the town's eclectic shops.

Carl and Marie Lawaetz Museum. For a trip back in time, tour this circa-1750 farm. Owned by the prominent Lawaetz family since 1896, just after Carl Lawaetz arrived from Denmark, the lovely two-story house is in a valley at La Grange. A Lawaetz family member shows you the four-poster mahogany bed Carl and Marie shared, the china Marie painted, the family portraits, and the fruit trees that fed the family for several generations. Initially a sugar plantation, it was subsequently used to raise cattle and

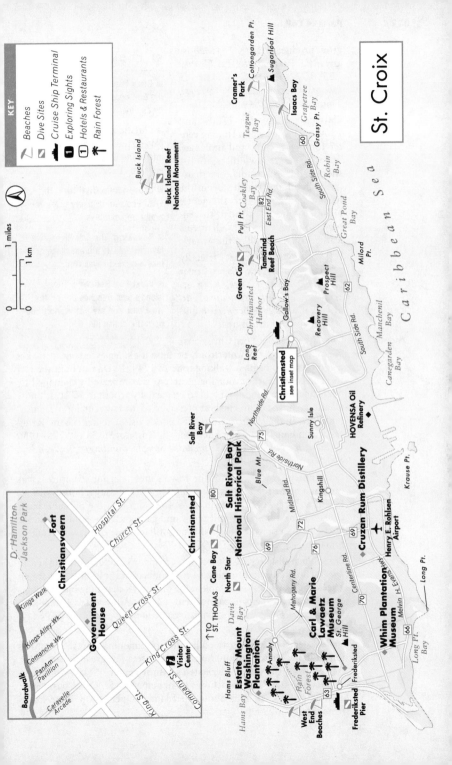

St. Croix

KEY

/ Beaches
☐ Dive Sites
⚓ Cruise Ship Terminal
◆ Exploring Sights
① Hotels & Restaurants
🌲 Rain Forest

0   1 miles
0   1 km

Buck Island

◆ Buck Island Reef
National Monument

Inset map (Christiansted):

D. Hamilton Jackson Park

Fort Christiansvaern

Hospital St.
Church St.

Kings Walk
Kings Alley Wk.
Comanche Wk.
PanAm Pavilion
Caravelle Arcade

Boardwalk

Government House

Queen Cross St.
King Cross St.
Company St.

① Visitor Center

Christiansted

**Main map labels:**

Cottongarden Pt.
Sugarloaf Hill
Cramer's Park
Isaacs Bay
Grapetree
Grassy Pt. Bay
Teague Bay
60
Robin Bay
South Side Rd.
Pull Pt. Coakley Bay
82
East End Rd.
Great Pond Bay
Green Cay
Tamarind Reef Beach
Christiansted Harbor
Gallow's Bay
Milord Pt.
Prospect Hill
62
Recovery Hill
Long Reef
Christiansted see inset map
South Side Rd.
Manchenil Bay
Caribbean Sea
Canegarden Bay
Krause Pt.
Sunny Isle
HOVENSA Oil Refinery ◆
Salt River Bay
Northside Rd.
75
Blue Mt.
Midland Rd.
Kingshill
Northside Rd.
72
76
Centerline Rd.
69
Cruzan Rum Distillery ◆
69
70
Henry E. Rohlsen Airport ◆
Whim Plantation Museum ◆
Melvin H. Evans Hwy.
66
Long Pt.
Long Pt. Bay

Salt River Bay National Historical Park
80
Cane Bay
North Star
Davis Bay
↑TO ST. THOMAS
Estate Mount Washington Plantation
Hams Bluff
Hams Bay
West End Beaches
63
Rain Forest
Annaly
Mahogany Rd.
St. George Hill
Carl & Marie Lawaetz Museum
Frederiksted
Frederiksted Pier

grow produce. ⊠*Rte. 76, Mahogany Rd., Estate Little La Grange* ☎*340/772–1539* ⊕*www.stcroix landmarks.com* 🖃*$10* ⊗*Tues., Thurs., and Sat. 10–4.*

Christiansted. In the 1700s and 1800s this town was a trading center for sugar, rum, and molasses. Today there are law offices, tourist shops, and restaurants, but many of the buildings, which start at the harbor and go up into the gentle hillsides, date from the 18th century. You can't get lost. All streets lead gently downhill to the water.

If you want some friendly advice, stop by the **Visitor Center** (⊠*Government House, King St.* ☎*340/773–0495* ⊕*www.usvito urism.vi*) weekdays between 8 and 5 for maps and brochures.

Fodor'sChoice
★
☾
The large, yellow **Fort Christiansvaern** dominates the waterfront. Because it's so easy to spot, it makes a good place to begin a walking tour. In 1749 the Danish built the fort to protect the harbor, but the structure was repeatedly damaged by hurricane-force winds and had to be partially rebuilt in 1771. It's now a national historic site, the best preserved of the few remaining Danish-built forts in the Virgin Islands. The park's visitor center is here. Rangers are on hand to answer questions. ⊠*Hospital St.* ☎*340/773–1460* ⊕*www.nps.gov/chri* 🖃*$3 (includes Steeple Building)* ⊗ *Weekdays 8–4:30, weekends 9–4:30.*

Government House, one of the town's most elegant structures, was built as a home for a Danish merchant in 1747. Today it houses offices. If you're here weekdays from 8 to 4:30, slip into the peaceful inner courtyard to admire the still pools and gardens. A sweeping staircase leads you to a second-story ballroom, still used for official government functions. ⊠*King St.* ☎*340/773–1404*

Cruzan Rum Distillery. A tour of the company's factory, established in 1760, culminates in a tasting of its products, all sold here at bargain prices. It's worth a stop to look at the distillery's charming old buildings even if you're not a rum connoisseur. ⊠ *West Airport Rd., Estate Diamond* ☎*340/692–2280* ⊕*www.cruzanrum.com* 🖃*$4* ⊗ *Weekdays 9–11:30 and 1–4:15.*

Frederiksted. The town is noted less for its remaining Danish structures than for the Victorian buildings erected after the great fire of 1878. Across from the pier, Federiksted's **visitor center** (⊠*200 Strand St.* ☎*340/772–0357*) has brochures from numerous St. Croix businesses, as well as a few exhibits about the island. You can stop in weekdays from 8 to 5.

ST. CROIX BEST BETS

■ **Buck Island.** The snorkeling trail here is fun, but go by catamaran.

■ **Christiansted.** The best shopping on the island as well as interesting historical sights are here.

■ **Cruzan Rum Distillery.** This West End rum distillery gives you a tour and samples.

■ **Kayaking.** The Salt River, with few currents, is a great place to take a guided kayak trip.

■ **West End Beaches.** The island's best beaches are on the west end, and are just a short hop from the cruise pier.

Sitting across from the waterfront in a historic building, the small **Caribbean Museum Center for the Arts** (⊠*10 Strand St.* ☎*340/772–2622* ⊕*www.cmcarts.org*) hosts an always-changing roster of exhibits. Many are cutting-edge multimedia efforts that you might be surprised to find in such an out-of-the way location. The openings are popular events. It's open Tuesday through Saturday from 10 to 4; admission is free.

Fort Frederiksted (⊠*Waterfront* ☎*340/772–2021*), completed in 1760, houses a number of interesting historical exhibits and an art gallery. Admission is $3, and it's open weekdays from 8:30 to 4. It's within earshot of the visitor center.

Salt River Bay National Historical Park and Ecological Preserve. This joint national and local park commemorates the area where Christopher Columbus's men skirmished with the Carib Indians in 1493 on his second visit to the New World. The peninsula on the bay's east side is named for the event: Cabo de las Flechas (Cape of the Arrows). Although the park is just in the developing stages, it has several sights with cultural significance. A ball court, used by the Caribs in religious ceremonies, was discovered at the spot where the taxis park. Take a short hike up the dirt road to the ruins of an old earthen fort for great views of Salt River Bay. The area also encompasses a coastal estuary with the region's largest remaining mangrove forest, a submarine canyon, and several endangered species, including the hawksbill turtle and the roseate tern. A visitor center sits just uphill to the west. The water at the beach can be on the rough side, but it's a nice place for sunning. ⊠*Rte. 75 to Rte. 80, Salt River* ☎*340/773–1460* ⊕*www.nps.gov/sari* ☉*Tues.–Thurs 9–4.*

☼ **Whim Plantation Museum.** The lovingly restored estate, with a windmill, ★ cook house, and other buildings, will give you a sense of what life was like on St. Croix's sugar plantations in the 1800s. The oval-shape greathouse has high ceilings and antique furniture and utensils. Notice its fresh, airy atmosphere—the waterless stone moat around the greathouse was used not for defense but for gathering cooling air. If you have kids, the grounds are the perfect place for them to run around, perhaps while you browse in the museum gift shop. It's just outside of Frederiksted. ⊠*Rte. 70, Estate Whim* ☎*340/772–0598* ⊕*www.stcroixlandmarks. com* ⛁$10 ☉*Mon.–Sat. 10–4.*

SHOPPING

The selection of duty-free goods on St. Croix is fairly good. The best shopping is in Christiansted, where most stores are in the historic district near the harbor. King Street, Strand Street, and the arcades that lead off them compose the main shopping district. The longest arcade is Caravelle Arcade, adjacent to the hotel of the same name. In Frederiksted, a handful of shops face the cruise-ship pier.

Fodor'sChoice **Royal Poinciana** (⊠*1111 Strand St., Christiansted* ☎*340/773–9892*), ★ an attractive shop, is filled with island seasonings and hot sauces, West Indian crafts, bath gels, and herbal teas. Shop here for tablecloths and paper goods in tropical brights. **Sonya's** (⊠*1 Company St., Christiansted* ☎*340/778–8605*) is owned and operated by Sonya Hough, who invented the hook bracelet that is popular among locals as well as visitors. With hurricanes hitting the island so frequently, she has added an interesting decoration to these bracelets: the swirling symbol used in weather forecasts to indicate these storms.

ACTIVITIES

BOAT TOURS

Almost everyone takes a day trip to Buck Island aboard a charter boat. Most leave from the Christiansted waterfront or from Green Cay Marina and stop for a snorkel at the island's eastern end before dropping anchor off a gorgeous sandy beach for a swim, a hike, and lunch. Sailboats can often stop right at the beach; a larger boat might have to anchor a bit farther offshore. A full-day sail runs about $100, with lunch included on most trips. A half-day sail costs about $65. **Big Beard's Adventure Tours** (⌧*Christiansted* ☎*340/773–4482* ⊕*www.bigbeards. com*) takes you on catamarans, either the *Renegade* or the *Flyer,* from the Christiansted waterfront to Buck Island for snorkeling before dropping anchor at a private beach for a barbecue lunch.

DIVING AND SNORKELING

In Frederiksted, **N2 the Blue** (⌧*Frederiksted Beach, Rte. 631, Frederiksted* ☎*340/772–3483 or 888/789–3483* ⊕*www.n2blue.com*) takes divers right off the beach near Coconuts restaurant, on night dives off the Frederiksted Pier, or on boat trips to wrecks and reefs.

GOLF

★ The spectacular 18-hole course at **Carambola Golf Club** (⌧*Rte. 80, Davis Bay* ☎*340/778–5638* ⊕*www.golfcarambola.com*), in the northwest valley, was designed by Robert Trent Jones Sr. It sits near Carambola Beach Resort. Greens fees are $90 for 18 holes, which includes the use of a golf cart.

HORSEBACK RIDING

Well-kept roads and expert guides make horseback riding on St. Croix pleasurable. At Sprat Hall, just north of Frederiksted, Jill Hurd runs **Paul and Jill's Equestrian Stables** (⌧*Rte. 58, Frederiksted* ☎*340/772–2880 or 340/332–0417* ⊕*www.paulandjills.com*). She will take you clip-clopping through the rain forest, across the pastures, along the beaches, and over the hilltops—explaining the flora, fauna, and ruins on the way. A 1½-hour ride costs $90.

KAYAKING

Caribbean Adventure Tours (⌧*Salt River Marina, Rte. 80, Salt River* ☎*340/778–1522* ⊕*www.stcroixkayak.com*) takes you on trips through Salt River Bay National Historical Park and Ecological Preserve, one of the island's most pristine areas. All tours run $45.

BEACHES

The waters aren't always gentle at **Cane Bay,** a breezy north-shore beach, but there are seldom many people around, and the scuba diving and snorkeling are wondrous. You can see elkhorn and brain corals, and less than 200 yards out is the drop-off called Cane Bay Wall. There are several unnamed **West End Beaches** along the coast road north of Frederiksted, but it's best if you don't stray too far from civilization. For safety's sake, it's best to visit with a group. The beach at the Rainbow Beach Club, a five-minute drive outside Frederiksted, has a bar, a casual restaurant, water sports, and volleyball.

WHERE TO EAT

$$$–$$$$ ✕**Blue Moon.** This terrific little bistro, which has a loyal local following,
ECLECTIC   offers a changing menu that draws on Cajun and Caribbean flavors.
Fodor'sChoice   Try the spicy gumbo with andouille sausage or crab cakes with a spicy
★   aioli for your appetizer. Chicken, shrimp, sausage, and peppers served over pasta makes a good entrée. The Almond Joy sundae should be your choice for dessert. There's live jazz on Wednesday and Friday. ✉*7 Strand St.* ☎*340/772–2222* ⊕*www.bluemoonstcroix.com* ▤*AE, MC, V* ☾*Closed Mon.*

$$–$$$ ✕**Rum Runners.** The view is as stellar as the food at this highly popular
CONTINENTAL   local standby. Sitting right on Christiansted boardwalk, Rum Runners
★   serves everything, including a to-die-for salad of crispy romaine lettuce
☾   and tender grilled lobster drizzled with lemongrass vinaigrette. More hearty fare includes baby back ribs cooked with the restaurant's special spice blend and Guinness stout. ✉*Hotel Caravelle, 44A Queen Cross St.* ☎*340/773–6585* ⊕*www.rumrunnersstcroix.com* ▤*AE, MC, V.*

ST. JOHN (CRUZ BAY)

Lynda Lohr   St. John's heart is Virgin Islands National Park, a treasure that takes up a full two-thirds of St. John's 20 square mi (53 square km). The park helps keep the island's interior in its pristine and undisturbed state, but if you go at midday, you'll probably have to share your stretch of beach with others, particularly at Trunk Bay. The island is booming, and while it can get a tad crowded at the ever-popular Trunk Bay Beach during the busy winter season, you won't find traffic jams or pollution. It's easy to escape from the fray, however: just head off on a hike. St. John doesn't have a grand agrarian past like her sister island, St. Croix, but if you're hiking in the dry season, you can probably stumble upon the stone ruins of old plantations. The less adventuresome can visit the repaired ruins at the park's Annaberg Plantation and Caneel Bay resort. Of the three U.S. Virgin Islands, St. John, which has 5,000 residents, has the strongest sense of community, which is primarily rooted in a desire to protect the island's natural beauty.

ESSENTIALS

Currency The U.S. dollar is the official currency of U.S. Virgin Islands; you'll find a few ATMs in Cruz Bay.

Internet ADM Wireless (✉*St. John Marketplace, 2nd fl., Cruz Bay* ☎*340/715-1469.* **Keep Me Posted** (✉*Cocoloba Shopping Center, Coral Bay* ☎*340/775-1727* ⊕*www.keepmepostedstjohn.com*).

Telephones Both Sprint and AT&T phones work in most of St. John (take care that you're not roaming on the Tortola cell network on the island's north coast, though). It's as easy to call home from St. John as from any city in the United States. On St. John, public phones are in front of the post office, east of the tender landing, and at the ferry dock.

COMING ASHORE

While smaller ships drop anchor at St. John, most people taking a cruise aboard a larger ship visit St. Thomas' sister island on a shore excursion or on an independent day trip from St. Thomas. If you prefer to not take a tour, ferries leave St. Thomas from the Charlotte Amalie waterfront and Red Hook. You'll have to take a taxi to reach the ferry dock.

If you're aboard a smaller ship that calls in St. John, your ship may simply pause outside Cruz Bay Harbor to drop you off or drop anchor if it's spending the day. You'll be tendered to shore at the main town of Cruz Bay. The shopping district starts just across the street from the tender landing. You'll find an eclectic collection of shops, cozy restaurants, and places where you can just sit and take it all in. The island has few sights to see. Your best bet is to take a tour of the Virgin Islands National Park. (If your ship doesn't offer such a tour, arrange one with one of the taxi drivers who will meet your tender.) The drive takes you past luscious beaches to a restored sugar plantation. With only a single day in port, you're better off just using the island's shared taxi vans rather than renting a car, but if you want to do some independent exploring, you can rent a car in Cruz Bay.

EXPLORING ST. JOHN

★ **Annaberg Plantation.** In the 18th century, sugar plantations dotted the steep hills of this island. Slaves and free Danes and Dutchmen toiled to harvest the cane that was used to create sugar, molasses, and rum for export. Built in the 1780s, the partially restored plantation at Leinster Bay was once an important sugar mill. Although there are no official visiting hours, the National Park Service has regular tours, and some well-informed taxi drivers will show you around. Occasionally you may see a living-history demonstration—someone making johnnycake or weaving baskets. For information on tours and cultural events, contact the St. John National Park Service Visitors Center. ⊠ *Leinster Bay Rd., Annaberg* ☎ *340/776–6201* ⊕ *www.nps.gov/viis* ☑ *Free* ☉ *Daily dawn–dusk.*

★ **Bordeaux Mountain.** St. John's highest peak rises to 1,277 feet. Route 10 passes near enough to the top to offer breathtaking vistas. Don't stray into the road here—cars whiz by at a good clip along this section. Instead, drive nearly to the end of the dirt road that heads off next to the restaurant and gift shop for spectacular views at Picture Point and the trailhead of the hike downhill to Lameshur. Get a trail map from the Park Service before you start. ⊠ *Rte. 10, Bordeaux.*

Cruz Bay. St. John's main town may be compact (it consists of only several blocks), but it's definitely a hub: the ferries from St. Thomas and the British Virgin Islands pull in here, and it's where you can get a taxi or rent a car to travel around the island. There are plenty of shops in

St. John

↑ TO JOST VAN DYKE

↖ TO TORTOLA

Windward Passage

The Narrows

— Mary Point

Whistling Cay

Francis Bay

Annaberg Plantation *Leinster Bay*

TO TORTOLA →

Francis Bay Maho Bay

Cinnamon Bay

Brown Bay

Sir Francis Drake Channel

Henley Cay

Trunk Bay

VIRGIN ISLANDS NATIONAL PARK

Centerline Rd.

20

Hawlover Bay

Newfound Bay

Hawksnest Beach

20

10

Palestina

East End Pt.

Coral Bay

Hurricane Hole

Caneel Bay

Coral Harbor

Round Bay

East End

← TO ST. THOMAS

Camelberg Pk.

Sanders Bay

East End Bay

Privateer Pt.

Cruz Bay

VIRGIN ISLANDS NATIONAL PARK

107

Coral Bay

Long Pt.

Privateer Bay

ephen's Cay

104

Bordeaux Mountain

Calabash

Lagoon Pt.

Great Cruz Bay

Fish Bay

Reef Bay

Lameshur Bay

John's Folly Bay

Leduck Island

Blasbalg Pt.

Rendezvous Bay

Dittlif Pt.

White Pt.

Chocolate Hole

Bovocoap Pt.

Dever's Bay

Salt Pond Bay

Drunk Bay

Salt Pond Peninsula

Ram Head

Caribbean Sea

KEY

⅂ Beaches

◥ Dive Sites

⛴ Ferry

····· Trail

0   1 mile

0   1 kilometer

which to browse, a number of watering holes where you can stop for a breather, many restaurants, and a grassy square with benches where you can sit back and take everything in. Look for the current edition of the handy, amusing "St. John Map" featuring Max the Mongoose. To pick up a useful guide to St. John's hiking trails, see various large maps of the island, and find out about current park service programs, including guided walks and cultural demonstrations, stop by the **V.I. National Park Visitors Center** (⊠ *Near baseball field, Cruz Bay* ☎ *340/776–6201* ⊕ *www.nps.gov/viis*). It's open daily from 8 to 4:30.

SHOPPING

In St. John the small shopping district runs from Wharfside Village near the ferry landing to Mongoose Junction, just up the street from the cruise-ship dock and tender landing, with lots of shops tucked in between.

Bamboula (⊠ *Mongoose Junction, North Shore Rd., Cruz Bay,* ☎ *340/693–8699*) owner Jo Sterling travels the world to find unusual housewares, rugs, bedspreads, accessories, and men's and women's clothes and shoes for this multicultural boutique. **Bougainvillea Boutique** (⊠ *Mongoose Junction, North Shore Rd., Cruz Bay* ☎ *340/693–7190*) is your destination if you want to look as if you stepped out of the pages of the resort-wear spread in an upscale travel magazine. Owner Susan Stair carries *very* chic men's and women's resort wear, straw hats, leather handbags, and fine gifts. **Caravan Gallery** (⊠ *Mongoose Junction, North Shore Rd., Cruz Bay* ☎*340/779–4566*), which is owned by Radha Speer, sells unusual jewelry that Radha has traveled the world to find. And the more you look, the more you see—folk art, tribal art, and masks for sale cover the walls and tables, making this a

★ great place to browse. **Pink Papaya** (⊠ *Lemon Tree Mall, King St., Cruz Bay* ☎*340/693–8535*) is where you can find the well-known work of longtime Virgin Islands resident M. L. Etre, plus a huge collection of one-of-a-kind gifts, including bright tablecloths, unusual trays, and unique tropical jewelry. **St. John**

ST. JOHN BEST BETS

■ **British Virgin Islands.** You can hop on a ferry from Cruz Bay and visit Tortola, Virgin Gorda, or Jost Van Dyke, depending on the ferry schedule.

■ **Hiking in the National Park.** Hiking trails that crisscross the terrain are easy enough for beginners and offer breathtaking scenery.

■ **Snorkeling Cruises.** The best snorkeling sites are reachable only by boat.

■ **Trunk Bay Beach.** St. John's national park beach is beautiful and has an underwater snorkeling trail.

Editions (⊠ *North Shore Rd., Cruz Bay* ☎*340/693–8444*) specializes swimsuits and nifty cotton dresses that go from beach to dinner with a change of shoes and accessories. Owner Molly Soper also carries attractive straw hats and inexpensive jewelry.

ACTIVITIES

DIVING AND SNORKELING

Cruz Bay Watersports (⊠ *Lumberyard Shopping Complex, Cruz Bay* ☎*340/776–6234* ⊠ *Westin St. John, Great Cruz Bay* ☎*340/776–6234* ⊕*www.divestjohn.com*) actually has two locations: in Cruz Bay at the Lumberyard Shopping Complex and at the Westin St. John Resort. Owners Marcus and Patty Johnston offer regular reef, wreck, and night dives and USVI and BVI snorkel tours. The company holds both PADI five-star facility and NAUI Dream Resort status.

Low Key Watersports (⊠ *Wharfside Village, Strand St., Cruz Bay* ☎*340/693–8999 or 800/835–7718* ⊕*www.divelowkey.com*) offers one- and two-tank dives and specialty courses. It's certified as a PADI five-star training facility.

FISHING

Well-kept charter boats—approved by the U.S. Coast Guard—head out to the north and south drops or troll along the inshore reefs, depending on the season and what's biting. The captains usually provide bait, drinks, and lunch, but you need to bring your own hat and sunscreen. Fishing charters run about $700 per day for the boat. **Capt. Byron Oliver** (☎*340/693–8339*) takes you out to the north and south drops.

HIKING

Although it's fun to go hiking with a Virgin Islands National Park guide, don't be afraid to head out on your own. To find a hike that suits your ability, stop by the park's visitor center in Cruz Bay and pick up the free trail guide; it details points of interest, trail lengths, and estimated hiking times, as well as any dangers you might encounter. Although the park staff recommends long pants to protect against thorns and insects, most people hike in shorts because it can get very hot. Wear sturdy shoes or hiking boots even if you're hiking to the beach. Don't forget to bring water and insect repellent.

Fodor's Choice ★ The **Virgin Islands National Park** (⊠ *1300 Cruz Bay Creek, St. John* ☎ *340/776–6201* ⊕ *www.nps.gov/viis*) maintains more than 20 trails on the north and south shores and offers guided hikes along popular routes. A full-day trip to **Reef Bay** is a must; it's an easy hike through lush and dry forest, past the ruins of an old plantation, and to a sugar factory adjacent to the beach. It can be a bit arduous for young kids, however. Take the $6 safari bus from the park's visitor center to the trailhead, where you can meet a ranger who'll serve as your guide. The park provides a boat ride back to Cruz Bay for $15 to save you the walk back up the mountain. The schedule changes from season to season; call for times and reservations, which are essential.

BEACHES

Cinnamon Bay Beach (⊠ *North Shore Rd., Rte. 20, Cinnamon Bay, about 4 mi [6 km] east of Cruz Bay*) faces beautiful cays and abuts the national park campground. The facilities are open to the public and include cool showers, toilets, a commissary, and a restaurant. You can rent water-sports equipment here—a good thing, because there's excellent snorkeling off the point to the right; look for the big angelfish and large schools of purple triggerfish. Afternoons on Cinnamon Bay can be windy so arrive early to beat the gusts. **Hawksnest Beach** (⊠ *North Shore Rd., Rte. 20, Hawksnest Bay, about 2 mi (3 km) east of Cruz Bay*) is the closest drivable beach to Cruz Bay, so it's often crowded with locals and visitors. Sea grape and waving palm trees line this narrow beach, and there are restrooms, cooking grills, and a covered shed for picnicking. **Trunk Bay Beach** (⊠ *North Shore Rd., Rte. 20, Trunk Bay, about 2½ mi [4 km] east of Cruz Bay*), St. John's most-photographed beach, is also the preferred spot for beginning snorkelers because of its underwater trail. Crowded or not, this stunning beach is one of the island's most beautiful. There are changing rooms with showers, bathrooms, a snack bar, picnic tables, a gift shop, phones, lockers, and snorkeling-equipment rentals. The parking lot often overflows, but you can park along the road.

Fodor's Choice ★

WHERE TO EAT

$–$$ ╳ **Sun Dog Cafe.** There's an unusual assortment of dishes at this charm-
ECLECTIC ing alfresco restaurant, which you'll find tucked into a courtyard in the upper reaches of the Mongoose Junction shopping center. Kudos to the white pizza with artichoke hearts, roasted garlic, mozzarella cheese, and

capers. The Jamaican jerk chicken salad and the black-bean quesadilla are also good choices. ✉ *Mongoose Junction, North Shore Rd., Cruz Bay* ☎ *340/693–8340* 🖃 *AE, MC, V* ◷ *No dinner.*

ST. KITTS (BASSETERRE)

Jordan Simon

Mountainous St. Kitts, the first English settlement in the Leeward Islands, crams some stunning scenery into its 65 square mi (168 square km). Vast, brilliant green fields of sugarcane (the former cash crop, now slowly being replanted) run to the shore. The fertile, lush island has some fascinating natural and historical attractions: a rain forest replete with waterfalls, thick vines, and secret trails; a central mountain range, dominated by the 3,792-foot Mt. Liamuiga, whose crater has long been dormant; and Brimstone Hill, known in the 18th century as the Gibraltar of the West Indies. St. Kitts and Nevis, along with Anguilla, achieved self-government as an Associated State of Great Britain in 1967. In 1983 St. Kitts and Nevis became an independent nation. English with a strong West Indian lilt is spoken here. People are friendly but shy; always ask before you take photographs. Also, be sure to wear wraps or shorts over beach attire when you're in public places.

ESSENTIALS

Currency Eastern Caribbean (E.C.) dollar (EC$2.67 to US$1). U.S. dollars are accepted practically everywhere, but you'll usually get change in E.C. currency.

Internet The Cable (✉ *Cayon St., Basseterre, St. Kitts* ☎ *869/469–1999*).

Telephones Phone cards, which you can buy in denominations of $5, $10, and $20, are handy for making local phone calls, calling other islands, and accessing U.S. direct lines. To make a local call, dial the seven-digit number. To call St. Kitts from the United States, dial the area code 869, then access code 465, 466, 468, or 469 and the local four-digit number.

COMING ASHORE

Cruise ships calling at St. Kitts dock at Port Zante, which is a deep-water port directly in Basseterre, the capital of St. Kitts. The cruise-ship terminal is right in the downtown area, two minutes' walk from sights and shops. Taxi rates on St. Kitts are fixed and should be posted right at the dock. If you'd like to go to Nevis, several daily ferries (30 to 45 minutes, $8 one-way) can take you to Charlestown in Nevis; the byzantine schedule is subject to change, so double-check times.

Taxi rates on St. Kitts are fairly expensive, and you may have to pay $32 for a ride to Brimstone Hill (for one to four passengers). A four-hour tour of St. Kitts runs about $80. It's often cheaper to arrange an island tour with one of the local companies than to hire a taxi driver to take your group around. Several restored plantation greathouses are known for their lunches; your driver can provide information and arrange drop-off and pickup. Before setting off in a cab, be sure to clarify whether the rate quoted is in E.C. or U.S. dollars.

EXPLORING ST. KITTS

Basseterre. On the south coast, St. Kitts's walkable capital is graced with tall palms and flagstone sidewalks; although many of the buildings appear run-down, there are interesting shops, excellent art galleries, and some beautifully maintained houses. Duty-free shops and boutiques line the streets and courtyards radiating from the octagonal **Circus,** built in the style of London's famous Piccadilly Circus.

There are lovely gardens on the site of a former slave market at **Independence Square** (⊠ *Off Bank St., Basseterre*). The square is surrounded on three sides by 18th-century Georgian buildings.

In the restored former Treasury Building, the **National Museum** presents an eclectic collection reflecting the history and culture of the island. It's a collaboration of the St. Christopher Heritage Society and the island government. ⊠ *Bay Rd., Basseterre* ☎ *869/465–5584* 🖙 *EC$1 residents, US$1 nonresidents* ⊘ *Weekdays 9–5, Sat. 9–1.*

Port Zante (⊠ *Waterfront, behind Circus, Basseterre*) is an ambitious 27-acre cruise-ship pier and marina in an area that has been reclaimed from the sea. The domed welcome center is an imposing neoclassical hodgepodge, with columns and stone arches, shops, walkways, fountains, and West Indian–style buildings housing luxury shops, galleries, and restaurants. A second pier, 1,434 feet long, has a draft that accommodates even leviathan cruise ships. The selection of shops and restaurants (Tiffany Bar and Deli is a find for fantastic local fare) is gradually expanding as well.

★ **Brimstone Hill.** The well-restored 38-acre fortress, a UNESCO World Heritage Site, is part of a national park dedicated by Queen Elizabeth in 1985. The steep walk up the hill from the parking lot is well worth it if military history and/or spectacular views interest you. After routing the French in 1690, the English erected a battery here, and by 1736 the fortress held 49 guns, earning it the moniker Gibraltar of the West Indies. In 1782, 8,000 French troops laid siege to the stronghold, which was defended by 350 militia and 600 regular troops of the Royal Scots and East Yorkshires. When the English finally surrendered, the French allowed them to march from the fort in full formation out of respect for their bravery (the English afforded the French the same honor when they surrendered the fort a mere year later). A hurricane severely damaged the fortress in 1834, and in 1852 it was evacuated and dismantled. The beautiful stones were carted away to build houses. The citadel has been partially reconstructed and its guns remounted. A seven-minute orientation film in the museum recounts the fort's history and restoration. The view from here includes Montserrat and Nevis to the southeast; Saba and St. Eustatius to the northwest; and St. Barths and St. Maarten to the north. Nature trails snake through the tangle of surrounding hardwood forest and savanna (a fine spot to catch the green vervet monkeys—inexplicably brought by the French and now outnumbering the residents—skittering about). ⊠ *Main Rd., Brimstone Hill* ☎ *869/465–2609* ⊕ *www.brimstone hillfortress.org* ⊠ *$8* ⊙ *Daily 9:30–5:30.*

★ **Romney Manor.** The ruins of this somewhat restored house (reputedly once the property of Thomas Jefferson) and surrounding cottages that duplicate the old chattel-house style are set in 6 acres of glorious gardens, with exotic flowers, an old bell tower, and an enormous, gnarled 350-year-old *saman* tree (sometimes called a rain tree). Inside, at **Caribelle Batik,** you can watch artisans hand-printing fabrics by the 2,500-year-old Indonesian wax-and-dye process known as batik. Look for signs indicating a turnoff for Romney Manor near Old Road.

St. Kitts Scenic Railway. The old narrow-gauge train that had transported sugarcane to the central sugar factory since 1912 is all that remains of the island's once-thriving sugar industry. Two-story cars bedecked in bright Kittitian colors circle the island in just under four hours.

ST. KITTS BEST BETS

■ **Brimstone Hill Fortress.** Stop here for some of the best views on St. Kitts.

■ **Nevis.** A trip to Nevis is a worthwhile way to spend the day.

■ **Plantation Greathouses.** Stop for a lunch at Ottley's or Rawlins Plantation.

■ **Rain-forest Hikes.** Several operators on the island lead day-long hikes through the rain forest.

■ **Romney Manor.** This partially restored manor house is made better by the chance to shop at Caribelle Batik and watch the elaborate wax-and-dye process.

Each passenger gets a comfortable, downstairs air-conditioned seat fronting vaulted picture windows and an upstairs open-air observation spot. The conductor's running discourse embraces not only the history of sugar cultivation but the railway's construction, local folklore, island geography, even other agricultural mainstays from papayas to pigs. You can drink in complimentary tropical beverages (including luscious guava daiquiris) along with the sweeping rain-forest and ocean vistas, accompanied by an a cappella choir's renditions of hymns, spirituals, and predictable standards like "I've Been Workin' on the Railroad." ⊠*Needsmust* ☎*869/465–7263* ⊕*www.stkittsscenicrailway.com* ⊠*$89* ⊙*Departures vary according to cruise-ship schedules but operate at least once daily Nov.–Apr.; call ahead.*

> ### STORAGE
>
> Take along a hanging shoe organizer for the closet to extend storage space for small items and to keep shoes off the floor. An over-the-door, pocket-style shoe organizer can be hung on the bathroom door. Slip bathroom necessities in the pockets so they are handy and out of the way.

SHOPPING

Most shopping plazas are in downtown Basseterre, on the streets radiating from the Circus. **All Kind of Tings,** a peppermint-pink edifice on Liverpool Row at College Street Ghaut, functions as a de facto vendors' market, where several booths sell local crafts and cheap T-shirts. Its courtyard frequently hosts folkloric dances, fashion shows, poetry readings, and steel-pan concerts. The **Pelican Mall**—a shopping arcade designed to look like a traditional Caribbean street—has 26 stores, a restaurant, tourism offices, and a bandstand near the cruise-ship pier. Directly behind Pelican Mall, on the waterfront, is **Port Zante,** the deepwater cruise-ship pier where a much-delayed upscale shopping-dining complex is becoming a 25-shop area (including the usual ubiquitous large jewelry concerns like Diamonds International and Kay's Jewelers); the **Amina Market** here is a fine source for cheap local crafts. If you're looking for inexpensive, island-y T-shirts and souvenirs, check out the series of vendors' huts behind Pelican Mall to the right of Port Zante as you face the sea. **Shoreline Plaza** is next to the Treasury Building, right on Basseterre's waterfront. **TDC Mall** is just off the Circus in downtown.

★ **Caribelle Batik** (⊠*Romney Manor, Old Road Town* ☎*869/465–6253*) sells gloriously colored batik wraps, kimonos, caftans, T-shirts, dresses,

★ wall hangings, and the like. **Kate Design** (⊠*Mount Pleasant House, St. Paul's* ☎*869/465–7740*) showcases the highly individual style of Kate Spencer, whose original paintings, serigraphs, note cards, and other

★ pieces are available from her studio outside Rawlins Plantation. The **Potter's House** (⊠*Camps Estate House, Camps Estate* ☎*869/465–5947*) is the atelier-home of Carla Astaphan, whose beautifully glazed ceramics and masks celebrate Afro-Caribbean heritage; she also carries marvelous Haitian pieces. **Spencer Cameron Art Gallery** (⊠*10 N. Independence Sq., Basseterre* ☎*869/465–1617*) has historical reproductions of Caribbean island charts and prints, in addition to owner Rosey Cameron's popular Carnevale clown prints and a wide selection of exceptional artwork by Caribbean artists. The gallery will mail anywhere.

ACTIVITIES

DIVING AND SNORKELING

St. Kitts has more than a dozen excellent dive sites. The surrounding waters feature shoals, hot vents, shallows, canyons, steep walls, and caverns at depths from 40 to nearly 200 feet, with hundreds of wrecks. **Dive St. Kitts** (⊠ *2 mi [3 km] east of Basseterre, Frigate Bay* ☎ *869/465–1189* ⊕ *www.divestkitts.com*), a PADI-NAUI facility, offers competitive prices; friendly, laid-back dive masters; and a more international clientele. The Bird Rock location features superb shore diving: common sightings 20 to 30 feet out include octopi, nurse sharks, manta and spotted eagle rays, and sea horses. Kenneth Samuel of **Kenneth's Dive Center** (⊠ *Bay Rd., Newtown* ☎ *869/465–2670* ⊕ *www.kenneths divecenter.com*), a PADI company, takes small groups of divers with C cards to nearby reefs. Rates average $70 for single-tank dives, $95 for double-tank dives; add $10 for equipment. Night dives, including lights, are $80–$90, and snorkeling trips (four-person minimum) are $40, drinks included. After 25 years' experience, former fisherman Samuel is considered an old pro (Jean-Michel Cousteau requested his guidance upon his first visit in the 1990s) and strives to keep groups small and prices reasonable. **Pro-Divers** (⊠ *Ocean Terrace Inn, Basseterre* ☎ *869/466–3483* ⊕ *www.prodiversstkitts.com*), is owned by Austin Macleod, a PADI-certified dive master–instructor, and offers resort and certification courses running $125–$420. He also takes groups to snorkeling sites accessible only by boat.

GOLF

The **Royal St. Kitts Golf Club** (⊠ *St. Kitts Marriott Resort, Frigate Bay* ☎ *869/466–2700 or 866/785–4653* ⊕ *www.royalstkittsgolfclub.com*) is an 18-hole, par-71 links-style championship course that underwent a complete redesign by Thomas McBroom to maximize Caribbean and Atlantic views and increase the challenge (there are now 12 lakes and 83 bunkers). Holes 15 through 17 actually skirt the Atlantic in their entirety, lending new meaning to the term "sand trap." The sudden gusts, wide but twisting fairways, and extremely hilly terrain demand pinpoint accuracy and finesse, yet holes such as 18 require pure power. Greens fees are $150 for Marriott guests in high season, $180 for nonguests with twilight and super-twilight discounts.

HIKING

Trails in the central mountains vary from easy to don't-try-it-by-yourself. Monkey Hill and Verchild's Peak aren't difficult, although the Verchild's climb will take the better part of a day. Don't attempt Mt. Liamuiga without a guide. You'll start at Belmont Estate—at the west end of the island—on horseback, then proceed on foot to the lip of the crater, at 2,600 feet. You can go down into the crater—1,000 feet deep and 1 mi (1.5 km) wide, with a small freshwater lake—clinging to vines and roots and scaling rocks, even trees. Expect to get muddy. There are several fine operators (each hotel recommends its favorite); tour rates range from $65 for a rain-forest walk to $90 for a volcano expedition, and usually include round-trip transportation from your hotel and picnic lunch.

CAUTION

Pack a small flashlight just in case there's an emergency. You don't want to be stumbling around in the dark.

★ Earl of **Duke of Earl's Adventures** (☎869/465–1899 or 869/663–0994) is as entertaining as his nickname suggests—and his prices are slightly cheaper than other operators ($45 for a rainforest tour including refreshments, $70 volcano expeditions include lunch). He genuinely loves his island and conveys that enthusiasm, encouraging hikers to swing on vines or sample unusual-looking fruits during his rain-forest trip. He also conducts a thorough volcano tour to the crater's rim. Greg Pereira of **Greg's Safaris** (☎869/465–4121 ⊕www.gregsafaris.com), whose family has lived on St. Kitts since the early 19th century, takes groups on half-day trips into the rain forest and on full-day hikes up the volcano and through the grounds of a private 18th-century greathouse. The rain-forest trips include visits to sacred Carib sites, abandoned sugar mills, and an excursion down a 100-foot coastal canyon containing a wealth of Amerindian petroglyphs. The Off the Beaten Track Plantation Tour provides a thorough explanation of the role sugar and rum played in the Caribbean economy and colonial wars. He and his staff relate fascinating historical, folkloric, and botanical information. Oliver Spencer of **Periwinkle Tours** (☎869/465–6314) leads rain-forest treks to the ruins of an abandoned coffee plantation taken over by spreading banyan trees, explaining folklore and flora, including herbal remedies, along the way. "Not one for crowds," he tries to keep groups small and personalized.

HORSEBACK RIDING

Wild North Frigate Bay and desolate Conaree Beach are great for riding, as is the rain forest. Guides from **Trinity Stables** (☎869/465–3226) offer beach rides ($40) and trips into the rain forest ($50). The latter is intriguing, as guides discuss plants' medicinal properties along the way (such as sugarcane to stanch bleeding) and pick oranges right off a tree to squeeze fresh juice. Otherwise, the staffers are cordial but shy, but this isn't a place for beginners' instruction.

BEACHES

The powdery white-sand beaches of St. Kitts, free and open to the public (even those occupied by hotels), are in the Frigate Bay area or on the lower peninsula.

★ **Banana/Cockleshell Bays,** twin connected eyebrows of glittering champagne-color sand—stretching nearly 2 mi (3 km) total at the southeastern tip of the island—feature majestic views of Nevis and are backed by lush vegetation and coconut palms. Lion Rock Beach Bar (order the knockout Lion Punch) and Reggae Beach Bar and Grill bracket either end of Cockleshell. Locals consider **Friar's Bay**, on the Caribbean (southern) side, the island's finest beach, where several hopping, happening bars serve terrific, inexpensive local food and cheap, frosty drinks. Chair rentals cost around $3, though if you order lunch you can negotiate a freebie. You can haggle with fishermen here to take you snorkeling off the eastern point, though live coral reefs protect both ends. The Caribbean side of **Frigate Bay** offers talcum-powder-fine beige sand framed by coconut palms and sea grapes, while the wilder Atlantic side (a 15-minute stroll)—the 4-mi-wide (6.5-km-wide) stretch sometimes called North Frigate Bay—is a favorite with horseback riders. South Frigate Bay is bookended by Sunset Café and Oasis BARS. In between are several other lively beach spots, including Cathy's (fabulous jerk ribs), the Monkey Bar, and Mr. X Shiggidy Shack.

WHERE TO EAT

$$$ — ╳ **Beach House.** Two refined refugees from Anguilla's captivating Cap
ECLECTIC — Juluca, Eustace "Guish" Guishard and executive chef George Reid, put
Fodor$Choice — the sin in scintillating at this outpost of chic on Turtle Beach. On the
★ — southwest peninsula, the Beach House preens like an advance scout for the army of chic. The 60-seat restaurant and oversized 30-seat lounge wouldn't be out of place in LA, featuring a rich color palette, plush yet comfy furnishings, hardwood floors, sea-grass carpets, and billowing white draperies forming cozy nooks throughout. George's eclectic menu showcases the Caribbean's sultry melting pot of culinary traditions— Spanish, Asian, French, African, and Dutch, taking the confusion out of fusion cuisine. Stunners such as oxtail-foie-gras ravioli in star-anise poultry broth garnished with chervil or cherrywood-smoked salmon with leek-fennel fondue and chardonnay-vanilla bean sauce provide textbook examples of how to juxtapose textures, flavors, even colors. Even the more casual, affordable lunch fare is gorgeously presented. ⊠ *Turtle Beach* ☎ *869/469–5299* ♙ *Reservations essential* ▤ *AE, MC, V.*

$–$$ — ╳ **Reggae Beach Bar and Grill.** Treats at this popular daytime watering
ECLECTIC — hole include honey-mustard ribs, coconut shrimp, grilled lobster (a best-buy special Friday nights), decadent bread pudding with rum sauce, and an array of tempting tropical libations. Business cards and pennants from around the world plaster the bar and the open-air space is decorated with a variety of nautical accoutrements, from fishnets and turtle shells to painted wooden crustaceans. You can snorkel here, spot hawksbill turtles and the occasional monkey, laze in a palm-shaded hammock, or rent a kayak or snorkel gear. Beach chairs are free. Locals come Sunday afternoons for dancing to live bands and for fun but fiercely contested volleyball. ⊠ *S.E. Peninsula Rd., Cockleshell Beach* ☎ *869/469–9086* ⊕ *www.reggaebeachbar.com* ▤ *AE, D, MC, V* ☻ *No dinner Mon.–Thurs.*

ST. LUCIA (CASTRIES)

Jane E. Zarem — Magnificent St. Lucia—with towering mountains, dense rain forest, fertile green valleys, and acres of banana plantations—lies in the middle of the Windward Islands. Nicknamed "the Helen of the West Indies" because of its natural beauty, St. Lucia is distinguished from its neighbors by its unusual geological landmarks, the Pitons—the twin peaks on the southwest coast that soar nearly ½ mi (1 km) above the ocean floor. They were named a World Heritage Site by UNESCO in 2004 and are the symbol of this island. Nearby, in the former French colonial capital of Soufrière, is a "drive-in" volcano, its neighboring sulfur springs that have rejuvenated bathers for nearly three centuries, and one of the most beautiful botanical gardens in the Caribbean. A century and a half of battles between the French and English resulted in St. Lucia's changing hands 14 times before 1814, when England established possession. In 1979 the island became an independent state within the British Commonwealth of Nations. The official language is English, although most people also speak a French-creole patois.

4

ESSENTIALS

Currency Eastern Caribbean (E.C.) dollar (EC$2.67 to US$1). U.S. dollars are generally accepted, but change is given in E.C. dollars.

Internet There are several Internet cafés in the Rodney Bay Marina. **Cyber Connections** (✉ *Rodney Bay Marina, Gros Islet* ☎ *758/450–9309*).

Telephones You can make direct-dial overseas and interisland calls from St. Lucia, and the connections are excellent. You can charge an overseas call to a major credit card with no surcharge by dialing 811. Phone cards can be purchased at many retail outlets.

COMING ASHORE

Most cruise ships dock at the capital city of Castries, on the island's northwest coast. Either of two docking areas is used: Pointe Seraphine, a port of entry and duty-free shopping complex, or Port Castries, a commercial wharf across the harbor. Ferry service connects the two piers. Smaller vessels occasionally call at Soufrière, on the island's southwest coast. Ships calling at Soufrière must anchor offshore and bring passengers ashore via tender. Tourist information booths are located at Pointe Seraphine and across from the commercial wharf in Castries and along the waterfront on Bay Street in Soufrière. Downtown Castries is within walking distance of the pier, and the produce market and adjacent crafts and vendors' markets are the main attractions. Soufrière is a sleepy West Indian town, but it's worth a short walk around the central square to view the French colonial architecture; many of the island's interesting natural sights are in or near Soufrière.

Taxis are available at the docks in Castries. Although they are unmetered, the standard fares are posted at the entrance to Pointe Seraphine. Taxi drivers are well informed and can give you a full tour—often an excellent one—thanks to government-sponsored training programs. From the Castries area, full-day island tours cost about $140 for up to four people; sightseeing trips to Soufrière, around $120. If you plan your own day, expect to pay the driver at least $20 per hour plus a 10% tip. Whatever your destination, negotiate the price with the driver before you depart—and be sure that you both understand whether the rate is quoted in E.C. or U.S. dollars.

EXPLORING ST. LUCIA

CASTRIES AND THE NORTH

🕐 **Castries.** The capital, a busy commercial city of about 65,000 people, wraps around a sheltered bay. Morne Fortune rises sharply to the south of town, creating a dramatic green backdrop. The charm of Castries lies almost entirely in its liveliness, since most of the colonial buildings were destroyed by four fires that occurred between 1796 and 1948. Freighters (exporting bananas, coconut, cocoa, mace, nutmeg, and citrus fruits) and cruise ships come and go daily, making Castries Harbour one of the Caribbean's busiest ports. Pointe Seraphine is a duty-free shopping complex on the north side of the harbor, about a 20-minute walk or two-minute cab ride from the city center; a launch ferries passengers across the harbor when ships are in port. Pointe Seraphine's attractive Spanish-style architecture houses more than 20 upscale duty-free shops, a tourist information kiosk, a taxi stand, and car-rental agencies.

Derek Walcott Square is a green oasis bordered by Brazil, Laborie, Micoud, and Bourbon streets. Formerly Columbus Square, it was renamed to honor the hometown poet who won the 1992 Nobel Prize for Literature—one of two Nobel laureates from St. Lucia (the late Sir W. Arthur Lewis won the 1979 Nobel Prize in economics). Some of the 19th-century buildings that have survived fire, wind, and rain can be seen on Brazil Street, the square's southern border. On the Laborie Street side, there's a huge, 400-year-old *samaan* tree with leafy branches that shade a good portion of the square.

Directly across Laborie Street from Derek Walcott Square is the Roman Catholic **Cathedral of the Immaculate Conception,** which was built in 1897. Though it's rather somber on the outside, its interior walls are decorated with colorful murals reworked by St. Lucian artist Dunstan St. Omer in 1985, just prior to Pope John Paul II's visit. This church has an active parish and is open daily for both public viewing and religious services.

At the corner of Jeremie and Peynier streets, spreading beyond its brilliant orange roof, is the **Castries Market.** Full of excitement and bustle, the market is open every day except Sunday. It's liveliest on Saturday morning, when farmers bring their fresh produce and spices to town, as they have for more than a century. Next door to the produce market is the **Craft Market,** where you can buy pottery, wood carvings, and handwoven straw articles. Across Peynier Street from the Craft Market, at the **Vendor's Arcade,** there are still more handicrafts and souvenirs.

🕐 **Pigeon Island National Park.** Jutting out from the northwest coast, Pigeon
★ Island is connected to the mainland by a causeway. Tales are told of the pirate Jambe de Bois (Wooden Leg), who once hid out on this 44-acre hilltop islet—a strategic point during the French and British struggles for control of St. Lucia. Now it's a national park and a venue for concerts, festivals, and family gatherings. There are two small beaches with calm waters for swimming and snorkeling, a restaurant, and picnic areas. Scattered around the grounds are ruins of barracks, batteries, and garrisons that date from 18th-century French and English battles. In the Museum and Interpretative Centre, housed in the restored British officers' mess,

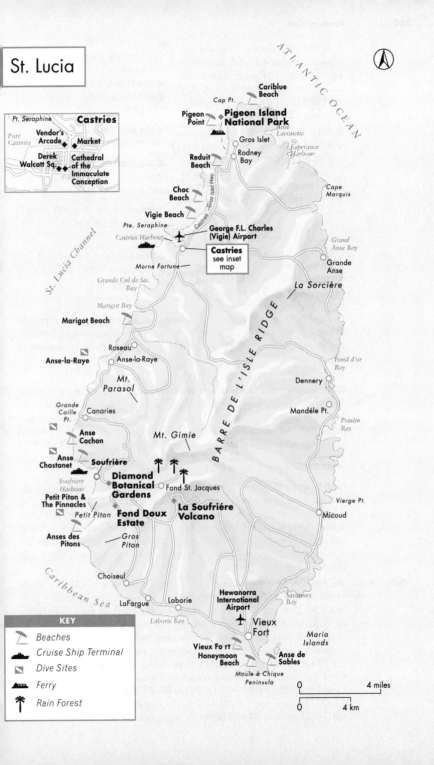

St. Lucia

ATLANTIC OCEAN

Castries

Pt. Seraphine
Port Castries

Vendor's Arcade ◆ ◆ Market

Derek Walcott Sq. ◆ ◆ Cathedral of the Immaculate Conception

Cap Pt.

Cariblue Beach

Pigeon Point ◆ **Pigeon Island National Park**

Gros Islet

Anse Lavouette

Rodney Bay

Reduit Beach

Esperance Harbour

St. Lucia Channel

Castries – Gros Islet Hwy.

Cape Marquis

Choc Beach

Vigie Beach

Pte. Seraphine

Castries Harbour

Castries

George F.L. Charles (Vigie) Airport

Castries see inset map

Morne Fortune

Grande Cul de Sac Bay

Grand Anse Bay

Grande Anse

Marigot Bay

La Sorcière

Marigot Beach

BARRE DE L'ISLE RIDGE

Roseau

Anse-la-Raye

Anse-la-Raye

Fond d'or Bay

Mt. Parasol

Dennery

Grande Caille Pt.

Canaries

Mandéle Pt.

Mt. Gimie

Praslin Bay

Anse Cochon

Anse Chastanet

Soufrière

Souffrière Harbour

Diamond Botanical Gardens

Fond St. Jacques

Vierge Pt.

Petit Piton & The Pinnacles

Petit Piton

Fond Doux Estate

La Soufrière Volcano

Micoud

Anses des Pitons

Gros Piton

Choiseul

Caribbean Sea

LaFargue

Laborie

Hewanorra International Airport

Savannes Bay

Laborie Bay

Vieux Fort

Maria Islands

Vieux Fort Honeymoon Beach

Moule à Chique Peninsula

Anse de Sables

KEY

🏖 *Beaches*
⛴ *Cruise Ship Terminal*
◻ *Dive Sites*
🚢 *Ferry*
🌴 *Rain Forest*

0 _____ 4 miles

0 _____ 4 km

a multimedia display explains the island's ecological and historical significance. ⊠ *Pigeon Island, St. Lucia National Trust, Rodney Bay* ☎ *758/452–5005* ⊕ *www.slunatrust.org* ⊠ *$4* ☉ *Daily 9–5.*

Rodney Bay. About 15 minutes north of Castries, the natural bay and an 80-acre man-made lagoon—surrounded by hotels and many popular restaurants—are named for British admiral George Rodney, who sailed the English Navy out of Gros Islet Bay in 1780 to attack and ultimately decimate the French fleet. Rodney Bay Marina is one of the Caribbean's premier yachting centers and the destination of the Atlantic Rally for Cruisers (transatlantic yacht crossing) each December. Yacht charters and sightseeing day trips can be arranged at the marina. The Rodney Bay Ferry makes hourly crossings between the marina and the shopping complex, as well as daily excursions to Pigeon Island.

SOUFRIERE AND THE SOUTH

☉ ★ **Diamond Botanical Gardens and Waterfall.** Water bubbling to the surface from underground sulfur springs streams downhill in rivulets to become Diamond Waterfall, deep within these splendid botanical gardens. For a small price, you can soak in one of the curative mineral baths. ⊠ *Soufrière Estate, Diamond Rd., Soufrière* ☎ *758/452–4759 or 758/454–7565* ⊠ *$2.75, outside bath $2.50, private bath $3.75* ☉ *Mon.–Sat. 10–5, Sun. 10–3.*

Fond Doux Estate. This plantation just outside Soufrière was one of the earliest French estates established by land grant (1745 and 1763); its 135 hilly acres still produce cocoa, citrus, bananas, coconut, and vegetables; the restored plantation house (built in 1864) is still in use. A tour can include lunch; souvenirs are sold at the boutique. ⊠ *Chateaubelair, Soufrière* ☎ *758/459–7545* ⊕ *www.fonddouxestate.com* ⊠ *$6, buffet lunch $14* ☉ *Daily 9–4.*

FodorsChoice ★ **The Pitons.** These two unusual mountains, named a UNESCO World Heritage Site in 2004, rise precipitously from the cobalt-blue Caribbean Sea just south of Soufrière. The Pitons are, in fact, the symbol of St. Lucia. Covered with thick tropical vegetation, the massive outcroppings were formed by lava from a volcanic eruption 30 to 40 million years ago. They are not identical twins since—confusingly—2,619-foot Petit Piton is taller than 2,461-foot Gros Piton, though Gros Piton is, as the word translates, broader. You can also climb Gros Piton. ☎ *758/450–2231, 758/450–2078 for St. Lucia Forest and Lands Department, 758/459–9748 for Pitons Tour Guide Association* ⊠ *Guide services $45* ☉ *Daily by appointment only.*

☺ **La Soufrière Drive-In Volcano.** As you approach, your nose will pick up
★ the strong scent of the sulfur springs. You actually drive up within a
few hundred feet of the gurgling, steaming mass, then follow a guide
around a fault in the substratum rock on foot. ⊠ *Bay St., Soufrière*
📞 *758/459–5500* 💰 *$1.25* ⊙ *Daily 9–5.*

Soufrière. The wharf is the center of activity in this sleepy town, the
oldest in St. Lucia and the former French colonial capital. It's located
1½ hours from Castries by car, 45 minutes by boat (take a boat if you
can). The **Soufrière Tourist Information Centre** (⊠ *Bay St., Soufrière*
📞 *758/459–7200*) provides information about area attractions. Note
that outside some of the popular attractions in and around Soufrière,
souvenir vendors can be persistent. Be polite but firm if you're not
interested in their wares.

SHOPPING

The island's best-known products are artwork and wood carvings;
clothing and household articles made from batik and silk-screen fabrics, designed and printed in island workshops; and clay pottery. You
can also take home straw hats and baskets and locally grown cocoa,
coffee, and spices. The only duty-free shopping is at **Pointe Seraphine**
or **La Place Carenage**, on opposite sides of the harbor. You must show
your passport and cabin key card to get duty-free prices. You'll want
to experience the **Castries Market** and scour the adjacent **Vendor's Arcade**
and **Craft Market** for handicrafts and souvenirs at bargain prices.

ACTIVITIES

DIVING AND SNORKELING

★ The coral reefs at Anse Cochon and Anse Chastanet, on the southwest
coast, are popular beach-entry dive sites. In the north, Pigeon Island
is the most convenient site. **Dive Fair Helen** (⊠ *Vigie Marina, Castries*
📞 *758/451–7716, 888/855–2206 in U.S. and Canada* ⊕ *www.dive
fairhelen.com*) is a PADI center that offers half- and full-day excursions to wreck, wall, and marine reserve areas, as well as night dives.
Scuba St. Lucia (⊠ *Anse Chastanet, Soufrière* 📞 *758/459–7755* ⊕ *www.
scubastlucia.com*) is a PADI five-star training facility. Daily beach and
boat dives and resort and certification courses are offered; underwater
photography and snorkeling equipment are available. Day trips from
the north of the island include round-trip speedboat transportation.

FISHING

Among the deep-sea creatures you can find in St. Lucia's waters are dolphin (the fish, not the mammal—also called dorado or mahimahi), barracuda, mackerel, wahoo, kingfish, sailfish, and white and blue marlin.
Sportfishing is generally done on a catch-and-release basis, but the captain
may permit you to take a fish back to your hotel to be prepared for your
dinner. Neither spearfishing nor collecting live fish in coastal waters is
permitted. Half- and full-day deep-sea fishing excursions can be arranged
at either Vigie Marina or Rodney Bay Marina. A half day of fishing
on a scheduled trip runs about $450 for one to six people. Beginners

are welcome. **Captain Mike's** (✉ *Vigie Marina, Castries* ☎*758/452–1216 or 758/452–7044* ⊕*www.capt mikes.com*) has a fleet of Bertram powerboats (31 to 38 feet) that accommodate as many as eight passengers; tackle and cold drinks are supplied. **Mako Watersports** (✉*Rodney Bay Marina, Rodney Bay* ☎*758/452–0412*) takes fishing enthusiasts out on the well-equipped six-passenger *Annie Baby*.

> ### BAG IT
>
> A mesh laundry bag or a "pop-up" mesh clothes hamper are two fairly light items that pack flat in your suitcase. The bag can hang from the closet, but either will keep your closet neat, allow damp clothing to dry out, and help you tote dirty clothes to the self-service laundry room so you can avoid high cleaning charges.

GOLF

St. Lucia Golf Club (✉*Cap Estate* ☎*758/452–8523* ⊕*www.stluciagolf.com*), the only public course, is at the island's northern tip and offers panoramic views of both the Atlantic and Caribbean. It's an 18-hole championship course (6,836 yards, par 71). You can rent clubs and shoes and arrange lessons at the pro shop and perfect your swing at the 350-yard driving range. Depending on the season, greens fees range from $90 for 9 holes in the off-season (April 15—December 15) to $140 for 18 holes in high season; carts are required and included; club and shoe rentals are available. Reservations are essential. Complimentary transportation from your cruise ship is provided for parties of three or more people.

HORSEBACK RIDING

Creole horses, a breed indigenous to South America and popular on the island, are fairly small, fast, sturdy, and even-tempered animals suitable for beginners. Established stables can accommodate all skill levels and offer countryside trail rides, beach rides with picnic lunches, plantation tours, carriage rides, and lengthy treks. Prices run about $40 for one hour, $50 for two hours, and $70 for a three-hour beach ride and barbecue. Transportation is usually provided between the stables and nearby hotels. Local people sometimes appear on beaches with their steeds and offer 30-minute rides for $10; ride at your own risk. **Country Saddles** (✉*Marquis Estate, Babonneau* ☎*758/450–5467 or 758/450–0197*), 45 minutes east of Castries, guides beginners and advanced riders through banana plantations, forest trails, and along the Atlantic coast. **International Riding Stables** (✉*Beauséjour Estate, Gros Islet* ☎*758/452–8139 or 758/450–8665*) offers English- and western-style riding. The beach-picnic ride includes time for a swim—with or without your horse. **Trim's National Riding Stable** (✉*Cas-en-Bas, Gros Islet* ☎*758/452–8273 or 758/450–9971*), the island's oldest riding stable, offers four sessions per day, plus beach tours, trail rides, and carriage tours to Pigeon Island.

BEACHES

All of St. Lucia's beaches are open to the public, but Pigeon Point, Reduit, and Vigie beaches are particularly accessible to cruise-ship passengers. **Pigeon Point** is within Pigeon Island National Park, on the

★ northwestern tip of St. Lucia; a restaurant serves snacks and drinks, but this is also a perfect spot for picnicking. **Reduit Beach,** a long stretch of golden sand framing Rodney Bay, is within walking distance of Rodney Bay Village. The Rex St. Lucian hotel, which faces the beach, has a water-sports center, where you can rent sports equipment and beach chairs and take windsurfing or waterskiing lessons. Many feel that Reduit is the island's finest beach. **Vigie Beach,** a 2-mi (3-km) strand running parallel to the George F. L. Charles Airport runway in Castries, continues on to become Malabar Beach, the beachfront in front of the Rendezvous resort.

WHERE TO EAT

$$ ✕ **Jacques.** Chef-owner Jacky Rioux creates magical dishes in his open-
FRENCH air garden restaurant (known for years as Froggie Jack's) overlooking
★ Vigie Cove. The cooking style is decidedly French, as is Rioux, but fresh produce and local spices create a fusion cuisine that's memorable at lunch or dinner. You might start with a bowl of creamy tomato-basil or pumpkin soup, a grilled portobello mushroom, or octopus and conch in curried coconut sauce. Main courses include fresh seafood, such as oven-baked kingfish with a white wine and sweet pepper sauce, or breast of chicken stuffed with smoked salmon in a citrus butter sauce. The wine list is also impressive. ⊠ *Vigie Marina, Castries* ☎ *758/458–1900* ⚐ *Reservations essential* ▤ *AE, MC, V* ⊗ *Closed Sun.*

$–$$ ✕ **The Still.** If you're visiting Diamond Waterfall, this is a great lunch
CARIBBEAN spot. The two dining rooms seat up to 400 people, so it's a popular stop for tour groups and cruise passengers. The emphasis is on local cuisine using vegetables such as christophenes, breadfruits, yams, and callaloo along with grilled fish or chicken, but there are also pork and beef dishes. All fruits and vegetables used in the restaurant are organically grown on the estate. ⊠ *The Still Plantation, Sir Arthur Lewis St., Soufrière* ☎ *758/459–7261* ▤ *MC, V.*

ST. MAARTEN (PHILLIPSBURG)

Elise Meyer   St. Martin/St. Maarten: one tiny island, just 37 square mi (59 square km), with two different accents and ruled by two sovereign nations. Here French and Dutch have lived side by side for hundreds of years, and when you cross from one country to the next there are no border patrols, no customs agents. In fact, the only indication that you have crossed a border at all is a small sign and a change in road surface. St. Martin/St. Maarten epitomizes tourist islands in the sun, where services are well developed but there's still some Caribbean flavor. The Dutch side is ideal for people who like plenty to do. The French side has a more genteel ambience, more fashionable shopping, and a Continental flair. The combination makes an almost ideal port. On the negative side, the island has been completely developed. It can be fun to shop, and you'll find an occasional bargain, but many goods are cheaper in the United States.

ESSENTIALS

Currency Legal tender on the Dutch side is the Netherlands Antilles florin (guilder), written NAf or ANG. At this writing, ANG 1.79 equals $1. On the French side, the currency is the euro (€1 to US$1.35 at this writing). There's little need to exchange money. Prices are usually quoted in both florins and dollars on the Dutch side and euros on the French side, but dollars are accepted all over the island.

Internet There is Wi-Fi service on the boardwalk behind Front Street if you have your own laptop. **Cyber Link** (✉ *53 Front St., Philipsburg*).

Telephones To phone from the Dutch side to the French, you first must dial (00–590–590) for local numbers, or (00–590–690) for cell phones, then the six-digit local number. To call from the French side to the Dutch, dial "00–599" then the seven-digit local number. Remember that a call from one side to the other is an international call.

At the Landsradio in Philipsburg, there are facilities for overseas calls and a USADirect phone, where you're directly in touch with an operator who will accept collect or credit-card calls. To call direct with an AT&T credit card or operator, dial 001–800/872–2881. On the French side, AT&T can be accessed by calling 080–099–00–11. If you need to use public phones, go to the special desk at Marigot's post office and buy a *télécarte*. There's a public phone at the tourist office in Marigot where you can make credit-card calls: the operator takes your card number (any major card) and assigns you a PIN, which you then use to charge calls to your card.

COMING ASHORE

Most cruise ships drop anchor off the Dutch capital of Philipsburg or dock in the marina at the southern tip of the Philipsburg harbor; a very few small or medium-size ships drop anchor in Marigot Bay and tender passengers ashore in the French capital. If your ship anchors, tenders will ferry you to the town pier in the middle of town, where taxis await passengers. If your ship docks at the marina, downtown is a 15-minute taxi ride away. The walk is not recommended. The island is small, and most spots aren't more than a 30-minute drive from Marigot or Phillipsburg.

Doing your own thing will be much less expensive here than a ship-sponsored tour, and since rental cars are cheap (starting at $30 per day for a local car rental), you can easily strike out as soon as your ship docks. This is the best thing to do if you just want to see the island and spend a little time at a beach. Taxis are government-regulated and fairly costly, so they aren't really an option if you want to do much exploring. Authorized taxis display stickers of the St. Maarten Taxi Association. Taxis are also available at Marigot. You may be able to negotiate a favorable deal with a taxi driver for a two- to three-hour island tour for as little as $50 plus $15 for each additional person.

St. Martin/
St. Maarten

KEY

≈ Beaches
🚢 Cruise Ship Terminal
🔲 Dive Sites

TO ANGUILLA ↗

TO ST. BARTHÉLEMY →

Creole Rock 🔲
Pt. des Froussards
Anse Marcel
Red Rock
Grandes Cayes
Bell Pt.
Ile Tintamarre →
Baie de Grand Case
French Cul de Sac
Galion Beach
Baie de Friars
Grand Case
Aéroport de l'Espérance
Baie Orientale
Green Key
Pt. Arago
Colombier
Pic du Paradis
Orléans
Butterfly Farm
Baie de l'Embouchure
Baie Rouge
Pte. du Bluff
Pt. du Plum
Baie de la Potence
Mt. Flagstaf
Terres Basses
Baie Nettle
Baie de Marigot
Marigot
ST. MARTIN
Sandy Ground
Babit Pt.
Baie Longue
Simpson Bay Lagoon
Musée de Staint-Martin
Dutch Cul-de-Sac
Bénéden Prinsen
Cupecoy Beach
Juliana International Sirport
Boven Prinsen
Dawn Beach
Mullet Bay
ST. MAARTEN
Maho Bay
Koolbaai
Guana Bay Point

Caribbean Sea
Simpson Bay
Annie
Salt Pond
Geneve Bay
Cole Bay
Great Bay
Philipsburg see inset map

Little Bay
Pt. Blanche

Great Salt Pond
Philipsburg
Post Office
Captain Hodge Pier
Wathey Sq.
Great Bay
Sint Maarten Museum
Bobby's Marina
Great Bay Marina

Proselyte Reef
ATLANTIC OCEAN

0 ___ 2 miles
0 ___ 3 km
TO ST. BARTHÉLEMY ↘

EXPLORING ST. MAARTEN/ST-MARTIN

★ **Butterfly Farm.** A serene, tropical environment envelops visitors in the terrarium-like Butterfly Sphere, where dozens of colorful butterflies flit. At any given time, some 40 species of butterflies, numbering as many as 600, flutter inside the garden under a tented net. Butterfly art and memorabilia are for sale in the gift shop. In case you want to come back, your ticket, which includes a guided tour, is good for your entire stay. ⊠ *Rte. de Le Galion, Quartier d'Orléans* ☎ *590/87–31–21* ⊕ *www.thebutterflyfarm.com* ⌑ *$12* ⊙ *Daily 9–3.*

French Cul de Sac. North of Orient Bay Beach, the French-colonial mansion of St. Martin's mayor is nestled in the hills. Little red-roof houses look like open umbrellas tumbling down the green hillside. The area is peaceful and good for hiking. There's construction, however, as the surroundings are slowly being developed. From the beach here, shuttle boats make the five-minute trip to **Ilet Pinel,** an uninhabited island that's fine for picnicking, sunning, and swimming.

Grand Case. The island's most picturesque town is set in the heart of the French side on a beach at the foot of green hills and pastures. Though it has only a 1-mi-long (1½-km-long) main street, it's known as the restaurant capital of the Caribbean. More than 27 restaurants serve French, Italian, Indonesian, and Vietnamese fare here. The budget-minded love the half-dozen lolos—kiosks at the far end of town that sell savory barbecue and seafood. Grand Case Beach Club is at the end of this road and has two beaches where you can take a dip.

Guana Bay Point. On the rugged, windswept east coast about 10 minutes north of Philipsburg, Guana Bay Point offers isolated, untended beaches and a spectacular view of St. Barths. However, because of the undercurrent, this should be more of a turf than a surf destination.

Marigot. This town's southern European flavor is most in evidence at its beautiful harborfront, with its shopping stalls, open-air cafés, and fresh-food vendors. From here, you can catch the ferry for Anguilla or St. Barths.

> ### ST. MAARTEN BEST BETS
>
> ■ **Beaches.** The island has 37 beautiful beaches, all open to the public.
>
> ■ **Butterfly Farm.** The terrarium-like Butterfly Farm is a treat for all ages.
>
> ■ **The 12-Metre Challenge.** Help sail an America's Cup yacht.
>
> ■ **Loterie Farm.** On the slopes of Pic du Paradis, an amazing eco-friendly preserve with fun activities.
>
> ■ **Shopping.** Both sides of the island are a shopper's paradise.

★ Though not much remains of the structure itself, **Le Fort Louis,** completed by the French in 1789, commands a sweeping view of Marigot, its harbor, and the English island of Anguilla, which alone makes it worth the climb. There are few signs to show the way, so the best way to find the fort is to go to Marigot and look up. ⊠ *Marigot.*

Philipsburg. The capital of Dutch St. Maarten stretches about a mile (1½ km) along an isthmus between Great Bay and the Salt Pond and has five parallel streets. Most of the village's dozens of shops and restaurants are on Front Street, narrow and cobblestoned, closest to Great Bay. It's generally congested when cruise ships are in port, because of its many duty-free shops and several casinos. Little lanes called *steegjes* connect Front Street with Back Street, which has fewer shops and considerably less congestion. Along the beach is a newly constructed ½-mi-long (1-km-long) boardwalk with restaurants and several Wi-Fi hot spots.

Wathey Square (pronounced watty) is in the heart of the village. Directly across from the square are the town hall and the courthouse, in the striking white building with the cupola. The structure was built in 1793 and has served as the commander's home, a fire station, a jail, and a post office. The streets surrounding the square are lined with hotels, duty-free shops, fine restaurants, and cafés. The **Captain Hodge Pier,** just off the square, is a good spot to view Great Bay and the beach that stretches alongside. The **Sint Maarten Museum** hosts rotating cultural exhibits and a permanent historical display called Forts of St. Maarten–St. Martin. The artifacts range from Arawak pottery shards to objects salvaged from the wreck of the HMS *Proselyte.* ⊠ *7 Front St., Philipsburg* ☎ *599/542–4917* ⊠ *Free* ⊗ *Weekdays 10–4, Sat. 10–2.*

★ **Pic du Paradis.** From Friar's Bay Beach, a bumpy, tree-canopied road leads inland to this peak. At 1,492 feet, it's the island's highest point.

There are two observation areas. From them, the tropical forest unfolds below and the vistas are breathtaking. The road is quite isolated, so it's best to travel in groups. It's also quite steep and not in particularly good shape, becoming a single lane as you near the summit; if you don't have a four-wheel-drive

> **CAUTION**
>
> Germicidal hand cleaner is a must-have for adventure excursions or where water might be at a premium. Bring a small bottle you can carry along with you.

vehicle, don't even try it. Parking at the top is iffy, and it's best if you turn around before you park. It may not be so easy later.

Near the bottom of Pic du Paradis is **Loterie Farm,** a peaceful 150-acre private nature preserve opened to the public in 1999 by American expat B. J. Welch. Designed to preserve island habitats, Loterie Farm offers a rare glimpse of Caribbean forest and mountain land. Welch has renovated an old farmhouse and welcomes visitors for hiking, mountain biking, ecotours, or less strenuous activities, such as meditation and yoga. Raves accompany lunch and dinner fare at the Hidden Forest Café since chef Julie Purkis took over the kitchen. The restaurant is open Tuesday through Sunday. The Loterie Farm's newest attraction, the Fly Zone, allows Tarzan wannabes to soar over the forest canopy via a series of ropes, cables, and suspended bridges. The Fly Zone boasts the longest zip lines in the western hemisphere. ⊠ *Rte. de Pic du Paradis* ☎ *590/87–86–16 or 590/57–28–55* ◫ *€5* ☉ *Daily sunrise–sunset.*

SHOPPING

It's true that the island sparkles with its myriad outdoor activities—diving, snorkeling, sailing, swimming, and sunning—but shopaholics are drawn to the sparkle within the jewelry stores. The huge array of such stores is almost unrivaled in the Caribbean. In addition, duty-free shops offer substantial savings—about 15% to 30% below U.S. and Canadian prices—on cameras, watches, liquor, cigars, and designer clothing. It's no wonder that each year 500 cruise ships make Philipsburg a port of call. On both sides of the island, be alert for idlers. They can snatch unwatched purses. Prices are in dollars on the Dutch side, in euros on the French side. As for bargains, there are more to be had on the Dutch side.

Philipsburg's **Front Street** has reinvented itself. Now it's mall-like, with redbrick walk and streets, palm trees lining the sleek boutiques, jewelry stores, souvenir shops, outdoor restaurants, and the old reliables—including McDonald's and Burger King. Here and there a school or a church appears to remind visitors there's more to the island than shopping. Back Street is where you'll find the **Philipsburg Market Place,** an open-air market where you can haggle for bargains on items such as handicrafts, souvenirs, and cover-ups. **Old Street,** near the end of Front Street, has stores, boutiques, and open-air cafés offering French crepes, rich chocolates, and island mementos. You can find an outlet mall amid the more upscale shops at the **Maho** shopping plaza. The **Plaza del Lago** at the Simpson Bay Yacht Club complex has an excellent choice of restaurants as well as shops.

On the French side, wrought-iron balconies, colorful awnings, and gingerbread trim decorate Marigot's smart shops, tiny boutiques, and bistros in the **Marina Royale** complex and on the main streets, **Rue de la Liberté** and **Rue de la République**. Also in Marigot are the pricey **West Indies Mall** and the **Plaza Caraïbes**, which house designer shops.

ACTIVITIES

For a wide range of water sports, including parasailing and water-skiing, head to Orient Beach, where a variety of operators have their headquarters.

DIVING AND SNORKELING

Although St. Maarten is not generally known as a dive destination, the water temperature here is rarely below 70°F (21°C). Visibility is often excellent, averaging about 100 feet to 120 feet. The island has more than 40 good dive sites, from wrecks to rocky labyrinths. For snorkelers, the area around Orient Bay, Caye Verte (Green Key), Ilet Pinel, and Flat Island is especially lovely and is officially classified, and protected, as a regional underwater nature reserve. You can take a half-day snorkeling trip for around $30.

Dive Safaris (⊠*Bobby's Marina, Yrausquin Blvd., Philipsburg* ☎*599/ 542–9001 or 599/545–2401* ⊕*www.divestmaarten.com*) has a shark-awareness dive where participants can watch professional feeders give reef sharks a little nosh. **Ocean Explorers Dive Shop** (⊠*113 Welfare Rd., Simpson Bay* ☎*599/544–5252* ⊕*www.stmaartendiving.com*) is St. Maarten's oldest dive shop, and offers different types of certification courses.

On the French side, **Blue Ocean** (⊠*Sandy Ground Rd., Baie Nettlé* ☎*590/ 87–89–73* ⊕*www.blueocean.ws*) is a PADI-certified dive center. At Grand Case Beach Club, **O2 Limits** (⊠*Bd. de Grand Case, Grand Case* ☎*690/50–04–00*) offers a variety of dives.

FISHING

You can angle for yellowtail snapper, grouper, marlin, tuna, and wahoo on deep-sea excursions. Costs range from $150 per person for a half day to $250 for a full day. Prices usually include bait and tackle, instruction for novices, and refreshments. Ask about licensing and insurance. **Big Sailfish Too** (⊠*Anse Marcel* ☎*690/27–40–90*) is your best bet on the French side of the island. **Lee's Deepsea Fishing** (⊠*Welfare Rd. 82, Simpson Bay* ☎*599/544–4233 or 599/544–4234* ⊕*www.leesfish.com*) organizes excursions, and when you return, Lee's Roadside Grill will cook your tuna, wahoo, or whatever else you catch and keep. **Rudy's Deep Sea Fishing** (⊠*14 Airport Rd., Simpson Bay* ☎*599/545–2177 or 599/522–7120* ⊕*www.rudysdeepseafishing.com*) has been around for years and is one of the more experienced sport-angling outfits.

GOLF

St. Maarten is not a golf destination. Although **Mullet Bay Golf Course** (⊠ *Airport Rd., north of airport* ☎ *599/545–3069*), on the Dutch side, is an 18-hole course, it's the island's *only* one. At this writing, only nine holes are open, as the beach side was damaged by a hurricane in 2008 hurricane, but it is serviceable, if you need a golf fix.

BEACHES

The island's 10 mi (16 km) of beaches are all open to cruise-ship passengers. You can rent chairs and umbrellas at most of the beaches, primarily from beachside restaurants. The best beaches are on the French side. Topless bathing is common on the French side. If you take a cab to a remote beach, be sure to arrange a specific time for the driver to return for you. Don't leave valuables unattended on the beach or in a rental car, even in the trunk.

★ **Baie de Friars** has a couple of simple good restaurants, calm waters, and a lovely view of Anguilla. To get to the beach, take National Road 7 from Marigot, go toward Grand Case to the Morne Valois hill, and turn left

★ on the dead-end road. True to its name, **Dawn Beach** is the place to be at sunrise. On the Atlantic side of Oyster Pond, just south of the French border, this is a first-class beach for sunning and snorkeling. To find it,

Fodor'sChoice follow the signs for the big Westin resort. Many consider **Baie Orientale**

★ the island's most beautiful beach, but its satiny white sand, underwater marine reserve, variety of water sports, beach bars, and hotels also make it one of the most crowded. The conservative north end is more family-oriented, while the liberal south end is clothing-optional and, as you approach the Club Orient resort, becomes full-on nudie territory. A

☾ protected nature reserve, **Ilet Pinel** is a five-minute ferry ride from French Cul de Sac ($6 per person round-trip). The water is clear and shallow, and the shore is sheltered. If you like snorkeling, don your gear and paddle along both sides of this pencil-shape speck in the ocean. A small boutique sells wraps, hats, and T-shirts.

WHERE TO EAT

$–$$ ✕**Enoch's Place.** The blue-and-white-stripe awning on a corner of the
CARIBBEAN Marigot Market makes this place hard to miss. But Enoch's cooking is what draws the crowds. Specialties include garlic shrimp, fresh lobster, and rice and beans (like your St. Martin mother used to make). Try the salt fish and fried johnnycake—a great breakfast option. The food more than makes up for the lack of decor, and chances are you'll be counting the days until you can return. ⊠ *Marigot Market, Front de Mer, Marigot* ☎ *590/29-29-88* ▭ *No credit cards* ☾ *Closed Sun. No dinner.*

$$ ✕**Taloula Mango's.** Ribs are the specialty at this casual beachfront res-
ECLECTIC taurant, but the jerk chicken and thin-crust pizza are not to be ignored.
★ There are also vegetarian options, like the tasty falafel. On weekdays lunch is accompanied by live music; every Friday during happy hour a DJ spins tunes. In case you're wondering, the restaurant got its name from the owner's golden retriever. ⊠ *Sint Rose Shopping Mall, off Front St. on beach boardwalk, Philipsburg* ☎ *599/542–1645* ▭ *AE, D, MC, V.*

ST. THOMAS (CHARLOTTE AMALIE)

Carol
Bareuther

St. Thomas is the busiest cruise port of call in the world. Up to eight giant ships may visit in a single day. Don't expect an exotic island experience: one of the three U.S. Virgin Islands (with St. Croix and St. John), St. Thomas is as American as any place on the mainland, complete with McDonald's and HBO. The positive side of all this development is that there are more tours here than anywhere else in the Caribbean, and every year the excursions get better. Of course, shopping is the big draw in Charlotte Amalie, but experienced travelers remember the days of "real" bargains. Today so many passengers fill the stores that it's a seller's market. On some days, there are so many cruise passengers on St. Thomas that you must book a ship-sponsored shore excursion if you want to do more than just take a taxi to the beach or stroll around Charlotte Amalie.

ESSENTIALS

Currency The U.S. dollar is the official currency of U.S. Virgin Islands, and ATMs are plentiful.

Internet Beans, Bytes and Websites (⊠ *Royal Dane Mall, behind Tavern on Waterfront, Charlotte Amalie* ☎ *340/775–5262* ⊕ *www.usvi.net/cybercafe*). **Cyber Zone** (⊠ *Port of Sale, Charlotte Amalie* ☎ *340/714–7743*).

Telephones Both GSM and Sprint phones work in St. Thomas. It's as easy to call home from St. Thomas and St. John as from any city in the United States. On St. Thomas, public phones are easily found, and AT&T has a telecommunications center across from the Havensight Mall and on the Waterfront in Charlotte Amalie across from Emancipation Gardens.

COMING ASHORE

Depending on how many ships are in port, cruise ships drop anchor in the harbor at Charlotte Amalie and tender passengers directly to the waterfront duty-free shops, dock at the Havensight Mall at the eastern end of the crescent-shaped bay, or dock at Crown Bay Marina a few miles west of town.

The distance from Havensight to the duty-free shops is 1½ mi (3 km), which can be walked in less than half an hour; a taxi ride there costs $6 per person ($5 for each additional person). Tourist information offices are at the Havensight Mall (across from Building No. 1) for docking passengers and downtown near Fort Christian (at the eastern end of the waterfront shopping area) for those coming ashore by tender. Both offices distribute free maps. From Crown Bay it's also a half-hour walk or a $5 per person cab ride ($4 for each additional person). Taxi drivers on St. Thomas do not typically do island tours, but there are myriad tour operators who will. You can rent a car in St. Thomas, but with all the tour options it's often easier and cheaper to take an organized excursion or just hop in a cab.

EXPLORING ST. THOMAS

Charlotte Amalie. St. Thomas's major burg is a hilly shopping town. There are also plenty of interesting historic sights—so take the time to see at least a few.

Built to commemorate the freeing of slaves in 1848, the **Emancipation Garden** was the site of a 150th anniversary celebration of emancipation. A bronze bust of a freed slave blowing a symbolic conch shell commemorates this anniversary. The gazebo here is used for official ceremonies. Two other monuments show the island's Danish-American connection—a bust of Denmark's King Christian and a scaled-down model of the U.S. Liberty Bell. ⊠ *Between Tolbod Gade and Fort Christian.*

St. Thomas's oldest standing structure, **Fort Christian** was built between 1672 and 1680 and now has U.S. National Landmark status. The clock tower was added in the 19th century. This remarkable building has, over time, been used as a jail, governor's residence, town hall, courthouse, and church. A multimillion-dollar renovation project completed in the spring of 2008 stabilized the structure and halted centuries of deterioration. Check out the **Virgin Islands Museum,** where you can see exhibits on the fascinating history of the region. The gift shop sells local crafts, books, and other souvenirs. ⊠ *Waterfront Hwy., east of shopping district* ☎ *340/776–4566.*

The historic **Frederick Lutheran Church** has a massive mahogany altar, and its pews—each with its own door—were once rented to families of the congregation. Lutheranism is the state religion of Denmark, and when the territory was without a minister, the governor—who had his own elevated pew—filled in. ⊠ *Norre Gade* ☎ *340/776–1315* ☉ *Mon.–Sat. 9–4.*

Built in 1867, the neoclassical white brick-and-wood **Government House** houses the offices of the governor of the Virgin Islands. Inside, the staircases are of native mahogany, as are the plaques hand-lettered in gold with the names of the governors appointed and, since 1970, elected. Brochures detailing the history of the building are available, but you may have to ask for them. ⊠ *Government Hill* ☎ *340/774–0294* ▭ *Free* ☉ *Weekdays 8–5.*

The pastoral-looking lime-green exterior of the **Legislature Building** conceals the vociferous political wrangling of the Virgin Islands Senate. Constructed originally by the Danish as a police barracks, the building was later used to billet U.S. Marines, and much later it housed a public school. You're welcome to sit in on sessions in the upstairs chambers. ⊠ *Waterfront Hwy., across from Fort Christian* ☎ *340/774–0880* ☉ *Daily 8–5.*

Fodor'sChoice ★ **Coral World Ocean Park.** This interactive aquarium and water-sports center lets you experience a variety of sea life and other animals. The park has several outdoor pools where you can pet baby sharks, feed stingrays, touch starfish, and view endangered sea turtles. There's also a walk-through aviary where colorful rainbow lorikeets might drink nectar from your hands. Other activities include the Sea Trek Helmet Dive that lets

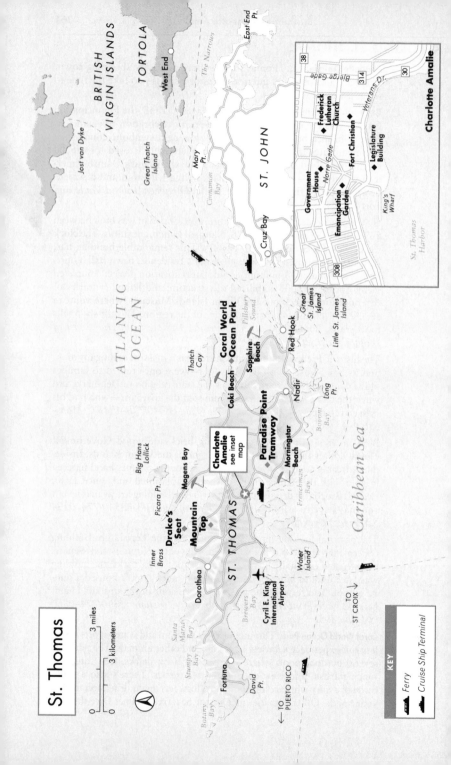

you walk along an underwater trail with a high-tech helmet that provides a continuous supply of air. A Shark Encounter program lets you observe juvenile sharks as they swim around you. A sea lion pool, which opened in 2007, is where you can get a big, wet, whiskered kiss. Also in 2007 the lorikeet exhibit opened. Buy a cup of nectar for $2 and let these parrot-look-alikes perch on your hand and drink. Coral World also has an offshore underwater observatory, an 80,000-gallon coral reef exhibit (one of the largest in the world), and a nature trail full of lush tropical flowers, ducks, and tortoises. Daily feedings take place at most exhibits. ⊠ *Coki Point, north of Rte. 38, Estate Frydendal* ☎ *340/775–1555* ⊕ *www.coral worldvi.com* ✆ *$21, Sea Lion Splash $106, Sea Trek $79, Shark Encounter $53* ☉ *Daily 9–5.*

ST. THOMAS BEST BETS

■ **Coral World Ocean Park.** This aquarium attraction is a great bet for families, and it's on one of best snorkeling beaches.

■ **Magen's Bay Beach.** St. Thomas has one of the most picture-postcard perfect beaches you'll ever see. It's great for swimming.

■ **St. John.** It's easy to hop on the ferry to St. John for a day of hiking, then relax for an hour or two on the beach afterward.

■ **Shopping.** Charlotte Amalie is one of the best places in the Caribbean to shop.

↻ **Drake's Seat.** Sir Francis Drake is supposed to have kept watch over his fleet and looked for enemy ships from this vantage point. The panorama is especially breathtaking (and romantic) at dusk, and if you arrive late in the day you can miss the hordes of day-trippers on taxi tours who stop here to take a picture and buy a T-shirt from one of the many vendors. ⊠ *Rte. 40, Estate Zufriedenheit.*

↻ **Paradise Point Tramway.** Fly skyward in a gondola to Paradise Point, an
★ overlook with breathtaking views of Charlotte Amalie and the harbor. There are several shops, a bar, a restaurant, and a wedding gazebo; kids enjoy the tropical bird show held daily at 10:30 AM, 1:30 PM, and 3:30 PM. A ¼-mi (½-km) hiking trail leads to spectacular views of St. Croix. Wear sturdy shoes, as the trail is steep and rocky. ⊠ *Rte. 30, across from Havensight Mall, Havensight,* ☎ *340/774–9809* ⊕ *www. paradisepointtramway.com* ✆ *$21; Sky Jump $30* ☉ *Thurs.–Tues. 9–5, Wed. 9–9.*

SHOPPING

The prime shopping area in **Charlotte Amalie** is between Post Office and Market squares; it consists of two parallel streets that run east–west (Waterfront Highway and Main Street) and the alleyways that connect them. Particularly attractive are the historic **A.H. Riise Alley, Royal Dane Mall, Palm Passage,** and pastel-painted **International Plaza. Vendors Plaza,** on the waterfront side of the Emancipation Garden in Charlotte Amalie, is a central location for vendors selling handmade earrings, necklaces, and bracelets; straw baskets and handbags; T-shirts; fabrics; African artifacts; and local fruits. Look for the many brightly colored umbrellas.

Havensight Mall, next to the cruise-ship dock, may not be as charming as downtown Charlotte Amalie, but it does have more than 60 shops. It also has an excellent bookstore, a bank, a pharmacy, a gourmet grocery, and smaller branches of many downtown stores. The shops at **Port of \$ale,** adjoining Havensight Mall (its buildings are pink instead of brown), sell discount goods. Next door to Port of \$ale is the **Yacht Haven Grande** complex, with many upscale shops.

East of Charlotte Amalie on Route 38, **Tillett Gardens** is an oasis of artistic endeavor across from the Tutu Park Shopping Mall. The late Jim and Rhoda Tillett converted this Danish farm into an artists' retreat in 1959. Today you can watch artisans produce silk-screen fabrics, candles, watercolors, jewelry, and other handicrafts. Something special is often happening in the gardens as well: the Classics in the Gardens program is a classical music series presented under the stars, Arts Alive is an annual arts-and-crafts fair held in November, and the Pistarckle Theater holds its performances here.

ACTIVITIES

DIVING AND SNORKELING

🅒 **Coki Beach Dive Club** (✉ *Rte. 388, at Coki Point, Estate Frydendal* ☎ *340/775–4220* ⊕ *www.cokidive.com*) is a PADI Gold Palm outfit run by avid diver Peter Jackson. Snorkel and dive tours in the fish-filled reefs off Coki Beach are available, as are classes from beginner to underwater photography. **Snuba of St. Thomas** (✉ *Rte. 388, at Coki Point, Estate Smith Bay* ☎ *340/693–8063* ⊕ *www.visnuba.com*) offers something for nondivers, a cross between snorkeling and scuba diving: a 20-foot air hose connects you to the surface. The cost is \$68. Children must be eight or older to participate.

FISHING

Fishing here is synonymous with blue marlin angling. If you're not into marlin fishing, try hooking sailfish in the winter, dolphinfish come spring, and wahoo in the fall. To really find the trip that will best suit you, walk down the docks at either American Yacht Harbor or Sapphire Beach Marina in the late afternoon and chat with the captains and crews. The **Charter Boat Center** (✉ *6300 Red Hook Plaza, Red Hook* ☎ *340/775–7990* ⊕ *www.charterboat.vi*) is a major source for sportfishing charters, both marlin and inshore. For inshore trips, **Peanut Gallery Charters** (✉ *Crown Bay Marina, Rte. 304, Estate Contant* ☎ *340/775–5274* ⊕ *www.fishingstthomas.com*) offers trips on its 18-foot *Dauntless* or 28-foot custom sportfishing catamaran.

GOLF

★ The **Mahogany Run Golf Course** (✉ *Rte. 42, Estate Lovenlund* ☎ *340/777–6006 or 800/253–7103* ⊕ *www.mahoganyrungolf.com*) attracts golfers for its spectacular view of the British Virgin Islands and the challenging 3-hole Devil's Triangle. At this Tom and George Fazio–designed, par-70, 18-hole course, there's a fully stocked pro shop, snack bar, and open-air clubhouse. Greens and half-cart fees for 18 holes are \$150. The course is open daily, and there are frequently informal weekend tournaments. It's the only course on St. Thomas.

BEACHES

All beaches in the USVI are public, but occasionally you'll need to stroll *Fodor'sChoice* through a resort to reach the sand. **Coki Beach** (⊠*Rte. 388, next to Coral* ★ *World Ocean Park*) is the best place on the island to snorkel and scuba ☾ dive. Fish, including grunts, snappers, and wrasses, are like an effervescent cloud you can wave your hand through. Ashore you can find conveniences like restrooms, changing facilities, mask and fin rentals, *Fodor'sChoice* and even fish food. **Magens Bay** (⊠*Rte. 35, at end of road on north side* ★ *of island*) is considered one of the most beautiful beaches in the world. ☾ The bottom of the bay is flat and sandy, so this is a place for sunning and swimming rather than snorkeling. There's a bar, snack shack, and beachwear boutique; bathhouses with restrooms, changing rooms, and saltwater showers are close by. There's entrance fee of $4 per person, ★ $2 per vehicle; children under age 12 are free. **Morningstar Beach** (⊠*Rte. 315, 2 mi [3 km] southeast of Charlotte Amalie, past Havensight Mall and cruise-ship dock*), between Marriott Frenchman's Reef and Morning Star Beach Resorts, has a concession that rents floating mats, snorkeling equipment, sailboards, and Jet Skis. Swimming is excellent; there ★ are good-size rolling waves year-round, but do watch the undertow. **Sapphire Beach** (⊠*Rte. 315, 2 mi [3 km] southeast of Charlotte Amalie, past Havensight Mall and cruise-ship dock*) gets steady breezes, making it a boardsailor's paradise. The swimming is great, as is the snorkeling, especially at the reef near Pettyklip Point. There's also a restaurant, bar, and water-sports rentals at Sapphire Beach Resort and Marina.

WHERE TO EAT

$$–$$$ ╳**Cuzzin's Caribbean Restaurant and Bar.** This is the place to sample bona CARIBBEAN   fide Virgin Islands cuisine. For lunch, order tender slivers of conch stewed in a rich onion and butter sauce, savory braised oxtail, or curried chicken. At dinner the island-style mutton, served in thick gravy and seasoned with locally grown herbs, offers a tasty treat that's deliciously different. Side dishes include peas and rice, boiled green bananas, fried plantains, and potato stuffing. In a 19th-century livery stable on Back Street, this restaurant is hard to find but well worth it if you like sampling local foods. ⊠*7 Wimmelskafts Gade, also called Back St.* ☎*340/777–4711* ▤*AE, MC, V.*

$$ ╳**Gladys' Cafe.** Even if the local specialties—conch in butter sauce, salt CARIBBEAN   fish and dumplings, hearty red bean soup—didn't make this a recom- *Fodor'sChoice* mended café, it would be worth coming for Gladys's smile. Her cozy ★ alleyway restaurant is rich in atmosphere with its mahogany bar and native stone walls, making dining a double delight. While you're here, pick up a $5 or $10 bottle of her special hot sauce. There are mustard-, oil and vinegar–, and tomato-based versions; the tomato-based sauce is the hottest. ⊠*Waterfront, at Royal Dane Mall* ⌂*28 Dronningens Gade, Charlotte Amalie* ☎*340/774–6604* ▤*AE* ☾*No dinner.*

ST. VINCENT (KINGSTOWN)

Jane E. Zarem   You won't find glitzy resorts or flashy discos in St. Vincent. Rather, you'll be fascinated by picturesque villages, secluded beaches, and fine sailing waters. St. Vincent is the largest and northernmost island in the Grenadines archipelago; Kingstown, the capital city of St. Vincent and the Grenadines, is the government and business center and major port. Except for one barren area on the island's northeast coast—remnants of the 1979 eruption of La Soufrière, one of the last active volcanoes in the Caribbean—the countryside is mountainous, lush, and green. St. Vincent's mountains and forests thwarted European settlement for many years. As colonization advanced elsewhere in the Caribbean, in fact, the island became a refuge for Carib Indians—descendants of whom still live in northeastern St. Vincent. After years of fighting and back-and-forth territorial claims, British troops prevailed by overpowering the French and banishing Carib warriors to Central America. Independent since 1979, St. Vincent and the Grenadines remains a member of the British Commonwealth.

ESSENTIALS

Currency Eastern Caribbean (E.C.) dollar (EC$2.67 to US$1). U.S. dollars are generally accepted, but change is given in E.C. dollars.

Internet E@gles Internet Cafe (⊠ *Halifax St., opposite the General Post Office, Kingstown, St. Vincent*).

Telephones Pay phones are readily available and best operated with the prepaid phone cards that are sold at many stores and can be used on many Caribbean islands. Telephone services are available at the Cruise Ship Complex in Kingstown. For an international operator, dial 115; to charge your call to a credit card, call 117.

COMING ASHORE

The Cruise Ship Complex at Kingstown, St. Vincent's capital city, accommodates two cruise ships; additional vessels anchor outside the harbor and bring passengers to the jetty by launch. The facility has about two-dozen shops that sell duty-free items and handicrafts. There's a communications center, post office, tourist information desk, restaurant, and food court.

Buses and taxis are available at the wharf. Taxi drivers are well equipped to take you on an island tour; expect to pay $25 per hour for up to four passengers. The ferry to Bequia (one hour each way) is at the adjacent pier. Renting a car for just one day isn't advisable, since car rentals are expensive (at least $55 per day) and require a $20 temporary driving permit on top of that. It's almost always more financially favorable to take a tour, though you don't have to limit yourself to those offered by your ship.

EXPLORING ST. VINCENT

🕐 **Botanic Gardens.** A few minutes north of Kingstown by taxi is St.
★ Vincent's famous Botanic Gardens. Founded in 1765, it's the oldest
botanical garden in the western hemisphere. Captain Bligh—of *Bounty*
fame—brought the first breadfruit tree to this island for landowners
to propagate. The prolific bounty of the breadfruit tree was used to
feed the slaves. You can see a direct descendant of this original tree
among the specimen mahogany, rubber, teak, and other tropical trees
and shrubs in the 20 acres of gardens. Two dozen rare St. Vincent parrots, confiscated from illegal collectors, live in the small aviary. Guides
explain all the medicinal and ornamental trees and shrubs; they also
appreciate a tip at the end of the tour. ✉ *Off Leeward Hwy., Montrose*
☎ 784/457–1003 💲$3 🕐 *Daily 6–6.*

★ **Falls of Baleine.** The falls are impossible to reach by car, so book an
escorted, all-day boat trip from Villa Beach or the Lagoon Marina. The
boat ride along the coast offers scenic island views. When you arrive,
you have to wade through shallow water to get to the beach. Then local
guides help you make the easy five-minute trek to the 60-foot falls and
the rock-enclosed freshwater pool the falls create—plan to take a dip.

🕐 **Fort Charlotte.** Started by the French in 1786 and completed by the Brit-
★ ish in 1806, the fort was named for King George III's wife. It sits on
Berkshire Hill, a dramatic promontory 2 mi (3 km) north of Kingstown
and 636 feet above sea level, with a stunning view of the capital city and
the Grenadines. Interestingly, cannons face inward—the fear of attack
by the French and their native allies was far greater than any threat
approaching from the sea, though, truth be told, the fort saw no action.
Nowadays the fort serves as a signal station for ships; its ancient cells
house historical paintings of the island by Lindsay Prescott.

Kingstown. The capital city of St. Vincent and the Grenadines is on the
island's southwestern coast. The town of 13,500 residents wraps around
Kingstown Bay; a ring of green hills and ridges, studded with homes,
forms a backdrop for the city. This is very much a working city, with
a busy harbor and few concessions to tourists. Kingstown Harbour is
the only deepwater port on the island.

A few gift shops can be found on and around **Bay Street,** near the harbor. Upper Bay Street, which stretches along the bay front, bustles with
daytime activity—workers going about their business and housewives
doing their shopping. Many of Kingstown's downtown buildings are
built of stone or brick brought to the island in the holds of 18th-century
ships as ballast (and replaced with sugar and spices for the return trip to
Europe). The Georgian-style stone arches and second-floor overhangs
on former warehouses create shelter from midday sun and the brief,
cooling showers common to the tropics.

Grenadines Wharf, at the south end of Bay Street, is busy with schooners loading supplies and ferries loading people bound for the Grenadines. The **cruise-ship complex,** south of the commercial wharf, has a
mall with a dozen or more shops, plus restaurants, a post office, communications facilities, and a taxi-minibus stand.

St. Vincent

St. Vincent Passage

Porter Pt.

Baleine Bay

Fancy

Commantawana Bay

Falls of Baleine

Owia

Owia Salt Pond

Espagnol Pt.

Sandy Bay

La Soufriére

Crater Lake

Larikai Bay

Caribbean Sea

Overland Village

Richmond

Richmond Peak

ATLANTIC OCEAN

Petit Bordel Bay

Chateaubelair Bay

Chateaubelair

Leeward Hwy.

Dark Head

Troumaka

Georgetown

Cumberland Bay

Grand Bonum

Wallilabou Bay

Barrouallie

Colonarie River

Colonarie

Peter's Hope

Sans Souci

Colonarie Bay

Leeward Hwy.

Greiggs

Mt. St. Andrew

Layou

Biabou

Buccament Bay

Questelle's Bay

Montreal Gardens

Mesopotamia

Grant's Bay

Botanical Garden

Yambou River

Anchor Reef, New Guinea Reef, The Forest

Kingstown

Ft. Charlotte

Kingstown Bay

Argyle Beach

E.T. Joshua Airport

Indian Bay

Vigie Hwy.

Argyle

Villa Beach

Villa

Calliaqua

Stubbs Bay

Young Island

Milligan Cay

Calliaqua Bay

St. Vincent
Bequia

The
Grenadines

0   2 miles
0   2 km

TO BEQUIA

An almost infinite selection of produce fills the **Kingstown Produce Market,** a three-story building that takes up a whole city block on Upper Bay, Hillsboro, and Bedford streets in the center of town. It's noisy, colorful, and open Monday through Saturday—but the busiest times (and the best times to go) are Friday and Saturday mornings. In the courtyard, vendors sell local arts and crafts. On the upper floors merchants sell clothing, household items, gifts, and other products.

St. George's Cathedral, on Grenville Street, is a pristine, creamy yellow Anglican church built in 1820. The dignified Georgian architecture includes simple wooden pews, an ornate chandelier, and beautiful stained-glass windows; one was a gift from Queen Victoria, who actually commissioned it for London's St. Paul's Cathedral in honor of her first grandson. When the artist created an angel with a red robe, she was horrified and sent it abroad. The markers in the cathedral's graveyard recount the history of the island. Across the street is **St. Mary's Cathedral of the Assumption** (Roman Catholic), built in stages beginning in 1823. The strangely appealing design is a blend of Moorish, Georgian, and Romanesque styles applied to black brick. Nearby, freed slaves built the **Kingstown Methodist Church** in 1841. The exterior is brick, simply decorated with quoins (solid blocks that form the corners), and the roof is held together by metal straps, bolts, and wooden pins. **Scots Kirk** (1839–80) was built by and for Scottish settlers but became a Seventh-Day Adventist church in 1952.

La Soufrière. The volcano, which last erupted in 1979, is 4,000 feet high and so huge in area that it covers virtually the entire northern third of the island. The eastern trail to the rim of the crater, a two-hour ascent, begins at Rabacca Dry River.

★ **Montreal Gardens.** Welsh-born landscape designer Timothy Vaughn renovated 7.5 acres of neglected commercial flower beds and a falling-down plantation house into a stunning yet informal garden spot. Anthurium, ginger lilies, birds of paradise, and other tropical flowers are planted in raised beds; tree ferns create a canopy of shade along the walkways. The gardens are in the shadow of majestic Grand Bonhomme Mountain, deep in the Mesopotamia Valley, about 12 mi (19 km) from Kingstown. ✉*Montreal St., Mesopotamia* ☎*784/458–1198* 💲*$3* ☉*Dec.–Aug., weekdays 9–4.*

ST. VINCENT BEST BETS

■ **Island Tour.** Tour the greater Kingstown area, then travel up the leeward coast to Wallilabou.

■ **Falls of Baleine.** An all-day boat trip to the 60-foot falls is a beautiful way to spend a day.

■ **Ferry to Bequia.** Laid-back Bequia is one hour by ferry from St. Vincent.

■ **Hiking.** Whether you hike in the rain forest or do the more difficult climb of La Soufrière, it's worth exploring some of the island's rugged terrain.

■ **Tobago Cays.** These uninhabited islands are the top destination for snorkeling.

4

☙ **Wallilabou Bay.** The *Pirates of the Caribbean* left its mark at Wallilabou (pronounced wally-la-*boo*), a location used for filming the recent movies. Many of the buildings and docks built as stage sets remain, giving the pretty bay an intriguingly historic appearance. You can sunbathe, swim, picnic, or buy your lunch at Wallilabou Anchorage. This is a favorite stop for day-trippers returning from the Falls of Baleine and boaters anchoring for the evening. Nearby there's a river with a small waterfall where you can take a freshwater plunge.

SHOPPING

The 12 blocks that hug the waterfront in **downtown Kingstown** comprise St. Vincent's main shopping district. Among the shops that sell goods to fulfill household needs are a few that sell local crafts, gifts, and souvenirs. Bargaining is neither expected nor appreciated. The **Cruise Ship Complex,** on the waterfront in Kingstown, has a collection of a dozen or so boutiques, shops, and restaurants that cater primarily to cruise-ship passengers but welcome all shoppers. St. Vincent is not a major duty-free shopping port, but you will find a few duty-free shops.

Nzimbu Browne (⊠ *McKie's Hill, Kingstown* ☎ 784/457–1677) is a self-taught Vincentian craftsman, artist, musician, and drum maker. He is best known for his original banana art, which he creates from dried banana leaves, carefully selecting and snipping varicolored bits and arranging them on pieces of wood to depict local scenes. Prices range from $15 or $20 for smaller items to several thousands of dollars for larger works sold in galleries. Browne has a kiosk in front of his home but often sets up shop on Bay Street, near the Cobblestone Inn. **St. Vincent Craftsmen's Centre** (⊠ *Frenches St., Kingstown* ☎ 784/457–2516), three blocks from the wharf, sells locally made grass floor mats, place mats, and other straw articles, as well as batik cloth, handmade West Indian dolls, hand-painted calabashes, and framed artwork. No credit cards are accepted. On the leeward coast about a half-hour's drive north of Kingstown, **Wallilabou Craft Centre** (⊠ *Leeward Highway, Wallilabou* ☎ 784/456–0078) was established in 1986 as a local cooperative, where villagers can learn various techniques for weaving straw and other natural fibers. Workers create baskets, handbags, hats, toys, and other items that are sold in the Kingstown market and make good souvenirs of a visit to St. Vincent.

ACTIVITIES

DIVING AND SNORKELING

Novices and advanced divers alike will be impressed by the marine life in the waters surrounding St. Vincent and the Grenadines—brilliant sponges, huge deepwater coral trees, and shallow reefs teeming with colorful fish. The best dive spots on St. Vincent are in the small bays along the coast between Kingstown and Layou; many are within 20 yards of shore and only 20 feet to 30 feet down.

Anchor Reef has excellent visibility for viewing a deep-black coral garden, schools of squid, seahorses, and maybe a small octopus. The **Forest,**

a shallow dive, is still dramatic, with soft corals in pastel colors and schools of small fish. **New Guinea Reef** slopes to 90 feet (28 meters) and can't be matched for its quantity of corals and sponges. The pristine waters surrounding the **Tobago Cays,** in the Southern Grenadines, will give you a world-class diving experience.

Dive Fantasea (⊠ *Villa Beach* ☎ *784/457–5560 or 784/457–5577*) offers dive and snorkeling trips to the St. Vincent coast and the Tobago Cays. **Dive St. Vincent** (⊠ *Young Island Dock, Villa Beach* ☎ *784/457–4714 or 784/547–4928* ⊕ *www.divestvincent.com*) is where NAUI- and PADI-certified instructor Bill Tewes and his staff offer beginner and certification courses and dive trips to the St. Vincent coast and the southern Grenadines.

FISHING

From Villa Beach or Indian Bay on St. Vincent, you can go on a full-day fishing trip or boat ride around the Grenadines for about $120–$140 per person, including all equipment and lunch. **Crystal Blue Charters** (⊠ *Indian Bay* ☎ *784/457–4532*) offers sportfishing charters on a 34-foot pirogue for both amateur and serious fishermen.

BEACHES

St. Vincent's origin is volcanic, so its beaches range in color from golden-brown to black. Swimming is recommended only in the lagoons and bays along the leeward coast. By contrast, beaches on Bequia and the rest of the Grenadines have pure white sand, palm trees, and crystal clear aquamarine water; some are even within walking distance of the jetty.

Indian Bay. South of Kingstown and just north of Villa Beach, this beach has golden sand but is slightly rocky; it's good for snorkeling.

Questelle's Bay. This beach (pronounced keet-*ells*), north of Kingstown and next to Campden Park, has a black-sand beach.

Villa Beach. The long stretch of sand in front of the row of hotels and restaurants along the Young Island Channel varies from 20–25 feet wide to practically nonexistent. The broadest, sandiest part is in front of Beachcombers Hotel, which is also the perfect spot for sunbathers to get lunch and liquid refreshments.

WHERE TO EAT

$ ✕**Beachcombers.** This friendly, laid-back restaurant and bar, which is
CARIBBEAN   perched above the best stretch of Villa Beach, welcomes cruise-ship passengers who want to spend a day swimming and sunbathing. The open-air deck with a view of Young Island, Bequia, and the sea beyond is the perfect place for lunch and liquid refreshments. Enjoy fresh seafood, salads, sandwiches, and more—washed down with a refreshing Hairoun beer, fruit punch, or tropical rum drink. ⊠ *Villa Beach* ☎ *784/458–4283* ⊟ *AE, D, MC, V.*

$–$$ ✕**Cobblestone Roof-Top Bar and Restaurant.** To reach what is perhaps the
CARIBBEAN   most pleasant, breeziest, and satisfying breakfast and luncheon spot in downtown Kingstown, diners must climb the equivalent of three flights of interior stone steps within the historic Cobblestone Inn. But getting

to the open-air roof-top restaurant is half the fun, as en route diners get an up close view of the 19th-century sugar (and later arrowroot) Georgian warehouse that is now a very appealing boutique inn. A full breakfast menu is available to hotel guests and the public alike. The luncheon menu ranges from homemade soups, salads (tuna, chicken, fruit, or tossed), sandwiches, or burgers and fries to full meals of roast beef, stewed chicken, or grilled fish served with rice, plantains, macaroni pie, and fresh local vegetables. Dee-licious! ⊠ *Upper Bay St., Kingstown* ☎ *784/456–1937* ⊟ *AE, D, MC, V* ⊘ *No dinner.*

SAN JUAN, PUERTO RICO

Mark Sullivan   Although Puerto Rico is a commonwealth of the United States, few cities in the Caribbean are as steeped in Spanish tradition as San Juan. Within a seven-square-block area in Old San Juan are restored 16th-century buildings, museums, art galleries, bookstores, and 200-year-old houses with balustraded balconies overlooking narrow, cobblestone streets. In contrast, San Juan's sophisticated Condado and Isla Verde areas have glittering hotels, fancy boutiques, casinos, and discos. Out in the countryside is 28,000-acre El Yunque National Forest, a rain forest with more than 240 species of trees growing at least 100 feet high. You can stretch your sea legs on dramatic mountain ranges, numerous trails, in vast caves, at coffee plantations, old sugar mills, and hundreds of beaches. No wonder San Juan is one of the busiest ports of call in the Caribbean. Like any other big city, San Juan has its share of petty crime, so guard your wallet or purse, especially in crowded markets and squares.

ESSENTIALS

Currency The U.S. dollar is the official currency of Puerto Rico.

Internet You can check your e-mail at **Cyber Net** (⊠ *1128 Av. Ashford, Condado* ☎ *787/724–4033* ⊠ *5980 Av. Isla Verde, Isla Verde* ☎ *787/728–4195*).

Telephones Calling the United States from Puerto Rico is the same as calling within the United States. You can use the long-distance telephone service office in the cruise-ship terminal, or you can use your calling card by dialing the toll-free access number of your long-distance provider from any pay phone. You'll find a phone center by the Paseo de la Princesa.

COMING ASHORE

Most cruise ships dock within a couple of blocks of Old San Juan; however, there is a second cruise pier across the bay, and if your ship docks there you'll need to take a taxi to get anywhere on the island. The Paseo de la Princesa, a tree-lined promenade beneath the city wall, is a nice place for a stroll—you can admire the local crafts and stop at the refreshment kiosks. A tourist information booth is in the cruise-terminal area. Major sights in the Old San Juan area are mere blocks from the piers, but be aware that the streets are narrow and steeply inclined in places.

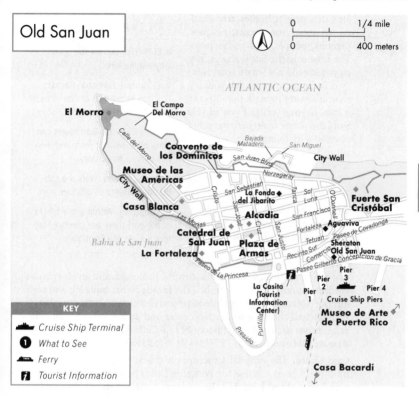

Old San Juan

0   1/4 mile
0   400 meters

ATLANTIC OCEAN

El Morro

El Campo Del Morro

Calle del Morro

Convento de los Dominicos

Museo de las Américas

City Wall

Casa Blanca

Las Monjas

Bajada Matadero

San Juan Blvd

San Miguel

City Wall

Norzagaray

La Fonda del Jibarito

Alcadia

San Sebastián

Sol

Luna

O'Donnell

Fuerte San Cristóbal

Cristo

San José

Cruz

San Justo

San Francisco

Fortaleza

Tetuan

Aguaviva

Paseo de Covadonga

Catedral de San Juan

Bahía de San Juan

La Fortaleza

Plaza de Armas

Recinto Sur

Comercio

Sheraton Old San Juan

Concepción de Gracia

Paseo de La Princesa

Paseo Gilberto

La Casita (Tourist Information Center)

Pier 1

Pier 2

Pier 3

Pier 4

Cruise Ship Piers

Museo de Arte de Puerto Rico

Puntilla

Presidio

Casa Bacardí

KEY

🚢 Cruise Ship Terminal
❶ What to See
⛴ Ferry
ℹ️ Tourist Information

4

It's particularly easy to get to Cataño and the Bacardí Rum Plant on your own; take the ferry (50¢) that leaves from the cruise piers every half hour and then a taxi from the other side. Taxis, which line up to meet ships, are the best option if you want to explore the city itself. White taxis labeled TAXI TURISTICO charge set fares of $10 to $19. Metered cabs authorized by the Public Service Commission charge an initial $1; after that, it's about 10¢ for each additional 1/13mi. If you take a metered taxi, insist that the meter be turned on, and pay only what is shown, plus a tip of 10% to 15%. You can negotiate with taxi drivers for specific trips, and you can hire a taxi for as little as $30 per hour for sightseeing tours. If you want to see more of the island but don't want to drive, then you may want to consider a shore excursion, though almost all trips can be booked more cheaply with local tour operators.

EXPLORING SAN JUAN

Old San Juan, the original city founded in 1521, contains authentic and carefully preserved examples of 16th- and 17th-century Spanish-colonial architecture. Graceful wrought-iron balconies decorated with lush hanging plants extend over narrow, cobblestone streets. Seven-teenth-century walls still partially enclose the old city. Designated a U.S. National Historic Zone in 1950, it is packed with shops, open-air cafés, private homes, tree-shaded squares, monuments, plaques, pigeons, people, and traffic jams. The area is particularly accesssible, so you should not waste your money on an expensive guided walking tour. It's faster to walk than to take a cab. If your feet fail you in Old San Juan (some streets are steep and covered with uneven cobblestones), climb aboard the free open-air trolleys. Take one from the stop across from Pier 4 or board anywhere along the route.

OLD SAN JUAN

Alcaldía. San Juan's city hall was built between 1604 and 1789. In 1841 extensive alterations were made so that it would resemble the city hall in Madrid, with arcades, towers, balconies, and an inner courtyard. Renovations have refreshed the facade of the building and some interior rooms, but the architecture remains true to its colonial style. A municipal tourist information center and an art gallery with rotating exhibits are on the first floor. ⊠ *153 Calle San Francisco, Plaza de Armas, Old San Juan* ☎*787/724–7171* ▢*Free* ◷ *Weekdays 8–4.*

Casa Blanca. The original structure on this site was a wooden house built in 1521 as a home for Ponce de León; he died in Cuba without ever having lived here. His descendants occupied its sturdier replacement, a lovely colonial mansion with tile floors and beam ceilings, for the next 250 years. A guide will show you around, and then you can explore on your own. The lush garden, recently reopened to the public, is a quiet place to unwind. ⊠ *1 Calle San Sebastián, Old San Juan* ☎*787/725–1454* ⊕*www.icp.gobierno.pr* ▢*$3* ◷ *Tues.–Sat. 9–noon and 1–4.*

Catedral de San Juan Bautista. The Catholic shrine of Puerto Rico had humble beginnings in the early 1520s as a thatch-top, wooden structure. Hurricane winds tore off the thatch and destroyed the church. It was reconstructed in 1540, when it was given a graceful circular staircase and vaulted Gothic ceilings. Most of the work on the present cathedral, however, was done in the 19th century. The remains of Ponce de León are in a marble tomb near the transept. ⊠ *151 Calle Cristo, Old San Juan* ☎*787/722–0861* ⊕*www.catedralsanjuan.com* ▢*$1 donation suggested* ◷ *Mon.–Sat. 8–5, Sun. 8–2:30.*

Convento de los Dominicos. Built by Dominican friars in 1523, this convent often served as a shelter during Carib Indian attacks and, more recently, as headquarters for the Antilles command of the U.S. Army. Now home to some offices of the Institute of Puerto Rican Culture, the beautifully restored building contains religious manuscripts, artifacts, and art. The institute also maintains a book and music shop on

SAN JUAN BEST BETS

■ **El Morro.** Explore the giant labyrinthine fort.

■ **El Yunque National Forest.** This rain forest east of San Juan is a great half-day excursion.

■ **Casa Bacardí.** Rum lovers can jump on the public ferry and then taxi over to the factory.

■ **Old San Juan.** Walk the cobblestone streets of Old San Juan.

■ **Shopping.** Within a few blocks of the port there are plenty of factory outlets and boutiques.

the premises. Classical concerts are held here occasionally. ✉ *98 Calle Norzagaray, Old San Juan* ☎ *787/721–6866* ⊕ *www.icp.gobierno.pr* 🖘 *Free $3* ☉ *Mon.–Sat. 9–5, Sun. 10:30–6.*

☉ **Fuerte San Cristóbal.** This stone fortress, built between 1634 and 1785, guarded the city from land attacks. Even larger than El Morro, San Cristóbal was known in the 17th and 18th centuries as the Gibraltar of the West Indies. ✉ *Calle Norzagaray at Calle Muñoz Rivera, Old San Juan* ☎ *787/729–6960* ⊕ *www.nps.gov/saju* 🖘 *$3; $5 includes admission to El Morro* ☉ *June–Nov., daily 9–5; Dec.–May, daily 9–6.*

☉ **Fuerte San Felipe del Morro.** On a rocky promontory at the northwestern Fodor'sChoice tip of the Old City is El Morro (which translates as "the promontory"), ★ a fortress built by the Spaniards between 1540 and 1783. Rising 140 feet above the sea, the massive six-level fortress covers enough territory to accommodate a 9-hole golf course. It is a labyrinth of dungeons, ramps, barracks, turrets, towers, and tunnels. Built to protect the port, El Morro has a commanding view of the harbor. You're free to wander throughout. Tours and a video are available in English. ✉ *Calle del Morro, Old San Juan* ☎ *787/729–6960* ⊕ *www.nps.gov/saju* 🖘 *$3; $5 includes admission to Fuerte San Cristóbal* ☉ *June–Nov., daily 9–5; Dec.–May, daily 9–6.*

★ **La Fortaleza.** Sitting on a hill overlooking the harbor, La Fortaleza was built as a fortress in 1533. Not a very good fortress, mind you. It was attacked numerous times and taken twice, by the British in 1598 and by the Dutch in 1625. When the city's other fortifications were finished, La Fortaleza was transformed into a palace. Guided tours of the extensive gardens and the circular dungeon are conducted on the hour in English, on the half hour in Spanish; both include a short video presentation. ✉ *Calle Recinto Oeste, Old San Juan* ☎ *787/721–7000* ⊕ *www.fortaleza. gobierno.pr* 🖘 *Free* ☉ *Weekdays 9–5.*

Museo de las Américas. On the second floor of the imposing former military barracks, Cuartel de Ballajá, the museum's permanent exhibit, "Las Artes Populares en las Américas," focusing on the popular and folk art of Latin America, contains religious figures, musical instruments, basketwork, costumes, and farming and other implements. ✉ *Calle Norzagaray at Calle del Morro, Old San Juan* ☎ *787/724–5052* ⊕ *www. museolasamericas.org* 🖘 *Free* ☉ *Tues.–Sun. 10–4.*

ELSEWHERE IN SAN JUAN

Casa Bacardí Visitor Center. Exiled from Cuba, the Bacardí family built a small distillery here in the 1950s. Today it's one of the world's largest, with the capacity to produce 100,000 gallons of spirits a day and 221 million cases a year. You can hop on a little tram to take a 45-minute tour of the bottling plant, distillery, and museum. Yes, you'll be given a free sample. If you don't want to drive, you can reach the factory by taking the ferry from Pier 2 for 50¢ each way and then a *público* (shared van) from the ferry pier to the factory for about $2 or $3 per person. ✉ *Rte. 888, Km 2.6, Cataño* ☎ *787/788–1500 or 787/788–8400* ⊕ *www.casabacardi.org* 🖘 *Free* ☉ *Mon.–Sat. 8:30–5:30, Sun. 10–5. Tours every 15–30 min.*

☾ **Museo de Arte de Puerto Rico.** One of the biggest museums in the Carib-
FodorsChoice bean, this 130,000-square-foot building was once San Juan Munici-
★ pal Hospital. The collection starts with works from the colonial era,
most of them commissioned for churches. Here you'll find works by
José Campeche, the island's first great painter. Also well represented
is Francisco Oller y Cestero, who was the first to move beyond religious subjects to paint local scenes. ✉*299 Av. José De Diego, San-
turce* ☎*787/977–6277* ⊕*www.mapr.org* ✉*$6* ☾*Tues.–Sat. 10–4,
Sun. noon–4.*

SHOPPING

San Juan is not a duty-free port, so you won't find bargains on electronics and perfumes. However, shopping for native crafts can be fun.
Popular souvenirs and gifts include *santos* (small, hand-carved figures
of saints or religious scenes), hand-rolled cigars, handmade lace, and
carnival masks.

★ **Mi Pequeño San Juan** (✉*107 Calle Cristo, Old San Juan* ☎*787/977–1636*)
specializes in tiny versions of the doorways of San Juan. These ceramics,
all done by hand right in the shop, are a wonderful souvenir of your
stay. You might even find the hotel where you stayed reproduced in plaster. **Nono Maldonado** (✉*1112 Av. Ashford, Condado* ☎*787/721–0456*)
is well known for his high-end, elegant linen designs. He should know
a thing or two about style—he worked for many years as the fashion
editor of *Esquire.*

ACTIVITIES

GOLF

Though there are no courses in San Juan proper, it's possible to do a
golf outing to one of Puerto Rico's stellar courses as a day trip. The
★ spectacular **Wyndham Rio Mar Beach Resort and Spa** (✉*6000 Río Mar
Bul., Río Grande* ☎*787/888–7060* ⊕*www.wyndhamriomar.com*) has
a clubhouse with a pro shop and two restaurants set between two
18-hole courses. The River Course, designed by Greg Norman, has
challenging fairways that skirt the Mameyes River. The Ocean Course
has slightly wider fairways than its sister; iguanas can usually be spotted sunning themselves near its 4th hole. If you're not a resort guest, be
sure to reserve tee times at least 24 hours in advance.

BEACHES

San Juan does not have the island's best beaches, but anyone can rent
a chair for the day at one of the public entry points.

When people talk of "beautiful Isla Verde beach," they're talking about
★ **Balneario de Carolina.** The long stretch of sand, which runs parallel to
Avenida Los Gobernadores, is shaded by palms and almond trees. East
of Old San Juan, **Playa del Condado** is overshadowed by an unbroken
string of hotels and apartment buildings. Beach bars, water-sports outfitters, and chair-rental places abound. You can access the beach from
several roads off Avenida Ashford, including Calle Cervantes and Calle

Candina. The stretch of sand near Calle Vendig (behind the Atlantic Beach Hotel) is especially popular with the gay community.

NIGHTLIFE

Almost every ship stays in San Juan late or even overnight to give passengers an opportunity to revel in the nightlife—the most sophisticated in the Caribbean.

CASINOS

By law, all casinos are in hotels. The atmosphere is refined, and many patrons dress to the nines, but informal attire (no shorts or tank tops) is usually fine. Casinos set their own hours, which change seasonally, but generally operate from noon to 4 AM, although the casino in the Conrad Condado Plaza Hotel and Casino is open 24 hours. Other hotels with casinos include the InterContinental San Juan Resort and Casino, the Ritz-Carlton San Juan Hotel, Spa and Casino, and the Sheraton Old San Juan Hotel and Casino.

BARS AND DANCE CLUBS

The oceanfront deck bar of the **Atlantic Beach Hotel** (⊠*1 Calle Vendig, Condado, San Juan* ☎*787/721–6100*), which is popular among San Juan's gay community, is famed for its early-evening happy hours, with pulsating tropical music, a wide selection of exotic drinks, and
★ ever-pleasant ocean breezes. **Candela** (⊠*110 San Sebastián, Old San Juan, San Juan* ☎*787/977–4305*), a lounge–art gallery housed in a historic building, hosts some of the most innovative local DJs on the island and often invites star spinners from New York or London. This is the island's best showcase for experimental dance music. At **Liquid** (⊠*San Juan Water and Beach Club, 2 Calle Tartak, Isla Verde* ☎*787/725–4664 or 787/725–4675*), the lobby lounge of San Juan's chicest boutique hotel, glass walls are filled with undulating water, and the fashionable patrons drink wild cocktails to pounding music. With a large dance and stage area and smokin' Afro-Cuban bands, **Rumba** (⊠*152 Calle San Sebastián, Old San Juan* ☎*787/725–4407*) is one of the best parties in town.

WHERE TO EAT

$$$ ✕**El Picoteo.** You could make a meal of the small dishes that dominate
SPANICH the menu at this tapas restaurant. You won't go wrong ordering the sweet sausage in brandy or the turnovers stuffed with lobsters and passing them around the table. If you're not into sharing, there are five different kinds of paella that arrive on huge plates. There's a long, lively bar inside; one dining area overlooks a pleasant courtyard, whereas the other takes in the action along Calle Cristo. ⊠*El Convento Hotel, 100 Calle Cristo, Old San Juan* ☎*787/723–9621* ⊟*AE, D, DC, MC, V.*

$ ✕**La Fonda del Jibarito.** Sanjuaneros have favored this casual, family-
CARIBBEAN run restaurant for years. The conch ceviche and chicken fricassee are among the specialties on the menu of comida criollo dishes. The back porch is filled with plants, and the dining room is filled with fanciful depictions of life on the street outside. The ever-present owner, Pedro

J. Ruiz, is filled with the desire to ensure that everyone is happy. ✉*280 Calle Sol, Old San Juan* ☎*787/725–8375* ⚠*Reservations not accepted* ▤*AE, MC, V.*

SANTO DOMINGO, DOMINICAN REPUBLIC

Eileen Robin-son Smith

Spanish civilization in the New World began in Santo Domingo's 12-block Zona Colonial (Colonial Zone). As you stroll its narrow streets, it's easy to imagine this old city as it was when the likes of Columbus, Cortés, and Ponce de León walked the cobblestones, when pirates sailed in and out of the harbor, and when colonists first started building the New World's largest city. Tourist brochures tout that "history comes alive here"—a surprisingly truthful statement. However, many tourists bypass the large, sprawling, and noisy city; it's their loss. The Dominican Republic's seaside capital—despite such detractions as poverty and sprawl, not to mention a population of some 2 million people—has some of the country's best hotels, restaurants, and nightlife (not to mention great casinos). Many of these are right on or near the Malecón and within the historic Zona Colonial area, which is separated from the rest of the city by Parque Independencia. If your ship calls or even embarks here, you'll be treated to a vibrant Latin cultural center unlike any other in the Caribbean.

ESSENTIALS

Currency The Dominican peso (RD$35 to US$1). Independent merchants willingly accept U.S. dollars, but you may need to change some money. Cambios (money exchange offices) are common, but you'll get the best rates at either a bank or a casino. Banco Popular has ATMS in the Zona Colonial, but you will be able to get only pesos.

Internet Look up, and you will see many Internet cafés on the Conde, usually with second-floor locations. In the Colonial Zone, a convenient place to check your e-mail is **Verizon Comunicaciones** (✉*256 Calle Conde, Zona Colonial* ☎*809/221–4249*), where you can also make phone calls. You will have to pay cash—pesos or dollars.

Telephones From the D.R. you need only dial 1 plus the area code and number to call the U.S. To make a local call, you must now dial 809 plus the seven-digit number. Phone cards, which are sold at gift shops and grocery stores, can give you considerable savings on your calls home. If you have a tri-band GSM phone, it should work on the island.

COMING ASHORE

Santo Domingo has two cruise-ship terminals. The Port of Don Diego is on the Ozuma River, facing the Avenida del Puerto, and across the street are steps that lead up to the main pedestrian shopping street of the Zona Colonial, Calle Conde. A lovely yellow-and-white building, with stained-glass windows and faux gas lights, it now has a small cafeteria, and potted palms soften the cordoned-off lines of passengers waiting to have their tickets checked and go through immigration. Just down the dock is an ATM machine; in front of that is a counter where you

Santo Domingo

(map of Santo Domingo showing Intramuros, Ozama River, Sans Souci, and streets. Labels include:)

Puente Mella
Calle Caracas
Calle Jacinto de la Concha
Calle Ravelo
C. Félix M. Ruiz
González
Av. Mella
G. Cabral
Celesti
Colón o parala
Ozama River
Juan Baptista Vicini
Calle Abreu
Enriquillo
Av. Duarte
Restauración
Calle Emiliano
Alcazar de Colón
San Souci Cruise Terminal
El Museo de la Casas Reales
Don Diego Cruise Terminal
Av. Mella
Calle Juan Pérez
Calle José Reyes
Calle Mercedes
Calle Hostos
Calle Arzobispo Meriño
Calle Isabella Católica
Calle Las Damas
Altagracia
Calle 16 de Agosto
Av. 30 de Marzo
Calle de las
Calle El Conde
C. Arzobispo Nouel
C. 19 de Marzo
Av. Duarte
Av. Bolívar
Calle Palo Hincado
Catedral Santa María la Menor
INTRAMUROS
Av. Independencia
Calle Padre Bellini
Calle Arzobispo Portes
José Gabriel García
Paseo Presidente Bellini
Ozama River
Calle Estrellela
Calle Pino
SANS SOUCI
Av. George Washington
◆ **El Malecón**

0 — 1/4 mile
0 — 400 meters

4

can get cold drinks and snacks. Across from it is a booth offering new self-guided audio tours. Should you want to go to the Malecón or shop in the modern city, $20 an hour is the going rate. Don't rent a car; it's expensive, and traffic and parking are stressful.

The new Sans Souci Terminal opened in spring 2008. Royal Caribbean ships docks here on Sunday. The complex is still a work in progress at this writing, and the shops and other infrastructure are not yet finished. It is diagonally across the river from Don Diego, on Avenida Francisco Alberto Caaman.

Just a few paces in front of the Don Diego cruise terminal is the office of **Audio Guide Dominicana** (⊕*www.jccolonialservice.com*). Tours come in three languages and include information on more than 29 historical points in the Colonial City and seven museums, plus a map and informative booklet. All museum entrances are included as well as a nonalcoholic beverage at Hard Rock Café. The total cost is US$29, and credit cards are accepted. The company will also store luggage and provide airport transfers.

AIRPORT TRANSFERS If you are embarking in Santo Domingo, you should fly into **Las Américas International Airport** (*SDQ* ⊠*Santo Domingo* ☎*809/549–0450*), about 15 mi (24 km) east of downtown. Transportation into the city is strictly by taxi; figure on $40 for a taxi to or from hotels on the Malecón or in the Zona Colonial. You'll be greeted by a melee of hawking taxi drivers and their English-speaking solicitors (who expect to be tipped, as do the freelance porters who will undoubtedly scoop up your luggage). If you are spending a night or two in Santo Domingo before a cruise, you can probably arrange a driver through your hotel, so you'll be met with someone holding a sign with your name (it's worth the extra $10 or so to avoid the hassle). If you're going straight to your cruise ship, consider taking the cruise line's prearranged transfer. When you disembark from your ship, expect long lines at check-in, and be sure to give yourself a full two hours for check-in and security. The government also collects a $10 U.S. departure tax.

SANTO DOMINGO BEST BETS

■ **Zona Colonial.** Santo Domingo's colonial zone is a World Heritage Site and a great place to stroll. It is a trip to the Old World; it is Spain in the 16th century.

■ **Dining.** Some of the D.R.'s best restaurants can be found in the capital. Take advantage of them if you have any extra time to spend here.

■ **Shopping.** The country's best shopping can be found in Santo Domingo. You can go souvenir shopping right on Calle Conde, a pedestrian street that is the main drag of the Zona Colonial.

EXPLORING SANTO DOMINGO

Numbers in the margin correspond to points of interest on the Santo Domingo map.

History buffs will want to spend a day exploring the many "firsts" of our continent. A horse-and-carriage ride throughout the Colonial Zone costs $20 an hour. The steeds are no thoroughbreds, but they clip right along, though any commentary will be in Spanish. You can also negotiate to use them as a taxi, say down to the Malecón. The drivers hang out in front of the Hostal Nicolas de Ovando hotel.

Alcazar de Colón. The castle of Don Diego Colón, built in 1517, has 40-inch-thick coral-limestone walls. The Renaissance-style structure, with its balustrade and double row of arches, has strong Moorish, Gothic, and Isabelline influences. The 22 rooms are furnished in a style to which the viceroy of the island would have been accustomed—right down to the dishes and the viceregal shaving mug. ⊠ *Plaza de España off Calle Emiliano Tejera at foot of Calle Las Damas, Zona Colonial* ☎ *809/682–4750* ⊡ *RD$60* ⊙ *Mon. and Tues.–Sat. 9–5, Sun. 9–4. Closed if no cruise ship in port.*

★ **Calle Las Damas.** The Street of the Ladies was named after the elegant ladies of the court who, in the Spanish tradition, promenaded in the evening. Here you can see a sundial dating from 1753 and the Casa de los Jesuitas, which houses a fine research library for colonial history as well as the **Institute for Hispanic Culture;** admission is free, and it's open weekdays from 8 to 4:30. If you follow the street going toward the Malecón, you will pass a picturesque alley fronted by a wrought-iron gate that has perfectly maintained colonial structures that are owned by the Catholic Church.

Catedral Santa María la Menor. The coral-limestone facade of the first cathedral in the New World towers over the south side of the Parque Colón. Spanish workmen began building the cathedral in 1514, but left to search for gold in Mexico. The church was finally finished in 1540. Its facade is composed of architectural elements from the late Gothic to the lavish Plateresque style. Inside, the high altar is made of hammered silver. At this writing, a museum was being built for the cathedral's treasures. ⊠ *Calle Arzobispo Meriño, Zona Colonial* ☎ *809/689–1920* 🖃 *Free* ⊙ *Mon.–Sat. 9–4; Sun. masses begin at 6 AM.*

El Malecón. Avenida George Washington, better known as the Malecón, runs along the Caribbean and has tall palms, cafés, hotels, and sea breezes.

★ **El Museo de las Casas Reales.** This is a remarkable museum that helps you understand the New World that was discovered by Columbus and the ensuing history of exploration and colonization in the 16th century. ⊠ *Calle Las Damas, right before Plaza de Espana, Zona Colonial* ☎ *809/682–4202* 🖃 *RD $30* ⊙ *Tues.–Sun. 9–5.*

BEACHES

If you are just in port for a day, you'll have a better time if you skip the beach and spend some time in the Zona Colonial and on the Malecón. If you are staying a couple of days, the closest good beach to Santo Domingo is **Playa Boca Chica** (⊠ *Autopista Las Americas, 21 mi [34 km] east of Santo Domingo, Boca Chica*), which is popular mainly with Dominicans and Europeans but is still one of the better places to go to the beach. The water is shallow but clear. You will be hasseled by an annoying parade of vendors and illicit proposals at the public beach. The best of the waterfront restaurants are Restaurant Boca Chica Marina and El Pelicano (it even has lovely showers and its own long stretch of beach).

SHOPPING

Exquisitely hand-wrapped cigars continue to be the hottest commodity coming out of the D.R. Only reputable cigar shops sell the real thing. Dominican rum and coffee are also good buys. *Mamajuana,* an herbal liqueur, is said to be the Dominican answer to Viagra. Look also for the delicate, faceless ceramic figurines that symbolize Dominican culture. Though locally crafted products are often very affordable, expect to pay for designer jewelry made of amber and larimar, an indigenous semiprecious stone the color of the Caribbean. Amber, a fossilization of resin from a prehistoric pine tree, often encasing ancient animal and plant life, from leaves to spiders to tiny lizards, is mined extensively. (Beware of fakes, which are especially prevalent in street stalls.)

One of the main shopping streets in the Zone is **Calle El Conde**, a pedestrian thoroughfare. With the advent of so many restorations, the dull and dusty stores with dated merchandise are giving way to some hip, new shops. However, many of the offerings, including local designer shops, are still of a caliber and cost that the Dominicans can afford. Some of the best shops are on **Calle Duarte**, north of the Colonial Zone, between Calle Mella and Avenida de Las Américas. **El Mercado Modelo,** a covered market, borders Calle Mella in the Colonial Zone; vendors here sell a dizzying selection of Dominican crafts. The **Malecón Center,** the latest complex, adjacent to the classy Hilton Santo Domingo, will eventually house 170 shops, boutiques, and services plus several movie theaters. In the tower above are luxury apartments and Sammy Sosa, in one of the penthouses. **Plaza Central** (⊠ *Avs. Winston Churchill and 27 de Febrero, Piantini* ☎ *809/541–5929*) is a major shopping center with high-end shops, including a Jenny Polanco shop (an upscale Dominican designer who has incredible white linen outfits, artistic jewelry, purses, and more).

NIGHTLIFE

★ Santo Domingo's nightlife is vast and ever changing. Check with the concierges and hip capitaleños. Get a copy of the free newspapers *Touring, Aqui o Guía de Bares Restaurantes*—available at the tourist office and at hotels—to find out what's happening. At this writing, there is still a curfew for clubs and bars; they must close at midnight during the week, and 2 AM on Friday and Saturday nights. There are some exceptions to the latter, primarily those clubs and casinos located in hotels. Sadly, the curfew has put some clubs out of business, but it has cut down on the crime and late-night noise, particularly in the Zone.

Doubles (⊠ *Calle Arzobispo Meriño 54, Zona Colonial* ☎ *809/688–3833*) looks like a friend's place—that is, if you have a French friend who has a hip sense of interior design and would mix rattan furniture, antiques, subdued lighting, and candles in a space that's centuries old. Spanish tiles add interest to this atmospheric piano bar. The **LED** (⊠ *Hispaniola Hotel and Casino, Av. Abraham Lincoln at Av. Independencia, Gazcue* ☎ *809/476–7733*) disco is in a hotel, so it is able to stay open later than the other clubs, and that in itself is what has made this a favorite of the young and well-to-do party set who take their music loud. Many a graduation is celebrated here until the wee small hours of the *mañana*.

WHERE TO EAT

$$–$$$ ✕ **Café Bellini.** This café has always had a panache far and above its

ITALIAN counterparts, for the Italian owners also have the adjacent furniture

★ design center. The modern, wicker-weave barrel chairs, and the contemporary art and light fixtures are all achingly hip. It has recently had a renovation and looks refreshed. The menu is the same at lunch and dinner. The democratic pricing usually offers a main course, such as the trio of raviolis (spinach, beet, and pumpkin), for about $10, which works for those on a slim budget. Also, know that an amuse-bouche, perhaps a tomato bruschetta, can usually suffice as an appetizer. The addition of grilled portobellos to a classic arugula-and-shaved-Parmesan salad is brilliant. Main courses are accompanied by pasta or grilled vegetables and potato. You can enjoy French and Italian liquors here (like pastis and grappa); dessert might be dark-chocolate mousse and fresh mango sorbet. Service is laudable, as is the music. ⊠ *Arzobispo Merino, corner of Padre Bellini, Zona Colonial* ☎ 809/686–3387 ⚑ *Reservations essential* ☐ *AE, MC, V* ☉ *Closed Sun. No lunch Mon.*

$$–$$$
FRENCH
★

✕ **La Residence.** This fine-dining enclave has always had the setting—Spanish colonial architecture, with pillars and archways overlooking a courtyard—and an esoteric lunch-dinner menu with high prices that did not always deliver. Now it has a French chef Denis Schetrit, who is serving classic yet innovative cuisine. He bows to more recent culinary trends while cleverly utilizing local produce and offering many moderately priced choices. The three-course, daily Menu del Chef is less than $28. It could be brochettes of spit-roasted duck, chicken au poivre, or vegetable risotto. You could start with a salad of panfried young squid for about and go bonkers over the dark- and white-chocolate terrine. Veer from the daily specials menu, and prices can certainly go higher but are still fair; even the grilled fillet and braised oxtail with foie gras sauce and wild mushrooms is reasonable. Anything that Chef Denis prepares is heaven on a plate. ⊠ *Hostal Nicolas Ovando, Calle Las Damas, Zona Colonial* ☎ 809/685–9955 ☐ *AE, MC, V.*

WHERE TO STAY

Since Santo Domingo is a port of embarkation for some ships, we list these hotel recommendations for those who want or need to stay overnight.

$–$$
★

▦ **Hilton Santo Domingo.** This has become *the* address on the Malecón for businesspeople, convention attendees, and leisure travelers. The six luxurious executive floors are wired for business, each with three phones, Internet ports, actual corner offices with imposing desks and ergonomic leather chairs, and DSL lines. Suites are geared for longer stays and have kitchenettes. Creature comforts are satisfied with the plush duvets, rain showers, and surround sound in the bathrooms, oversize flat-screen TVs, and gorgeous sea views. Service might just be the best in the country, and rates are surprisingly moderate, particularly with online packages that include a lavish and healthful buffet breakfast. **Pros:** Sunday brunch is one of the city's top tickets; great music in the lobby lounge; best service in Santo Domingo. **Cons:** little about the property is authentically Dominican; hotel can be large and impersonal. ⊠ *Av. George Washington 500, Gazcue* ☎ 809/685–0000 ⊕ *hiltoncaribbean.com/santodomingo* ⇆ *228 rooms, 32 suites* ⚑ *In-room: safe, refrigerator, Internet. In-hotel: 2 restaurants, bars, pool, gym, spa, Internet terminal, Wi-Fi* ☐ *AE, D, MC, V* ⦿ *EP.*

$$$–$$$$
Fodor'sChoice
★

▦ **Hostal Nicolas Ovando.** This luxury hotel, sculpted from the residence of the first Governor of the Americas, is the best thing to happen in the Zone since Diego Columbus's palace was finished in 1517. Formerly a Sofitel, it was rebranded by its parent group, Accor, and is now part of its collection of luxury hotels, M Gallery. Colonial rooms have canopied king-size beds, tall ceilings, original stone window benches, and shutters. Some prefer the sunny (smaller) rooms in the contemporary annex; with river views, these are smart examples of French minimalist style. Overlooking the river, the pool is shaded by trees and tropical plantings, and swimmers leave the sun for a fitness break in the gym. The bar is a social scene, particularly when the music man plays at cocktail hour, which includes complimentary hors d'oeuvres. If not, he can be found in the laudable restaurant, La Residence. **Pros:** lavish breakfast buffet; beautifully restored historic section. **Cons:** inconsistent service in the lovely restaurant. ⊠ *Calle Las Damas, Zona Colonial* ☎ *809/685–9955 or 800/763–4835* ⊕ *www.sofitel.com* 🛏 *100 rooms, 4 suites* ♿ *In-room: safe, refrigerator. In-hotel: restaurant, room service, bars, pool, gym, laundry service, Internet terminal, Wi-Fi, parking (free), some pets allowed* ⊟ *AE, MC, V* ⦿ *BP.*

SANTO TOMÁS DE CASTILLA, GUATEMALA

Jeff Van Fleet   Guatemala's short Caribbean shoreline doesn't generate the buzz of that of neighboring Belize and Mexico. The coast weighs in at a scant 74 mi (123 km), and this mostly highland country, which wears its indigenous culture on its sleeve, has historically looked inland rather than to the sea. You'll be drawn inland, too, with a variety of shore excursions. This is the land of the Maya, after all. But there's plenty to keep you occupied here in the lowlands. Tourist brochures tout the Caribbean coast as "The Other Guatemala." The predominantly indigenous and Spanish cultures of the highlands give way to an Afro-Caribbean tradition that listens more closely to the rhythms of far-off Jamaica rather than taking its cue from Guatemala City. Think of it as mixing a little reggae with your salsa.

ESSENTIALS

Currency The Guatemalan quetzal, named for the brightly plumed bird that is the symbol of the country (Q8.10 to US$1). Take care of any banking matters in the cruise terminal in Santo Tomás de Castilla. You'll find ATMs in Puerto Barrios and Livingston but nowhere else in this region.

Internet The Terminal de Cruceros in Santo Tomás de Castilla has Internet computers for your use, the easiest option if you're a day visitor.

Telephones Guatemalan phone numbers have eight digits. There are no city or area codes. Simply dial the number for any in-country call. Most towns have offices of Telgua, the national telephone company, where you can place both national and international calls. Avoid the ubiquitous public phones with signs promising FREE CALLS TO THE USA. The number back home being called gets socked with a hefty bill.

COMING ASHORE

Cruise ships dock at the modern, spacious Terminal de Cruceros, where you'll find a bank, post office, money exchange, telephones, Internet access, a lively craft market, and an office of INGUAT, Guatemala's national tourist office. A marimba band serenades you with its clinking xylophone-like music; a Caribbean ensemble dances for you (and may even pull you in to take part).

Taxis, both vehicular and water, take you to various destinations in the area. Plan on paying $2 to Santo Tomás de Castilla proper, and $5 to Puerto Barrios. Boats transport cruise visitors to Livingston, charging about $5 for the 20-minute trip. The Amantique Bay Resort provides water taxis from port to resort of $8 per person. Vehicular taxis charge $15 per head to travel by land to the resort.

EXPLORING SANTO TOMÁS DE CASTILLA

Amatique Bay. "Bahía de Amatique" denotes the large bay that washes the Caribbean coast of Guatemala and southern Belize, but for most travelers the name is inexorably linked with the **Amatique Bay Resort and Marina,** part of the Clarion chain, and the region's only five-star hotel. The 61-room resort opens itself up for day visitors, and many cruise passengers stop by for a drink, a meal, or an entire day of swimming, watersliding, kayaking, horseback riding, or bicycling. ⊠ *6 mi (10 km) north of Santo Tomás* ☎ *7948–1800, 2421–3333 in Guatemala City* ⊕ *www.amatiquebay.net.*

Copán. The famous Mayan ruins of Copán lie just across the border from this region in neighboring Honduras, but are accessible enough from Santo Tomás to be an excursion on many itineraries. Bring your passport, since this entails an international border crossing. For more information, see ⇨ Copán *in* Roatán, Honduras. ⊠½ *mi (1 km) east of Copán Ruinas* ☎*No phone* ⊠*$15* ⊘*Daily 8–4.*

Livingston. Visitors compare Livingston with Puerto Barrios across the bay, and the former wins hands down, for its sultry, seductive Caribbean flavor. Wood houses, some on stilts, congregate in this old fishing town, once an important railroad hub, but today inaccessible by land from the outside world. Livingston proudly trumpets its Garífuna heritage, a culture unique to Central America's eastern coast and descended from the intermarriage of African slaves with Caribbean indigenous peoples. Music and dance traditions and a Caribbean-accented English remain, even if old-timers lament the creeping outside influences, namely Spanish, rap, and reggae. ⊠*15 mi (25 km) by water northwest of Santo Tomás.*

Puerto Barrios. Puerto Barrios maintains the atmosphere of an old banana town, humid and a tad down at the heels, perhaps longing for better days. Santo Tomás has replaced it as the country's largest port, and you'll likely zip through the Caribbean coast's biggest city on your way to somewhere else, but the cathedral and municipal market are worth a look if you find yourself here. Water taxis depart from the municipal docks for Livingston, across the bay, where you start your trip up the Río Dulce. ⊠*3 mi (5 km) north of Santo Tomás de Castilla.*

Quiriguá. Construction began on the Guatemalan lowlands' most important Mayan ruins about AD 500. Its hieroglyhics tell its story: Quiriguá served at the time as a satellite state under the control of Copán, about 30 mi (50 km) away in present-day Honduras. By the height of its power in the 7th century, Quiriguá had overpowered Copán, but just as quickly, fell back into submissive status. Quiriguá's ruins still today live in the shadow of their better-known neighbor across the border, and of the Tikal ruins in the northern part of Guatemala, but a visit here is rewarding for the carvings of *stelae,* the ornate sculptures depicting the city's rulers, and the largest such works in Central America. (Quiriguá's stelae stand 33 feet [10 meters] tall, dwarfing those of Copán.) Ease of access from the Caribbean coast makes Quiriguá well worth a visit, too. ⊠*54 mi (90 km) southwest of Santo Tomás* ⊠*$4* ⊘*Daily 8–4.*

Río Dulce. The natural crown jewel of this region is the 13,000-hectare (32,000-acre) national park that protects the river leading inland from Livingston to Lago de Izabal, Guatemala's largest lake. Pelicans, herons, egrets, and terns nest and fly along the Río Dulce, which cuts through a heavily forested limestone canyon. Excursions often approach the park by land, but we recommend making the trip upriver from Livingston to immerse yourself in the entire Indiana Jones experience. ⊠*Southwest of Livingston.*

Once an important Mayan trade route, the Río Dulce later became the route over which the conquistadors sent the gold and silver they plundered back to Spain. All this wealth attracted Dutch and English pirates, who attacked both the ships and the warehouses on shore. In hopes of curtailing these buccaneers, colonists built a series of fortresses on the river's northern banks. In 1955 the Guatemalan government reconstructed the ruined fortress of **Castillo de San Felipe de Lara**

(⊠*Southwest of Fronteras* ☎*No phone* 💰*Q10*). Spanish colonists constructed the fortress in 1595 to guard the inland waterway from pirate incursions. It was used as a prison between 1655 and 1660. You can reach it by the road leading west from Río Dulce or by a short boat ride. A 1999 earthquake in this region destroyed the river pier as well as damaging portions of the fort. If you wish to visit, rather than simply see the structure from the water, you'll need to approach the park overland rather than upriver.

A short launch from Fronteras takes you to **Hacienda Tijax** (⊠*Northeast of Fronteras* ☎*7930–5505*), an old rubber plantation, now a reforestation project, which offers hiking and kayaking, and a chance to view the cultivation of orchids and spices.

Santo Tomás de Castilla. Belgian immigrants settled Santo Tomás in the 19th century, but little remains of their heritage today, save for the preponderance of French and Flemish names in the local cemetery. Most visitors move on. Santo Tomás has experienced a small renaissance as the country's most important port, receiving growing numbers of cruise and cargo ships, and serving as the headquarters of the Guatemalan navy.

Fodor'sChoice ★ **Tikal.** The high point of any trip to Guatemala is a visit to Central America's most impressive ruins. There's nothing quite like the sight of the towering temples, ringed on all sides by miles of virgin forest, but you need a lot of quetzales to get here, since you'll travel by plane from the airstrip outside Santo Tomás to the small airport in Santa Elena, near the ruins. Although this region was home to Mayan communities as early as 600 BC, Tikal wasn't established until around 200 BC. By AD 500 it's estimated that the city covered more than 18 square mi (47 square km) and had a population of close to 100,000. For almost 1,000 years Tikal remained engulfed by the jungle. Excavation began in earnest in the mid-1800s. Today, after more than 150 years of digging, researchers say that Tikal includes some 3,000 buildings. Countless more are still covered by the jungle. Temple IV, the tallest-known structure built by the Maya, offers an unforgettable view from the top. ⊠*Parque Nacional Tikal* ☎*No phone* 💰*Q50* 🕙*Daily 6–6.*

SANTO TOMÁS BEST BETS

■ **Quiriguá.** If you want to see Maya ruins but don't want to spend an entire day on the bus, nearby Quiriguá can be impressive.

■ **Copán.** In neighboring Honduras, this Maya site is a worthwhile day trip from Santo Tomás.

■ **Riding on the Río Dulce.** The ride on this river is one of Guatemala's most beautiful boat trips.

4

SHOPPING

The rest of Guatemala overflows with indigenous crafts and art, but the famous market towns of the highlands are nowhere to be found in Caribbean region. Quite honestly, your best bet for shopping is the Terminal de Cruceros at Santo Tomás de Castilla, and you'll have plenty of opportunity to buy before you board your ship. What you'll find here comes from Guatemala's highlands—the Caribbean has never developed a strong artisan tradition—with a good selection of fabrics, weavings, woodwork, and basketry to choose from. Markets in Puerto Barrios and Livingston, the only real urban areas you'll encounter in this region, are more geared to the workaday needs of residents rather than visitors.

ACTIVITIES

BEACHES AND WATER SPORTS

A beach culture has just never developed in this region of Guatamala the way it has in neighboring Belize and Mexico. The only real beach in the region is found within the confines of the **Amantique Bay Resort and Marina** (⊠*6 mi [10 km] north of Santo Tomás* ☎*7948–1800, 2421–3333 in Guatemala City* ⊕*www.amatiquebay.net*), which is the only place here that has a resort feel to it. Day visitors partake of swimming, waterslides, and kayaking. The resort's launch will bring you over from the cruise-ship terminal in Santo Tomás.

HIKING AND KAYAKING

Hacienda Tijax (⊠*Northeast of Fronteras* ☎*7930–5505* ⊕*tijax.com*), inland, near the point where the Río Dulce meets Lake Izabal, provides kayaking and hiking for day visitors.

TOBAGO (SCARBOROUGH)

Vernon
O'Reilly
Ramesar

The smaller and quieter of the sister islands that make up Trinidad and Tobago offers pristine beaches and friendly people. Tobago has long been a favorite of European visitors, who enjoy the rustic feel of the island and the laid-back pace. There are numerous fine restaurants, though many are not located in Scarborough, where cruise ships dock. The culinary thrill here is exploring the local cuisine that can be found at food stalls across the island, and you could easily make eating the focus of your shore excursion and be all the happier for it. No trip here is complete without trying the quintessential Tobago dish, curry crab and dumplings. This can be a slow (and messy) experience, but it fits in perfectly with the pace of life on the island.

ESSENTIALS

Currency The Trinidad and Tobago dollar (TT$6.26 to $1US). Most places catering to tourists will accept U.S. currency, but the exchange rate may vary wildly from place to place.

Hours Most shops are open weekdays from 8 to 4:30, Saturday from 8 to noon; malls stay open later during the week, often until at least 6 or 7 PM, and operate all day Saturday.

Internet J-Puter Tech (⊠*20 Burnett St., Scarborough, Tobago* ☎*868/639–3393*).

Telephones Pay phones are located in the cruise terminal. To make an international call from a pay phone, you must first purchase a prepaid "companion" card, which is readily available from most convenience shops at or near the port, then simply follow the instructions on the card. Cards are available in various denominations.

COMING ASHORE

Scarborough, Tobago's lazy and hilly capital, is where all cruise ships dock. The cruise terminal is at the base of the city, near the market, many colorful shops, and fast-food restaurants. There are shops selling items specifally marketed to tourists right at the port, but a short stroll around the streets of downtown can yield considerably more interesting treasures.

While you can easily walk into town, the island's best beaches and restaurants are in Crown Point. Because of the narrow roads and hilly terrain—not to mention aggressive drivers who like to drive very fast—it is not advisable to rent a car. But if you choose to drive yourself, remember that driving is on the left, British style. Taxis flock to the port whenever a cruise ship arrives. Authorized taxis always have a license plate starting with the letter "H" (for "hire"). Although rates are technically fixed, it is never a bad idea to negotiate with the driver.

TOBAGOS BEST BETS

■ **Bird-Watching.** For such a small island, the diversity of bird life is fascinating.

■ **Buccoo Reef.** The reef at the southwestern tip of the island is teeming with life.

■ **Beaches.** If you're craving an excellent Caribbean beach, this is one place where you can take your pick of beaches, each lovelier than the last.

■ **Golf.** The island has one excellent and one very good golf course.

EXPLORING TOBAGO

Ft. King George. On Mt. St. George, a short drive up the hill from Scarborough, Tobago's best-preserved historic monument clings to a cliff high above the ocean. Ft. King George was built in the 1770s and operated until 1854. It's hard to imagine that this lovely, tranquil spot commanding sweeping views of the bay and landscaped with lush tropical foliage was ever the site of any military action, but the prison, officers' mess, and several stabilized cannons attest otherwise. Just to the left of the tall wooden figures dancing a traditional Tobagonian jig is the former barrack guardhouse, now housing the small **Tobago Museum.** Exhibits include weapons and other pre-Columbian artifacts found in the area; the fertility figures are especially interesting. Upstairs are maps and photographs of Tobago's past. Be sure to check out the gift display cases for the perversely fascinating jewelry made from embalmed and painted lizards and sea creatures; you might find it hard to resist a pair of bright-yellow shrimp earrings. The **Fine Arts Centre** at the foot of the Ft. King George complex shows the work of local artists. ⊠ *84 Fort St., Scarborough* ☎ *868/639–3970* ✉ *Fort free, museum TT$2* ☉ *Weekdays 9–5.*

★ **Kimme's Sculpture Museum.** The diminutive and eccentric German-born sculptress Luise Kimme fell in love with the form of Tobagonians and has devoted her life to capturing them in her sculptures. Her pieces can exceed 12 feet in height and are often wonderfully whimsical. Much of her work is done in wood (none of it local), but there are many

Tobago

bronze pieces as well. The museum itself is a turreted structure with a commanding view of the countryside. Most locals refer to it as "The Castle." There are numerous signs in Mt. Irvine directing visitors to the museum. ⊠ *Mt. Irvine* ☎ *868/639–0257* ⊕ *www.luisekimme.com* ⊠ *TT$5* ☺ *Sun. 10 AM–2 PM or by appointment.*

Scarborough. Around Rockley Bay on the island's leeward hilly side, this town is both the capital of Tobago and a popular cruise-ship port, but it conveys the feeling that not much has changed since the area was settled two centuries ago. It may not be one of the delightful pastel-color cities of the Caribbean, but Scarborough does have its charms, including several interesting little shops. Whatever you do, be sure to check out the busy Scarborough Market, an indoor and outdoor affair featuring everything from fresh vegetables to live chickens and clothing. Note the red-and-yellow Methodist church on the hill, one of Tobago's oldest churches.

SHOPPING

Souvenir seekers will do better in Trinidad than in Tobago, but determined shoppers should manage to find a few things to take home. Scarborough has the largest collection of shops, and Burnett Street, which climbs sharply from the port to St. James Park, is a good place to browse. **Cotton House** (⊠ *Bacolet St., Scarborough* ☎ *868/639–2727*) is a good bet for jewelry and imaginative batik work. Paula Young runs her shop like an art school. You can visit the upstairs studio; if it's not too busy, you can even make a batik square at no charge. **Forro's Homemade Delicacies** (⊠ *The Andrew's Rectory, Bacolet St., opposite fire station, Scarborough* ☎ *868/639–2485*) sells its own fine line of homemade tamarind chutney, lemon and lime marmalade, hot sauce, and guava and golden-apple jelly. Eileen Forrester, wife of the Anglican archdeacon of Trinidad and Tobago, supervises a kitchen full of good cooks who boil and bottle the condiments and pack them in little straw baskets—or even in bamboo. Most jars are small, easy to carry, and inexpensive. **Souvenir and Gift Shop** (⊠ *Port Mall, Wrightson Rd., Scarborough* ☎ *868/639–5632*) stocks straw baskets and other crafts.

ACTIVITIES

BIRD-WATCHING

★ Some 200 varieties of birds have been documented on Tobago: look for the yellow oriole, scarlet ibis, and the comical motmot—the male of the species clears sticks and stones from an area and then does a dance complete with snapping sounds to attract a mate. The flora is as vivid as the birds. Purple-and-yellow *poui* trees and spectacular orange immortelles splash color over the countryside, and something is blooming virtually every season. Pat Turpin and Renson Jack at **Pioneer Journeys** (☎ *868/660–4327 or 868/660–5175* ✎ *pturpin@tstt.net.tt*) can give you information about their bird-watching tours of Bloody Bay rain forest and Louis d'Or River valley wetlands. Naturalist and ornithologist David Rooks operates **Rooks Nature Tours** (⊠ *462 Moses Hill, Lambeau* ☎ *868/756–8594* ⊕ *www.rookstobago.com*), offering bird-watching walks inland and trips to offshore bird colonies. He's generally considered to be the best guide on the island.

BOAT TOURS

Tobago offers many wonderful spots for snorkeling. Although the reefs around Speyside in the northeast are becoming better known, **Buccoo Reef,** off the island's southwest coast, is still the most popular—perhaps too popular. Over the years the reef has been damaged by the ceaseless boat traffic and by the thoughtless visiting divers who take pieces of coral as souvenirs. Still, it's worth experiencing, particularly if you have children. Daily 2½-hour tours by glass-bottom boats let you snorkel at the reef, swim in a lagoon, and gaze at Coral Gardens—where fish and coral are as yet untouched. Most dive companies in the Black Rock area also arrange snorkeling tours. There's also good snorkeling near the **Arnos Vale Hotel** and the **Mt. Irvine Bay Hotel.**

Hew's Glass Bottom Boat Tours (⊠ *Pigeon Point* ☎ *868/639–9058*) are perfect excursions for those who neither snorkel nor dive. Boats leave daily at 11:30 AM.

GOLF

FodorsChoice The 18-hole, PGA-designed championship par-72 course at **Tobago Plan-** ★ **tations Golf and Country Club** (⊠ *Lowlands* ☎ *868/631–0875*) is set amid rolling greens and mangroves. It offers some amazing views of the ocean as a bonus. Greens fees are $85 for one round, $150 for two rounds (these rates include a golf cart and taxes). This is the newer of the two main courses on the island and is by far the most popular. The course is well maintained and contains areas of mangrove and forest that are home to many bird species.

BEACHES

You won't find manicured country-club sand here. But those who enjoy feeling as though they've landed on a desert island will relish the untouched quality of these shores.

Bacolet Beach (⊠ *Windward Rd. east of Scarborough*) was the setting for the films *Swiss Family Robinson* and *Heaven Knows, Mr. Allison*. Though used by the Blue Haven Hotel, like all local beaches it's open to the public. If you are not a guest at the hotel, access to the beach is down a track next door to the hotel. The bathroom and changing facilities on the beach are for hotel guests only. **Great Courland Bay** (⊠ *Leeward Rd. northeast of Black Rock, Courland*), near Ft. Bennett, has clear, tranquil waters. Along the sandy beach—one of Tobago's longest—you can find several glitzy hotels. A marina attracts the yachting crowd. **King's Bay** (⊠ *Delaford*) is the most visually satisfying of the swimming sites off the road from Scarborough to Speyside—the bay hooks around so severely you can feel like you're in a lake. The crescent-shape beach is easy to find because it's marked by a sign about halfway between the two towns. Just before you reach the bay, there's a bridge with an unmarked turnoff that leads to a gravel parking lot; beyond that, a landscaped path leads to a waterfall with a rocky pool. **Pigeon Point Beach** (⊠ *Pigeon Point*) is often displayed on Tobago travel brochures. Although the beach is public, it abuts part of what was once a large coconut estate, and you must pay a token admission (about TT$18) to enter the grounds and use the facilities. **Store Bay** (⊠ *Crown Point*), where boats depart for Buccoo Reef, is little more than a small sandy cove between two rocky breakwaters, but the food stands here are divine: several huts licensed by the tourist board to local ladies who sell roti, pelau, and the world's messiest dish—crab and dumplings. Near the airport, just walk around the Crown Point Hotel to the beach entrance.

WHERE TO EAT

$–$$
CARIBBEAN
Fodor'sChoice
★

✕ **Blue Crab Restaurant.** The Sardinha family have been serving the best local lunches at their home since the 1980s. The ebullient Alison entertains and hugs diners while her husband, Ken, does the cooking. The food is hearty and usually well seasoned in the creole style. The only bad news here is that the restaurant is rarely open for dinner; the good news is that you may not have room for dinner after lunch. ⊠ *Robinson and Main Sts., Scarborough* ☎ 868/639–2737 ▭ *AE, MC, V* ⊗ *Closed weekends. No dinner.*

$$–$$$
ECLECTIC

✕ **Café Iguana.** This funky little restaurant and art gallery is a popular gathering place evenings as it serves some of the best cocktails on the island. The menu is eclectic, but there is a distinct Tobago touch to everything and an emphasis on local ingredients. The crayfish, though messy to eat, is not to be missed. The art on the walls is available for sale—you might want to exercise restraint with the cocktails before deciding to become an art investor. ⊠*Store Bay Local Rd. at Milford Rd., Crown Point* ☎*868/631–8205* ▤*AE, MC, V* ☉*Closed Wed.*

TORTOLA (ROAD TOWN)

Lynda Lohr

Once a sleepy backwater, Tortola is definitely busy these days, particularly when several cruise ships tie up at the Road Town dock. Passengers crowd the streets and shops, and open-air jitneys filled with cruise-ship passengers create bottlenecks on the island's byways. That said, most folks visit Tortola to relax on its deserted sands or linger over lunch at one of its many delightful restaurants. Beaches are never more than a few miles away, and the steep green hills that form Tortola's spine are fanned by gentle trade winds. The neighboring islands glimmer like emeralds in a sea of sapphire. Tortola doesn't have many historic sights, but it does have abundant natural beauty. Beware of the roads, which are extraordinarily steep and twisting, making driving demanding. The best beaches are on the north shore.

ESSENTIALS

Currency The U.S. dollar is the official currency. Some places accept cash only, but major credit cards are widely accepted. You'll find ATMs in Road Town.

Internet Trellis Bay Cybercafé (⊠ *Trellis Bay, Tortola* ☎ *284/495–2447*).

Telephones To call anywhere in the BVI once you've arrived, dial all seven digits. A local call from a pay phone costs 25¢, but such phones are sometimes on the blink. An alternative is a Caribbean phone card, available in $5, $10, and $20 denominations. They're sold at most major hotels and many stores, and can be used to call within the BVI as well as all over the Caribbean, and to access USA-Direct from special phone-card phones. If you're coming ashore at the cruise-ship dock, you'll find pay phones right on the dock. If a tender drops you right in Road Town at the ferry dock, phones are located in the terminal.

AT&T has service in nearby St. John, USVI, so it's possible to get service from there in some spots in Road Town and along the waterfront highway that leads to the West End. You may not have to pay international roaming charges on some U.S. cell-phone plans if you can connect with this network.

COMING ASHORE

Large cruise ships usually anchor in Road Town Harbor and bring passengers ashore by tender. Small ships can sometimes tie up at Wickham's Cay dock. Either way, it's a short stroll to Road Town. If your ship isn't going to Virgin Gorda, you can make the 12-mi (19 km) trip by ferry from the dock in Road Town in about 30 minutes for about $30 round-trip, but you'll still have to take a taxi to get to the Baths for swimming and snorkeling, so it's not necessarily a bad deal to go on your ship's shore excursion.

There are taxi stands at Wickham's Cay and in Road Town. Taxis are unmetered, and there are minimums for travel throughout the island, so it's usually cheaper to travel in groups. Negotiate to get the best fares, as there is no set fee schedule. If you are in the islands for just a day, it's usually more cost-effective to share a taxi with a small group than to rent a car, since you'd have to pay an agency at Wickham's Cay or in Road Town car-rental charges of at least $50 a day. You must be at least age 25 to rent a car.

EXPLORING TORTOLA

Road Town, the laid-back capital of the BVI, looks out over Road Town Harbour. It takes only an hour or so to stroll down Main Street and along the waterfront, checking out the traditional West Indian buildings painted in pastel colors and sporting high-pitched, corrugated-tin roofs; bright shutters; and delicate fretwork trim. If you don't feel particularly energetic, just choose a seat on one of the benches in Sir Olva Georges Square, on Waterfront Drive, and watch the people come and go from the ferry dock and customs office across the street.

☾ ★ **Dolphin Discovery.** Get up close and personal with dolphins as they swim in a spacious seaside pen. There are two different programs that provide a range of experiences. In the Royal Swim, dolphins tow participants around the pen. The less expensive Encounter allows you to touch the dolphins. ⊠ *Prospect Reef Resort, Road Town* ☎ *284/494–7675* ⊕ *www.dolphindiscovery.com* ☒ *Royal Swim $139, Adventure $99, Discovery $79* ☾ *Royal Swim daily at 10 and noon, Adventure and Discovery daily at 11 and 1*

Fort Burt. The most intact historic ruin on Tortola was built by the Dutch in the early 17th century to safeguard Road Harbour. It sits on a hill at the western edge of Road Town and is now the site of a small hotel and restaurant. The foundations and magazine remain, and the structure offers a commanding view of the harbor. ⊠ *Waterfront Dr., Road Town* ☎ *No phone* ☒ *Free* ☾ *Daily dawn–dusk.*

★ **J. R. O'Neal Botanic Gardens.** Take a walk through this 4-acre showcase of lush plant life. There are sections devoted to prickly cacti and succulents, hothouses for ferns and orchids, gardens of medicinal herbs, and plants and trees indigenous to the seashore. From the tourist office in Road Town, cross Waterfront Drive and walk one block over to Main Street and turn right. Keep walking until you see the high school. The gardens are on your left. ⊠ *Botanic Station, Road Town* ☎ *284/494–3904* ☒ *$3* ☾ *Mon.–Sat. 9–4:30.*

★ **Old Government House Museum.** The seat of government until 1987, this gracious building now displays a nice collection of items from Tortola's past. The rooms are filled with period furniture, hand-painted china, books signed by Queen Elizabeth II on her 1966 and 1977 visits, and numerous items reflecting Tortola's seafaring legacy. ⊠ *Waterfront Dr., Road Town* ☎ *284/494–4091* ☒ *$3* ☾ *Weekdays 9–3, Sat. 9–1.*

★ **Sage Mountain National Park.** At 1,716 feet, Sage Mountain is the highest peak in the BVI. From the parking area, a trail leads you in a loop not only

Tortola

0   1   2 miles
0   1   2 km

JOST VAN DYKE
Little Jost Van Dyke
Little Harbour
Black Pt.

Long Bay
West End
Apple Bay
Carrot Bay
Cane Garden Bay
Todman Pk.
Brewers Bay
Frenchman's Cay

ST. JOHN

Sage Mountain National Park

Dolphin Discovery

TORTOLA

Trunk Bay
Josiah's Bay

Road Town
see inset map

Fort Shirley

Road Harbour

Road

East End
Monkey Pt.
Towing Pt.

Fat Hogs Bay
Buck Island
Beef Island
Beef Island Int'l Airport

Little Camanoe

Great Camanoe

North Bay
Kitto Ghut

Purser's Marina Cay

Scrub Island

West Dog

Guana Island
North Bay
Long Pt.

Sir Francis Drake Channel

Dead Chest

Peter Island
Great Harbour
Rock Hole
White Bay
Big Reef Bay

Spanish Town

Cockroach Island
George Dog
Great Dog

KEY
Ferry
Cruise Ship Terminal

Inset — Road Town

J.R. O'Neal Botanic Gardens

Blyden Yard

Wickhams Cay 1
Wickhams Cay 2

Port Purcell
Free Bottom

Road Bay

Peter Island Ferry

Romasco Place
Sir Olva Georga's Plaza
Ferry Dock
Customs House

Fort Burt

Old Government House

Road Town

Road Reef

0   1/4 miles
0   1/4 kilometers

to the peak itself (and extraordinary views) but also to a small rain forest that is sometimes shrouded in mist. Most of the forest was cut down over the centuries to clear land for sugarcane, cotton, and other crops; to create pastureland; or simply to utilize the stands of timber. In 1964 this park was established to preserve what remained. Up here you can see mahogany trees, white cedars, mountain guavas, elephant-ear vines, mamey trees, and giant bullet woods, to say nothing of such birds as mountain doves and thrushes. Take a taxi from Road Town or drive up Joe's Hill Road and make a left onto Ridge Road toward Chalwell and Doty villages. The road dead-ends at the park. ⊠ *Ridge Rd., Sage Mountain* ☎ *284/494–3904* ⊕ *www.bvina-tionalparkstrust.org* ⌨ *$3* ⊙ *Daily dawn–dusk.*

SHOPPING

Many shops and boutiques are clustered along and just off Road Town's **Main Street.** You can shop in Road Town's **Wickham's Cay I** adjacent to the marina. The **Crafts Alive Market** on the Road Town waterfront is a collection of colorful West Indian–style buildings with shops that carry items made in the BVI. You might find pretty baskets or interesting pottery or perhaps a bottle of home-brewed hot sauce. There's an ever-growing number of art and clothing stores at **Soper's Hole** in West End.

ACTIVITIES

DIVING AND SNORKELING

Clear waters and numerous reefs afford some wonderful opportunities for underwater exploration. In some spots visibility reaches 100 feet, but colorful reefs teeming with fish are often just a few feet below the sea surface. In 1867 the **RMS** *Rhone,* a 310-foot royal mail steamer, split in two when it sank in a devastating hurricane. It's so well preserved that it was used as an underwater prop in the movie *The Deep.* You can see the crow's nest and bowsprit, the cargo hold in the bow, and the engine and enormous propeller shaft in the stern. Every dive outfit in the BVI runs scuba and snorkel tours to this part of the BVI National Parks Trust; if you only have time for one trip, make it this one. Rates start at around $60 for a one-tank dive and $90 for a two-tank dive.

Blue Waters Divers (⊠ *Nanny Cay* ☎ *284/494–2847* ⊠ *Soper's Hole, West End* ☎ *284/495–1200* ⊕ *www.bluewaterdiversbvi.com*) teaches resort, open-water, rescue, and advanced diving courses, and also makes daily dive trips. If you're chartering a sailboat, the company's boat will meet your boat at Peter, Salt, Norman, or Cooper Island for a rendezvous dive. Rates include all equipment as well as instruction. Reserve two days in advance.

> **CAUTION**
>
> Check the balance of your shipboard account before the end of your cruise. You'll avoid a long line at the Purser's Desk that last morning after the final bill arrives.

Dive Tortola (⊠ *Prospect Reef Resort, Road Town* ☎ *284/494–9200* ⊕ *www.divetortola.com*) offers beginner and advanced diving courses and daily dive trips. Trainers teach open-water, rescue, advanced diving, and resort courses. Dive Tortola also offers a rendezvous diving option for folks on charter sailboats.

FISHING

Most of the boats that take you deep-sea fishing for bluefish, wahoo, swordfish, and shark leave from nearby St. Thomas, but local anglers like to fish the shallower water for bonefish. A half day runs about $480, a full day around $850. Call **Caribbean Fly Fishing** (⊠ *Nanny Cay* ☎ *284/494–4797* ⊕ *www.caribflyfishing.com*).

SAILING

Fodor'sChoice ★ ☾ The BVI are among the world's most popular sailing destinations. They're close together and surrounded by calm waters, so it's fairly easy to sail from one anchorage to the next. **Aristocat Charters** (⊠ *West End* ☎ *284/499–1249* ⊕ *www.aristocatcharters.com*) sets sail daily to the Indians and Peter Island aboard a 48-foot catamaran. **White Squall II** (⊠ *Village Cay Marina, Road Town* ☎ *284/494–2564* ⊕ *www.white squall2.com*) takes you on regularly scheduled day sails to the Baths at Virgin Gorda, Cooper, the Indians, or the Caves at Norman Island on an 80-foot schooner.

BEACHES

Tortola's north side has several perfect palm-fringed white-sand beaches that curl around turquoise bays and coves. Nearly all are accessible by car (preferably one with four-wheel-drive), albeit down bumpy roads that corkscrew precipitously. Facilities run the gamut from absolutely none to a number of beachside bars and restaurants as well as places to rent water-sports equipment.

Brewers Bay is good for snorkeling, and you can find a campground with showers and bathrooms and beach bar tucked in the foliage right behind the beach. The beach is easy to find, but the paved roads leading down the hill to it can be a bit daunting. You can get there from either Brewers Bay Road East or Brewers Bay Road West. **Cane Garden Bay** has exceptionally calm, crystalline waters—except when storms at sea turn the water murky. Snorkeling is good along the edges. The beach is a laid-back, even somewhat funky place to put down your towel. It's the closest beach to Road Town—one steep uphill and downhill drive—and one of the BVI's best-known anchorages (unfortunately, it can be very crowded). **Long Bay West** is a stunning, mile-long stretch of white sand.

Although Long Bay Resort sprawls along part of it, the entire beach is open to the public. The water isn't as calm here as at Cane Garden or Brewers Bay, but it's still swimable. Rent water-sports equipment and enjoy the beachfront restaurant at the resort. Turn left at Zion Hill Road; then travel about half a mile.

WHERE TO EAT

$$–$$$ ✕**CafeSito.** Don't be put off by the pedestrian decor. The chef at this
ECLECTIC   shopping-center spot conjures up delicious dishes that run the gamut from burgers to fresh fish to chicken alfredo. It's the place to go for pizza smothered with everything from the standard cheese and tomato to the more unusual chicken and bacon. In winter the staff will deliver anything from its menu straight to your hotel. ⊠ *Wickham's Cay I, Waterfront Dr., Road Town* ☎*284/494–7412* ▭*MC, V.*

$$ ✕**Roti Palace.** You might be tempted to pass this tiny spot on Road
CARIBBEAN   Town's Main Street when you see the plastic tablecloths and fake flow-
★   ers, but owner Jean Leonard's reputation for dishing up fantastic roti is known far and wide. Flatbread is filled with curried potatoes, onions and lobster, chicken, beef, conch, goat, or vegetables. Ask for the bone out if you order the chicken, to save yourself the trouble of fishing them out of your mouth. ⊠ *Main St., Road Town* ☎*284/494–4196* ▭*No credit cards* ⊗ *Closed Sun. No dinner.*

TRINIDAD (PORT OF SPAIN)

Vernon
O'Reilly-
Ramesar

Trinidad, the big sister in the twin-island republic of Trinidad and Tobago, is the most southerly in the Caribbean and a melting pot of African, Indian, European, and South American cultures, which happily exist together. But it's not a typical Caribbean island, since it is a major energy producer and relies very little on tourism for income. But Trinidadians do know how to party, and the island's population is always celebrating or preparing for some sort of festival, the biggest of which is undoubtedly Carnival, which takes over much of Port of Spain every year for two days of bacchanalian excess. Those expecting pristine white beaches may find the island disappointing, but lovers of the rain forest and wildlife will find paradise.

ESSENTIALS

Currency The Trinidad and Tobago dollar (TT$6.26 to $1US). Most places catering to tourists will accept U.S. currency, but the exchange rate may vary wildly from place to place.

Internet Computer Planet Ltd. (⊠ *Corner of Ariapita Ave. and Luis St., Port of Spain, Trinidad* ☎ *868/622–6888).*

Telephones Pay phones are located in the cruise terminal. To make an international call from a pay phone, you must first purchase a prepaid "companion" card, which is readily available from most convenience stores, then simply follow the instructions on the card. Cards are available in various denominations. Phones and calling cards are also available from the main phone company, TSTT, which has an office on Independence Square about a 10-minute walk from the port.

COMING ASHORE

Port of Spain is a bustling and sprawling metropolis with seemingly endless traffic jams. The capital of the twin-island republic is a work in progress, with government investing billions of dollars into upgrading the port area and many other parts of the city. The scale of this project means that the port will be a construction zone for some time to come, but the end result is expected to be a mile-long facility designed to offer a range of facilities and services to visitors.

Because of the driving habits of Trinidadians and the often confusing road signs and narrow roads, it is not advisable to rent a car. Taxis flock to the port whenever a cruise ship arrives. Authorized taxis always have a license plate starting with the letter "H" (for "hire"). Though rates are technically fixed, it is never a bad idea to negotiate with the driver.

EXPLORING TRINIDAD

Caroni Bird Sanctuary. This large swamp with mazelike waterways is bordered by mangrove trees, some plumed with huge termite nests. If you're lucky, you may see lazy caimans idling in the water and large snakes hanging from branches on the banks taking in the sun. In the middle of the sanctuary are several islets that are home to Trinidad's national bird, the scarlet ibis. ⊠ *½ hr from Port of Spain; take Churchill Roosevelt Hwy. east to Uriah Butler south; turn right and in about 2 mins, after passing Caroni River Bridge, follow sign for sanctuary* ⊠*$10* ⊗*Daily dawn–dusk.*

Chaguaramas Military History and Aerospace Museum. On the former U.S. military base, this is a must-see for history buffs. The exhibits are in a large hangarlike shed without air-conditioning, so dress appropriately. Exhibits cover everything from Amerindian history to the Cold War, but the emphasis is on the two World Wars. There's a decidedly charming and homemade feel to the place; in fact, most exhibits were made by the curator and founder, Commander Gaylord Kelshall of the TandT Coast Guard. The museum is set a bit off the main road, but is easily spotted thanks to the turquoise BWIA L1011 jet parked out front (Trinidad and Tobago's former national airline). ⊠ *Western Main Rd., Chaguaramas* ☎*868/634–4391* ⊠*TT$20* ⊗*Mon.–Sat. 9–5.*

Dattatreya Yoga Centre. This impressive temple site was constructed by artisans brought in from India. It is well worth a visit to admire the intricate architectural details of the main temple, learn about Trinidad Hinduism, and marvel at the towering 85-foot statue of the god Hanuman. This is a religious site, so appropriate clothing is required (no shorts), and shoes must be left outside the temple door. The temple is half an hour from Port of Spain; take Churchill Roosevelt Highway east to Uriah Butler south; turn right until the Chase Village flyover; follow the signs south to Waterloo; then follow signs to the temple. ⊠*Datta Dr. at Orangefield Rd., Carapichaima* ☎*868/673–5328* ⊠*Free* ⊗*Daily dawn–dusk, services daily.*

Port of Spain. Most organized tours begin at the port. If you're planning to explore on foot, which will take two to four hours, start early in the

Trinidad

KEY
~ Beaches
🚢 Ferry

TO TOBAGO →

Caribbean Sea

Dragon's Mouth

Chaguaramas

Las Cuevas Bay
Cyril Bay
Tyrico Bay
Maracas Bay

Blanchisseuse Bay
Matelot

Grande Rivière
Salibea Bay
Toco
Galera Pt.

Mt. Oropuche
Redhead
Balandra Bay

San Juan
El Tucuche
Tunapuna
El Cerro del Aripo
Matura
Saline Bay

Port of Spain
Arima
Valencia

Caroni Bird Sanctuary

Piarco Int'l Airport

Sangre Grande
Matura Bay

Dattatreya Yoga Centre

Chaguaramas Military History & Aerospace Museum

Manzanilla Beach

Gulf of Paria

Couva
California
Tabaquite

Flanigin Town

Cocos Bay
Guataro Pt.

San Fernando
Oropuche Lagoon

Tableland
Rio Claro

Pierreville

La Brea
Irois Bay

Princes Town
New Grant

Mayaro Bay

Point Fortin
Cedros Bay

Penal
Pointe-a-Pierre
Basse Terre
Moruga

Guayaguayare
Galeota Pt.
Guayaguayare Bay

Fullarton
Islote Pt.
Icacos Pt.
Erin Bay
San Francique
Erin Pt.

ATLANTIC OCEAN

0   10 miles
0   10 kilometers

day; by midday the port area can be as hot and packed as Calcutta. It's best to end your tour on a bench in the Queen's Park Savannah, sipping a cool coconut water bought from one of the vendors operating out of flatbed trucks. For about 50¢ he'll lop the top off a green coconut with a deft swing of the machete and, when you've finished drinking, lop again, making a bowl and spoon of coconut shell for you to eat the young pulp. As in most cities, take extra care at night; women should not walk alone. Local police advise tourists and locals to avoid the neighborhoods just east of Port of Spain.

The town's main dock, **King's Wharf,** entertains a steady parade of cruise and cargo ships, a reminder that the city started from this strategic harbor. When hurricanes threaten other islands, it's not unusual to see as many as five large cruise ships taking advantage of the safety of the harbor. It's on Wrightson Road, the main street along the water on the southwest side of town. The national government has embarked on a massive development plan, which means that most of the wharf area is an active construction zone. The plan is to turn the area into a vibrant and attractive commercial and tourism zone. Many spanking-new high-rises have already been built, but the area is likely to be a work in progress for several years.

Across Wrightson Road and a few minutes' walk from the south side of King's Wharf, the busy **Independence Square** has been the focus of the downtown area's major gentrification. On its south side the cruiseship complex, full of duty-free shops, forms an enclave of international anonymity with the Crowne Plaza Trinidad. On the eastern end of the square is the Cathedral of the Immaculate Conception; it was by the sea when it was built in 1832, but subsequent landfill around the port gave it an inland location.

Frederick Street, Port of Spain's main shopping drag, starting north from the midpoint of Independence Square, is a market street of scents and sounds—perfumed oils sold by sidewalk vendors and music tapes being played from vending carts—and crowded shops. Although it may be tempting to purchase CDs from these street vendors, they are selling pirated material and doing so robs local artists of their livelihood.

At Prince and Frederick streets, **Woodford Square** has served as the site of political meetings, speeches, public protests, and occasional violence. It's dominated by the magnificent Red House, a Renaissance-style building that takes up an entire city block. Trinidad's House of Parliament takes its name from a paint job done in anticipation of Queen Victoria's Diamond Jubilee in 1897. The original Red House was burned to the ground in a 1903 riot, and the present structure was built four years later. The chambers are open to the public.

If the downtown port area is the pulse of Port of Spain, the great green expanse of **Queen's Park Savannah,** roughly bounded by Maraval Road, Queen's Park West, Charlotte Street, and Saddle Road, is the city's soul. You can walk straight north on Frederick Street and get there within 20 minutes. Its 2-mi (3-km) circumference is a popular jogger's track. The northern end of the Savannah is devoted to plants. A rock garden, known as the the Hollows, and a fishpond add to the rusticity. In the middle of the Savannah you will find a small graveyard where members of the Peschier family—who originally owned the land—are buried. While the perimeter of the Savannah is busy and safe, you shouldn't walk across the park, as there have been occasional reports of muggings.

A series of astonishing buildings constructed in several 19th-century styles—known collectively as the **Magnificent Seven**—flanks the western side of the Savannah. Notable are Killarney, patterned (loosely) after Balmoral Castle in Scotland; Whitehall, constructed in the style of a Venetian palace; Roomor, a flamboyantly baroque colonial house with a preponderance of towers, pinnacles, and wrought-iron trim; and the Queen's Royal College, in German Renaissance style, with a prominent

---

TRINIDADS BEST BETS

■ **Maracas Beach.** Trinidad's most popular beach has some of the island's best food huts.

■ **Caroni Bird Sanctuary.** This maze of swamps is one of the island's top birding spots.

■ **National Museum and Art Gallery.** A fascinating look into the island's history and culture.

■ **Port of Spain.** Madly busy and hectic, this is still an interesting place if you can stand the crowds.

tower clock that chimes on the hour. Sadly, several of these fine buildings have fallen into advanced decay.

🕭 Head over to the southeast corner of the Savannah to see the **National Museum and Art Gallery,** especially its Carnival exhibitions, the Amerindian collection and historical re-creations, and the fine 19th-century paintings of Trinidadian artist Cazabon. ⊠*117 Upper Frederick St., Port of Spain* ☎*868/623–5941* ⊠*Free* ☉*Tues.–Sat. 10–6.*

The cultivated expanse of parkland north of the Savannah is the site of the president's and prime minister's official residences and also the **Emperor Valley Zoo and Botanical Gardens.** A meticulous lattice of walkways and local flora, the parkland was first laid out in 1820 for Governor Ralph Woodford. In the midst of the serene wonderland is the 8-acre zoo, which exhibits mostly birds and animals of the region—from the brilliantly plumed scarlet ibis to slithering anacondas and pythons; you can also see (and hear) the wild parrots that breed in the surrounding foliage. The zoo draws a quarter of a million visitors a year. The admission price is a steal, and tours are free. ⊠*Botanical Gardens, Port of Spain* ☎*868/622–3530 or 868/622–5343* ⊠*Zoo TT$4, gardens free* ☉*Daily 9:30–5:30.*

SHOPPING

★ Trinidad offers the choice of shopping in the hectic downtown core of Port of Spain, where the prices are generally cheaper, or in any of a number of air-conditioned malls, where the atmosphere is calmer and the prices are higher. Local calypso and steelband music CDs are a popular choice, as is rum produced on the island.

The tourism office can provide a list of local artisans who specialize in everything from straw and cane work to miniature steel pans.

ACTIVITIES

GOLF
The best course in Trinidad is the 18-hole course at **St. Andrew's Golf Club** (⊠*Moka, Saddle Rd., Maraval, Port of Spain* ☎*868/629–2314*), just outside Port of Spain. Greens fees are approximately $50 for 9 holes. The most convenient tee times are available on weekdays.

BEACHES

★ **Maracas Bay.** This long stretch of sand has a cove and a fishing village at one end. It's *the* local favorite, so it can get crowded on weekends. Lifeguards will guide you away from strong currents. Parking sites are ample, and there are snack bars and restrooms. Try a shark-and-bake ($3, to which you can add any of dozens of toppings, such as tamarind sauce and coleslaw) at one of the beach huts or in the nearby car park (Richard's is by far the most popular). Take the North Coast Road from Maraval (it intersects with Long Circular Road right next to KFC Maraval) over the Northern Range; the beach is about 7 mi (11 km) from Maraval. ⊠*North Coast Rd.*

WHERE TO EAT

$$–$$$ ✕**Veni Mangé.** The best lunches in town are served in this traditional
CARIBBEAN West Indian house. Credit Allyson Hennessy—a Cordon Bleu–trained
Fodor'sChoice chef and local television celebrity—and her friendly, flamboyant sister
★ and partner, Rosemary (Roses) Hezekiah. Despite Allyson's training,
☯ home cooking is the order of the day here. The creative creole menu
changes regularly, but there's always an unusual and delicious vegetarian entrée. Veni's version of Trinidad's national dish, callaloo, is
considered one of the best on the island. The *chip chip* (a small local
clam) cocktail is deliciously piquant and is a restaurant rarity. ✉*67A
Ariapita Ave., Woodbrook, Port of Spain* ☏*868/624–4597* ⚓*Reservations essential* ▤*AE, MC, V* ☯*Closed weekends. No dinner Mon.,
Tues., or Thurs.*

$$–$$$ ✕**The Verandah.** Owner and hostess Phyllis Vieira has been hosting din-
CARIBBEAN ers since the 1980s and prides herself on her "free-style Caribbean"
Fodor'sChoice menu, which is one of the best-kept secrets on the island. But the rea-
★ sonable prices and consistently excellent cuisine make this a secret we
can no longer keep. The open verandah, interior, and courtyard of this
beautiful gingerbread-style colonial house provide a suitable setting for
the menu, which changes weekly and is brought to you on a blackboard
by the attentive, white-garbed staff. ✉*10 Rust St., St. Clair, Port of
Spain* ☏*868/622–6287* ⚓*Reservations essential* ▤*No credit cards*
☯*Closed Sun. No dinner Mon.–Wed. and Fri.*

VIRGIN GORDA

Lynda Lohr   Virgin Gorda, or "Fat Virgin," received its name from Christopher
Columbus. The explorer envisioned the island as a pregnant woman in
a languid recline with Gorda Peak being her big belly and the boulders
of the Baths her toes. Different in topography from Tortola, with its
arid landscape covered with scrub brush and cactus, Virgin Gorda has
a slower pace of life, too. Goats and cattle own the right-of-way, and
the unpretentious friendliness of the people is winning. The top sight
(and beach for that matter) is the Baths, which draws scores of cruise-
ship passengers and day-trippers to its giant boulders and grottoes that
form a perfect snorkeling environment. While ships used to stop only
in Tortola, saving Virgin Gorda for shore excursions, smaller ships are
coming increasingly to Virgin Gorda directly.

ESSENTIALS

Currency The U.S. dollar is the official currency here. Some places accept cash
only, but major credit cards are widely accepted. First Caribbean International,
which has an ATM, isn't far from the ferry dock in Spanish Town.

Internet At this writing, there are no Internet cafés on Virgin Gorda.

Telephones To call anywhere in the BVI once you've arrived, dial all seven
digits. A local call from a pay phone costs 25¢, but such phones are sometimes
on the blink. An alternative is a Caribbean phone card, available in $5, $10,
and $20 denominations. They're sold at most major hotels and many stores,
and can be used to call within the BVI, as well as all over the Caribbean, and

to access USADirect from special phone-card phones. If you're coming ashore at the cruise-ship dock, you'll find pay phones right on the dock. You'll find pay phones in Spanish Town at the public dock, Virgin Gorda Yacht Harbor, and the Post Office, all located near spots where cruise-ship tenders land. If Leverick Bay is your destination, you'll find pay phones in the marina. Passengers coming ashore in North Sound will find pay phones at the Gun Creek public dock.

COMING ASHORE

Ships often dock off Spanish Town, Leverick Bay, or in North Sound and tender passengers to the ferry dock. A few taxis will be available at Leverick Bay and at Gun Creek in North Sound—you can set up an island tour for about $45 for two people—but Leverick Bay and North Sound are far away from the Baths, the island's must-see beach, so a shore excursion is often the best choice. If you are tendered to Spanish Town, then it's possible to take a shuttle taxi to the Baths for as little as $4 per person each way. If you are on Virgin Gorda for just a day, it's usually more cost-effective to share a taxi with a small group than to rent a car, since you'd have to pay car-rental charges of at least $50 a day. You must be at least age 25 to rent a car.

EXPLORING VIRGIN GORDA

There are few roads on Virgin Gorda, and most byways don't follow the scalloped shoreline. The main route sticks resolutely to the center of the island, linking the Baths at the tip of the southern extremity with Gun Creek and Leverick Bay at North Sound and providing exhilarating views. The craggy coast, scissored with grottos and fringed by palms and boulders, has a primitive beauty. If you drive, you can hit all the sights in one day. Stop to climb Gorda Peak, in the island's center.

Fodor's Choice **The Baths.** At Virgin Gorda's most celebrated sight, giant boulders are
★ scattered about the beach and in the water. Some are almost as large as
☼ houses and form remarkable grottoes. Climb between these rocks to swim in the many placid pools. Early morning and late afternoon are the best times to visit if you want to avoid crowds. If it's privacy you crave, follow the shore northward to quieter bays—Spring Bay, the Crawl, Little Trunk, and Valley Trunk—or head south to Devil's Bay. ✉ *Off Tower Rd., The Baths* ☎ *284/494–3904* ⊕ *www.bvinationalparkstrust. org* 💰 *$3* ⏱ *Daily dawn–dusk.*

Copper Mine Point. Here stand a tall stone shaft silhouetted against the sky and a small stone structure that overlooks the sea. These are the ruins of a copper mine established 400 years ago and worked first by the Spanish, then by the English, until the early 20th century. The route is not well marked, so turn inland near LSL Restaurant and look for the hard-to-see sign pointing the way. ✉ *Copper Mine Rd.* ☎ *No phone* ⊕ *www.bvinationalparkstrust.org* 💰 *Free.*

Spanish Town. Virgin Gorda's peaceful main settlement, on the island's southern wing, is so tiny that it barely qualifies as a town at all. Also known as the Valley, Spanish Town has a marina, some shops, and a couple of car-rental agencies. Just north of town is the ferry slip. At the

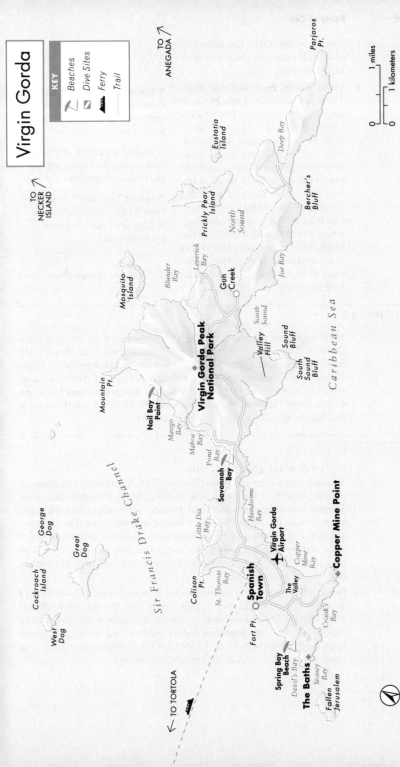

Virgin Gorda

KEY

- Beaches
- Dive Sites
- Ferry
- Trail

TO NECKER ISLAND ↗

TO ANEGADA ↗

0 — 1 miles
0 — 1 kilometers

← TO TORTOLA

West Dog
Cockroach Island
Great Dog
George Dog

Sir Francis Drake Channel

Mosquito Island
Blunder Bay
Prickly Pear Island

North Sound

Eustatia Island
Deep Bay
Bercher's Bluff

Mountain Pt.
Nail Bay Point
Mango Bay
Mahoe Bay
Pond Bay
Savannah Bay

Virgin Gorda Peak National Park

Leverick Bay
Gun Creek
Joe Bay
South Sound

Valley Hill
Sound Bluff
South Sound Bluff
South Bluff

Caribbean Sea

Colison Pt.
Little Dix Bay
St. Thomas Bay
Handsome Bay

Fort Pt.
Spanish Town
The Valley
Virgin Gorda Airport
Copper Mine Bay
Copper Mine Point

Spring Bay Beach
The Baths
Devil's Bay
Stoney Bay
Crook's Bay
Fallen Jerusalem

Virgin Gorda Yacht Harbour you can stroll along the dock and do a little shopping.

★ **Virgin Gorda Peak National Park.** There are two trails at this 265-acre park, which contains the island's highest point, at 1,359 feet. Small signs on North Sound Road mark both entrances; sometimes, however, the signs are missing, so keep your eyes open for a set of stairs that disappears into the trees. It's about a 15-minute hike from either entrance up to a small clearing, where you can climb a ladder to the platform of a wooden observation tower and a spectacular 360-degree view. ✉ *North Sound Rd., Gorda Peak* ☎ *No phone* ⊕ *www.bvinational parkstrust.org* 🎫 *Free.*

SHOPPING

Most boutiques are within hotel complexes—one of the best is at Little Dix Bay. There is a respectable and diverse scattering of shops in the bustling yacht harbor complex in Spanish Town. **Blue Banana** (✉ *Virgin Gorda Yacht Harbour, Spanish Town* ☎ *284/495–5957*) carries a large selection of gifts, clothing, and accessories. **Margo's Boutique** (✉ *Virgin Gorda Yacht Harbour, Spanish Town* ☎ *284/495–5237*) is the place to buy handmade silver, pearl, and shell jewelry.

ACTIVITIES

DIVING AND SNORKELING

The dive companies are all certified by PADI. Costs vary, but count on paying about $75 for a one-tank dive and $110 for a two-tank dive. There are some terrific snorkel and dive sites off Virgin Gorda, including areas around the Baths, the North Sound, and the Dogs. The Chimney at Great Dog Island sports a coral archway and canyon covered with a wide variety of sponges. At Joe's Cave, an underwater cavern on West Dog Island, huge groupers, eagle rays, and other colorful fish accompany divers as they swim.

☾ **DiveBVI** (✉ *Virgin Gorda Yacht Harbour, Spanish Town* ☎ *284/495–5513 or 800/848–7078* ✉ *Leverick Bay Resort and Marina, Leverick Bay* ☎ *284/495–7328* ⊕ *www.divebvi.com*) offers expert instruction, certification, and day trips. **Sunchaser Scuba** (✉ *Bitter End Yacht Club, North Sound* ☎ *284/495–9638 or 800/932–4286* ⊕ *www.sunchaserscuba. com*) offers resort, advanced, and rescue courses.

FISHING

The sportfishing here is so good that anglers come from all over the world. **Charter Virgin Gorda** ✉ *Leverick Bay, North Sound* ☎ *284/495–7421* ⊕ *www.charter virgingorda.com*) offers a choice of trips aboard its 46-foot Hatteras, the Mahoe Bay, for full-day marlin hunting. Plan to spend $800 to $1,200.

> **CAUTION**
>
> If you pick an outside cabin, check to make sure your view of the sea is not obstructed by a lifeboat. The ship's deck plan will help you figure it out.

SAILING AND BOATING

The BVI waters are calm, and terrific places to learn to sail. You can also rent sea kayaks, waterskiing equipment, dinghies, and powerboats, or take a parasailing trip.

If you just want to sit back, relax, and let the captain take the helm, choose a sailing or power yacht from **Double "D" Charters**(✉ *Virgin Gorda Yacht Harbour, Spanish Town* ☎ *284/499–2479* ⊕ *www.doubledbvi. com*). Rates are $60 for a half-day trip and $95 for a full-day island-hopping excursion. Private full-day cruises or sails for up to eight people run $950. If you'd rather rent a Sunfish or Hobie Wave, check out **Leverick Bay Watersports** (✉ *Leverick Bay, North Sound* ☎ *284/495–7376* ⊕ *www.watersportsbvi.com*).

BEACHES

★ The best beaches are easily reached by water, although they're also accessible on foot, usually after a moderately strenuous 10- to 15-minute hike. Anybody going to Virgin Gorda should experience swimming or snorkeling among its unique boulder formations, which can be visited at several beaches along Lee Road. The most popular of these spots is the Baths, but there are several others nearby that are easily reached. **The Baths** is usually crowded midday with day-trippers. Public bathrooms and a handful of bars and shops are close to the water and at the start of the path that leads to the beach. Beach lockers are available to keep belongings safe. Admission is $3. **Savannah Bay** is a wonderfully private beach close to Spanish Town. It may not always be completely deserted, but it's a long stretch of soft, white sand. There are no facilities. **Spring Bay Beach,** just off Tower Road, gets much less traffic than the nearby Baths and has the similarly large, imposing boulders that create interesting grottos for swimming. The snorkeling is excellent, and the grounds include swings and picnic tables.

WHERE TO EAT

$$
AMERICAN
╳**Bath and Turtle.** You can sit back and relax at this informal tavern with a friendly staff—although the noise from the television can sometimes be a bit much. Well-stuffed sandwiches, homemade pizzas, pasta dishes, and daily specials like conch soup round out the casual menu. Local musicians perform Wednesday and Friday night. ✉ *Virgin Gorda Yacht Harbour, Spanish Town* ☎ *284/495–5239* ▭ *AE, MC, V.*

$$ ✕ **Top of the Baths.** At the entrance to the Baths, this popular restaurant
AMERICAN   starts serving at 8 AM. Tables are on an outdoor terrace or in an open-
✧   air pavilion; all have stunning views of the Sir Francis Drake Chan-
nel. Hamburgers, coconut chicken sandwiches, and fish-and-chips are
among the offerings at lunch. For dessert, the key lime pie is excellent.
The Sunday barbecue, served from noon until 3 PM, is an island event.
⊠ *The Valley* ☎ *284/495–5497* ⊟ *AE, MC, V* ⊗ *No dinner.*

INDEX